PREPARING
FOR WORSHIP

PREPARING FOR WORSHIP

The Essential Handbook for Worship Leaders

Michael Perry

Marshall Pickering
An Imprint of HarperCollins*Publishers*

Marshall Pickering is an Imprint of
HarperCollins*Religious*
Part of HarperCollins*Publishers*
77–85 Fulham Palace Road, London W6 8JB

First published in Great Britain
in 1995 by Marshall Pickering

1   3   5   7   9   10   8   6   4   2

A catalogue record for this book is
available from the British Library

ISBN 0 551 02895-5

Typeset by Harper Phototypesetters Limited
Northampton, England
Printed and bound in Great Britain by
HarperCollinsManufacturing Glasgow

For
the musicians
who as joint editors
have helped me
with the compilation
of worship books –

David Iliff
David Peacock
Noël Tredinnick
Norman Warren

with admiration and thanks

CONTENTS

The Bible in Worship

ACKNOWLEDGEMENTS

I would like to acknowledge the help given in writing this book by the following:

- Christopher Idle for a fair proportion of the Bible index to hymns
- Kathleen Bowe for Hebrew help with the responsive Psalms
- Charlotte Hails and Helen Hancox for database work
- Valerie Parker and Ann Jenner for typing
- Bunty Grundy for copyright clearance and information
- David Peacock of Jubilate, Andrew Maries of Music and Worship Foundation, and Jane Hicks of *Deo* Magazine for encouragement to write various articles which grapple with current issues for worship leaders and which are the basis of chapters in this book
- Jane, Gill, Peter, Chris, Rupert and Brian – my staff colleagues in Tonbridge for their stimulus to thinking and for their pastoral care of me
- The choirs, ministers and musicians of the churches where I have served, for their patient tolerance of my experiments
- Experts who have encouraged me in the preparation of liturgical (prayer) material, especially Colin Buchanan, Michael Perham and Trevor Lloyd
- The publishers who have allowed me to explore new areas and have sponsored my work: in particular HarperCollins, Hodder & Stoughton, Hope Publishing (USA), Baker Book House (USA) and Stainer & Bell
- Colleagues in the Christian copyright world and in the Christian Music Publishers Association, who have corrected my scripts and provided professional information, notably Geoff Booker of Christian Copyright Licensing, Rob Lamont of Sovereign Lifestyle, Geoff Shearn of The Worship Service, and Julian Elloway of Oxford University Press

Copyright attributions will be found appended to hymns, songs etc. quoted in the text.

Michael Perry
1995

PREFACE

'All the Levites who were musicians – Asaph, Heman, Jeduthun and their sons and relatives – stood on the east side of the altar, dressed in fine linen and playing cymbals, harps and lyres. They were accompanied by one hundred and twenty priests sounding trumpets. The trumpeters and singers joined in unison, as with one voice, to give praise and thanks to the LORD. Accompanied by trumpets, cymbals and other instruments, they raised their voices in praise to the LORD and sang:
"He is good;
his love endures for ever."

Then the temple of the LORD was filled with a cloud, and the priests could not perform their service because of the cloud, for the glory of the LORD filled the temple of God.'
2 Chronicles 5.12-14

The divine irony here must be appreciated. Was there ever a more significant dedication of a religious building? Imagine the spectacle! Consider the preparations – the rehearsals, the organisation of so many professionals . . . ! And yet, what happened defeated them all . . . but was supremely worship. Musicians, worship leaders, priests were redundant; the glory of the Lord took over.

Our preparation for worship can only go so far. It is doomed

1

if the Spirit of the Lord is not in it. On the other hand, God is sovereign; he can 'take over' any kind of worship, provided that those who lead and those who participate are open to his grace. God's requisitioning of our worship is independent of culture. He can take over a cathedral Eucharist or a prayer rally. He honours dedication, integrity of purpose and hearts open to receive him. Our responsibility as ministers and worship leaders, planners, writers, composers, performers, accompanists, is to provide the circumstances in which God is approachable and to 'prepare his way before him'.

This resource book offers practical advice and useful material; it may be found helpful, even invaluable. But it is the worship of the heart and the witness of the life with which God is concerned. I have therefore ventured to suggest that prayerfulness is the priority in preparing for worship, followed closely by a caring attitude towards those who are being led into God's presence, and an over-riding biblical basis for nurturing and nourishing through praise and prayer.

St Paul, in his memorable twelfth chapter of Romans uses terms and words with deliberate double intention. 'Offer yourselves as a living sacrifice', he says, 'which is your spiritual service' or, more literally, 'logical worship'. Logical because of God's glory (the end of chapter 11) and because of his mercy towards us in Christ (chapter 12, verse 1). 'Service' here translates '*latreia*', a word used to describe both temple worship and practical service. Paul implies a continuity between prayer and praise and our everyday life in Christ.

There is a current tendency to describe a sequence or 'flow' of songs as 'a time of worship'. I think we must struggle to find another expression; though I know that once such descriptions are ingrained they are difficult to erase. Surely, the whole service is worship. For St Paul, the whole of life in Christ is worship. Therefore, for the Christian, worship must connect! What we do in church on Sunday – or at Christian conferences, camps and other gatherings – must relate to our everyday behaviour. Sunday worship must be translatable into Monday-to-Saturday terms.

2

This has implications for evangelism too. If the language of our Sunday worship is disconnected from the language we live by, we are proclaiming to all who venture near us that God is for church services only. I believe that to be obscure is an indulgence we cannot allow ourselves. So this resource book is built on the assumption that we will want to connect.

The Bible itself is earthy in its description and written to communicate. And this resource book encourages us to make use of all that the Bible offers for worship. I would like to commend its provisions to those who, like me, pastor churches, or who prepare, lead and accompany worship, and to all who aspire to such ministry one day. May God bless you as you serve him – and may you find him 'taking over' your worship, and making it far deeper, richer and holier than you or I could ever contrive it to be by our own skills.

1

WORSHIP
PROVISION

What must our worship include?

'In the year that King Uzziah died, I saw the Lord seated on a throne, high and exalted, and the train of his robe filled the temple. Above him were seraphs, each with six wings: With two wings they covered their faces, with two wings they covered their feet, and with two they were flying. And they were calling to one another:

"Holy, holy, holy is the LORD Almighty;
the whole earth is full of his glory!"

At the sound of their voices the doorposts and thresholds shook and the temple was filled with smoke.

"Woe to me!" I cried. "I am ruined! For I am a man of unclean lips, and I live among a people of unclean lips, and my eyes have seen the King, the LORD Almighty."

Then one of the seraphs flew to me with a live coal in his hand, which he had taken with tongs from the altar. With it he touched my mouth and said, "See, this has touched your lips; your guilt is taken away and your sin atoned for."

Then I heard the voice of the Lord . . . '

Isaiah 6.1-8.

Isaiah's experience in the temple undoubtedly conditioned his whole life. The narrative exemplifies true worship – its content and its outcome. The Sanctus – 'Holy, holy, holy is the

Lord . . . ', repeated in Revelation 4, has become a central act
of praise in the historic churches. How pregnant with praise
are those few words in Isaiah.6:

> 'Holy, holy, holy is the LORD Almighty;
> the whole earth is full of his glory!'

It is not without significance that Christians down the
centuries have found value in repeated biblical patterns of
words. There is all the difference in the world between 'vain'
repetition, and meaningful repetition. We could not even say
'Amen' without some degree of repetition. And it is clear
from the well-honed phrasing of various passages in the New
Testament – now visible in modern editions by typographical
arrangement in poetic style – that Christians from the very
earliest time have used established texts in worship. (Much
will be said later about the Psalms – the hymn book of the
Hebrew and the Christian alike). For instance the hymn of
Philippians 2:

> . . . being found in appearance as a man,
> he humbled himself
> and became obedient to death –
> even death on a cross . . .

. . . or the credal statement of 2 Timothy 2:

> If we died with him,
>   we will also live with him;
> if we endure,
>   we will also reign with him.

. . . or the pæans of praise of Revelation, for example in
chapter 4:

'You are worthy, our Lord and God,
   to receive glory and honour and power,
for you created all things,
   and by your will they were created
   and have their being.'

We must not overlook the significance of these liturgical texts and others like them, nor should we neglect the biblical implications for our worship. In this regard, what was right for the first Christians is undoubtedly right for us too. Our worship provision must include scriptural common prayer, especially elements based on the hallowed liturgical texts of the Bible.

It was at this point that Isaiah had a vision of God. Many of us will recall an overwhelming sense of God's presence during praise in worship. On one such occasion in my experience we had in fact been using the popular song form of the *Sanctus*,

Holy, holy, holy is the Lord,
holy is the Lord God almighty.
Holy, holy, holy is the Lord,
holy is the Lord God almighty
   who was and is and is to come!
Holy, holy, holy is the Lord!
© controlled

A woman – sane, sensible and self-controlled – came up to me after the service and said, 'I could have died in there tonight.' The sense of heaven and the presence of God had been so powerful. Our worship provision must give people opportunity to sense God's majesty and to express their adoration.

For Isaiah the experience was physical – 'the doorposts and thresholds shook, and the temple was filled with smoke'. Sometimes people will exhibit physical manifestations as God touches their deepest need. This can be confusing – even embarrassing – for any who have not witnessed it before. But we must not deny what may well be a work of the Spirit of God until we have had opportunity to test its fruit. St Paul's

Thessalonian injunction, 'Do not put out the Spirit's fire' (1 Thessalonians 5.19) was in the context of ministry and worship. Our worship provision must allow people to react not just cerebrally, but with emotion – even physically – to their experience of God.

Isaiah was in considerable distress as a result of his encounter with God. The reason was an overwhelming consciousness of sin – both in himself, and as a member of the community. When leaders default, nations feel unclean; we recall the atmosphere of the United States of America during the Watergate episode. In one petulant incident, King Uzziah had arrogated to himself the divinely-appointed role of the priests (2 Chronicles 26). As a result he had contracted a contagious disease akin to leprosy which, in the terms of his day, made him 'unclean'. This 'uncleanness' had haunted the land; so that Isaiah had to admit, 'I live among a people of unclean lips.' Our worship provision must help people to face up to their sin, and to their part in the community's sin, in the light of God's holiness.

I am consciously writing for ministers and worship leaders of all denominations and none. For this reason I am trying not to be too Anglican in my expression – even though I owe my experience of God and my call to ministry to that church. But we all have good news to share, and much to learn from each other. Later in this book I want to offer some serendipities – happy discoveries about the service of bread and wine which Jesus commended to us. Even its title is divisive. And to some the word 'sacrament' smacks of superstitious priest-craft and error. Permit me to use that term in any sense you will allow to describe what happened to Isaiah next. God – albeit in picture – did a physical thing to communicate forgiveness and purging; the seraph took from the altar a live coal and touched Isaiah's lips; meeting Isaiah at his very point of need.

I recall one Sunday returning home from a distance, none too pleased with myself, and wanting to hear the words of assurance of God's forgiveness with which many Anglican services begin. I was too late – I had missed the 'absolution'. I crept into the back of the congregation feeling that I should not go forward to receive the bread and wine – for that was the form of service that evening. However, I did go – and held out my open hands. It was as the bread touched me that I knew I was forgiven. What words had not been able to do, the physical consciousness of the bread – the token and reality of God's love for me in Christ – was able to achieve. I think it is like that for more people than we realise – to whom sacrament or symbol conveys most effectively the assurance of Christ's saving work upon the cross.

Many in our denomination, concerned for evangelism and for accessibility in our worship, are anxious because Communion (using the Prayer Book term for now) has become the only main service in many churches, thereby impeding evangelism. They feel that it is unfriendly to the newcomer – something that is done by the 'in' crowd; that visitors do not understand. This is especially worrying when children and whole families are present.

It needs to be said that it is not like this everywhere, and all-age Communion services need not be exclusive. In two, at least, of the churches of which I have oversight, the local practice is to invite everyone forward for prayer at the distribution; to deploy sufficient ministers to make individual prayer care possible, and to give communion within this ministry to those who want it. Hence the normality becomes 'being prayed for', the option is receiving bread and wine. Everyone feels cared for; no-one feels excluded.

Worst of all is the relegation of this service – so central in the mind of Jesus, and so effective in ministry – to a corner of the occasional Sunday. We need to look at it again as a divine opportunity for reassurance, nourishment and prayer within worship, change its form if necessary, and give it a role and position which God can honour in welcoming all comers to the love-feast of Jesus. Our worship provision must include opportunity to receive communion as part of a prayerful ministry of assurance.

Why is it that of all the stories about Jesus ('If every one of them were written down, I suppose that even the whole world would not have room for the books that would be written' – John 21.25), St Luke records Jesus' breaking of bread at Emmaus (Luke 24.30-35)? Surely because the early Christian world community, within which Luke was writing, valued this story not just as an historical event (so were all the others, never written), but as true to their ongoing experience of ministry and worship. When the words of Jesus were spoken and the Scripture was expounded, their 'hearts burned within them'; when they were at the table together and 'broke bread and gave thanks', Jesus 'was recognised in the breaking of bread'. 'Word and sacrament' have long been seen as the balanced provision for a worshipping people. Our worship provision must include meals and fellowship, the discovery of Jesus' presence among us and the sharing of testimony.

In the Isaiah 6 account, God speaks to Isaiah three times, in effect. Once via the seraph, to reassure and forgive. Then in very general terms, 'Whom shall I send? And who will go for us?' This general interrogation reminds me comically of the question we ministers ask at a wedding ceremony: 'Who gives this woman to be married to this man?' (Incidentally, it's a folk custom – neither existing in the Book of Common Prayer, nor in recent services. Some will regard it as sexist and impugning the independence of the woman to be married. But still brides want it!) We ask the question to the assembled company, but know full well exactly where the person who is to 'give the bride away' is standing! There is a sense in which such general questions in a worship context allow people to retain integrity; to respond as and when they want to. God did not say directly to Isaiah, 'Shall I send you? And will you go for me?'

What can we learn from this? Surely that worship must include challenge, unequivocal and eloquent – but allow the Spirit of God to bear it to the individual conscience. Isaiah's response is now positive and enthusiastic; it could not have been so when he was still weighed down by his own sinful inadequacy. How the assurance of forgiveness liberates people for service! Our worship provision must always include challenge.

9

The third utterance of God is specific. Isaiah is told what his task will be. It's certainly not going to be easy: 'Go and tell this people, "Be ever hearing but never understanding . . ."' Isaiah communes with God as he utters the prayer, 'How long, O Lord?' The worship service is often the place where people come to terms with God's calling – even receiving their life's vocation – where they commune with God about the dimensions of it, where they respond in obedience and go out to serve him. Any challenge from the preacher needs to be followed by space for response – often during the quiet music of worship, sometimes in silence. We must leave space after the word has been declared for quiet communing with God. Our worship provision must include space for individual response in prayer.

Isaiah's task was to take him out of the temple into the world of human sinfulness, obduracy and error: 'Go and tell this people' . . . God was concerned for his people – and, as the later chapters of Isaiah witness, for the kingdoms of the world. We are commissioned in church to go out. The wider world needs to be the subject of prayer, challenge and commitment – even in its most frightening and unpleasant aspects. There is a danger that some of our worship is becoming too 'internalised'. All will admit this cannot be healthy, but it is ministers and worship leaders who can do something about it. Here, people with wider experience of the world can be of great help – supplying information and topics for prayer, challenging the church with plans for social action. Our worship provision must be world-conscious.

Isaiah's response to God's call was made at the place where he received Communion. We, thoughtlessly, hurry people away from the spot by clumsy queuing arrangements which we inherit by weary tradition or devise to meet deadlines of convenience. Some denominations receive Communion together – this too needs careful handling. For Anglicans, the rail or step is approached, and we are fed in sequence as the ministers revolve. It would be much better to administer from static positions – not necessarily to standing communicants, but at the rail or step as usual, though simply serving people as they arrive, and allowing them to stay as long as they wish for prayer. This needs rather more ministers ministering, and planned time – including music – during reception. But it meets deep needs. Our worship provision must always include time for humble devotion and silent meeting with God.

Isaiah shared his testimony with his disciples, and wrote it down for posterity. We may want to invite worshippers to respond in a variety of ways. Privately, in a public gesture, in conversation with a minister, in receiving prayer ministry, or in testimony and in writing like Isaiah. What matters is that we give people the opportunity to tell others what God is doing for them. Our worship provision must always include opportunity for individual witness to God's call.

Isaiah 6 is a remarkable chapter, but no one Bible passage can tell us everything about worship. We have already looked at 2 Chronicles 5 and Luke 24. There are significant references to 'giving' within worship in both Old and New Testaments (Deuteronomy 16, 2 Chronicles 31, etc.) upon which Jesus comments (Matthew 5.23). There are dedication services for buildings (2 Chronicles 6 etc.), and acts of contrition abound.

A model of public biblical exposition is given in Nehemiah 8 where, flanked by civic and religious officials, Ezra reads the law from a purpose-built rostrum. There is responsorial liturgy, the people bow down in worship, there are classes for exegesis led by experts; the people weep for their sins. They are exhorted to rejoice in the presence of God. Our worship provision must offer prominence for declaring the word of God, clarity of exposition, careful application, group teaching, and celebration.

Most delightfully, there are instructions for individual worshippers in an unexpected place, Ecclesiastes 5:

'Guard your steps when you go to the house of God. Go near to listen, rather than to offer the sacrifice of fools, who do not know that they do wrong.

11

Do not be quick with your mouth,
   do not be hasty in your heart
   to utter anything before God.
God is in heaven
   and you are on earth,
   so let your words be few.

When you make a vow to God, do not delay in fulfilling
it. He has no pleasure in fools; fulfil your vow. It is better
not to vow than to make a vow and not fulfil it. Do not let
your mouth lead you into sin. And do not protest to the
temple messenger, "My vow was a mistake". . . stand
in awe of God.'

Our worship provision should enable people to approach
God reverently, and allow space for listening to God in
prayer.

Notice the reference to vows, and the charming description
of the worshipper reneging on his covenant in front of the
church treasurer (the 'temple messenger'). There are many
references to vows in the Psalms, too. We may have underesti-
mated the need for the making of vows to be part of our
services of worship. We have emphasised the immediate
economic necessity of the collection to the disadvantage of
the long-term need for life commitment to the kingdom of
God. Vows are more vital than cash. Our worship provision
must enable the making of (practical) vows.

The chapters which follow explore many of these aspects of
our worship, and suggest ways and means to make proper
provision for the people in our care as ministers and worship
leaders – a glorious and responsible task under the hand of
almighty God.

2

LEADERSHIP
AND CHANGE

Achieving the object with grace

We all want our churches full, we all want people to enjoy themselves, we all want them to say to us, 'Well done. That was great!' But then there's God. What matters, of course, is that God is happy with our leadership. Or, rather, happy that he can still lead despite us!

As I prayed on my own before a Church Council meeting, I found myself saying, 'Lord, bless my church.' And in my heart I felt God was saying to me, 'It's not *your* church.' This was humbling, for I was quite proud of my role. But it was also a great relief; for if we come to see that our churches are not our churches, but God's, we can then believe that God has the final responsibility. We are not answerable for God's plans; and, as long as we yield to him, we shall see the kind of success he wants. Not simply the realisation of our own dubious ambitions, but the fulfilling of his programme. Moreover, we will then be disposed to trust others with leadership as long as we know that they too are God-driven. Even if they do not share our point of view!

It is not wrong to enjoy compliments and encouragement (though we should always evaluate what is said by where it comes from). Ignatius Loyola's prayer suggests we should not 'seek any reward save that of knowing that we do thy (God's) will'. He may well have been renowned for self-discipline, but there is an inhumanity here, and a lack of realism. We are created to affirm each other and to be affirmed;

nowhere is this more important than in Christian circles today, since we live among people who suffer the symptoms of rejection. Loyola's sentiments here conflict with the New Testament, which sees reward as very much part of our Christian faith. Jesus promises rewards to those who serve well and with dedication, Paul asserts that workers are worthy of their wages; he presses on to 'claim the prize' etc. For Paul, it is salvation, not approbation, that we cannot earn. For the minister/worship leader however, approbation and reward must come supremely from God.

VISION AND PATIENCE

When I began my present job, people were constantly asking me, 'Michael, what's your vision for the church here?' Initially, I said, 'I don't know!' Which was hard, because I felt they would think me indecisive. But I had learned this lesson from others: first to meet all those who would work with me and to take soundings. Only when I had received their insights, appreciated their aspirations, and prayed the whole thing through with them, could I begin to offer a 'vision' based on what I had heard and really understood. The total vision that eventually emerged had been received by the whole 'body of Christ', and was the more easily 'owned' by them because they had been part of this openness to God. All of us had been praying and listening together.

'Look before you leap' is probably good advice to all of us when we enter upon a new period of leadership. People sometimes say, 'If you don't make changes when you first arrive, you'll never make them.' I think this is a highly dangerous attitude; it succeeds only if a majority wants the changes, or clearly sees the point of them. Of course, there are always one or two issues of principle which need to be discussed prior to accepting a job. On these you can act straight away, provided such action has been agreed with your new employer/superior/trustees/Church Council etc. Otherwise, it is best to respect local wisdom until you know

14

better – and until you can take most people with you in your decision.

Sometimes, having to be patient is very galling. In one church, we regularly used a hymn book I disliked intensely. But I learned why others liked it, and realised that the problem was not always the melodies, but the unsuitability of the arrangements for the musical culture I was working in.

Living with worship you dislike can also be embarrassing if you are a leader – particularly when friends who know your views turn up in your congregation and can't believe you haven't implemented changes. 'What hypocrisy!', they must be thinking. This is the time to live close to God, tell him your frustrations, and wait for the opportunity he gives for change. Meanwhile, he will be teaching you new things – even if it's just patience and tolerance, or even if he is simply dealing with your pride!

CHANGE WITH LOVE

Jesus refers to some who 'take the kingdom of God by force'. There is an immense danger in having a 'vision' which is not God's vision, and forcing it upon those for whom you are responsible. Taste in worship – music and words – is often more cultural than theological. The following must be considerations when changes are to be made:

- Clarity and comprehension for the visitor.
- Accessibility for children present.
- Nourishment value: worship words that tell God how wonderful he is, but don't say why, will not feed people.
- A pathway for devotion: people want to (and need to) worship with their hearts as well as their heads.
- The comfort of the present congregation, so that they may worship God individually with minimal distraction.
- Fulfilment for musicians – choir or worship group, instrumentalists, organists.

15

And there must be, within or around worship services, opportunities for:

- Perceiving the majesty and holiness of God.
- Hearing God's voice in our hearts – receiving his word of challenge, forgiveness and love; and also receiving his assurance of our own worth. For some people, both of these may well come as effectively by symbol/sacrament.
- Getting right with God – repentance, obedience, commitment etc.
- Individual response: expressions of love towards God.
- Fellowship with each other.
- Petition and intercession.

As to the listening which must be done when change is contemplated, this should be in order of priority, from steps 1 to 5. The reverse is too often fatally true!

1. Listening to God.
2. Listening to the needs of the *potential* congregation – those whom we would like to see in church.
3. Listening to the needs of the present congregation – what they desire for their comfort.
4. Listening to the needs of singers/music group and how they feel these can be fulfilled.
5. Listening to personal preferences of leaders/accompanists – what they believe they can do best, or feel confident about.

Finally, change should always be in the direction of increased opportunity for ministry, and of wider prayerfulness in activity.

LISTENING TO GOD

Of all these steps, listening to God is the most important. This has become a fashionable subject in Christian renewal circles: easily talked about, less easy to understand and practise.

Christians who are fully prophetic – who speak the will of God 'up front' – are rare. God seems to give this role to the few who are able to do it and still bring glory to him and not them. (Although we are urged to cultivate this gift, for many of us it will be in the quiet conversation that we can be prophetic.) But discovering confirmation of our obedience to God's will 'looking back' is possible for all of us – if we will watch and listen.

The leader of worship must therefore stay as close to the Lord as possible at all times – especially in advance of key decisions and crucial opportunities for ministry. But it is after the event that we also need to reflect with the mind of Christ. What is he saying to us through the things that went wrong? What is he confirming in the things that went right? Such questioning has to happen before God in prayer.

A few years ago, a church in which I was working faced a 'cash-flow' problem – a euphemism for uneven giving! The Church Council had asked the ministers to preach throughout the summer not about money, but about the generosity of God, (a very wise request, as it turned out). There was to be one sermon touching directly upon giving, and I was to preach it. This was to be the final challenge to renewed commitment.

When that evening came, much of the fellowship was present and there was a great air of expectancy. My sermon was prepared. Before the service I stood at the back of the church talking to one of our church officers – a godly man. He fairly bit my head off – about nothing in particular. I could not understand it – here was a senior member of the Church Council who should have known how vital it was that night for me to remain in a relaxed frame of mind. Yet he was getting me wound up with an irrelevance ten minutes before the service was to begin. How could he be so thought-less? I retired hurt to the vestry, where we were to pray. Without explaining what had happened, I asked one of the other ministers to pray for me. It was something in the prayer that gave me a perfect understanding of what was wrong. The man I had been speaking to had just lost his job;

17

and here was I about to challenge people to increase their giving!

That prayer had three results: first, I changed my sermon in order to express sympathy with those who would not be able to give more money. Second, I relaxed because I knew what was wrong, and I could love the man in his need. Third – the long-term result – I rarely begin a service now without asking someone to pray for me. If you are a worship leader – minister or musician, have someone pray for you, and be sure to listen to what they are praying. God will often touch your heart through their prayer, and you will go into worship knowing what you have to do and say.

The truth is that preachers do not know what is in the hearts of those who are listening to them; only God knows. Therefore, without God's Spirit there is going to be no communication and no real application of the word of God to the point of need. This must apply not only to sermons and addresses, but also to music and liturgy. How crass to make people jump up and down when in their hearts they are in deep mourning! Or, conversely, to depress others with false contrition on a day when they want to thank God with unspeakable joy! How do we know? Only God's Spirit can connect our ministry with our people's needs. So, take time for prayer – especially that cleansing prayer which frees the conscience from guiltiness through the blood of Christ. Isn't it amazing how evil attacks come just before we are to lead important worship? We shouldn't be surprised, just glad to fight for the Lord – and prepared to face the enemy of our souls.

LISTENING TO THE NEEDS OF THE POTENTIAL CONGREGATION

Prejudices are a real block to blessing in a church. It may be the people's prejudice: for example, the congregation that won't accept any change but can't see that it is dying. But it can also be the leader's prejudice: the minister who wants everything his (or her) way, or the musician who believes in 'high standards' – except where love is concerned. In our churches we must teach and learn cultural unselfishness.

Every minister, musician or other leader of worship desires for their church progress in evangelism, and a deepening of life in Christ that issues in joy, confidence and caring concern for others. That is at the first level. But there is also the personal ambition that besets every one of us – we also want to be loved and appreciated, complimented and rewarded. More honourably, we want to be satisfied in our own hearts that we have done a good job.

Radical changes in worship patterns are fraught with dangers especially in congregations unused to trying new things. Imagine the difference between a town church served by a series of enthusiastic young ministers/musicians, and a rural church deeply rooted in the local community, often served by the same minister/musician for many years.

The town congregation is quite accustomed to being regaled with new ideas of all sorts. It has not only acquired an inbuilt tolerance, but has learned that the purpose of good change is to meet the developing needs of the church – especially in relation to fresh generations. Even in this climate it is sadly possible for leaders and musicians to make changes clumsily, and without wisdom or love.

The rural congregation tends to be far more conservative. They may have received faithful pastoral care from one minister, or musical leadership from one accompanist, over a long period of time. They are unaccustomed to change and feel threatened by it. They prize their isolation from rowdy secular development, and see the church as the supreme link with the general tradition which they are bent on conserving. Any intending leader of such a congregation, bent on change, must take this into account.

In town or in country, the measure of trust in the previous leadership must also be reckoned with. If you are a member of a church, and its minister has shown you the love of Christ, taught you the way of salvation, nourished you in your faith, cared for your children and married and buried friends or family, you are not going to see his/her views on worship challenged without some hesitation – to say the least. Or if the organist has played for your daughter's wedding and your husband's funeral, you may feel inclined to give his/her successor a hard time!

LISTENING TO THE NEEDS OF THE PRESENT CONGREGATION

If as a minister or worship leader you intend to make a major change without incurring a major disharmony, your people must be able to trust you; they must feel you love them (as your predecessor did), or at least that you are a person of peace, and would not willingly hurt them.

Recently I was involved in the appointment of a vicar. Part of my duty prior to the appointment was to hear the Church Council's views on the style of leadership and pastoral care they wanted. One council member in particular appeared difficult to please in the area of worship; she was expressing very conservative opinions. On the one hand, this was a large 'village' church; on the other, it was seeing something of a boom in renewal worship, and needed further changes to meet the needs of young families. I knew that, in the light of the church's needs as I understood them, I would not be able to meet her traditional specification. Eventually I proposed a minister who had previously shown considerable skill at reconciling the conflicting interests of 'village' consciousness and renewal. He was appointed, and I heard that he was going down well with the church. Six months into the ministry of the new incumbent I was asked over to preach while he was on holiday. The church looked very healthy, and this was borne out by every casual conversation I had, and especially by a chat with the ultra-conservative lady. 'How is it going?' I asked her, somewhat nervously. She replied, 'We know he loves us.' Love covers a multitude of changes (and sins!).

Paving the way for worship change is an art in itself. Attention should be given to the cultural predispositions of those who are to receive the change. I am at present responsible for five churches: every so often we have a joint service when members of the congregations merge. We try to meet the musical (and liturgical) challenge these joint services offer. In trying to blend very different cultural traditions we have made some happy discoveries which have themselves taught us how to achieve painless change elsewhere.

How, for instance do you persuade an extremely conservative congregation actually to enjoy the renewal songs which they have always associated with happy-clappy casual Christianity? We asked a member of the traditional congregation, a professional 'cellist, warmly regarded for her musical associations and reliable taste, to play – and later accompany – some of the quieter melodies which renewal/charismatic congregations regularly enjoy. The conservative congregation had never sung this sort of thing before, and the renewal congregation had only heard them with guitars etc. Both cultures learned from the other, liked what they heard and found a new unity.

LISTENING TO THE NEEDS OF THE MUSICIANS

Another illustration involves musical sensibilities. Musicians shouldn't need telling this, but musically illiterate ministers and other worship leaders certainly do. Do not let your choice of music make artists redundant. I had strong representations from the choir in one of our churches that a worship leader was choosing songs which had no parts for them to sing – and hence they felt awkward and redundant. For instance, they felt their weekly choir practice was practically wasted if they were all going to sing the same note! An enterprising musician's reaction might well have been to teach that choir how to rediscover the skills of spontaneous harmonisation. Or, and this is the other possibility, to arrange the proposed worship songs in four-part (Soprano, Alto, Tenor, Bass) or three part (Soprano, Alto, Men) harmony.

I should have spotted what was happening. Once I realised, I made sure that the choir – a sizeable and spiritual group – were given sufficient parts and challenging material. And I welcomed the suggestion from the offending worship leader that he might assist at one of the other churches where there was no choir, and where his insensitivity would go unnoticed. The choir director has since begun a collection of the quieter song material arranged in parts. They enjoy it, and the congregation love it too. As many ministers and worship leaders are discovering, quiet songs in the renewal idiom can effectively be used as an accompaniment to the ministry of communion. This gives them one natural place in a traditional context. Another is the 'vesper' slot at the end of a traditional service, after the Blessing. We have now largely lost the vesper tradition, and with it, the one opportunity for the congregation to end a service reflectively in prayer. Too often, the organist cannot wait to spring into his latest magisterial voluntary so demonstrating prowess or, at least, drowning out the talking as people leave.

CHANGE IN THE DIRECTION OF PRAYERFULNESS

By ending a service quietly, a gentle ministry of prayer, reconciliation and healing can take place. This is facilitated by a medley of quieter songs, or by a reprise of some of the quieter songs or hymns that have been used earlier, and have led to the frame of mind in which worshippers find themselves at its end.

A more general point can be made here. There is a sort of received wisdom that 'going out with a bang' is the most effective way of concluding a service. If anything, probably the opposite is true. Finishing on a tender, even sad, note has a great impact on the emotions and a much more lasting effect on the memory (whether we like it or not). Think of the plays and operas with sad endings: *Romeo and Juliet*, *Othello*, *Tosca*, *Madam Butterfly* – many more. Think of Tchaikovsky's Sixth (*Pathètique*) Symphony.

We published in our *Psalms for Today*[1] an exquisite arrangement of Psalm 103 by Philip Moore, master of music at York

---

[1] *Psalms for Today*, published 1990 by Hodder & Stoughton Ltd, London.

Minster. I first heard this as a recessional piece at the Sunday Morning service of the Church of England General Synod meeting at York. The archbishops, bishops and other church dignitaries were there – ample excuse for celebration at the end. But when all was complete the choir disappeared into the distance to the faint echoes of 'Lord, you are full of compassion and mercy'. Breathtaking! I copied this idea when launching *Psalms for Today* at Westminster Abbey – with precisely the same effect. People were so touched by the atmosphere of worship, and quite stunned by this unaccompanied and plaintive melody. The impact was far greater than any trumpeting climax.

Twice I have tried the same thing at – wait for it – the annual carol service. Apparently completing the occasion with stentorian renditions of 'Hark the Herald' or 'O come, all ye faithful', the choir has then recessed (once by candlelight) to a lyrical 'Away in a manger' using John Barnard's beautiful descant (available in *Carols for Today*[2] and *Carol Praise*[3]). People came out of those services visibly and deeply touched with a very proper emotion.

Finally, taking up the mention above of individual ministry and prayer: this too can be threatening at first to a traditional congregation, but is irenically introduced during the Communion ministry. In all five of our very different congregations it has been similarly possible to pray spontaneously or by request for those who come to receive – one of the advantages of not passing the bread and wine round. A healing ministry can go on happily alongside reception of communion if those who do not want it are given permission to leave the service when they need to. In this way the same effect is achieved as when 'a time of ministry' is declared after the service. Except that no-one panics, and people accept it who might otherwise fight shy. Once again, the music can be quiet worship songs, or gentle traditional anthems.

[2] *Carols for Today*, published 1986 by Hodder & Stoughton Ltd, London.
[3] *Carol Praise*, published 1987 by HarperCollins*Publishers* Ltd, London.

3

MUSICIANS
AND MINISTERS

Understanding each other for the good of the Church

One rendering of James 3.2 is 'No man is perfect'. A sexist remark if ever I heard one! Seriously, it wasn't meant like that – but it's true! No human being is perfect. And we have to live with each other: 'doing nothing out of selfish ambition or vain conceit, but in humility considering others better than ourselves'. In music, as in every other sphere of Christian leadership, 'each of us should look not only to our own interests, but also to the interests of others' (texts from Philippians 2.3-4). Interestingly, this advice appears as an introduction to the finest and most important Christian hymn/song ever written.

The debate therefore ought not to be 'What do I like?', but 'What is in the interests of others?' In the final analysis, to know what is in the interests of others we need the mind of Christ; we need God's perspective.

We stand little chance of discerning God's will unless we pray. So the first thing to do for minister and musician (or music group – I'll use these terms to express the relationship) is to check that both are praying about it; this can best be done by praying for each other, for each other's roles, decisions and choices; and by praying together.

Then there needs to be an accord about the culture of the congregation. Or, more importantly, about what ought to be the congregation. What is right in one locality/culture, might be entirely unsuitable for another. What is appropriate for the present congregation (particularly for entrenched members) might not be appropriate for the future congregation (where newcomers have not yet found their voice in the councils of the church).

An important issue between minister and musician is the 'placing' of music within worship. For instance, a worship song is not a stand-alone hymn. Using it as such will only lead to annoyance and frustration. Better place it in a 'flow' or, even more evocatively, as a response to prayer, reading or sermon, or as preparation for these things.

Skill and wisdom are required for introducing new items (and not too many at once). As we have seen, a traditional congregation can be wooed into singing a renewal type song if it is first played on a classical instrument such as a 'cello. An SATB (Soprano, Alto, Tenor and Bass sections) choir is more likely to accept a modern worship song if it is arranged in parts (for examples, see *Sing Mission Praise*[1]). Conversely, hymns can be re-introduced to churches which have an exclusive worship song diet if arrangements suitable for keyboard, synthesiser, guitar etc. are available (for examples, see *Hymns for the People*[2]).

But do ministers and musicians know these things – or ever share them and talk about it? Too often ministers and musicians disagree because they are working on entirely different agendas. The musician's anxieties might be as follows:

- Will I look a twit if I play/sing this?
- Will the choir/music group thank me for including it?
- Is it old hat?
- Does it set my teeth (or my wife's/husband's teeth) on edge?
- Can I get it right in time for Sunday?
- How many hymns is that in Long Metre/songs by the same song writer etc.?
- Oh no, not that again!

---

[1]*Sing Mission Praise*, published 1995 by HarperCollins*Publishers* Ltd, London.
[2]*Hymns for the People*, published 1993 by HarperCollins*Publishers* Ltd, London.

- Does it fit with the rest of the music?
- It won't work on this organ.
- We've always done it the other way and we're very happy with it.
- I need time to sort out the music/make a transparency etc.

On the other hand, the Minister's concerns might be:

- Dare I put in more than one new song without getting hammered by the churchwarden?
- What will match my sermon/be suitable for Holy Communion etc.?
- Do the words say what is needed there?
- Is it really suitable for visitors?
- Is it long enough to take the collection?
- But it's an *advent* hymn!
- I've got it planned for next month's guest service.
- I need a solid one there to give the congregation confidence.
- I need a lively one here to get the young people going.
- My daughter likes it.
- It's Mrs Smith's anniversary; this hymn meant a lot to her and I want to be kind.

Of course, these priorities are not equally honourable – but if any creative planning is going to emerge they've got to be considered – by both sides together!

It would be good if minister and musician sat down at intervals and explained exactly what they were both trying to do. In my experience there are often very good reasons why this doesn't happen. The musician knows how busy the minister is and doesn't like to be a bother. The minister appreciates that the musician does a good job, so 'if it's not broke, don't fix it'.

But there can are also be some sinister feelings on both sides:

Minister: I'm the professional here, and I'm not appreciated.

Musician: I've got another job to do as well as this one.

Musician: The kind of stuff the minister wants me to play makes my hair curl.

Minister: We'll never have a viable Family Service while the musician is so inflexible.

Minister: He doesn't realise I have got a hundred and one things to do before next Sunday.

Musician: He doesn't realise this is my last chance to sort it out before next Sunday.

Minister: I don't understand music anyway.

Musician: He doesn't understand music anyway.

In fact, the situation is quite perilous. It has been known for musicians to protest elaborately. Sometimes they have done it musically: for instance by playing the item they don't like in the way it deserves. I once remember an organist who introduced 'Three blind mice' into 'Standing on the promises'. And another who switched from organ to piano in the middle of a hymn on Easter Sunday – because he had *told* the Church Council that a note wasn't working on the dulciana!

But ministers, too, can be obdurate. Sacked choirs abound. Songs are excluded – or songs are everywhere, etc. In really violent clashes, the minister usually wins because of his stronger position in the church structure. The musician is probably wise not to underestimate the regard in which the minister is held because of his (unseen) pastoral caring. A rebellion rarely gets anywhere, except unpleasantly into the press. The minister is wise not to underestimate the damage that can be caused through a musical upset.

Jesus' advice is (paraphrasing Matthew 5.23-24): When you come to worship in church, if you realise your musician/ minister has anything against you, leave your service sheet where it is and go and make it up with him. Then come and start the service.

In the last resort, if any relationships become intolerable – between worship leader and worship group, choir leader and choir, or minister and musician/accompanist – it is important to discover what really lies behind the difference. Someone outside the situation needs to be involved; which often requires humility on the part of the principal antagonists. The Church of England has its churchwardens (or archdeacon, whose job it is to help); free churches have their senior deacons, circuit superintendents etc.; these are the people to bring in to the dispute. They may well be able to discover the true problem and, in any case, their involvement can be an insurance against a public row which only serves to disgrace the church.

4

FEEDING
THE FLOCK

The need for nourishment in musical worship

Accounts of Christians imprisoned for their faith reveal their dependence on psalms, hymns and spiritual songs. Deprived of Bibles, and reliant on memory, they are enabled by the rhythm and rhyme of a hymn, or song, and its association with a tune, to recall the text in a way they cannot recall prose. And, with the text, the teaching it includes.

The texts of hymns and songs strike deep into our consciousness because of their form, and because we repeat them over and over again. They are allied in our memory to tunes, metres and rhymes. Sermons, on the other hand, are not preached in verse, or to music – so far as I am aware! And preachers do not ask us to repeat their words after them. (Though this is precisely what the rabbinical teachers of Jesus' day did. And there is no reason to assume that Jesus himself taught any less effectively – indeed, the didactic form of many of his preserved sayings would seem to confirm this. We preachers may need to learn from his style!) On the whole, sermons are less easily remembered. How important it is, then, that we recognise the teaching role of hymns, psalms and songs in our worship today! Through them God speaks to us. Or he can, if the texts we choose allow.

All those who choose items for worship will want their congregations and groups to be properly fed in order for them to grow and mature in the faith. The chart below is a

HYMN/SONG DIET SHEET

Father?					Does it speak of God the Father?
Son?					Does it speak of God the Son?
Holy Spirit?					Does it speak of God the Holy Spirit?
Act in history?					Does it celebrate God's saving acts?
Relating Act to the present?					Does it?
Scripture base?					Is it based on Scripture?
Scripture allusion?					Is Scripture usefully quoted?
Relating Scripture to the present?					Does it?
Act of God in life?					Does it draw on our Christian experiences of God?
Relating Act to the present?					Does it?
Act of God in Creation?					Does it wonder at sky, trees, animals, etc?
Relating Act to the present?					Does it?
Confessing our sins/failures?					Does it allow us to do this?
Intercession for others?					Is this element present?
Thanksgiving?					Can we use the song/hymn to thank God?
Adoration?					Is this expressed unsentimentally?
Relating worship to reality?					Does it?
Challenging?					Does it ask us to do something?
Eye-opening?					Does it show us something we have not seen before?
Educating?					Does it teach us things we need to know?
Nurturing?					Does it feed us so we can grow as believers?
Response possible?					Does it provide words for us to say 'Yes'?
Memorable?					Does it stick in the mind?
Permanent value?					Is it something we will value later in life?
Effect of tune?					Does the tune help, or wreck, the words?
Scope for nourishment?					Will it 'build up the Body'?

'Diet Sheet'. It was designed for worship leaders. You may only need to use it once to get the point!

Take Graham Kendrick's 'Servant King' ('From heaven you came'), for instance, and use the checklist to see what that song offers in terms of nourishment. Plenty. Nearly two thirds of the boxes warrant a tick. A good main course. Then, examine the same writer's equally popular – and excellent for its purpose – 'Shine, Jesus, shine'. Very few ticks. A wonderful sweet, but no protein (that's not what it's for).

Meat and vegetables can be boring; all jelly and cream makes you sick! All 'Servant King' type songs in a service and no 'Shine, Jesus, shine' would be too 'heavy'; all 'Shine, Jesus, shine' and no 'Servant King' would be undernourishing. Worship leaders (and ministers) need to realise this, and offer a balanced diet. Above all they must ensure that their congregations and groups are fed. They must allow God to speak; to teach, nourish and challenge. God-ward texts alone will not do this.

SPEAKING TO GOD

Many of our contemporary worship songs are love songs: praising God from the heart. I believe that many worshippers who express a dislike for the contemporary song idiom are not upset by what they are, but by *where they are put*. There is a suspicion that songs of adoration placed in a string at the beginning of a service are there to get you in the mood, not to worship the Lord. This could be a fair criticism. There is an authentic use of worship songs prior to receiving from God – either in word (address or sermon), in sacrament (usually Holy Communion), in silence or in specific ministries of prayer.

But songs may also be used effectively in *response* to God's expressed love for us. 'We love him because he first loved us.' So let's place them, for instance, after a Scripture reading which tells of God's self-sacrifice in Christ, or his generosity towards us: 'Such love . . .' Other songs ask him to speak to us: 'Open our eyes, Lord . . .' Place them before a Scripture reading or address. Yet others tell God we want to dedicate our lives to him. Put them after an address, or within a time of prayer.

Besides which, a stream of compliments *without substantiation* is fatuous. Richard Bewes writes, 'If I say to my dentist, "Denise, you're simply marvellous, amazing, wonderful," she will think me very strange. But if I tell her, "Your drilling technique is flawless and your fillings never wear out," that is praise indeed'. Many find it hard to say to God from cold, 'I love you, praise you, thank you . . . ' etc. But if the same songs (separately or together) come after a substantial statement about what God has done for them, the feel is entirely different.

'I love you, Lord, because you first loved me.'
'I praise you Lord, because you are faithful.'
'I thank you, Lord, because you have redeemed me.'

The really useful song or hymn goes on to relate abstracts – my love for God, his love for me, his majesty, faithfulness etc., to the practical – what he has done. Such a hymn or song will relate faith to salvation history, and explain the consequences in my life. By and large, it is the 'hymn' which contains the logical outworking of grace; the 'song' may be content with mere applause! Both are valid and desirable, but we need hymns as well as songs if we are going to speak to God with true gratitude and appreciation.

LISTENING TO GOD

Songs of adoration have a very important place – but not as 'stand-alone' hymns, which must have some substance and nourishment value. A hymn has a logical sequence and works out the implications for us of God's acts of creation and redemption. Sometimes, items *called* 'songs' more appropriately fall into this category. In fact 'The Servant King' is more of a hymn than a song. A hymn, partly because of its length, but mainly because of its content, functions as a 'stand-alone'

HYMNS AND SONGS IN WORSHIP
What is their real function?

This is how we think of hymns and songs . . .

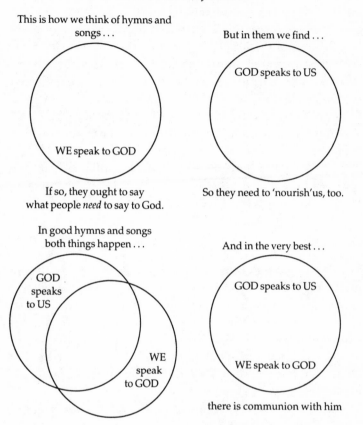

WE speak to GOD

But in them we find . . .

GOD speaks to US

If so, they ought to say what people *need* to say to God.

So they need to 'nourish' us, too.

In good hymns and songs both things happen . . .

GOD speaks to US

WE speak to GOD

And in the very best . . .

GOD speaks to US

WE speak to GOD

there is communion with him

Sometimes we are selfish about what we like, and this is what we forget . . .

GOD speaks to US

WE speak to GOD

OTHERS listen and learn

Visitors are confused and excluded by our 'in' language.

33

item in a worship service. Placing a single song in a service as if it were a hymn – unsupported by *factual* information about what God has done or what is demanded of us – is so unsatisfying! And endless repetition of the song merely to give it the length of a hymn simply aggravates the problem for those who need something more substantial. Traditionally, a hymn requires a much greater attention to careful and reflective wording: syntax must be right; scansion perfect; rhyme true. Songs, which are – often intentionally – more transient, do not warrant such accuracy, and would sound stilted if so constructed.

Hymns, psalms and songs are different animals – all three are essential to the worship economy; but each must be treated with respect and properly deployed.

. . . IN PSALMS

The Psalms are the church's primary book of hymns and spiritual songs. From them we can learn of God's creative and saving acts, of his glory and majesty – but also of his love for each of us. With them we can say 'I love you, Lord'. Contemporary, intimate, relevant, the Psalms speak to God, and God speaks through the Psalms, but we have all but lost them from our worship. They are a prime source of nourishment in musical worship, and yet . . .

Anglican chant (a great cathedral experience) has killed the Psalms for many, if not most, Anglicans. The only book in the Bible omitted from the Lectionary (now common to several denominations) is . . . the Psalms. So we rarely hear them read. In any case, for most Anglicans, the predominance of Communion services, with the optional psalm rubric widely neglected, makes the use of psalms in Anglican worship less likely than in the days of the dominance of Matins.

The majority of free churches, historically confined to metrical psalms, often in the *same* metre, have never really emerged from their frustration with this format, although some of the greatest non-conformist hymns were psalm-based. Roman Catholic interest in psalms has widened but the development came after the new liturgies were set. Many churches have yet to discover the liberty of contemporary psalm forms (see the 'Psalm Index to Hymns, Songs and Psalm Versions', p. 78).

A number of contemporary songs and hymns are based on the Psalms. These offer vitamins! They should be given priority in the repertoire. And Anglicans should put them (rather than non-psalm hymns) in the Psalm 'spot' in the service. Singer-songwriters can do worse than start from a psalm as a basis for writing and composing.

We can scarcely call ourselves people of the Bible if we systematically miss out a whole book in our worship. Or if we ignore in our singing the Bible's richest worship resource.

. . . IN HYMNS

During the past forty years, English hymnody has blossomed. Much of the new material is an excellent main course nourishment. You will find it to some extent in *Hymns and Psalms*[1], *Hymns Ancient and Modern New Standard*[2], *Baptist Praise and Worship*[3] and *Church Family Worship*[4], but supremely in *Hymns for Today's Church*[5] (choir music format), or *Hymns for the People*[6] (contemporary music format).

The Americans have imported large quantities of English texts by authors from the United Kingdom, and are calling it 'the Hymn Explosion'. Churches in the United Kingdom have scarcely noticed it at all and are suffering as a consequence.

One reason for the loss is the move away from organ accompaniment and worship led by choirs singing in four-part harmony. With guitars, synthesisers and a variety of solo instruments (flutes, clarinets, violins etc.) in the lead, tradi-

[1] *Hymns and Psalms*, published 1983 by the Methodist Publishing House, London.
[2] *Hymns Ancient and Modern New Standard*, published 1983 by The Canterbury Press, Norwich.
[3] *Baptist Praise and Worship*, published 1991 by Oxford University Press, Oxford.
[4] *Church Family Worship*, published 1986 by Hodder & Stoughton, London.
[5] *Hymns for Today's Church*, published 1982 by Hodder & Stoughton, London.
[6] *Hymns for the People*, published 1993 by HarperCollins*Publishers* Ltd, London.

tional arrangements simply don't work. David Peacock, Roger Mayor, Christopher Norton and others redress the balance in *Hymns for the People*. At last we can use the spirituality and depth of hymns again – in the new culture.

Another reason for sidelining hymns is the feeling that they belong to the past. Often they do! Updating hymns is nothing new. Every new major hymn book has done it. Even John Wesley did it. But the new song books somehow went backwards, and by including archaic versions made the God of hymns look like the God of yesterday – just at the wrong moment. Among the song books, we had to wait for *Let's Praise!*[7] before the tide turned and durable contemporary versions of standard hymns were reintroduced.

Back to diet! Some of our songs have high fibre content – but not many, because they are designed to do another (albeit, vital) job – to express love for God, not to grow mature Christians. We need to use hymns again – to nourish people. So let's use a wide range of the very best, in the most relevant version, arranged in the most suitable musical idiom – and start feeding the flock.

In many cases, ministers and worship leaders are simply not aware of contemporary hymn writers. Here are some examples of their styles. All these writers are capable of writing vigorous hymns or songs, but I have chosen some of the more thoughtful and profound texts in order to provide a contrast with songs of praise. In nearly all cases, references are given to *Hymns for the People* because it is a book that may well enable a worship leader in a renewal situation to bring hymns into the repertoire of a music group, and so into the diet of the congregation. David Mowbray's contribution is taken from *The Wedding Book*[8]. However, the hymn chosen is an excellent example of his style.

[7] *Let's Praise! 1 and 2*, published 1988, 1994 by HarperCollins*Publishers* Ltd, London.
[8] *The Wedding Book*, published 1989 by HarperCollins*Publishers* Ltd, London.

Feeding the Flock

Timothy Dudley-Smith

1. Had he not loved us
       he had never come,
    yet is he love
       and love is all his way;
    low to the mystery
       of the virgin's womb
    Christ bows his glory –
       born on Christmas Day.

2. Had he not loved us
       he had never come;
    had he not come
       he need have never died,
    nor won the victory
       of the vacant tomb,
    the awful triumph
       of the Crucified.

3. Had he not loved us
       he had never come;
    still were we lost
       in sorrow, sin and shame,
    the doors fast shut
       on our eternal home –
    which now stand open,
       for he loved and came.

Brian Foley

1. There is no moment of my life,
    no place where I may go,
    no action
       which God does not see,
    no thought he does not know.

2. Before I speak,
       my words are known,
    and all that I decide.
    To come or go:
       God knows my choice,
    and makes himself my guide.

3. If I should close my eyes
       to him,
    he comes to give me sight;
    if I should go where all is dark,
    he makes my darkness light.

4. He knew my days
       before all days,
    before I came to be;
    he keeps me, loves me,
       in my ways –
    no lover such as he.

Christopher Idle

1. My Lord,
      you wore no royal crown;
   you did not wield
      the powers of state,
   nor did you need
      a scholar's gown
   or priestly robe,
      to make you great.

2. You never used
      a killer's sword
   to end an unjust tyranny;
   your only weapon
      was your word,
   for truth alone
      could set us free.

3. You did not live a world away
   in hermit's cell or desert cave,
   but felt our pain
      and shared each day
   with those you came to seek
      and save.

4. You made no mean or cunning
      move,
   chose no unworthy
      compromise,
   but carved a track
      of burning love
   through tangles of deceit
      and lies.

5. You came unequalled,
      undeserved,
   to be what I was meant to be;
   to serve
      instead of being served,
   to pay for my iniquity.

6. So when I stumble,
   set me right;
   command my life
      as you require;
   let all your gifts be my delight
   and you, my Lord,
      my one desire.

© *Christopher Idle/Jubilate Hymns,*Hymns for the People, 204

Fred Kaan

1. Put peace
      into each other's hands
   and like a treasure hold it;
   protect it like a candle-flame,
   with tenderness enfold it.

2. Put peace
      into each other's hands
   with loving expectation;
   be gentle in your words
      and ways,
   in touch with God's creation.

3. Put peace
      into each other's hands,
   like bread we break
      for sharing;
   look people warmly in the eye:
   our life is meant for caring.

4. As at communion,
      shape your hands
   into a waiting cradle;
   the gift of Christ receive,
      revere,
   united round the table.

5. Put Christ
    into each other's hands:
    he is love's deepest measure;
    in love make peace,
       give peace a chance
    and share it like a treasure.

David Mowbray

1. Where may that love be found
   uplifting and complete,
   a love which bears and braves
     all things,
   which death cannot defeat?

2. A parent for a child
   will often mountains move;
   a husband caring for a wife
   reflects this strength of love.

3. In Christ upon the Cross,
   Love's depths we see revealed;
   a sacrifice for others' sake,
   as God the Father willed.

4. No greater love than this
   dare we expect to find,
   that seeks
     the good of the beloved
   and leaves self-love behind.

5. Give us, Lord Christ, your help
   to tread this narrow way,
   to live your resurrection life
   and enter into joy!

Michael Perry

1. The hands of Christ,
      the caring hands,
   they nailed them
      to a cross of wood;
   the feet that climbed
      the desert road
   and brought the news
      of peace with God,
   they pierced them through.

2. The kingly Christ,
      the saviour king,
   they hailed him
      with a cruel crown;
   the lips that spoke the truth
      alone,
   that made the way to heaven
      known,
   they mocked with wine.

3. Too late for life,
      in death too late
   they tried to maim him
      with a spear;
   for sacrilege
      they could not bear –
   the Sabbath comes,
      so they must tear
   the heart from God.

4. To him be praise,
      all praise to him
   who died
      upon the cross of pain;
   whose agonies
      were not in vain –
   for Christ the Lord
      is risen again
   and brings us joy!

© *Michael Perry/Jubilate Hymns* Hymns for the People, 272

Fred Pratt Green

1. For the fruits of his creation,
      thanks be to God;
   for his gifts to every nation,
      thanks be to God;
   for the ploughing, sowing,
      reaping,
   silent growth
      while we are sleeping,
   future needs in
      earth's safe keeping,
   thanks be to God.

2. In the just reward of labour,
      God's will is done;
   in the help
      we give our neighbour,
      God's will is done;
   in our world-wide task
      of caring
   for the hungry and despairing,
   in the harvests we are sharing,
      God's will is done.

3. For the harvests of the Spirit,
      thanks be to God;
   for the good we all inherit,
      thanks be to God;
   for the wonders that astound us,
   for the truths that still confound us,
   most of all, that love has found us,
      thanks be to God.

Fred Pratt Green © 1970 Stainer & Bell Ltd Hymns for the People, 82

Michael Saward

1. Lord of the cross of shame,
   set my cold heart aflame
   with love to you,
   my saviour and my master;
   who on that lonely day
   bore all my sins away,
   and saved me
   from the judgement
      and disaster.

2. Lord of the empty tomb,
   born of a virgin's womb,
   triumphant over death,
   its power defeated;
   how gladly now I sing
   your praise, my risen king,
   and worship you,
   in heaven's splendour
      seated.

3. Lord of my life today,
   teach me to live and pray
   as one who knows
   the joy of sins forgiven;
   so may I ever be,
   now and eternally,
   one with my fellow-citizens
      in heaven.

© *Michael Saward/Jubilate Hymns* Hymns for the People, *181*

Brian Wren

1. I come with joy
      to meet my Lord,
   forgiven, loved and free;
   in awe and wonder to recall
   his life laid down for me.

2. I come with Christians
      far and near
   to find, as all are fed,
   the new community of love
   in Christ's communion bread.

3. As Christ breaks bread
      and bids us share,
   each proud division ends;
   the love that made us
      makes us one,
   and strangers now are friends.

4. And thus with joy
      we meet our Lord;
   his presence, always near,
   is in such friendship
      better known:
   we see and praise him here.

5. Together met, together bound,
   we'll go our different ways;
   and as his people in the world
   we'll live and speak his praise.

© *Brian Wren/Oxford University Press* Hymns for the People, *132*

One of the joys of using hymnody is that you are able to match hymn with subject, or with Bible story, or with Bible passage, more comprehensively than with most songs (there are notable exceptions). When I was compiling the Bible index for a major song book ten years ago, I was sadly surprised at the reliance of so many songs on so few verses from Scripture. These were the predominant texts that held up much of the song worship:

Isaiah 9.6 – 'Wonderful Counsellor, Prince of Peace' etc.
Philippians 2.10-11 – 'Every knee bow . . . every tongue confess'
Revelation 4 and 5 – 'Holy, holy . . . You are worthy . . . Worthy is the Lamb' etc.

Things are improving now – but not much!

How refreshing it is to find a hymn like the one that follows! It is quite unique (do you know another hymn on the trial of Jesus?), it is simple, yet profound, and it relates the gospel story to our own situation – as well as worshipping God.

1. He stood before the court
    on trial instead of us;
    he met its power to hurt,
    condemned to face the cross:
    our King, accused
    of treachery;
    our God, abused
    for blasphemy!

2. These are the crimes that tell
    the tale of human guilt;
    our sins, our death, our hell –
    on these the case is built:
    to this world's powers
    their Lord stays dumb;
    the guilt is ours,
    no answers come.

3. The sentence must be passed,
    the unknown prisoner killed;
    the price is paid at last,
    the law of God fulfilled:
    he takes our blame,
    and from that day
    the accuser's claim
    is wiped away.

4. Shall we be judged and tried?
    In Christ our trial is done;
    we live, for he has died,
    our condemnation gone:
    in Christ are we
    both dead and raised,
    alive and free –
    his name be praised!

© *Christopher Idle/Jubilate Hymns* Hymns for the People, 112

5

CHOOSING HYMN AND SONG BOOKS

Our responsibility to communicate

This chapter is addressed particularly to those who have the responsibility for choosing a new hymn or song book, and to those who decide which version of a hymn or song to use when they print out overhead projection view-foils, service sheets; or who compile hymn, song and prayer books for local or conference use. There may well be readers who cannot agree with the trend of this chapter – they may even take offence. Nevertheless, I hope they will patiently read through to the end where I set out both the successes and the failures of 'updating' worship language.

NEW TESTAMENT PRINCIPLES

I suppose that if our church is only for the faithful of long years past, if evangelism is no part of our thinking, then idiosyncrasies and obscurities in our worship do not matter, and we can indulge ourselves without confusing anyone else. Sadly, there are regular worshippers who do not want the discomfort of visitors in services. I remember a parishioner demanding at a Church Annual Meeting, 'Who are all these strangers in church'! I even remember a churchwarden's indignant wife telling me she was 'disgusted' and was going home, because there were 'far too many people' at a service. When such a person expresses a view, everyone should be asked to examine the motive.

If you are reading this book it is most unlikely that you will think in this way. You will be keen to match the needs of the outsider, rather than the taste of the insider. As a consequence you will find yourself asking the 'insider' to be patient and yielding. Faithful worshippers will sometime have to forego their preferences; the alternative is an exclusive church now, and a dead church in the next generation.

When it comes to understanding worship, St Paul gives the visitor a high priority:

'If I do not know the language being spoken, the man who uses it will be a foreigner to me and I will be a foreigner to him. But in church worship I would rather speak five words that can be understood, in order to teach others, than speak thousands of words in strange tongues. If then, the whole church meets together and everyone starts speaking in strange tongues – if some ordinary people or unbelievers come in, won't they say that you are all crazy? But if all speak God's message, when some unbeliever or ordinary person comes in he will be convinced of his sin by what he hears. He will be judged by all he hears, his secret thoughts will be brought into the open, and he will bow down and worship God, confessing, "Truly God is here with you!"'
1 Corinthians 14 GNB

Obviously, these passages are culled from another context – the debate about publicly speaking in tongues, and about interpretation. But the *principle* holds good; we are obliged to examine *all* we say, or sing, in public worship to see if it is *comprehensible*. This was also the great principle of the 1662 *Book of Common Prayer* in England – it was compiled so that its liturgy could be 'understood of the people.' To that end,

'Alterations were made . . for the more proper expressing of some words or phrases of ancient usage in terms more suitable to the language of the present times, and the clearer explanation of some other words and phrases, that were either of doubtful signification, or otherwise liable to misconstruction.'

Cranmer's *Preface* to the 1662 *Book of Common Prayer.*

All those who stand in the heritage of the Reformation must surely see what has to be done. Others might feel that the 'element of mystery' should be retained in our worship. I would want to reply 'Yes' if by mystery they mean 'awe' and a sense of the presence of God. But 'No' if they mean a 'mystique' something gnostic, exclusive. For the New Testament writers, God's mysteries are not closed secrets now, but declared secrets. Far from promoting 'mystery' in worship, it is the Christian task – especially the minister's task – to *open the secrets* of God to a waiting world:

If anyone doubts this, here are some excerpts that will bear me out:

Romans 16.25-26: Now to him who is able to establish you by my gospel and the proclamation of Jesus Christ, according to the revelation of the mystery hidden for long ages past, but now revealed and made known through the prophetic writings by the command of the eternal God, so that all nations might believe and obey him.

Ephesians 1.9, 10: God . . . made known to us the mystery of his will according to his good pleasure, which he purposed in Christ, to be put into effect when the times will have reached their fulfilment – to bring all things in heaven and on earth together under one head, even Christ.

Ephesians 3.8, 9: Although I am less than the least of all God's people, this grace was given me: to preach to the Gentiles the unsearchable riches of Christ, and to make plain to everyone the administration of this mystery, which for ages past was kept hidden in God, who created all things.

Ephesians 6.19: Pray also for me, that whenever I open my mouth, words may be given me so that I will fearlessly make known the mystery of the gospel,

Colossians 1.25-27: . . . the commission God gave me to present to you the word of God in its fulness – the mystery that has been kept hidden for ages and generations, but is now disclosed to the saints. To them God has chosen to make known among the Gentiles the glorious riches of this mystery, which is Christ in you, the hope of glory.

Colossians 2.2: My purpose is that they may be encouraged in heart and united in love, so that they may have the full riches of complete understanding, in order that they may know the mystery of God, namely, Christ,

Colossians 4.3: And pray for us, too, that God may open a door for our message, so that we may proclaim the mystery of Christ, for which I am in chains.

1 Timothy 3.16: Beyond all question, the mystery of godliness is great: He appeared in a body, was vindicated by the Spirit, was seen by angels, was preached among the nations, was believed on in the world, was taken up in glory.

There will always be a sense of awe when God's Spirit touches the heart of the worshipper; but this divine action should never be contrived. To fulfil the Christian task of making the gospel available we must make the language and idiom of worship accessible to the culture of the people we serve. If this is *only* the traditional congregation there will be no need for change. If, however, we want to open the doors of our church and reach out into a culture which is rapidly changing and often alien to traditional religious language, then exclusive patterns of worship simply won't do. And since we are the 'people of the word' and conveying verbal truths, the *wording* of our worship will require attention first of all.

I can remember the sense of liberation for many of us when, in the early 1960s it became acceptable to address God as 'you' in our prayers, rather than 'thou'. At the same time, there were many who could not face this change. For others, it was a new version of the Bible which helped them to see God was real – and for today. But there are those who have never left the Authorised Version behind – a few of whom wish to deny even to a new generation the liberty of the Jerusalem Bible, or the Good News Bible, or the New International Version.

After some years of experiment, the Church of England (having worked in partnership with other Christian denominations) brought in the *Alternative Service Book 1980* (*ASB*). The experiments (*Series 2, Series 3* etc.) had helped acceptance of the new texts. In particular, the central ('eucharistic') prayer of the Communion service made possible a wider act of thanksgiving for all God's mercies in Christ. The heavily penitential emphasis of the 1662 *Book of Common Prayer* Communion service renders it very difficult to use in the context of, say, joyful celebration at Christmas or at Easter. (The Church of England has not yet found a counterpart to the 1662 service for occasions when a penitential atmosphere *is* desired at Holy Communion.)

Since 1980 the Liturgical Commission of the Church of England has published further 'accessible' forms of service: *Patterns for Worship*[1], and *A Service of the Word*[2] being of particular significance. The *ASB* is authorised for use until the year 2000 – which year is therefore a liturgical milestone. The Liturgical Commission and the General Synod are looking at the possibility of several more eucharistic prayers – especially one (at least) shorter one which is also suitable for occasions when children are present at worship.

None of this work is easy – it requires theological judgement and sensitivity as well as an imaginative and creative approach, and an eye to the future. In this chapter we

---

[1] *Patterns for Worship*, published 1989 by Church House Publishing, London.
[2] *A Service of the Word*, published in 1994 by Church House Publishing, London.

consider why such development is necessary, and ask the questions: should revision of language extend to Bible versions and prayer provision alone, or should it encompass hymns and songs too.

EIGHT REASONS FOR REVISION

Why has principle of 'accessibility' required revision of Bible versions and liturgy? Here are some answers:

1. Language changes its meaning with the passing of time.
2. Our 'image' of God should be contemporary as well as historical.
3. Faith and reality should not be divided in people's thinking.
4. A 'private' language makes for an exclusive church.
5. Casual affirmations about God suggest casual beliefs.
6. Evangelism, education, memorability all require clear statement.
7. All-age worship emphasises this need.
8. Involvement and spontaneity demand an easy identity with the language of worship.

Language changes its meaning – sometimes substantially. I discovered a priceless example in the church on the Duke of Wellington's estate at Stratfield Saye in Hampshire:

> Sacred to ye memory of Mr. John Howsman,
> Rector of this church,
> who here continued a paynful preacher
> by the space of 41 years
> and died the 9th of March, 1626.
> The earth his corps but heavn his soule containes.
> His mournefull wyfe Mary erected this.

In this illustration, 'paynful' no longer means 'diligent'. Conventions of syntax have changed, so the positioning of 'by the space of 41 years' might humorously be read now as suggesting sermons were that long! 'Mournefull' no longer effectively implies 'sorrowing', but has a connotation which is less kind to Mary's general personality.

A classic instance of a word changing its meaning from a positive to a negative sense comes in the *Book of Common Prayer* 'Prayer for the Church Militant', where we are required to pray for 'indifferent' judges. This once meant judges who would give fair and equal judgements in all cases – 'in-different'. But we are now left praying for 'indifferent' judges i.e. those who couldn't care less!

With Bible versions for worship, it is now accepted that 'translation' into a modern idiom is a proper and right thing to do.

How Daniel's prayer benefits from updating!

O Lord, righteousness belongeth unto thee, but unto us confusion of faces, as at this day; to the men of Judah, and to the inhabitants of Jerusalem, and unto all Israel, that are near, and that are far off, through all the countries whither thou hast driven them, because of their trespass that they have trespassed against thee. O Lord, to us belongeth confusion of face, to our kings, to our princes, and to our fathers, because we have sinned against thee.
Daniel 9.7, Authorised Version

→ Lord, you are righteous, but this day we are covered with shame – the men of Judah and people of Jerusalem and all Israel, both near and far, in all the countries where you have scattered us because of our unfaithfulness to you. O Lord, we and our kings, our princes and our fathers are covered with shame because we have sinned against you.
Daniel 9.7, New International Version

Let's suppose we had left John 17.1 as Wycliffe's Bible first translated it:

> 'These thingis Jesus spak; and whanne he hadde cast up hise eyen into hevene, he seide: Fadir, the our cometh; clarifie thi sone, that thi sone clarifie thee; as thou hast yovun to hym power on ech fleische, that al thing that thou hast yovun to hym, he yyve to hem everlastynge liif'

Would this not be irresponsible? Psychologically, we would be saying, 'Our faith is a thing of the past alone; our God is a

God of the past alone.' Practically, we would be placing a barrier of confusion between the modern reader and the truth. We would be in danger of 'killing' Scripture; as far as most people were concerned, the Bible would be dead to them and they would be dead to the Bible.

REVISING THE LANGUAGE OF HYMNS

There is a sad graveyard of hymns and Christian poetry – rich material that could have been saved for our generation if only someone had revised or translated it. See what gems there are in the second stanza of this Christian poem by Chaucer:

Love Unfeigned

O younge freshe folkes, he or she,
In which that love upgroweth
  with your age,
Repaireth home
  from worldly vanity,
And of your heart upcasteth
  the viságe
To thilke God that after his imáge
You made, and thinketh all n'is
  but a fair
This world, and passeth
  soon as flowers fair.

And loveth him,
  the which that right for love
Upon a cross,
  our soules for to buy,
First starf, and rose,
  and sit in heaven above;
For he n'ill falsen no wight,
  dare I say,
That will his heart
  all wholly on him lay.
And since he best to love is,
  and most meek,
What needeth feignèd loves
  for to seek?

But now it is lost to most – unless, of course, someone comes along and successfully updates it!

Here is a *hymn* that is on the way out ('The day of Resurrection'):

Our hearts be pure from evil,
  That we may see aright
The Lord in rays eternal
  Of resurrection-light;
And, listening to his accents,
  May hear so calm and plain
His own 'All hail,' and, hearing,
  May raise the victor strain.

It has a good pedigree – written by J M Neale in 1872, after a hymn by St John of Damascus in the eighth century. But it has the disease of internal decay. Not only have the words shifted in meaning, but also the atmosphere is unfamiliar. We have options. Let it die – or bring it back to life with a revision. In this case, it may have to die. But that can't be true of all our hymns as they age. We should lose such a wealth of material.

Hymn revision is seen by some as a criminal act perpetrated upon *poetry* by interfering editors. The truth is that nearly every hymn book editor has had to attempt the revision of hymnody. Without this painstaking work we should have been deprived of many of the historic hymns that have become so famous. 'Rock of ages' is an example – already drastically different from the many stanzas originally written.

How about this contrast?

A. *John Cennick's original*	→ **B.** *What we now sing – a revision*
Lo! He cometh.	Lo! he comes
Countless trumpets	with clouds descending
Blow before his bloody sign!	Once for favoured sinners slain.

We couldn't possibly sing the *original*!

I believe we have to regard the words of hymns and songs as the *vehicle* of our praises God-wards, and the *vehicle* of God's word and truth in the other direction. We do not value hymns and songs primarily for the poetry's sake; though we need more, not less, true poetry in our worship – certainly more *visual* language. Poetry, though undeniably important, must remain secondary to truth and integrity of worship. Therefore any hymn or song writer – with John Ellerton, the author of 'The day thou gavest, Lord, is ended' – should be able to say gladly:

'Anyone who presumes to lay his offering of a song of praise upon the altar, not for his own but for God's glory, cannot be too thankful for the devout, thoughtful and scholarly criticism of those whose object it is to make his work less unworthy of it sacred purpose.'

There have been notable hymn writers who have stood out against revision; John Wesley is a prime example. But he was not beyond adjusting the work of Isaac Watts (with admirable result) and even the poetry of Dryden (for which he was fined)!

My own conviction that discerning revision was right came as I witnessed a televised *Songs of Praise* choir singing with apparent sincerity words from Herbert's 'King of glory, king of peace' quite unintelligible to the average viewer:

'And that love may never cease, I will move Thee,'
and,
'Thou didst note my working breast . . .'

. . . at which the whole front row of the girls' choir collapsed in giggles before the cameras. Does this sort of thing honour our faith and our Lord? This was television. What about in church? Does it matter if we sing obscurities in church worship? There are all too many in our 'received' hymnody.

DO WE VALUE HYMNS?

If we value hymns – and I most certainly do – then we have to realise that many hymns will die unless they are given life-saving treatment. It is simply not good enough for ministers and worship leaders to look at archaic language in hymnody and say, 'That doesn't bother me.' For not only does the use in church of archaic and nonsensical phrasing convey a careless-ness about what we believe, it eventually proves the fatal wound that takes hymns out of circulation. They will fall into disuse far more easily than the *Book of Common Prayer*, because there are no *laws* about hymns, and no-one *has* to use them.

In the list of archaisms that follows, you can identify the hymn from its first line in italics. My comments in bold type do not disparage the writer or the poem. In the example above, Herbert was not in control of later changes of meaning, nor is it easy to say if his poetry in this instance should have been used as a hymn at all. I want simply to indicate the impression likely to be conveyed by careless use of words to the *uninitiated*. Of course, we could stop to explain difficult lines every time we announce a hymn. But visitors to our churches should not have to be tutored in obscurities like this; our teaching energy should be saved for explaining the gospel.

The obscure

Full soon were we down-ridden
A safe stronghold our God is still . . .

Can it be that thou regardest
Angel voices . . .

But naught changeth thee
Immortal invisible . . .

Of the poor wealth thou wouldst reckon as thine
O worship the Lord . . .

There is a book who runs may read
There is a book . . .

He wants not friends that hath thy love
He wants not . . .

All shall frame to bow them low before thee, Lord.
The Lord will come and not be slow

Thy blessèd unction from above
Come, Holy Ghost . . .

Who sweeps a room as for thy laws makes that and the action fine
Teach me, my God and king . . .

This life he disesteemeth
The duteous day now closes

Knitting severed friendships up where partings are no more
Ten thousand times ten thousand . . .

The comic

. . . All in white shall wait around.
Once in royal . . .

What though the spicy breezes
From Greenland's icy . . .

Each in his office wait
Ye servants of the Lord . . .

Thou didst note my working breast
King of glory . . .

Twixt us and thee, our bosom guest, be but the veil withdrawn
When came in flesh the incarnate Lord . . .

Though feeble their lays
O worship the king . . .

Be present, aweful Father to give away this bride
Be present . . .

They cannot rise and come to
church with us, for they are dead
*Within the churchyard side by
side . . .*

Who is he in yonder cot,
bending to his toilsome lot
Who is he in yonder stall . . .

Let evening blush to own a star
Jesus, and shall it ever be . . .

Christian, dost thou feel them,
how they work within?
Christian, dost thou see them . . .

Are big with mercy, and shall
break in blessings on your head
God moves in a mysterious way

Come, my soul, thy suit prepare
Come, my soul

No foot may shrink in fear
O Master, when thou callest . . .

Shake off dull sloth
Awake, my soul . . .

When heated in the press
As pants the heart

(Sheds)
Bridal glory round her shed
Blessed city (English Hymnal) . . .

Shed within its walls alway
Christ is made our sure foundation

Chilly dewdrops nightly shed
Forty days . . .

(Trains)
Swell the triumph of his train
Lo, he comes . . .

Who follows in their train?
The Son of God goes forth . . .

The slothful cannot join his train
Behold, the Bridegroom . . .

(Worms)
For such a worm as I
Alas, and did my saviour . . .

The confusing

Without a city wall
There is a green hill . . .

Fading is the wordling's pleasure
Glorious things of thee are spoken

The 'untrue' (because language has changed)

. . . dreary . . . through the desert
thou didst go
Lead us, heavenly Father . . .

The Son of God his glory hides
with parents mean . . .
The Son of God . . .

I am aware of the reactions I get when I speak or write
publicly about this issue; some people find it is exactly what
they have always wanted to say. Others feel the foundations
of their faith are being attacked. And between these pole positions are the rest – even the indifferent.

To the lovers of hymns let me say: at a time when hymnody
is being lost to many churches, it is unwise for us to be
complacent. We need to discover why. There are musical

reasons, of course. But also many hymns are sunk by lines which make people cringe or titter. Ministers and worship leaders have simply stopped choosing them – so they are frankly unknown to all who join the church subsequently.

To those who still feel that archaic language does not bother them, let me say: try coming back to a church which sings such obscurities after a period of using contemporary versions! It can be excruciating.

EVANGELISM AS A PRIORITY

The classic opportunity for Christians to confuse the general public comes at Christmas. During this season, we are told, nearly one third of our population attends a service of worship – as against 5% maximum during the rest of the year. So what does the entrenched traditional choir do? Why, it proclaims the good news in song!

Adam lay ybounden,	Willie, take your little drum,
Bounden in a bond;	With your whistle, Robin, come.
Four thousand winter	When we hear the fife and drum,
Thought he not too long.	Tu-re-lu-re-lu, pat-a-pat-a-pan.

I dream that the minister then steps forward and says to the bewildered guest congregation, 'If you would like to know more about these things, why don't you join our regular study group on a Wednesday evening?' Do you think he'd get a crowd?

Choirs like this are best given an Advent Carol Service when they can sing such antiquities to the faithful – a sort of concert not advertised to the general public! Having said that, a comprehensible Advent Carol service can be an evangelistic opportunity, too.

But it's not the traditional purist alone who causes the problem. Much *new* material that passes for worship songs falls into the same trap. Words and allusions which come from the Authorised Version of the Bible, but are no longer present in current versions, help to make God seem remote.

An example would be the pervasive use of the word 'magnify'. Its Christian currency derives from the song of Mary in Luke 1 – the *Magnificat* in the Authorised Version and the 1662 *Book of Common Prayer* – but in modern speech it is redundant. To everyone except the initiated Christian, 'magnify' means either what you do with a magnifier, or what you do when you make out that your little difficulty is bigger than it really is; as in, 'He's magnifying the problem.' Therefore, for most people now, to 'magnify' is either falsifying or disparaging. To 'magnify the Lord' is to make him out either to be bigger or greater than he really is. The first is nonsense, and the second is impossible.

Similarly, the Christian communicators do not see the pitfalls of the word 'blessed' (when pronounced bless-ed, as often in songs and hymns where it is spread across two 'beats', thus requiring two syllables). In the world outside the church, 'bless-ed' is now commonly used only in derogatory senses, such as:

'He is a bless-ed nuisance.'
'What a bless-ed idiot!' (a swear word)
'She's rather bless-ed' (implying religiosity or super-piety)

So what is the newcomer going to make of a prayer which begins 'Bless-ed Lord'?

Of course, if all the people in your church have been brought up on a diet of this language, then using terms like 'magnify', 'bless-ed' and all the other archaisms, doesn't matter – they'll know what is meant . . . But new generations are emerging, whose parents and grandparents never went to church. They don't even know Bible stories, let alone Authorised Version language! If we are keen to have them with us, we should avoid exclusive 'in' words and phrases at all costs; there is enough for newcomers to learn anyway – indispensable terms like 'grace', 'faith', 'works', 'Communion', etc. that we shall need to explain. Accepting 'magnify', 'bless-ed' etc. is not necessary to salvation!

We mentioned that all hymn books have revised hymns.

But not all hymn books have tackled the two pressing contemporary issues in revision, the revision of:

A. Archaic language in respect of the personal pronouns 'thee', 'thou' and their verbal counterparts.

B. Exclusive language in respect of 'man', 'mankind' etc.

ARCHAIC PRONOUNS AND VERBS

One of the main objections to the revision of 'thee', 'thou', 'thy' etc. is that they are necessary *reverential* terms for the Deity. To be fair, that is neither their origin nor intention in hymnody, in written prayers or in the Bible. In the Bible and in prayers we now happily revise to 'you' and 'your'. Why not in hymns too?

The prejudice is most clearly visible when it is argued that 'thee', 'thou', 'thy' should stay in all cases – even where the Deity is not involved. For example, who is being addressed here?

> Jesus lives! *thy* terrors now
> Can, O Death, no more appall us;
> Jesus lives! by this we know
> *Thou*, O grave, canst not enthral us.
> Alleluya!

In this case 'thy' is Death and 'thou' is grave, surely neither deserving of the reverence we give to God.

In fact it is not the 'thee's' and 'thou's', but the accompanying 'should'sts' and 'did'sts' which in hymnody play havoc with the modern mind.

Once we have agreed – if we do – that the words of hymns and songs may need revision from time to time, the question is: How should it be done?

PRINCIPLES OF REVISION

In the early 1970s, the 'Jubilate' team – under the chairmanship of the then Vicar/Rector of All Souls' Church Langham Place in London, Michael Baughen, soon to be Bishop of Chester – embarked on such a process. The results of our work are to be seen primarily in *Hymns for Today's Church*[3], but also in subsequent books like *Church Family Worship*[4], *Carols for Today*[5] and *Hymns for the People*[6]. Like most pioneer enthusiasts, we probably went too far and limited the popularity of *Hymns for Today's Church* by a thoroughgoing policy of excluding all archaism. The second edition of *Hymns for Today's Church*, and the subsequent books redressed this to a large extent. It is undeniable that many dying hymns were released from their shrouds by virtue of this project.

Jubilate hymn versions have now begun appearing in publications and on radio and television programmes quite unconnected with the revisers. If we can translate hymnody across musical cultures – as *Hymns for the People* does so effectively, we may yet see the revival of hymnody that ministers with a pastoral heart long for. Only time will tell if we are not too late.

The principle on which the Jubilate revisers worked was one of *minimum disruption*. That meant attempting to find an assonant word to replace an archaic one; for example:

Fill thou my life	→	Fill now my life
Seek thou this soul of mine	→	Seek out this soul of mine
And the city's crowded clangour	→	and the city's crowded clamour
For such a worm as I	→	for such a one as I
Poor and mean and lowly	→	poor and meek and lowly
Mild, obedient	→	kind, obedient
Our meat the body of the Lord	→	to eat the body of the Lord

[3] *Hymns for Today's Church*, published 1982 by Hodder & Stoughton Ltd, London.
[4] *Church Family Worship*, published 1986 by Hodder & Stoughton Ltd, London.
[5] *Carols for Today*, published 1986 by Hodder & Stoughton Ltd, London.
[6] *Hymns for the People*, published 1993 by HarperCollins*Publishers* Ltd, London.

Unbosom all our cares	➜	unburden all our cares
I'm not ashamed to own my Lord	➜	I'm not ashamed to name my Lord

On the whole we tried not to alter memorable lines – especially the first. One such alteration, from 'Thine be the glory' to 'Yours be the glory' has proved our greatest disaster, since critics of the whole process have used this more than any other change to berate *Hymns for Today's Church*. 'O come, all you faithful' was quickly restored to 'O come, all ye faithful' in the second edition and in all subsequent books. And there is good reason: for one thing, it is a folk possession and lots of uncommitted churchgoers are around at Christmas. For another, it is almost impossible to get the 'ye' out of your memory, so that you sing 'ye' even if you read 'you'. Moreover, there isn't a good reason for discomforting people here because neither the 'ye' nor the verb renders the line incomprehensible.

On the other hand, there are one or two occasions where a change to the first line makes a substantial improvement. For instance, the removal of the archaic 'Ghost' was a procedure long accepted with 'The Grace . . .' in Anglican churches who use or used the *Book of Common Prayer* services. To do this in 'Come Holy Ghost, our souls inspire' allows us to translate more accurately the original *Veni creator Spiritus*. Here archaisms are indicated by **bold italics**.

Come Holy *Ghost*,
  our souls inspire
And *lighten* with celestial fire.
Thou the anointing Spirit *art*,
Who dost Thy sevenfold gifts
  impart.

Thy *blessèd unction* from above
Is comfort, life and fire of love.
Enable with perpetual light
The *dulness* of our blinded sight.

Anoint and cheer our *soilèd* face
With the *abundance*
  of Thy grace.
Keep far our *foes*,
  give peace at home:
Where *Thou* art guide,
  no *ill* can come.

Teach us to know the Father, Son,
And *Thee of both to be but* One,
That, through the ages all along,
This may be our endless song;
  Praise to *Thy* eternal merit,
  Father, Son, and Holy Spirit.
Amen.

?St. Rabanus Maurus (c 776-856)
(tr. J. Cosin 1627)

→ Creator Spirit, come, inspire
  our lives with light
    and heavenly fire;
  now make us willing to receive
  the sevenfold gifts
    you freely give.

Your pure anointing from above
is comfort, life, and fire of love:
so heal with your eternal light
the blindness
  of our human sight.

Anoint and cheer
  our saddened face
with all the fulness of your grace;
remove our fears,
  give peace at home –
where you are guide,
  no harm can come.

Teach us to know the Father, Son,
and you with them
  the Three-in-One;
that through the ages all along
this shall be our endless song:
  Praise to your eternal merit,
  Father, Son, and Holy Spirit.
Amen.

After R Maurus (c.776-856) and
J Cosin (1594-1671),
© in this version Jubilate Hymns

Another instance is the rescue of a dying hymn – dying because William Cowper's imagery of c.1770 is just too stark and exaggerated for our taste today; so the hymn is quietly dropped even though it has much to teach.

There is a fountain
  filled with blood
Drawn from Emmanuel's veins;
And sinners,
  plunged beneath that flood,
Lose all their guilty stains.

→ There is a fountain opened wide
  where life and hope begin;
  for Christ the Lord was crucified
  to cleanse us from our sin.

The reference to the blood of Christ is not lost, but transposed to a later verse where it can be restated with no less doctrinal certainty, but with greater contemporary care.

Here is a general example – 'Amazing grace' – of how delicate revision can eliminate archaisms and help understanding. Archaic forms are in **_bold italics_**. Note that 'the veil' is an allusion to the veil of the Temple in Hebrews 10.20 etc. – which term, by its disappearance in later versions of the Bible, has left hymn and song references to 'veil' without obvious meaning for a generation that has discarded the Authorised Version.

Amazing grace!
  How sweet the sound,
That saved a wretch like me;
I once was lost,
  but now am found,
Was blind but now I see.

'Twas grace
  that taught my heart to fear,
And grace my fears relieved;
How precious
  did that grace appear
The hour I first believed!

Through many dangers,
  toils and snares
_I am_ already come;
'Tis grace hath brought me safe
  thus far,
And grace will lead me home.

The Lord hath promised good
  to me,
His word my hope secures;
He will my shield and **_portion_** be
As long as life endures.

Yes, when this flesh and heart
  shall fail
And mortal life shall cease,
I shall possess **_within the veil_**
A life of joy and peace.

→ Amazing grace –
  how sweet the sound –
that saved a wretch like me!
I once was lost,
  but now am found;
was blind, but now I see.

God's grace
  first taught my heart to fear,
his grace my fears relieved;
how precious did that grace
  appear
the hour I first believed!

Through every danger,
  trial and snare
I have already come;
for grace has brought me safe
  thus far,
and grace will lead me home.

The Lord has promised good
  to me,
his word my hope secures;
my shield and stronghold
  he shall be
as long as life endures.

And when this earthly life
  is past,
and mortal cares shall cease,
I shall possess with Christ at last
eternal joy and peace.

'MAKING WOMEN VISIBLE'

The title here was one chosen by the Church of England's Liturgical Commission for the report which set out their reasons for 'inclusivising' the denomination's prayers. The debate about 'inclusive language' has been touched upon elsewhere. My own view is that we should not be unduly concerned in the United Kingdom about inclusive language in respect of the Deity. God as Father so dominates the Bible that it will never be possible or right to eliminate the male reference. However, American hymn circles are far more conscious than we are of this issue, and it is difficult for a hymn-writer to get male God language published.

Inclusive language in respect of *other people*, however, is a different matter. Many women quite reasonably dislike being spoken of as 'brothers', 'men', 'man' etc. They feel excluded in such statements – sometimes unconsciously until they realise what is happening. On this basis the 'sensitivity principle' of St Paul must apply to exclusive language – however much others may claim not to be bothered. St Paul's principle is illustrated by the passages which follow, from 1 Corinthians and Romans. (The quotation here is from the New International Version, which has the offending word 'brother' – new versions will undoubtedly 'inclusivise', as the Good News Bible already has in its new edition.) The principle is this: that, when there is no over-riding spiritual issue at stake, we do not allow our freedom from scruples and taboos to upset those who have them.

From 1 Corinthians 8.9-12: Be careful . . that the exercise of your freedom does not become a stumbling-block to the weak. When you sin against your brothers in this way and wound their weak conscience, you sin against Christ.

From Romans 14.7-22: For none of us lives to himself alone and none of us dies to himself alone. If your brother is distressed because of what you eat, you are no longer acting in love. Do not by your eating destroy your brother for whom Christ died. Let us therefore make every effort to do what leads to peace and to mutual edification. So whatever you believe about these things keep between yourself and God. Blessed is the man who does not condemn himself by what he approves.

From Romans 15.1-7: We who are strong ought to bear with the failings of the weak and not to please ourselves. Each of us should please his neighbour for his good, to build him up. For even Christ did not please himself but, as it is written: 'The insults of those who insult you have fallen on me.' May the God who gives endurance and encouragement give you a spirit of unity among yourselves as you follow Christ Jesus, so that with one heart and mouth you may glorify the God and Father of our Lord Jesus Christ. Accept one another, then, just as Christ accepted you, in order to bring praise to God.

St Paul requires us as Christians to be sensitive where others are vulnerable, and not to give unnecessary offence, even though the issue is of no consequence to us and we can't see why others should find it a problem.

There is more than one way in which this principle of 'inclusivising' can be applied, as this selection of inclusivised lines from popular carols shows. Sometimes the sense will change – if this is theologically correct, and if archaism can be removed with the same touch of the brush, then it should be permissible. After all, the original writer manoeuvred his words and ideas to reach a proper rhythm and rhyme – the exact words and doctrinal precision had to be secondary to the construction of the verse.

Good Christian *men*, rejoice	→	Good Christians all, rejoice
man is blessed for evermore	→	we are blessed for evermore
born that *man* no more may die	→	born that we no more may die
born to raise the *sons* of earth	→	born to raise us from the earth
the wonder God had wrought for *man*	→	the wonder of our God made man

6

PRESENTATION

*Setting out hymns and songs on overhead projection
transparencies, song- and service-sheets*

Since our objective is simple and clear communication, we
need to do some thinking about how we set out hymns and
songs. Most churches at some time will need to prepare
service sheets or overhead projection view foils; many
churches do it all the time and have for the most part abandoned congregational hymn and song books. Such freedom
carries with it considerable responsibility. And there are
hazards. What are the best principles for setting out psalms,
hymns, songs and prayers in these media?

First, consider the difference in presentation between these
versions of 'The Lord's Prayer':

A.
Our Father which art in heaven,
Hallowed be thy Name, Thy
kingdom come, Thy will be done,
in earth as it is in heaven. Give us
this day our daily bread; And
forgive us our trespasses, As we
forgive them that trespass against
us; And lead us not into temptation, But deliver us from evil. For
thine is the the kingdom, the
power and the glory; For ever and
ever. Amen.
Book of Common Prayer

B.
Our Father in heaven,
hallowed be your name,
your kingdom come,
your will be done,
on earth as in heaven.
Give us today our daily bread.
Forgive us our sins
as we forgive those
    who sin against us.
Lead us not into temptation
but deliver us from evil.

For the kingdom, the power,
and the glory are yours
now and for ever. Amen.
The Alternative Service Book 1980

Notice, first of all, that breaks in sense are indicated in **A.** by capital letters; but in **B.** by speech-equivalent lines. In the *Book of Common Prayer* (**A.**) these divisions were to enable repetition in sensible phrases after the minister. But, when said as a unity by a whole congregation, they also enabled the people to keep together as they spoke – to pause and breathe as one. When in our century new service books were devised it was thought more effective to divide congregational prayers into lines, rather than to use capital letters to make the breaks. This is much more effective, and should be adhered to when printing out prayers for *people* to say together. Notice that the initial capital letters are now dropped.

Another useful convention has been to place in **bold** type the words that the people say (sometimes just the '**Amen.**'); and, conversely, to use ordinary Roman type for the minister's part. The minister's part is not set out in lines, so that it contrasts with the lines spoken by the people:

> Come close to God and he will come close to you. The Lord our God is worthy to receive glory and honour and power, for he has created and redeemed us:
> **Heavenly Father,**
> **in our worship**
> **help us to sing your praise,**
> **confess our sins,**
> **hear your word**
> **and bring our prayers to you,**
> **through Jesus Christ our Lord. Amen.**
> From *Church Family Worship*[1]

The minister – theoretically – will have had time to read and digest his or her part of the prayer; so that decisions about phrasing will have been made. To the congregation, however, the thoughts will be fresh, and this breaking into lines gives guidance as to sense and emphasis. Even more importantly, the minister is only one voice—he/she has only to keep in

[1] *Church Family Worship*, published 1986 by Hodder & Stoughton Ltd, London.

step with him/herself. The congregation, on the other hand, speak together; they need to know where to pause and to breathe. So these are good principles and worth adhering to when setting out prayers – and songs. Speech-equivalent lines make the meaning clear, and keep the worshippers together. For example, form **D.** is much less helpful to the congregation than form **E.**:

D.
Lord of my life today,
teach me to live and pray
as one who knows the joy of
sins
forgiven;
so may I ever be,
now and eternally,
one with my fellow-citizens
in heaven.
 	
© *Michael Saward/Jubilate Hymns*
Reprinted under CCL 2487
	E.
	Lord of my life today,
	teach me to live and pray
	as one who knows
	    the joy of sins forgiven;
	so may I ever be,
	now and eternally,
	one with my fellow-citizens
	    in heaven.
	
	© *Michael Saward/Jubilate Hymns*
	Reprinted under CCL 2487

It's also a matter of clarity. On this pattern, where there does need to be a 'turn-over' – a line bent round because of undue length – it makes for easy reading (a) to take it back to an indent, and not to the margin, and (b) to make the break at a sensible point; i.e. not as in **F.**, but as in **G.**:

F. Ascribe greatness to our God the rock: His work is perfect and all His ways are just. *Copyright control*	**G.** Ascribe greatness to our God, the rock: His work is perfect and all his ways are just. *Copyright control*

CAPITALS V. LOWER CASE LETTERS

Notice also how the initial letters of the lines in F. cause hiccups in the flow of the song, as does the capitalisation of 'His'. The more professional (and pastoral) song and hymn books are now following contemporary 'prayer' style, and removing the irritating capital letters from the beginning of lines. Unfortunately, the educational world has not yet caught up with this, and many schools are still insisting that children capitalise their lines in poetry, even though contemporary poets have long abandoned the tradition.

You might think that the capitalisation of 'You' and 'Your' when speaking of God was essential, but note how all prayer books (including the old ones) and all Bibles (AV/KJV, NEB/RNEB, TEV/GNB, NIV etc.) *do not capitalise personal pronouns for God.* No 'You's' or 'Thee's' (unless, of course, they begin a new sentence or speech) – only 'you's' and 'thee's'. If you don't believe it, look at your Bible!

Why, then, do we need to capitalise pronouns in hymns and songs when the Bibles don't? You may initially feel there's a slight loss of reverence in removing the capital from 'Your' when referring to God. But there's everything to be gained in terms of flow of text and comprehensibility. And God is worshipped in Spirit and in truth, not in letter. It is the Spirit who must be allowed to speak through the texts of the songs and hymns we reproduce for worship; and the truth that must be absolutely *clear* to all who read.

SERVICE SHEETS

Modern word processing packages allow for the construction of simple and effective service sheets – clean, and with the 'printed' feel about them. See the illustration overleaf. Here, hymns, songs, prayers and congregational response material have all been treated similarly. The need for instructions like 'Minister', and 'People' has been eliminated by the use of Roman and bold type. This not only improves clarity, but also cuts out marginal notes, which means that a 10 or 11 point

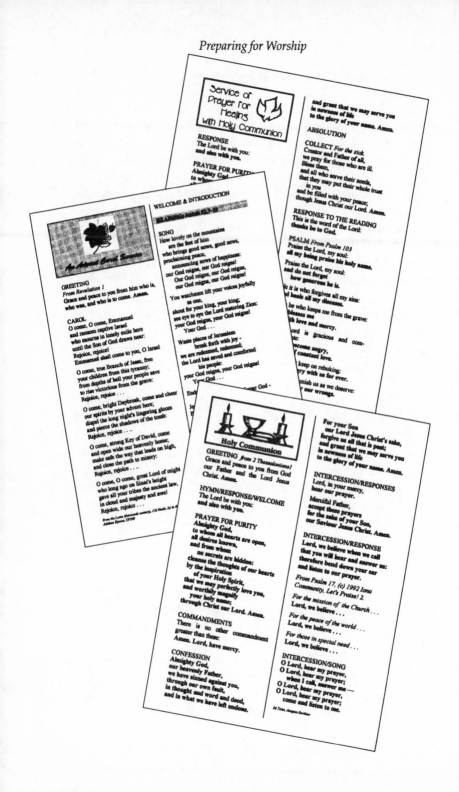

Service of Prayer for Healing with Holy Communion

RESPONSE
The Lord be with you:
and also with you.

PRAYER FOR PURITY
Almighty God,
to whom...

and grant that we may serve you
in newness of life
to the glory of your name. Amen.

ABSOLUTION

COLLECT *For the sick.*
Creator and Father of all,
we pray for those who are ill.
Bless them,
and all who serve their needs,
that they may put their whole trust
in you
and be filled with your peace;
through Jesus Christ our Lord. Amen.

RESPONSE TO THE READING
This is the word of the Lord:
thanks be to God.

PSALM *From Psalm 103*
Praise the Lord, my soul:
all my being praise his holy name.

Praise the Lord, my soul:
and do not forget
how generous he is.

...le it is who forgives all my sins:
...d heals all my diseases.

...he who keeps me from the grave:
...blesses me
...th love and mercy.

...ord is gracious and com-
...te:
...ecome angry,
...constant love.

...keep on rebuking:
...ry with us for ever.

...nish us as we deserve:
...r our wrongs.

WELCOME & INTRODUCTION

SONG
How lovely on the mountains
are the feet of him
who brings good news, good news,
proclaiming peace,
announcing news of happiness:
our God reigns, our God reigns!
Our God reigns, our God reigns,
our God reigns, our God reigns!

You watchmen lift your voices joyfully
as one,
shout for your king, your king;
see eye to eye the Lord restoring Zion:
your God reigns, your God reigns!
Your God ...

Waste places of Jerusalem
break forth with joy -
we are redeemed, redeemed,
the Lord has saved and comforted
his people:
your God reigns, your God reigns!
Your God ...

End... ...God -

Je...
B...

GREETING
From Revelation 1
Grace and peace to you from him who is,
who was, and who is to come. Amen.

CAROL
O come, O come, Emmanuel
and ransom captive Israel
who mourns in lonely exile here
until the Son of God draws near:
Rejoice, rejoice!
Emmanuel shall come to you, O Israel

O come, true Branch of Jesse, free
your children from this tyranny;
from depths of hell your people save
to rise victorious from the grave:
Rejoice, rejoice ...

O come, bright Daybreak, come and cheer
our spirits by your advent here;
dispel the long night's lingering gloom
and pierce the shadows of the tomb:
Rejoice, rejoice ...

O come, strong Key of David, come
and open wide our heavenly home;
make safe the way that leads on high,
and close the path to misery:
Rejoice, rejoice ...

O come, O come, great Lord of might,
who long ago on Sinai's height
gave all your tribes the ancient law,
in cloud and majesty and awe!
Rejoice, rejoice ...

From the Latin (thirteenth century), J M Neale, (v) in R... Jubilate Hymns, CP288

Holy Communion

GREETING *from 2 Thessalonians 1*
Grace and peace to you from God
our Father and the Lord Jesus
Christ. Amen.

HYMN/RESPONSE/WELCOME
The Lord be with you:
and also with you.

PRAYER FOR PURITY
Almighty God,
to whom all hearts are open,
all desires known,
and from whom
no secrets are hidden:
cleanse the thoughts of our hearts
by the inspiration
of your Holy Spirit,
that we may perfectly love you,
and worthily magnify
your holy name;
through Christ our Lord. Amen.

COMMANDMENTS
There is no other commandment
greater than these:
Amen. Lord, have mercy.

CONFESSION
Almighty God,
our heavenly Father,
we have sinned against you,
through our own fault,
in thought and word and deed,
and in what we have left undone.

For your Son
our Lord Jesus Christ's sake,
forgive us all that is past;
and grant that we may serve you
in newness of life
to the glory of your name. Amen.

INTERCESSION/RESPONSES
Lord, in your mercy,
hear our prayer.

Merciful Father,
accept these prayers
for the sake of your Son,
our Saviour Jesus Christ. Amen.

INTERCESSION/RESPONSE
Lord, we believe when we call
that you will hear and answer us:
therefore bend down your ear
and listen to our prayer.

*From Psalm 17, (c) 1992 Iona
Community, Let's Praise! 2*

For the mission of the Church ...
Lord, we believe ...

For the peace of the world ...
Lord, we believe ...

For those in special need ...
Lord, we believe ...

INTERCESSION/SONG
O Lord, hear my prayer,
O Lord, hear my prayer;
when I call, answer me —
O Lord, hear my prayer,
O Lord, hear my prayer;
come and listen to me.

(c) Taizé, Ateliers Bucélier

type face can be used in double columns on a A5 page. In this way, a full service can be included on four sides (one sheet of A4 folded). A service, such as a carol service, with more items would require double this – two pages of A4 folded to give eight sides. Even so, such a format allows considerable saving of paper and duplicating (or photocopying) costs. The CCL copyright licence number would appear on the final page.

Another possible format is three columns vertically on an A4 sheet. This yields a little more room for continuous songs or hymns. The centre rule is available in word processors such as Microsoft *Word for Windows*™. Illustrations can be scanned in from copyright-free art work; or public domain illustrations can be obtained. This, and coloured paper, helps to identify sheets when there is more than one around. The Communion service illustrated is printed on card.

For the information of those who already use *Windows*™ type word processors, the settings for the *Advent Carol Service* paper are:

Paper size: 5.83" by 8.27" (this is the setting even though the paper being fed is A4)
Orientation: Landscape
Margins: 0.4" all round (some printers question this, but usually can be over-ridden.
Point size: 10pt Roman
Columns: 2 (column spacing 0.2")
Tab settings: four at 0.1" intervals from the margin.

The page setup can also be recorded as a document template or macro for regular use.

Each page was printed separately on the left half of an A4 sheet in landscape orientation. Odd numbered pages were then folded in half and tucked round the blank side of the landscape A4 (see diagram):

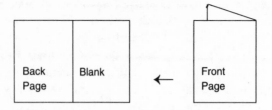

This saves any gluing or pasting prior to photocopying, and obviates the need for expensive and time-consuming desk-top publishing software.

Until it is possible to obtain disks or CD-Roms of complete song, hymn and prayer books, it will make sense (subject to copyright restrictions) to store psalms, songs, hymns and prayer material in computer files for re-use. It is very helpful to store material in the same text format as illustrated here. Worship items can be pasted across from one document to another without clashes in appearance. *WorshipMaster*™² offers a resource for this – at a price! It is hoped that publishers will soon be persuaded to make their books available on disk so that compiling service sheets is merely a matter of going by the numbers in the book.

²*WorshipMaster*™, published 1993 by Hodder & Stoughton Ltd, London, and Oxford University Press, Oxford

7

USING THE
PSALMS

The basic Christian song/hymn book

The Psalms are an inheritance of the Christian Church, and its basic hymn book. Many if not most of the hymns we sing – certainly the lasting ones – owe their existence to a psalm. Psalms are the encouragement of our spiritual growth, the reminder of God's omnipotence and ever-presence; they are the celebration of our life in Christ and the consolation of our dying.

How were the Psalms first used? A good proportion of them have notes as to their dedication or origin, and about how they are to be performed. Terms which apparently refer to instruments and tunes are obscure so that, on the whole, their interpretation is conjectural. There is little doubt about 'with stringed instruments' (Psalm 4); but 'for the flutes' is just one possible rendering of a phrase which occurs only in Psalm 5. The sense of the Hebrew 'choral' directions is similarly uncertain. But they do suggest energy, variety, and special use for certain occasions. Nehemiah indicates a responsive (antiphonal) form of saying or singing. In praise and thanksgiving, one section responded to the other:

'And the leaders of the Levites were Hashabiah, Sherebiah, Jeshua the son of Kadmiel, and their associates who stood opposite them to give praise and thanksgiving, one section responding to the other, as prescribed by David the man of God.'
Nehemiah 12.24.

71

Most of our evidence for the purpose and early use of psalms comes from the text itself. For instance, there is a huge difference between a psalm of individual confidence or sorrow, and a psalm of communal thanksgiving.

Individual psalms – for instance, the laments – are often packed by the psalmist with human experiences, evidently to meet the pastoral situation of various individuals. Whoever was the contemporary custodian of the psalms at temple or shrine, meeting-place or (later) synagogue, would thus be equipped to articulate the unexpressed needs of the worshipper – not only in public services, but also in private counselling. There are psalms available for those who mourn, psalms for those going on pilgrimages, psalms for the sick and oppressed, psalms for the victims of aggression . . . and so on.

At the other end of the scale are the great communal worship songs – many apparently tied to a recurring event or festival. The clearest example is Psalm 118. Here it is, set out for responsive use in the Jubilate Liturgical Format:

Psalm 118

'M' – minister; 'W' – worshipper, advancing from the back; 'C' – choir/chorus; 'D' – director in flat tone.

ᴹGive thanks to the Lord, for he is good:
his love endures for ever.

ᴹAll those who fear the Lord shall say:
his love endures for ever.

ᵂOpen for me the gates of the Temple; I will go in and give thanks to the Lord.

ᴹThis is the gate of the Lord, only the righteous can come in.

ᵂI will give thanks because you heard me; you have become my salvation.

ᶜThe stone which the builders rejected as worthless turned out to be the most important of all:

ᴬᴸᴸThe Lord has done this –
what a wonderful sight it is!

ᴹThis is the day of the Lord's victory – let us be happy, let us celebrate:

ᴬᴸᴸ**O Lord, save us,
O Lord, grant us success.**

ᴹMay God bless the one who comes in the name of the Lord:

ᴬᴸᴸ**The Lord is God –
he has been good to us!**

ᴹFrom the Temple of the Lord, we bless you.

^DWith branches in your hands, start the procession and march round the altar:

^WYou are my God and I will give you thanks:

^{ALL}**You are my God, and I will exalt you.**

^MGive thanks to the Lord, for he is good:

^{ALL}**His love endures for ever. Amen.**

The temple congregation and chorus ('C') give thanks, and sing 'his love endures for ever'; the symbolic would-be worshipper ('W') stands at the door and asks for entrance. Persons in authority ('M') assert: 'This is the gate of the Lord; only the righteous can come in'. God's goodness and salvation is declared by the worshipper. There is a blessing: 'May God bless the one who comes in the name of the Lord'. Then action begins; the master of ceremonies ('D') orders: 'With branches in your hands, start the festival and march round the altar'. How did we ever imagine that this psalm might be treated as a straight poem, let alone that it should be chanted – including the stage instructions – in complete ignorance of its intended setting and without distinction of one part from another?

THE WAY PSALMS HAVE BEEN USED

In the Church of England

The practice of chanting pointed psalms only came into general use in parish churches during the latter part of the nineteenth century. This style is found beautiful and helpful by many, but it has to be acknowledged that more worshippers are defeated by the technicalities of pointing and wish consequently to discontinue the use of psalms.

The move towards Parish Communion as the main Sunday service has reduced the opportunity for psalm and canticle singing. Morning and Evening Prayer (Matins and Evensong) traditionally provided for three or four canticles to be sung, and because these services are used less often, the Psalter has become much less well-known. It is not widely appreciated that the Psalms do not appear in the Church's Lectionary as readings; and therefore, in churches that order their worship by the Lectionary, the Psalms is the only book in the Bible which is never read in a service!

The Church of England has in fact lost part of the genius of its heritage. The recital of the psalms at the offices according to a regular pattern dates back to very early times. The *Book of Common Prayer* Psalter provides for the public reading of every psalm once a month. But quite apart from tradition, the persistent omission of the Psalms deprives the Church of a pillar of its spirituality. As a consequence the Church is unable to offer the resources of the Psalms, which so squarely face up to the human condition, as it tries to meet the needs of the present secular generation. Where is the remedy?

In the Free Churches

Today's Free Churches, whose forebears developed metrical psalmody, received from them a host of psalm texts. But they did not feel the obligation to use them systematically, as Anglicans used the *Psalter*. In the eighteenth century, the flowering of hymnody in the Free Churches tended to eclipse the metrical psalms – although Spurgeon's *Our Own Hymn-book*[1] (1866) devoted its first 150 numbers to a complete metrical psalter, and *Wesley's Hymns*[2] still had a large selection of metrical psalms. Many of the traditional texts are rigidly Long Metre or Common Metre, and this gives them a bland, even monotonous, feel. Their dated appeal, and the absence of any system of psalm use in the less structured worship of the Free Churches led to their gradual demise. Once again, the losers are the congregation, because they no longer have that close acquaintance with the spirituality of the Psalms which is the inheritance of all Christendom.

In the Roman Catholic Church

Until the Second Vatican Council, the Roman Catholic Church used almost exclusively Gregorian psalm-tones, with

---

[1] *Our Own Hymn-book*, C. H. Spurgeon, published 1866, London.
[2] *Wesley's Hymns*, published 1889.

antiphons before and after each psalm. This world-wide practice employed the Latin text whenever a monastic or neo-monastic office was sung. The exception was the Gélineau form of vernacular psalmody which is now little used; although it is more prevalent in the United States than in the United Kingdom. At Mass, a psalm-verse or two would be sung during the Gradual or Alleluia between the readings (again with a Latin text), using either very florid plainchant or, less often, polyphonic or faux bourdon settings. These chants were reserved for the choir.

Since Vatican II, the Sunday and Weekday Lectionary has contained a responsive psalm after the first reading at Mass. A congregational response occurs every four or six lines; the normal practice is for the congregation to sing the refrain, and for a cantor – or a group of cantors – to sing the verses. A substantial majority of the psalm-tones used are of the 'reciting note with termination' type. There is now an increasing use of psalm tunes (tones in regular metres).

As regards translation, the Grail version is almost universal for the English-speaking world (the USA also uses the NAB). Specific examples of the Gélineau form (for which the Grail text was designed) still appeal, though the generality does not. It was probably ahead of its time, becoming available before the use of the vernacular at Mass. By the time that departure was authorised, taste and opinion had moved on; the text, however, has remained.

Less than half of English-speaking Catholic congregations sing any psalms at all, the responsive psalm being said. And, although various styles of psalm are attempted by forward-looking Catholics, these are often employed for exits, entrances, Communion etc. and do not occupy the traditional positions in the service.

For monastic, or neo-monastic, offices today, most communities sing the Psalms in English, using similar tones to those mentioned above; some communities still preserve some Latin psalmody to Gregorian tones mixed in with vernacular psalmody (though not normally within the same office).

It is remarkable, then, that each tradition – Roman Catholic,

Free Church, and Anglican – has lost a significant element of the 'word' service developed by the early Church from their Hebrew inheritance. There are riches to be discovered! Recent musical publications present ministers and worship leaders with an opportunity to put the matter right. (See 'Finding the material you need', p. 266).

Spoken Psalms

As chanted and severely metrical psalms have dropped out of use, so concerned ministers and worship leaders have tried to compensate by 'saying' them with the congregation – either together or antiphonally. Many have been discouraged by the feeling that this 'doesn't work'. The main reason is that their source of psalms is either a set which has been punctuated ('pointed') for chanting – a style confusing to the uninitiated majority – or the text of a church Bible. Neither of these is designed for congregational use. For one thing, the Psalms in their full text are not all equally suitable for common worship. For another, they are devised to be read by one person as prose, and therefore do not have the rhythm about them which will keep a congregation together.

The way forward

In the section 'Spoken Prayer and Praise' (p. 362), a selection of liturgical, or 'Spoken', psalms will be found. By careful division into parts, these texts offer the more congregational psalms in lively and authentic form. This is the spirit in which they will have been used in Hebrew worship – and, indeed, in the synagogue worship of Jesus' day.

Another way forward is for ministers and worship leaders to discover which of the hymns and songs they currently use are already psalm versions, and to use them in conjunction with a reading of the psalm they depict. Alternatively, in liturgical churches, at least the psalm-based hymn or song can be used in the 'psalm slots' provided by the rubrics in the denominational prayer book.

Today there is a wealth of psalm material – paraphrases of the psalms designed for a whole variety of singing methods:

Taizé, Wild Goose, Jubilate, St Thomas More Centre, and various song-styles. An index follows immediately which will give the worship leader opportunity to select from over 600 hymns and songs for a suitable *Psalm position* in the 'word' part of the service. Most of the items listed correspond with a good section of the psalm in question. Those marked '*' are either more loosely based, or simply contain an important allusion to verses from the psalm. Where a liturgical (spoken) version follows, the psalm is marked †.

8

PSALMS INDEX TO HYMNS, SONGS AND PSALM VERSIONS

**indicates hymns which only allude to the Psalm, or are
less obviously based on the text
†indicates that a spoken or 'liturgical' version of the
psalm is available in this book*

A&M	*Hymns A&M New Standard Edition*[1]
BPW	*Baptist Praise and Worship*[2]
CFW	*Church Family Worship*[3]
CP	*Carol Praise*[4]
H&P	*(Methodist) Hymns and Psalms*[5]
HFP	*Hymns for the People*[6]
HTC	*Hymns for Today's Church*[7] ('s' indicates song supplement)
Iona	*Psalms of Patience, Protest and Praise*[8]
JP	*Junior Praise*[9]
LP	*Let's Praise! 1 and 2*[10]
MP	*Mission Praise* (combined edition: numbers for earlier editions are given in brackets)[11]
NEH	*New English Hymnal*[12]
O&N	*Hymns Old and New*[13]
PFT	*Psalms for Today*[14]
SF	*Songs of Fellowship*[15] (including hymns)
SFP	*Songs from the Psalms*[16]
WP	*World Praise*[17]
WSAM	*Worship Songs Ancient and Modern*[18]

Taizé psalm versions are now included in many English publications, including *Psalms for Today* and *Songs from the Psalms*. They are listed here within other publications which have congregational books.

R indicates that a responsorial psalm is available in *Responsorial Psalms*[19]

[1]*Hymns Ancient and Modern New Standard*, published 1983 by The Canterbury Press, Norwich.

[2]*Baptist Praise and Worship*, published 1991 by Oxford University Press, Oxford.

[3]*Church Family Worship*, published 1986 by Hodder & Stoughton Ltd, London.

[4]*Carol Praise*, published 1987 by HarperCollins*Publishers* Ltd, London.

[5]*Hymns and Psalms*, published 1983 by The Methodist Publishing House, London.

[6]*Hymns for the People,* published 1993 by HarperCollins*Publishers* Ltd, London.

[7]*Hymns for Today's Church*, published 1982 by Hodder & Stoughton Ltd, London.

[8]*Psalms of Patience, Protest and Praise*, published 1994 by Wild Goose Publications, Iona.

[9]*Junior Praise*, published 1986 by HarperCollins*Publishers* Ltd, London.

[10]*Let's Praise! 1 and 2,* published 1988, 1994 by HarperCollins*Publishers* Ltd, London.

[11]*Mission Praise,* published 1982, 1986, 1990 by HarperCollins*Publishers* Ltd, London.

[12]*New English Hymnal,* published 1989 by The Canterbury Press, Norwich.

[13]*Hymns Old and New*, published 1989 by Kevin Mayhew, Bury St Edmunds.

[14]*Psalms for Today*, published 1990 by Hodder & Stoughton Ltd, London.

[15]*Songs of Fellowship*, published 1991 by Kingsway's Thankyou Music, Eastbourne.

[16]*Songs from the Psalms*, published 1990 by Hodder & Stoughton Ltd, London.

[17]*World Praise*, published 1993, 1995 by HarperCollins*Publishers* Ltd, London.

[18]*Worship Songs Ancient and Modern*, published 1992 by The Canterbury Press, Norwich.

[19] *Responsorial Psalms*, published 1994 by HarperCollins*Publishers* Ltd, London.

Psalm 1 R

Blessed are they who listen not –
PFT 1c.

Bless-ed is the man – CFW 138.

Blessed is the man – SFP 1e.

God is with the righteous – SFP 1f.

Happy is the one – Iona 4.

If we love the word of God – PFT 1a,
SFP 1a.

The Law of God is life to choose –
PFT 1b.

When we walk with God, we are
blessed – SFP 1d.

Psalm 3 R

Christian soldiers, onward go* –
CFW 530, HTC 524.

How many are against me, Lord –
PFT 3a.

O Lord, how many are my foes –
SFP 3b.

Psalm 4

Answer me – LP 239.

O God, defender of the poor – PFT 4a.

O righteous Lord – LP 380, SFP 4b.

Psalm 5

Lord, as I wake I turn to you –
A&M 485, CFW 162, H&P 634,
HFP 174, HTC 267, NEH 236, PFT 5,
WP 46.

Psalm 6

Hear me, Lord, and draw near –
Iona 6.

O gracious Lord, be near me – PFT 6.

Psalm 7 R

I have no strength but yours – SFP 7b.

I will give thanks to the Lord most
high – PFT 7.

Psalm 8† R

Lord, how majestic is your name –
PFT 8a.

O Lord our Governor – PFT 8c.

O Lord, our Lord – Iona 8.

O Lord, our Lord, how majestic –

CP 217, LP 150, MP 508 (MP3 727),
SFP 8d.

Sovereign Lord, in all the earth –
SFP 8e.

With wonder, Lord, we see your
works – A&M 531, CFW 271,
H&P 353, PFT 8b.

Psalm 9 R

All hail the power of Jesus' name* –
A&M 140, BPW 29, H&P 252,
HFP 7, HTC 587, LP 2, MP 13
(MP1 51), NEH 332, O&N 13, SF 9.

I long to praise the Lord – WP73.

I praise you, Lord, with all my heart –
PFT 9, SFP 9.

Psalm 10 R

All heaven declares – LP 234, MP 14
(MP3 649), SF 10.

In my hour of grief or need – PFT 10.

Your Kingdom come* – BPW 644,
CFW 67, CP 355, HTC 334.

Psalm 11 R

Bright the vision that delighted –
A&M 96, BPW 71, H&P 445,
HTC 578, NEH 343, O&N 55.

I find my refuge in the Lord – PFT 11.

Psalm 12

God will arise because the weak –
PFT 12a.

The promises of God are pure –
PFT 12b.

Psalm 13

Forgotten for eternity – SFP 13b.

How long, O Lord – HFP 128, LP 304,
SFP 13c.

How long will you forget me, Lord? –
CFW 222, PFT 13a.

Psalm 14

God made me for himself to serve
him* – HTC 361.

The fool whose heart declares in pride
– PFT 14.

Psalm 15 R

Lord, who may dwell within your
house – PFT 15a.
Lord, who may venture where you
dwell – PFT 15b.

Psalm 16 R

I set the Lord before my eyes –
PFT 16a.
I will come and bow down – CP 130,
LP 85, SFP 16c.
In your presence is fulness of joy –
SFP 16b.
O Lord, you are the centre of my life –
LP 378.
You will show me the path of life –
SFP 16d.

Psalm 17 R

Be thou/O Lord my guardian and my
guide* – A&M 217, CFW 124,
HTC 374, NEH 64, O&N 45,
WSAM 9.
Lord of all my footsteps – PFT 17.
O Lord our guardian and our guide* –
CFW 124, HTC 374.

Psalm 18 R

How I love you (you are the one)* –
LP 69, MP 246 (MP2 398), SF 190.
I love you, Lord, my strength and rock
– PFT 18b.
I love you, O Lord, my rock – SFP 18c.
I love you, O Lord, you alone –
BPW 341, CFW 248, HFP 134,
HTC 475, LP 78, MP 286 (MP3 691),
PFT 18a.
Thee will I love – O Lord, my love –
HTC 485.
You are the one (How I love you)* –
LP 69, MP 246 (MP2 398), SF 190.

Psalm 19 R

Christ, whose glory fills the skies* –
A&M 4, CFW 134, H&P 457,
HFP 51, HTC 266, MP 79 (MP2 320),
O&N 71.
Everywhere the skies declare –
SFP 19d.

Glory and praise to God – H&P 581,
PFT 19b.
God's glory fills the heavens with
hymns – PFT 19c.
May our worship be acceptable –
LP 134, MP 461 (MP3 720), SFP 19f.
May the words of my mouth –
SFP 19e.
May the words of my mouth – Iona 11.
The heavens declare the glory (Silver)
– HTC 254, MP 648 (MP2 598).
The heavens declare thy glory, Lord –
A&M 168, H&P 481.
We look into your heavens and see –
PFT 19a.
You, Lord, have the message* –
LP 446.

Psalm 20 R

Bless the Lord, our father's God –
CFW 56, HTC 610.
May the Lord answer you – SFP 20b.
May the Lord God hear you pray –
PFT 20a.
May the Lord God hear your prayer –
LP 358, SFP 20c.
Some trust in chariots – SFP 20d.

Psalm 21

Unto the hills around – HTC 48.
With all your heart rejoice, and sing –
PFT 21.

Psalm 22 R

In the presence of your people –
CFW 334, LP 92, MP 341 (MP1 108),
SF 244, SFP 22b.
O Lord my God, O Lord my God –
HFP 223, LP 375, SFP 22c.
Why, God, have you forsaken me –
PFT 22a.

Psalm 23 R

Because the Lord is my shepherd –
HFP 27, LP 243.
Faithful Shepherd, feed me –
CFW 571, HTC 29, NEH 282,
O&N 106.
How bright these glorious spirits

shine* – A&M 306, HTC 572,
NEH 227.

In heavenly love abiding* – BPW 555,
H&P 678, HFP 141, HTC 458,
MP 331 (MP1 106), O&N 234,
SF 238.

My faithful shepherd is the Lord –
CFW 560.

My lips shall praise you – LP 361.

My shepherd is the Lord – Iona 12.

O Lord my shepherd, lead me in your
ways – PFT 23b.

The God of love my shepherd is –
A&M 110, H&P 43, NEH 77,
O&N 491.

The King of love my Shepherd is –
A&M 126, BPW 394, CFW 27,
H&P 69, HFP 274, HTC 44, Iona 241,
MP 649 (MP1 221), NEH 457, SF 533,
SFP 23d.

The Lord is my shepherd – PFT 23c.

The Lord is my shepherd – H&P 44,
Iona 244.

The Lord is my shepherd, he knows –
SFP 23e.

The Lord my shepherd rules my life –
A&M 426, BPW 395, CFW 137,
H&P 70, HFP 278/279,
HTC 45/591, LP 203, MP 660
(MP1 227), PFT 23a, SF 537, SFP 23a.

Psalm 24† R

Fling wide the gates – CFW 291,
CP 86, PFT 24b.

Fling wide your doors – LP 36,
SFP 24h.

Glory, glory, glory to the King – CP 98,
SFP 24i.

Lift up your heads, eternal gates –
PFT 24a.

Lift up your heads, O you gates –
CP 162, SF 337, SFP 24e.

Lift up your heads, you gates of brass
– H&P 227, HTC 509.

Lift up your heads, you mighty gates
– A&M 483, CP 163, H&P 240,
NEH 8.

The earth and its fullness – LP 413,
SFP 24g.

The earth is the Lord's – LP 128,
MP 642 (MP3 748), SF 528, SFP 24f.

The earth is the Lord's and all that is –
PFT 24c.

This earth belongs to God – CFW 584,
CP 312, HFP 290, LP 208, SFP 24d.

Psalm 25 R

A mighty fortress is our God* –
A&M 114, HFP 96, HTC 523, MP 2
(MP2 284), SF 25.

A safe stronghold our God is still* –
A&M 114, BPW 375, H&P 661,
HFP 96, HTC 523, MP 2 (MP2 284),
O&N 32, SF 25.

All my soul to God I raise – PFT 25a.

God is our fortress and our rock* –
A&M 114, HFP 96, HTC 523, MP 2
(MP2 284), SF 25.

I lift my soul to you – LP 309.

I lift my soul to you, O God – Iona 14.

Lord, in your mercy remember me –
WP 145.

Remember, remember your mercy –
HFP 246, LP 171, SFP 25d.

Show us your ways, O Lord –
H&P 133, SFP 25b.

Teach me your way (Undivided heart)
– LP 195, SFP 86b.

To you, O Lord, I lift up my soul –
SFP 25c.

Psalm 26 R

To lead a blameless life, O Lord –
PFT 26.

Psalm 27 R

As the deer pants for the water –
LP 240, MP 37 (MP2 303), SF 27,
SFP 42d.

Christ is the world's true light* –
A&M 346, BPW 618, H&P 456,
HTC 323, NEH 494.

God is my strong salvation – PFT 27a.

Safe in the hands of God who made
me – SFP 27b.

The Lord is my light – LP 414,
WP 148(76).

Psalm 28 R

O Lord, my rock, to you I cry – PFT 28.

Psalm 29 R

Bring your tributes to the Lord of hosts – SFP 29c.
Let all in heaven and earth unite – PFT 29a.
The God of heaven thunders – SFP 29b.

Psalm 30 R

I worship you, O Lord – PFT 30a.
You have changed my sadness – SFP 30b.

Psalm 31 R

How great is the goodness you have shown – SFP 31b.
I come to you for shelter, Lord – PFT 31a.
In you, O Lord, I found refuge – Iona 16.

Psalm 32 R

Happy is the one – LP 57, SFP 32b.
How glad are those with peace of mind – PFT 32a.

Psalm 33† R

All you that are righteous, shout – SFP 33b.
Bring songs of joy to God the Lord – PFT 33a.
Thanks to God whose word was spoken* – A&M 423, BPW 106, CFW 621, H&P 483, HTC 255.

Psalm 34 R

Holy, holy, holy, Lord – LP 66, SFP 34e.
I'll praise the Lord for ever and ever – PFT 34b, WSAM 38.
O magnify the Lord with me – LP 379.
O taste and see that the Lord is good – CFW 28, LP 381, SF 447, SFP 34c.
Praise to the Lord – SFP 34d.
Silver and gold – MP 598 (MP1 199), O&N 142.
Tell his praise in song and story – BPW 563, HTC 41, PFT 34a.
Through all the changing scenes – A&M 209, BPW 544, CFW 576, H&P 73, HFP 292, HTC 46, MP 702 (MP1 246), NEH 467, O&N 541.

Psalm 35 R

Psalm 36† R

Immortal, invisible – A&M 199, BPW 383, CFW 267, H&P 9, HFP 137, HTC 21, LP 88, MP 327 (MP1 103), NEH 377, O&N 227, SF 234.
No fear of God before the eyes – PFT 36.

Psalm 37 R

Commit your way to God the Lord – PFT 37a.
Delight yourself in the Lord – LP 268, MP 112 (MP2 337), SFP 37c, WP181.
The steadfast love of the Lord – CFW 373, Iona 250, MP 666 (MP1 229), O&N 517, SF 549, SFP 37b.

Psalm 38 R

Lord, will you turn from your anger – PFT 38.

Psalm 39 R

Silent, I have waited – PFT 39.

Psalm 40† R

I waited, I waited on the Lord – LP 313, SFP 40c.
I waited patiently for God – Iona 18.
I waited patiently for the Lord – SFP 40b.
Patiently waiting for you – WP 80.
Rejoice today with one accord* – HTC 347, NEH 444.
Take my life and let it be – A&M 249, BPW 358, CFW 151, H&P 705, HFP 266, HTC 554, LP 193, MP 624 (MP1 212), O&N 470, SF 519.
To the Lord I looked in patience – PFT 40a.

Psalm 42 R

Be thou my vision/Lord be my vision
– A&M 343, BPW 521, H&P 378,
HFP 175, HTC 545, MP 51 (MP1 17),
NEH 339, O&N 46, SF 42.
Just as a lost and thirsty deer –
HFP 163, Iona 22, SFP 42c.
Like the deer, athirst and questing –
PFT 42a.
Lord be my vision/Be thou my vision
– A&M 343, BPW 521, HFP 175,
HTC 545, MP 51 (MP1 17),
NEH 339, SF 42.
My soul longs for you – WP 22.
O put your trust in God the living God
– PFT 42b.
The deer longs – WP 147.
You holy angels bright* – BPW 23,
HFP 313, HTC 353.

Psalm 43 R

Bind us together, Lord – BPW 471,
CFW 119, HTC S4, Iona 17, LP 12,
MP 54 (MP1 21), O&N 47, SF 43.
O Father, send your light – SFP 43c.
O Light and Truth of God* – PFT 43a.
When my bitter foes surround –
PFT 43b.

Psalm 44

We have heard, O Lord our God –
LP 431, PFT 44, SFP 44.

Psalm 45 R

Let those with voices sing – PFT 45.

Psalm 46† R

Be still and know that I am God –
BPW 280, Iona 22, LP 245, MP 48
(MP1 16), O&N 42, SF 41,
SFP 46c/46e.
Blessed be the name of the Lord –
LP 248, O&N 49, SF 46.
Emmanuel, God is with us* – CP 79,
SFP 46d.
God is our strength and refuge –
BPW 308, CFW 77, CP 106, HFP 95,
HTC 527, LP 47, MP 188 (MP2 372),
PFT 46/46b.

Immortal Love, for ever full* –
A&M 133, BPW 198, H&P 392,
HTC 105, MP 328 (MP4 819),
NEH 378, O&N 228.
Jesus is our refuge – WP 28.

Psalm 47† R

Clap your hands all you nations –
Iona 24.
Clap your hands, all you people –
Iona 26, SFP 47c.
Clap your hands, clap your hands –
SFP 47e.
Clap your hands, clap your hands –
CP 55.
Clap your hands, you people, shout –
CP 56.
God is the King of all the earth –
PFT 47b.
Sing praises to our God, sing praises –
SFP 47d.
Take heart and praise our God –
CFW 78, CP 284, MP 623 (MP3 740),
PFT 47a.

Psalm 48

Bless the Lord . . . King of kings –
BPW 33, CFW 80, CP 36, LP 14,
MP 57 (MP1 26), SF 48.
City of God, Jerusalem – CFW 595,
HTC 187.
Great is the Lord, his praise is great –
CFW 488, PFT 48a.
How great is God almighty –
CFW 313, SFP 48b.

Psalm 49

O people, listen – hear God's wisdom
– PFT 49b.
What riches on this earth – PFT 49a.

Psalm 50 R

God speaks – the Lord of all the earth
– PFT 50b.
Let God, who called the worlds to be –
PFT 50a.
Let the giving of thanks – Iona 27.

Psalm 51 R

Create in me a pure heart – LP 267.
Create in us clean hearts – LP 266.
Give me a new heart, O God – LP 275.
God, be merciful to me – PFT 51a.
Have mercy, Lord, as you promise –
  SFP 51c.
Have mercy on me O God – PFT 51b.
Praise the Lord, you heavens, adore
  him – A&M 195, CFW 284, H&P 15,
  HFP 240, HTC 583, NEH 437,
  O&N 421.

Psalm 52 R

Why in the dawning of another day –
  PFT 52.

Psalm 53

I believe there is a God – LP 306.
Only the fool will say – PFT 53, SFP 53.

Psalm 54 R

I am not skilled to understand –
  H&P 221, HTC 432, MP 257
  (MP2 406).
Save me, O God, hear my prayer –
  PFT 54.
Still near me, O my Saviour, stand* –
  HTC 464.

Psalm 55

By your side – LP 252, SF 55.
O for the wings to fly afar – PFT 55.

Psalm 56 R

Be merciful to me, O God – PFT 56a.
In my day of fear – Iona 30.
When I'm afraid I will trust in God –
  SFP 56b.

Psalm 57 R

Be gracious to me, Lord – PFT 57a.
I will give thanks to you – SFP 57b.
O God of Jacob, by whose hand* –
  HTC 35.

Psalm 58

The Lord is King! lift up thy voice –
  A&M 107, BPW 322, CFW 290, H&P
  58, HFP 276, HTC 183, O&N 499.

Psalm 60

We are a land divided – PFT 60.

Psalm 61 R

From the earth wherever I may be –
  WP 129.
Hear my cry, O God – MP 227
  (MP2 392), O&N 188.
Hear my cry, O Lord – SFP 61c.
Listen to my prayer, Lord – BPW 556,
  HTC 365, PFT 61a, SFP 61a.
O God, hear me calling – PFT 61b.

Psalm 62 R

God has spoken – by his prophets* –
  BPW 100, H&P 64, HFP 94,
  HTC 248.
I rest in God alone – LP 79, MP 291
  (MP3 690), SFP 62c.
In silent stillness – WP 71.
My soul is at rest in God alone –
  PFT 62b.
O Lord, you are my confidence – WP
  33.
On God alone I wait silently – Iona 33.
Rest in God, our God most mighty –
  PFT 62a.

Psalm 63 R

Because your love is better than life –
  CFW 79, MP 53 (MP1 19), SFP 63d.
Glory to you, my God, this night –
  A&M 10, BPW 108, H&P 642,
  HTC 274, Iona 52, MP 176
  (MP2 366), NEH 244, O&N 147.
God is my great desire – PFT 63a.
I hunger and I thirst – H&P 730,
  HTC 409.
I seek you, Lord God, I yearn for you –
  SFP 63c.
O God, you are my God – PFT 63b.
O God, you are my God alone –
  Iona 34.
O Lord, I want to sing your praises –
  LP 373.
Thy loving-kindness is better –
  MP 706 (MP1 241), O&N 547.
Your loving-kindness is better than
  life – SFP 63e.

Psalm 65† R

God whose praise is sung in Zion –
PFT 65a.

The earth is yours, O God – CFW 514,
HTC 290, SFP 65c.

You are to be praised O God in Zion –
PFT 65b.

Psalm 66†

Praise our God with shouts of joy –
HFP 238, PFT 66a.

Shout with joy to God, all the earth –
SFP 66b.

Psalm 67† R

God of mercy, God of grace –
A&M 179, BPW 48, CFW 527,
HFP 97, HTC 293, NEH 366,
O&N 156, WSAM 32.

Kyrie eleison (Look around you)* –
LP 113.

Let God be gracious to us and bless us
– PFT 67c.

Let the people praise you, O God –
HFP 169, LP 339, SFP 67e.

Look around you (Kyrie eleison) –
LP 113.

May God be gracious, may we see his
face – PFT 67b.

May God be gracious to us – HTC 330.

May God be gracious to us and bless
us – SFP 67d.

Mercy, blessing, favour, grace –
PFT 67a.

The Son of God proclaim* – A&M 427,
BPW 455, H&P 627, HFP 280,
HTC 415, O&N 513.

Psalm 68

Come, bless the Lord – MP 88
(MP1 32), O&N 81, SF 68.

Let all the world in every corner sing*
– A&M 202, BPW 54, CFW 49,
H&P 10, HTC 342, MP 404
(MP1 135), NEH 394, O&N 283.

Let God arise – CFW 534, CP 159,
LP 127, MP 405 (MP2 467), SF 323.

Let God arise, and let his enemies –
SFP 68b.

Let God arise! his enemies be gone –
PFT 68a.

Thy Kingdom come, O God* –
A&M 177, CFW 67, H&P 783,
HTC 334, NEH 499, O&N 546.

Psalm 69 R

How firm a foundation* – BPW 380,
HFP 125, HTC 430, MP 243
(MP1 76), O&N 202.

Jesus, lover of my soul* – BPW 345,
H&P 528, HFP 154, HTC 438,
MP 372 (MP1 120), SF 297.

When my sorrows cover me – LP 436,
SFP 69b.

When the waters cover me – PFT 69a.

Psalm 70

Come quickly, Lord, to rescue me –
PFT 70, WSAM 16.

Psalm 71

From time beyond my memory –
PFT 71a, SFP 71a.

I will praise you with the harp –
SFP 71b.

Lord, be my vision* – HFP 175,
HTC 545, LP 114, MP 51 (MP1 17).

Our confidence is in the Lord – LP 387,
SF 452.

You are the Lord – LP 444.

Psalm 72

Jesus shall reign* – A&M 143,
BPW 313, CFW 415, H&P 239,
HFP 156, HTC 516, LP 97, MP 379
(MP1 123), NEH 388, O&N 266,
SF 301.

O God, with holy righteousness –
Iona 37.

The Lord will come and not be slow* –
A&M 29, H&P 245, NEH 15,
O&N 504.

To those who rule our land – PFT 72.

Psalm 73 R

Surely God the Lord is good – PFT 73.

Psalm 75

O God, we thank you that your name
– PFT 75.
Thank you, O Lord of earth and
heaven* – HTC 43.

Psalm 76 R

Silent the earth when God arose* –
PFT 76.

Psalm 77 R

Crown him with many crowns* –
A&M 147, BPW 37, CFW 198,
H&P 255, HFP 69, HTC 174, LP 36,
MP 109 (MP1 39), NEH 352,
O&N 97, SF 77.
I cried out for heaven to hear me –
PFT 77.

Psalm 78

Thy hand, O God, has guided* –
A&M 171, BPW 398, CFW 130,
H&P 784, HFP 315, HTC 536,
MP 705 (MP1 247), NEH 485,
O&N 545.
We will tell each generation –
PFT 78.

Psalm 80† R

Bless the Lord, the God of our fathers
– LP 15.
God of eternity, Lord of the ages* –
HTC 495.
God of hosts, you chose a vine –
PFT 80.
Great Shepherd of your people –
A&M 164, H&P 490, HTC 363.
Out of darkness let light shine –
HTC 447.

Psalm 81

Sing merrily to God – PFT 81.

Psalm 82 R

God is king – be warned, you mighty
– PFT 82.
O Lord, all the world belongs to you –
BPW 636, LP 148, O&N 368.
Who can sound the depths of sorrow –

HFP 312, LP 225, MP 766 (MP3 754),
SF 604.

Psalm 83

Before Jehovah's awesome/aweful
throne* – A&M 197, H&P 61,
HTC 15.
Do not keep silent, O God – Iona 40.

Psalm 84 R

As water to the thirsty – HFP 20,
HTC 470.
How lovely is your dwelling-place
(various versions) – LP 70, SFP 84d,
SFP 84e, PFT 84a, PFT 84c
O Lord, the mansions where you
dwell – PFT 84b.
One thing I ask, one thing I seek –
LP 385, SF 440.
Only one thing I ask – LP 384.
We love the place, O God* – A&M 160,
CFW 497, HFP 301, HTC 558,
MP 731 (MP2 618), NEH 471,
O&N 563.

Psalm 85 R

Grant to us your peace, Lord (Dona
nobis pacem) – LP 52, SFP 85b,
WSAM 2.
God of mercy, God of grace –
A&M 179, BPW 48, CFW 527,
HFP 97, HTC 293, NEH 366,
O&N 156, WSAM 32.
When this land knew – CFW 55,
PFT 85a.

Psalm 86

Hear me, O Lord, and respond to my
prayer – HFP 116, PFT 86a.

Psalm 87

For all your boundless gifts – PFT 87.

Psalm 88

O Lord, the God who saves me –
PFT 88.

Psalm 89 R

I will sing of the Lord for ever –

SFP 89b.

Timeless love! We sing the story –
CFW 372, H&P 60, HTC 47, MP 707
(MP1 250), PFT 89a.

When all your mercies, O my God –
A&M 109, BPW 361, CFW 383,
H&P 573, HFP 306, HTC 39, MP 751
(MP4 842), NEH 472, O&N 574.

Psalm 90 R

God everlasting, at your word* –
PFT 90b.

Lord, you have been our dwelling-
place – SFP 90d.

O God, our help in ages past –
A&M 99, CFW 50, H&P 358,
HFP 220, HTC 37, MP 498
(MP2 503), NEH 417, O&N 360,
SF 415.

O Lord, the refuge of each generation
– HFP 225, LP 377, SFP 90c.

Our God eternal, reigning – PFT 90a.

You have been a shelter, Lord –
LP 448.

Psalm 91 R

From fears and phantoms of the night
– HFP 251.

I will dwell in his secret place –
SFP 91b.

I will live within the shadow –
SFP 91c.

Safe in the shadow of the Lord –
CFW 395, HTC 445, MP 583
(MP2 549), PFT 91a, WSAM 68.

Whoever lives beside the Lord –
Iona 42, WP 162.

Psalm 92 R

How good it is to give thanks to you –
SFP 92c.

It is good to give thanks to the Lord –
SFP 92b.

It is good to give thanks to the Lord –
SFP 106b.

Make music to the Lord most high –
PFT 92a.

Sweet is the work, my God, my King –
H&P 514, HTC 377, MP 620

(MP2 568).

Psalm 93†

Clothed in kingly majesty – CFW 355,
CP 57, HFP 55, PFT 93a.

God is King! The Lord is reigning –
PFT 93b.

Rejoice, the Lord is King – A&M 139,
BPW 317, CFW 301, H&P 243,
HFP 245, HTC 180, MP 575
(MP1 195), NEH 443, O&N 432,
SF 482.

Sing we praise to God the King –
CFW 333.

Psalm 95† R

Come, let us praise the Lord –
BPW 119, LP 259, MP 92 (MP3 653),
SFP 95g.

Come, let us sing for joy – LP 24, SF 71,
SFP 95h.

Come, let us sing out with joy –
SFP 95d.

Come, let us sing to the Lord –
CFW 393.

Come, let us worship our Redeemer –
CP 68, MP 97 (MP3 654).

Come now with joyful – WP 21.

Come, sing praises to the Lord –
CFW 115, SFP 95f.

Come with all joy to sing to God –
CFW 205, HTC 16, PFT 95a.

Come, worship God who is worthy –
BPW 36, CFW 606, HTC 18,
PFT 95b.

Joy, joy, ring out your joy – SFP 95i.

Let us sing to the God of salvation –
BPW 15, CFW 186, HFP 172,
SFP 95e.

O come, let us sing out to the Lord –
PFT 95c.

O come, let us sing to the Lord –
CFW 493.

You are the rock of my salvation –
LP 445.

Psalm 96†

Joy to the world* – BPW 315,
CFW 664, CP 153, H&P 77, HFP 161,

HTC 197, LP 102, MP 393 (MP3 708),
O&N 273, SF 314.

O give thanks to the Lord, for his love
– LP 371.

O sing out to the Lord a new song –
SFP 96d.

O sing to the Lord a new song –
PFT 96b.

Sing a new song of glory and
salvation – PFT 96a.

Sing out to the Lord a new song –
SFP 96c.

Sing to the Lord with a song – LP 185,
SFP 96e.

This is the day that the Lord has
made* – BPW 21, CFW 201,
HTC 379.

This is the day the Lord hath made* –
A&M 22, H&P 577, NEH 257,
O&N 529.

Psalm 97† R

The everlasting Lord is King – PFT 97.

The Lord is King! lift up thy voice –
A&M 107, BPW 322, CFW 290,
H&P 58, HFP 276, HTC 183,
O&N 499.

Thee Lord reigns – LP 417, MP 659
(MP2 584), NEH 266, SFP 99b.

Psalm 98† R

Blow upon the trumpet – CP 37,
HFP 31, HTC 186.

Joy to the world* – BPW 315,
CFW 664, CP 153, H&P 77, HFP 161,
HTC 197, LP 102, MP 393 (MP3 708),
O&N 273, SF 314.

Lift up your hearts to the Lord –
CP 164, HTC 366, SFP 98d.

New songs of celebration render* –
A&M 498, H&P 491, HTC 343.

O sing to the Lord a new song –
PFT 98c.

Sing a new song to the Lord –
CFW 420, CP 271, H&P 57,
HTC 349, Iona 454, MP 599
(MP1 203), O&N 450, PFT 98b,
WSAM 73.

Sing to God new songs of worship –

CFW 249, HTC 352, LP 187, MP 600
(MP2 560), PFT 98a, SFP 98a.

Your hand, O God, has guided* –
A&M 171, BPW 398, CFW 130,
H&P 784, HFP 315, HTC 536, Iona
298, MP 705 (MP1 247).

Psalm 99†

God is King – the nations tremble –
PFT 99a.

He is exalted – WP 184.

Let us praise the Lord our God –
LP 342, WP 7.

Psalm 100 R

All people that on earth do dwell –
A&M 100, BPW 2, CFW 367, H&P 1,
HFP 9, HTC 14, Iona 4, LP 235,
MP 201 (MP1 6), NEH 334, O&N 16,
SF 13.

Before Jehovah's awesome/aweful
throne* – A&M 197, H&P 61,
HTC 15.

Come, rejoice before him (Jubilate
Deo) – LP 260, SFP 100h.

Come, rejoice before your maker –
BPW 35, CFW 96, HTC 17,
PFT 100a.

Come, rejoice in God – LP 261,
SFP 100i.

Give to our God immortal praise –
A&M 460, BPW 47, H&P 22,
HTC 31, MP 171 (MP2 363).

I will enter his gates with
thanksgiving – BPW 11, MP 307
(MP1 97), O&N 248, SF 268,
SFP 100e.

Jubilate (O shout to the Lord) – LP 154.

Jubilate Deo – BPW 13, O&N 274.

Jubilate, everybody – BPW 14, Iona
145, MP 394 (MP1 130), O&N 274,
SF 315, SFP 100g, WSAM 46.

O be glad in the Lord and rejoice –
CFW 443, SFP 100j.

O be joyful in the Lord – SFP 100n.

O shout to the Lord (Jubilate) – LP 154,
PFT 100c.

O shout to the Lord in triumph –
SFP 100f.

Shout for joy and sing – SFP 100k.

Shout for joy and sing, serve the Lord – LP 179.

Shout for joy, and sing your praises – LP 401.

Shout, shout joyfully – LP 180, SFP 100m.

Sing, all creation, sing to God – PFT 100b.

With joyful shouts acclaim the Lord – PFT 100d.

Psalm 101

With heart and hands washed clean – PFT 101.

Psalm 102

Father on high to whom we pray* – BPW 499, HTC 296.

Hear my prayer, O Lord – SFP 102b.

Lord Jesus, think of me – A&M 129, H&P 533, HTC 316, NEH 70, O&N 303.

You laid the foundations of earth – PFT 102a.

Psalm 103† R

Bless the Lord . . . he's healed – LP 247.

Bless the Lord, my soul – SFP 103d.

Bless the Lord, my soul – BPW 32.

He has shown you – LP 58, MP 215 (MP3 675).

O bless the Lord (O my soul) – SFP 103f, WSAM 59.

Praise my soul, the King of heaven – A&M 192, BPW 65, CFW 459, H&P 13, HFP 237, HTC 38, Iona 204, LP 163, MP 560 (MP1 187), NEH 436, O&N 418, SF 466, WP 208.

Praise the Lord and bless his name – PFT 103a.

Praise the Lord O my soul – PFT 103b.

Praise to the Lord, the Almighty – A&M 207, BPW 68, CFW 89, H&P 16, HFP 242, HTC 40, MP 564 (MP1 192), NEH 440, O&N 424, SF 470.

The Lord is full of compassion and mercy – PFT 103c.

Psalm 104† R

All things I see, Lord, call to me – PFT 104a.

Bless the Lord, O my soul – SFP 103e.

Bless the Lord, O my soul – SFP 103g.

Bless the Lord, O my soul – SFP 103h.

Bless the Lord, O my soul – SFP 104d.

I will sing out to the Lord as long – SFP 104e.

O bless the Lord, my soul – BPW 129, HTC 34.

O bless the Lord, my soul, I sing – PFT 104b.

O worship the King – A&M 101, BPW 63, CFW 351, H&P 28, HFP 230, HTC 24, LP 155, MP 528 (MP1 178), NEH 433, O&N 405, SF 456, WP 104.

The majesty of mountains – PFT 104c, SFP 104c.

Psalm 105† R

God be in my head* – A&M 236, BPW 592, H&P 694, HFP 91, HTC 543, NEH 328, O&N 149.

Holy, holy, holy, Lord God almighty – HTC 7.

Let the hearts of those who seek – SFP 105b.

Saviour, again to thy dear name* – A&M 15, CFW 553, H&P 643, HTC 281, MP 584 (MP4 833), NEH 250, O&N 441.

The Lord has led forth – CFW 121, LP 200, MP 654 (MP3 741), SF 535, SFP 105a.

Psalm 106

Alleluia! Love eternal – PFT 106a.

Psalm 107† R

Gabi, gabi (Praise the Father)* – LP 164.

Give God thanks for he is gracious – PFT 107.

Praise the Father (Gabi, gabi)* – LP 164.

Praise the Lord (Alabad) – WP 3.

Psalm 108 R

Come, O Fount of every blessing* –
H&P 517, HTC 337.
My heart is ready, O my God –
PFT 108a.
Through our God we shall do
valiantly* – CFW 540, CP 315,
LP 209, MP 703 (MP2 600), SF 558,
SFP 108b.

Psalm 110

This is the word of God's decree –
PFT 110.

Psalm 111 R

God's holy ways are just and true –
PFT 111A.
Hallelujah, praise the Lord – SFP 111b.

Psalm 112 R

How blessed are those who live by
faith – PFT 112.
They who stand in awe of God are
happy – HFP 288.

Psalm 113 R

From the rising of the sun – BPW 43,
CFW 139, Iona 49, MP 163 (MP1 54),
O&N 138, SF 121, SFP 113b.
God of God, the uncreated* – CP 105,
HTC 56.
Servants of the living Lord – PFT 113a.
Ye servants of God, your master
proclaim – A&M 149, H&P 278,
HFP 314, HTC 520, MP 784
(MP1 278), NEH 476, O&N 591,
SF 620.

Psalm 114 R

When Israel broke their cruel chains –
PFT 114.

Psalm 115 R

Father, let us dedicate* – CFW 73,
HTC 257.
Not to us be glory given – PFT 115.

Psalm 116† R

How can I repay the Lord – PFT 116b.

I love the Lord, he heard my voice –
PFT 116a.

Psalm 117†

By every nation, race and tongue* –
HTC 579, LP 19.
Every nation, praise the Lord –
CFW 97.
From all who live beneath the skies –
A&M 98, CFW 419, H&P 489,
HTC 580, SF 119.
Holy is God, holy and strong –
SFP 117c.
O praise the Lord God (Laudate
Dominum) – LP 153, NEH 426,
SFP 104f.
Praise him, you nations – PFT 117b.
Praise the Lord, all nations, praise –
PFT 117a.
Praise the Lord, all you nations –
WP 90.
Praise your Maker – Iona 44.

Psalm 118† R

God is the strength of my life (Show
us) – LP 48.
Let us gladly with one mind* –
BPW 56, CFW 280, HTC 23.
Open the gates of righteousness –
PFT 118a.
Show us your strength (God is the
strength) – LP 48.

Psalm 119 R

All your commandments, Father
almighty – SFP 119d.
Blessed are those whose way is
blameless – PFT 119c.
How can we sing with joy – BPW 86,
HFP 124, HTC 362.
Jesus, priceless treasure – H&P 259,
HTC 461.
Oft in danger, oft in woe* – A&M 210,
CFW 530, H&P 715, HTC 524,
MP 533 (MP2 524), NEH 434,
O&N 356.
Show me how much you love me,
Lord – LP 402, SFP 119f.
The will of God to mark my way –

CFW 607, HFP 277, PFT 119a.
With all my heart – LP 435, MP 772
(MP3 755), SF 610.
With all my heart I seek – PFT 119b.
Your word is a lamp – LP 232,
SFP 119e.

Psalm 121 R

I lift my eyes to the quiet hills –
BPW 595, MP 281 (MP2 416),
PFT 121b.
I lift up my eyes to the hills –
PFT 121d.
I look up to the mountains – LP 81,
SFP 121f.
I see the mountains far away –
PFT 121a.
I will lift up my eyes – SFP 121h.
I will lift up my eyes to the hills –
PFT 121c.
I'll lift my eyes to the hills – SFP 121g.
Lifting my eyes up to the hills –
Iona 46.
When I look towards the hills –
SFP 121e.

Psalm 122† R

From the sun's rising – HFP 86, LP 41,
MP 164 (MP3 666), SF 122.
I rejoiced to hear them say – PFT 122a.
I was glad when they said to me –
CFW 559, SFP 122c.
Jerusalem! How glad I was –
PFT 122b.
Let us go to the house of the Lord –
LP 340, SF 331, SFP 122d.
What joy to hear the pilgrims say –
SFP 122e.

Psalm 123

Holy Lord, have mercy on us all –
SFP 123c.
I lift my eyes to you – PFT 123a.
Master, we lift our eyes, expecting –
PFT 123b.

Psalm 124†

If the Lord had not been near –
PFT 124a.

If the Lord had not been on our side –
SFP 124b.

Psalm 125

God the Father of creation – BPW 376,
CFW 277, HTC 427.
Those who rely on the Lord – PFT 125.

Psalm 126† R

Laughter and song – PFT 126a.
Sound on the trumpet – CP 280,
SFP 126d.
When God delivered Israel – SFP 126c.
When the Lord, he turned again –
SFP 126e.
When the Lord turned again the
fortunes – PFT 126b.

Psalm 127 R

Glorious things of thee/you are
spoken – A&M 172, BPW 480,
CFW 183, H&P 817, HTC 494,
MP 173 (MP1 59), NEH 362,
O&N 143, SF 127.
If God is building when we build –
PFT 127a.
Unless the Lord builds the house –
LP 426.
Unless the Lord constructs the house –
SFP 127c.
Unless the Lord has built the house –
PFT 127b.
Yours be the glory* – BPW 260,
CFW 263, HFP 316, HTC 167, Iona
299, LP 233, MP 689 (MP1 238).

Psalm 128†

Bless all who trust in God – PFT 128b.
Blessed are those who fear the Lord –
PFT 128a.
I should be getting to know you –
LP 311.
O blessed are those who fear the Lord
– SFP 128c.

Psalm 130 R

From deep despair to you I call –
HFP 81, SFP 130d.
From the very depths I cry – SFP 130e.

I call to you (My soul waits) – LP 75,
SFP 130f.

O Lord, hear my prayer – SFP 130g.

O Lord, hear my prayer – BPW 600,
LP 149, SF 423.

Out of our failure to create – PFT 130a.

Out of the depths I cry – PFT 130c.

Out of the direst depths – Iona 48.

Up from the depths I cry to God –
PFT 130b.

Psalm 131 R

Before the Lord my soul is bowed –
PFT 131a.

For you the pride from my heart –
Iona 50.

God has spoken to his people* –
CFW 611, CP 103, HTC 13, LP 53,
MP 182 (MP2 367), SF 131.

Lord, this thing I ask you – PFT 131b.

The pride from my heart – Iona 50.

Psalm 132

As David took no rest until – PFT 132.

God is good – CFW 377, Iona 55,
LP 49, MP 185 (MP2 370), SF 132.

Psalm 133 R

Behold how pleasant it shall be –
PFT 133b.

How good a thing it is – CFW 116,
HTC 497, PFT 133a.

Jesus Christ, sovereign King – LP 326.

Lord, we come in your name – LP 351.

Men and women, let us walk – LP 359,
WP 70.

Oh isn't it good – LP 146.

Spirit of God most high – CFW 480,
HFP 264, HTC 242.

Psalm 134†

Bless the Lord as day departs –
HTC 608, PFT 134a.

Come bless the Lord all you servants –
PFT 134c.

Come bless the Lord, all you servants
– SFP 134d.

Come, praise the Lord – PFT 134b.

Come, praise the Lord – CFW 486,
HTC 609, O&N 90.

You servants of God, your master
proclaim* – A&M 149, BPW 76,
HFP 314, HTC 520, MP 784
(MP1 278), SF 620.

You servants of the Lord – CP 353,
HTC 598.

Psalm 135 R

Bless the Lord, creation sings –
CFW 163, HTC 604.

God is working his purpose out –
H&P 769, HTC 191, Iona 57, MP 189
(MP2 373), NEH 495, O&N 154,
SF 135.

Psalm 136†

Give thanks to God, for he is good –
SFP 136b.

Give thanks to God, the Lord of all –
PFT 136a.

Give to our God immortal praise –
A&M 460, BPW 47, H&P 22,
HTC 31, MP 171 (MP2 363).

Let us with a gladsome mind –
A&M 204, CFW 280, H&P 27,
HTC 23, Iona 154, MP 415
(MP2 471), NEH 397, O&N 288,
SF 333.

O give thanks to the Lord for he is
good – SFP 136c.

Psalm 137

Babylon, by the rivers of sorrow –
SFP 137c.

Beside the streams of Babylon –
Iona 52.

By flowing waters of Babylon –
SFP 137b.

By rivers of sorrow we sat – PFT 137a.

By the Babylonian rivers – WP 14.

By the waters – WP 15.

God of glory – CFW 337, CP 104,
LP 51, MP 191 (MP2 376), SF 137.

Psalm 138

All the kings of the earth – WP 140.

God of grace, I turn my face – LP 278,
SF 138.

I will praise you Lord with all my
heart – SFP 138b.
I'll praise you, Lord – PFT 138a.

Psalm 139 R

Lord all-knowing – CFW 394,
PFT 139b.
O Lord, my God, you know all my
ways – LP 376, WSAM 61.
O Lord, you know my mind –
SFP 139c.
Search me, O God – Iona 212, LP 396,
MP 587 (MP1 200), O&N 442,
SFP 139e.
There is no moment of my life –
BPW 133, CFW 164, H&P 428,
HFP 286, PFT 139a.
You are before me, Lord – LP 440,
SFP 139d.

Psalm 140 R

Psalm 141

My prayers rise like incense – WP 107.
O Lord, come quickly when I call –
PFT 141.

Psalm 142 R

When I lift up my voice – LP 434,
SFP 142b.
You are my refuge – PFT 142a,
SFP 142a.

Psalm 143†

Father of mercies, in your word –
A&M 167, BPW 99, CFW 601,
HTC 247.
Hear me, O Lord, in my distress –
PFT 143a.
How good is the God we adore –
BPW 338, CFW 84, HFP 126, HTC
450, MP 244 (MP1 77), O&N 203.
I offer up my song – LP 310.
Jesus, the joy of loving hearts* –
BPW 439, H&P 258, HFP 158,
HTC 413, MP 383 (MP1 128),
O&N 269.
My Lord, I did not choose you* –
HFP 202, HTC 107.

O Lord, I bring myself to you –
SFP 143b.

Psalm 144

O Lord my love, my strength, my
tower – HTC 485.
Rejoice, O land, in God your Lord* –
A&M 296, HTC 331, NEH 493,
O&N 431.
We exalt you, mighty Lord – WP 141.

Psalm 145 R

All creatures of our God and King –
A&M 105, BPW 28, CFW 283,
H&P 329, HFP 5, HTC 13, MP 7
(MP2 287), NEH 263, O&N 5.
Great is the Lord, and most worthy –
LP 280, MP 199 (MP3 671), SF 145,
SFP 48c.
I will exalt you O God my king –
PFT 145b.
King of glory, King of peace* –
A&M 194, BPW 53, CFW 157,
H&P 499, HFP 165, HTC 603,
MP 397 (MP2 462), NEH 391,
O&N 278.
Nothing can trouble – LP 364.
To God our great salvation – PFT 145a.
We come to praise you, Father –
SFP 145d.

Psalm 146 R

Great is the Lord and mighty in power
– SF 146, SFP 147c.
I'll praise my maker while I've breath*
– BPW 127, H&P 439, HTC 20,
MP 320 (MP2 427).
Praise the God of our salvation –
PFT 146.

Psalm 147† R

Fill your hearts with joy and gladness
– BPW 40, CFW 513, HFP 77,
HTC 30, Iona 339, MP 147
(MP2 353), O&N 122, PFT 147a.
How good it is to sing – SFP 147d.
Magnificat (Come, glorify)* – LP 356.
O let the Church rejoice* – CFW 467,
PFT 147b.

Sing to God with joy – Iona 54.
The Lord is building Jerusalem* –
SFP 147e.

Psalm 148† R

All things that are – PFT 148c.
Bless the Lord, created things –
HFP 28.
Easter song (By every nation, race)* –
HTC 579, LP 19.
Glory to God above – Iona 57.
O bless the Lord, the God of salvation
– LP 368.
O praise ye the Lord, praise him –
A&M 203, CFW 490, HFP 257,
HTC 354, MP 518 (MP2 519),
NEH 427, O&N 389, SF 445.
Praise God from whom (revised)* –
HTC 585.
Praise God from whom (traditional)*
– BPW 113, CFW 345, HFP 235,
HTC 586, Iona 199, MP 557
(MP1 185), O&N 416, SF 462,
WSAM 20.
Praise him, praise him, praise him –
H&P 506, HFP 236, HTC 25, Iona
202, PFT 148b.
Praise the Lord . . . from the heavens –
LP 162.
Praise the Lord, dark and light –
SFP 148e.
Praise the Lord of heaven – H&P 507,
HFP 239, PFT 148a, SFP 148f.
Praise the Lord our God – CFW 515,
HTC S31, SFP 148g.
Praise the Lord, praise the Lord –
SFP 148d.
Praise the Lord, you heavens – HTC
583.
Praise to the Lord, sing alleluia –
LP 165.
Sing praise to the Lord – BPW 70,
CFW 490, HFP 257, HTC 354,

LP 184, MP 518 (MP2 519).

Psalm 149 R

Bring to the Lord a glad song –
BPW 30, CFW 54, HFP 37, HTC 336,
LP 17, PFT 149a, SFP 149a.
Give praise to the Lord – WP 123.
Sing a new song, alleluia – CFW 535,
SFP 149b.
Sing of the Lord's goodness –
HFP 256, LP 183, WSAM 77.

Psalm 150

Give praise to the Lord – WP 123.
Hail to the Lord's anointed* –
A&M 142, BPW 142, CP 113,
H&P 125, HFP 107, HTC 190,
MP 204 (MP1 64), NEH 55,
O&N 179, SF 150.
Let everything that has breath –
PFT 150b.
Let us praise the Lord – WP 125.
New songs of celebration render* –
A&M 498, H&P 491, HTC 343.
O praise God in his sanctuary –
PFT 150c.
O praise ye the Lord, praise him –
HTC 354.
Praise God within his holy place –
SFP 150d.
Praise him in his sanctuary – SFP 150e.
Praise him on the trumpet – CFW 468,
Iona 200, LP 161, MP 558 (MP2 539),
SF 464, SFP 150g.
Praise the Lord, his glories show –
H&P 14, HTC 345.
Praise the Lord, sing him a new song –
SFP 150f, PFT 150a.
Praise the Lord with joyful cry –
H&P 508.
Sing praise to the Lord – HTC 354.

9

DEALING WITH COPYRIGHT

Musical freedom under the law

MONEY OUT OF WORSHIP?

Some Christians feel that since worship is a gift of God, songs and hymns – vehicles of worship – should not be claimed by anyone as a personal possession. Hence there should be no copyrights and certainly no royalties to pay. However, this argument could apply to all who give their skills and time to the Church – no pay for ministers, directors of music etc. (Some may already have this problem!) Jesus says the worker is worthy of his hire (Luke 10.7) and should be allowed to benefit by what he produces. Paul agrees, while at the same time saying that he prefers not to be a burden to a church which he is visiting and serving (2 Corinthians 11.9; 2 Thessalonians 3.8).

Many writers and composers I know keep this healthy balance by dedicating a good proportion of the income they receive from royalties either to general church work, or towards future creative projects which in their turn will benefit the church as a whole. We must allow creative artists the freedom of choice as to where to channel the money their work generates. We may not make the decision for them – either by arguing that they should not benefit, or by reproducing their work without proper compensation.

Whatever our feelings might be, as the law in the United Kingdom stands no copyright work may be copied without the permission of the copyright holder or their agent, or reproduced visually (photocopied, for instance) without the agreement of the publisher who owns the copyright inherent in typography or music setting.

Christians must honour the law. The problem is how to be correct and yet to retain flexibility in exploring new music.

A SERVICE TO YOUR CHURCH

In the early 1980s, major copyright holders – some of them artists, some agents on behalf of copyright holders, most publishers – got together to see if there were practical ways forward to help the churches reproduce copyright songs and hymns without massive complications of research, and chronic disparities in payments. Out of this was born the Christian Music Association (CMA). Following the United Kingdom development, the Americans took the same route - but went further. Christian Copyright Licensing (CCL) came into being in the United States. The American churches do not favour words copies of hymn books - since their publishing markets, and therefore print-runs are so large, music or melody editions proliferate. Hence, CCL was licensing printed music reproduction right from the start, whereas we are only now seeing the beginnings of music licensing.

More recently it was perceived that a single transatlantic body could represent with greater efficiency English language songs and hymns. CMA stepped aside, and the English Christian Music Publishers Association authorised CCL to act on their behalf. The Christian Music Publishers Association (CMPA) is the body representing publishers and major copyright holders which acts on their behalf in relating to CCL and in educating the churches both as to their responsibility, and as to how to obtain permissions easily.

DON'T BE AFRAID

Churches need not be afraid of getting in touch with CCL. They are not a police force, and are very keen to be perceived as friendly and understanding. So if you have been reproducing songs and hymns illegally, do not be timid! CCL will not prosecute (though some secular publishers might well do so if the American experience is anything to go by). CCL charges for their licence are in proportion to a church's average congregation. Licences are also available for copyright hymn and worship song use in schools.

At the time of writing, only the reproduction of words is covered by a CCL licence, though many of the participating publishers and copyright owners hope that shortly a 'bolt-on' licence might become available for those who wish to reproduce music from books. Reproducing music from 'octavos' – single sheet songs or anthem settings could never be covered by this sort of blanket licence scheme. If you want to reproduce out-of-stock anthems or, say, one item only of a communion setting, then get in touch with the publisher. You may well be allowed to do this for a small fee.

TYPES OF COPYRIGHT

Copyright in the United Kingdom subsists in works of authors who are living or who died less than seventy years ago – prior to 1st July 1995 it was fifty years. Copyright is secured simply by the communication of a work (or an idea) to someone else. If you are an author or composer there is no need to register your copyright, apart from a safe procedure of posting the item to a friend so that, at a later date you can establish when and by whom it was written (see 'Writing for Worship', p. 108). In the United States the situation is somewhat more complicated: material has to be registered with the Library of Congress and the copyrights can be re-entered in successive years (hence the multiple dates on some hymns and songs emanating from the United States).

As regards copyright in the print setting, some publishers are very co-operative about allowing churches to reproduce their typography without the complications of charge or enquiry. Others are less happy, particularly about the reproduction of music, though publishers who are getting revenue through CCL anyway for the use of words material would not seek to inhibit the churches from using it.

PRACTICAL TIPS

It is important – especially for the encouragement of up-and-coming composers and writers – that use of songs and hymns is properly reported to the licensing authority (CCL). Sometimes it is very difficult at the end of a reporting period to remember what the church has used if you have not kept a proper record. One way of doing this easily is to place a box or tray by the photocopier, asking that everyone who reproduces any copyright item would put one copy of what they have done in the receptacle.

Another way to help those who do the copying is to have 'Able' labels (or similar) produced with the CCL membership and membership number clearly declared. Again, the labels can be placed near the copier for sticking on to the original prior to reproduction.

Don't just tick the listed songs on the reporting sheets. Add others you have used or their writers will not be paid. Do not be afraid of reporting to CCL songs of which the copyright is uncertain – this will be helpful to the owner.

Special licences are available for major events such as conferences, pop festivals etc. These need to be negotiated directly with CCL.

DO YOU EVER RECORD EVENTS, OR CHARGE FOR ADMISSION?

Many churches tape-record services, either as souvenirs for those who come or as compensation for those who have been unable to attend – not least the housebound. The Mechanical Copyright Protection Society (MCPS), of whom most writers and composers are members, will issue relatively inexpensive licences to churches (called 'Miscellaneous Licences'). This saves the enormous hassle of writing down every item on their form and applying for separate permission. Churches who hold a Christian Copyright Licence may soon be able to obtain the necessary permissions through CCL. [At the time of writing, negotiations are in progress, so your first recourse might be to CCL rather than MCPS.]

Copyright holders are legally entitled to performance royalties when hymns and songs are used – but the common policy is that this right is waived in the area of worship services. However, if you intend to *charge* for a concert or recital that is a different matter. Permission must be obtained and royalties paid, usually through the Performing Rights Society (PRS). A way for a church to satisfy this requirement if the use is simply of songs and hymns, is not to charge for entrance but to cost into a printed programme royalty payments for songs and hymns reproduced there, which will reach the copyright owner through the normal reporting system under the licence. Again, it is likely that during the lifetime of this book, CCL will be licensed to collect performance royalties on behalf of PRS. So CCL membership will become the 'one-stop' source of assistance for churches wishing to reproduce words and music, to record worship, and to stage concerts etc.

EXCEPTIONS TO THE RULE

It would not be proper to conclude this chapter without mentioning that there are still some publishers and copyright holders who are not members of a licence scheme. This is a decreasing number, but they are equally entitled to compensation. Your choice is either not to use their material in print, or else to get in touch with them independently to obtain permission. In fact, very few publishers of Christian songs and hymns are not covered by the licence you get - CCL will supply a list of member publishers. It is the secular publishers who may have just one or two items of interest to the church, who do not feel the need to co-operate, and whose charges can be high.

Information about the Christian Copyright Licence may be obtained from CCL at 26 Gildredge Road, Eastbourne, East Sussex BN21 4SA (01323 417711; Fax 01323 417722).

Permission for tape recording may be obtained from the Mechanical Copyright Protection Society (MCPS) at Elgar House, 41 Streatham High Road, London SW16 1ER. (0181 769 4400; Fax 0181 769 8792) - or soon from CCL if your church is a member.

Enquiries about performance royalties (free permission granted for worship services where no formal admission charge is made) should be addressed to The Performing Rights Society (PRS) at 29/33 Berners Street, London W1P 4AA (0171 580 5544; Fax 0171 631 4138).

Major Copyright holders and Agencies for Hymns and Songs
Please note: many song copyrights change hands frequently

A & C Black	Howard Road, Eaton Socon, Huntingdon, Cambridgeshire PE19 3EZ
A.P. Watt Ltd	20 John Street, London WC1N 2DR. (0171 405 6774, Fax: 0171 831 2154)
American Catholic Press	16160 S Seton Drive, South Holland, Illinois 60473, USA
Anfield Music Ltd.	201 Monument Road, Edgbaston, Birmingham B16 8UU (0121 454 4671)
Banks Music Publications	The Old Forge, Sand Hulton, York YO4 1LB
Baptist Union of GB and Ireland	4 Southampton Row, London WC1
Bible Society	Stonehill Green, Westlea, Swindon SN5 7DG, Wiltshire. (01793 418100, Fax: 01793 418118)
Birdwing Music	c/o CopyCare Ltd, P.O. Box 77, Hailsham, East Sussex BN27 3EF (01323 840942, Fax: 01323 849355)
Blandford Music	Cassell (Publishers) Plc, Villiers House, 41-47 Strand, London WC2N 5JE (0171 839 4900, Fax: 0171 839 1804)
BMG Music	BMG Music, Bedford House, 69-74 Fulham High Street, London SW6 3JW (0171 973 0011, Fax: 0171 973 0337)
Bob Kilpatrick Music	c/o CopyCare Ltd., P.O. Box 77, Hailsham, East Sussex BN27 3EF (01323 840942, Fax: 01323 849355)
Boosey & Hawkes	Boosey & Hawkes, The Hyde, Edgware Road, London NW9 6JN (0181 205 3861, Fax: 0181 205 8530)
Bourne Music	Bourne Music, Standbrook House, 2/5 Old Bond Street, London W1X 3TB (0171 493 6412, Fax: 0171 493 6583)
Breitkopf und Härtel	Buch- und Musikverlag, Walkmuhlstrasse 52, Postf. 1707, 6200, Wiesbaden 1, Germany (0049 0611 49030)
Calamus	30 North Terrace, Mildenhall, Suffolk IP28 7AB (01638 716579, Fax: 01638 716579)
Cambridge University Press	The Edinburgh Building, Shaftesbury Road, Cambridge CB2 9RU (01223 312393, Fax: 01223 315052)
Canterbury Press Ltd.	St Mary's Works, St Mary's Plain, Norwich, Norfolk NR3 3BH (01603 616563, Fax: 01603 624483)
Cassell Plc	Villiers House, 41/47 Strand, London WC2N 5JE (0171 839 4900, Fax: 0171 839 1804)

Central Board of Finance	Central Board of Finance, Church House, Great Smith Street, London SW1P 3NZ (0171 222 9011, Fax: 0171 799 2714)
CFC	Christian Fellowship of Columbia, 4600 Christian Fellowship Road, Columbia, Missouri 65203, USA
Chatto & Windus Ltd.	20 Vauxhall Bridge Road, London SW1V 2SA (0171 973 9740)
Cherry Lane Music Co. Inc.	c/o CopyCare Ltd, P.O. Box 77, Hailsham, East Sussex BN27 3EF (01323 840942, Fax: 01323 849355)
Christian Conference of Asia	96, 2nd District, Pak Tin Village, Mei Tin Road, Shatin, N.T. Hong Kong (001 852 691 1068, Fax: 852 692 3805)
Christian Copyright Licensing Ltd.	26 Gildredge Road, Eastbourne, East Sussex BN21 4SA (01323 417711, Fax: 01323 417722)
Christian Music Ministries	c/o Sovereign Lifestyle Music, P.O. Box 356, Leighton Buzzard, Bedfordshire LU7 8WP (01525 385578, Fax: 01525 372743)
Church Hymnal Corporation	The Church Hymnal Corporation, 800 Second Avenue (at 42nd St), New York, NY 10017, USA
Church Pastoral Aid Society	Athena Drive, Tachbrook Park, Warwick CV34 6NG, (01926 334242, Fax: 01926 337613)
Cliff College Publishing	Calver, Sheffield S30 1XG (011246 582321, Fax: 011246 583739)
Collins	HarperCollins, 77-85 Fulham Palace Road, Hammersmith, London W6 8JB (0181 741 7070, Fax: 0181 307 4064)
CopyCare	CopyCare Ltd, P.O. Box 77, Hailsham, East Sussex BN27 3EF (01323 840942, Fax: 01323 849355)
Coronation Music Publishing	c/o Kingsway's Thankyou Music, P.O. Box 75, Eastbourne, East Sussex BN23 6NW (01323 410930, Fax: 01323 411970)
CRC Publications	2850 Kalamazoo Avenue S.E, Grand Rapids, Michigan 49560, USA (001 616 246 0797)
David Higham Associates	5-8 Lower John Street, Golden Square, London W1R 3PE (0171 437 7888, Fax: 0171 437 1072)
Daybreak Music Ltd.	4 Regency Mews, Silverdale Road, Eastbourne, East Sussex BN20 7AB (01323 643341)
Eaton Music	c/o BMG Music, Bedford House, 69–74 Fulham High Street, London SW6 3JW (0171 973 0011, Fax: 0171 973 0337)

Elkin Music Services	William Elkin Music Services, Station Road Industrial Estate, Salhouse, Norwich, NR13 6NY (01603 721302, Fax: 01603 721801)
EMI Music	EMI Music UK, 127 Charing Cross Road, London WC2H 0EA (0171 434 2131, Fax: 0171 734 1568)
Faber Music Ltd.	3 Queen Square, London WC1N 3AU (0171 278 7436, Fax: 0171 278 3817)
Forlaget Filadelfia	Dagenhuset, 105 36 Stockholm, Sweden,
Franciscan Communications	1229 South Santee Street, Los Angeles, California 90015, USA (001 213 746 2916, Fax: 213 747 9126)
Galliard	Stainer & Bell Ltd., P.O. Box 110, Victoria House, 23 Gruneisen Road, London N3 1DZ (0181 343 3303, Fax: 0181 343 3024)
GIA Publications	GIA Publications Inc, 7404 S. Mason Avenue, Chicago, Illinois 60638, USA (001 708 496 3800, Fax: 708 496 2130)
HarperCollins	77-85 Fulham Palace Road, Hammersmith, London W6 8JB (0181 741 7070, Fax: 0181 307 4064)
High-Fye Music	c/o Campbell Connelly, 8-9 Frith Street, London W1V 5TZ (0171 434 0066, Fax: 0171 287 6329)
Hinshaw Music	PO Box 470, Chappell Hill, North Carolina 27514, USA
Hodder & Stoughton	Hodder Headline, 338 Euston Road, London NW1 3BH (0171 873 6000, Fax: 0171 873 6024)
Hope Publishing Company	Carol Stream, Illinois 60188, USA (001 708 665 3200, Fax: 001 708 665 2552)
Hymns Ancient and Modern	St Mary's Works, St Mary's Plain, Norwich, Norfolk NR3 3BH (01603 616563, Fax: 01603 624483)
Integrity Music	Integrity Music, c/o Kingsway's Thankyou Music, PO Box 75, Eastbourne, East Sussex BN23 6NW. (0323 410930, Fax: 01323 411970)
International Music Publications	Woodford Trading Estate, Southend Road, Woodford Green, Essex IG8 8HN (0181 551 6131, Fax: 0181 551 3919)
Iona	The Iona Community, (Wild Goose Publications), Pearce Institute, 840 Govan Road, Glasgow G51 3UU (041 445 4561, Fax: 0141 445 4295)
Josef Weinberger	Josef Weinberger, 12/14 Mortimer Street, London W1N 7RD (0171 580 2827, Fax: 0171 436 9616)
Jubilate Hymns Ltd.	61 Chessel Avenue, Southampton, SO19 4DY

	(01703 630038, Fax: 01703 232057)
Kevin Mayhew Ltd.	Rattlesden, Bury St. Edmunds, Suffolk IP30 0SZ
	(01449 737978)
Kingsway's Thankyou Music	Kingsway's Thankyou Music, PO Box 75, Eastbourne, East Sussex BN23 6NW
	(01323 410930, Fax: 01323 411970)
Leosong Copyright Service	Suite 8, Westmead House, 123 Westmead Road, Sutton, Surrey SM1 4JH
	(0181 770 7177, Fax: 0181 770 9272)
Little Misty Music	Little Misty Music, P.O. Box 8, Perth PH2 7EX, Scotland
Make Way Music	P.O. Box 263, Croydon, Surrey CR9 5AP
	(0181 741 8686, Fax: 0181 741 8644)
Maranatha Music	c/o CopyCare Ltd., P.O. Box 77, Hailsham, East Sussex BN27 3EF.
	(01323 840942, Fax: 01323 849355)
Marshall Pickering	c/o HarperCollins, 77-85 Fulham Palace Road, Hammersmith, London W6 8JB
	(0181 741 7070, Fax: 0181 307 4064)
MCA Music Ltd.	Unit 9, Elsinore House, 77 Fulham Palace Road, Hammersmith, London W6 8JA
	(0181 741 8686, Fax: 0181 741 8644)
McCrimmon Publishing	McCrimmon Publishing, 10-12 High Street, Great Wakering, Essex SS3 0EQ
	(01702 218956)
National Christian Education Council	1020 Bristol Road, Selly Oak, Birmingham, B29 6LB
	(0121 472 4242, Fax: 0121 472 7575)
New Song Ministries	RRI, Box 454, Evin, Tennessee 37061, USA
Novello and Co.	Novello and Co., 8/9 Frith Street, London W1V 5TZ
	(0171 434 0066, Fax: 0171 287 6329)
Oregon Catholic Press	5536 N.E. Hassalo, Portland, Oregon 97213, USA
	(001 503 281 1191, Fax: 001 503 282 3486)
Overseas Missionary Fellowship	Belmont, The Vine, Sevenoaks, Kent TN13 3TZ
	(01732 450747)
Oxford University Press [London]	3 Park Road, London NW1 6XN
	(0171 724 7484, Fax: 0171 723 5033)
Oxford University Press [Oxford]	Walton Street, Oxford OX2 6DP
	(01865 56767)
Polygram Music	Bond House, 347-454 Chiswick High Road, Chiswick, London W4 4HS
	(0181 742 5600, Fax: 0181 742 5607)
Religious and Moral Education Press	Hennock Road, Exeter EX2 8RP

Restoration Music	P.O. Box 356, Leighton Buzzard, Bedfordshire LU7 8WP
	(01525 385578, Fax: 01525 372743)
Royal School of Church Music	Addington Palace, Croydon, Surrey CR9 5AD
	(0181 654 7676)
Rt Rev Timothy Dudley-Smith	9 Ashlands, Ford, Salisbury, Wiltshire SP4 6DY
	(01722 326417)
Salvationist Publishing & Supplies	117/121 Judd Street, King's Cross, London WC1H 9NN
	(0171 387 1656, Fax: 0171 383 3420)
Scripture Gift Mission	Radstock House, 3 Eccleston Street, London SW1W 9LZ
Scripture Union	130 City Road, London EC1V 2NJ,
	(0171 782 0013)
Sea Dream Music	236 Sebert Road, Forest Gate, London E7 0NP
	(0181 534 8500)
Search Press	Wellwood, North Farm Road, Tunbridge Wells, Kent TN2 3DR
Serious Music UK	11 Junction Road, Oldfield Park, Bath BA2 3NQ
	(01225 483223, Fax: 01225 483201)
Sovereign Lifestyle Music	P.O. Box 356, Leighton Buzzard, Bedfordshire LU7 8WP
	(01525 385578, Fax: 01525 372743)
St Thomas More Group	30 North Terrace, Mildenhall, Suffolk IP28 7AB
	(01638 716579, Fax: 01638 716579)
Stainer & Bell	Stainer & Bell Ltd, P.O. Box 110, Victoria House, 23 Gruneisen Road, London N3 1DZ
	(0181 444 9135, Fax: 0181 343 3024)
Stanmore Music	c/o Mgt Brace Copyright Bureau, Suite 8, Westmead House, 123 Westmead Road, Sutton, Surrey SM1 4JH
Tempo Music Publications	3773 West 95th Street, Leawood, KS 66206, USA
	(001 913 381 5088)
Thankyou Music	Kingsway's Thankyou Music, P.O. Box 75, Eastbourne, East Sussex BN23 6NW
	(0323 410930, Fax: 01323 411970)
The Dohnavur Fellowship	The Dohnavur Fellowship, 15 Elm Drive, North Harrow, Middlesex HA2 7BS
	(0181 427 2189)
The Worship Service	c/o CopyCare Ltd., P.O. Box 77, Hailsham, East Sussex BN27 3EF
	(01323 840942, Fax: 01323 849355)
TKO Publishing	Copyright Permissions, Roland Rogers, 79 Sherbrooke Road, London SW6 7QL
	(0171 736 5520)
United Reformed Church	86 Tavistock Place, London WC1H 9RX

	(0171 837 7661, Fax: 0171 833 9262)
Wild Goose Productions	The Iona Community, Community House, Pearce Institute, 840 Govan Road, Glasgow G51 3UU
	(0141 445 4561, Fax: 0141 445 4295)
William Elkin Music Services	Station Road Industrial Est., Salhouse, Norwich NR13 6NY
	(01603 721302, Fax: 01603 721801)
Word Music (UK)	c/o CopyCare Ltd, P.O.Box 77, Hailsham, East Sussex BN27 3EF
	(01323 840942, Fax: 01323 849355)
Word of God Music	c/o CopyCare Ltd., P.O. Box 77, Hailsham, East Sussex BN27 3EF
	(01323 840942, Fax: 01323 849355)

10

WRITING FOR WORSHIP

Some guidance on hymn and song writing

'HYMN'OR 'SONG'? WHAT'S THE DIFFERENCE?

We can make some general distinctions between 'hymns', and 'songs'which helps us when talking about writing them. Hymns develop a logical theme; songs can be adoration alone. Hymns are acceptable if they have a careful structure; songs are of a more spontaneous (disposable?) nature and appeal even if there are obvious faults. To confuse us all, some of the current 'song'material is more hymn-like. For instance, I would think most of us who enjoy both hymns and songs would use 'The Servant King' or 'Praise you, Lord' in a hymn slot.

Generally hymns are 'stand-alone', long term, teaching aids as well as worship items, and need considerable care in construction if they are to gain acceptance. Songs are more spontaneous expressions of worship and do not necessarily need such care in construction.

WHAT MAKES A GREAT HYMN?

Some hymns last, others fade away. Some texts come out of obscurity and suddenly find a tune.[1] What makes a great hymn?

---

[1]'Let all the world in every corner sing', written by George Herbert (1593–1632) acquired its celebrated tune 'Luckington' three centuries later – composed by Basil Harwood (1859–1949).

Let's take the hymn by Francis Pott (1832-1909) in its unrevised form, popular for a generation and still in wide use:

Angel voices ever singing
round thy throne of light –
angel harps for ever ringing
rest not day or night:
thousands only live to bless thee
and confess thee, Lord of might.

Thou who art beyond the farthest
mortal eye can scan,
can it be that thou regardest
songs of sinful man?
Can we know that thou art near us
and will hear us? Yes, we can!

What can we learn?
1. See how the words match the beat beautifully all the way through – the 'declamation' is right.
2. The effect is sensational. The 'crunch' comes in the last line: 'Lord of might', 'Yes, we can!' Weak last lines can kill a hymn; especially the last line of all. Strong last lines make them. A striking first line is the next most important feature.
3. The rhymes are good: 'Light, night, might' and 'scan, man, can'. Note that verse 2 has half rhymes in the other lines: 'farthest, regardest'. This carries on in later verses. Half rhymes are both acceptable and effective if carefully handled. It is totally wrong rhymes that kill.
4. Internal rhymes add bite and class to the construction: '. . . bless thee, and confess thee . . .', '. . . near us, and will hear us . . . ' Fascinating and convincing, but very hard work to master.
5. The movement is good. Each verse is an obvious sequence – it goes somewhere – with a convincing climax. Not just a jumble of ideas which are good in themselves but have no obvious connection, let alone satisfying logical sequence.

6. The hymn breathes conviction.

What makes a good song?

Now for a song. What makes this one by Martyn Nystrom[2] so successful?

> As the deer pants for the water
> so my soul longs after you;
> you alone are my heart's desire,
> and I long to worship you.
> > You alone are my strength, my shield,
> > to you alone may my spirit yield;
> > you alone are my heart's desire
> > and I long to worship you.

Why is this so popular?
1. Because of the tune. This is more important with songs because they are not normally written in a conventional metre, so the tune has to gain acceptance, not just the words.
2. Because it says what worshippers need to say to God.
3. Because it's a psalm and has Scriptural resonances so that people will find natural uses for it.
4. Because it flows in thought as well as melody: 'I yearn for you, Lord; I love you, Lord – and only you, so I want to give myself to you.'
5. Because it is visual. We can see the deer gasping for water; and feel it ourselves.

HOW TO BEGIN WRITING

Study the greats

The best way of starting to write hymns is to study the greats; the Watts and the Wesleys, for instance. How do they do it? How do they achieve their effect. Analyse them for effective rhymes, punchy last lines, clever picture language, faithful-

[2]First verse quoted here by kind permission of the copyright holders, Restoration Music/Sovereign Music UK.

ness to the Bible, consistency of theme, logical progression, careful attention to emphasis . . . and so on.

Get your idea first

It may be that using a psalm or other Bible text will provide a perfectly adequate structure. Try to write for a need, and certainly pray about it. At all costs avoid a conglomeration of unconnected pious thoughts. With hymns especially, the logic needs to flow.

Use the best source material

If you look through a modern Bible version you will almost certainly find some passages set in poetic form; loose-ended lines that correspond with the thought pattern of the poetry. Here is where to start hymn or song writing. Supremely, the Psalms do make a wonderful start: and how our contemporaries need to rediscover the Psalms! So we are doing people a real service if we use them as a basis for our work. Many hymn writers have 'Christianised' the Psalms; made them a basis for a Christ-centred statement of worship. We should feel free to use the Psalms in this way. Indeed, the New Testament writers do it; so what better example do we need?

Settle on a good first line

'Love is his word, love is his way' (Luke Connaughton)
'We have a gospel to proclaim' (Eddie Burns)
'A purple robe, a crown of thorn' (Timothy Dudley-Smith)

Often, the first line can make or break a hymn. The best first lines are unusual, striking, confident, and (once again) say what the worshipper wants to say. They need to speak the spirit of the hymn or song – to say where it's going.

Work towards a punchy last line

'. . . most of all, that love has found us, thanks be to God' (Fred Pratt Green)
'. . . and stand complete at last' (Charles Wesley)

Study other people's last lines – where they are effective and provide a satisfying completeness to the whole. Especially study the last lines of popular contemporary hymns – this will best tell you what works today. Avoid 'inverted' lines at all costs – unless that is the pattern of every last line, in each verse. The last *word* itself is often extremely important. A weak or inconclusive finish can wreck the spirit of worship!

Decide if it is to be a song or a hymn

The margins of these two species overlap but, as we have suggested earlier, a hymn is both a worship and a teaching vehicle; it needs a logical flow. In order to last it will also need a tighter syntax, a consistent metre and, in most cases, a rhyming structure. Songs may have within them expressions which will date, since most songs are 'disposable' and so linked in metre to their tune that the words die when the tune becomes unfashionable – or deserted for newer songs.

Choose a useful metre/tune

Match the metre/tune to your theme. A 'severe' metre can mar a delicate expression of, say, penitence or faith. A frivolous metre cannot serve a grand subject, though much of this will vary as current culture changes. If you are writing a hymn, at all costs avoid overworked melodies – especially when the metre is poorly represented by other viable tunes; a hymn book editor can only include 'Woodlands' to two texts at most. And one of them is going to be 'Tell out, my soul'!

Write down the alphabet

Write down the alphabet vertically on the right edge of a piece of paper. This is the easiest, quickest, and best alternative to using a rhyming dictionary. You can run your eye down the column trying (in your mind) vowels against the consonants you see, and consonants against the vowels you see. Murmuring the results to yourself may jog your memory as to a possible rhyme. (See the alphabet printed opposite.)

Sing your words

Sing your words to the tune you intend to use, and see if the tune makes you emphasise the right things. And do the

RHYMING
Using a vertical alphabet

Rhyming dictionaries are a blessing to the would-be hymn or song writer—especially in early days. Eventually you find you can just look at a word, and *you* know that finding a rhyme is hopeless! If you are like me, you frequently lose or forget your rhyming dictionary. An alternative—often quicker—way is to write down an alphabet vertically on a spare sheet of paper. I find that using right hand margin is best for me (as far, right). First, read each key letter down the column, and say it with the ending you need, making single syllable words. Then do it again for words which have a syllable prefix to the key letter as in 'delight' (right); then again for words which have a single letter before the key letter, as in 'bright' (right). Finally, try for 'half' rhymes. Make sure no-one is listening, because it will sound daft! (Please note: the table below, left is by way of illustration; not all the possible words are listed.)

	a		a
	b	right	b
in	c	ite	c
	d		d
	e		e
	f	light	f
	g		g
	h	eight	h
	i		i
	j		j
	k		k
de	l	ight, plight etc	l
	m	ight	m
u	n	ite	n
	o		o
s	p	ite	p
re	q	uite	q
b	r	ight, right etc	r
	s	ight	s
	t	ight	t
	u		u
in	v	ite	v
	w		w
e	x	ite	x
	y		y
	z		z

syllables fit? Or do you have to gabble a line in some verses, where you have sung it without rush in another. Has the tune got the right feel for the words? Is the metre firm enough, or flexible enough?

Check for the 'Cringe' factor!

It's all too easy to write words that sound funny when you see what they *could* mean. And it's easy to write 'clichés'; phrases that everybody uses too often – or to take bits of other people's songs and make them your own. (See the examples given in the Check List below.)

Be honest about rhymes and metre

Have you turned sentences on their head just to get a rhyme – or do the rhymes come naturally, as they should? Are the rhymes in the right line – in each verse; do the verses match in this respect? Are they real rhymes (or matching half rhymes)? Does your writing really 'scan'; and do the word breaks come in the same place in each verse?

Use the Check List

The Check List that follows has illustrations of the above pitfalls, and many others, waiting to trap the unwary lyricist. Go through it with your songs and hymns – be much more strict about your hymn texts if you want them to last, as well as to be acceptable to a hymn publisher:

Check List

*Make sure you eliminate from your song/hymn these
unhealthy features!*

1. Unplanned inversions:

Up with which I will not put

But inversions can be effective if
intended – and especially if
matched in the same place in each
verse.

2. Forced rhymes:

*So let us pray
and sing alway.*

3. Untrue rhymes:

*Remember always to be kind
whatever you may do
to animals or humankind*
and they'll be kind to you.*

*'unkind' is not a true rhyme for
'kind'

4. Unmatched half rhymes:

i. *I sometimes feel
my songs are cool.*
(Half rhyme – well, a quarter!)

ii. *When work is poor
I just write more.* (Full rhyme)

iii. *My tunes are best –
I do not jest.* (Full rhyme)

iv. *My words are worst
when done in haste.* (Half
rhyme)

5. Faulty rhyming scheme:

*This verse is rhyming A, A, B –
it's satisfying – you'll agree!
And what a good last line!*

*The second's rhyming A, B, A –
and though while on its own it's fine
it just won't match this way.*

6. Ambiguous rhymes:

*To heaven and to glory
the church is moving now;
marching rank on rank,
progressing row by row.*

**7. Faulty 'scansion' (count the
number of syllables in matching
lines):**

*At school I never learned to count
and now when writing get confused –
the words look just the right amount,
but I can't think
how many syllables I've used.*
(Sing to 'New every morning')

**8. Bad 'declamation' (wrong
syllables emphasised):**

*My count of syllables is right (8)
a work of art is this my song; (8)
the concept's really rather bright – (8)
Emphases however are wrong. (8)*
(Sing to 'New every morning')

9. Weak final lines:

*Praise, praise all praises be –
glory, glory, majesty:
sing, sing, my grateful heart
worshipping in every part.*
('The groans that other songs
can't produce!')

10. Unmatched division of lines:

Number one * here is divided,
number two * is just the same,
four lines in * I was misguided,
split it lat * er – I'm to blame . . .
(Sing to 'Hark a thrilling voice is
sounding')

11. Over-used (*every part*, above, is one) or 'borrowed' expressions:

A thousand tongues, amazing grace!
abide with me, sing songs of praise
for forty days and forty nights –
who cares? They have no copyrights.

It's very easy to mimic currently
popular songs, or to remember
phrases from hymns and steal
them for your own work. This is
offensive to many, and not
something that Christians can do
honourably.

12. Unplanned repetition of words or ideas:

Fill my joyful lips with praise,
let me overflow with joy

As against planned repetition:

Fill my longing heart with joy;
joyful let my praises be . . .

13. Inconsequential logic/convenient rhymes:

To you I will always sing
because you are a king.

14. Archaisms (bold italic):

*I will **magnify**, magnify*
***thy** blessed laws*
*among**st** your people.*

Some writers rely on archaism to
make any impression at all! It is
salutary to read the *Book of
Mormon*, which is impressive only
in its archaic language – 'Yea, and
verily etc.'; if you updated it, the
whole edifice would collapse.

15. Mixed persons:

Yes, he is wonderful,
he is my all:
I will praise you.

The Psalmists actually do this and
get away with it! It's worth a try
at imitating them – but don't
move from 'third person' to
'second person' without being
conscious of the confusion you
are causing; it has to be done very
well!

16. Visual subtleties:

Come, see and taste! The shepherd
will guide his wayward sheep.

Clever lines like this may look
right in print, but they sing
differently!

17. Inconsequential sense patterns:

I am lost in sin, so I praise you . . .

18. Nonsense:

Bridal glory round her shed
(From 'Blessed city, heavenly
Salem')

It wasn't nonsense when it was
written. It's just that language has
changed. But to create nonsense
for the sake of a rhyme, or filling
the tune, is irresponsible.

19. Exclusive Language:

Lord, you came for love of men . . .

You, as a writer – or even women you know – may not be troubled by 'exclusive language'. But there are other considerations:

(a) The words 'men' and 'man' are perceptibly changing their meaning (see above example) and we have to think what we are communicating; and, indeed, how long we hope our writing will last!

(b) There are enough people who feel excluded by such phrasing for us not only to take their objections seriously, but also to apply the biblical principles of concern for the sensitive so clearly set out in Romans and 1 Corinthians.

(c) American hymn- (as against song-) book editors will by and large refuse to publish material which is 'exclusive' in this sense. And, as the American church is so march larger than the church in the United Kingdom it is wise for us to listen to their needs if we are wanting the widest use of our created material. In this regard, it may help you to think of inclusive language as a matter of *translation* from English idiom into American English idiom.

20. Hilarities:

Usually not spotted until someone else reads it. Try sending your work to someone who can draw!

21. 'Cringe' factor:

One man's meat is another man's poison: be careful how you import cultures.

Repeats like

Hallelu, lu, lu, lu . . .

appear to many worshippers, to be not only banal but irreverent.

Once, when I was teaching hymn-writing, someone gave me the example:

I'm on the pil-, pil-, pilgrim way . . . !

22. 'Pi':

I really want to magnify your bless-ed name.

Avoid a religious super-piety; try not to use language which is only understood by an inner circle of Christians – the élite! Always be aware of the visitor. Our responsibility is to declare the mystery of the gospel, not to create it! (1 Corinthians 14.23 f).

23. (Badly) mixed metaphor:

Example:

You are my rock sweeter than honey

Yes, visual imagery *is* important, but try to avoid mixing metaphors. Don't thereby cut out all the 'picture' and 'object' interest.

24. Syntax errors:

Poetry should not be an excuse for bad grammar or sentence construction. To check on your hymn or song, read it as prose – or even type it out in prose format if you are not sure. Always punctuate hymns and songs as if they were normal sentences.

25. Morbidity:

There are too few songs about Jesus' sacrifice on the cross but, in recent song/hymn drafts that I have seen, agonised description has swamped theological meaning. It also is very easy unintentionally to bring poetry about death and suffering to the edge of humour.

Leave it to simmer!

Leave your work in a drawer overnight before anyone else has seen it. Sometimes in the morning you will never believe what you wrote the night before! Don't be discouraged; it happens to everybody.

Send it to a friend

Next, send the result to someone whose work you admire. (Also, communicating it to someone else will establish your copyright.) If it's a hymn, send it to a friendly musician as well as to a writer, to see if it works with an established tune. Get them to be absolutely honest with you. Send it also to an *American* friend if you want to gain universal currency for your English, and therefore need to avoid mistakes in idiom. Incidentally, if you do prepare material for the United States, and have a computer, it is sometimes possible to obtain American student versions of word-processing software including American spell-checker and grammar, cheaper than you can buy the American spell-checker alone as a separate item.

Don't force it on your church/fellowship

When you get your work back, make improvements as best you can. Now live with it for a while; to see if you are really satisfied. Your local church will *want* to like it – for your sake. Remember they are prejudiced in your favour, and may find it difficult to be honest! So don't force it on them until (a) someone who can be objective has approved it, and (b) there is a good reason apart from their acquaintance with you for using it in a particular service.

Send it to publishers

You will not lose your copyright by doing this; and there is absolutely no harm in sending individual songs to every publisher at once! On the other hand . . . publishers of Christian songs and hymns have so many submissions of this kind that you may not hear from them. There are other ways:

- Telephone the publisher, say you write songs/hymns, and ask what sort of item they are looking for at the moment. They may have in mind, say, a youth book, or a carol book and may well be able to give you some guidance on the most acceptable material.
- Watch out for competitions. Television and radio companies run these from time to time. They often have a very indifferent entry, and you may well score by sending in your material. Certainly a large number of items featuring in competition programmes have become popular. Be careful, however, of any publisher's competition where you are required to agree that they buy your copyright if you are successful. Many a good hymn/song writer now regrets selling copyrights.
- Try sending material to *Deo* or any similar magazine – or even to denominational newspapers.
- Try the United States! Send to a publisher like Hope Publishing Company (hymns, anthems, settings for choirs, handbells) or Integrity or Word (USA) for songs.[3] Certainly with hymns that you intend for the United States you must avoid 'exclusive' language: speaking of people as 'men'. This now applies to the United Kingdom too. And avoid overmuch concentration on God as 'he'; they are sensitive to this, whereas we are not. As far as songs are concerned you need not worry half as much about language. However, with songs you

[3]See list of copyright holders' addresses on pp. 102–107.

need to send the music; hymns are probably best sent as text only, because USA music taste is different – especially their music arrangements. Also, only send one thing at a time – your best; because a committee will be looking at material from all quarters and will just not be able to cope with a pack of English hymns/songs.

Don't give up your copyright

Whatever happens, don't give up your copyright unless you have to. For one thing, if your work does become popular, the publisher who has bought the copyright will be the major beneficiary, not you – or whatever charitable object you decide to give your royalties to. For another, your work may get buried. Let me explain.

Publishers/agents have been known to buy in copyrights and then refuse to let book editors have them under a 'pro rata' royalty agreement. A 'pro rata' agreement is where the publisher of a book contracts to pay the owner (or agent) of a copyright an agreed fraction of the selling price of (or net receipts from) the book. For instance, if a book *'Glory Praise'* has 100 items and sells for £10, the agreement might be for '10% pro rata'. 10% of the projected income on the book is then available for the copyright owners (or agents) – £1 per book. Since there are 100 items, however, this £1 per book must be divided by 100 – 1p per item, per book. Such is a 'pro rata' agreement. If, however, the publisher or agent to whom you have sold your copyright demands a fixed sum larger than this 1p (or a higher percentage than makes economic sense), the publisher of *Glory Praise* has a decision to make. Either the *Glory Praise* publisher will pay up, and find the money somewhere else, or your item will be left out of the book. In practice, book publishers will pay over the odds only for items which they cannot afford to be without, and these are nearly always songs/hymns that are already established as popular favourites, so your new song/hymn doesn't stand a chance. Then, when the busy owner of your precious work finds that it is not selling, he/she will forget all about it – so it is that works get buried.

The best way forward is to use an agent on a fixed period basis of, say, five years. If the arrangement is a disaster you can always retrieve it when the five year period is up. Such agents (who may also be publishers in their own right – but equally may not) will charge anything between 15% and 75% fee on royalties received for you. Some will allow you to make separate direct arrangements with other publishers, most will not. Some will want world rights, others will not include the United States. If they want to include the United States, make sure they are efficient in that market. Write for the list of publishers and agents held by the Christian Music Publishers Association which now represents publishers as different as Thankyou Music and Oxford University Press.

Finally, don't give up when your work is heavily criticised or rejected! There are classic stories of rejection by publishers of works which eventually became best-sellers. For instance, various publishers turned down the original *Youth Praise*[4] in the 1960s. It was eventually rescued by the Church Pastoral Aid Society and became an absolute bestseller and a mould-breaker, the true parent in the United Kingdom of all the current song books. As an editor, I remember criticising far too heavily Garth Hewitt's early work – we remain good friends, but he never lets me forget it! Similarly, my own *Dramatised Bible*[5] was turned down by the first publishers I went to both in the United Kingdom and in the United States, but now seems to be flourishing in both places and more – for which I am truly grateful. Again, hymns I wrote for English books were never published here, but have since appeared in the United States, where the market is far bigger. So don't ever lose heart!

[4] *Youth Praise*, published 1964 by The Church Pastoral Aid Society, London.
[5] *The Dramatised Bible*, published 1989 by HarperCollins*Publishers* Ltd, London.

Establishing Copyright – Question and Answer

Q. I haven't got a clue about claiming my copyright . . . how do I register it? Is putting a date on it with my name enough? Also, although the song was completed a year ago I've actually been sharing it around for a while since then. Would copyright be from then, or from completion?

A. In this country, at least, copyright is established when a signed work is communicated to another person – the point of this is that if there were any dispute later as to who had origi-nated a successful item there would at least be a witness in the contention. The true date of origination would of course be needed, so ultimate proof of ownership would be afforded if the item were sent through the post in a sealed envelope – then the postmark would verify the date.

My guess is that few successful writers actually bother to do more than let a friend see the text and music in the normal course of getting a second opinion. No self-respecting publisher would want to print a falsely claimed song anyway. So, advice: send your work to an able writer/musician to get their comment. Then you will have the double benefit of establishing copyright and getting advice. Ask your correspondent to keep a copy filed away.

As to which date the copyright stems from: theoretically each version of the song has its own date. In practice, though, once the song is more or less right and ready to communicate that is the date you will want to put on it.

The copyright will then belong to your estate for seventy years after your death. Incidentally, any royalties you receive are taxable – even if you give them away to a charity! The only way to avoid tax is to give away the copyright itself to the charity.

11

BIBLE INDEX TO HYMNS, SONGS AND PSALMS

Genesis

Genesis 1

All things bright and beautiful
Give to our God immortal praise
God, that madest earth and heaven
God who made the earth
Let us with a gladsome mind
Morning has broken
Songs of praise the angels sang
Thanks to God whose word was spoken
1 All-creating heavenly Giver
1 At the name of Jesus
1 Before the ending of the day
1 Before the heaven and earth
1 Come, praise the Lord
1 Creation creed (The Lord is a mighty)
1 Creator of the earth and skies
1 Eternal Father, strong to save
1 God/Thou, whose almighty word
1 I believe in God the Father
1 I bind myself to God today
1 My God, how wonderful you are
1 My Lord of light who made the worlds
1 O God, our help in ages past
1 Out of darkness let light shine
1 Send out the gospel! Let it sound
1 Shout for joy, loud and long
1 The Lord is a mighty King
1 Thou/God, whose almighty word
1 We believe in God Almighty
2 Christ on whom the Spirit rested
2 Come to us, creative Spirit
2 Creator Spirit, come, inspire

2 O Holy Spirit, come to bless
2 Send out the gospel! Let it sound
2 Spirit divine, attend/inspire our prayers
2 Spirit of God, rest on your people
3 First of the week and finest day
3 God of light and life's creation
3 God/Thou, whose almighty word
3 He who created light
3 I'll praise my maker while I've breath
3 Lights to the world (The earth was dark)
3 Morning has broken
3 Ring out the bells (Past three a clock)
3 Songs of praise the angels sang
3 Spirit divine, attend/inspire our prayers
3 The earth was dark
3 The Son of God proclaim
3 This is the day of light
3 Thou/God, whose almighty word
5 Morning has broken
6 Now praise the protector of heaven
9 O worship the King
12 We plough the fields, and scatter
14 All hail the power of Jesus' name
14 Give to our God immortal praise
14 O Christ of all the ages, come
14 Out of darkness let light shine
26 Creation creed (The Lord is a mighty)
26 Lord God, your love has called us here

26 O Lord of every shining
    constellation
26 Spirit of God within me
26 The Lord is a mighty King
26 The Lord made man, the Scriptures
    tell
28 Shout for joy, loud and long
31 All things bright and beautiful
31 Angel voices ever singing

Genesis 2
    Remember, Lord, the world you
    made
2 Love divine, all loves excelling
3 This is the day, this is the day
4 I believe in God the Father
4 Morning has broken
7 Breathe on me, breath of God
7 O Breath of Life, come sweeping
   through
7 O worship the King
8 Name of all majesty
8 The Lord made man, the Scriptures
   tell
24 Eternal Father, Lord of life
24 Great God, we praise the mighty
    love
24 Happy the home that welcomes
    you
24 Jesus, Lord, we pray
24 Jesus the Lord

Genesis 3
    All hail the power of Jesus' name
    Come sing the praise of Jesus
    Praise to the Holiest in the height
    Spirit of God within me
    The Lord made man, the Scriptures
    tell
    Welcome, happy morning
15 Jesus, the name high over all
15 Join all the glorious names
15 You choirs of new Jerusalem
16 Joy to the world
17 Creation creed (The Lord is a
    mighty)
17 The Lord is a mighty King
17 These were the words
19 In Christ shall all be made alive
19 Jesus, your blood and
    righteousness
19 O worship the King
19 Spirit of God within me
19 The Lord is King! lift up thy voice
23 Had he not loved us

23 Lift high the cross, the love of
    Christ
24 Had he not loved us

Genesis 4
8 Christ is the world's Light, he and
   none other
10 Can we/man by searching find out
    God
21 Angel voices ever singing
21 Come to us, creative Spirit
21 God is here! As we his people
21 Lord, speak to me that I may speak

Genesis 5
1 Lord God, your love has called us
   here
1 O Lord of every shining
   constellation
1 Spirit of God within me
1 The Lord made man, the Scriptures
   tell
22 Forth in thy/your name, O Lord, I
    go
22 Immortal Love, for ever full
22 Like a mighty river flowing
22 Oh for a closer walk with God

Genesis 6
9 Forth in thy/your name, O Lord, I
   go
9 Immortal Love, for ever full
9 Oh for a closer walk with God

Genesis 7
    Lord of our life

Genesis 8
8 Oh for a closer walk with God
22 Great is your faithfulness
22 Lord of the changing year

Genesis 9
6 Lord God, your love has called us
   here
6 Spirit of God within me
6 The Lord made man, the Scriptures
   tell
12 O love that wilt not let me go
16 O love that wilt not let me go

Genesis 11
1 All my hope on God is founded
1 Creator of the earth and skies

Genesis 12
8 Jehovah Jireh

Genesis 14
8 In the streets of every city
18 Before the eternal King and Priest
22 He is lovely

Genesis 15
1 Lord, be thy word my rule
1 Lord, make your word my rule
1 On Jordan's bank, the Baptist's cry
1 Timeless love! We sing the story
5 These were the words

Genesis 16
13 Awake, my soul, and with the sun

Genesis 18
25 Great God, what do I see and hear
25 The Lord is King! lift up thy voice
27 Lord, teach us how to pray aright

Genesis 22
8 Jesus, Lamb of God and source of life
8 New every morning is the love
8 See, amid the winter's snow
8 Today, if you hear his voice
16 The God of Abraham praise

Genesis 24
42 The God of Abraham praise
45 Like a mighty river flowing

Genesis 26
24 The God of Abraham praise

Genesis 28
12 O happy band of pilgrims
13 God of Abraham, lead us
20 O God of Jacob, by whose hand

Genesis 29
35 Now praise the protector of heaven
35 Praise the Lord, his glories show
35 Praise the Lord, you heavens, adore him
35 To God be the glory

Genesis 31
13 O God of Jacob, by whose hand
42 The God of Abraham praise
53 The God of Abraham praise

Genesis 32
30 Author of life divine
30 Here, O my Lord, I see thee face to face
30 It is a thing most wonderful
30 Jerusalem on high
36 O love that wilt not let me go

Genesis 35
19 O little town of Bethlehem

Genesis 37
9 Praise, my soul, the King of heaven

Genesis 39
3 Praise to the Lord, the Almighty

Genesis 49
9 You choirs of new Jerusalem

Exodus

Exodus 2
23 Tell his praise in song and story
23 Through all the changing scenes

Exodus 3
5 Be still, for the presence of the Lord
5 In your arms of love
5 Jesus, where'er thy people meet
5 Lord Jesus, when your people meet
5 The Lord made man, the Scriptures tell
6 God of Abraham, lead us
6 Holy, holy, holy, Lord God almighty
6 The God of Abraham praise
7 I, the Lord of sea and sky
13 Bless the Lord, our fathers' God
14 Alleluia to the King of kings
14 Before the throne of God above
14 Ten thousand times ten thousand
14 The God of Abraham praise
15 The God of Abraham praise

Exodus 4
5 The God of Abraham praise
10 There is a fountain
22 Praise be to Christ in whom we see

Exodus 6
3 Before Jehovah's awesome/aweful throne
5 Jesus, where'er thy people meet
5 Lord Jesus, when your people meet

125

7 God whose love we cannot measure

Exodus 12
3 Christ the Lord is risen again
3 Hail, our once-rejected Jesus
3 Hail, thou once despised Jesus
3 Jesus, Lamb of God and source of life
3 Lord, enthroned in heavenly splendour
3 No weight of gold or silver
3 Now lives the Lamb of God
3 The day of resurrection
3 You choirs of new Jerusalem
11 On earth an army is marching
11 Singabahambayo (On earth an army)
14 Come on and celebrate
14 Jesus came, the heavens adoring
47 Come on and celebrate

Exodus 13
21 Glorious things of thee/you are spoken
21 Guide me, O my great Redeemer
21 Guide me, O thou great Jehovah
21 Through the night of doubt and sorrow

Exodus 14
22 Lead us, heavenly Father, lead us

Exodus 15
The Lord is my strength and my song
1 I will sing unto the Lord
2 Christians, lift up your hearts (Word)
2 Christ's church shall glory in his power
2 I love you, O Lord, you alone
2 Stand up and bless the Lord
2 With all my heart
13 Guide me, O my great Redeemer
13 Guide me, O thou great Jehovah
18 And he shall reign
18 Christ triumphant
18 Crown him with many crowns
18 Hail Redeemer! King divine
18 Hail to the Lord's anointed
18 In the tomb so cold
18 Jesus shall reign
18 Rejoice, the Lord is King
18 The day thou gavest, Lord, is ended
18 The Lord is King! lift up thy voice
18 The people who in darkness walked
20 God of Abraham, lead us
21 O praise ye the Lord, praise him
21 Sing praise to the Lord
26 Jesus, lover of my soul

Exodus 16
7 I cannot tell why he whom angels worship
10 Be still, for the presence of the Lord
14 Dear Lord and Father of mankind
14 Glorious things of thee/you are spoken
14 I hunger and I thirst
14 Lord, enthroned in heavenly splendour
14 Lord, speak to me that I may speak
14 O God, unseen yet ever near
31 Dear Lord and Father of mankind
31 Glorious things of thee/you are spoken
31 I hunger and I thirst
31 Lord, enthroned in heavenly splendour
31 Lord, speak to me that I may speak
31 O God, unseen yet ever near
35 Children of the heavenly King

Exodus 17
5 Father, hear the prayer we offer
5 Guide me, O my great Redeemer
5 Guide me, O thou great Jehovah
5 I hunger and I thirst
5 Lord, enthroned in heavenly splendour
7 Come with all joy to sing to God
15 Jehovah Jireh

Exodus 19
4 Let saints on earth together sing
4 The God of Abraham praise
6 Church of God, elect and glorious
6 Forth in the peace of Christ
9 O come, O come, Emmanuel
16 Let us love and sing and wonder
18 Let us love and sing and wonder
20 O come, O come, Emmanuel

Exodus 20
1 Father of all, whose laws have stood
1 O come, O come, Emmanuel

11 This is the day, this is the day

Exodus 22
29 To you, O Lord, our hearts we raise

Exodus 23
14 Come on and celebrate
16 Come, you thankful people, come
16 For the fruits of his creation
16 To you, O Lord, our hearts we raise

Exodus 24
 6 Oh for a heart to praise my God
15 Glorious things of thee/you are
    spoken
15 Guide me, O my great Redeemer
15 Guide me, O thou great Jehovah
16 Let us love and sing and wonder

Exodus 25
 2 All-creating heavenly Giver
 2 Take my life and let it be
17 Jesus, where'er thy people meet
17 Lord Jesus, when your people
    meet
31 He walks among the golden lamps

Exodus 30
 7 Jesus shall reign
12 No weight of gold or silver

Exodus 31
 1 All-creating heavenly Giver
 1 Angel voices ever singing
 1 Christ, from whom all blessings
    flow
 1 Come to us, creative Spirit

Exodus 33
 9 Glorious things of thee/you are
    spoken
 9 Guide me, O my great Redeemer
 9 Guide me, O thou great Jehovah
13 It is the cry of my heart
13 Teach me your way (Undivided
    heart)
13 Undivided heart (Teach me your
    way)
14 I will sing the wondrous story
14 To be in your presence
18 Holy, holy, holy, Lord God
    almighty
18 O worship the King
21 Rock of ages, cleft for me
21 We shall stand

22 Rock of ages, cleft for me

Exodus 34
 6 Father most holy, merciful and
    loving
 6 Give to our God immortal praise
 6 God of mercy, God of grace
 6 Praise to the Lord, the Almighty
 6 The Lord my shepherd rules my
    life
18 Come on and celebrate
30 Come, praise the name of Jesus

Exodus 35
 2 This is the day, this is the day
 5 All-creating heavenly Giver
 5 Take my life and let it be
21 All-creating heavenly Giver
21 Take my life and let it be
30 All-creating heavenly Giver
30 Angel voices ever singing
30 Christ, from whom all blessings
    flow
30 Come to us, creative Spirit
35 Beauty for brokenness (God of the
    poor)

Exodus 37
 6 Jesus, where'er thy people meet
 6 Lord Jesus, when your people
    meet
17 He walks among the golden lamps

Exodus 40
34 Glorious things of thee/you are
    spoken
34 Guide me, O my great Redeemer
34 Guide me, O thou great Jehovah

Leviticus
Leviticus 1
 2 Come, let us worship the Christ

Leviticus 2
12 To you, O Lord, our hearts we raise

Leviticus 3
    Not all the blood of beasts
    What offering shall we give

Leviticus 4
    Not all the blood of beasts
    What offering shall we give

Leviticus 5
6 Come, let us worship the Christ

Leviticus 6
4 We plough the fields, and scatter
13 O Lord, who came from realms above
13 O thou who camest from above
13 Send out the gospel! Let it sound

Leviticus 7
2 Glory be to Jesus
2 Oh for a heart to praise my God

Leviticus 9
24 O Lord, who came from realms above
24 O thou who camest from above
24 Send out the gospel! Let it sound

Leviticus 11
44 One holy apostolic church
45 Purify my heart

Leviticus 12
6 Come, let us worship the Christ

Leviticus 14
13 Glory in the highest, to the God
14 Only by grace
14 There is only one Lord
24 Glory in the highest, to the God

Leviticus 16
21 Not all the blood of beasts
21 What offering shall we give
30 Come, thou/most Holy Spirit, come
30 Jesus, lover of my soul
30 Just as I am
30 Oh for a heart to praise my God
30 Rock of ages, cleft for me
30 The heavens declare the glory

Leviticus 17
11 Not all the blood of beasts
11 O come, our all-victorious Lord
11 What offering shall we give

Leviticus 19
2 One holy apostolic church
10 Beauty for brokenness (God of the poor)
11 Father of all, whose laws have stood
18 For the fruits of his creation
18 Welcome to another day

Leviticus 20
26 Holiness is your life in me
26 Purify my heart

Leviticus 21
8 Purify my heart

Leviticus 23
10 To you, O Lord, our hearts we raise
22 Beauty for brokenness (God of the poor)
22 For the fruits of his creation

Leviticus 26
12 God whose love we cannot measure
13 Jesus, we celebrate your victory

Numbers

Numbers 6
8 Take my life and let it be
12 Glory in the highest, to the God
14 Hail the day that sees him rise
25 God of eternity, Lord of the ages
25 God of mercy, God of grace
25 Out of darkness let light shine
25 The Son of God proclaim

Numbers 9
15 Glorious things of thee/you are spoken
15 Guide me, O my great Redeemer
15 Guide me, O thou great Jehovah

Numbers 10
29 Amazing grace
35 Thy/your Kingdom come, O God

Numbers 11
9 Dear Lord and Father of mankind

Numbers 14
21 God is working his purpose out

Numbers 18
20 Be thou my vision/Lord be my vision
20 Lord be my vision/Be thou my vision

Numbers 20
2 Come with all joy to sing to God
7 Father, hear the prayer we offer
7 Guide me, O my great Redeemer
7 Guide me, O thou great Jehovah

7 I hunger and I thirst
7 Lord, enthroned in heavenly
 splendour
8 Rock of ages, cleft for me

Numbers 21
8 Bread of heaven, on you we feed
16 Holy Spirit, truth divine
16 Jesus, lover of my soul

Numbers 23
21 Look, ye saints, the sight is
 glorious

Numbers 24
16 A child this day is born
17 Bethlehem, the chosen city of our
 God
17 O come, O come, Emmanuel

Numbers 29
12 Come on and celebrate

Numbers 33
48 Guide me, O my great Redeemer
48 Guide me, O thou great Jehovah

Numbers 35
34 Blessed are the pure in heart
34 Hark! the herald-angels sing
34 Love divine, all loves excelling

Deuteronomy
Deuteronomy 1
33 Glorious things of thee/you are
 spoken
33 Guide me, O my great Redeemer
33 Guide me, O thou great Jehovah

Deuteronomy 3
27 There is a land of pure delight

Deuteronomy 4
10 O come, O come, Emmanuel
11 O Lord, the clouds are gathering
13 Father of all, whose laws have
 stood
22 Guide me, O my great Redeemer
22 Guide me, O thou great Jehovah
29 Jesus, where'er thy people meet
29 Lord Jesus, when your people
 meet
29 You can trust his promises
34 Show your power, O Lord
35 Holy, holy, holy, Lord God

 almighty
36 Stir my heart, O Lord
39 Awake, my soul, and with the sun
39 Glory to you, my God, this night
39 Praise God from whom all
 blessings flow

Deuteronomy 5
4 O come, O come, Emmanuel
6 Father of all, whose laws have
 stood
22 Holy, holy, holy, Lord God almighty

Deuteronomy 6
4 God has spoken, by his prophets
5 Christian, seek not yet repose
5 Father of all, whose laws have
 stood
5 Happy are they, they who love God
5 I love you, O Lord, you alone
5 My God, I love you
5 O Lord my love, my strength, my
 tower
5 Thee will I love, O Lord, my love
5 Welcome to another day
5 You can trust his promises
13 All heaven declares
16 Come with all joy to sing to God

Deuteronomy 7
6 Church of God, elect and glorious
7 City of God, Jerusalem
21 Be bold, be strong

Deuteronomy 8
7 Praise God for the harvest of farm
15 Guide me, O my great Redeemer
15 Guide me, O thou great Jehovah
15 O God of Jacob, by whose hand
15 Rock of ages, cleft for me
15 The God of Abraham praise

Deuteronomy 10
9 Be thou my vision/Lord be my
 vision
14 Hail the day that sees him rise
17 God of gods, we sound his praises
21 How can we sing with joy
21 To God be the glory

Deuteronomy 11
31 Guide me, O my great Redeemer
31 Guide me, O thou great Jehovah

Deuteronomy 14
2 Church of God, elect and glorious

Deuteronomy 15
7 Beauty for brokenness (God of the poor)

Deuteronomy 16
15 Come on and celebrate

Deuteronomy 18
2 Be thou my vision/Lord be my vision
13 Oh for a heart to praise my God
15 Ascended Christ
15 Christmas for God's holy people
15 Father of heaven, whose love profound
15 How sweet the name of Jesus sounds
15 Join all the glorious names
18 Ascended Christ
18 Christmas for God's holy people

Deuteronomy 24
19 For the fruits of his creation

Deuteronomy 26
1 To you, O Lord, our hearts we raise
2 We plough the fields, and scatter
7 Bless the Lord, our fathers' God
16 You can trust his promises

Deuteronomy 28
2 Praise God from whom all blessings flow
58 Praise the Lord, you heavens, adore him
65 Love divine, all loves excelling

Deuteronomy 29
4 Great Shepherd of your people
5 Guide me, O my great Redeemer
5 Guide me, O thou great Jehovah
15 I will seek your face, O Lord
29 O God, you give to all mankind

Deuteronomy 30
2 You can trust his promises
6 You can trust his promises
10 You can trust his promises
12 Immortal Love, for ever full

Deuteronomy 31
6 How firm a foundation

Deuteronomy 32
4 A mighty fortress is our God
4 A safe stronghold our God is still
4 God is our fortress and our rock
4 Rejoice, the Lord is King
10 For your mercy and your grace
10 The God of Abraham praise
11 Glory to you, my God, this night
11 Listen to my prayer, Lord
11 O God of Jacob, by whose hand
15 Come with all joy to sing to God
15 Come, worship God who is worthy
18 O Father of the fatherless (Father me)
39 Before Jehovah's awesome/aweful throne
39 The right hand of God is writing
39 There is none like you
48 There is a land of pure delight

Deuteronomy 33
2 O God most high
3 Jesus, King of kings
27 By your side
27 Eternal light, shine in my heart
27 Father, I want you to hold me
27 God is our strength and refuge
27 In heavenly love abiding
27 In your arms of love
27 Jesus, priceless treasure
27 O Father of the fatherless (Father me)
27 What a friend we have in Jesus
29 We rest on thee/trust in you

Deuteronomy 34
1 There is a land of pure delight
12 Show your power, O Lord

Joshua
Joshua 1
5 How firm a foundation
6 Lift up your heads, you gates of brass
9 Be bold, be strong
9 Children of the heavenly King
9 Guide me, O my great Redeemer
9 Guide me, O thou great Jehovah
9 The God of Abraham praise
9 There is a land of pure delight
9 Thine/Yours be the glory

Joshua 2
24 Rejoice, rejoice, Christ is in you

130

Joshua 3
Guide me, O my great Redeemer
Guide me, O thou great Jehovah
The God of Abraham praise
Thine/Yours be the glory
11 You are crowned with many
    crowns

Joshua 4
Guide me, O my great Redeemer
Guide me, O thou great Jehovah
The God of Abraham praise
Thine/Yours be the glory

Joshua 5
15 In your arms of love
15 Jesus, where'er thy people meet
15 Lord Jesus, when your people
    meet
15 The Lord made man, the Scriptures
    tell

Joshua 6
2 Rejoice, rejoice, Christ is in you

Joshua 7
19 Christ is the world's Light, he and
    none other
19 To God be the glory

Joshua 13
33 Be thou my vision/Lord be my
    vision

Joshua 21
22 God of gods, we sound his praises
44 Lord Jesus, think of me

Joshua 22
4 Lord Jesus, think of me
5 You can trust his promises

Joshua 24
14 Glory to you, my God, this night
14 Go forth and tell
14 In full and glad surrender
17 God of Abraham, lead us

Joshua 34
9 Breathe on me, Spirit of Jesus

Judges
Judges 3
9 Rejoice today with one accord
9 Tell his praise in song and story

9 Through all the changing scenes
15 Rejoice today with one accord
15 Tell his praise in song and story
15 Through all the changing scenes

Judges 5
3 O bless the God of Israel

Judges 6
8 God of Abraham, lead us
14 Christian soldiers, onward go
14 Go forth and tell
14 Oft in danger, oft in woe
24 Jehovah Jireh

Judges 7
15 In heavenly armour we'll enter the
    land
15 The battle belongs to the Lord

Judges 11
27 Great God, what do I see and hear
27 Judge eternal, throned in
    splendour

Judges 20
1 For I'm building a people of power

Judges 21
25 Lord, as I wake I turn to you

Ruth
Ruth 2
12 Glory to you, my God, this night
12 Jesus, lover of my soul
12 Listen to my prayer, Lord
12 O God of Jacob, by whose hand
20 Let saints on earth together sing

1 Samuel
1 Samuel 1
13 Like a mighty river flowing

1 Samuel 2
1 Holy is the name of God
1 Rejoice today with one accord
1 Tell out my soul
2 Holy, holy, holy, Lord God
    almighty
2 Rock of ages, cleft for me
2 Timeless love! We sing the story
6 Before Jehovah's awesome/aweful
    throne
10 Sing a new song to the Lord
10 Sing to God new songs of worship

35 Ascended Christ
35 Before the throne of God above
35 Christmas for God's holy people
35 How sweet the name of Jesus
 sounds
35 Join all the glorious names
35 Lord, enthroned in heavenly
 splendour
35 Where high the heavenly temple
 stands

1 Samuel 3
 Speak, Lord, in the stillness
 1 Bless the Lord as day departs
 9 Lord, speak to me that I may
 speak
 9 Speak, Lord, in the stillness

1 Samuel 4
 4 Bless the Lord, our fathers' God

1 Samuel 6
20 I will seek your face, O Lord

1 Samuel 7
 3 All heaven declares

1 Samuel 10
24 God save our gracious Queen

1 Samuel 11
13 Rejoice today with one accord

1 Samuel 12
23 Lord, teach us how to pray aright
24 Church of God, elect and glorious
24 You can trust his promises

1 Samuel 15
29 All hail the power of Jesus' name
29 Come, O/thou long-expected
 Jesus
29 Faithful vigil ended
29 Lord, now let your servant depart

1 Samuel 17
 Ye/you servants of God, your
 master proclaim
26 Let saints on earth together sing
26 Lift up your heads, you gates of
 brass
47 In heavenly armour we'll enter the
 land
47 The battle belongs to the Lord

1 Samuel 20
42 Like a mighty river flowing

1 Samuel 23
18 Like a mighty river flowing

1 Samuel 24
 6 Earth was waiting, spent and
 restless
 6 Hail to the Lord's anointed

1 Samuel 25
32 O bless the God of Israel

1 Samuel 30
 6 I love you, O Lord, you alone
 6 Now let us learn of Christ
 6 Soldiers of Christ, arise
 6 Stand up! stand up for Jesus
 6 We rest on thee/trust in you

2 Samuel
2 Samuel 1
14 Earth was waiting, spent and
 restless
14 Hail to the Lord's anointed

2 Samuel 6
 2 Bless the Lord, our fathers' God
14 When the Spirit of the Lord
21 Come on and celebrate
21 O give thanks to the Lord, all you

2 Samuel 7
 6 Lord, you need no house
13 The day thou gavest, Lord, is
 ended
18 Amazing grace
21 Teach me your way (Undivided
 heart)
21 Undivided heart (Teach me your
 way)
26 Christ is the King! O friends
 rejoice
27 We love the place, O God
28 Amazing grace

2 Samuel 12
 1 Give praise for famous men

2 Samuel 16
16 God save our gracious Queen

2 Samuel 22
 I love you, O Lord, you alone

1 Kings 9
5 The day thou gavest, Lord, is ended

1 Kings 18
17 Give praise for famous men
36 The God of Abraham praise
45 O Lord, the clouds are gathering

1 Kings 19
11 Be still, for the presence of the Lord
11 Dear Lord and Father of mankind
11 Lord Jesus, let these eyes of mine
12 Dear Lord and Father of mankind
12 Lord, you sometimes speak in wonders

1 Kings 21
17 Give praise for famous men

1 Kings 22
17 Restless souls, why do you scatter
17 Risen Lord, whose name we cherish
17 Souls of men, why will ye scatter

2 Kings
2 Kings 2
19 Guide me, O my great Redeemer
19 Guide me, O thou great Jehovah

2 Kings 3
12 Give praise for famous men

2 Kings 4
26 All shall be well

2 Kings 5
10 Jesus, lover of my soul
10 Just as I am
10 Rock of ages, cleft for me
14 River, wash over me

2 Kings 7
9 Christians, awake, salute the happy morn
9 God rest you/ye merry, gentlemen
9 Infant holy, infant lowly
9 O little town of Bethlehem

2 Kings 11
12 God save our gracious Queen

2 Kings 19
15 Bless the Lord, our fathers' God

15 See, amid the winter's snow

2 Kings 20
3 Oh for a heart to praise my God

2 Kings 23
21 Come on and celebrate

2 Kings 25
21 O God most high

1 Chronicles
1 Chronicles 13
6 Bless the Lord, our fathers' God
6 See, amid the winter's snow

1 Chronicles 15
16 Angel voices ever singing
16 Bring to the Lord a glad song
16 Come to us, creative Spirit
16 New songs of celebration render
16 O praise ye the Lord, praise him
16 Sing a new song to the Lord
16 Sing praise to the Lord
16 You holy angels bright

1 Chronicles 16
8 Church of God, elect and glorious
10 Glorious things of thee/you are spoken
10 Jesus, Jesus, holy and anointed one
29 O worship the Lord in the beauty
29 Oh for a heart to praise my God
29 Worship the Lord in the beauty
29 You are the God of our fathers
29 You holy angels bright
31 All creation join to say
31 Christ the Lord is risen today
31 I cannot tell why he whom angels worship
31 Joy to the world
31 Light's glittering morning fills the sky
31 Love's redeeming work is done
31 New songs of celebration render
31 O give thanks to the Lord, for his love
31 Praise the Lord, his glories show
31 Rejoice, the Lord is King
31 Sing a new song to the Lord
31 Sing heaven, shout for joy
31 Sing to God new songs of worship
31 The day of resurrection
31 The Lord is King! lift up thy voice

134

31 This is the day that the Lord has made

34 All people that on earth do dwell

34 Give to our God immortal praise

34 Let us gladly with one mind

34 O give thanks to the Lord, for his love

35 Lord of our life

35 Praise the Lord, you heavens, adore him

42 Songs of praise the angels sang

1 Chronicles 17

5 Lord, you need no house

9 The right hand of God is writing

11 Hail to the Lord's anointed

11 The day thou gavest, Lord, is ended

16 Amazing grace

20 Holy, holy, holy, Lord God almighty

20 Timeless love! We sing the story

24 Christ is the King! O friends rejoice

26 Amazing grace

1 Chronicles 20

6 He who would valiant be

6 Who would true valour see

1 Chronicles 21

26 O Lord, who came from realms above

26 O thou who camest from above

26 Send out the gospel! Let it sound

1 Chronicles 22

15 Beauty for brokenness (God of the poor)

19 You can trust his promises

1 Chronicles 23

30 The day thou gavest, Lord, is ended

1 Chronicles 28

7 Hail to the Lord's anointed

7 The day thou gavest, Lord, is ended

9 Jesus, the joy of loving hearts

9 Jesus, the very thought of thee

9 Jesus, where'er thy people meet

9 Lord Jesus, when your people meet

20 How firm a foundation

1 Chronicles 29

3 Take my life and let it be

10 All glory, laud/praise and honour

10 Father most holy, merciful and loving

10 Here from all nations

12 Lord, you need no house

14 All-creating heavenly Giver

14 Come, let us with our Lord arise

14 Father God in heaven (Kum ba yah)

14 Here, Lord, we come to you

14 Lord, you need no house

14 O Lord of heaven and earth and sea

15 Abide with me, fast falls the eventide

15 Immortal, invisible

15 O God, our help in ages past

16 All we've received (We are your church)

20 Bless the Lord, our fathers' God

2 Chronicles

2 Chronicles 1

11 Who can measure heaven and earth

2 Chronicles 2

5 Come with all joy to sing to God

6 God our Father and creator

6 Hail the day that sees him rise

6 In the bleak mid-winter

6 Lord, who left the highest heaven

6 Ring out the bells (Past three a clock)

2 Chronicles 3

10 Holy, holy, holy, Lord God almighty

10 In the bleak mid-winter

2 Chronicles 5

12 Angel voices ever singing

12 Bring to the Lord a glad song

12 Come to us, creative Spirit

12 New songs of celebration render

12 O praise ye the Lord, praise him

12 Sing a new song to the Lord

12 Sing praise to the Lord

12 You holy angels bright

13 All people that on earth do dwell

13 Give to our God immortal praise

13 Let us gladly with one mind

13 Let us with a gladsome mind

2 Chronicles 6

4 O bless the God of Israel
14 Awake, my soul, and with the sun
14 Glory to you, my God, this night
14 God of light and life's creation
14 Holy, holy, holy, Lord God
   almighty
14 Praise God from whom all
   blessings flow
14 Timeless love! We sing the story
18 Angel voices ever singing
18 God our Father and creator
18 Hail the day that sees him rise
18 In the bleak mid-winter
18 Lord, who left the highest heaven
18 This is the day that the Lord has
   made
20 Great Shepherd of your people
21 We love the place, O God
26 You're worthy of my praise
38 O God most high
41 Thy/your Kingdom come, O God
42 And now, O Father, mindful of the
   love

2 Chronicles 7

14 I will seek your face, O Lord
14 If my people

2 Chronicles 13

12 Christ is the world's true light
12 Christian soldiers, onward go
12 For all the saints who from their
   labour
12 Join all the glorious names
12 Lift high the cross, the love of
   Christ
12 Oft in danger, oft in woe
12 Soldiers of Christ, arise
12 We rest on thee/trust in you

2 Chronicles 14

11 We rest on thee/trust in you

2 Chronicles 15

4 Jesus, the joy of loving hearts
4 Jesus, the very thought of thee
4 Jesus, where'er thy people meet
4 Lord Jesus, when your people
   meet
4 Rejoice today with one accord
4 Tell his praise in song and story
4 Through all the changing scenes
15 O happy day that fixed my choice

2 Chronicles 18

16 Restless souls, why do you scatter
16 Risen Lord, whose name we cherish
16 Souls of men, why will ye scatter

2 Chronicles 20

6 You are the God of our fathers
12 We rest on thee/trust in you
15 In heavenly armour we'll enter the
   land
15 The battle belongs to the Lord
20 I do not hold life so dear
21 O worship the Lord in the beauty
21 Worship the Lord in the beauty
21 You are the God of our fathers

2 Chronicles 23

11 God save our gracious Queen

2 Chronicles 24

19 God has spoken, by his prophets

2 Chronicles 26

Almighty God, our heavenly
Father

2 Chronicles 29

11 You are the God of our fathers
30 Come let us join our cheerful
   songs
30 All people that on earth do dwell
30 Alleluia, alleluia! hearts to heaven
30 As with gladness men of old
30 Bring to the Lord a glad song
30 Come all you good people
30 Come with all joy to sing to God
30 Fill your hearts with joy and
   gladness
30 Glad music fills the Christmas sky
30 Jesus Christ is risen today
30 Let us gladly with one mind
30 Let us with a gladsome mind
30 O praise ye the Lord, praise him
30 Rejoice today with one accord
30 Sing praise to the Lord
30 Songs of praise the angels sang
30 When morning gilds the skies
30 You are worthy, Lord you are
   worthy
30 You holy angels bright

2 Chronicles 30

9 All things bright and beautiful
9 Father most holy, merciful and
   loving

9 Give to our God immortal praise
9 Praise to the Lord, the Almighty
9 The Lord my shepherd rules my life
16 Oh for a heart to praise my God
23 Come on and celebrate

2 Chronicles 32
8 Stand up! stand up for Jesus

2 Chronicles 35
11 Glory be to Jesus
11 Oh for a heart to praise my God

2 Chronicles 36
23 Alleluia, sing to Jesus
23 Angels from the realms of glory
23 Come and see the shining hope
23 Come sing the praise of Jesus
23 Faithful vigil ended
23 Jesus comes with clouds descending
23 Lo! He comes with clouds descending
23 O little town of Bethlehem
23 Soldiers of the cross, arise

Ezra
Ezra 3
11 All people that on earth do dwell
11 Come, rejoice before your maker
11 Give to our God immortal praise
11 Let us gladly with one mind
11 Let us with a gladsome mind
11 Look, ye saints, the sight is glorious
11 Shout for joy, loud and long

Ezra 5
2 God has spoken, by his prophets

Ezra 7
10 Help us, O Lord, to learn
25 I bind myself to God today

Ezra 8
21 Thy/your way, not mine, O Lord

Ezra 10
1 We love the place, O God

Nehemiah
Nehemiah 1
6 Lord, we believe when we call
6 We your people

Nehemiah 4
9 Christian, seek not yet repose
9 Forth in thy/your name, O Lord, I go
9 Stand up! stand up for Jesus

Nehemiah 8
10 O joy of God, we seek you in the morning

Nehemiah 9
5 No other name
5 Stand up and bless the Lord
5 You holy angels bright
6 Give to our God immortal praise
6 Hail the day that sees him rise
6 Heavenly hosts in ceaseless worship
6 I will build my church
6 Lord, who left the highest heaven
6 O Father of the fatherless (Father me)
6 This is the day that the Lord has made
11 How firm a foundation
12 Guide me, O my great Redeemer
12 Guide me, O thou great Jehovah
13 O bless the Lord, my soul
15 Guide me, O my great Redeemer
15 Guide me, O thou great Jehovah
15 Lord, enthroned in heavenly splendour
19 O Jesus, I have promised

Nehemiah 12
43 Rejoice, the Lord is King
46 Songs of praise the angels sang

Esther
Esther 3
8 A mighty fortress is our God
8 A safe stronghold our God is still
8 God is our fortress and our rock
8 Who honours courage here

Esther 7
Tell out my soul

Esther 9
22 Hail to the Lord's anointed
22 O worship the Lord in the beauty
22 Worship the Lord in the beauty

Job
Job 1
1 Oh for a heart to praise my God

Job 4
3 When the King shall come again
19 Spirit of God within me

Job 5
10 I, the Lord of sea and sky
15 Beauty for brokenness (God of the poor)
18 O come, our all-victorious Lord
18 The right hand of God is writing

Job 6
6 Here I am

Job 9
4 You are beautiful beyond description
8 Give to our God immortal praise
9 He is lovely

Job 10
9 In Christ shall all be made alive
9 Jesus, your blood and righteousness
9 O worship the King
9 Rejoice, rejoice, Christ is in you
9 Spirit of God within me
9 The Lord is King! lift up thy voice

Job 11
7 Can we/man by searching find out God
8 Oh the bitter shame and sorrow
17 Within our darkest night
18 To be in your presence

Job 12
12 Who can measure heaven and earth

Job 13
15 O God beyond all praising

Job 14
1 Immortal, invisible
1 O God, our help in ages past
7 Revive thy work/your church, O Lord
7 We give immortal praise

Job 15
7 O God, our help in ages past

Job 16
22 O God, our help in ages past

Job 17
15 Unto the hills around

Job 19
6 O come, our all-victorious Lord
25 I know that my Redeemer lives, comfort
25 Jesus Christ our great Redeemer
26 How sweet the name of Jesus sounds
26 It is a thing most wonderful
26 My God, how wonderful you are
26 Once in royal David's city

Job 23
2 Can we/man by searching find out God
10 Awake, my soul, and with the sun

Job 25
1 You are beautiful beyond description

Job 26
10 Eternal Father, strong to save

Job 28
12 Who can measure heaven and earth

Job 29
2 Oh for a closer walk with God
4 Like a mighty river flowing
14 O Father of the fatherless (Father me)

Job 32
8 Stir my heart, O Lord

Job 33
4 Breathe on me, breath of God
4 O Breath of Life, come sweeping through
4 O Father of the fatherless (Father me)
4 Stir my heart, O Lord

Job 35
5 Like a mighty river flowing
7 O Lord of heaven and earth and sea
10 Through the night of doubt and sorrow
10 Wise men, they came to look for wisdom

138

10 Within our darkest night

Job 36
28 I, the Lord of sea and sky
31 We plough the fields, and scatter

Job 37
 5 My peace I leave I leave with you
 6 I, the Lord of sea and sky
 6 We plough the fields, and scatter
12 We plough the fields, and scatter

Job 38
 2 I, the Lord of sea and sky
 4 I, the Lord of sea and sky
 5 Who can measure heaven and
    earth
 7 O little town of Bethlehem
 7 Songs of praise the angels sang
 8 Eternal Father, strong to save
37 You are beautiful beyond
    description

Job 40
 4 Jesus, lover of my soul
 4 Rock of ages, cleft for me

Job 41
11 O Lord of heaven and earth and
    sea

Job 42
 3 It is a thing most wonderful

Psalms
Psalm 1
 2 Father of mercies, in your word
 2 Lord, be thy word my rule
 2 Lord, make your word my rule
 3 Light has dawned
 6 Thy/your way, not mine, O Lord

Psalm 2
 2 Earth was waiting, spent and
    restless
 2 Hail to the Lord's anointed
 2 Ride on, ride on in majesty
 9 Thy/your Kingdom come, O God

Psalm 3
 1 Christian soldiers, onward go
 1 Oft in danger, oft in woe
 3 Faithful vigil ended
 7 Thy/your Kingdom come, O God

Psalm 4
   O righteous Lord
 1 Answer me
 1 O Lord, hear my prayer
 5 Lord, who left the highest heaven
 7 Fill your hearts with joy and
    gladness
 7 Lead us, heavenly Father, lead us
 7 You are worthy, Lord you are
    worthy
 8 Answer me
 8 Glory to you, my God, this night

Psalm 5
   Lord, as I wake I turn to you
 3 Angel voices ever singing
 3 Great is your faithfulness
 3 Holy, holy, holy, Lord God almighty
 3 O happy day that fixed my choice
 8 The Lord my shepherd rules my
    life
 8 Timeless love! We sing the story
11 Jesus, Jesus, holy and anointed one
11 Shout for joy, loud and long

Psalm 6
 3 The Church's one foundation

Psalm 7
 6 Thy/your Kingdom come, O God
17 Bright the vision that delighted
17 With all my heart

Psalm 8
 1 Bright the vision that delighted
 1 Immortal, invisible
 1 Lord, how majestic you are
 1 O Lord, our Lord, how majestic
 1 You are the Lord
 3 All glory, laud/praise and honour
 4 I wonder as I wander
 4 Not the grandeur of the mountains
 4 O God beyond all praising
 5 Jesus, you are the radiance
 5 You are crowned with many
    crowns

Psalm 9
 2 Jesus, Jesus, holy and anointed one
 2 Take my life and let it be
 2 With all my heart
 4 In the Lord I'll ever be thankful
 7 O give thanks to the Lord, for his
    love
 7 Rock of ages, cleft for me

7 The Lord is King! lift up thy voice
10 Nothing can trouble
11 Jesus, we enthrone you

Psalm 10
12 Thy/your Kingdom come, O God
16 The Lord is King! lift up thy/your
   voice
17 Angel voices ever singing

Psalm 11
4 Bright the vision that delighted

Psalm 12
  Who can sound the depths of
   sorrow
6 The heavens declare the glory

Psalm 13
  How long, O Lord
1 The Church's one foundation

Psalm 14
1 God made me for himself to serve
   him
1 I believe there is a God
1 Sing to God new songs of worship

Psalm 15
  God be in my head
2 It is the cry of my heart

Psalm 16
  O Lord, you are the centre of my
   life
2 Lord, you need no house
5 Be thou my vision/Lord be my
   vision
8 Forth in thy/your name, O Lord, I
   go
9 Holy Spirit, truth divine
11 As I hold out my hand
11 I will come and bow down
11 In heavenly love abiding
11 Lead us, heavenly Father, lead us
11 Now to him who is able
11 Send me, Lord (Thuma mina)
11 Soften my heart, Lord, I want to
   meet
11 Thuma mina (Send me, Lord)
11 To be in your presence

Psalm 17
  Be thou/O Lord my guardian and
   my guide

  O Lord our guardian and our
   guide
6 O Lord, hear my prayer
8 Glory to you, my God, this night
8 Jesus, lover of my soul
8 Listen to my prayer, Lord
8 Living under the shadow of his
   wing
8 O God of Jacob, by whose hand
15 Send me, Lord (Thuma mina)
15 Speak, Lord, in the stillness
15 Thuma mina (Send me, Lord)

Psalm 18
  Blessed be the name of the Lord
  I love you, O Lord, you alone
  O worship the King
1 By your side
1 How I love you (you are the one)
1 I love you, O Lord, you alone
1 Jesus, Jesus, holy and anointed one
1 O Lord my love, my strength, my
   tower
1 Open our eyes, Lord
1 Thank you for the cross
1 Thee will I love, O Lord, my love
1 We are here to praise you
1 With all my heart
1 You are the one (How I love you)
2 A mighty fortress is our God
2 A safe stronghold our God is still
2 Amazing grace
2 Christ's church shall glory in his
   power
2 For all the saints who from their
   labour
2 God is our fortress and our rock
2 God is our strength and refuge
2 Guide me, O my great Redeemer
2 Guide me, O thou great Jehovah
2 Jesus, you have lifted me
2 Listen to my prayer, Lord
2 Safe in the shadow of the Lord
2 The God of Abraham praise
2 Unto the hills around
2 We rest on thee/trust in you
2 You are the rock of my salvation
4 Jesus, lover of my soul
6 Nothing can trouble
6 Rejoice today with one accord
6 Tell his praise in song and story
6 Through all the changing scenes
9 O Lord, the clouds are gathering
9 O worship the King
27 Tell out my soul

26 I, the Lord of sea and sky
28 The Lord is King! lift up thy voice
33 God, we praise you! God, we bless
 you

Psalm 23
 Because the Lord is my shepherd
 In heavenly love abiding
 The God of love my shepherd is
 The King of love my Shepherd is
 The Lord my shepherd rules my life
1 Faithful Shepherd, feed me
1 Here from all nations
1 How bright these glorious spirits
 shine
1 In heavenly love abiding
2 Father, hear the prayer we offer
2 In Christ shall all be made alive
2 In heavenly love abiding
3 As I hold out my hand
3 My Father, for another night
3 My lips shall praise you
3 O worship the Lord in the beauty
3 Send me, Lord (Thuma mina)
3 Spirit divine, attend/inspire our
 prayers
3 Thuma mina (Send me, Lord)
3 Worship the Lord in the beauty
4 I bind myself to God today
4 I will sing the wondrous story
4 In heavenly love abiding
4 O sacred head, once wounded
4 Within our darkest night
5 My God, now is your table spread
5 The trumpets sound, the angels
 sing
6 Lord of our growing years
6 Praise to the Lord, the Almighty

Psalm 24
 Crown him with many crowns
 Fling wide your doors
 The earth and its fulness
 The earth is the Lord's
 This earth belongs to God
1 Come with all joy to sing to God
1 Come, worship God who is
 worthy
1 The earth is yours, O God
1 This earth belongs to God
1 You are the Lord
6 O God of Jacob, by whose hand
7 Alleluia, alleluia! hearts to heaven
7 At the name of Jesus
7 Fling wide the gates

7 God of gods, we sound his
 praises
7 God, we praise you! God, we bless
 you
7 Hail the day that sees him rise
7 King of glory, King of peace
7 Lift up your heads, O you gates
7 Lift up your heads to the coming
 King
7 Lift up your heads, you gates of
 brass
7 Lift up your heads, you mighty
 gates
7 Make way, make way
7 Stand up! stand up for Jesus
7 We have come as the family of God
8 Glory, glory, glory to the King
8 O come, O come, Emmanuel
8 The Lord is King he is mighty in
 battle

Psalm 25
 I lift my soul to you
 Remember, remember your
 mercy
3 You are the Lord
4 As I hold out my hand
4 At the name of Jesus
4 It is the cry of my heart
4 Lord of our life
4 Praise the Lord, you heavens,
 adore him
4 Teach me your way (Undivided
 heart)
4 Tell out my soul
4 Thy/your way, not mine, O Lord
4 Undivided heart (Teach me your
 way)
6 Restore, O Lord
8 God is good
12 As I hold out my hand
12 Thy/your way, not mine, O Lord
14 Blessed are the pure in heart
21 You are the Lord

Psalm 26
3 It is the cry of my heart
8 We love the place, O God

Psalm 27
 The Lord is my light
1 Christ is the world's true light
1 O come, all ye/you faithful
4 All heaven declares
4 I will seek your face, O Lord

4 O God beyond all praising
4 The King of love my Shepherd is
4 The Lord my shepherd rules my life
5 Nothing can trouble
5 Rock of ages, cleft for me
6 Lord, enthroned in heavenly
 splendour
7 What a friend we have in Jesus
8 Fight the good fight with all
 thy/your might
9 Tell out my soul
11 Teach me your way (Undivided
 heart)
11 Thy/your way, not mine, O Lord
11 Undivided heart (Teach me your
 way)

Psalm 28
7 Amazing grace
7 Guide me, O my great Redeemer
7 Guide me, O thou great Jehovah
7 O worship the King
7 Unto the hills around
7 We plough the fields, and scatter
7 We rest on thee/trust in you
9 God, we praise you! God, we bless
 you

Psalm 29
2 Fill now/thou my life, O Lord my
 God
2 Give him the glory (lift your voice)
2 Lift your voice and sing
2 O worship the Lord in the beauty
2 Oh for a heart to praise my God
2 Worship the Lord in the beauty
2 You are the God of our fathers
3 You are the Lord
4 You are beautiful beyond
 description
5 Child of the stable's secret birth
9 Let us gladly with one mind
9 Let us with a gladsome mind
9 The Kingdom of God
11 Shalom, shalom

Psalm 30
2 Shout for joy, and sing your praises
5 All shall be well
5 Lord Jesus, think of me
5 O joy of God, we seek you in the
 morning
5 O love that wilt not let me go
5 O worship the Lord in the beauty
5 The Church's one foundation

5 Worship the Lord in the beauty

Psalm 31
2 A mighty fortress is our God
2 A safe stronghold our God is still
2 Christ's church shall glory in his
 power
2 For all the saints who from their
 labour
2 God is our fortress and our rock
2 God is our strength and refuge
2 I love you, O Lord, you alone
2 Jesus, you have lifted me
2 Listen to my prayer, Lord
2 Lord, we believe when we call
2 O Lord my love, my strength, my
 tower
2 Rock of ages, cleft for me
2 Safe in the shadow of the Lord
2 Thee will I love, O Lord, my love
3 Faithful one, so unchanging
3 How sweet the name of Jesus
 sounds
3 Rock of ages, cleft for me
4 Be thou my vision/Lord be my
 vision
5 O bless the Lord, my soul
6 How firm a foundation
7 Nothing can trouble
20 Rock of ages, cleft for me
20 Soften my heart, Lord, I want to
 meet
23 Tell his praise in song and story

Psalm 32
1 Happy is the one
4 Fill your hearts with joy and
 gladness
4 You are worthy, Lord you are
 worthy
7 How sweet the name of Jesus
 sounds
7 Nothing can trouble
11 Shout for joy, and sing your praises

Psalm 33
1 Magnificat (Come, glorify)
1 Shout for joy, and sing your praises
4 Praise to the Holiest in the height
6 Shout for joy, loud and long
6 Thanks to God whose word was
 spoken
9 Shout for joy, loud and long
9 Thanks to God whose word was
 spoken

12 Rejoice, O land, in God your Lord
21 Jesus, Jesus, holy and anointed one

Psalm 34
   O magnify the Lord with me
   O taste and see that the Lord is
     good
   Silver and gold
   Tell his praise in song and story
   Through all the changing scenes
1 Holy, holy, holy, Lord
1 Love divine, all loves excelling
1 My lips shall praise you
1 You holy angels bright
3 Christ is the King! O friends
   rejoice
3 God of glory
3 Let us praise the Lord our God
8 Jesus, the name high over all
8 Praise to the Lord, sing alleluia
8 You can trust his promises
10 Nothing can trouble
14 O come, Christians, wonder
15 I bind myself to God today
18 God of heaven
18 In the Lord I'll ever be thankful
22 O bless the Lord, my soul

Psalm 35
3 On Jordan's bank, the Baptist's cry
18 Ye/you servants of God, your
    master proclaim

Psalm 36
5 Immortal, invisible
7 Jesus, lover of my soul
7 Living under the shadow of his
   wing
7 Not the grandeur of the mountains
8 See the feast our God prepares
9 Such love
9 You are the Lord

Psalm 37
   Delight yourself in the Lord
4 Born of the water
4 I want to serve the purpose of God
4 Jesus our hope, our heart's desire
4 O Lord, who came from realms
   above
4 O thou who camest from above
6 All shall be well
7 Be still, for the presence of the Lord
26 The King is among us
31 Help us, O Lord, to learn

34 You are the Lord
39 Nothing can trouble

Psalm 38
13 Lord, I was blind; I could not see

Psalm 39
7 All my hope on God is founded
7 Jesus, lover of my soul
12 O Lord, hear my prayer

Psalm 40
   I waited, I waited on the Lord
1 Rejoice today with one accord
1 Tell his praise in song and story
2 Amazing grace
2 We shall stand
3 Jesus put this song into our hearts
5 Tell out my soul
8 Help us, O Lord, to learn
9 Take my life and let it be
10 Ye/you servants of God, your
    master proclaim

Psalm 41
1 Nothing can trouble
4 Almighty God, our heavenly
   Father
4 Praise, my soul, the King of heaven
10 Praise, my soul, the King of heaven
12 To be in your presence

Psalm 42
1 As the deer pants for the water
1 Just as a lost and thirsty deer
1 As water to the thirsty
2 As water to the thirsty
2 I offer up my song
2 My Lord, I did not choose you
4 We plough the fields, and scatter
8 Be thou my vision/Lord be my
   vision
8 Lord of our life
8 Through the night of doubt and
   sorrow
8 Wise men, they came to look for
   wisdom
11 Praise, my soul, the King of heaven
11 Praise to the Lord, the Almighty
11 You holy angels bright

Psalm 43
3 Lord, thy word abideth
3 Lord your word shall guide us

144

Psalm 44

We have heard, O Lord our God
1 Thy/Your hand, O God, has guided
4 All creatures of our God and King
4 God has spoken to his people
4 Let all the world in every corner sing
4 Oh for a thousand tongues to sing
4 Rejoice today with one accord
11 Risen Lord, whose name we cherish
18 Loving Shepherd of your sheep
18 My God, accept my heart this day
26 Thy/your Kingdom come, O God

Psalm 45

1 Take my life and let it be
2 Fairest Lord Jesus
3 Name of all majesty
3 The strife is past/o'er, the battle done
4 Ride on, ride on in majesty
4 Show your power, O Lord
6 Join all the glorious names
6 The day thou gavest, Lord, is ended
7 My heart is full of adoration

Psalm 46

Be still and know that I am God
1 A mighty fortress is our God
1 A safe stronghold our God is still
1 God is our fortress and our rock
1 God is our strength and refuge
1 I love you, O Lord, you alone
1 Immortal Love, for ever full
1 Nothing can trouble
1 O Lord my love, my strength, my tower
1 Thee will I love, O Lord, my love
2 Jesus, priceless treasure
6 Onward, Christian soldiers
7 Emmanuel, God is with us
7 O God of Jacob, by whose hand
10 Be still and know that I am God
10 Be still, for the presence of the Lord
10 This is the day of light
11 O God of Jacob, by whose hand

Psalm 47

1 Clap your hands, clap your hands
1 Clap your hands, you people, shout

1 Take heart and praise our God
2 You are the Lord
5 Ascended Christ
5 Christ in majesty ascending
5 Look, ye saints, the sight is glorious
5 See the conqueror mounts in triumph
5 The Lord is King! lift up thy voice
6 Magnificat (Come, glorify)
9 The God of Abraham praise

Psalm 48

Great is the Lord, and most worthy
1 City of God, Jerusalem
1 Glorious things of thee/you are spoken
8 City of God, Jerusalem
8 Glorious things of thee/you are spoken
11 God has spoken to his people
14 O Jesus, I have promised

Psalm 49

7 Father of heaven, whose love profound
7 No weight of gold or silver
7 O bless the Lord, my soul
7 Praise, my soul, the King of heaven

Psalm 50

1 Christ is the world's true light
1 From the sun's rising
1 God has spoken, by his prophets
1 Jesus shall reign
1 Thanks to God whose word was spoken
2 O God beyond all praising
15 Nothing can trouble

Psalm 51

Create in me a pure heart
Create in us clean hearts
Give me a new heart, O God
2 Come, thou/most Holy Spirit, come
2 Jesus, lover of my soul
2 My Lord, what love is this
2 Rock of ages, cleft for me
2 The heavens declare the glory
4 Almighty God, our heavenly Father
6 Teach me your way (Undivided heart)

6 Undivided heart (Teach me your way)
7 It's your blood that cleanses me
8 I want to serve the purpose of God
10 My trust I place in God's good grace
10 O Breath of Life, come sweeping through
10 Oh for a heart to praise my God
14 Lord of our life
14 Praise the Lord, you heavens, adore him
15 All things bright and beautiful
15 My lips shall praise you
17 Blessed are the pure in heart
17 Brightest and best of the sons
17 Great Shepherd of your people
17 How do we start (That the world may)

Psalm 52
1 Praise to the Lord, the Almighty
9 Praise the Lord, his glories show

Psalm 53
1 God made me for himself to serve him
1 How can we sing with joy
1 I believe there is a God

Psalm 54
1 I am not skilled to understand
1 Still near me, O my Saviour, stand
2 O Lord, hear my prayer
6 And can it be
6 Oh for a heart to praise my God

Psalm 55
1 O Lord, hear my prayer
17 What a friend we have in Jesus
22 All creatures of our God and King
22 Fight the good fight with all thy/your might
22 God has spoken to his people
22 Great Shepherd of your people
22 O worship the Lord in the beauty
22 What a friend we have in Jesus
22 Worship the Lord in the beauty

Psalm 56
3 Have faith in God, my heart
3 Safe in the shadow of the Lord
13 Today, if you hear his voice

Psalm 57
1 Glory to you, my God, this night
1 Jesus, lover of my soul
1 Listen to my prayer, Lord
1 O God of Jacob, by whose hand
5 Father most holy, merciful and loving
7 Awake, my soul, and with the sun
7 Come, O Fount of every blessing

Psalm 58
11 Great God, what do I see and hear
11 The Lord is King! lift up thy voice

Psalm 59
16 A mighty fortress is our God
16 A safe stronghold our God is still
16 Be thou my vision/Lord be my vision
16 For all the saints who from their labour
16 God is our fortress and our rock
16 God is our strength and refuge
16 Holy, holy, holy, Lord God almighty
16 I love you, O Lord, you alone
16 Be thou my vision/Lord, be my vision
16 Nothing can trouble
16 Safe in the shadow of the Lord

Psalm 60
4 In heavenly armour we'll enter the land
4 Soldiers of the cross, arise
4 Stand up! stand up for Jesus
4 The battle belongs to the Lord
12 The victory of our God is won

Psalm 61
Hear my cry, O God
Listen to my prayer, Lord
1 What a friend we have in Jesus
3 All my hope on God is founded
3 Be thou my vision/Lord be my vision
4 Glory to you, my God, this night
4 Jesus, lover of my soul
4 O God of Jacob, by whose hand
5 Awake, my soul, and with the sun
8 With all my heart

Psalm 62
I rest in God alone

146

2 A mighty fortress is our God
2 A safe stronghold our God is still
2 Christ's church shall glory in his power
2 For all the saints who from their labour
2 God is our fortress and our rock
2 Jesus, you have lifted me
2 Listen to my prayer, Lord
2 On Jordan's bank, the Baptist's cry
2 Safe in the shadow of the Lord
6 Rock of ages, cleft for me
11 God has spoken, by his prophets

Psalm 63

O Lord, I want to sing your praises
Thy loving-kindness is better
1 As water to the thirsty
1 Father of mercies, in your word
1 I hunger and I thirst
1 I offer up my song
1 Jesus, priceless treasure
1 Jesus, the joy of loving hearts
1 My Lord, I did not choose you
5 My lips shall praise you
5 See the feast our God prepares
5 Songs of praise the angels sang
7 Glory to you, my God, this night
7 Jesus, lover of my soul
7 Listen to my prayer, Lord
7 O God of Jacob, by whose hand

Psalm 64

1 What a friend we have in Jesus
2 Jesus, lover of my soul
2 Rock of ages, cleft for me

Psalm 65

2 Christ is made the sure foundation
2 Christ is our cornerstone
2 Father God in heaven (Kum ba yah)
2 Father, hear the prayer we offer
2 Listen to my prayer, Lord
2 What a friend we have in Jesus
4 My Lord, I did not choose you
5 Bread of life
5 Lord of our life
5 Praise the Lord, you heavens, adore him
5 Show your power, O Lord
7 Eternal Father, strong to save
8 All creatures of our God and King
8 God has spoken to his people
9 I, the Lord of sea and sky
9 The earth is yours, O God

9 We plough the fields, and scatter
12 To you, O Lord, our hearts we raise

Psalm 66

Praise our God with shouts of joy
1 All people that on earth do dwell
1 Before Jehovah's awesome/aweful throne
2 Oh for a thousand tongues to sing
3 Rejoice, the Lord is King
5 God is our strength and refuge
9 How firm a foundation
10 Purify my heart
19 Tell his praise in song and story

Psalm 67

God of mercy, God of grace
Let the people praise you, O God
May God be gracious to us
1 God of eternity, Lord of the ages
1 Kyrie eleison (Look around you)
1 Look around you
1 Out of darkness let light shine
1 The Son of God proclaim

Psalm 68

What a friend we have in Jesus
1 Let God arise
1 Thy/your Kingdom come, O God
10 Beauty for brokenness (God of the poor)
18 Songs of praise the angels sang
19 Lord of our life
19 Praise the Lord, you heavens, adore him
24 All creatures of our God and King
24 God has spoken to his people
24 Let all the world in every corner sing
24 Oh for a thousand tongues to sing
24 Rejoice today with one accord
28 God is the strength of my life (Show us)
28 Show us your strength
32 Magnificat (Come, glorify)
33 God of God, the uncreated
33 Of the Father's love begotten

Psalm 69

When my sorrows cover me
1 How firm a foundation
6 Nothing can trouble
20 I cannot tell why he whom angels worship

21 Sing, my tongue, the glorious
  battle
34 All creatures of our God and King
34 Holy, holy, holy, Lord God
  almighty

Psalm 70
21 All hail the power of Jesus' name

Psalm 71
  Our confidence is in the Lord
2 Lord, we believe when we call
3 A mighty fortress is our God
3 A safe stronghold our God is still
3 Be thou my vision/Lord be my
  vision
3 Christ's church shall glory in his
  power
3 Faithful one, so unchanging
3 For all the saints who from their
  labour
3 God is our fortress and our rock
3 God is our strength and refuge
3 I love you, O Lord, you alone
3 Jesus, you have lifted me
3 Listen to my prayer, Lord
3 Safe in the shadow of the Lord
4 Hail to the Lord's anointed
5 Lord of our growing years
5 Sovereign Lord, I am yours
5 You are the Lord
8 All I am will sing out (Jag vill ge
  dig)
9 His eyes will guide my footsteps
16 Forth in thy/your name, O Lord, I
  go
16 Go forth and tell
16 God is working his purpose out
16 Jesus, the name high over all
16 Soldiers of Christ, arise
16 Stand up! stand up for Jesus
19 To God be the glory

Psalm 72
  Hail to the Lord's anointed
  Jesus shall reign
  The Lord will come and not be
  slow
5 Give to our God immortal praise
5 Jesus shall reign
8 Jesus shall reign
10 All hail the power of Jesus' name
18 O bless the God of Israel
19 God is working his purpose out

Psalm 73
1 God is good
24 Lord of all power, I give you my
  will
25 Jesus, priceless treasure
25 Jesus, the very thought of thee
25 O Jesus, King, most wonderful
25 O Lord my love, my strength, my
  tower
25 Thee will I love, O Lord, my love
28 Draw near and take the body of the
  Lord
28 Lord, teach us how to pray aright

Psalm 74
2 God of Abraham, lead us
22 Thy/your Kingdom come, O God

Psalm 75
1 Now thank we all our God
1 Thank you, O Lord of earth and
  heaven
1 When all your mercies, O my God
9 With all my heart

Psalm 76
4 You are the Lord
7 I will seek your face, O Lord
9 Christ on whom the Spirit rested
11 Awake, my soul, and with the sun

Psalm 77
1 Through all the changing scenes
2 Nothing can trouble
8 Praise the Lord, you heavens,
  adore him
14 Guide me, O my great Redeemer
14 Guide me, O thou great Jehovah
19 How firm a foundation
19 O Jesus, I have promised
20 Like a shepherd I will feed you
20 Thy/Your hand, O God, has
  guided

Psalm 78
14 Guide me, O my great Redeemer
14 Guide me, O thou great Jehovah
20 Rock of ages, cleft for me
24 Dear Lord and Father of mankind
35 A mighty fortress is our God
35 A safe stronghold our God is still
35 God is our fortress and our rock
37 Oh for a heart to praise my God
52 Guide me, O my great Redeemer
52 Guide me, O thou great Jehovah

52 Like a shepherd I will feed you
52 Thy/Your hand, O God, has
    guided

Psalm 79
5 The Church's one foundation
9 Lord of our life
9 Praise the Lord, you heavens,
    adore him
13 All people that on earth do dwell
13 Thy/Your hand, O God, has
    guided

Psalm 80
   Who can sound the depths of
    sorrow
1 Bless the Lord, our fathers' God
1 Bless the Lord, the God of our
   fathers
1 God is the strength of my life
   (Show us)
1 Great Shepherd of your people
1 Show us your strength (God is the
   strength)
3 All my hope on God is founded
3 God of eternity, Lord of the ages
3 God of mercy, God of grace
3 Out of darkness let light shine
7 God of mercy, God of grace
18 O Breath of Life, come sweeping
    through
19 God of mercy, God of grace

Psalm 81
1 Come let us join our cheerful songs
1 O God of Jacob, by whose hand
1 Shout for joy, and sing your praises
2 Christ is our cornerstone
2 Let all the world in every corner
   sing
2 Songs of praise the angels sang
6 Cast your burdens on to Jesus
7 Nothing can trouble

Psalm 82
   Who can sound the depths of
    sorrow
1 O Lord, all the world belongs to
   you
4 Hail to the Lord's anointed
8 Thy/your Kingdom come, O God

Psalm 83
2 A mighty fortress is our God
2 A safe stronghold our God is still

2 God is our fortress and our rock
2 Who honours courage here
13 Come, you thankful people, come
13 Judge eternal, throned in
    splendour
18 Before Jehovah's awesome/aweful
    throne
18 O Lord, all the world belongs to
   you
18 You are the Lord

Psalm 84
   One thing I ask, one thing I seek
   Only one thing I ask
1 How lovely is your dwelling-place
1 We love the place, O God
2 As water to the thirsty
2 Father of mercies, in your word
2 I hunger and I thirst
2 Jesus, priceless treasure
2 Jesus, the joy of loving hearts
2 My Lord, I did not choose you
3 Let all the world in every corner
   sing
3 Oh for a thousand tongues to sing
3 Rejoice today with one accord
3 The Lord made man, the Scriptures
   tell
4 Love divine, all loves excelling
7 God of gods, we sound his praises
7 Soldiers of Christ, arise
8 O Lord, hear my prayer
9 And now, O Father, mindful of the
   love
10 We love the place, O God
11 Here, O my Lord, I see thee face to
   face
11 Timeless love! We sing the story

Psalm 85
   Dona nobis pacem II (Grant to us)
   Grant to us your peace, Lord
    (Dona nobis)
1 Rejoice, O land, in God your Lord
4 Lord of our life
4 Praise the Lord, you heavens,
   adore him
6 O Breath of Life, come sweeping
   through
6 Revive thy work/your church, O
   Lord
7 Come, most/thou Holy Spirit,
   come
8 Shalom, shalom
12 God of mercy, God of grace

Psalm 86
>   Hear me, O Lord, and respond to my prayer
>   The Lord will come and not be slow
6   O Lord, hear my prayer
6   Tell his praise in song and story
6   Through all the changing scenes
6   What a friend we have in Jesus
7   Nothing can trouble
8   Come, let us glorify the Lord
11   It is the cry of my heart
11   Teach me your way (Undivided heart)
11   Undivided heart (Teach me your way)
12   Fill thou/now my life, O Lord my God
15   Not the grandeur of the mountains

Psalm 87
3   Glorious things of thee/you are spoken
4   Born by the Holy Spirit's breath
4   Born of the water
4   It was a man who was born
4   This is the truth which we proclaim
7   Praise God from whom all blessings flow

Psalm 88
1   Be thou my vision/Lord be my vision
2   Lord, we believe when we call
2   O Lord, hear my prayer
13   Holy, holy, holy, Lord God almighty

Psalm 89
1   Timeless love! We sing the story
1   When all your mercies, O my God
7   You are beautiful beyond description
9   Eternal Father, strong to save
9   I, the Lord of sea and sky
16   Jesus, Jesus, holy and anointed one
26   Come, worship God who is worthy
26   Rock of ages, cleft for me
28   I am trusting thee/you, Lord Jesus
46   The Church's one foundation

Psalm 90
>   O God, our help in ages past
>   O Lord, the refuge of each

generation
>   You have been a shelter, Lord
1   O God, our help in ages past
5   Immortal, invisible
13   The Church's one foundation
14   Now to him who is able

Psalm 91
>   From fears and phantoms of the night
>   Safe in the shadow of the Lord
1   O God, our help in ages past
2   A mighty fortress is our God
2   A safe stronghold our God is still
2   For all the saints who from their labour
2   God is our fortress and our rock
2   God is our strength and refuge
2   I love you, O Lord, you alone
3   Amazing Grace
4   Glory to you, my God, this night
4   Jesus, lover of my soul
4   Listen to my prayer, Lord
4   O God of Jacob, by whose hand
5   Lighten our darkness
5   Nothing can trouble
5   We shall stand
11   I bind myself to God today
11   Tell his praise in song and story
11   Through all the changing scenes
12   Praise, my soul, the King of heaven

Psalm 92
>   Sweet is the work, my God, my King

Psalm 93
1   Clothed in kingly majesty
1   God of glory
1   O give thanks to the Lord, for his love
1   Rejoice, the Lord is King
1   The Lord is King! lift up thy voice
1   Ye/you servants of God, your master proclaim
2   The day thou gavest, Lord, is ended
3   I love you, O Lord, you alone
3   Jesus, lover of my soul
4   You are the Lord
5   How sure the Scriptures are

Psalm 94
2   Great God, what do I see and hear
2   The Lord is King! lift up thy voice

3 The Church's one foundation
22 Jesus, you have lifted me
22 Rock of ages, cleft for me

Psalm 95
Come, let us praise the Lord
Come with all joy to sing to God
Come, worship God who is
worthy
Let us sing to the God of salvation
1 Come, let us sing for joy
1 Come, let us worship our
Redeemer
1 Let all the world in every corner
sing
1 Let us praise the Lord our God
1 Magnificat (Come, glorify)
1 You are the rock of my salvation
2 Angel voices ever singing
2 Christ is our cornerstone
2 I will sing unto the Lord
2 Songs of praise the angels sang
5 I, the Lord of sea and sky
5 Three-in-One and One-in-Three
6 He is lovely
6 O come, let us worship and bow
down
6 O worship the Lord in the beauty
6 Worship the Lord in the beauty
7 Cast your burdens on to Jesus
7 How sure the Scriptures are
7 Tell all the world of Jesus
7 Thy/Your hand, O God, has
guided
7 Today, if you hear his voice
7 Your hand, O God, has guided

Psalm 96
Sing to the Lord with a song
1 Bring to the Lord a glad song
1 Magnificat (Come, glorify)
1 New songs of celebration render
1 O give thanks to the Lord, for his
love
1 Sing a new song to the Lord
1 Sing to God new songs of worship
2 Bless the Lord, creation sings
2 Bless the Lord, our fathers' God
2 Join all the glorious names
2 Stand up and bless the Lord
(Montgomery)
6 All heaven declares
8 O worship the Lord in the beauty
8 To God be the glory
8 Worship the Lord in the beauty

9 O worship the Lord in the beauty
9 Oh for a heart to praise my God
9 Worship the Lord in the beauty
9 You are the God of our fathers
10 O give thanks to the Lord, for his
love
10 The Lord is King! lift up thy voice
10 Ye/you servants of God, your
master proclaim
10 You are the Lord
11 All creation join to say
11 Christ the Lord is risen today
11 I cannot tell why he whom angels
worship
11 Joy to the world
11 Light's glittering morning fills the
sky
11 Love's redeeming work is done
11 New songs of celebration render
11 Praise the Lord, his glories show
11 Sing a new song to the Lord
11 Sing to God new songs of worship
11 The day of resurrection
11 This is the day that the Lord has
made

Psalm 97
The Lord reigns
1 Rejoice, the Lord is King
1 The day thou gavest, Lord, is
ended
1 The Lord is King! lift up thy voice
1 You are the Lord
2 O worship the King
5 You are crowned with many
crowns
5 You are the Lord
5 You sat down
8 God has spoken to his people
9 Father most holy, merciful and
loving
9 You are the Lord

Psalm 98
Blow upon the trumpet
Joy to the world
New songs of celebration render
Sing a new song to the Lord
Sing to God new songs of worship
1 Bring to the Lord a glad song
1 Joy to the world
1 Lift up your hearts to the Lord
1 Magnificat (Come, glorify)
1 Sing a new song to the Lord
1 Thy/Your hand, O God, has guided

151

4 All people that on earth do dwell
4 Joy to the world
4 Shout for joy, and sing your praises
5 Angel voices ever singing
5 Christ is our cornerstone
5 O praise ye the Lord, praise him
5 Sing praise to the Lord
5 Songs of praise the angels sang
6 Blow upon the trumpet
6 Shout for joy, and sing your
   praises
7 A great and mighty wonder
7 Let the heavens shout for joy
7 Let the world sing Jesus reigns
9 Hail to the Lord's anointed

Psalm 99
1 Bless the Lord, our fathers' God
1 Bless the Lord, the God of our
   fathers
1 O give thanks to the Lord, for his
   love
1 Rejoice, the Lord is King
1 The Lord is King! lift up thy voice
2 He is exalted, the King is exalted
5 Let us praise the Lord our God

Psalm 100
   All people that on earth do dwell
   Before Jehovah's awesome/aweful
      throne
   Bring to the Lord a glad song
   Come, rejoice before him (Jubilate
      Deo)
   Come, rejoice before your maker
   Come, rejoice in God
   Jubilate (O shout to the Lord)
   O shout to the Lord (Jubilate)
   Shout for joy and sing, serve the
      Lord
   Shout, shout joyfully
1 Shout for joy, and sing your praises
3 Thy/Your hand, O God, has
   guided
4 Come, let us with our Lord arise
4 O give thanks to the Lord, all you
4 O worship the Lord in the beauty
4 Worship the Lord in the beauty
5 Give to our God immortal praise
5 I'll praise my maker while I've
   breath
5 Let us gladly with one mind

Psalm 101
2 Oh for a heart to praise my God

6 Rejoice, O land, in God your Lord

Psalm 102
1 Father God in heaven (Kum ba
   yah)
1 Father on high to whom we pray
1 Lord Jesus, think of me
1 O Lord, hear my prayer
1 What a friend we have in Jesus
2 Lord, we believe when we call
27 Christ is the King! O friends rejoice
27 I know that my Redeemer lives,
   comfort
27 Jesus, priceless treasure
27 O Christ, the same, through all
27 There's a song for all the children

Psalm 103
   Bless the Lord . . . he's healed
   O bless the Lord, my soul
   Praise, my soul, the King of heaven
   Praise to the Lord, the Almighty
1 Bless the Lord . . . King of kings
1 He has shown you
1 Praise to the Lord, the Almighty
2 O bless the Lord, O my soul
3 Shout for joy, and sing your praises
3 Songs of thankfulness and praise
3 Thine/Yours for ever! God of love
4 You are the Lord
8 O Lord, your tenderness
13 We plough the fields, and scatter
14 In Christ shall all be made alive
14 Lead us, heavenly Father, lead us
14 O worship the King
14 The Lord is King! lift up thy voice
15 Immortal, invisible
17 Lord of all goodness
17 Loved with everlasting love
19 Ye/you servants of God, your
   master proclaim
20 You holy angels bright
21 Praise God from whom all
   blessings flow
22 Bless the Lord, creation sings
22 Come to us, creative Spirit
22 Holy, holy, holy, Lord God
   almighty
29 All creatures of our God and King

Psalm 104
   O worship the King
1 All hail the power of Jesus' name
1 O bless the Lord, my soul
10 The earth is yours, O God

13 I, the Lord of sea and sky
14 God, whose farm is all creation
23 Forth in thy/your name, O Lord, I go
24 Immortal, invisible
24 The works of the Lord are created
29 Immortal, invisible
30 O Breath of Life, come sweeping through
30 O give thanks to the Lord, for his love
31 Angel voices ever singing
33 How sweet the name of Jesus sounds
33 There is a fountain
33 With all my heart

Psalm 105

1 Holy, holy, holy, Lord God almighty
1 Saviour, again to thy dear name
2 God be in my head
2 Take my life and let it be
3 Nothing can trouble
39 Glorious things of thee/you are spoken
39 Guide me, O my great Redeemer
39 Guide me, O thou great Jehovah
40 Alleluia, sing to Jesus
40 Bread of heaven, on you we feed
40 Draw near and take the body of the Lord
40 Guide me, O my great Redeemer
40 Guide me, O thou great Jehovah
40 In the quiet consecration
40 Light of the minds that know him
40 Speak, Lord, in the stillness
40 To you, O Lord, our hearts we raise
43 The Lord has led forth

Psalm 106

1 All people that on earth do dwell
1 Come, rejoice before your maker
1 Give to our God immortal praise
1 Just as I am
1 Let us gladly with one mind
1 Let us with a gladsome mind
1 O give thanks to the Lord, for his love
4 Love divine, all loves excelling
15 God of grace and God of glory
20 Faithful vigil ended
20 Lord, now let your servant depart
21 Tell out my soul
22 Show your power, O Lord

48 Jesus shall reign
48 O bless the God of Israel
48 Praise to the Lord, the Almighty
48 Wake, O wake, and sleep no longer

Psalm 107

1 All people that on earth do dwell
1 Come, rejoice before your maker
1 Give to our God immortal praise
1 Let us gladly with one mind
1 Let us with a gladsome mind
1 O give thanks to the Lord, for his love
1 Praise the Father (Gabi, gabi)
1 When I survey the wondrous cross
3 Lift high the cross, the love of Christ
6 Nothing can trouble
6 Rejoice today with one accord
6 Tell his praise in song and story
6 Through all the changing scenes
9 As water to the thirsty
9 Judge eternal, throned in splendour
9 My Lord, I did not choose you
9 Tell out my soul
9 The trumpets sound, the angels sing
10 And can it be
10 Come sing the praise of Jesus
10 Hark the glad sound! The Saviour comes
10 I'll praise my maker while I've breath
10 Jesus shall reign
10 Jesus, the name high over all
10 O sacred head, once wounded
10 Oh for a thousand tongues to sing
10 The Kingdom of God
10 When Jesus walked upon this earth
15 Jesus, lover of my soul
15 Lord, thy word abideth
15 Lord your word shall guide us
16 Hark the glad sound! The Saviour comes
16 Lift up your heads, you gates of brass
29 Bless the Lord, creation sings
29 Eternal Father, strong to save
29 I cannot tell why he whom angels worship
29 Jesus calls us! In/o'er the tumult
29 O changeless Christ, for ever new
29 O Jesus, I have promised

29 Son of God, eternal Saviour
29 Timeless love! We sing the story

Psalm 108
1 Come, O Fount of every blessing
2 Awake, my soul, and with the sun
5 Father most holy, merciful and
   loving
13 Through our God we shall do
   valiantly

Psalm 109
26 God, we praise you! God, we bless
   you
26 I know that my Redeemer lives,
   comfort
26 Jesus, Saviour of the world
26 Through all the changing scenes
26 Where high the heavenly temple
   stands

Psalm 110
1 All hail the power of Jesus' name
1 Rejoice, the Lord is King
4 Ascended Christ
4 Before the eternal King and Priest
4 Christ triumphant
4 Christmas for God's holy people
4 Father of heaven, whose love
   profound
4 How sweet the name of Jesus
   sounds
4 Join all the glorious names
4 To us a child of royal birth
4 Where high the heavenly temple
   stands
7 It came upon the midnight clear
7 Lord, enthroned in heavenly
   splendour

Psalm 111
2 Before the throne of God above
7 Lord, enthroned in heavenly
   splendour
8 Not the grandeur of the mountains
9 A great and mighty wonder
9 Alleluia, raise the anthem
9 Come, let us worship the Christ
9 Come, ye faithful, raise the anthem
9 Jesus came, the heavens adoring
9 Lord Jesus Christ (Living Lord)
9 See, amid the winter's snow
9 The works of the Lord are created
9 Thy/Your hand, O God, has
   guided

9 To God be the glory
9 We share a new day's dawn
9 When the King shall come again
10 Who can measure heaven and earth

Psalm 112
They who stand in awe of God are
   happy
4 Light has dawned
7 O happy day that fixed my choice

Psalm 113
From the rising of the sun
1 God of God, the uncreated
1 Of the Father's love begotten
3 Christ is the world's true light
3 From the sun's rising
3 The day thou gavest, Lord, is
   ended
5 Timeless love! We sing the story
7 Tell out my soul

Psalm 114
7 Be still, for the presence of the Lord
8 Glorious things of thee/you are
   spoken
8 Rock of ages, cleft for me
8 When the King shall come again

Psalm 115
1 Father, let us dedicate
5 He is lovely
9 A mighty fortress is our God
9 A safe stronghold our God is still
9 God is our fortress and our rock
15 Bless the Lord as day departs
15 Come, praise the Lord
18 Bless the Lord, creation sings

Psalm 116
4 Nothing can trouble
5 Beauty for brokenness (God of the
   poor)
8 O Father of the fatherless (Father
   me)
12 Lord of all goodness
12 Not all the blood of beasts
12 O Lord of heaven and earth and
   sea
12 What offering shall we give
14 Awake, my soul, and with the sun
17 All my hope on God is founded
17 For the beauty of the earth
17 O God beyond all praising
17 To you, O Lord, our hearts we raise

3 Only by grace
4 You are beautiful beyond
   description
5 O God beyond all praising
6 Lighten our darkness
7 Restless souls, why do you scatter
7 Souls of men, why will ye scatter

Psalm 131
3 All my hope on God is founded
3 My hope is built on nothing less
3 Through the night of doubt and
   sorrow

Psalm 132
8 Thy/your Kingdom come,
   O God
9 A debtor to mercy alone
9 And can it be
9 Look, ye saints, the sight is
   glorious
9 My hope is built on nothing less
9 Shout for joy, loud and long

Psalm 133
  How good a thing it is
1 Bind us together, Lord
1 Jesus Christ, sovereign King
1 Lord, we come in your name
1 Men and women, let us walk
1 Oh isn't it good
1 Spirit of God most high
3 Lord, we come in your name

Psalm 134
  Bless the Lord as day departs
  Come, bless the Lord
  Come, praise the Lord
3 He is lovely

Psalm 135
  Rejoice today with one accord
1 How sweet the name of Jesus
   sounds
2 Come, praise the Lord
5 Come with all joy to sing to God
5 Come, worship God who is
   worthy
13 Hail to the Lord's anointed
19 Bless the Lord, creation sings

Psalm 136
  All people that on earth do dwell
  Give to our God immortal praise
  Let us with a gladsome mind

2 God of gods, we sound his praises
5 The works of the Lord are created
7 I, the Lord of sea and sky
26 Not the grandeur of the mountains

Psalm 137
1 O come, O come, Emmanuel
3 Alleluia, sing to Jesus
5 City of God, Jerusalem

Psalm 138
1 King of glory, King of peace
2 No other name
4 All hail the power of Jesus' name
7 Nothing can trouble
7 Thy/Your hand, O God, has
   guided

Psalm 139
  O Lord, my God, you know all my
   ways
  Search me, O God
  There is no moment of my life
  You are before me, Lord
1 God of grace, I turn my face
2 Awake, my soul, and with the sun
2 How sure the Scriptures are
6 It is a thing most wonderful
10 Guide me, O thou great Jehovah
12 Saviour, again to thy dear name
16 Forth in thy/your name, O Lord, I
   go
23 Lord, the light (Shine, Jesus, shine)

Psalm 140
5 Amazing grace
7 Guide me, O my great Redeemer
7 Guide me, O thou great Jehovah

Psalm 141
1 What a friend we have in Jesus
2 Jesus shall reign
2 Let our praise to you
2 May our worship be as fragrance
2 The day thou gavest, Lord, is
   ended
3 Saviour, again to thy dear name
8 Sovereign Lord, I am yours
9 Amazing grace

Psalm 142
  What a friend we have in Jesus
  When I lift up my voice

Psalm 143

1 O Lord, hear my prayer
6 As water to the thirsty
6 Father of mercies, in your word
6 I hunger and I thirst
6 I offer up my song
6 Jesus, priceless treasure
6 Jesus, the joy of loving hearts
6 My Lord, I did not choose you
9 Jesus, lover of my soul
9 Rock of ages, cleft for me
10 How good is the God we adore
10 O Jesus, I have promised

Psalm 144

1 Rock of ages, cleft for me
2 A mighty fortress is our God
2 A safe stronghold our God is still
2 Amazing grace
2 Christ's church shall glory in his
  power
2 For all the saints who from their
  labour
2 God is our fortress and our rock
2 Guide me, O my great Redeemer
2 Guide me, O thou great Jehovah
2 I love you, O Lord, you alone
2 O Lord my love, my strength, my
  tower
2 Safe in the shadow of the Lord
2 The God of Abraham praise
2 Thee will I love, O Lord, my love
2 Unto the hills around
5 Jesus, where'er thy people meet
5 Lord Jesus, when your people
  meet
14 O God most high
15 Rejoice, O land, in God your Lord

Psalm 145

1 All creatures of our God and King
1 God has spoken to his people
1 God of glory
1 Let all the world in every corner
  sing
1 Oh for a thousand tongues to sing
1 Rejoice today with one accord
2 King of glory, King of peace
2 Tell all the world of Jesus
3 King of the universe, Lord of the
  ages
6 Show your power, O Lord
7 Come on and celebrate
7 Sing of the Lord's goodness
7 When all your mercies, O my God

10 All creatures of our God and King
10 Holy, holy, holy, Lord God
  almighty
10 Ye/you servants of God, your
  master proclaim
12 The strife is past/o'er, the battle
  done
13 The day thou gavest, Lord, is
  ended
14 Nothing can trouble
17 Children of the heavenly King
21 Holy, holy, holy, Lord God
  almighty
21 Praise to the Lord, the Almighty

Psalm 146

I'll praise my maker while I've
  breath
2 How sweet the name of Jesus
  sounds
2 There is a fountain
2 You holy angels bright
5 O God of Jacob, by whose hand
6 He is lovely
6 O Lord of heaven and earth and
  sea
7 Hail to the Lord's anointed
7 Jesus shall reign
7 Jesus, the name high over all
7 Jesus, your name is power
7 Judge eternal, throned in
  splendour
7 Oh for a thousand tongues to sing
7 Tell out my soul
7 The Kingdom of God
10 And he shall reign
10 The Lord is King! lift up thy voice

Psalm 147

Fill your hearts with joy and
  gladness
You are worthy, Lord you are
  worthy
2 City of God, Jerusalem
3 God of heaven
3 I cannot tell why he whom angels
  worship
3 No weight of gold or silver
3 Shout for joy, and sing your praises
5 King of the universe, Lord of the
  ages
7 Magnificat (Come, glorify)
8 I, the Lord of sea and sky
8 Like a mighty river flowing
15 Shout for joy, loud and long

158

Psalm 148
  All creatures of our God and King
  Bless the Lord, creation sings
  God has spoken to his people
  O bless the Lord, the God of
    salvation
  O praise ye the Lord, praise him
  Praise God from whom all
    blessings flow
  Praise him, praise him, praise him
  Praise the Lord .. from the heavens
  Praise the Lord, his glories show
  Praise the Lord of heaven
  Praise the Lord, you heavens,
    adore him
  Praise to the Lord, sing alleluia
  Sing praise to the Lord
1 O praise ye the Lord, praise him
1 Sing praise to the Lord
2 God of God, the uncreated
2 Of the Father's love begotten
3 By every nation, race and tongue
3 Easter song (By every nation, race)
3 Praise, my soul, the King of heaven
5 Bless the Lord, created things
5 Holy, holy, holy, Lord God
    almighty
7 All creatures of our God and King
11 All hail the power of Jesus' name
11 All people that on earth do dwell
13 No other name
13 You are the God of our fathers

Psalm 149
  Bring to the Lord a glad song
  Sing of the Lord's goodness
1 New songs of celebration render
1 Sing a new song to the Lord
1 Sing to God new songs of worship
4 Angel voices ever singing

Psalm 150
  Bring to the Lord a glad song
  O praise ye the Lord, praise him
  Praise the Lord, his glories show
  Sing of the Lord's goodness
  Sing praise to the Lord
1 The King is among us
3 Angel voices ever singing
3 Come to us, creative Spirit
3 New songs of celebration render
3 Praise him on the trumpet
3 Sing a new song to the Lord
3 Sing to God new songs of worship
6 All creatures of our God and King

6 God has spoken to his people
6 Holy, holy, holy, Lord God
    almighty
6 Jesus Christ the Lord is born
6 Praise to the Lord, the Almighty
6 Unto us a boy is born

Proverbs
Proverbs 1
20 Spirit of God within me

Proverbs 2
6 Who can measure heaven and
    earth

Proverbs 3
5 I am trusting thee/you, Lord Jesus
5 Like a river glorious
5 Lord, you are more precious
5 O worship the King
5 Safe in the shadow of the Lord
5 You can trust his promises
6 As I hold out my hand
6 Let saints on earth together sing
9 To you, O Lord, our hearts we
    raise
13 Who can measure heaven and
    earth
19 The works of the Lord are created
24 Almighty Lord, the holy One
24 Before the ending of the day
24 Glory to you, my God, this night
24 Round me falls the night
26 Christ is made the sure foundation

Proverbs 4
18 Christ, whose glory fills the skies
18 From you all skill and science flow
18 Light has dawned

Proverbs 5
21 Awake, my soul, and with the sun
21 How sure the Scriptures are

Proverbs 6
4 As sons of the day and daughters

Proverbs 8
1 Spirit of God within me
22 Who can measure heaven and earth
23 Alleluia, raise the anthem
23 Come, ye faithful, raise the anthem

Proverbs 11
4 Great God, what do I see and hear

Proverbs 13
14 Father, hear the prayer we offer
14 Guide me, O my great Redeemer
14 Guide me, O thou great Jehovah
14 I hunger and I thirst
14 Jesus, lover of my soul
14 O Jesus, King, most wonderful

Proverbs 14
31 Beauty for brokenness (God of the poor)

Proverbs 15
11 Guide me, O my great Redeemer
11 Guide me, O thou great Jehovah
24 Father eternal, Lord of the ages

Proverbs 16
9 Thy/your way, not mine, O Lord
24 Jesus, Jesus, holy and anointed one

Proverbs 17
6 Tell out my soul
6 The King is among us

Proverbs 18
10 Be thou my vision/Lord be my vision
10 How sweet the name of Jesus sounds
10 Listen to my prayer, Lord
10 Safe in the shadow of the Lord

Proverbs 21
12 Great Shepherd of your people

Proverbs 22
2 He is lovely

Proverbs 23
11 Alleluia, sing to Jesus
11 I know that my Redeemer lives, comfort
11 Lord, enthroned in heavenly splendour
26 All my hope on God is founded
26 My God, accept my heart this day

Proverbs 25
25 As water to the thirsty

Proverbs 27
1 Father, although I cannot see
20 Guide me, O my great Redeemer
20 Guide me, O thou great Jehovah

Proverbs 29
18 Lord, be my vision/Be thou my vision

Proverbs 30
8 We plough the fields, and scatter
11 Now thank we all our God

Ecclesiastes
Ecclesiastes 2
1 Glorious things of thee/you are spoken

Ecclesiastes 3
3 Spirit of God, rest on your people
11 All things bright and beautiful
11 King of the universe, Lord of the ages
11 O God, you give to all mankind
20 In Christ shall all be made alive
20 Jesus, your blood and righteousness
20 O worship the King
20 The Lord is King! lift up thy voice

Ecclesiastes 4
12 Bind us together, Lord

Ecclesiastes 5
2 Father God in heaven (Kum ba yah)
7 You are beautiful beyond description
12 Almighty Lord, the holy One
12 Glory to you, my God, this night

Ecclesiastes 7
20 At even(ing), ere/when the sun was set

Ecclesiastes 9
10 Awake, my soul, and with the sun

Ecclesiastes 10
17 Rejoice, O land, in God your Lord

Ecclesiastes 11
6 We plough the fields, and scatter
9 Lord of our growing years

Ecclesiastes 12
1 His eyes will guide my footsteps
1 Lord of our growing years
2 O Lord, the clouds are gathering
2 Today, if you hear his voice
5 O God, our help in ages past

13 Awake, my soul, and with the sun
13 O God beyond all praising
13 Powerful in making us wise to salvation

Song of Songs

Song of Songs 1
3 How sweet the name of Jesus sounds
15 Fairest Lord Jesus

Song of Songs 2
10 Tell me, why do you weep
16 Jesus, my Lord, my God, my all
16 Loved with everlasting love
16 O happy day that fixed my choice
17 Abide with me, fast falls the eventide

Song of Songs 4
6 Abide with me, fast falls the eventide
15 Glorious things of thee/you are spoken
15 I hunger and I thirst
15 Jesus, lover of my soul

Song of Songs 5
2 Wake, O wake, and sleep no longer
8 Jesus, priceless treasure
15 When the Lord in glory comes
16 He is lovely

Song of Songs 6
3 How sweet the name of Jesus sounds

Song of Songs 8
6 At the name of Jesus
6 Christian, do you not hear the Lord
6 Gracious Spirit, Holy Ghost
6 Hark, my soul! it is the Lord
6 Holy Spirit, gracious guest
6 Jesus, Lord, we pray
6 Revive thy work/your church, O Lord
6 Within our darkest night

Isaiah

Isaiah 1
3 Christmas for God's holy people
3 God rest you/ye merry, gentlemen
3 Good Christian men/Christians all rejoice

3 Infant holy, infant lowly
3 Once in royal David's city
4 Judge eternal, throned in splendour
12 Strengthen for service, Lord, the hands
17 I'll praise my maker while I've breath
18 My Lord, what love is this
24 Tell out my soul

Isaiah 2
3 Rejoice, O land, in God your Lord
4 Christ is the world's true light
4 Crown him with many crowns
4 My peace I leave with you
4 O Lord, the clouds are gathering
4 Thy/your Kingdom come, O God
5 Children of the heavenly king
5 Today, if you hear his voice
11 Father most holy, merciful and loving
19 Name of all majesty
19 Restore, O Lord

Isaiah 4
11 O Father of the fatherless (Father me)
25 Change my heart, O God

Isaiah 5
9 Within our darkest night

Isaiah 6
Bright the vision that delighted
Holy, holy, holy (Santo, santo)
We see the Lord
1 Bright the vision that delighted
1 Holy, holy, holy (Andy Park)
1 Light of gladness, Lord of glory
2 Holy, holy, holy, Lord God almighty
2 Immortal, invisible
2 Let all mortal flesh keep silence
2 Lift high the cross, the love of Christ
2 My God, how wonderful you are
3 God of gods, we sound his praises
3 God we praise you
3 God, we praise you! God, we bless you
3 Holy, holy, holy is the Lord
3 Holy, holy, holy, Lord
3 Holy, holy, holy, Lord God almighty
3 In awe and wonder, Lord our God

3 Let our praise to you
3 The God of Abraham praise
3 You are the God of our fathers
6 Lord, I was blind; I could not see
6 Stand up and bless the Lord
7 Take my life and let it be
8 At the supper, Christ the Lord
8 Father almighty, we your humble servants
8 For the bread which you have broken
8 Forth in the peace of Christ
8 How shall they hear
8 I, the Lord of sea and sky
8 Jesus, send more labourers
8 Let us talents and tongues employ
8 O Lord, who came from realms above
8 O thou who camest from above
8 Send me, Lord (Thuma mina)
8 Take my life and fill me, O Lord
8 Thuma mina (Send me, Lord)

Isaiah 7
14 A child is born for us today
14 A great and mighty wonder
14 Christmas for God's holy people
14 Emmanuel, Emmanuel, his name is called
14 Emmanuel, Emmanuel, we call your name
14 Emmanuel, Emmanuel, wonderful counsellor
14 Emmanuel, God is with us
14 Emmanuel . . . he is here
14 God of God, the uncreated
14 God we praise you
14 Had he not loved us
14 Hark! the herald-angels sing
14 Immanuel, O Immanuel
14 Jesus, King of kings
14 Jesus, Lamb of God and source of life
14 Lord, you were rich beyond all splendour
14 O come, all ye/you faithful
14 O come, O come, Emmanuel
14 O little town of Bethlehem
14 O Trinity, O Trinity
14 The darkness turns to dawn
14 The virgin Mary had a baby boy
14 Thou who wast rich

Isaiah 8
8 Emmanuel, Emmanuel, wonderful

counsellor
8 Hark! the herald-angels sing
12 Through all the changing scenes

Isaiah 9
His name is wonderful
2 A child is born for us today
2 Christ, whose glory fills the skies
2 God whose love we cannot measure
2 In the darkness of the night
2 Into darkness light has broken
2 Light has dawned
2 O come, O come, Emmanuel
2 O little town of Bethlehem
2 O Spirit of the living God
2 People walking in the dark
2 The darkness turns to dawn
2 The people who in darkness walked
2 Within our darkest night
3 The race that long in darkness pined
6 A child is born for us
6 A child is born for us today
6 A child is born in Bethlehem
6 A great and mighty wonder
6 A messenger named Gabriel
6 Christ is the world's true light
6 Come and hear the joyful singing
6 Come, let us with our Lord arise
6 Emmanuel, Emmanuel, wonderful counsellor
6 Emmanuel . . . he is here
6 For unto us a child is born (Hadden)
6 God of gods, we sound his praises
6 Hark the glad sound! The Saviour comes
6 Hark! the herald-angels sing
6 It came upon the midnight clear
6 Jerusalem on high
6 King of kings . . . glory, alleluia
6 Long, long ago it happened
6 Look to the skies, there's a celebration
6 Lord, enthroned in heavenly splendour
6 No more weeping (Paschal procession)
6 O bless the Lord, O my soul
6 O Christ, at your first Eucharist
6 O Lord, our Lord, how majestic
6 O Prince of peace, whose promised birth

6 O thou, who at thy Eucharist didst pray
6 Peace to you
6 Prince of peace, counsellor
6 Rejoice, rejoice, a saviour has come
6 See, to us a child is born
6 Songs of praise the angels sang
6 The darkness turns to dawn
6 The God of Abraham praise
6 These were the words
6 To people of goodwill
6 To us a child of royal birth
6 Wonderful counsellor, Jesus
6 Ye/you servants of God, your master proclaim
6 You are the King of glory
6 You are the mighty King
7 And he shall reign
7 Hail to the Lord's anointed
7 Jesus has sat down
7 King of kings, Lord of lords, lion
7 Praise God for the harvest of farm and
7 The King of glory comes (King of Kings)
7 To us a child of royal birth

Isaiah 10
17 Lord, now let your servant depart

Isaiah 11
1 All hail the power of Jesus' name
1 Bethlehem, the chosen city of our God
1 O come, O come, Emmanuel
1 Songs of thankfulness and praise
2 Come, Holy Ghost, our souls inspire
2 Creator Spirit, come, inspire
9 God is working his purpose out
9 May the mind of Christ my Saviour
10 In heavenly armour we'll enter the land
10 Jesus, hope of every nation
10 The battle belongs to the Lord
16 When the King shall come again

Isaiah 12
God brings us comfort where his anger
We shall draw water joyfully
1 Praise God today
2 Before Jehovah's awesome/aweful throne

2 Christians, lift up your hearts (Word)
2 Christ's church shall glory in his power
2 I love you, O Lord, you alone
2 Stand up and bless the Lord
4 No other name
4 To God be the glory
4 Ye/you servants of God, your master proclaim
6 Happy day of great rejoicing

Isaiah 13
7 Thy/Your hand, O God, has guided
10 Songs of thankfulness and praise

Isaiah 17
10 Lord of our life
10 Rock of ages, cleft for me
10 Tell out my soul

Isaiah 18
4 Lord, we come in your name

Isaiah 22
22 O come, O come, Emmanuel

Isaiah 24
15 God of glory

Isaiah 25
See the feast our God prepares
1 God of glory
4 Jesus, lover of my soul
4 Listen to my prayer, Lord
7 Arise, shine (Darkness like a shroud)
7 Darkness like a shroud
8 Alleluia, alleluia! hearts to heaven
8 Christian soldiers, onward go
8 From you all skill and science flow
8 Here from all nations
8 How bright these glorious spirits shine
8 I know that my Redeemer lives, comfort
8 O come, O come, Emmanuel
8 O Father of the fatherless (Father me)
8 Oft in danger, oft in woe
8 The strife is past/o'er, the battle done
8 This day above all days
9 Let us rejoice and be glad

9 We trust in you, our shield

Isaiah 26
1 Glorious things of thee/you are spoken
3 Like a mighty river flowing
3 Like a river glorious
3 Loved with everlasting love
3 Not the grandeur of the mountains
3 Peace, perfect peace
4 Beyond all knowledge is your love divine
4 Glorious things of thee/you are spoken
4 It passeth knowledge
4 Rock of ages, cleft for me
19 Great God, what do I see and hear

Isaiah 28
16 Christ is made the sure foundation
16 Christ is our cornerstone
16 How firm a foundation
16 O Christ the great foundation
16 Oh heaven is in my heart
16 The Church's one foundation

Isaiah 29
16 Change my heart, O God
18 Lord, I was blind; I could not see
19 Beauty for brokenness (God of the poor)
19 Shout for joy, and sing your praises
23 Holy is the name of God
23 You are beautiful beyond description

Isaiah 30
21 The right hand of God is writing
23 We plough the fields, and scatter
27 O Spirit of the living God

Isaiah 32
1 The God of Abraham praise
2 How sweet the name of Jesus sounds
2 Jesus, lover of my soul
2 Listen to my prayer. Lord
2 Rock of ages, cleft for me
15 Born in song
15 For I'm building a people of power
15 We your people

Isaiah 33
2 O Lord, the clouds are gathering
2 On Jordan's bank, the Baptist's cry

5 You are crowned with many crowns
6 Christ is made the sure foundation
11 Born of the water
11 I believe in God the Father
11 Lord of the church, we pray for our renewing
11 Spirit divine, attend/inspire our prayers
20 Glorious things of thee/you are spoken
20 Jerusalem, my happy home
20 Jerusalem on high
22 Judge eternal, throned in splendour

Isaiah 34
1 To God be the glory
4 Loved with everlasting love
4 Songs of thankfulness and praise
8 Jesus, the name high over all

Isaiah 35
Joy to the world
Let the desert sing
When the King shall come again
1 Joy to the world
1 Let the desert sing
1 When the King shall come again
5 His eyes will guide my footsteps
5 Lord, I was blind; I could not see
5 My song is love unknown
5 Oh for a thousand tongues to sing
5 We declare that the Kingdom of God
6 I hunger and I thirst
6 O God, unseen yet ever near
10 Children of the heavenly King
10 Man of Sorrows, what a name

Isaiah 37
4 My God, how wonderful you are
16 Bless the Lord, our fathers' God
16 See, amid the winter's snow

Isaiah 40
1 I, the Lord of sea and sky
3 Alleluia . . . prepare the way
3 Clear the road (Prepare the way)
3 Make way, make way
3 On Jordan's bank, the Baptist's cry
3 Prepare the way (Clear the road)
3 Prepare the way for Jesus to return
3 Prepare the way of the Lord
3 Prepare the way, the way for the Lord

3 The bells ring out at Christmas-
time
3 When the King shall come again
5 I cannot tell why he whom angels
worship
6 Immortal, invisible
6 On Jordan's bank, the Baptist's cry
11 Faithful Shepherd, feed me
11 How sweet the name of Jesus
sounds
11 Like a shepherd I will feed you
11 Praise him! praise him, Jesus our
13 You are beautiful beyond
description
18 Timeless love! We sing the story
20 Lord, you need no house
21 Have you not heard
26 Like a shepherd I will feed you
26 Soldiers of Christ, arise
26 Tell out my soul
28 Fight the good fight with all
thy/your might
28 We plough the fields, and scatter
29 O Spirit of the living God
30 Father in heaven, grant to your
children
31 Like a shepherd I will feed you
31 The God of Abraham praise

Isaiah 41

1 God rest you/ye merry, gentlemen
4 God has spoken, by his prophets
10 How firm a foundation
13 Like a shepherd I will feed you
14 All glory, laud/praise and honour
14 Alleluia, sing to Jesus
14 Child in the manger
14 Crown him with many crowns
14 Draw near and take the body of the
Lord
14 Father in heaven, grant to your
children
14 Father most holy, merciful and
loving
14 Father of heaven, whose love
profound
14 Father of mercies, in your word
14 For your mercy and your grace
14 From all who live beneath the skies
14 God of God, the uncreated
14 Guide me, O my great Redeemer
14 Guide me, O thou great Jehovah
14 Hail Redeemer! King divine
14 I believe in God the Father
14 I know that my Redeemer lives,

comfort
14 Jesus, hope of every nation
14 O worship the King
14 Of the Father's love begotten
14 Oh for a heart to praise my God
14 Oh for a thousand tongues to sing
14 Our great Redeemer, as he
breathed
14 Sing, my tongue, the glorious
battle
14 Tell all the world of Jesus
14 Thou art coming, O my Saviour
14 Wake, O wake, and sleep no longer
14 You are coming, O my Saviour
18 Let the desert sing
18 When the King shall come again

Isaiah 42

1 God is here! As we his people
5 Give to our God immortal praise
5 I believe in God the Father
5 O Breath of Life, come sweeping
through
5 O Father of the fatherless (Father
me)
6 Come, praise the name of Jesus
6 Faithful vigil ended
6 Jesus, hope of every nation
6 Lord, now let your servant depart
7 All we've received (We are your
church)
7 Come sing the praise of Jesus
7 Hark the glad sound! The Saviour
comes
7 I'll praise my maker while I've
breath
7 Jesus shall reign
7 Jesus, the name high over all
7 O God most high
7 Oh for a thousand tongues to sing
7 The Kingdom of God
7 When Jesus walked upon this
earth
7 Will you come and follow me
8 No other name
10 Bring to the Lord a glad song
10 New songs of celebration render
10 Sing a new song to the Lord
10 You holy angels bright
16 His eyes will guide my footsteps
16 Jesus, lover of my soul
16 O Jesus, I have promised
16 O love that wilt not let me go
18 Lord, I was blind; I could not see
18 Oh for a thousand tongues to sing

18 When the King shall come again

Isaiah 43
1 Fear not for I am with you
1 From the distant east and the farthest
1 How firm a foundation
1 Do not be afraid
2 How firm a foundation
5 City of God, Jerusalem
5 God has spoken to his people
10 We shall stand
11 Holy, holy, holy, Lord God almighty
11 Rock of ages, cleft for me
25 Hail to the Lord's anointed
25 The Lord my shepherd rules my life

Isaiah 44
3 For I'm building a people of power
3 We your people
5 Oh for a heart to praise my God
6 Christ upon the mountain peak
6 God has spokenóby his prophets
6 Holy, holy, holy, Lord God almighty
6 How good is the God we adore
6 Rock of ages, cleft for me
6 Timeless love! We sing the story
8 A mighty fortress is our God
8 A safe stronghold our God is still
8 God is our fortress and our rock
8 Rock of ages, cleft for me
8 We shall stand
10 Lord, you need no house
21 God is here! As we his people
22 Hail to the Lord's anointed
22 No weight of gold or silver
23 All creation join to say
23 Christ the Lord is risen today
23 I cannot tell why he whom angels worship
23 Light's glittering morning fills the sky
23 Love's redeeming work is done
23 Praise the Lord, his glories show
23 The day of resurrection
23 This is the day that the Lord has made
24 Give to our God immortal praise

Isaiah 45
2 Hark the glad sound! The Saviour comes

2 Lift up your heads, you gates of brass
5 Holy, holy, holy, Lord God almighty
6 Christ is the world's true light
6 From the sun's rising
6 Jesus shall reign
6 The day thou gavest, Lord, is ended
8 The Spirit of the Lord
9 Change my heart, O God
9 Jesus, you are changing me
12 I, the Lord of sea and sky
12 Like a shepherd I will feed you
18 Bread of heaven, on you we feed
22 Angels from the realms of glory
22 We have a gospel
23 All creation join to say
23 All praise to Christ, our Lord aand King
23 Angels from the realms of glory
23 At the name of Jesus
23 Before the heaven and earth
23 Christ is risen! hallelujah/alleluia
23 Christ the Lord is risen today
23 Look, ye saints, the sight is glorious
23 Love's redeeming work is done
23 Thou art coming, O my Saviour
23 You are coming, O my Saviour
23 You can trust his promises

Isaiah 46
4 His eyes will guide my footsteps
5 Timeless love! We sing the story

Isaiah 48
10 How firm a foundation
10 Purify my heart
12 Christ upon the mountain peak
12 God has spoken, by his prophets
12 How good is the God we adore
18 Like a mighty river flowing
18 Like a river glorious
18 Praise the Father, God of justice
21 Father, hear the prayer we offer
21 Guide me, O my great Redeemer
21 Guide me, O thou great Jehovah
21 I hunger and I thirst
21 Lord, enthroned in heavenly splendour
21 Rock of ages, cleft for me

Isaiah 49
1 God is working his purpose out
2 Like a river glorious

166

2 Rock of ages, cleft for me
2 Still near me, O my Saviour, stand
6 Come, praise the name of Jesus
6 Faithful vigil ended
6 Jesus, hope of every nation
6 Lord, now let your servant depart
7 All my heart this night rejoices
9 Faithful Shepherd, feed me
9 The King of love my Shepherd is
9 The Lord my shepherd rules my life
10 Here from all nations
10 How bright these glorious spirits shine
15 Christian, do you not hear the Lord
15 Hark, my soul! it is the Lord
15 Soften my heart, Lord, soften my heart
16 A debtor to mercy alone
16 Before the throne of God above
22 City of God, Jerusalem
26 I cannot tell why he whom angels worship

Isaiah 50

4 Open our eyes, Lord
4 Teach me your way (Undivided heart)
4 Undivided heart (Teach me your way)
6 Downtrodden Christ
6 O sacred head, once wounded
6 See, Christ was wounded for our sake
7 We shall stand
8 He lives in us, the Christ of God

Isaiah 51

3 Name of all majesty
3 On Jordan's bank, the Baptist's cry
3 The Lord made man, the Scriptures tell
5 God is working his purpose out
6 Great God, what do I see and hear
6 In the bleak mid-winter
6 Loved with everlasting love
6 Songs of praise the angels sang
11 Children of the heavenly King
11 Let the desert sing
11 When the King shall come again
13 Songs of praise the angels sang
17 Wake, O wake, and sleep no longer

Isaiah 52

How lovely on the mountains

1 City of God, Jerusalem
1 Wake, O wake, and sleep no longer
3 So freely flows the endless love
7 Go, tell it on the mountain
7 Hail to the Lord's anointed
7 How lovely on the mountains
7 Rejoice, the Lord is King
7 Take my life and let it be
14 Lord, I was blind; I could not see
14 O sacred head, once wounded

Isaiah 53

Ah, holy Jesus, how have you offended
Christ triumphant
Come, let us worship the Christ
He was pierced for our transgressions
No weight of gold or silver
O sacred head, once wounded
See, Christ was wounded for our sake
2 Lord, I was blind; I could not see
2 They killed him as a common thief
3 Emmanuel . . . he is here
3 How do we start (That the world may)
3 Look, ye saints, the sight is glorious
3 Lord Christ, we praise your sacrifice
3 Man of Sorrows, what a name
4 Come, let us kneel before him
4 He is born, our Lord and Saviour
4 I really want to worship you (You laid aside)
4 Jesus Christ is risen today
4 O sacred head, once wounded
4 Praise him! praise him, Jesus our
4 Thank you for the cross
4 You laid aside your majesty
5 Come and see, come and see
5 I believe in Jesus
5 I believe there is a God
5 In the streets of every city
5 It's your blood that cleanses me
5 The price is paid
6 Before Jehovah's awesome/aweful throne
6 Come and see, come and see
6 Hail, our once-rejected Jesus
6 Hail, thou once despised Jesus
6 Help me to understand it, Lord
6 I will sing the wondrous story
6 Restless souls, why do you scatter

6 Souls of men, why will ye scatter
6 Thank you for the cross
6 The King of love my Shepherd is
7 He stood before the court
7 I cannot tell why he whom angels worship
7 Jesus, Lamb of God and source of life
7 Led like a lamb (You're alive)
8 I, the Lord of sea and sky
9 My song is love unknown
10 We give immortal praise
11 Christ triumphant
11 From heaven ou came (The Servant King)
11 God, we praise you! God, we bless you
12 Broken for me
12 He gave his life in selfless love
12 I come with joy to meet my Lord
12 O Christ of all the ages, come
12 We sing the praise of him who died

Isaiah 54
7 Soften my heart, Lord, soften my heart
8 Loved with everlasting love
10 Hail to the Lord's anointed
10 Soften my heart, Lord, soften my heart
17 In heavenly armour we'll enter the land
17 No weapon formed, or army or King
17 The battle belongs to the Lord

Isaiah 55
 All who are thirsty
1 Alleluia! We sing your praises
1 Haleluya! Pelo tsa rona
1 Rock of ages, cleft for me
1 So freely flows the endless love
1 Come to the waters
2 The trumpets sound, the angels sing
6 Tell his praise in song and story
10 We plough the fields, and scatter
11 At even(ing), ere/when the sun was set
11 I am trusting thee/you, Lord Jesus
12 A great and mighty wonder
12 Blow upon the trumpet
12 Forth in the peace of Christ
12 Sing to God new songs of worship
12 You shall go out with joy

Isaiah 56
5 The head that once was crowned
7 Here within this house of prayer
7 We love the place, O God

Isaiah 57
15 All glory be to God on high
15 Blessed are the pure in heart
15 Hark! the herald-angels sing
15 Holy is the name of God
15 Jesus, the very thought of thee
15 Jesus, where'er thy people meet
15 Lord Jesus, when your people meet
15 Love divine, all loves excelling
15 O little town of Bethlehem
15 Oh for a heart to praise my God
15 Our great Redeemer, as he breathed
19 Shalom, shalom
19 Thy/your kingdom come, O God

Isaiah 58
6 Hail to the Lord's anointed
6 What a friend we have in Jesus
7 Judge eternal, throned in splendour
7 Tell out my soul
8 Light has dawned
8 Today, if you hear his voice
11 Guide me, O my great Redeemer

Isaiah 59
1 Jesus, where'er thy people meet
1 Lord Jesus, when your people meet
2 How can we sing with joy
17 Be thou my vision/Lord be my vision
17 Christian soldiers, onward go
17 Oft in danger, oft in woe
17 Soldiers of Christ, arise
17 Soldiers of the cross, arise
17 Stand up! stand up for Jesus
19 God has spoken to his people
19 Jesus shall reign
20 O come, O come, Emmanuel

Isaiah 60
1 Arise, shine
1 Arise, shine (Darkness like a shroud)
1 Behold, the darkness (Arise, shine)
1 Darkness like a shroud
1 Faithful vigil ended
1 Lord, now let your servant depart

168

2 Lighten our darkness
3 All hail the power of Jesus' name
3 All my heart this night rejoices
3 Angels from the realms of glory
3 Light has dawned
3 To him we come
3 Welcome your King
4 City of God, Jerusalem
6 Brightest and best of the sons
6 Hail to the Lord's anointed
6 O come, all ye/you faithful
6 O worship the Lord in the beauty
6 Wise men, they came to look for wisdom
6 Worship the Lord in the beauty
18 Glorious things of thee/you are spoken
19 As with gladness men of old
19 O little town of Bethlehem
19 Today, if you hear his voice

Isaiah 61

1 A child is born in Bethlehem
1 And can it be
1 Christian, do you not hear the Lord
1 Come sing the praise of Jesus
1 God has chosen me
1 God is working his purpose out
1 God of glory
1 God of heaven
1 God we praise you
1 Hail to the Lord's anointed
1 Hark, my soul! it is the Lord
1 Hark the glad sound! The Saviour comes
1 I cannot tell why he whom angels worship
1 I'll praise my maker while I've breath
1 Jesus has sat down
1 Jesus, Lamb of God and source of life
1 Jesus shall reign
1 Jesus, the name high over all
1 Let all the earth hear his voice
1 Make way, make way
1 O bless the God of Israel
1 Oh for a thousand tongues to sing
1 Praise the Father (Gabi, gabi)
1 The Kingdom of God
1 The Spirit of the Lord
1 We declare that the Kingdom of God
1 When Jesus walked upon this earth

2 We declare that the Kingdom of God
3 Beauty for brokenness (God of the poor)
3 Hail to the Lord's anointed
10 A debtor to mercy alone
10 And can it be
10 God of grace, I turn my face
10 Here, O my Lord, I see thee face to face
10 Jesus, your blood and righteousness
10 My hope is built on nothing less
10 O Father of the fatherless (Father me)

Isaiah 62

2 Oh for a heart to praise my God
5 O Christ the great foundation
5 The Church's one foundation
6 Pass through the gates
10 Make way, make way
25 Oh the valleys shall ring

Isaiah 63

1 I love you, O Lord, you alone
1 Ye/you servants of God, your master proclaim
7 Soften my heart, Lord, soften my heart
9 You are the Lord
10 The Spirit came, as promised
12 How firm a foundation

Isaiah 64

1 Jesus comes with clouds descending
1 Jesus, where'er thy people meet
1 Lo! He comes with clouds descending
1 Lord Jesus, when your people meet
4 Lord of all power, I give you my will
8 Change my heart, O God
8 Jesus, you are changing me

Isaiah 65

17 It came upon the midnight clear
17 Songs of praise the angels sang

Isaiah 66

1 Jesus, where'er thy people meet
1 Lord Jesus, when your people meet
1 Lord, you need no house

2 Come down, O Love divine
2 Love divine, all loves excelling
2 Oh for a heart to praise my God
2 Praise the Father, God of justice
12 In your arms of love
12 Like a mighty river flowing
12 Like a river glorious
12 Praise the Father, God of justice
12 There is none like you
14 The right hand of God is writing
22 It came upon the midnight clear
22 Songs of praise the angels sang
72 Lord, the light (Shine, Jesus, shine)

Jeremiah
Jeremiah 1
5 My Lord, I did not choose you
7 Lord, speak to me that I may speak
9 God be in my head
9 Lord Jesus, let these eyes of mine
9 Take my life and let it be

Jeremiah 2
2 Guide me, O my great Redeemer
2 Guide me, O thou great Jehovah
11 Faithful vigil ended
11 Lord, now let your servant depart
13 Father, hear the prayer we offer
13 Glorious things of thee/you are spoken
13 I hunger and I thirst
13 Jesus, lover of my soul
13 Lord of the church, we pray for our renewing
13 Rock of ages, cleft for me
13 Such love

Jeremiah 6
1 Blow upon the trumpet

Jeremiah 9
5 He who would valiant be
5 Who would true valour see
15 All hail the power of Jesus' name
23 When I survey the wondrous cross
24 Eternal light, shine in my heart
24 Light of the minds that know him

Jeremiah 10
7 God of eternity, Lord of the ages
7 King of the universe, Lord of the ages
10 My God, how wonderful you are
10 Praise, my soul, the King of heaven

Jeremiah 12
3 Forth in thy/your name, O Lord, I go

Jeremiah 14
8 Christ's church shall glory in his power
8 Jesus, hope of every nation
8 O God, our help in ages past
20 Almighty God, our heavenly Father

Jeremiah 15
16 Breathe on me, Spirit of Jesus
16 Lord, I was blind; I could not see

Jeremiah 16
19 A mighty fortress is our God
19 A safe stronghold our God is still
19 God is our fortress and our rock
19 God is our strength and refuge

Jeremiah 17
4 How do we start (That the world may)
7 All my hope on God is founded
7 Jesus, lover of my soul
8 Light has dawned
13 Father, hear the prayer we offer
13 Glorious things of thee/you are spoken
13 Guide me, O my great Redeemer
13 Guide me, O thou great Jehovah
13 I hunger and I thirst
13 Jesus, hope of every nation
13 Jesus, lover of my soul
13 Lord of the church, we pray for our renewing
13 O God, our help in ages past
13 Such love

Jeremiah 18
3 Change my heart, O God
4 Jesus, you are changing me

Jeremiah 19
1 Change my heart, O God

Jeremiah 22
29 Rejoice, O land, in God your Lord

Jeremiah 23
5 A child is born in Bethlehem
5 All hail the power of Jesus' name
5 O come, O come, Emmanuel

41 Come, praise the Lord
41 Lift up your hearts to the Lord
41 O God beyond all praising
41 Rejoice, the Lord is King
58 O bless the Lord, my soul

Lamentations 4
4 Beauty for brokenness (God of the poor)

Lamentations 5
19 And he shall reign
19 In the tomb so cold

Ezekiel
Ezekiel 1
26 Ride on, ride on in majesty

Ezekiel 3
1 Lord, speak to me that I may speak
17 Go, tell it on the mountain

Ezekiel 10
1 Bright the vision that delighted
1 Ride on, ride on in majesty
4 Be still, for the presence of the Lord

Ezekiel 11
19 O Spirit of the living God
19 Oh for a heart to praise my God

Ezekiel 12
2 God has spoken to his people

Ezekiel 16
9 Rock of ages, cleft for me

Ezekiel 17
6 Rock of ages, cleft for me
23 The right hand of God is writing

Ezekiel 18
16 Praise the Father (Gabi, gabi)
31 Oh for a heart to praise my God

Ezekiel 21
27 Ye/you servants of God, your master proclaim

Ezekiel 26
4 All my hope on God is founded

Ezekiel 32
7 Songs of thankfulness and praise

Ezekiel 34
5 Risen Lord, whose name we cherish
6 Before Jehovah's awesome/aweful throne
6 Come, O Fount of every blessing
6 Lord, speak to me that I may speak
6 O Christ, at your first Eucharist
6 O thou, who at thy Eucharist didst pray
6 Restless souls, why do you scatter
6 Souls of men, why will ye scatter
6 The King of love my Shepherd is
12 Now to him who is able
24 Jerusalem the golden
26 Hail to the Lord's anointed
31 All people that on earth do dwell
31 Come, rejoice before your maker
31 Come with all joy to sing to God
31 Come, worship God who is worthy

Ezekiel 36
2 Spirit of God, rest on your people
21 The Lord my shepherd rules my life
25 Jesus, lover of my soul
25 Rock of ages, cleft for me
26 Lord have mercy, Lord have mercy
26 O Spirit of the living God
26 Oh for a heart to praise my God
28 God whose love we cannot measure
35 Name of all majesty
35 The Lord made man, the Scriptures tell

Ezekiel 37
I hear the sound of rustling
1 O Trinity, O Trinity
1 Revive thy work/your church, O Lord
1 Spirit of God most high
1 This is the day of light
4 Spirit of God most high
9 Breathe on me, breath of God
9 Here within this house of prayer
9 O Breath of Life, come sweeping through
9 O Spirit of the living God
9 We are his children
10 Rejoice, rejoice, Christ is in you
14 Stir my heart, O Lord
26 A debtor to mercy alone
26 Hail to the Lord's anointed

26 My hope is built on nothing less

Ezekiel 38
15 Rejoice, rejoice, Christ is in you

Ezekiel 39
7 Holy is the name of God
29 We your people

Ezekiel 43
2 He walks among the golden lamps
2 You are the God of our fathers

Ezekiel 44
3 Jerusalem the golden

Ezekiel 46
2 Jerusalem the golden

Ezekiel 47
3 I will sing the wondrous story
5 River, wash over me
9 Jesus, lover of my soul
9 River, wash over me
12 Guide me, O my great Redeemer
12 Guide me, O thou great Jehovah
12 Jerusalem the golden
12 Jesus, lover of my soul

Ezekiel 48
31 Jerusalem, my happy home
31 Wake, O wake, and sleep no longer
35 God of eternity, Lord of the ages
35 Jehovah Jireh
35 We love the place, O God

Daniel
Daniel 2
20 Immortal, invisible
20 Who can measure heaven and earth
23 Bless the Lord, our fathers' God
28 Father God in heaven (Kum ba yah)
44 The day thou gavest, Lord, is ended
47 God of gods, we sound his praises

Daniel 3
Bless the Lord, creation sings
Father of all, whose laws have stood
Give praise for famous men
Oh for a closer walk with God
17 Glory to you, my God, this night

17 You servants of the Lord

Daniel 4
37 Be thou my vision/Lord be my vision
37 Bless the Lord, our fathers' God
37 Christmas for God's holy people
37 Praise, my soul, the King of heaven
37 Shepherds came, their praises bringing

Daniel 5
23 O Lord of heaven and earth and sea
23 Unto the hills around
24 The right hand of God is writing
30 Tell out my soul

Daniel 6
10 Prayer is the soul's sincere desire
20 O Spirit of the living God
20 Ye/you servants of God, your master proclaim
26 The day thou gavest, Lord, is ended

Daniel 7
9 Immortal, invisible
9 O worship the King
9 O worship the Lord in the beauty
9 Such love
10 I cannot tell why he whom angels worship
10 Ten thousand times ten thousand
13 And he shall reign
13 Great God, what do I see and hear
13 Jesus came, the heavens adoring
13 Jesus comes with clouds descending
13 Lo! He comes with clouds descending
14 Hail to the Lord's anointed
14 The day thou gavest, Lord, is ended
18 The head that once was crowned

Daniel 8
25 Alleluia, raise the anthem
25 Come, ye faithful, raise the anthem

Daniel 9
5 We your people
7 Here, O my Lord, I see thee face to face
7 Jesus, lover of my soul
8 Almighty God, our heavenly Father

173

9 When all your mercies, O my God
19 O Lord, the clouds are gathering
24 Hail to the Lord's anointed
24 New songs of celebration render

Daniel 10
5 He walks among the golden lamps
6 Won, the victor's crown
19 Lift up your heads, you gates of brass
19 Soldiers of Christ, arise
19 Stand up! stand up for Jesus
19 We rest on thee/trust in you

Daniel 11
36 God of gods, we sound his praises

Daniel 12
2 Oh heaven is in my heart
3 For all the saints who from their labour
3 Once in royal David's city

Hosea

Hosea 2
19 O Christ the great foundation
19 The Church's one foundation
19 You are the Lord
23 Church of God, elect and glorious
23 The right hand of God is writing

Hosea 5
14 You choirs of new Jerusalem
15 I will seek your face, O Lord

Hosea 6
1 How do we start (That the world may)

Hosea 10
12 Tell his praise in song and story

Hosea 11
1 Christian, do you not hear the Lord
1 Hark, my soul! it is the Lord
1 When all your mercies, O my God
4 Bind us together, Lord
8 Soften my heart, Lord, soften my heart

Hosea 13
4 Father of all, whose laws have stood
4 Holy, holy, holy, Lord God almighty

14 Abide with me, fast falls the eventide
14 All creation join to say
14 Christ the Lord is risen today
14 Light's glittering morning fills the sky
14 Love's redeeming work is done
14 Risen Lord, whose name we cherish
14 The strife is past/o'er, the battle done
14 Thine/Yours be the glory

Hosea 14
4 Christian, do you not hear the Lord
4 Hark, my soul! it is the Lord
4 So freely flows the endless love
8 Praise God from whom all blessings
9 Give to our God immortal praise
9 How can we sing with joy
9 Praise to the Holiest in the height
9 Rejoice, O land, in God your Lord

Joel

Joel 2
1 Blow upon the trumpet
1 We are his children
2 O Lord, the clouds are gathering
13 How can we sing with joy
13 How do we start (That the world may)
15 Blow upon the trumpet
20 To God be the glory
21 Rejoice, O land, in God your Lord
28 Pour out, I will pour out my Spirit
28 The King is among us
28 The Spirit came, as promised
28 We your people
31 Blow upon the trumpet
31 Songs of thankfulness and praise
32 In awe and wonder, Lord our God
32 Jesus, the joy of loving hearts
32 Saviour, again to thy dear name
32 There is power in the name of Jesus

Joel 3
2 Angels from the realms of glory
10 My peace I leave I leave with you
16 O God, our help in ages past
17 Glorious things of thee/you are spoken
18 Jesus, lover of my soul

174

Amos

Amos 3
3 Men and women, let us walk

Amos 4
12 Great God, what do I see and hear
12 O Spirit of the living God
13 I, the Lord of sea and sky
13 O worship the Lord in the beauty
13 Worship the Lord in the beauty

Amos 5
6 Tell his praise in song and story
8 I, the Lord of sea and sky
8 O worship the Lord in the beauty
8 Worship the Lord in the beauty
24 Hail to the Lord's anointed
24 O Lord, the clouds are gathering

Amos 7
2 O Lord, the clouds are gathering
10 Give praise for famous men
10 God has spoken, by his prophets

Amos 8
11 Lord, we long for you (Heal our nation)

Amos 9
6 O worship the Lord in the beauty
6 Worship the Lord in the beauty
15 The right hand of God is writing

Obadiah

Obadiah
21 Come and see the shining hope
21 Soldiers of the cross, arise

Jonah

Jonah 1
9 I, the Lord of sea and sky
9 O Lord of heaven and earth and sea
11 Lead us, heavenly Father, lead us

Jonah 2
2 I love you, O Lord, you alone
2 Listen to my prayer, Lord
9 Rock of ages, cleft for me
9 With all my heart

Jonah 3
1 God has spoken, by his prophets
10 Soften my heart, Lord, soften my heart

Micah

Micah 2
13 Jesus, we celebrate your victory

Micah 4
3 Christ is the world's true light
3 Crown him with many crowns
3 My peace I leave I leave with you
3 Thy/your Kingdom come, O God
8 Like a shepherd I will feed you

Micah 5
2 While shepherds watched
2 A messenger named Gabriel
2 Bethlehem, the chosen city of our God
2 Bethlehem, what greater city
2 Calypso Carol (See him lying on a bed of straw)
2 Christians, awake, salute the happy morn
2 Christmas for God's holy people
2 Come all you good people
2 God rest you/ye merry, gentlemen
2 Hark! the herald-angels sing
2 I cannot tell why he whom angels worship
2 Jesus Christ the Lord is born
2 O come, all ye/you faithful
2 O little town of Bethlehem
2 See, amid the winter's snow
2 See him lying on a bed of straw
2 Songs of thankfulness and praise
2 The first nowell the angel did say
2 Unto us a boy is born
2 We have a gospel to proclaim
2 While shepherds watched
2 Wise men, they came to look for wisdom
4 From east to west, from shore to shore
4 How sweet the name of Jesus sounds

Micah 6
6 Brightest and best of the sons
6 Not all the blood of beasts
6 What offering shall we give
7 King of glory, King of peace
8 Forth in thy/your name, O Lord, I go
8 He has shown you
8 Immortal Love, for ever full
8 Oh for a closer walk with God

Micah 7
7 Lord of our life
7 Praise the Lord, you heavens,
   adore him
8 God whose love we cannot
   measure
8 Within our darkest night
20 Tell out my soul

Nahum
Nahum 1
3 O worship the King
3 The works of the Lord are created
7 Amazing grace
7 Unto the hills around
15 Come on and celebrate
15 Hail to the Lord's anointed
15 Take my life and let it be

Habakkuk
Habakkuk 1
12 God of gods, we sound his praises
12 Jesus comes with clouds
   descending
12 Lo! He comes with clouds
   descending

Habakkuk 2
14 God is working his purpose out
14 May the mind of Christ my
   Saviour
14 You are the God of our fathers
20 From all who live beneath the
   skies
20 Let all mortal flesh keep silence

Habakkuk 3
2 O Breath of Life, come sweeping
   through
2 Revive thy work/your church, O
   Lord
2 You are beautiful beyond
   description
3 Bright the vision that delighted
17 A mighty fortress is our God
17 A safe stronghold our God is still
17 God is our fortress and our rock
18 In the Lord I'll ever be thankful
18 Tell out my soul
19 Christians, lift up your hearts
   (Word)
19 Christ's church shall glory in his
   power
19 Guide me, O my great Redeemer
19 Guide me, O thou great Jehovah

19 I love you, O Lord, you alone
19 Stand up and bless the Lord

Zephaniah
Zephaniah 1
18 No weight of gold or silver

Zephaniah 3
   The Lord your God is in your
   midst
9 Saviour, again to thy dear name
14 Glorious things of thee/you are
   spoken
16 Thy/Your hand, O God, has
   guided
16 When the King shall come again
17 Be bold, be strong

Haggai
Haggai 2
4 Stand up! stand up for Jesus
7 Christ is the world's true light
7 Come, O/thou long-expected
   Jesus
7 Earth was waiting, spent and
   restless
7 Ten thousand times ten thousand
8 Son of God, eternal Saviour
23 My Lord, I did not choose you

Zechariah
Zechariah 2
13 Be still, for the presence of the Lord
13 From all who live beneath the skies
13 Let all mortal flesh keep silence

Zechariah 3
8 O come, O come, Emmanuel
8 Songs of thankfulness and praise

Zechariah 4
14 You are crowned with many
   crowns
14 You are the Lord

Zechariah 6
5 You are crowned with many
   crowns
5 You are the Lord
5 You sat down

Zechariah 8
12 Praise God from whom all
   blessings flow
12 We plough the fields, and scatter

13 Be bold, be strong
17 Father of all, whose laws have stood
22 Angels from the realms of glory

Zechariah 9
9 All glory, laud/praise and honour
9 Ride on, ride on in majesty
9 Shout for joy, and sing your praises
14 Blow upon the trumpet
16 Now to him who is able
17 Through all the changing scenes
17 When all your mercies, O my God

Zechariah 10
3 How sweet the name of Jesus sounds
4 Oh heaven is in my heart
6 Soften my heart, Lord, soften my heart

Zechariah 12
1 O Father of the fatherless (Father me)
10 Jesus comes with clouds descending
10 Lo! He comes with clouds descending
10 O dearest Lord, your sacred head
10 Sing lullaby
10 Sing, my tongue, the glorious battle
10 Spirit of faith, by faith be mine
10 The hands of Christ, the caring hands
10 We your people

Zechariah 13
1 Guide me, O thou great Jehovah
1 Guide me, O my great Redeemer
1 Jesus, lover of my soul
1 Rock of ages, cleft for me
1 There is a fountain
2 For I'm building a people of power
7 Ah, holy Jesus, how have you offended
7 Risen Lord, whose name we cherish
9 How firm a foundation
9 You're worthy of my praise

Zechariah 14
8 Glorious things of thee/you are spoken
8 Lord of the church, we pray for our

renewing
8 Such love
9 Christ is the world's true light
9 You are the Lord

Malachi

Malachi 1
11 Christ is the world's true light
11 Jesus shall reign
11 The day thou gavest, Lord, is ended
14 You servants of the Lord

Malachi 3
1 Clear the road (Prepare the way)
1 Love divine, all loves excelling
1 Make way, make way
1 Prepare the way (Clear the road)
2 Purify my heart
2 Restore, O Lord
3 God we praise you
6 Abide with me, fast falls the eventide
6 Fight the good fight with all thy/your might
6 God has spoken, by his prophets
6 How good is the God we adore
6 I hear the words of love
10 Christ is our cornerstone

Malachi 4
1 Come, you thankful people, come
2 All creation join to say
2 All shall be well
2 Christ the Lord is risen today
2 Christ, whose glory fills the skies
2 God/Thou, whose almighty word
2 Hark! the herald-angels sing
2 Judge eternal, throned in splendour
2 Love's redeeming work is done
2 The heavens declare the glory (Silver)
2 The people who in darkness walked
2 Thou/God, whose almighty word
2 You are the God of our fathers
4 Christ upon the mountain peak
4 Our Saviour Christ once knelt in prayer
4 When Jesus led his chosen three

Matthew

Matthew 1
Holy child, how still you lie
1 All glory, laud/praise and honour

1 Earth was waiting, spent and restless
1 Hail to the Lord's anointed
1 O bless the God of Israel
1 This is the day that the Lord has made
11 Small wonder the star
16 I cannot tell why he whom angels worship
18 O come, all ye/you faithful
20 Rejoice, rejoice, for the king Messiah
21 All hail the power of Jesus' name
21 At the name of Jesus
21 Come, O/thou long-expected Jesus
21 Good Christian men/Christians all rejoice
21 How sweet the name of Jesus sounds
21 I'm not ashamed to own/name my Lord
21 Jesus, my Lord, my God, my all
21 Jesus, the name high over all
21 Jesus, the very thought of thee
21 Jesus, where'er thy people meet
21 Lord Jesus, when your people meet
21 Mary had a baby, yes Lord
21 Name of all majesty
21 No weight of gold or silver
21 Oh for a thousand tongues to sing
21 To the name of our salvation
22 God of God, the uncreated
22 Of the Father's love begotten
23 A child is born for us today
23 A great and mighty wonder
23 Angels from the realms of glory
23 Christians, awake, salute the happy morn
23 Christmas for God's holy people
23 Come all you good people
23 Earth was waiting, spent and restless
23 Emmanuel, Emmanuel, his name is called
23 Emmanuel, Emmanuel, we call your name
23 Emmanuel, Emmanuel, wonderful counsellor
23 Emmanuel, God is with us
23 Emmanuel . . . he is here
23 Father eternal, Lord of the ages
23 God of God, the uncreated
23 God we praise you

23 God, we praise you! God, we bless you
23 Had he not loved us
23 Hail, our once-rejected Jesus
23 Hail, thou once despised Jesus
23 Hark! the herald-angels sing
23 Hark! the voice of love and mercy
23 Immanuel, O Immanuel
23 Jesus, King of kings
23 Jesus, Lamb of God and source of life
23 Let us talents and tongues employ
23 Lord of the cross of shame
23 Lord, you were rich beyond all splendour
23 O come, all ye/you faithful
23 O come, O come, Emmanuel
23 O little town of Bethlehem
23 O Trinity, O Trinity
23 Of the Father's love begotten
23 Shout aloud, girls and boys
23 Silent night, holy night
23 Sing, my tongue, the glorious battle
23 The darkness turns to dawn
23 The virgin Mary had a baby boy
23 Thou who wast rich
24 As Joseph was awaking
35 Dear Lord and Father of mankind

Matthew 2

 As with gladness men of old
 Mary came with meekness
1 A baby was born in Bethlehem
1 A song was heard at Christmas
1 All my heart this night rejoices
1 Angels from the realms of glory
1 As with gladness men of old
1 Be still and know that I am God
1 Behold, the great creator makes
1 Brightest and best of the sons
1 Calypso Carol (See him lying on a bed of straw)
1 Come and join the celebration
1 Ding, dong, ring out the carillon
1 Glory in the highest heaven
1 Hail to the Lord's anointed
1 Holy child, how still you lie
1 In the bleak mid-winter
1 Jesus Christ the Lord is born
1 Land of hope and glory (Glory in the highest)
1 Love came down at Christmas
1 O come, all ye/you faithful
1 O leave your sheep

Matthew 3

11 Spirit divine, attend/inspire our prayers
12 Come, you thankful people, come
13 I bind myself to God today
13 Songs of thankfulness and praise
16 Christ on whom the Spirit rested
16 God/Thou, whose almighty word
16 Lead us, heavenly Father, lead us
16 Like the murmur of the dove's song
16 O Lord of heaven and earth and sea
16 Oh for a closer walk with God
16 Spirit divine, attend/inspire our prayers
16 Thou/God, whose almighty word
17 Name of all majesty

Matthew 4

1 Be still and know that I am God
1 Forty days and forty nights
1 God save and bless our nation
1 Lead us, heavenly Father, lead us
2 O happy band of pilgrims
2 Who is he, in yonder stall
10 All heaven declares
15 Faithful vigil ended
15 Jesus, hope of every nation
15 Lord, now let your servant depart
16 Christ, whose glory fills the skies
16 Light has dawned
16 O bless the God of Israel
16 O Spirit of the living God
16 The darkness turns to dawn
16 The people who in darkness walked
17 Crown him with many crowns
17 The Kingdom of God
18 Dear Lord and Father of mankind
19 Be still and know that I am God
19 Dear Lord and Father of mankind
19 From heaven you came (The Servant King)
19 Will you come and follow me
19 You're worthy of my praise
23 God/Thou, whose almighty word
23 Songs of thankfulness and praise
23 The Kingdom of God
23 Thou/God, whose almighty word

Matthew 5

1 Lord Jesus, once you spoke to men
1 O changeless Christ, for ever new
4 Oh for a thousand tongues to sing
5 Christ on whom the Spirit rested
6 I hunger and I thirst

6 Lord, we long for you (Heal our nation)
6 Revive thy work/your church, O Lord
8 Blessed are the pure in heart
8 Breathe on me, breath of God
8 Jesus lives! Thy/Your terrors now
8 Oh for a heart to praise my God
9 Make me a channel of your peace
9 Put peace into each other's hands
12 Christ is surely coming
13 All we've received (We are your church)
13 Here I am
13 Here in this place
14 All we've received (We are your church)
14 Christ triumphant
14 God of eternity, Lord of the ages
14 Lights to the world (The earth was dark)
14 The earth was dark
15 Christ is the King! O friends rejoice
15 Make me a channel of your peace
15 Risen Lord, whose name we cherish
16 Church of God, elect and glorious
16 Help us, O Lord, to learn
22 Christ is the world's Light, he and none other
24 I come with joy to meet my Lord
24 Spirit of God most high
24 We plough the fields, and scatter
35 Jerusalem on high
44 O Lord, all the world belongs to you
48 Oh for a heart to praise my God

Matthew 6

6 Prayer is the soul's sincere desire
9 Blessed be the Lord (Father in heaven)
9 Father God, I wonder
9 Father God in heaven (Kum ba yah)
9 Father in heaven, grant to your children
9 Father in heaven, how we love you
9 Father in heaven, our voices we raise
9 I will sing your praises (Father God)
9 Our Father in heaven
9 We will crown him (Father in heaven)

10 Abba, Father
10 Before the ending of the day
10 Christ is the King! O friends rejoice
10 Come, O/thou long-expected Jesus
10 For the bread which you have broken
10 For the fruits of his creation
10 Jesus, King of kings
10 Jesus, send more labourers
10 Lord, teach us how to pray aright
10 O Christ, at your first Eucharist
10 O Father of the fatherless (Father me)
10 O thou, who at thy Eucharist didst pray
10 Prayer is the soul's sincere desire
10 Reign in me
10 Rejoice, O land, in God your Lord
10 Remember, Lord, the world you made
10 Son of God, eternal Saviour
10 The Kingdom of God
10 Thy/your Kingdom come, O God
11 O God of Jacob, by whose hand
11 To you, O Lord, our hearts we raise
11 We plough the fields, and scatter
12 Forgive our sins as we forgive
12 Glory to you, my God, this night
12 Heal me, hands of Jesus
12 Make me a channel of your peace
13 A mighty fortress is our God
13 A safe stronghold our God is still
13 Almighty Lord, the holy One
13 Be thou/O Lord my guardian and my guide
13 Christian, seek not yet repose
13 God is our fortress and our rock
13 Lighten our darkness
13 O Jesus, I have promised
13 O Lord our guardian and our guide
13 Unto the hills around
13 Who honours courage here
19 Glorious things of thee/you are spoken
19 O Lord of heaven and earth and sea
24 Lord, be my vision/Be thou my vision
26 We plough the fields, and scatter
28 Immortal, invisible
29 He walks among the golden lamps
33 Seek ye first the Kingdom of God

Matthew 7

7 Jesus, the joy of loving hearts
7 Jesus, the very thought of thee
7 Jesus, where'er thy people meet
7 Lord Jesus, when your people meet
7 Seek ye first the Kingdom of God
11 For the beauty of the earth
11 We plough the fields, and scatter
13 As with gladness men of old
13 Faithful Shepherd, feed me
13 I will sing the wondrous story
13 The Son of God rides out to war
14 As with gladness men of old
16 O Trinity, O Trinity
24 My hope is built on nothing less
24 Rock of ages, cleft for me

Matthew 8

2 We give God thanks for those who knew
3 Heal me, hands of Jesus
3 There is none like you
3 We give God thanks for those who knew
8 I am not worthy, holy Lord
8 Word of justice
11 City of God, Jerusalem
16 At even(ing), ere/when the sun was set
16 With loving hands
19 Lord, who left the highest heaven
20 My song is love unknown
22 Be still and know that I am God
22 From heaven you came (The Servant King)
22 You're worthy of my praise
23 Bless the Lord, creation sings
23 Child of the stable's secret birth
23 God, whose farm is all creation
23 I cannot tell why he whom angels worship
23 Jesus, Saviour of the world
23 Light of the minds that know him
23 O changeless Christ, for ever new
23 O Jesus, I have promised
23 Son of God, eternal Saviour
23 Timeless love! We sing the story
23 We plough the fields, and scatter
26 Holy Spirit, truth divine
26 I cannot tell why he whom angels worship
26 Jesus, lover of my soul
26 This is the day of light
27 We plough the fields, and scatter

28 Jesus, the name high over all
28 Songs of thankfulness and praise
28 When Jesus walked upon this
   earth

Matthew 9

2 O come, our all-victorious Lord
2 Songs of thankfulness and praise
6 On Jordan's bank, the Baptist's cry
9 And can it be
9 Be still and know that I am God
9 From heaven you came (The
   Servant King)
9 Jesus calls us! In/o'er the tumult
9 You're worthy of my praise
10 Jesus came, the heavens adoring
10 The Kingdom of God
13 At the name of Jesus
13 He gave his life in selfless love
13 Shout for joy, loud and long
20 Immortal Love, for ever full
20 Open our eyes, Lord
20 We give God thanks for those who
   knew
31 Oh for a thousand tongues to sing
35 We believe in God Almighty
36 Love divine, all loves excelling
36 Restless souls, why do you scatter
36 Soften my heart, Lord, soften my
   heart
36 Souls of men, why will ye scatter
37 Here I am
38 Come, you thankful people, come
38 For the fruits of his creation
38 How shall they hear
38 Jesus, send more labourers
38 Send more labourers
38 Send out the gospel! Let it sound

Matthew 10

1 Songs of thankfulness and praise
1 When Jesus walked upon this
   earth
7 Crown him with many crowns
8 Jesus, the name high over all
8 Oh for a thousand tongues to sing
8 Son of God, eternal Saviour
9 Send me out from here, Lord
16 Put peace into each other's hands
22 O Jesus, I have promised
32 For all the saints who from their
   labour
32 I'm not ashamed to own/name my
   Lord
34 In silent pain the eternal Son

38 Be still and know that I am God
38 Light of the minds that know him
38 Praise to the Holiest in the height
38 Take up your cross, the Saviour
   said
38 The Son of God rides out to war
38 You're worthy of my praise

Matthew 11

4 Oh for a thousand tongues to sing
4 The Kingdom of God
5 God we praise you
5 God/Thou, whose almighty word
5 He gave his life in selfless love
5 Here in this place
5 His eyes will guide my footsteps
5 Jesus, a stranger
5 Jesus has sat down
5 Jesus, the name high over all
5 Let the desert sing
5 Lord, I was blind; I could not see
5 My song is love unknown
5 Oh for a thousand tongues to sing
5 He gave his life in selfless love
5 Thou/God, whose almighty word
5 When the King shall come again
19 Alleluia, sing to Jesus
19 Here within this house of prayer
19 O Christ, the same, through all
19 We come as guests invited
25 O Lord of heaven and earth and
   sea
25 Thank you, O Lord of earth and
   heaven
28 Cast your burdens on to Jesus
28 Father in heaven, grant to your
   children
28 Forth in thy/your name, O Lord, I
   go
28 Here, O my Lord, I see thee face to
   face
28 How sweet the name of Jesus
   sounds
28 I cannot tell why he whom angels
   worship
28 Jesus shall reign
28 Jesus, we celebrate your victory
28 Just as I am
28 Lord Jesus, think of me
28 To be in your presence
28 What a friend we have in Jesus
29 He is lovely

Matthew 12

13 As I hold out my hand

182

15 At even(ing), ere/when the sun
   was set
18 Name of all majesty
22 Jesus, a stranger
23 Hail to the Lord's anointed
28 Songs of thankfulness and praise
28 The Kingdom of God
28 When Jesus walked upon this
   earth
42 He walks among the golden lamps
46 In Christ there is no East or West
50 Love is his word

Matthew 13
 3 Christ's church shall glory in his
   power
13 Great Shepherd of your people
17 God of God, the uncreated
17 Of the Father's love begotten
18 Christ's church shall glory in his
   power
24 Come, you thankful people, come
24 Happy are they, they who love
   God
24 He gave his life in selfless love
25 Come, you thankful people, come
30 From the sun's rising
31 Hail to the Lord's anointed
31 The day thou gavest, Lord, is
   ended
31 The Kingdom of God
34 For all the saints who from their
   labour
43 Jesus, priceless treasure
44 Be thou my vision/Lord be my
   vision
44 Give praise for famous men
44 Lord, thy word abideth
44 Lord, your word shall guide us
46 Like a mighty river flowing
54 We believe in God Almighty

Matthew 14
 3 As we break the bread
14 Beauty for brokenness (God of the
   poor)
14 Soften my heart, Lord, soften my
   heart
15 Jesus calls us! In/o'er the tumult
15 Let us talents and tongues employ
19 Break thou/now the bread of life
23 Bless the Lord, creation sings
23 Eternal Father, strong to save
23 I cannot tell why he whom angels
   worship

23 Jesus, Saviour of the world
23 Light of the minds that know him
23 O changeless Christ, for ever new
23 O Jesus, I have promised
23 Timeless love! We sing the story
29 Just as I am
32 Son of God, eternal Saviour
33 I believe in Jesus
33 The Son of God proclaim
35 Who is he, in yonder stall
36 Immortal Love, for ever full
36 Open our eyes, Lord

Matthew 15
13 Lord, I was blind; I could not see
14 Risen Lord, whose name we
   cherish
26 My God, now is your table spread
30 God/Thou, whose almighty word
30 He gave his life in selfless love
30 He who created light
30 His eyes will guide my footsteps
30 Let the desert sing
30 My song is love unknown
30 Oh for a thousand tongues to sing
30 Thou/God, whose almighty word
30 When the King shall come again
31 Here in this place
31 In the streets of every city
31 My song is love unknown
31 Oh for a thousand tongues to sing
31 We give God thanks for those who
   knew
32 As we break the bread
32 Let us talents and tongues employ
32 Soften my heart, Lord, soften my
   heart
36 Break thou/now the bread of life

Matthew 16
 6 There is a Redeemer
18 All creation join to say
18 Christ the Lord is risen today
18 Christ's church shall glory in his
   power
18 For I'm building a people of power
18 I will build my church
18 Light's glittering morning fills the
   sky
18 Love's redeeming work is done
18 O Christ the great foundation
18 Onward, Christian soldiers
18 Won, the victor's crown
21 The strife is past/o'er, the battle
   done

23 Spirit of God most high
24 Be still and know that I am God
24 Light of the minds that know him
24 New every morning is the love
24 Praise to the Holiest in the height
24 Take up your cross, the Saviour said
24 The Son of God rides out to war
24 Will you come and follow me
24 You're worthy of my praise
27 At the name of Jesus
27 Christ is surely coming
27 He is Lord

Matthew 17
   Christ upon the mountain peak
1 Be thou my vision/Lord be my vision
1 Christ upon the mountain peak
1 Come, praise the name of Jesus
1 Our Saviour Christ once knelt in prayer
1 When Jesus led his chosen three
2 Christ, whose glory fills the skies
2 Lord, the light (Shine, Jesus, shine)
3 Jesus restore to us again
5 Lord Jesus, once you spoke to men
5 Name of all majesty
7 Heal me, hands of Jesus
7 We give God thanks for those who knew
20 Gracious Spirit, Holy Ghost
20 Holy Spirit, gracious guest
20 Rejoice, rejoice, Christ is in you
21 Forty days and forty nights

Matthew 18
12 Before Jehovah's awesome/aweful throne
12 I cannot tell why he whom angels worship
12 I will sing the wondrous story
12 O Father of the fatherless (Father me)
12 The King of love my Shepherd is
14 Amazing grace
20 We love the place, O God
21 Alas! and did my Saviour bleed
21 Father God in heaven (Kum ba yah)
21 Forgive our sins as we forgive
21 Heal me, hands of Jesus
32 Such love

Matthew 19
3 Heal me, hands of Jesus
5 Eternal Father, Lord of life
5 Great God, we praise the mighty love
5 Happy the home that welcomes you
5 Jesus, Lord, we pray
5 Jesus the Lord
5 Will you come and follow me
14 God is here! As we his people
17 There is only one Lord
18 Father of all, whose laws have stood
21 Be still and know that I am God
21 Be thou my vision/Lord be my vision
21 Glorious things of thee/you are spoken
21 In heavenly love abiding
21 O Lord of heaven and earth and sea
21 Will you come and follow me
21 You're worthy of my praise
22 Take my life and let it be
26 Rejoice, rejoice, Christ is in you
27 Children of the heavenly King
28 Angels from the realms of glory
29 He who would valiant be
29 Oh heaven is in my heart
29 Who honours courage here
29 Who would true valour see

Matthew 20
1 Forth in thy/your name, O Lord, I go
17 Jesus, come! for we invite you
19 Come and see, come and see
19 The price is paid
19 The strife is past/o'er, the battle done
19 This is the day, this is the day
22 Child of the stable's secret birth
22 He gave his life in selfless love
28 A purple robe, a crown of thorn
28 All-creating heavenly Giver
28 All shall be well
28 Christ the Lord is risen again
28 Empty he came
28 Father of heaven, whose love profound
28 From heaven you came (The Servant King)
28 God of gods, we sound his praises
28 Have you not heard

27 Songs of thankfulness and praise
29 Christ is ascending! let creation sing
29 Loved with everlasting love
29 When the sun is darkened
30 Great God, what do I see and hear
30 I cannot tell why he whom angels worship
30 Jesus came, the heavens adoring
30 Jesus comes with clouds descending
30 Let the heavens shout for joy
30 Let the world sing Jesus reigns
30 Lo! He comes with clouds descending
30 Ten thousand times ten thousand
30 You are crowned with many crowns
31 Blow upon the trumpet
31 Hark! A thrilling voice is sounding
31 Jesus the Saviour comes
31 Lift up your hearts to the Lord
31 Lord of our life
31 My hope is built on nothing less
31 Rejoice, the Lord is King
31 These are the facts
31 This joyful Eastertide
31 When the Lord in glory comes
35 And he shall reign
35 Great God, what do I see and hear
35 In the bleak mid-winter
35 Loved with everlasting love
35 Praise him, praise him, praise him
35 Songs of praise the angels sang
35 The day thou gavest, Lord, is ended
35 You can trust his promises
42 You servants of the Lord

Matthew 25
1 Christ is the King! O friends rejoice
1 Wake, O wake, and sleep no longer
1 You servants of the Lord
4 Tell me, why do you weep
6 Sound on the trumpet
10 Here, O my Lord, I see thee face to face
14 All-creating heavenly Giver
14 All for Jesus, all for Jesus
14 Awake, my soul, and with the sun
14 Come to us, creative Spirit
14 Let us talents and tongues employ
21 Lord Jesus, think of me
31 Angels from the realms of glory
31 At the name of Jesus

31 Come, you thankful people, come
31 Tell all the world of Jesus
31 Thy/your Kingdom come, O God
35 There's a spirit in the air

Matthew 26
2 Love is his word
7 Open our eyes, Lord
15 Christ is the world's Light, he and none other
19 Love is his word
24 Jesus is King
26 Alleluia, raise the anthem
26 Bread of the world in mercy broken
26 Broken for me
26 Christians, lift up your hearts (Word)
26 City of God, Jerusalem
26 Come, let us with our Lord arise
26 Come, ye faithful, raise the anthem
26 Faithful Shepherd, feed me
26 First of the week and finest day
26 For the bread which you have broken
26 Glory be to Jesus
26 God is here! As we his people
26 God our Father, bless your people
26 Here is bread
26 I know that my Redeemer lives, comfort
26 Let all mortal flesh keep silence
26 Look, Lord, in mercy as we pray
26 Lord God, your love has called us here
26 Love is his word
26 Now lives the Lamb of God
26 O changeless Christ, for ever new
26 O God of Jacob, by whose hand
26 Peace be with you all, we sing
26 Tell his praise in song and story
26 Thank you, O Lord of earth and heaven
26 The Church's one foundation
26 The King of love my Shepherd is
26 The Kingdom of God
26 The Lord my shepherd rules my life
26 The Son of God proclaim
26 There's a spirit in the air
26 Thou art coming, O my Saviour
26 Through all the changing scenes
26 Thy/Your hand, O God, has guided
26 Wake, O wake, and sleep no longer

18 Ascended Christ
18 Christians, lift up your hearts (Praise)
18 Jesus lives! Thy/Your terrors now
18 Sent by the Lord am I
18 You choirs of new Jerusalem
19 From the sun's rising
19 Go forth and tell
19 I believe in God the Father
19 I bind myself to God today
19 Lord, your church on earth
19 No more weeping (Paschal procession)
19 Now through the grace of God
19 O Spirit of the living God
19 Oh for a thousand tongues to sing
19 Send me out from here, Lord
19 We are his children
20 Alleluia, sing to Jesus
20 Don't be afraid
20 Let us talents and tongues employ
20 We love the place, O God
38 Praise to the Holiest in the height

Mark

Mark 1
1 I believe in Jesus
1 Name of all majesty
1 The Son of God proclaim
1 We have a gospel to proclaim
2 On Jordan's bank, the Baptist's cry
3 Alleluia . . . prepare the way
3 Clear the road (Prepare the way)
3 Make way, make way
3 My Lord, he is a-coming soon
3 Prepare the way (Clear the road)
3 Prepare the way of the Lord
3 The bells ring out at Christmas-time
4 On Jordan's bank, the Baptist's cry
5 River, wash over me
9 I bind myself to God today
9 I cannot tell why he whom angels worship
9 Songs of thankfulness and praise
10 Christ on whom the Spirit rested
10 God/Thou, whose almighty word
10 Lead us, heavenly Father, lead us
10 Like the murmur of the dove's song
10 O Lord of heaven and earth and sea
10 Oh for a closer walk with God
10 Spirit divine, attend/inspire our prayers
10 Thou/God, whose almighty word

11 Welcome, welcome, saviour born
12 At even(ing), ere/when the sun was set
12 Forty days and forty nights
12 Lead us, heavenly Father, lead us
13 Be still and know that I am God
13 Lead us, heavenly Father, lead us
14 Crown him with many crowns
14 The kingdom of God
15 I want to serve the purpose of God
15 The kingdom of God
16 Dear Lord and Father of mankind
16 Jesus calls us! In/o'er the tumult
17 Be still and know that I am God
17 Dear Lord and Father of mankind
17 From heaven you came (The Servant King)
17 Will you come and follow me
17 You're worthy of my praise
18 Children of the heavenly king
24 There is a redeemer
28 Oh for a thousand tongues to sing
32 At even(ing), ere/when the sun was set
32 With loving hands
40 We give God thanks for those who knew
41 Heal me, hands of Jesus
41 Soften my heart, Lord, soften my heart
41 We give God thanks for those who knew
45 Oh for a thousand tongues to sing

Mark 2
4 You're worthy of my praise
5 Born of the water
5 O come, our all-victorious Lord
5 Songs of thankfulness and praise
14 And can it be
14 Be still and know that I am God
14 Jesus calls us! In/o'er the tumult
15 Jesus came, the heavens adoring
15 The kingdom of God
17 At the name of Jesus
17 He gave his life in selfless love
17 Shout for joy, loud and long
19 Here, O my Lord, I see thee face to face

Mark 3
5 As I hold out my hand
11 I believe in Jesus
11 The Son of God proclaim
27 Songs of thankfulness and praise

27 When Jesus walked upon this
  earth
27 Who honours courage here
31 In Christ there is no East or West
31 Love is his word
35 Love is his word

Mark 4

3 Christ's church shall glory in his
  power
9 God has spoken to his people
12 Great Shepherd of your people
21 Christ is the king! O friends rejoice
21 Make me a channel of your peace
23 God has spoken to his people
26 Come, you thankful people, come
26 For the fruits of his creation
30 Hail to the Lord's anointed
30 The kingdom of God
35 Bless the Lord, creation sings
35 Eternal Father, strong to save
35 I cannot tell why he whom angels
  worship
35 Jesus calls us! In/o'er the tumult
35 Jesus, Saviour of the world
35 Light of the minds that know him
35 O changeless Christ, for ever new
35 O Jesus, I have promised
35 Son of God, eternal saviour
39 Child of the stable's secret birth
39 Holy Spirit, truth divine
39 Jesus, lover of my soul
39 This is the day of light
41 Timeless love! We sing the story
41 We plough the fields, and scatter

Mark 5

12 Jesus, the name high over all
15 Dear Lord and Father of mankind
15 Rock of ages, cleft for me
19 To God be the glory
25 Immortal Love, for ever full
27 Heal me, hands of Jesus
27 Open our eyes, Lord
27 We give God thanks for those who
  knew
34 Forth in the peace of Christ

Mark 6

3 Lord of all hopefulness, Lord of all
  joy
3 O Christ, the Master Carpenter
3 When the Lord in glory comes
7 Alleluia! We sing your praises
7 Haleluya! Pelo tsa rona

7 No more weeping (Paschal
  procession)
7 Sent by the Lord am I
8 Send me out from here, Lord
12 Songs of thankfulness and praise
17 Give praise for famous men
29 Lord, you need no house
34 Restless souls, why do you scatter
34 Soften my heart, Lord, soften my
  heart
34 Souls of men, why will ye scatter
35 As we break the bread
35 Let us talents and tongues employ
41 Break thou/now the bread of life
45 Eternal Father, strong to save
45 I cannot tell why he whom angels
  worship
45 Jesus calls us! In/o'er the tumult
45 Jesus, Saviour of the world
45 Light of the minds that know
  him
45 O changeless Christ, for ever new
45 O Jesus, I have promised
45 Son of God, eternal saviour
55 Who is he, in yonder stall
56 Immortal Love, for ever full
56 Open our eyes, Lord
56 We give God thanks for those who
  knew

Mark 7

27 My God, now is your table spread
33 We give God thanks for those who
  knew
37 All things bright and beautiful
37 Christ on whom the Spirit rested
37 Let the desert sing
37 Lord, I was blind; I could not see
37 Oh for a thousand tongues to sing
37 When the King shall come again

Mark 8

Take up your cross, the Saviour
  said
1 As we break the bread
1 Let us talents and tongues employ
2 Soften my heart, Lord, soften my
  heart
18 Great Shepherd of your people
22 We give God thanks for those who
  knew
23 Heal me, hands of Jesus
23 Jesus, a stranger
29 There is a redeemer
34 At the name of Jesus

34 Be still and know that I am God
34 I'm not ashamed to own/name my Lord
34 Light of the minds that know him
34 New every morning is the love
34 Praise to the Holiest in the height
34 Take up your cross, the Saviour said
34 The Son of God rides out to war
34 Will you come and follow me
34 You're worthy of my praise

Mark 9
1 Rejoice, O land, in God your Lord
2 Be thou my vision/Lord be my vision
2 Christ upon the mountain peak
2 Come, praise the name of Jesus
2 Our Saviour Christ once knelt in prayer
2 When Jesus led his chosen three
3 Christ, whose glory fills the skies
5 Jesus we are here (Jesu tawa pano)
7 Lord Jesus, once you spoke to men
7 Name of all majesty
24 Christ, whose glory fills the skies
29 Forty days and forty nights
36 What a friend we have in Jesus
49 How firm a foundation

Mark 10
7 Eternal Father, Lord of life
7 Great God, we praise the mighty love
7 Happy the home that welcomes you
7 Jesus, Lord, we pray
7 Jesus the Lord
7 Will you come and follow me
16 Away in a manger
17 He who would valiant be
17 Who honours courage here
17 Who would true valour see
18 God is good
19 Father of all, whose laws have stood
21 Be still and know that I am God
21 Be thou my vision/Lord be my vision
21 Glorious things of thee/you are spoken
21 In heavenly love abiding
21 O Lord of heaven and earth and sea
21 Will you come and follow me

22 Take my life and let it be
27 Rejoice, rejoice, Christ is in you
28 Children of the heavenly king
30 Oh heaven is in my heart
38 Child of the stable's secret birth
38 He gave his life in selfless love
45 A purple robe, a crown of thorn
45 All-creating heavenly Giver
45 All shall be well
45 Christ the Lord is risen again
45 Empty he came
45 Father of heaven, whose love profound
45 From heaven you came (The Servant King)
45 God came among us, he became a man
45 God of gods, we sound his praises
45 Have you not heard
45 He came to earth, not to be served
45 I am not worthy, holy Lord
45 Jesus our hope, our heart's desire
45 Jesus, Saviour of the world
45 My Lord, you wore no royal crown
45 O bless the Lord, my soul
45 O come, O come, Emmanuel
45 Praise my soul, the king of heaven
45 Tell his praise in song and story
45 There is a green hill far away
45 When Jesus walked upon this earth
45 Within a crib my saviour lay
51 Jesus, a stranger
52 Creator of the earth and skies

Mark 11
1 All glory, laud/praise and honour
1 My song is love unknown
1 Ride on, ride on in majesty
8 All glory, laud/praise and honour
9 Hark, the glad sound
9 Hark the glad sound! The Saviour comes
9 Holy, holy, holy, Lord
9 Hosanna, hosanna, hosanna
9 I will sing unto the Lord
9 Let trumpets sound
9 Lord, enthroned in heavenly splendour
9 My song is love unknown
9 Ride on, ride on in majesty
9 Sanna
9 This is the day that the Lord has made
9 This is the day, this is the day

9 Who is he, in yonder stall
9 You are the King of glory
17 God our Father and creator
17 Here within this house of prayer
17 We love the place, O God
22 Have faith in God, my heart
23 Gracious Spirit, Holy Ghost
23 Holy Spirit, gracious guest
25 Father God in heaven (Kum ba yah)
25 Forgive our sins as we forgive
25 Heal me, hands of Jesus
27 We love the place, O God

Mark 12
6 Name of all majesty
6 O bless the Lord, my soul
10 Christ is made the sure foundation
10 Christ is our cornerstone
10 Oh heaven is in my heart
26 God of Abraham, lead us
26 The God of Abraham praise
28 Love came down at Christmas
28 Welcome to another day
29 Father of all, whose laws have stood
30 You can trust his promises
33 You can trust his promises
35 All hail the power of Jesus' name
35 Hail to the Lord's anointed
36 Rejoice, the Lord is King
41 Take my life and let it be

Mark 13
1 All my hope on God is founded
8 Jesus, priceless treasure
10 How shall they hear
10 Send out the gospel! Let it sound
10 We have a gospel to proclaim
13 O Jesus, I have promised
20 Church of God, elect and glorious
20 Jerusalem the golden
21 You're worthy of my praise
24 Christ is ascending! let creation sing
24 From the Father's throne on high
24 Songs of thankfulness and praise
25 Loved with everlasting love
26 And he shall reign
26 Great God, what do I see and hear
26 He is Lord
26 I cannot tell why he whom angels worship
26 Jesus came, the heavens adoring
26 Jesus comes with clouds

descending
26 Let the heavens shout for joy
26 Let the world sing Jesus reigns
26 Lo! He comes with clouds descending
27 Ten thousand times ten thousand
31 Great God, what do I see and hear
31 In the bleak mid-winter
31 Loved with everlasting love
31 Praise him, praise him, praise him
31 Songs of praise the angels sang
31 The day thou gavest, Lord, is ended
31 You can trust his promises
33 Christian, seek not yet repose
33 Forth in thy/your name, O Lord, I go
33 Stand up! stand up for Jesus
33 You servants of the Lord
35 He is Lord

Mark 14
1 Love is his word
3 Consider how he loves you (Sweet Perfume)
3 Open our eyes, Lord
10 Christ is the world's Light, he and none other
12 Christ the Lord is risen again
15 Come, risen Lord, as guest
16 Love is his word
20 Here is bread
22 Bread of the world in mercy broken
22 Broken for me
22 For the bread which you have broken
22 Love is his word
22 Peace be with you all, we sing
22 The Son of God proclaim
25 He gave his life in selfless love
25 Here is bread
25 Here, O my Lord, I see thee face to face
25 One shall tell another (New Wine)
25 He gave his life in selfless love
25 We're going to shine like the sun
27 Ah, holy Jesus, how have you offended
27 Risen Lord, whose name we cherish
30 Ah, holy Jesus, how have you offended
34 Praise to the Holiest in the height
34 Stay with me, remain here with me
36 Abba, Father

36 From heaven you came (The
  Servant King)
36 He gave his life in selfless love
36 When you prayed beneath the trees
38 Christian, seek not yet repose
38 Forth in thy/your name, O Lord, I
  go
38 Stand up! stand up for Jesus
38 Stay with me, remain here with me
43 When you prayed beneath the
  trees
47 My Lord, you wore no royal crown
59 He stood before the court
50 In silent pain the eternal Son
55 He stood before the court
58 God our Father and creator
61 I cannot tell why he whom angels
  worship
61 When you prayed beneath the
  trees
62 And he shall reign
62 God we praise you
62 Great God, what do I see and hear
62 Jesus came, the heavens adoring
62 Jesus comes with clouds
  descending
62 Jesus has sat down
62 Jesus is king
62 Led like a lamb (You're alive)
62 Lo! He comes with clouds
  descending
66 Ah, holy Jesus, how have you
  offended

Mark 15
1 Be still and know that I am God
1 He stood before the court
6 My song is love unknown
7 At the foot of the cross
13 My song is love unknown
14 Ah, holy Jesus, how have you
  offended
14 The hands of Christ, the caring
  hands
14 When you prayed beneath the
  trees
15 The price is paid
16 A purple robe, a crown of thorn
16 Ah, holy Jesus, how have you
  offended
16 Empty he came
16 Man of Sorrows, what a name
16 O sacred head, once wounded
16 Sing, my tongue, the glorious
  battle

17 A purple robe, a crown of thorn
17 Child of the stable's secret birth
17 Come and see, come and see
17 It is a thing most wonderful
17 Jesus, child of Mary
17 Look, ye saints, the sight is
  glorious
17 Lord Jesus, for my sake you come
17 My Lord of light who made the
  worlds
17 O dearest Lord, your sacred head
17 O sacred head, once wounded
17 The hands of Christ, the caring
  hands
17 The head that once was crowned
17 When I survey the wondrous cross
19 The Son of God proclaim
20 Lord Jesus Christ (Living Lord)
21 When you prayed beneath the
  trees
22 There is a green hill far away
23 All hail the power of Jesus' name
23 Sing, my tongue, the glorious
  battle
23 The hands of Christ, the caring
  hands
24 At the foot of the cross
24 He gave his life in selfless love
24 I believe in God the Father
24 I believe there is a God
24 In silent pain the eternal Son
24 He gave his life in selfless love
24 Thank you for the cross
25 Downtrodden Christ
26 Look, ye saints, the sight is glorious
27 Lead us, heavenly Father, lead us
27 We saw thee not
27 We were not there to see you come
29 God our Father and creator
31 Come and see, come and see
32 All glory, laud/praise and honour
32 The first nowell the angel did say
33 Alas! and did my saviour bleed
33 Downtrodden Christ
33 It was raining (light a candle)
33 Light a candle
33 My God, I love you
33 They killed him as a common thief
33 When you prayed beneath the trees
36 The hands of Christ, the caring
  hands
37 Hark! the voice of love and mercy
37 It is a thing most wonderful
37 When you prayed beneath the
  trees

Luke 2

15 Christians, awake, salute the
     happy morn
15 Christmas for God's holy people
15 Come all you good people
15 Come and praise the Lord our King
15 God rest you/ye merry, gentlemen
15 Holy child, how still you lie
15 In the bleak mid-winter
15 Mary came with meekness
15 O come, all ye/you faithful
15 O Prince of peace, whose promised
     birth
15 See, amid the winter's snow
15 See him lying on a bed of straw
15 Shepherds came, their praises
     bringing
15 Shepherds, leave your drowsy
     sheep
15 Shepherds, leave your flocks
15 There's a saviour to see on
     Christmas
16 Away in a manger
16 Baby Jesus, sleeping softly
16 Calypso Carol (See him lying on a
     bed of straw)
16 Christ is born within a stable
16 Christians, awake, salute the
     happy morn
16 Come all you good people
16 Come and hear the joyful singing
16 Come and join the celebration
16 Come now with awe
16 Girls and boys, leave your toys
16 Glad music fills the Christmas sky
16 God rest you/ye merry, gentlemen
16 In the bleak mid-winter
16 Lift your heart and raise your voice
16 Lord, speak softly to my soul
16 Lord, the light (Shine, Jesus, shine)
16 O come all you children to
     Bethlehem
16 Off to David's town they go
16 Play your pipe, bang your drum
16 See him lying on a bed of straw
16 See the dawn appearing
16 Shepherds came, their praises
     bringing
16 Silent night, holy night
16 Soft the evening shadows fall
16 Where's everybody going
16 Who is he, in yonder stall
17 Holy child, how still you lie
18 See, amid the winter's snow
19 Come ride with kings
19 Glad music fills the Christmas sky

19 Praise to God and peace on earth
19 The stars danced, the angels sang
20 Christians, make a joyful sound
20 Mary and Joseph, praise with
     them
20 Ring out the bells (Past three a
     clock)
20 When God from heaven to earth
     came down
21 All hail the power of Jesus' name
21 At the name of Jesus
21 How sweet the name of Jesus
     sounds
21 I'm not ashamed to own/name my
     Lord
21 Jesus, my Lord, my God, my all
21 Jesus, the name high over all
21 Jesus, the very thought of thee
21 Jesus, where'er thy people meet
21 Lord Jesus, when your people
     meet
21 Name of all majesty
21 Oh for a thousand tongues to sing
21 To the name of our salvation
25 Come, O/thou long-expected
     Jesus
29 Faithful vigil ended
29 Forth in the peace of Christ
29 Greetings, Christian friends
29 Holy child, how still you lie
29 Jesus, hope of every nation
29 Lord, now let your servant depart
29 Lord, now let your servant go
29 Now at last
29 Peace be with you all, we sing
30 Rejoice, rejoice, for the king
     Messiah
32 Come, O/thou long-expected
     Jesus
32 Come, praise the name of Jesus
32 Consider how he loves you
32 Lighten our darkness
32 Lights to the world (The earth was
     dark)
32 The earth was dark
34 Child of gladness, child of sorrow
34 This Child, secretly comes in the
     night
35 This is the truth which we
     proclaim
38 See, amid the winter's snow
39 I cannot tell why he whom angels
     worship
39 Lord, who left the highest heaven
39 Once in royal David's city

34 There is a redeemer
40 At even(ing), ere/when the sun was set
40 Heal me, hands of Jesus
40 We give God thanks for those who knew
40 With loving hands
41 I believe in Jesus
41 The Son of God proclaim
41 There is a redeemer

Luke 5

5 Forth in thy/your name, O Lord, I go
8 I am not worthy, holy Lord
8 Jesus, lover of my soul
11 Children of the heavenly king
12 We give God thanks for those who knew
13 Heal me, hands of Jesus
13 We give God thanks for those who knew
20 Born of the water
20 O come, our all-victorious Lord
20 Songs of thankfulness and praise
27 Be still and know that I am God
28 And can it be
28 Children of the heavenly king
29 Jesus came, the heavens adoring
29 The kingdom of God
32 At the name of Jesus
32 He gave his life in selfless love
32 Shout for joy, loud and long
34 Here, O my Lord, I see thee face to face
72 From heaven you came (The Servant King)

Luke 6

6 We believe in God Almighty
10 As I hold out my hand
12 Dear Lord and Father of mankind
17 Lord Jesus, once you spoke to men
17 O changeless Christ, for ever new
17 Songs of thankfulness and praise
17 When Jesus walked upon this earth
19 God/Thou, whose almighty word
20 Beauty for brokenness (God of the poor)
20 We're going to shine like the sun
21 Lord, we long for you (Heal our nation)
21 O happy band of pilgrims
21 The trumpets sound, the angels sing
27 O Lord, all the world belongs to you
37 Make me a channel of your peace
38 Good King Wenceslas looked out
39 Risen Lord, whose name we cherish
47 My hope is built on nothing less
47 You can trust his promises
48 Rock of ages, cleft for me
68 You, Lord, have the message

Luke 7

6 I am not worthy, holy Lord
7 Word of justice
16 O bless the God of Israel
21 God/Thou, whose almighty word
21 He gave his life in selfless love
21 His eyes will guide my footsteps
21 Jesus, the name high over all
21 Let the desert sing
21 Lord, I was blind; I could not see
21 My song is love unknown
21 Oh for a thousand tongues to sing
21 He gave his life in selfless love
21 Thou/God, whose almighty word
21 When the King shall come again
22 God we praise you
22 He gave his life in selfless love
22 Here in this place
22 Jesus, a stranger
22 Jesus has sat down
22 Lord, I was blind; I could not see
22 My song is love unknown
22 Oh for a thousand tongues to sing
22 The kingdom of God
34 Alleluia, sing to Jesus
34 Here within this house of prayer
34 O Christ, the same, through all
34 We come as guests invited
37 Consider how he loves you
38 Open our eyes, Lord
42 Such love
47 Like a mighty river flowing
48 Born of the water
50 Peace be with you all, we sing

Luke 8

1 I want to serve the purpose of God
5 Christ's church shall glory in his power
8 God has spoken to his people
14 Jesus calls us! In/o'er the tumult
16 Christ is the king! O friends rejoice
16 Make me a channel of your peace

34 We give God thanks for those who knew

Luke 11

1 Lord Jesus Christ (Living Lord)
1 Lord, teach us how to pray aright
1 Lord, teach us to pray
1 Prayer is the soul's sincere desire
2 Before the ending of the day
2 Blessed be the Lord (Father in heaven)
2 Christ is the king! O friends rejoice
2 Come, O/thou long-expected Jesus
2 Father God, I wonder
2 Father God in heaven (Kum ba yah)
2 Father in heaven, grant to your children
2 Father in heaven, how we love you
2 Father in heaven, our voices we raise
2 For the bread which you have broken
2 For the fruits of his creation
2 I will sing your praises (Father God)
2 Jesus, King of kings
2 Jesus, send more labourers
2 Look, Lord, in mercy as we pray
2 Lord, teach us how to pray aright
2 O Christ, at your first Eucharist
2 O thou, who at thy Eucharist didst pray
2 Our Father in heaven
2 Prayer is the soul's sincere desire
2 Reign in me
2 Rejoice, O land, in God your Lord
2 Remember, Lord, the world you made
2 Son of God, eternal saviour
2 The kingdom of God
2 Thy/your kingdom come, O God
2 We will crown him (Father in heaven)
2 Our Father which art in heaven
3 O God of Jacob, by whose hand
3 To you, O Lord, our hearts we raise
3 We plough the fields, and scatter
4 A mighty fortress is our God
4 A safe stronghold our God is still
4 Almighty Lord, the holy One
4 Forgive our sins as we forgive
4 Glory to you, my God, this night
4 God is our fortress and our rock

4 Heal me, hands of Jesus
4 Lighten our darkness
4 O Jesus, I have promised
4 Unto the hills around
4 Who honours courage here
9 Jesus, the joy of loving hearts
9 Jesus, the very thought of thee
9 Jesus, where'er thy people meet
9 Lord Jesus, when your people meet
13 We plough the fields, and scatter
20 Songs of thankfulness and praise
20 The kingdom of God
20 When Jesus walked upon this earth
28 How sure the Scriptures are
28 Rejoice, O land, in God your Lord
30 Jesus, come! for we invite you
31 He walks among the golden lamps
33 Christ is the king! O friends rejoice
33 Make me a channel of your peace
42 The kingdom of God
46 I cannot tell why he whom angels worship
46 What a friend we have in Jesus
50 God has spoken, by his prophets
51 Glory be to Jesus

Luke 12

8 I'm not ashamed to own/name my Lord
16 God of grace and God of glory
24 We plough the fields, and scatter
27 He walks among the golden lamps
27 We plough the fields, and scatter
29 In heavenly love abiding
33 Glorious things of thee/you are spoken
33 In heavenly love abiding
33 O Lord of heaven and earth and sea
34 Be thou my vision/Lord be my vision
35 Bless the Lord as day departs
35 Christ is the king! O friends rejoice
35 You servants of the Lord
40 He is Lord
49 O Lord, who came from realms above
49 O thou who camest from above
49 Send out the gospel! Let it sound

Luke 13

11 Come and see, come and see
12 Freedom and life are ours
16 Hark the glad sound! The Saviour comes

202

22 From heaven you came (The Servant King)

22 Glorious things of thee/you are spoken

22 In heavenly love abiding

22 O Lord of heaven and earth and sea

22 Will you come and follow me

25 Take my life and let it be

27 Rejoice, rejoice, Christ is in you

28 Children of the heavenly king

30 Oh heaven is in my heart

32 The price is paid

33 The strife is past/o'er, the battle done

38 All glory, laud/praise and honour

38 Earth was waiting, spent and restless

38 Hail to the Lord's anointed

38 This is the day that the Lord has made

42 Break thou/now the bread of life

Luke 19

5 Abide with me, fast falls the eventide

9 This is the day that the Lord has made

10 Christians, make a joyful sound

10 He gave his life in selfless love

10 Holy child, how still you lie

10 My Lord, you wore no royal crown

10 He gave his life in selfless love

28 All glory, laud/praise and honour

28 My song is love unknown

28 Ride on, ride on in majesty

38 All glory be to God on high

38 Glory be to God in heaven

38 Glory in the highest, to the God

38 Holy, holy, holy, Lord

38 Hosanna, hosanna, hosanna

38 I will sing unto the Lord

38 O come, all ye/you faithful

38 This is the day that the Lord has made

38 We have a gospel to proclaim

38 Who is he, in yonder stall

41 Soften my heart, Lord, soften my heart

46 God our Father and creator

46 Here within this house of prayer

46 We love the place, O God

Luke 20

13 Name of all majesty

13 O bless the Lord, my soul

17 Christ is made the sure foundation

17 Christ is our cornerstone

17 Oh heaven is in my heart

37 God of Abraham, lead us

37 The God of Abraham praise

41 All hail the power of Jesus' name

41 Hail to the Lord's anointed

43 Rejoice, the Lord is King

Luke 21

1 Take my life and let it be

5 All my hope on God is founded

25 Come and see the shining hope

25 Hark! A thrilling voice is sounding

25 Jesus, priceless treasure

25 Songs of thankfulness and praise

27 Be still, for the presence of the Lord

27 Great God, what do I see and hear

27 I cannot tell why he whom angels worship

27 Jesus came, the heavens adoring

27 Jesus comes with clouds descending

27 Lo! He comes with clouds descending

27 You are crowned with many crowns

28 A great and mighty wonder

28 In heavenly armour we'll enter the land

28 Jesus, your blood and righteousness

28 Lift up your heads to the coming King

28 See, amid the winter's snow

28 The battle belongs to the Lord

31 Crown him with many crowns

33 Great God, what do I see and hear

33 In the bleak mid-winter

33 Loved with everlasting love

33 Praise him, praise him, praise him

33 Songs of praise the angels sang

33 The day thou gavest, Lord, is ended

33 You can trust his promises

36 Christian, seek not yet repose

36 Forth in thy/your name, O Lord, I go

36 Stand up! stand up for Jesus

36 Stay with me, remain here with me

Luke 22

1 Love is his word

204

3 Christ is the world's Light, he and
none other
7 Christ the Lord is risen again
12 Come, risen Lord, as guest
14 Love is his word
15 Love is his word
18 He gave his life in selfless love
18 Here is bread
18 Here, O my Lord, I see thee face to
face
18 One shall tell another (New Wine)
19 Bread of the world in mercy
broken
19 Broken for me
19 Father in heaven, grant to your
children
19 For the bread which you have
broken
19 Lord Jesus Christ (Living Lord)
19 Love is his word
19 Peace be with you all, we sing
19 The Son of God proclaim
20 Alleluia! We sing your praises
20 Haleluya! Pelo tsa rona
20 I believe there is a God
20 It's your blood that cleanses me
20 My Lord, what love is this
20 See this bread
20 Show me your hands
24 It's your blood that cleanses me
26 Empty he came
26 My Lord, you wore no royal crown
26 O Lord, all the world belongs to
you
26 When Jesus walked upon this
earth
27 A child is born for us
28 I want Jesus to walk with me
30 He gave his life in selfless love
30 Here, O my Lord, I see thee face to
face
30 He gave his life in selfless love
32 I hear the words of love
34 Ah, holy Jesus, how have you
offended
35 Send me out from here, Lord
39 Praise to the Holiest in the height
40 O Jesus, I have promised
42 Abba, Father
42 Before the ending of the day
42 Child of the stable's secret birth
42 Christ is the king! O friends rejoice
42 Father God in heaven (Kum ba
yah)
42 For the fruits of his creation

42 From heaven you came (The
Servant King)
42 He gave his life in selfless love
42 Jesus, King of kings
42 Look, Lord, in mercy as we pray
42 Lord, as I wake I turn to you
42 Lord, teach us how to pray aright
42 O Christ, at your first Eucharist
42 O Father of the fatherless (Father
me)
42 O thou, who at thy Eucharist didst
pray
42 Prayer is the soul's sincere desire
42 He gave his life in selfless love
42 Son of God, eternal saviour
42 Thy/your way, not mine, O Lord
44 I believe there is a God
44 My God, I love you
44 Praise to the Holiest in the height
44 When you prayed beneath the
trees
49 My Lord, you wore no royal crown
51 Heal me, hands of Jesus
51 My Lord, you wore no royal crown
52 When you prayed beneath the
trees
53 Holy child, how still you lie
53 Soldiers of Christ, arise
53 When morning gilds the skies
53 When you prayed beneath the
trees
54 Ah, holy Jesus, how have you
offended
63 A purple robe, a crown of thorn
63 Ah, holy Jesus, how have you
offended
63 Man of Sorrows, what a name
63 Sing, my tongue, the glorious
battle
66 He stood before the court
69 Glory in the highest, to the God
69 God we praise you
69 Jesus has sat down
69 Jesus is king
69 Led like a lamb (You're alive)
69 Once in royal David's city
70 I believe in Jesus

Luke 23
1 Be still and know that I am God
1 He stood before the court
4 Man of Sorrows, what a name
4 Through all our days we'll sing
11 Come and see, come and see
21 My song is love unknown

205

John

John 1

1 King of kings, Lord of lords, lion
1 Of the Father's love begotten
1 Songs of thankfulness and praise
1 The darkness turns to dawn
1 The King of glory comes (King of
     Kings)
1 The Son of God proclaim
1 When things began to happen
1 Word of the Father everlasting
2 God of God, the uncreated
3 Alleluia, raise the anthem
3 Come, let us worship the Christ
3 Come, ye faithful, raise the anthem
3 My God, how wonderful you are
3 The Son of God proclaim
4 Christ is the world's Light, he and
     none other
4 God is love, his the care
4 He holds the key to our salvation
4 Jesus, the joy of loving hearts
4 Out of darkness let light shine
4 Speak, Lord, in the stillness
4 Such love
4 The darkness turns to dawn
4 You are the mighty king
5 Come to set us free (Advent
     entrance song)
5 God whose love we cannot
     measure
5 Let all mortal flesh keep silence
5 Light shining in the darkness
5 Lighten our darkness
5 Lord, the light (Shine, Jesus, shine)
9 Christ is the world's Light, he and
     none other
9 Christ is the world's true light
9 Christ, whose glory fills the skies
9 Light of the world (You are the
     light)
9 You are the light of the world
10 Come, let us worship the Christ
10 Happy day of great rejoicing
10 My song is love unknown
11 Ah, holy Jesus, how have you
     offended
11 Child in the manger
11 I really want to worship you (You
     laid aside)
11 My song is love unknown
11 You laid aside your majesty
12 Christ is born for us today
12 Come, Lord Jesus
14 A great and mighty wonder
14 All hail the power of Jesus' name
14 Alleluia, raise the anthem

14 Angels from the realms of glory
14 Behold, the great creator makes
14 Christ triumphant
14 Christians, awake, salute the
     happy morn
14 Christmas for God's holy people
14 Come and sing the Christmas story
14 Come, let us worship the Christ
14 Come, praise the name of Jesus
14 Come, ye faithful, raise the anthem
14 Father, now behold us
14 Father of all, whose laws have stood
14 Father of heaven, whose love
     profound
14 God came among us, he became a
     man
14 Hark! the herald-angels sing
14 I bind myself to God today
14 Jesus is king
14 Jesus, Lamb of God and source of
     life
14 Jesus, lover of my soul
14 Jesus restore to us again
14 Joy to the world
14 Lord, enthroned in heavenly
     splendour
14 O come, all ye/you faithful
14 Praise be to Christ in whom we see
14 Thanks to God whose word was
     spoken
14 The darkness turns to dawn
14 This is the day that the Lord has
     made
14 This is the day, this is the day
14 We have a gospel to proclaim
16 How sweet the name of Jesus
     sounds
16 Love divine, all loves excelling
16 O Spirit of the living God
17 O bless the Lord, my soul
18 All glory be to God on high
18 Glory be to God in heaven
18 Holy, holy, holy, Lord God almighty
18 O come, all ye/you faithful
18 Ye/you servants of God, your
     master proclaim
23 On Jordan's bank, the Baptist's cry
23 Prepare the way, the way for the
     Lord
23 The bells ring out at Christmas-
     time
29 Come let us join our cheerful songs
29 All glory be to God on high
29 Before the throne of God above
29 Christ the Lord is risen again

29 Come and see the shining hope
29 Come, let us worship the Christ
29 Crown him with many crowns
29 Glory be to God in heaven
29 Glory be to Jesus
29 Glory in the highest, to the God
29 Great and wonderful your deeds
29 Hail, our once-rejected Jesus
29 Hail Redeemer! king divine
29 Hail the day that sees him rise
29 Hail, thou once despised Jesus
29 Hark! A thrilling voice is sounding
29 Hark! the voice of love and mercy
29 Heavenly hosts in ceaseless worship
29 Here from all nations
29 Here, O my Lord, I see thee face to face
29 Here within this house of prayer
29 How bright these glorious spirits shine
29 I bless the Christ of God
29 Jesus comes with clouds descending
29 Jesus, Lamb of God and source of life
29 Jesus, priceless treasure
29 Jesus, the name high over all
29 Just as I am
29 Let creation bless the Father
29 Let us love and sing and wonder
29 Lo! He comes with clouds descending
29 Lord, enthroned in heavenly splendour
29 Man of Sorrows, what a name
29 My Lord, what love is this
29 No weight of gold or silver
29 Not all the blood of beasts
29 Now lives the Lamb of God
29 O Sacrifice of Calvary
29 O Trinity, O Trinity
29 Saviour Christ, in praise we name him
29 See, amid the winter's snow
29 Sing, my tongue, the glorious battle
29 Ten thousand times ten thousand
29 There is a redeemer
29 We have a gospel to proclaim
29 What offering shall we give
29 Ye/you servants of God, your master proclaim
32 Christ on whom the Spirit rested
32 God/Thou, whose almighty word

32 Lead us, heavenly Father, lead us
32 Like the murmur of the dove's song
32 O Lord of heaven and earth and sea
32 Oh for a closer walk with God
32 Spirit divine, attend/inspire our prayers
32 Thou/God, whose almighty word
34 I believe in Jesus
36 Christ the Lord is risen again
36 Glory be to Jesus
36 Jesus, the name high over all
36 No weight of gold or silver
36 See, amid the winter's snow
36 There is a redeemer
38 We saw thee not
38 We were not there to see you come
41 There is a redeemer
43 Be still and know that I am God
43 From heaven you came (The Servant King)
43 Will you come and follow me
45 Christ upon the mountain peak
45 I cannot tell why he whom angels worship
45 Our Saviour Christ once knelt in prayer
45 We saw thee not
45 We were not there to see you come
45 When Jesus led his chosen three
49 All glory, laud/praise and honour
49 I believe in Jesus
49 The first nowell the angel did say
49 The Son of God proclaim
50 O Father, we bless your name (Panama Praise)

John 2
1 Jesus, come! for we invite you
1 Jesus, Lord, we pray
1 Lord Jesus Christ, invited guest
1 Songs of thankfulness and praise
8 Before the eternal King and Priest
9 Here in this place
9 Jesus, a stranger
9 The trumpets sound, the angels sing
16 Come to us, creative Spirit
18 God our Father and creator
23 Love is his word
23 Oh for a thousand tongues to sing

John 3

3 Born by the Holy Spirit's breath
3 Born of the water
3 Hark! the herald-angels sing
3 It was a man who was born
3 O Father, we bless your name (Panama Praise)
3 O praise ye the Lord, praise him
3 Sing praise to the Lord
3 This is the truth which we proclaim
5 Born of the water
7 Hark! the herald-angels sing
7 O Father, we bless your name (Panama Praise)
8 Born of the water
8 I believe in God the Father
8 Lord of the church, we pray for our renewing
8 Our great Redeemer, as he breathed
8 Spirit divine, attend/inspire our prayers
8 Spirit of God within me
8 We are his children
13 He came down that we may have love
14 Downtrodden Christ
14 Lift high the cross, the love of Christ
14 Man of Sorrows, what a name
14 Sing, my tongue, the glorious battle
14 When Christ was lifted from the earth
14 When you prayed beneath the trees
14 With loving hands
15 Oh heaven is in my heart
16 All my heart this night rejoices
16 Calypso Carol (See him lying on a bed of straw)
16 Christ is the world's Light, he and none other
16 Christians, make a joyful sound
16 Come ride with kings
16 For God so loved the world (Kendrick)
16 For God so loved the world (Londonderry)
16 Give thanks with a grateful heart
16 It is a thing most wonderful
16 Name of all majesty
16 O come, all ye/you faithful
16 Peace be with you all, we sing
16 Ring the bells, ring the bells
16 See him lying on a bed of straw

16 To God be the glory
17 Give to our God immortal praise
17 We give immortal praise
19 The light of Christ has come
21 Eternal light, eternal light
29 Here, O my Lord, I see thee face to face
29 Wake, O wake, and sleep no longer
30 Oh the bitter shame and sorrow
31 O Lord, who came from realms above
31 O thou who camest from above
33 God is love, his the care
36 Christ is the world's Light, he and none other
36 Oh heaven is in my heart

John 4

10 Come, O Fount of every blessing
10 Glorious things of thee/you are spoken
10 Here, Lord, we come to you
10 Holy Spirit, truth divine
10 I hunger and I thirst
10 Jesus, lover of my soul
10 Jesus, the joy of loving hearts
10 Lord of the church, we pray for our renewing
10 Rock of ages, cleft for me
10 Such love
14 Jesus, lover of my soul
19 Ascended Christ
19 Christmas for God's holy people
19 Father of heaven, whose love profound
19 How sweet the name of Jesus sounds
19 Join all the glorious names
20 God of light and life's creation
21 God is here! As we his people
21 Jesus, where'er thy people meet
21 Lord Jesus, when your people meet
35 Here I am
35 Send more labourers
42 Calypso Carol (See him lying on a bed of straw)
42 Christians, awake, salute the happy morn
42 I cannot tell why he whom angels worship
42 Jesus our hope, our heart's desire
42 Jesus, Saviour of the world
42 See him lying on a bed of straw
46 Jesus, a stranger

48 Alleluia! We sing your praises
48 Break thou/now the bread of life
48 Come, let us worship Christ
48 Haleluya! Pelo tsa rona
48 We come as guests invited
49 Dear Lord and Father of mankind
50 Alleluia, sing to Jesus
50 I, the Lord of sea and sky
51 Guide me, O my great Redeemer
51 Guide me, O thou great Jehovah
51 He came down that we may have love
51 Here is bread
51 Jesus, the joy of loving hearts
51 See this bread
51 Speak, Lord, in the stillness
53 Almighty God, we thank you for feeding
53 Before the eternal King and Priest
53 Bread of heaven, on you we feed
53 Glory be to Jesus
53 I believe there is a God
53 In the quiet consecration
53 It's your blood that cleanses me
53 My God, now is your table spread
53 O God, unseen yet ever near
53 O joy of God, we seek you in the morning
53 O Sacrifice of Calvary
53 We love the place, O God
54 I believe there is a God
54 We come as guests invited
58 Alleluia, sing to Jesus
58 Dear Lord and Father of mankind
58 I, the Lord of sea and sky
63 O Father of the fatherless (Father me)
63 Speak, Lord, in the stillness
68 Bread of the world in mercy broken
68 Creator of the earth and skies
68 See this bread
69 There is a redeemer
69 We have come as the family of God

John 7
37 Just as I am
38 Glorious things of thee/you are spoken
38 I hunger and I thirst
38 Jesus, lover of my soul
38 Lord of the church, we pray for our renewing
38 Such love
42 Be still and know that I am God

42 Once in royal David's city
52 Eternal Father, strong to save
52 Hail, our once-rejected Jesus
52 Hail, thou once despised Jesus
52 Immortal Love, for ever full
52 O changeless Christ, for ever new

John 8
12 I am the Bread of Life
12 Arise, shine (Darkness like a shroud)
12 Christ is the world's Light, he and none other
12 Christ is the world's true light
12 Christ, whose glory fills the skies
12 Come and sing the Christmas story
12 Come, let us worship Christ
12 Come, let us worship the Christ
12 Come, light of the world
12 Consider how he loves you (Sweet Perfume)
12 Darkness like a shroud
12 God is love, his the care
12 Jesus, King of kings
12 My Lord, you wore no royal crown
12 O come, all ye/you faithful
12 O Jesus, King, most wonderful
28 Downtrodden Christ
28 Lift high the cross, the love of Christ
28 Man of Sorrows, what a name
28 Sing, my tongue, the glorious battle
28 When Christ was lifted from the earth
28 When you prayed beneath the trees
28 With loving hands
31 Spirit of God within me
36 Freedom and life are ours
58 Before the throne of God above
58 Ten thousand times ten thousand
58 The God of Abraham praise

John 9
1 Amazing grace
1 Church of God, elect and glorious
1 Come, Holy Ghost, our souls inspire
1 Creator Spirit, come, inspire
1 Father of mercies, in your word
1 God/Thou, whose almighty word
1 He gave his life in selfless love
1 His eyes will guide my footsteps
1 I'll praise my maker while I've breath

1 Jesus, lover of my soul
1 Just as I am
1 Let the desert sing
1 Lord, I was blind; I could not see
1 My Lord, I did not choose you
1 My song is love unknown
1 O Holy Spirit, giver of life
1 Oh for a thousand tongues to sing
1 Spirit of God within me
1 Thou/God, whose almighty word
1 When the King shall come again
2 He healed the darkness of my
 mind
5 I am the Bread of Life
5 Arise, shine (Darkness like a
 shroud)
5 Christ is the world's Light, he and
 none other
5 Christ is the world's true light
5 Christ, whose glory fills the skies
5 Come, let us worship Christ
5 Come, let us worship the Christ
5 Come, light of the world
5 Darkness like a shroud
5 God is love, his the care
5 Jesus, King of kings
5 Lights to the world (The earth was
 dark)
5 My Lord, you wore no royal
 crown
5 O come, all ye/you faithful
5 O Jesus, King, most wonderful
5 The earth was dark
6 Break thou/now the bread of life
19 Jesus, a stranger
24 To God be the glory
25 Amazing grace
25 He healed the darkness of my
 mind
25 Lord, I was blind; I could not see
25 One thing I know, that Christ has
 healed
30 All I am will sing out (Jag vill ge dig)
39 Jesus, a stranger
39 Rejoice, the Lord is King

John 10
1 Ah, holy Jesus, how have you
 offended
1 All people that on earth do dwell
1 Before Jehovah's awesome/aweful
 throne
1 Blow upon the trumpet
1 Come, rejoice before your maker
1 Come with all joy to sing to God

1 Come, worship God who is
 worthy
1 Faithful Shepherd, feed me
1 God is here! As we his people
1 Great Shepherd of your people
1 Happy are they, they who love
 God
1 Here from all nations
1 How bright these glorious spirits
 shine
1 How sweet the name of Jesus
 sounds
1 I cannot tell why he whom angels
 worship
1 In heavenly love abiding
1 Jesus, where'er thy people meet
1 Lord Jesus, when your people
 meet
1 Lord, now let your servant depart
1 Loving Shepherd of your sheep
1 O Christ, at your first Eucharist
1 O thou, who at thy Eucharist didst
 pray
1 Restless souls, why do you scatter
1 See, Christ was wounded for our
 sake
1 Souls of men, why will ye scatter
1 Ten thousand times ten thousand
1 The King of love my Shepherd is
1 The Lord my shepherd rules my
 life
10 Christ is the world's Light, he and
 none other
10 Jesus Christ gives life and gladness
11 How sweet the name of Jesus
 sounds
11 Now to him who is able
12 Thy/your kingdom come, O God
15 Good Christians all, rejoice and
 sing
15 I come with joy to meet my Lord
15 Jesus, Saviour of the world
16 Risen Lord, whose name we
 cherish
21 Spirit of God, rest on your people
27 Loving Shepherd of your sheep
28 For God so loved the world
 (Kendrick)
28 O Father of the fatherless (Father me)
28 Oh heaven is in my heart
30 God has spoken, by his prophets
35 Glorious things of thee/you are
 spoken
36 Give to our God immortal praise
36 I believe in Jesus

36 Name of all majesty
36 We give immortal praise

John 11
    Come, let us with our Lord arise
    Come sing the praise of Jesus
    Eternal light, shine in my heart
    God our Father and creator
    Great God, what do I see and hear
    Hark! the herald-angels sing
    Here within this house of prayer
    In Christ shall all be made alive
    Jesus Christ the Lord is born
    Jesus, the name high over all
    Jesus, your blood and
        righteousness
    Lord, I was blind; I could not see
    Now lives the Lamb of God
    O Trinity, O Trinity
    Oh for a thousand tongues to sing
    Revive thy work/your church, O
        Lord
    Spirit of God most high
    The God of Abraham praise
    These are the facts
    Unto us a boy is born
    We give immortal praise
    Welcome, happy morning
    You choirs of new Jerusalem
20 Jesus, good above all other
25 Christ is the world's Light, he and
    none other
25 Christ's church shall glory in his
    power
25 Good Christian men/Christians all
    rejoice
25 Light of the minds that know him
25 Thou art the way; by thee alone
25 You are the way, to you alone
26 Breathe on me, breath of God
27 I believe in Jesus
27 The Son of God proclaim
27 There is a redeemer
35 It is a thing most wonderful
35 Soften my heart, Lord, soften my
    heart
40 Christian, do you not hear the Lord
40 Hark, my soul! it is the Lord
40 I cannot tell why he whom angels
    worship
43 He who created light
43 Jesus, your blood and
    righteousness
43 Lord, I was blind; I could not see
43 Oh for a thousand tongues to sing

43 Revive thy work/your church, O
    Lord
43 Show me your hands
50 Jesus, good above all other
52 Christ is the king! O friends rejoice
52 For I'm building a people of power
52 Risen Lord, whose name we cherish

John 12
 3 Consider how he loves you (Sweet
    Perfume)
 3 How good a thing it is
13 All glory, laud/praise and honour
13 Hark, the glad sound
13 Holy, holy, holy, Lord
13 Hosanna, hosanna, hosanna
13 I will sing unto the Lord
13 Let trumpets sound
13 Lord, enthroned in heavenly
    splendour
13 My song is love unknown
13 Ride on, ride on in majesty
13 Sanna
13 The first nowell the angel did say
13 This is the day, this is the day
13 We have a gospel to proclaim
13 Who is he, in yonder stall
15 Ride on, ride on in majesty
20 Open our eyes, Lord
22 Give him the glory (lift your voice)
22 Lift your voice and sing
24 As we break the bread
26 Be still and know that I am God
28 Father, let us dedicate
28 Great God, we praise the mighty
    love
29 Christ upon the mountain peak
31 A mighty fortress is our God
31 A safe stronghold our God is still
31 God is our fortress and our rock
32 And now, O Father, mindful of the
    love
32 Christian, seek not yet repose
32 Downtrodden Christ
32 Lift high the cross, the love of
    Christ
32 Man of Sorrows, what a name
32 Sing, my tongue, the glorious
    battle
32 When you prayed beneath the trees
32 With loving hands
35 Children of the heavenly king
36 As sons of the day and daughters
42 Risen Lord, whose name we
    cherish

26 Spirit of God within me
26 Spirit of holiness
27 Christ is the world's Light, he and
   none other
27 How can I be free from sin
27 My peace I leave I leave with you
30 A mighty fortress is our God
30 A safe stronghold our God is still
30 God is our fortress and our rock

John 15
   A new commandment that I give
      to you
1 Bread of heaven, on you we feed
1 I hunger and I thirst
1 O God, unseen yet ever near
4 In the quiet consecration
5 Come, let us worship the Christ
5 Come, thou/most holy Spirit,
   come
5 For the fruits of his creation
5 May we, O Holy Spirit, bear your
   fruit
5 O Trinity, O Trinity
5 Spirit of holiness
5 Thine/Yours be the glory
5 We come as guests invited
7 You can trust his promises
8 We shall stand
10 Be still and know that I am God
10 In heavenly love abiding
12 Eternal Father, Lord of life
12 Let there be love
12 Love is his word
12 O Father, we bless your name
   (Panama Praise)
13 Be still and know that I am God
13 Good Christians all, rejoice and
   sing
13 I come with joy to meet my Lord
13 Jesus, Saviour of the world
13 May our worship be as fragrance
13 My song is love unknown
13 Tell all the world of Jesus
14 Lord God, your love has called us
   here
14 The Son of God proclaim
14 What a friend we have in Jesus
15 Born of the water
15 Bread of life
15 We come as guests invited
16 My Lord, I did not choose you
16 We shall stand
26 Away with our fears
26 Christ in majesty ascending

26 Come down, O Love divine
26 Come, thou/most holy Spirit,
   come
26 Creator Spirit, come, inspire
26 Father most holy, merciful and
   loving
26 Jesus restore to us again
26 Our great Redeemer, as he
   breathed
26 River, wash over me
26 Spirit of faith, by faith be mine
26 Spirit of God, rest on your people
26 Spirit of holiness
26 There is a redeemer

John 16
7 My Lord of light who made the
   worlds
11 A mighty fortress is our God
11 A safe stronghold our God is still
11 God is our fortress and our rock
13 Creator Spirit, come, inspire
13 God/Thou, whose almighty word
13 Holy Spirit, truth divine
13 Jesus restore to us again
13 River, wash over me
13 Spirit of faith, by faith be mine
13 Spirit of God, rest on your people
13 Spirit of God within me
13 Spirit of holiness
13 There is a redeemer
13 Thou/God, whose almighty word
14 Spirit of God, show me Jesus
20 City of God, Jerusalem
20 Come sing the praise of Jesus
20 Jerusalem, my happy home
20 Loved with everlasting love
20 Now thank we all our God
20 O love that wilt not let me go
22 Rejoice, rejoice, Christ is in you
33 Light of the world (You are the
   light)
33 Tell all the world of Jesus
33 You are the light of the world

John 17
   O thou, who at thy Eucharist didst
      pray
2 O Father of the fatherless (Father
   me)
3 Come, Holy Ghost, our souls
   inspire
3 Creator Spirit, come, inspire
3 Eternal light, shine in my heart
3 Oh heaven is in my heart

30 Lord Jesus, for my sake you come
30 Love's redeeming work is done
30 Man of Sorrows, what a name
30 Ride on, ride on in majesty
30 They killed him as a common thief
30 Who is he, in yonder stall
31 The hands of Christ, the caring hands
34 I believe there is a God
34 It's your blood that cleanses me
34 Lord, enthroned in heavenly splendour
34 My God, I love you
34 O Christ, the Master Carpenter
34 O dearest Lord, your sacred head
34 Rock of ages, cleft for me
34 Sing lullaby
34 Sing, my tongue, the glorious battle
34 The hands of Christ, the caring hands
34 When I survey the wondrous cross
35 It is a thing most wonderful
37 Jesus comes with clouds descending
37 Lo! He comes with clouds descending
37 O dearest Lord, your sacred head
37 Sing lullaby
37 Sing, my tongue, the glorious battle
37 The hands of Christ, the caring hands
38 Alleluia, alleluia! hearts to heaven
38 Baptised in water
38 Christ the Lord is risen again
38 Have you not heard
38 Holy child, how still you lie
38 Low in the grave he lay (Christ arose)
38 Name of all majesty
38 See, Christ was wounded for our sake
38 Sing lullaby
38 This is the truth which we proclaim
38 Welcome, happy morning
41 In the tomb so cold
41 My song is love unknown
41 They killed him as a common thief
42 Lord, you need no house
42 They killed him as a common thief

John 20
1 All creation join to say
1 Christ the Lord is risen today

1 Comes Mary to the grave
1 First of the week and finest day
1 Good Christians all, rejoice and sing
1 Led like a lamb (You're alive)
1 Light's glittering morning fills the sky
1 Love's redeeming work is done
2 Had he not loved us
2 Lord of the cross of shame
2 Ring out the bells (Past three a clock)
2 Thou art the way; by thee alone
2 You are the way, to you alone
6 Thine/Yours be the glory
11 Comes Mary to the grave
11 Led like a lamb (You're alive)
11 Thine/Yours be the glory
14 No more weeping (Paschal procession)
14 Who is he, in yonder stall
16 Comes Mary to the grave
16 Oh for a thousand tongues to sing
16 Thine/Yours be the glory
17 Christ is going to the Father
19 Alleluia, alleluia! hearts to heaven
19 Christ is the world's Light, he and none other
19 First of the week and finest day
19 I believe in Jesus
19 Jesus, stand among us at the
19 Jesus, stand among us in thy risen power
19 Peace be with you all, we sing
19 They killed him as a common thief
20 Breathe on me, Spirit of Jesus
20 Crown him with many crowns
21 At the supper, Christ the Lord
21 Father almighty, we your humble servants
21 For the bread which you have broken
21 How shall they hear
21 Let us talents and tongues employ
21 O joy of God, we seek you in the morning
22 Breathe on me, breath of God
22 Here within this house of prayer
22 Jesus, stand among us in thy risen power
22 Lead us, heavenly Father, lead us
22 O Breath of Life, come sweeping through
22 Our great Redeemer, as he breathed

218

1 O Spirit of the living God
1 O thou who camest from above
1 O Trinity, O Trinity
1 Our great Redeemer, as he
   breathed
1 Ring out the bells (Past three a
   clock)
1 Spirit divine, attend/inspire our
   prayers
1 Spirit of God most high
1 Spirit of God within me
1 The Spirit came, as promised
3 O Spirit of the living God
3 Spirit divine, attend/inspire our
   prayers
4 Come, Holy Spirit
4 Lord of the church, we pray for our
   renewing
20 Blow upon the trumpet
20 Christ is ascending! let creation
   sing
20 Songs of thankfulness and praise
21 In awe and wonder, Lord our God
21 Jesus, the joy of loving hearts
21 Saviour, again to thy dear name
21 There is power in the name of Jesus
21 To the name of our salvation
23 I believe there is a God
23 When you prayed beneath the
   trees
24 I believe in Jesus
24 Low in the grave he lay (Christ
   arose)
25 Forth in thy/your name, O Lord, I
   go
26 I believe in God the Father
27 There is a redeemer
28 Breathe on me, Spirit of Jesus
28 Now to him who is able
28 Send me, Lord (Thuma mina)
28 Spirit divine, attend/inspire our
   prayers
28 Thuma mina (Send me, Lord)
28 To be in your presence
30 Tell all the world of Jesus
32 Comes Mary to the grave
33 Christ the Lord is risen again
33 Glory in the highest, to the God
33 Jesus has sat down
33 Man of Sorrows, what a name
33 Once in royal David's city
34 God we praise you
35 Rejoice, the Lord is King
36 All creation join to say
36 Christ the Lord is risen today

36 Go forth and tell
36 Love's redeeming work is done
36 We believe in God the Father
38 Born of the water
38 Oh for a thousand tongues to sing
38 There is power in the name of Jesus
39 Happy day of great rejoicing
39 You can trust his promises
42 Oh isn't it good
46 Here is bread
46 Peace be with you all, we sing

Acts 3
   Peter and John went to pray
1 Let the desert sing
1 Oh for a thousand tongues to sing
1 When the King shall come again
6 Jesus, your name is power
6 Oh for a thousand tongues to sing
6 There is power in the name of Jesus
13 Away with our fears
13 God of Abraham, lead us
13 Lord, enthroned in heavenly
   splendour
14 My song is love unknown
15 Author of life divine
15 Come, let us with our Lord arise
15 I believe in Jesus
15 Lord, enthroned in heavenly
   splendour
15 O Christ, the same, through all
15 O Prince of peace, whose promised
   birth
15 Thine/Yours be the glory
16 Jesus, the name high over all
16 Oh for a thousand tongues to sing
16 There is power in the name of Jesus
18 Child in the manger
18 God has spoken, by his prophets
19 How can we sing with joy
21 It came upon the midnight clear
21 Name of all majesty
21 O praise ye the Lord, praise him
21 Sing praise to the Lord
22 Ascended Christ
22 Christmas for God's holy people
22 Father of heaven, whose love
   profound
22 How sweet the name of Jesus
   sounds
22 Join all the glorious names
25 Born of the water
25 God of heaven
25 This is the truth which we
   proclaim

Acts 4

2 He is risen
2 Jesus Christ is risen today
2 Sing alleluia to the Lord
10 Comes Mary to the grave
10 Jesus, your name is power
10 Oh for a thousand tongues to sing
11 Christ is made the sure foundation
11 Oh heaven is in my heart
11 Still near me, O my Saviour, stand
12 Christ is the world's Light, he and none other
12 I tell you (Leben)
12 Immortal Love, for ever full
12 In awe and wonder, Lord our God
12 Jesus Christ is the Lord of all
12 Jesus, the name high over all
12 No other name
12 Oh for a thousand tongues to sing
12 There is power in the name of Jesus
12 To the name of our salvation
18 Oh for a thousand tongues to sing
24 I'll praise my maker while I've breath
24 O Lord of heaven and earth and sea
24 Sovereign Lord, I am yours
24 You are the Lord
27 A messenger named Gabriel
27 Ah, holy Jesus, how have you offended
27 Child in the manger
27 God rest you/ye merry, gentlemen
27 Holy child, how still you lie
27 Jesus, Jesus, holy and anointed one
27 O little town of Bethlehem
27 Silent night, Holy night
29 Christ on whom the Spirit rested
29 Christians, lift up your hearts (Praise)
29 O Spirit of the living God
30 O Father, we bless your name (Panama Praise)
30 The right hand of God is writing
31 Jesus restore to us again
31 Lord of the church, we pray for our renewing
32 God our Father, bless your people
32 Oh isn't it good

Acts 5

12 O Father, we bless your name (Panama Praise)
21 I believe in Jesus
30 A song was heard at Christmas

30 Alas! and did my saviour bleed
30 By your cross
30 Comes Mary to the grave
30 Downtrodden Christ
30 Help me to understand it, Lord
30 I believe there is a God
30 We sing the praise of him who died
30 When you prayed beneath the trees
31 Christ the Lord is risen again
31 I believe there is a God
31 Jesus has sat down
31 Low in the grave he lay (Christ arose)
31 Man of Sorrows, what a name
31 Once in royal David's city
31 Ten thousand times ten thousand
42 There is a redeemer

Acts 6

7 A mighty fortress is our God
7 A safe stronghold our God is still
7 God is our fortress and our rock

Acts 7

2 God of grace and God of glory
32 God of Abraham, lead us
33 Be still, for the presence of the Lord
33 In your arms of love
33 Jesus, where'er thy people meet
33 Lord Jesus, when your people meet
33 The Lord made man, the Scriptures tell
49 Jesus, where'er thy people meet
49 Lord Jesus, when your people meet
49 Lord, you need no house
54 Give praise for famous men
54 The Son of God rides out to war
55 I am not skilled to understand
55 Once in royal David's city
56 Glory in the highest, to the God
56 God we praise you
56 Jesus has sat down
59 Jesus, lover of my soul

Acts 8

4 We have a gospel to proclaim
12 How sweet the name of Jesus sounds
12 Jesus, your name is power
12 The kingdom of God
12 Ye/you servants of God, your master proclaim
32 He stood before the court

32 He was pierced for our
transgressions
32 I cannot tell why he whom angels
worship
32 Jesus, Lamb of God and source of
life
32 See, Christ was wounded for our
sake
39 O God, unseen yet ever near

Acts 9
17 Breathe on me, Spirit of Jesus
20 I believe in Jesus
20 The Son of God proclaim
27 Jesus, your name is power
27 There is power in the name of Jesus
27 Ye/you servants of God, your
master proclaim
28 Be bold, be strong
31 We believe in God the Father

Acts 10
 2 Beauty for brokenness (God of the
poor)
31 Beauty for brokenness (God of the
poor)
36 All hail the power of Jesus' name
36 Christ be the Lord of all our days
36 God is here! As we his people
36 Infant holy, infant lowly
36 Once in royal David's city
36 We believe in God the Father
36 You are crowned with many
crowns
36 You sat down
38 Jesus, Jesus, holy and anointed one
38 Songs of thankfulness and praise
39 By your cross
39 I believe there is a God
39 When you prayed beneath the
trees
40 Comes Mary to the grave
40 I believe in Jesus
40 Low in the grave he lay (Christ
arose)
40 The strife is past/o'er, the battle
done
41 I believe in Jesus
44 Come, Holy Spirit
44 He came down that we may have
love
48 How sweet the name of Jesus
sounds

Acts 11
15 Come, Holy Spirit
15 He came down that we may have
love
18 O come, our all-victorious Lord
26 Filled with the Spirit's power

Acts 12
 2 Give praise for famous men
 6 And can it be
 7 And can it be
 7 Jesus shall reign
 7 Jesus, the name high over all
23 To God be the glory
24 A mighty fortress is our God
24 A safe stronghold our God is still
24 God is our fortress and our rock

Acts 13
29 Lord, the light (Shine, Jesus, shine)
30 I believe in Jesus
30 Low in the grave he lay (Christ
arose)
32 We have a gospel to proclaim
35 There is a redeemer
37 Comes Mary to the grave
38 Songs of thankfulness and praise
39 God of gods, we sound his praises
46 Be bold, be strong
47 Faithful vigil ended
47 Jesus, hope of every nation
47 Lights to the world (The earth was
dark)
47 Lord, now let your servant depart
47 The earth was dark
48 He who created light
52 Breathe on me, Spirit of Jesus
52 Lord of the church, we pray for our
renewing

Acts 14
 3 Be bold, be strong
 3 O Father, we bless your name
(Panama Praise)
15 I'll praise my maker while I've
breath
15 O Lord of heaven and earth and
sea
17 Breathe on me, Spirit of Jesus
17 Fill your hearts with joy and
gladness
17 Lord of the changing year
17 You are worthy, Lord you are
worthy
22 How firm a foundation

22 O happy band of pilgrims

Acts 15
11 All hail the power of Jesus' name
11 Amazing grace
12 O Father, we bless your name (Panama Praise)

Acts 16
7 Spirit of faith, by faith be mine
18 Jesus, your name is power
18 There is power in the name of Jesus
25 O praise ye the Lord, praise him
25 Sing praise to the Lord
25 The day thou gavest, Lord, is ended
26 Lord, I was blind; I could not see
31 There is power in the name of Jesus
34 Breathe on me, Spirit of Jesus

Acts 17
6 O Lord, all the world belongs to you
23 All my hope on God is founded
23 There is a redeemer
24 I, the Lord of sea and sky
24 Jesus, where'er thy people meet
24 Lord Jesus, when your people meet
24 Lord, you need no house
25 Here, Lord, we come to you
25 I know that my Redeemer lives, comfort
25 O Father of the fatherless (Father me)
25 O Lord of heaven and earth and sea
25 Roar the waves
28 Let creation bless the Father
28 We are his children

Acts 18
9 How firm a foundation

Acts 19
5 How sweet the name of Jesus sounds
6 Come, Holy Spirit
8 Be bold, be strong
13 There is power in the name of Jesus
17 How sweet the name of Jesus sounds
17 Oh for a thousand tongues to sing

Acts 20
7 Here is bread
11 Peace be with you all, we sing
21 O come, our all-victorious Lord
22 The God of Abraham praise
24 Forth in thy/your name, O Lord, I go
28 Lord, you can make our spirits shine
28 O thou who makest souls to shine
28 The first nowell the angel did say
28 There is a green hill far away
28 To God be the glory
29 Thy/your kingdom come, O God
32 As sons of the day and daughters
35 O Master Christ, draw near to take

Acts 21
13 How sweet the name of Jesus sounds

Acts 22
16 Jesus, the joy of loving hearts
16 My Lord, what love is this
16 Saviour, again to thy dear name
22 Jerusalem on high

Acts 26
18 Consider how he loves you (Sweet Perfume)
18 Creator of the earth and skies
18 God whose love we cannot measure
18 Hail to the Lord's anointed
18 Holy child, how still you lie
20 How can we sing with joy
23 Faithful vigil ended
23 Jesus, hope of every nation
23 Lord, now let your servant depart

Acts 27
23 Glory to you, my God, this night
23 I love you, O Lord, you alone
35 Here is bread
35 Peace be with you all, we sing

Acts 28
8 The right hand of God is writing
31 Be bold, be strong

Romans
Romans 1
  Had we not sinned
3 Earth was waiting, spent and restless
4 I believe in Jesus

4 Spirit of faith, by faith be mine
4 The Son of God proclaim
4 There is power in the name of Jesus
7 Peace to you
16 I'm not ashamed to own/name my Lord
16 Show me your hands
16 There is power in the name of Jesus
17 My hope is built on nothing less
17 There is a green hill far away
20 I believe in God the Father
25 Jesus shall reign

Romans 2
Had we not sinned
2 We shall stand
7 Oh heaven is in my heart
16 Rejoice, the Lord is King
16 We believe in God the Father

Romans 3
Had we not sinned
21 There is a green hill far away
24 Alleluia, raise the anthem
24 And can it be
24 Come, ye faithful, raise the anthem
24 God, we praise you! God, we bless you
24 King of glory, King of peace
24 There is a green hill far away
25 Alleluia, raise the anthem
25 And can it be
25 Come, ye faithful, raise the anthem
25 I believe there is a God
25 It's your blood that cleanses me
25 There is a green hill far away
25 To God be the glory
26 Before the throne of God above
30 King of glory, King of peace
30 There is only one Lord

Romans 4
Had we not sinned
11 And can it be
25 I believe in Jesus

Romans 5
1 Bread of heaven, on you we feed
1 Child of the stable's secret birth
1 Christ is the world's Light, he and none other
1 I bless the Christ of God
1 I hear the words of love
1 O Prince of peace, whose promised birth

1 The hands of Christ, the caring hands
2 I am a new creation
2 Rejoice, the Lord is King
4 Through all the changing scenes
5 Born in song
5 Christians, lift up your hearts (Praise)
5 Come down, O Love divine
5 Happy day of great rejoicing
5 In heavenly love abiding
5 Jesus, we celebrate your victory
5 Lead us, heavenly Father, lead us
5 Lord Jesus Christ (Living Lord)
5 Lord of all hopefulness, Lord of all joy
5 Lord of the cross of shame
5 Love divine, all loves excelling
5 May the mind of Christ my saviour
5 Oh heaven is in my heart
5 Spirit of holiness
5 Take my life and fill me, O Lord
5 The darkness turns to dawn
6 And can it be
6 Glorious things of thee/you are spoken
6 Rock of ages, cleft for me
8 In awe and wonder, Lord our God
8 Jesus lives! Thy/Your terrors now
8 Jesus, my Lord, my God, my all
8 So freely flows the endless love
8 The kingdom of God
8 We give immortal praise
9 I am trusting thee/you, Lord Jesus
9 King of glory, King of peace
9 The victory of our God is won
9 There is only one Lord
10 Be thou my vision/Lord be my vision
10 Born of the water
10 My God, I love you
10 O Spirit of the living God
10 Spirit of God most high
11 Ah, holy Jesus, how have you offended
11 To God be the glory
12 Praise to the Holiest in the height
12 The Lord made man, the Scriptures tell
17 And can it be
17 Jesus Christ the Lord is born
17 Unto us a boy is born
18 O Father of the fatherless (Father me)
20 Jesus, lover of my soul

21 Hark! the voice of love and mercy

Romans 6

3 Baptised in water
3 Christians, lift up your hearts (Word)
3 Have you not heard
4 Baptised in water
4 Born of the water
4 I believe in Jesus
4 Jesus Christ the Lord is born
4 Unto us a boy is born
5 Born of the water
5 Bread of the world in mercy broken
5 He stood before the court
5 Through the night of doubt and sorrow
6 I believe in God the Father
6 I believe there is a God
6 Jesus, we celebrate your victory
6 Lord, for the years
7 Oh for a heart to praise my God
8 All my heart this night rejoices
8 Born of the water
8 Now let us from this table rise
9 All shall be well
9 God came among us, he became a man
9 Now lives the Lamb of God
9 The strife is past/o'er, the battle done
9 This day above all days
9 We know that Christ is raised
10 All my heart this night rejoices
10 God made me for himself to serve him
10 He gave his life in selfless love
11 And can it be
11 He is risen
12 Now lives the Lamb of God
13 I want to serve the purpose of God
13 In full and glad surrender
13 Take my life and let it be
18 Freedom and life are ours
18 How can I be free from sin
18 Oh for a heart to praise my God
22 How can I be free from sin
22 Ye/you servants of God, your master proclaim
23 And now, O Father, mindful of the love
23 Christ is the world's Light, he and none other
23 Oh heaven is in my heart

Romans 7

7 Father of all, whose laws have stood
7 Powerful in making us wise to salvation
18 Jesus, lover of my soul
25 The strife is past/o'er, the battle done

Romans 8

Born by the Holy Spirit's breath
He lives in us, the Christ of God
1 And can it be
1 He stood before the court
1 I am a new creation
1 I'm accepted
2 Freedom and life are ours
2 Holy Spirit, truth divine
2 Spirit of faith, by faith be mine
2 Spirit of God within me
3 Give to our God immortal praise
3 He stood before the court
3 Name of all majesty
3 To God be the glory
3 We give immortal praise
5 Born of the water
6 Oh for a thousand tongues to sing
6 Take my life and let it be
9 Come down, O Love divine
9 So freely flows the endless love
9 Spirit of God within me
10 Rejoice, rejoice, Christ is in you
10 These are the facts
11 Father of heaven, whose love profound
11 O Father of the fatherless (Father me)
13 Alleluia, alleluia! hearts to heaven
13 Firmly I believe, and truly
15 Abba, Father
15 Father God, I wonder
15 I will sing your praises (Father God)
15 We are here to praise you
15 We worship God
16 Thanks to God whose word was spoken
17 Born of the water
17 The head that once was crowned
17 The king is among us
17 We are his children
19 Christ is the world's true light
19 Creation creed (The Lord is a mighty)
19 Let creation bless the Father

19 The Lord is a mighty king
23 Freedom is coming (Oh freedom is coming)
23 In the streets of every city
25 Help us to help each other, Lord
25 In heavenly love abiding
26 God the Father of creation
26 Lord, teach us how to pray aright
28 Father, although I cannot see
29 New every morning is the love
29 O Jesus, King, most wonderful
29 Spirit of God within me
30 King of glory, King of peace
31 The price is paid
32 O Lord of heaven and earth and sea
32 To God be the glory
33 Church of God, elect and glorious
33 Jerusalem the golden
33 The Church's one foundation
34 Glory in the highest, to the God
34 God we praise you
34 Hail the day that sees him rise
34 Jesus has sat down
34 Jesus is king
34 Jesus lives! Thy/Your terrors now
34 Jesus, your blood and righteousness
34 Once in royal David's city
35 Had he not loved us
35 In heavenly love abiding
35 It is a thing most wonderful
35 Loved with everlasting love
35 O love that wilt not let me go
35 A safe stronghold our God is still
37 Christian soldiers, onward go
37 Come on and celebrate
37 Oft in danger, oft in woe
37 Soldiers of Christ, arise
37 Thine/Yours be the glory
38 A debtor to mercy alone
38 Have faith in God, my heart
38 Jesus lives! Thy/Your terrors now
38 Oh for a heart to praise my God
38 Still near me, O my Saviour, stand
38 The strife is past/o'er, the battle done
39 Oh for a heart to praise my God

Romans 9

4 Born of the water
5 Lord of the church, we pray for our renewing
5 The God of Abraham praise

9 Soften my heart, Lord, soften my heart
16 My Lord, I did not choose you
21 Change my heart, O God
21 Jesus, you are changing me
25 Church of God, elect and glorious
33 How firm a foundation
33 I'm not ashamed to own/name my Lord

Romans 10

1 Jesus our hope, our heart's desire
1 O Lord, who came from realms above
1 O thou who camest from above
6 Immortal Love, for ever full
8 Jesus restore to us again
9 Comes Mary to the grave
9 He is Lord
9 I believe in Jesus
9 I will build my church
9 Jerusalem, my happy home
9 Jesus Christ is the Lord of all
9 Low in the grave he lay (Christ arose)
9 Name of all majesty
9 O Jesus, King, most wonderful
9 O Spirit of the living God
9 We have a gospel to proclaim
9 You're worthy of my praise
11 How firm a foundation
11 I'm not ashamed to own/name my Lord
12 Lord of the church, we pray for our renewing
12 To him we come
12 You are crowned with many crowns
12 You sat down
13 Jesus, the joy of loving hearts
13 Saviour, again to thy dear name
13 There is power in the name of Jesus
13 To the name of our salvation
14 Go forth and tell
14 How shall they hear
15 Hail to the Lord's anointed
15 Take my life and let it be
18 The heavens declare the glory

Romans 11

7 Today, if you hear his voice
8 O Spirit of the living God
9 Spirit of God most high
32 O come, our all-victorious Lord
33 Be thou my vision/Lord be my vision

33 Calypso Carol (See him lying on a bed of straw)
33 Praise to the Holiest in the height
33 See him lying on a bed of straw
33 You are beautiful beyond description
35 O Lord of heaven and earth and sea
36 Christ be the Lord of all our days
36 Jesus shall reign
36 O Lord of heaven and earth and sea
36 The kingdom of God

Romans 12

1 All we've received (We are your church)
1 Almighty God, we thank you for feeding
1 Father almighty, we your humble servants
1 Help me to understand it, Lord
1 I offer up my song
1 I want to give my all (I want to serve)
1 I want to serve you (I want to give)
1 In full and glad surrender
1 Lord Christ, we praise your sacrifice
1 May our worship be as fragrance
1 O Holy Spirit, come to bless
1 Sovereign Lord, I am yours
1 Take my life and let it be
1 When I survey the wondrous cross
2 Forth in thy/your name, O Lord, I go
2 King of glory, King of peace
2 Lord, help me to know your presence
2 O Breath of Life, come sweeping through
2 O Lord, who came from realms above
2 O Lord, your tenderness
2 O thou who camest from above
2 Take my life and let it be
4 As sons of the day and daughters
4 Christ, from whom all blessings flow
4 Christ's church shall glory in his power
4 Come, risen Lord, as guest
4 God our Father and creator
4 Men and women, let us walk
4 O Christ, at your first Eucharist

4 O thou, who at thy Eucharist didst pray
4 One holy apostolic church
4 Onward, Christian soldiers
5 For I'm building a people of power
6 All-creating heavenly Giver
6 Ascended Christ
6 Christ, from whom all blessings flow
6 Christ on whom the Spirit rested
6 Come, let us worship the Christ
6 God our Father and creator
6 God the Father, name we treasure
6 Let every Christian pray
6 O Trinity, O Trinity
6 Spirit of holiness
6 The Spirit came, as promised
9 As sons of the day and daughters
10 From heaven you came (The Servant King)
10 Let there be love
10 O Father, we bless your name (Panama Praise)
11 To him we come
15 Make me a channel of your peace

Romans 13

8 Alas! and did my saviour bleed
8 Let there be love
8 O Father, we bless your name (Panama Praise)
9 Father of all, whose laws have stood
9 For the fruits of his creation
9 Freedom and life are ours
9 Love came down at Christmas
9 Welcome to another day
11 Hark! A thrilling voice is sounding
11 My Lord, he is a-coming soon
11 Spirit of God most high
11 We are his children
12 Christian soldiers, onward go
12 First of the week and finest day
12 Oft in danger, oft in woe
12 Soldiers of Christ, arise
12 Soldiers of the cross, arise
12 Stand up! stand up for Jesus
13 Today, if you hear his voice
14 Dear Lord and Father of mankind

Romans 14

4 You sat down
8 All my heart this night rejoices
8 Born of the water

8 God made me for himself to serve
   him
8 God of light and life's creation
8 Jesus lives! Thy/Your terrors now
9 Let saints on earth together sing
11 All creation join to say
11 All praise to Christ, our Lord and
   king
11 Angels from the realms of glory
11 At the name of Jesus
11 Before the heaven and earth
11 Christ is risen! hallelujah/alleluia
11 Christ the Lord is risen today
11 Look, ye saints, the sight is glorious
11 Love's redeeming work is done
11 Thou art coming, O my Saviour
11 You are coming, O my Saviour
17 Away with our fears
17 Filled with the Spirit's power
17 O joy of God, we seek you in the
   morning
17 The kingdom of God
19 Help us to help each other, Lord
19 Make me a channel of your peace

Romans 15
2 Born of the water
2 Fill thou/now my life, O Lord my
   God
2 Help us to help each other, Lord
5 We worship God
6 Christ is the king! O friends rejoice
6 Help us, O Lord, to learn
6 Through all the changing scenes
7 When Christ was lifted from the
   earth
9 With all my heart
10 Rejoice, rejoice, Christ is in you
10 Rejoice, rejoice, rejoice
12 All hail the power of Jesus' name
12 Angels from the realms of glory
12 Great and wonderful your deeds
12 Jesus, hope of every nation
12 King of the universe, Lord of the
   ages
12 O come, O come, Emmanuel
13 Breathe on me, Spirit of Jesus
13 Father eternal, Lord of the ages
13 In heavenly love abiding
13 Now to him who is able
17 O come, all ye/you faithful
19 Almighty God, we thank you for
   feeding
19 We have a gospel to proclaim
33 Peace be with you all, we sing

Romans 16
16 Let us greet one another
20 Join all the glorious names
24 May the mind of Christ our
   saviour
25 Now to him who is able
26 God of God, the uncreated
26 Of the Father's love begotten
27 O come, all ye/you faithful
27 Who can measure heaven and
   earth

1 Corinthians
1 Corinthians 1
2 Church of God, elect and glorious
2 Holiness is your life in me
3 Peace to you
4 Father almighty, we your humble
   servants
8 As sons of the day and daughters
8 Jesus the saviour comes
10 Christ, from whom all blessings
   flow
10 O Christ, at your first Eucharist
10 O thou, who at thy Eucharist didst
   pray
10 Take my life and let it be
13 Onward, Christian soldiers
18 I believe there is a God
21 Calypso Carol (See him lying on a
   bed of straw)
21 See him lying on a bed of straw
24 Be thou my vision/Lord be my
   vision
24 Wise men, they came to look for
   wisdom
25 Child in a stable
25 You are beautiful beyond
   description
26 The wise may bring their learning
27 Jesus, child of Mary
30 Before the throne of God above
30 How can I be free from sin
30 Jesus, your blood and
   righteousness
30 Lift your heart and raise your voice
30 The God of Abraham praise
30 We rest on thee/trust in you
31 Glorious things of thee/you are
   spoken

1 Corinthians 2
2 Forth in thy/your name, O Lord, I
   go
2 I believe in God the Father

228

11 Have you not heard

1 Corinthians 9
24 Christ's church shall glory in his power
24 Fight the good fight with all thy/your might
24 Jesus, the very thought of thee
24 O Lord my love, my strength, my tower
24 Thee will I love, O Lord, my love
24 You holy angels bright

1 Corinthians 10
4 For all the saints who from their labour
4 For your mercy and your grace
4 How sweet the name of Jesus sounds
4 I hunger and I thirst
4 Lord, enthroned in heavenly splendour
4 Mwamba ni Yesu (Who is the rock)
4 Rock of ages, cleft for me
4 Who is the rock (Mwamba ni Yesu)
10 Bread of the world in mercy broken
10 I come with joy to meet my Lord
16 Bread of life
16 He gave his life in selfless love
16 Here is bread
16 I believe there is a God
16 I come with joy to meet my Lord
16 It's your blood that cleanses me
16 No weight of gold or silver
16 Peace be with you all, we sing
16 Put peace into each other's hands
16 We break this bread
17 Come, risen Lord, as guest
17 For I'm building a people of power
17 Here is bread
17 I come with joy to meet my Lord
17 O Christ, at your first Eucharist
17 O thou, who at thy Eucharist didst pray
17 Sing of the Lord's goodness
17 The Church's one foundation
17 We break this bread
17 We come as guests invited
26 Come with all joy to sing to God
26 Come, worship God who is worthy
31 Awake, my soul, and with the sun
31 My Father, for another night

1 Corinthians 11
7 Lord God, your love has called us here
7 O Lord of every shining constellation
7 Spirit of God within me
7 The Lord made man, the Scriptures tell
12 Christ be the Lord of all our days
12 O Lord of heaven and earth and sea
18 I come with joy to meet my Lord
18 The Church's one foundation
23 Here is bread
23 Love is his word
23 We come as guests invited
24 Broken for me
24 Father in heaven, grant to your children
24 Lord Jesus Christ (Living Lord)
24 Love is his word
24 The Son of God proclaim
25 Alleluia! We sing your praises
25 For the bread which you have broken
25 Haleluya! Pelo tsa rona
25 I believe there is a God
25 It's your blood that cleanses me
25 See this bread
25 Show me your hands
25 We come as guests invited
26 Bread of life
26 He gave his life in selfless love
26 Here is bread
26 Here, Lord, we take the broken bread
26 I come with joy to meet my Lord
26 He gave his life in selfless love

1 Corinthians 12
1 All-creating heavenly Giver
1 Ascended Christ
1 Christ, from whom all blessings flow
1 Christ on whom the Spirit rested
1 Come, let us worship the Christ
1 God our Father and creator
1 God the Father, name we treasure
1 Let every Christian pray
1 O Trinity, O Trinity
1 Spirit of holiness
1 The Spirit came, as promised
3 He is Lord
3 I will build my church
3 Jesus Christ is the Lord of all

9 Jesus, saviour, holy child
9 Like a flicker in the darkness
9 Lord, you left your throne
9 Lord, you were rich beyond all
  splendour
9 My Lord, you wore no royal crown
9 Once in royal David's city
9 See him lying on a bed of straw
9 The darkness turns to dawn
9 Thou who wast rich
9 Welcome, welcome, saviour born
9 When the Lord came to our land

2 Corinthians 9
15 All my hope on God is founded

2 Corinthians 10
17 Glorious things of thee/you are
   spoken

2 Corinthians 11
31 Oh for a thousand tongues to sing

2 Corinthians 12
9 Ascended Christ
9 Father, hear the prayer we offer
9 Immanuel, O Immanuel
9 Lord of all power, I give you my
  will
9 One thing I know, that Christ has
  healed
9 Rejoice, rejoice, Christ is in you
9 Still near me, O my Saviour, stand
10 Give thanks with a grateful heart

2 Corinthians 13
12 Filled with the Spirit's power
12 Let us greet one another
12 May the mind of Christ our
   saviour
13 May the grace of Christ our
   saviour

2 Corinthians 15
47 Praise to the Holiest in the height

Galatians
Galatians 1
1 Comes Mary to the grave
1 I believe in Jesus
1 Low in the grave he lay (Christ
  arose)
3 Peace to you
4 I believe in Jesus
4 I believe there is a God

4 I know it was your love for me
5 Send out the gospel! Let it sound
5 We have a gospel to proclaim

Galatians 2
6 To him we come
19 Born of the water
19 God made me for himself to serve
   him
19 He stood before the court
19 Now let us from this table rise
19 These are the facts
19 Through the night of doubt and
   sorrow
20 And can it be
20 Come on and celebrate
20 I am trusting thee/you, Lord Jesus
20 I believe in Jesus
20 I bind myself to God today
20 Jesus loves me! This I know
20 Lord, for the years
20 My God, I love you
20 No weight of gold or silver

Galatians 3
1 I believe there is a God
1 When I survey the wondrous cross
8 To him we come
13 A song was heard at Christmas
13 Alas! and did my saviour bleed
13 Downtrodden Christ
13 When I survey the wondrous cross
13 When you prayed beneath the
   trees
14 I believe in God the Father
18 You can trust his promises
19 Born of the water
24 King of glory, King of peace
25 We worship God
27 And can it be
27 God of grace, I turn my face
28 In Christ there is no East or West
28 Jesus is the Lord of living
28 To him we come
29 All hail the power of Jesus' name

Galatians 4
1 All hail the power of Jesus' name
1 Christ be the Lord of all our days
1 God is here! As we his people
1 Once in royal David's city
4 Hail to the Lord's anointed
4 Sing, my tongue, the glorious
  battle

234

5 Father God, I wonder
5 I will sing your praises (Father God)
5 To us a child of royal birth
6 Abba, Father
6 Born by the Holy Spirit's breath
6 I believe in God the Father
7 Jesus, we celebrate your victory
9 In Christ shall all be made alive
9 Loving Shepherd of your sheep
9 My God, how wonderful you are
9 When Christ was lifted from the earth
26 City of God, Jerusalem
26 God of eternity, Lord of the ages
26 Jerusalem, my happy home
26 Jerusalem on high
26 Jerusalem the golden

Galatians 5
1 Freedom and life are ours
1 Now let us learn of Christ
7 Fight the good fight with all thy/your might
13 Freedom and life are ours
22 Come, let us worship the Christ
22 Come, most/thou holy Spirit, come
22 Come, praise the name of Jesus
22 Come, thou/most Holy Spirit, come
22 For the fruits of his creation
22 God our Father and creator
22 Here within this house of prayer
22 Lead us, heavenly Father, lead us
22 May we, O Holy Spirit, bear your fruit
22 O Holy Spirit, giver of life
22 O Trinity, O Trinity
22 Spirit of holiness
24 Alleluia, alleluia! hearts to heaven
24 Firmly I believe, and truly
24 Lord, for the years
25 Christians, lift up your hearts (Praise)
25 O Father of the fatherless (Father me)

Galatians 6
2 Help us to help each other, Lord
14 I believe there is a God
14 I'm not ashamed to own/name my Lord
14 In the cross of Christ I glory
14 When I survey the wondrous cross

15 Christ on whom the Spirit rested
15 Jesus, come! for we invite you
15 Love divine, all loves excelling
15 No weight of gold or silver
15 The Church's one foundation
15 We worship God
16 Shalom, shalom

Ephesians
Ephesians 1
2 Peace to you
3 Come, O Fount of every blessing
3 Lead us, heavenly Father, lead us
4 As with gladness men of old
4 Come to set us free (Advent entrance song)
4 Holiness is your life in me
4 I'm accepted
4 My Lord, I did not choose you
5 Born of the water
5 Father God, I wonder
5 I will sing your praises (Father God)
5 The king is among us
5 We worship God
6 Holy child, how still you lie
6 Let us praise the Lord our God
7 All-holy Father, king of endless glory
7 Alleluia, raise the anthem
7 Born of the water
7 Calypso Carol (See him lying on a bed of straw)
7 Come, ye faithful, raise the anthem
7 Give thanks with a grateful heart
7 How can I be free from sin
7 I believe in Jesus
7 Jesus, my Lord, my God, my all
7 Jesus, the name high over all
7 O Lord of heaven and earth and sea
7 Praise be to Christ in whom we see
7 Restless souls, why do you scatter
7 See him lying on a bed of straw
7 Souls of men, why will ye scatter
7 They killed him as a common thief
7 Thy/Your hand, O God, has guided
7 To God be the glory
8 Shalom, shalom
11 Calypso Carol (See him lying on a bed of straw)
11 See him lying on a bed of straw
13 Baptised in water
13 Born of the water

13 Father in heaven, grant to your
   children
13 Freedom and life are ours
13 Take me, Lord, just as I am
13 The Spirit came, as promised
13 We come as guests invited
14 Oh heaven is in my heart
16 Father almighty, we your humble
   servants
17 Come, Holy Ghost, our souls
   inspire
17 Creator Spirit, come, inspire
17 Fire of God, titanic Spirit
17 God/Thou, whose almighty word
17 Holy Spirit, truth divine
17 Light of the minds that know him
17 Now let us learn of Christ
17 Now praise the protector of
   heaven
17 O Holy Spirit, giver of life
17 Spirit of God, rest on your people
17 Spirit of God within me
17 Thou/God, whose almighty word
18 Be thou my vision/Lord be my
   vision
18 Born of the water
18 Give thanks with a grateful heart
18 In heavenly love abiding
20 Come and see, come and see
20 God we praise you
20 I believe in Jesus
20 Jesus has sat down
20 Low in the grave he lay (Christ
   arose)
20 Once in royal David's city
20 Praise be to Christ in whom we see
20 The head that once was crowned
21 And he shall reign
21 Ascended Christ
21 Jesus, the name high over all
21 Join all the glorious names
22 All creation join to say
22 Christ is made the sure foundation
22 Christ the Lord is risen today
22 God of eternity, Lord of the ages
22 God our Father and creator
22 Jesus Christ, sovereign King
22 Let saints on earth together sing
22 Lord of the church, we pray for our
   renewing
22 Love's redeeming work is done
22 O Christ the great foundation
22 The Son of God proclaim
23 Jesus Christ, sovereign King

Ephesians 2

4 How good is the God we adore
4 On a night when all the world
4 Tell all the world of Jesus
4 You, O Lord, rich in mercy
5 All I am will sing out (Jag vill ge
   dig)
5 Amazing grace
5 How can I be free from sin
5 Lord, I was blind; I could not see
5 O come, Christians, wonder
5 Only by grace
6 All creation join to say
6 Christ the Lord is risen today
6 Comes Mary to the grave
6 Hail the day that sees him rise
6 Love's redeeming work is done
6 See the conqueror mounts in
   triumph
7 Born of the water
7 Give thanks with a grateful heart
7 How sweet the name of Jesus
   sounds
7 Jesus, my Lord, my God, my all
7 Jesus, the name high over all
8 All hail the power of Jesus' name
8 Amazing grace
8 How can I be free from sin
8 I bless the Christ of God
8 Lord, as I wake I turn to you
8 Lord God, your love has called us
   here
8 My hope is built on nothing less
8 Only by grace
8 So freely flows the endless love
9 Rock of ages, cleft for me
13 Be thou my vision/Lord be my
   vision
13 I believe there is a God
13 It's your blood that cleanses me
13 No weight of gold or silver
13 To him we come
14 Christ is the world's true light
14 Church of God, elect and glorious
14 I come with joy to meet my Lord
14 In Christ there is no East or West
16 All heaven declares
16 O Spirit of the living God
16 Peace, perfect peace
17 Christ is the world's Light, he and
   none other
18 Only by grace
18 To God be the glory
19 Men and women, let us walk
19 We have come as the family of God

236

20 Christ is made the sure foundation
20 Christ is our cornerstone
20 O Christ the great foundation
20 Oh heaven is in my heart
20 The Church's one foundation
21 The Spirit came, as promised

Ephesians 3
3 Calypso Carol (See him lying on a bed of straw)
3 See him lying on a bed of straw
4 Now let us learn of Christ
5 Spirit of God, rest on your people
6 As sons of the day and daughters
6 For I'm building a people of power
6 Men and women, let us walk
8 Be thou my vision/Lord be my vision
8 Born of the water
8 Can we/man by searching find out God
8 Give thanks with a grateful heart
9 Come, let us worship the Christ
9 O Christ, the same, through all
12 Oh heaven is in my heart
12 Only by grace
14 All-creating heavenly Giver
14 Father and God, from whom our world
14 The God of Abraham praise
15 Let saints on earth together sing
15 O Father of the fatherless (Father me)
16 Born of the water
16 Come down, O Love divine
16 Lord, as the day begins
16 Lord, teach us how to pray aright
16 Our great Redeemer, as he breathed
16 Spirit divine, attend/inspire our prayers
16 The Spirit came, as promised
16 These are the facts
17 Forth in the peace of Christ
17 How firm a foundation
17 May we, O Holy Spirit, bear your fruit
17 Oh heaven is in my heart
17 On Jordan's bank, the Baptist's cry
17 Reign in me
17 River, wash over me
17 To us a child of royal birth
18 Beyond all knowledge is your love divine
18 By your side
18 Father of all, whose laws have stood
18 Had he not loved us
18 It is a thing most wonderful
18 It passeth knowledge
18 Just as I am
18 Oh the deep, deep love of Jesus
18 So freely flows the endless love
19 Christ, from whom all blessings flow
19 Come down, O Love divine
19 God whose love we cannot measure
19 How good is the God we adore
19 Jesus Christ, sovereign King
19 Jesus, the very thought of thee
19 Lord, speak to me that I may speak
19 Lord, you were rich beyond all splendour
19 Not the grandeur of the mountains
19 Such love
19 Tell all the world of Jesus
19 The King of love my Shepherd is
19 Thou who wast rich
20 Jesus, come! for we invite you
20 Now to him who is able
21 In my life, Lord
21 May the fragrance of Jesus
21 Restore, O Lord
21 Revive thy work/your church, O Lord
21 To God be the glory
21 When morning gilds the skies
23 All we've received (We are your church)

Ephesians 4
One is the body
1 Church of God, elect and glorious
1 We worship God
2 Come down, O Love divine
2 Put peace into each other's hands
3 The Spirit came, as promised
4 Christ's church shall glory in his power
4 Come, risen Lord, as guest
4 Father on high to whom we pray
4 For I'm building a people of power
4 Here is bread
4 Look, Lord, in mercy as we pray
4 One holy apostolic church
4 Onward, Christian soldiers
4 The Church's one foundation
4 Through the night of doubt and sorrow

4 Thy/Your hand, O God, has guided
5 Christ is the world's true light
5 Glory in the highest, to the God
5 One thing I know, that Christ has healed
5 Thy/Your hand, O God, has guided
5 We worship God
6 Jesus Christ is the Lord of all
6 You are crowned with many crowns
6 You sat down
7 Come, let us worship the Christ
8 Ascended Christ
8 Christ in majesty ascending
8 God of gods, we sound his praises
8 My Lord of light who made the worlds
8 O Holy Spirit, come to bless
8 Revive thy work/your church, O Lord
8 Songs of praise the angels sang
8 The king is among us
10 He came down that we may have love
11 Revive thy work/your church, O Lord
13 I believe in Jesus
13 Jesus put this song into our hearts
15 God of eternity, Lord of the ages
15 Help us to help each other, Lord
15 Now let us learn of Christ
15 O Christ the great foundation
15 Praise be to Christ in whom we see
16 Praise the Father, God of justice
20 Now let us learn of Christ
22 City of God, Jerusalem
23 Change my heart, O God
23 Come, let us with our Lord arise
24 And can it be
25 For I'm building a people of power
28 Father of all, whose laws have stood
28 Take my life and let it be
29 Help us to help each other, Lord
30 Baptised in water
30 Father in heaven, grant to your children
30 I believe in God the Father
30 Oh for a closer walk with God
30 The Spirit came, as promised
31 Risen Lord, whose name we cherish
32 All creatures of our God and King

32 Forgive our sins as we forgive
32 God has spoken to his people
32 He is lovely
32 Heal me, hands of Jesus
32 Make me a channel of your peace
32 Now let us learn of Christ
32 Soften my heart, Lord, soften my heart

Ephesians 5
2 Eternal light, eternal light
2 May the fragrance of Jesus
2 Now let us learn of Christ
2 There is a green hill far away
8 Almighty Lord, the holy One
8 As sons of the day and daughters
8 Consider how he loves you (Sweet Perfume)
8 God whose love we cannot measure
8 Today, if you hear his voice
11 First of the week and finest day
12 Lift up your hearts to the Lord
14 Awake, my soul, and with the sun
14 Christians, awake, salute the happy morn
14 Hark! A thrilling voice is sounding
14 On Jordan's bank, the Baptist's cry
14 Today, if you hear his voice
14 Wake, O wake, and sleep no longer
14 We are his children
16 Awake, my soul, and with the sun
18 Breathe on me, Spirit of Jesus
18 The Spirit came, as promised
19 Angel voices ever singing
19 Born in song
19 Let all the world in every corner sing
19 Songs of praise the angels sang
20 Father almighty, we your humble servants
20 How sweet the name of Jesus sounds
20 My Father, for another night
20 When all your mercies, O my God
21 We worship God
23 God of eternity, Lord of the ages
23 God our Father and creator
23 Help us to help each other, Lord
23 Let saints on earth together sing
23 Lord of the church, we pray for our renewing
23 O Christ the great foundation
23 Praise be to Christ in whom we see

6 You laid aside your majesty
7 All the way, all the way
7 And can it be
7 Behold, the great creator makes
7 Christ triumphant
7 Come and sing the Christmas story
7 Come to set us free (Advent entrance song)
7 For God so loved the world (Londonderry)
7 From east to west, from shore to shore
7 From heaven you came (The Servant King)
7 God of heaven
7 He became poor
7 I am not skilled to understand
7 Jesus, child of Mary
7 Jesus Christ gives life and gladness
7 Jesus, saviour, holy child
7 Lord, you left your throne
7 Lord, you were rich beyond all splendour
7 Lullaby, baby, lie still and slumber
7 My song is love unknown
7 O come, all ye/you faithful
7 O Lord, all the world belongs to you
7 Thanks to God whose word was spoken
7 Thou who wast rich
8 By your cross
8 Holy child, how still you lie
8 Hush you, my baby
8 I believe there is a God
8 Meekness and majesty (This is your God)
8 Name of all majesty
8 The kingdom of God
9 All hail the power of Jesus' name
9 Ascended Christ
9 Christ the Lord is risen again
9 Christ triumphant
9 God has exalted him
9 I believe in Jesus
9 I believe there is a God
9 Immortal Love, for ever full
9 Jesus, Name above all names
9 Jesus shall take the highest honour
9 Jesus, the name high over all
9 Join all the glorious names
9 Let praises ring, let praises ring
9 Man of Sorrows, what a name
9 Name of all majesty

9 No other name
9 Reigning in all splendour
9 Revive thy work/your church, O Lord
9 The head that once was crowned
9 There is power in the name of Jesus
9 To the name of our salvation
9 We believe in God the Father
9 We trust in you, our shield
9 We worship and adore you
10 All creation join to say
10 All hail the power of Jesus' name
10 Angels from the realms of glory
10 At the name of Jesus
10 Christ is risen! hallelujah/alleluia
10 Christ the Lord is risen today
10 Give him the glory (lift your voice)
10 He is Lord
10 I will build my church
10 Lift up your heads, you gates of brass
10 Lift your voice and sing
10 Look, ye saints, the sight is glorious
10 Love's redeeming work is done
10 Mighty in victory, glorious in majesty
10 Oh for a thousand tongues to sing
10 Ye/you servants of God, your master proclaim
11 Glory be to God in heaven
11 Glory in the highest, to the God
11 Holy child, how still you lie
11 Jesus Christ is the Lord of all
11 Name of all majesty
11 O Jesus, King, most wonderful
11 O Spirit of the living God
11 Stand up! stand up for Jesus
11 Thou art coming, O my Saviour
11 We have come as the family of God
11 You are coming, O my Saviour
11 You're worthy of my praise
12 Let all mortal flesh keep silence
13 Speak, Lord, in the stillness
16 Lord, for the years
16 Speak, Lord, in the stillness
16 We love the place, O God
17 O Lord, who came from realms above
17 O thou who camest from above

Philippians 3
1 Rejoice, rejoice, Christ is in you
1 Rejoice, rejoice, rejoice
1 Rejoice, the Lord is King

7 Can we/man by searching find out God
7 I tell you (Leben)
7 We sing the praise of him who died
7 When I survey the wondrous cross
8 Light of the minds that know him
8 To him we come
9 And can it be
9 Here, O my Lord, I see thee face to face
9 Jesus, the name high over all
9 Jesus, your blood and righteousness
9 My hope is built on nothing less
10 Born of the water
10 Christ's church shall glory in his power
10 Come, let us with our Lord arise
10 Jesus, the very thought of thee
10 O happy band of pilgrims
13 Lord, for the years
13 One thing I know, that Christ has healed
14 Child of the stable's secret birth
14 Christ's church shall glory in his power
14 Fight the good fight with all thy/your might
14 Jesus, the very thought of thee
14 You holy angels bright
20 Church of God, elect and glorious
20 Lord of the cross of shame
20 O come, all ye/you faithful

Philippians 4
1 Fight the good fight with all thy/your might
4 As sons of the day and daughters
4 Don't be afraid
4 Rejoice in the Lord always
4 Rejoice, rejoice, Christ is in you
4 Rejoice, rejoice, rejoice
4 Rejoice, the Lord is King
5 In the Lord I'll ever be thankful
5 Put peace into each other's hands
5 We are his children
6 Cast your burdens on to Jesus
6 Consider how he loves you (Sweet Perfume)
6 Father, I want you to hold me
6 Jesus, we celebrate your victory
6 The Lord is King! lift up thy voice
6 We plough the fields, and scatter
6 What a friend we have in Jesus
7 Heal me, hands of Jesus

7 How can I be free from sin
7 In the cross of Christ I glory
7 Like a mighty river flowing
7 May the mind of Christ my saviour
7 My peace I leave with you
7 Now to him who is able
7 O joy of God, we seek you in the morning
9 Behold, the great creator makes
9 How can I be free from sin
11 Beauty for brokenness (God of the poor)
13 Go forth and tell
13 Soldiers of Christ, arise
19 Come, you thankful people, come
20 To God be the glory
21 Let us greet one another

Colossians

Colossians 1
2 Peace to you
3 Father almighty, we your humble servants
4 Gracious Spirit, Holy Ghost
4 Help us to help each other, Lord
4 Holy Spirit, gracious guest
4 O Lord, who came from realms above
4 O thou who camest from above
5 In heavenly love abiding
7 Take me, Lord, just as I am
9 Breathe on me, Spirit of Jesus
9 Speak, Lord, in the stillness
11 Lord, teach us how to pray aright
11 We rest on thee/trust in you
12 Oh heaven is in my heart
12 Praise to God the father
12 The God of Abraham praise
13 Holy child, how still you lie
13 Soldiers of Christ, arise
13 Thanks be to God who gives us
13 When morning gilds the skies
14 All-holy Father, king of endless glory
14 Alleluia, raise the anthem
14 Come, ye faithful, raise the anthem
14 How can I be free from sin
14 O Lord of heaven and earth and sea
14 Restless souls, why do you scatter
14 Souls of men, why will ye scatter
14 To God be the glory
15 Come, let us worship the Christ
15 O Christ, the same, through all
15 O come, all ye/you faithful

241

15 Praise be to Christ in whom we see
15 Rejoice with heart and voice
15 See, amid the winter's snow
15 The brightness of God's glory
15 Who is this child
16 At the name of Jesus
16 God of God, the uncreated
16 I believe in God the Father
16 My God, how wonderful you are
16 See, amid the winter's snow
16 Shepherds, leave your drowsy
   sheep
18 All we've received (We are your
   church)
18 Be thou my vision/Lord be my
   vision
18 God of eternity, Lord of the ages
18 God our Father and creator
18 Jesus Christ, sovereign King
18 Let saints on earth together sing
18 Lord, enthroned in heavenly
   splendour
18 Lord of the church, we pray for our
   renewing
18 O Christ the great foundation
18 The Son of God proclaim
19 Hark! the herald-angels sing
20 All heaven declares
20 Be thou my vision/Lord be my
   vision
20 Glory be to Jesus
20 Hark! the herald-angels sing
20 In Christ there is no East or West
20 Lord, enthroned in heavenly
   splendour
20 O Spirit of the living God
20 Peace, perfect peace
21 My God, I love you
22 Born of the water
22 I come with joy to meet my Lord
22 Jesus the saviour comes
22 Only by grace
22 Spirit of God most high
23 How firm a foundation
27 Calypso Carol (See him lying on a
   bed of straw)
27 Come and sing the Christmas
   story
27 In my life, Lord
27 Jesus, you are changing me
27 Lord, help me to know your
   presence
27 Rejoice, rejoice, Christ is in you
27 See him lying on a bed of straw
29 Now let us learn of Christ

Colossians 2
2 Father in heaven, grant to your
   children
3 Be thou my vision/Lord be my
   vision
3 Glorious things of thee/you are
   spoken
3 Jesus, priceless treasure
7 Father and God, from whom our
   world
8 O God most high
10 O Father of the fatherless (Father me)
12 Baptised in water
12 Comes Mary to the grave
12 Have you not heard
12 I believe in Jesus
12 This is the truth which we
   proclaim
14 I believe there is a God
14 Sing lullaby
14 Such love
14 When I survey the wondrous cross
14 When you prayed beneath the
   trees
15 Holy child, how still you lie
15 Jesus, we celebrate your victory
15 Low in the grave he lay (Christ
   arose)
15 Name of all majesty
19 Help us to help each other, Lord
19 Praise the Father, God of justice
19 Restless souls, why do you scatter
19 Souls of men, why will ye scatter
20 How can I be free from sin

Colossians 3
1 Alleluia, alleluia! hearts to heaven
1 Child of the stable's secret birth
1 God we praise you
1 In heavenly love abiding
1 Jesus has sat down
1 Jesus lives! Thy/Your terrors now
1 Let all mortal flesh keep silence
1 Lord, as the day begins
1 Lord of the cross of shame
1 Now let us learn of Christ
1 Once in royal David's city
1 This is the truth which we
   proclaim
3 Before the throne of God above
3 Jesus, you have lifted me
4 Hail, our once-rejected Jesus
4 Hail, thou once despised Jesus
5 Alleluia, alleluia! hearts to heaven
5 Firmly I believe, and truly

242

16 These are the facts
16 This joyful Eastertide
16 When the Lord in glory comes
17 We worship God

1 Thessalonians 5
4 As sons of the day and daughters
5 Almighty Lord, the holy One
5 O Holy Spirit, come to bless
8 Be thou my vision/Lord be my vision
8 Christian, seek not yet repose
8 Christian soldiers, onward go
8 Oft in danger, oft in woe
8 Soldiers of Christ, arise
8 Soldiers of the cross, arise
10 Be thou my vision/Lord be my vision
10 From heaven you came (The Servant King)
10 Jesus lives! Thy/Your terrors now
11 Help us to help each other, Lord
17 Love divine, all loves excelling
17 The day thou gavest, Lord, is ended
18 Father almighty, we your humble servants
19 I believe in God the Father
19 Lord of the church, we pray for our renewing
19 My Lord of light who made the worlds
19 O Lord, who came from realms above
19 O thou who camest from above
19 Peace be with you all, we sing
19 Spirit divine, attend/inspire our prayers
23 God be in my head
23 My hope is built on nothing less
25 We give God thanks for those who knew
26 Let us greet one another

2 Thessalonians
2 Thessalonians 1
1 You sat down
2 Peace to you
3 Father almighty, we your humble servants
3 O Lord, who came from realms above
3 O thou who camest from above
4 O happy band of pilgrims
11 In my life, Lord

11 Speak, Lord, in the stillness
12 How sweet the name of Jesus sounds
12 O come, all ye/you faithful

2 Thessalonians 2
13 Father almighty, we your humble servants
13 My Lord, I did not choose you
16 Come on and celebrate
16 There is a green hill far away

2 Thessalonians 3
1 We give God thanks for those who knew
5 Change my heart, O God
6 As sons of the day and daughters

1 Timothy
1 Timothy 1
2 Bless the Lord as day departs
2 We believe in God Almighty
7 Immortal, invisible
12 Go forth and tell
14 Jesus, lover of my soul
14 Lord Jesus Christ (Living Lord)
15 Good Christian men/Christians all rejoice
15 This is the day that the Lord has made
16 Oh heaven is in my heart
17 Come, ye/you faithful, raise the strain
17 Happy are they, they who love God
17 Immortal, invisible
17 My God, I love you
17 Spring has come for us today
18 Christian soldiers, onward go
18 Fight the good fight with all thy/your might
18 Oft in danger, oft in woe

1 Timothy 2
1 The Lord is King! lift up thy voice
5 Jesus Christ is the Lord of all
6 A purple robe, a crown of thorn
6 All-creating heavenly Giver
6 All shall be well
6 Father of heaven, whose love profound
6 God of gods, we sound his praises
6 Have you not heard
6 I am not worthy, holy Lord
6 Jesus our hope, our heart's desire

244

6 Praise my soul, the king of heaven
6 There is a green hill far away
6 Within a crib my saviour lay
8 Bless the Lord as day departs
8 Come, praise the Lord
8 Take my life and let it be

1 Timothy 3
3 Put peace into each other's hands
16 Behold, the great creator makes
16 Hark! the herald-angels sing
16 O come, all ye/you faithful
16 The darkness turns to dawn

1 Timothy 4
4 All things bright and beautiful
4 I believe in God the Father
6 We come as guests invited
6 We love the place, O God
10 Jesus, the very thought of thee

1 Timothy 5
10 Meekness and majesty (This is your God)

1 Timothy 6
Fight the good fight with all thy/your might
10 How do we start (That the world may)
11 Come, praise the name of Jesus
12 Christian soldiers, onward go
12 Fight the good fight with all thy/your might
12 Oft in danger, oft in woe
12 You holy angels bright
13 O Father of the fatherless (Father me)
15 Ascended Christ
15 Christ the Lord is risen again
15 Come, ye/you faithful, raise the strain
15 Crown him with many crowns
15 Give to our God immortal praise
15 He became poor
15 He came to earth, not to be served
15 Hosanna, hosanna, hosanna
15 Jesus, King of kings
15 Judge eternal, throned in splendour
15 King of kings .. glory, alleluia
15 King of kings, Lord of lords, lion
15 King of the universe, Lord of the ages
15 Look, ye saints, the sight is glorious

15 No more weeping (Paschal procession)
15 Spring has come for us today
15 The head that once was crowned
15 The King of glory comes (King of Kings)
15 The victory of our God is won
16 Alleluia, raise the anthem
16 Come, ye faithful, raise the an them
16 Hail, gladdening Light
16 Immortal, invisible
17 Be thou my vision/Lord be my vision
17 Immortal, invisible
17 O Lord of heaven and earth and sea
19 Fight the good fight with all thy/your might

2 Timothy
2 Timothy 1
2 Bless the Lord as day departs
5 Now thank we all our God
6 O Lord, who came from realms above
6 O thou who camest from above
7 Almighty God, we thank you for feeding
8 I'm not ashamed to own/name my Lord
9 God of God, the uncreated
9 Of the Father's love begotten
10 Crown him with many crowns
10 Guide me, O my great Redeemer
10 Guide me, O thou great Jehovah
10 Jesus Christ the Lord is born
10 Name of all majesty
10 O Holy Spirit, giver of life
10 O Lord of every shining constellation
10 Unto us a boy is born
12 I'm not ashamed to own/name my Lord

2 Timothy 2
3 Christian soldiers, onward go
3 For all the saints who from their labour
3 Oft in danger, oft in woe
3 Onward, Christian soldiers
3 Soldiers of Christ, arise
3 Soldiers of the cross, arise
3 Stand up! stand up for Jesus
3 To him we come

5 Fight the good fight with all
thy/your might
5 O Lord my love, my strength, my
tower
5 Thee will I love, O Lord, my love
5 Won, the victor's crown
11 All my heart this night rejoices
11 Through the night of doubt and
sorrow
12 And he shall reign
12 Christ is made the sure foundation
12 Hail the day that sees him rise
12 Jesus lives! Thy/Your terrors now
12 Stand up! stand up for Jesus
12 The head that once was crowned
19 Father in heaven, grant to your
children
21 In full and glad surrender
21 Take my life and let it be
24 Dear Lord and Father of mankind
26 O God most high

2 Timothy 3
15 Lord, thy word abideth
15 Lord, your word shall guide us
15 Powerful in making us wise to
salvation
16 Lord, for the years
16 Lord, you sometimes speak in
wonders

2 Timothy 4
1 We believe in God the Father
7 All creation join to say
7 Christ the Lord is risen today
7 Fight the good fight with all
thy/your might
7 For all the saints who from their
labour
7 Love's redeeming work is done
7 Soldiers of Christ, arise
7 You holy angels bright
8 And can it be
8 Rejoice, the Lord is King
17 Go forth and tell
18 Give to our God immortal praise
18 Now thank we all our God

Titus
Titus 1
2 God of God, the uncreated
2 In heavenly love abiding
2 Of the Father's love begotten
4 Bless the Lord as day departs

Titus 2
13 A mighty fortress is our God
13 A safe stronghold our God is still
13 God is our fortress and our rock
14 Church of God, elect and glorious

Titus 3
2 Put peace into each other's hands
5 All hail the power of Jesus' name
5 Lord God, your love has called us
here
5 O Breath of Life, come sweeping
through
5 O Father of the fatherless (Father
me)
5 Rock of ages, cleft for me
5 This is the truth which we
proclaim
7 Calypso Carol (See him lying on a
bed of straw)
7 God, we praise you! God, we bless
you
7 King of glory, King of peace
7 Oh heaven is in my heart
7 See him lying on a bed of straw
15 Let us greet one another

Philemon
Philemon
5 O Lord, who came from realms
above
5 O thou who camest from above
6 Born of the water
16 Jesus is the Lord of living
16 Jesus, we celebrate your victory

Hebrews
Hebrews 1
The brightness of God's glory
1 God has spoken, by his prophets
1 It came upon the midnight clear
1 Thanks to God whose word was
spoken
2 God has spoken to his people
2 I believe in God the Father
2 Lord, you sometimes speak in
wonders
2 Rejoice with heart and voice
2 The darkness turns to dawn
3 Come, let us worship the Christ
3 Glory in the highest, to the God
3 God we praise you
3 God, we praise you! God, we bless
you
3 Hail, our once-rejected Jesus

Hebrews 2

Hebrews 3

Hebrews 4

12 A safe stronghold our God is still
12 Arise, shine (Darkness like a shroud)
12 Darkness like a shroud
12 God is our fortress and our rock
12 How sure the Scriptures are
12 Lord, your word shall guide us
12 Now in reverence and awe
13 Awake, my soul, and with the sun
13 Come and see, come and see
13 God of grace, I turn my face
14 Before the throne of God above
14 I believe in Jesus
14 Jesus is king
14 Join all the glorious names
14 Lord, enthroned in heavenly splendour
14 Where high the heavenly temple stands
15 At even(ing), ere/when the sun was set
15 Holy child, how still you lie
15 Immanuel, O Immanuel
15 Lead us, heavenly Father, lead us
15 Thanks be to God who gives us
15 What a friend we have in Jesus
16 Abide with me, fast falls the eventide
16 And can it be
16 Be bold, be strong
16 Let us draw near to God
16 O God of Jacob, by whose hand
25 I know it was your love for me

Hebrews 5

2 He is lovely
2 Holy child, how still you lie
2 Lead us, heavenly Father, lead us
2 Once in royal David's city
7 It is a thing most wonderful
7 Where high the heavenly temple stands
8 A debtor to mercy alone
8 Lead us, heavenly Father, lead us
8 Meekness and majesty (This is your God)
10 O Trinity, O Trinity
12 Break thou/now the bread of life

Hebrews 6

5 Tell his praise in song and story
5 Through all the changing scenes
6 Lord of the cross of shame
12 Born of the water
13 The God of Abraham praise

17 My hope is built on nothing less
19 God has spoken, by his prophets
19 In heavenly love abiding
19 Jesus is king
19 My hope is built on nothing less
20 Glory be to Jesus

Hebrews 7

1 Christ triumphant
2 King of glory, King of peace
3 I believe in Jesus
16 The brightness of God's glory
19 Beyond all knowledge is your love divine
19 Draw near and take the body of the Lord
19 It passeth knowledge
20 My hope is built on nothing less
25 All-creating heavenly Giver
25 Alleluia, sing to Jesus
25 Before the throne of God above
25 Christ the Lord is risen again
25 Hail, our once-rejected Jesus
25 Hail the day that sees him rise
25 Hail, thou once despised Jesus
25 I know that my Redeemer lives, comfort
25 Jesus is king
25 Lord, enthroned in heavenly splendour
25 Now through the grace of God
25 O Sacrifice of Calvary
25 Oh the deep, deep love of Jesus
25 Son of God, eternal saviour
25 Thank you for the cross
27 He gave his life in selfless love
27 Jesus Christ is risen today
27 Lord, enthroned in heavenly splendour

Hebrews 8

1 Before the throne of God above
1 Christ triumphant
1 God we praise you
1 God, we praise you! God, we bless you
1 Hail, our once-rejected Jesus
1 Hail, thou once despised Jesus
1 Jesus has sat down
1 Jesus our hope, our heart's desire
1 Join all the glorious names
1 Lord, enthroned in heavenly splendour
1 Meekness and majesty (This is your God)

1 Rejoice, the Lord is King
1 Saviour Christ, in praise we name him
1 See the conqueror mounts in triumph
1 The Lord is King! lift up thy voice
1 You sat down
10 God of heaven
10 Help us, O Lord, to learn
10 Thou art the way; by thee alone
10 You are the way, to you alone

Hebrews 9

5 My God, how wonderful you are
11 Jesus calls us! in/o'er the tumult
11 Join all the glorious names
12 All praise to Christ, our Lord and king
12 Come, let us worship the Christ
12 Eternal light, eternal light
12 He gave his life in selfless love
12 I believe there is a God
12 It's your blood that cleanses me
12 Not all the blood of beasts
12 Restless souls, why do you scatter
12 He gave his life in selfless love
12 Souls of men, why will ye scatter
12 The Church's one foundation
12 The first nowell the angel did say
12 They killed him as a common thief
12 What offering shall we give
13 Glory be to Jesus
14 At the name of Jesus
14 Come, let us worship the Christ
14 Heal me, hands of Jesus
14 Here, O my Lord, I see thee face to face
14 How do we start (That the world may)
14 I believe there is a God
14 Jesus Christ the Lord is born
14 Jesus, priceless treasure
14 Light has dawned
14 No weight of gold or silver
14 O come, our all-victorious Lord
14 O Trinity, O Trinity
14 Unto us a boy is born
15 Freedom and life are ours
15 Oh heaven is in my heart
19 Oh for a heart to praise my God
21 Oh for a heart to praise my God
22 Baptised in water
22 Heal me, hands of Jesus
22 I believe there is a God
22 It's your blood that cleanses me

22 Light has dawned
24 Christ the Lord is risen again
24 Hail the day that sees him rise
28 Alas! and did my saviour bleed
28 And now, O Father, mindful of the love
28 Lord, enthroned in heavenly splendour
28 My Lord, what love is this
28 No weight of gold or silver
28 Not all the blood of beasts
28 See, Christ was wounded for our sake
28 We sing the praise of him who died
28 What offering shall we give

Hebrews 10

4 Not all the blood of beasts
4 What offering shall we give
10 And now, O Father, mindful of the love
10 Lord, enthroned in heavenly splendour
10 Not all the blood of beasts
10 What offering shall we give
12 And now, O Father, mindful of the love
12 Glory in the highest, to the God
12 God we praise you
12 Jesus has sat down
12 Jesus is king
12 Lord, teach us how to pray aright
12 My Lord, what love is this
13 Rejoice, the Lord is King
16 Help us, O Lord, to learn
19 And can it be
19 Holiness is your life in me
19 I believe there is a God
19 It's your blood that cleanses me
19 Let us draw near to God
20 Lord, enthroned in heavenly splendour
20 O changeless Christ, for ever new
22 Draw near and take the body of the Lord
22 Glory be to Jesus
22 Heal me, hands of Jesus
22 In silent pain the eternal Son
22 Let us draw near to God
22 Lord, teach us how to pray aright
22 O Jesus, I have promised
22 Oh for a heart to praise my God
22 Spirit divine, attend/inspire our prayers
22 The Lord is King! lift up thy voice

23 You can trust his promises
29 Spirit of faith, by faith be mine
34 I want to serve the purpose of God

Hebrews 11
3 Shout for joy, loud and long
3 Thanks to God whose word was spoken
5 Like a mighty river flowing
6 I do not hold life so dear
10 As with gladness men of old
10 Children of the heavenly king
10 Christ is made the sure foundation
10 City of God, Jerusalem
10 Crown him with many crowns
10 Glorious things of thee/you are spoken
10 Jerusalem, my happy home
10 Jerusalem on high
10 Jerusalem the golden
10 Wake, O wake, and sleep no longer
11 You can trust his promises
13 Guide me, O my great Redeemer
13 Guide me, O thou great Jehovah
13 He who would valiant be
13 O God of Jacob, by whose hand
13 O happy band of pilgrims
13 Who would true valour see
14 Children of the heavenly king
14 Jerusalem the golden
14 There is a land of pure delight
14 Through the night of doubt and sorrow
14 To you, O Lord, our hearts we raise
28 Oh for a heart to praise my God
34 Give thanks with a grateful heart
35 Give praise for famous men
35 The Son of God rides out to war

Hebrews 12
1 Fight the good fight with all thy/your might
1 Give praise for famous men
1 O Lord my love, my strength, my tower
1 Thee will I love, O Lord, my love
1 You holy angels bright
2 Christ the Lord is risen again
2 Glory in the highest, to the God
2 God we praise you
2 He gave his life in selfless love
2 I believe there is a God
2 Jesus Christ is risen today
2 Jesus has sat down
2 Jesus lives! Thy/Your terrors now

2 Lord of the cross of shame
2 Lord, teach us how to pray aright
2 May the mind of Christ my saviour
2 Now let us learn of Christ
2 He gave his life in selfless love
2 Such love
2 The God of Abraham praise
2 The head that once was crowned
2 The Son of God proclaim
2 Wake, O wake, and sleep no longer
2 When I survey the wondrous cross
10 Such love
12 Quiet my mind
12 When the King shall come again
14 Holiness is your life in me
18 Let us love and sing and wonder
22 Glorious things of thee/you are spoken
24 Glory be to Jesus
24 Oh for a heart to praise my God
26 Restore, O Lord
28 A mighty fortress is our God
28 A safe stronghold our God is still
28 God is our fortress and our rock
28 Lord, teach us how to pray aright
28 Rejoice, the Lord is King

Hebrews 13
5 How firm a foundation
5 Jesus, priceless treasure
6 Be bold, be strong
6 Let us draw near to God
8 Christ is the king! O friends rejoice
8 Father God, we worship you, evermore
8 I know that my Redeemer lives, comfort
8 O Christ, the same, through all
8 Praise my soul, the king of heaven
8 There's a song for all the children
12 Glory be to Jesus
12 I believe there is a God
12 It's your blood that cleanses me
13 There is a green hill far away
15 All my hope on God is founded
15 For the beauty of the earth
15 How sweet the name of Jesus sounds
15 My lips shall praise you
15 O God beyond all praising
15 To you, O Lord, our hearts we raise
15 We are here to praise you
15 You're worthy of my praise
18 The day thou gavest, Lord, is ended

18 We give God thanks for those who knew
20 Behold, the great creator makes
20 Great Shepherd of your people
20 Jesus, where'er thy people meet
20 Lord Jesus, when your people meet
20 Yours be the glory
21 And now, O Father, mindful of the love

James

James 1
6 Just as I am
11 Immortal, invisible
12 And can it be
12 My Lord of light who made the worlds
12 Stand up! stand up for Jesus
17 Abide with me, fast falls the eventide
17 Awake, my soul, and with the sun
17 Fight the good fight with all thy/your might
17 For the beauty of the earth
17 From you all skill and science flow
17 Glory to you, my God, this night
17 How good is the God we adore
17 Immortal, invisible
17 Lord, you need no house
17 O God beyond all praising
17 O Lord of heaven and earth and sea
17 Praise God from whom all blessings flow
17 We plough the fields, and scatter
17 When all your mercies, O my God
18 It was a man who was born
18 When things began to happen
21 Come, let us with our Lord arise
27 Beauty for brokenness (God of the poor)
27 I'll praise my maker while I've breath

James 2
1 Light of gladness, Lord of glory
1 Praise we offer, Lord of glory
5 Born of the water
5 Give thanks with a grateful heart
5 Happy are they, they who love God
5 The kingdom of God
8 Beauty for brokenness (God of the poor)
8 Welcome to another day

19 Jesus Christ is the Lord of all

James 3
9 Lord God, your love has called us here
9 O Lord of every shining constellation
9 Spirit of God within me
9 The Lord made man, the Scriptures tell
15 Wise men, they came to look for wisdom
16 How can we sing with joy
17 Come, thou/most holy Spirit, come
17 May we, O Holy Spirit, bear your fruit
17 O Holy Spirit, giver of life
17 Put peace into each other's hands
18 Put peace into each other's hands

James 4
6 Tell out my soul
7 Jesus, the name high over all
7 The price is paid
7 Who honours courage here
8 Draw near and take the body of the Lord
8 Lord, teach us how to pray aright
8 O Jesus, I have promised
8 The Lord is King! lift up thy voice
10 Tell out my soul
12 Great God, what do I see and hear
12 Judge eternal, throned in splendour
12 Rejoice, the Lord is King
12 Thank you for the cross
12 There is only one Lord

James 5
3 Be thou my vision/Lord be my vision
4 God of gods, we sound his praises
4 God, we praise you! God, we bless you
9 Great God, what do I see and hear
9 Judge eternal, throned in splendour
9 Rejoice, the Lord is King
11 O Lord, your tenderness
11 Restless souls, why do you scatter
11 Souls of men, why will ye scatter
13 Songs of praise the angels sang
14 Come, thou/most Holy Spirit, come

1 Peter

1 Peter 1

1 The Church's one foundation
2 Church of God, elect and glorious
2 Clear the road (Prepare the way)
2 Glory be to Jesus
2 I am trusting thee/you, Lord Jesus
2 Jerusalem the golden
2 Oh for a heart to praise my God
2 Prepare the way (Clear the road)
2 Purify my heart
2 There is only one Lord
2 To the name of our salvation
3 Born of the water
3 Father in heaven, grant to your children
3 Hark! the herald-angels sing
3 In heavenly love abiding
3 It was a man who was born
3 O Christ the great foundation
3 O praise ye the Lord, praise him
3 Sing praise to the Lord
3 This is the truth which we proclaim
4 Glorious things of thee/you are spoken
4 Oh heaven is in my heart
4 There is a land of pure delight
6 O love that wilt not let me go
6 Restore, O Lord
7 How firm a foundation
7 How sure the Scriptures are
7 Lord, you are more precious
7 Purify my heart
7 Restore, O Lord
7 The head that once was crowned
8 Away with our fears
8 Breathe on me, Spirit of Jesus
8 Jesus, the joy of loving hearts
8 Not all the blood of beasts
8 O Jesus, King, most wonderful
8 To God be the glory
8 What offering shall we give
9 Lift high the cross, the love of Christ
12 And can it be
12 Glad music fills the Christmas sky
12 Now in reverence and awe
12 Ride on, ride on in majesty
12 The works of the Lord are created
13 A mighty fortress is our God
13 A safe stronghold our God is still
13 God is our fortress and our rock
15 One holy apostolic church
16 Holiness is your life in me

16 Purify my heart
18 How firm a foundation
18 No weight of gold or silver
18 The Church's one foundation
19 Alleluia, raise the anthem
19 Christ the Lord is risen again
19 Come, let us worship the Christ
19 Come, ye faithful, raise the anthem
19 I believe there is a God
19 It's your blood that cleanses me
19 Jesus, Lamb of God and source of life
19 Jesus, priceless treasure
19 No weight of gold or silver
19 O Trinity, O Trinity
19 Only by grace
19 There is a green hill far away
20 Alleluia, raise the anthem
20 Christ, our king before creation
20 Come, ye faithful, raise the anthem
20 God of God, the uncreated
20 Of the Father's love begotten
21 Comes Mary to the grave
21 Gracious Spirit, Holy Ghost
21 Help us to help each other, Lord
21 Holy Spirit, gracious guest
21 I believe in Jesus
21 Low in the grave he lay (Christ arose)
22 Eternal Father, Lord of life
22 Let there be love
22 Love is his word
22 O Father, we bless your name (Panama Praise)
24 Immortal, invisible
25 God has spoken, by his prophets
25 Jesus restore to us again
25 Jesus, the joy of loving hearts

1 Peter 2

  Christ is made the sure foundation
  Christ is our cornerstone
3 Tell his praise in song and story
3 Through all the changing scenes
4 Christ is made the sure foundation
4 Jesus Christ gives life and gladness
4 To him we come
5 Christ is made the sure foundation
5 Jesus Christ, sovereign King
6 Christ is made the sure foundation
6 Christ is our cornerstone
6 How firm a foundation
6 Oh heaven is in my heart
9 Christian, do you not hear the Lord
9 Church of God, elect and glorious

252

11 Father God in heaven (Kum ba yah)
11 In my life, Lord
11 Lift up your heads, you gates of brass
11 Now let us learn of Christ
11 Soldiers of Christ, arise
11 The kingdom of God
11 To God be the glory
12 How firm a foundation
12 O happy band of pilgrims
13 Forty days and forty nights
14 Spirit of faith, by faith be mine
17 The kingdom of God
17 We have come as the family of God

1 Peter 5
1 Christian, do you not hear the Lord
1 Hark, my soul! it is the Lord
2 Lord, you can make our spirits shine
2 O thou who makest souls to shine
4 And can it be
4 My Lord of light who made the worlds
4 Stand up! stand up for Jesus
5 Dear Lord and Father of mankind
5 Tell out my soul
5 We worship God
7 All creatures of our God and King
7 Cast your burdens on to Jesus
7 Fight the good fight with all thy/your might
7 God has spoken to his people
7 Here, O my Lord, I see thee face to face
7 I cannot tell why he whom angels worship
7 Jesus, we celebrate your victory
7 Tell all the world of Jesus
7 What a friend we have in Jesus
8 Who honours courage here
10 God of grace and God of glory
10 Immanuel, O Immanuel
10 Lord of all hopefulness, Lord of all joy
10 Love divine, all loves excelling
10 Now let us learn of Christ
10 Praise my soul, the king of heaven
10 We rest on thee/trust in you
12 I am a new creation
14 Let us greet one another

2 Peter
2 Peter 1
3 Come, praise the name of Jesus
4 Christ, from whom all blessings flow
16 Christ upon the mountain peak
16 Meekness and majesty (This is your God)
16 Our Saviour Christ once knelt in prayer
17 When Jesus led his chosen three
19 Brightest and best of the sons
19 Christ is the world's true light
19 Christ, whose glory fills the skies
19 Come to set us free (Advent entrance song)
19 Eternal light, shine in my heart
19 Jesus came, the heavens adoring
19 Jesus, stand among us at the
19 Light has dawned
19 The day thou gavest, Lord, is ended
19 Thy/your kingdom come, O God
21 God has spoken, by his prophets
21 Powerful in making us wise to salvation
21 We believe in God Almighty

2 Peter 2
1 Jesus, Saviour of the world
1 The first nowell the angel did say
1 We give immortal praise
9 Father God in heaven (Kum ba yah)
9 Let us love and sing and wonder
19 Freedom and life are ours

2 Peter 3
5 Shout for joy, loud and long
5 Thanks to God whose word was spoken
5 The Son of God proclaim
8 O God, our help in ages past
9 You can trust his promises
11 Holiness is your life in me
12 Forth in thy/your name, O Lord, I go
12 In the bleak mid-winter
13 It came upon the midnight clear
13 Songs of praise the angels sang
14 My hope is built on nothing less
18 Born of the water
18 Glory be to Jesus
18 Great Shepherd of your people
18 Now let us learn of Christ

19 Heal me, hands of Jesus
22 Lord Jesus Christ (Living Lord)
22 Powerful in making us wise to
   salvation
23 Let there be love
23 Now let us learn of Christ

1 John 4
2 Behold, the great creator makes
2 Hark! the herald-angels sing
2 Jesus Christ gives life and gladness
2 O come, all ye/you faithful
2 The darkness turns to dawn
4 He that is in us
4 Stand up! stand up for Jesus
6 Jesus restore to us again
6 Spirit of faith, by faith be mine
6 You sat down
7 Beloved, let us love: for love is of
   God
7 Eternal Father, Lord of life
7 Let there be love
7 Love is his word
7 O Father, we bless your name
   (Panama Praise)
8 God is love, his the care
8 Hail to the Lord's anointed
8 Love came down at Christmas
8 Shout for joy, loud and long
8 We sing the praise of him who died
9 Give to our God immortal praise
9 I'm accepted
9 Name of all majesty
9 O come, all ye/you faithful
9 The head that once was crowned
9 To God be the glory
9 We give immortal praise
10 Alleluia, my Father
10 Clear the road (Prepare the way)
10 Hallelujah, my Father
10 I believe in Jesus
10 I believe there is a God
10 Love divine, all loves excelling
10 Love was born at Christmas
10 Prepare the way (Clear the road)
10 So freely flows the endless love
10 Thank you for the cross
10 There is a green hill far away
10 To God be the glory
12 Ye/you servants of God, your
   master proclaim
13 He is risen
13 He lives in us, the Christ of God
13 In the quiet consecration
14 Calypso Carol (See him lying on a

bed of straw)
14 Christians, awake, salute the
   happy morn
14 I cannot tell why he whom angels
   worship
14 Jesus our hope, our heart's desire
14 Jesus, Saviour of the world
14 See him lying on a bed of straw
15 All praise to Christ, our Lord and
   king
15 At the name of Jesus
15 Before the heaven and earth
15 I believe in Jesus
15 The Son of God proclaim
15 Thou art coming, O my Saviour
15 You are coming, O my Saviour
16 God is love, his the care
17 And can it be
17 Jesus, your blood and
   righteousness
18 Beyond all knowledge is your love
   divine
18 Don't be afraid
18 It passeth knowledge
18 Jesus, we celebrate your victory
18 My lips shall praise you
18 We share a new day's dawn
19 All I am will sing out (Jag vill ge
   dig)
19 Beloved, let us love: for love is of
   God
19 My God, I love you
19 My Lord, I did not choose you
19 Now let us learn of Christ
19 There is a green hill far away
20 Christ is the world's Light, he and
   none other
20 Let there be love

1 John 5
6 I believe there is a God
6 It's your blood that cleanses me
6 Rock of ages, cleft for me
6 The Church's one foundation
10 I believe in Jesus
11 Calypso Carol (See him lying on a
   bed of straw)
11 Eternal light, shine in my heart
11 O Father of the fatherless (Father
   me)
11 See him lying on a bed of straw
12 I believe in Jesus
13 Oh heaven is in my heart
14 Be bold, be strong
15 Angel voices ever singing

16 Deck yourself, my soul, with gladness
16 In silent pain the eternal Son
16 Peace be with you all, we sing
16 Risen Lord, whose name we cherish
17 At your feet we fall
17 Christ upon the mountain peak
17 God has spoken, by his prophets
17 How good is the God we adore
18 Alleluia, alleluia! hearts to heaven
18 Alleluia, raise the anthem
18 Come, ye faithful, raise the anthem
18 I believe in God the Father
18 I believe there is a God
18 I know that my Redeemer lives, comfort
18 O Christ the great foundation
18 Praise to God and peace on earth
18 Rejoice, the Lord is King
18 We have a gospel to proclaim
20 Christ is the king! O friends rejoice
20 Risen Lord, whose name we cherish

Revelation 2

1 He walks among the golden lamps
1 In silent pain the eternal Son
1 Risen Lord, whose name we cherish
2 O happy band of pilgrims
4 At even(ing), ere/when the sun was set
4 Thy/your kingdom come, O God
7 All creation join to say
7 Christ the Lord is risen today
7 For all the saints who from their labour
7 From you all skill and science flow
7 Love's redeeming work is done
8 Alleluia, alleluia! hearts to heaven
8 Alleluia, raise the anthem
8 Christ upon the mountain peak
8 Come, ye faithful, raise the anthem
8 God has spoken, by his prophets
8 How good is the God we adore
8 I know that my Redeemer lives, comfort
8 O Christ the great foundation
9 Give thanks with a grateful heart
10 Jesus, Lord, we pray
10 My Lord of light who made the worlds
10 Stand up! stand up for Jesus
12 He walks among the golden lamps

17 Dear Lord and Father of mankind
17 Oh for a heart to praise my God
17 The head that once was crowned
18 I believe in Jesus
27 Thy/your kingdom come, O God
28 Christ be the Lord of all our days
28 Come to set us free (Advent entrance song)
28 For your mercy and your grace
28 Thy/your kingdom come, O God

Revelation 3

1 Come, Holy Ghost, our souls inspire
1 Creator Spirit, come, inspire
1 He walks among the golden lamps
1 Risen Lord, whose name we cherish
2 We are his children
4 Jerusalem the golden
4 The victory of our God is won
7 Go forth and tell
7 He walks among the golden lamps
7 O come, O come, Emmanuel
8 Rejoice, O land, in God your Lord
10 At the name of Jesus
11 Come, let us worship the Christ
11 Come, you thankful people, come
11 Jesus comes with clouds descending
11 Jesus, where'er thy people meet
11 Lo! He comes with clouds descending
11 Lord Jesus, when your people meet
11 We are his children
12 Children of the heavenly king
12 Christ is made the sure foundation
12 City of God, Jerusalem
12 God is our strength and refuge
12 I'm not ashamed to own/name my Lord
12 Jerusalem, my happy home
12 Jerusalem on high
12 Jerusalem the golden
12 Oh for a heart to praise my God
12 We love the place, O God
12 You choirs of new Jerusalem
14 Welcome, happy morning
17 God of grace and God of glory
17 Jesus, lover of my soul
17 Just as I am
17 Lord, I was blind; I could not see
17 Rock of ages, cleft for me

5 Songs of thankfulness and praise
5 The King of glory comes (King of Kings)
5 You choirs of new Jerusalem
6 All heaven declares
6 And he shall reign
6 Father in heaven, our voices we raise
6 No weight of gold or silver
6 There is a redeemer
6 We will crown him (Father in heaven)
8 Jesus comes with clouds descending
8 Jesus shall reign
8 Lo! He comes with clouds descending
8 Wake, O wake, and sleep no longer
8 Ye/you servants of God, your master proclaim
9 Alleluia, sing to Jesus
9 And he shall reign
9 By every nation, race and tongue
9 Easter song (By every nation, race)
9 Fill now/thou my life, O Lord my God
9 Fill thou/now my life, O Lord my God
9 Glory and honour
9 Hail, gladdening Light
9 I believe there is a God
9 It's your blood that cleanses me
9 Light of gladness, Lord of glory
9 Lord of the church, we pray for our renewing
9 The first nowell the angel did say
9 The victory of our God is won
9 There is a green hill far away
9 To God be the glory
9 We give immortal praise
10 Church of God, elect and glorious
10 Forth in the peace of Christ
11 Angel voices ever singing
11 I cannot tell why he whom angels worship
11 Jesus comes with clouds descending
11 Lo! He comes with clouds descending
11 Oh for a thousand tongues to sing
11 Ten thousand times ten thousand
11 Wake, O wake, and sleep no longer
12 Come let us join our cheerful songs
12 Come and see, come and see
12 Give him the glory (lift your voice)
12 Great and wonderful your deeds

12 Hail, our once-rejected Jesus
12 Hail, thou once despised Jesus
12 Heavenly hosts in ceaseless worship
12 Here from all nations
12 Holy, holy, holy is the Lord
12 Jesus, Lamb of God and source of life
12 Let us love and sing and wonder
12 Lift your voice and sing
12 Majesty
12 No other name
12 The price is paid
12 Ye/you servants of God, your master proclaim
13 Come let us join our cheerful songs
13 All glory, laud/praise and honour
13 Alleluia to the King of kings
13 Bless the Lord, created things
13 Father most holy, merciful and loving
13 Glory in the highest, to the God
13 Hail the day that sees him rise
13 Hark! the voice of love and mercy
13 Now to him who is able
13 Onward, Christian soldiers
13 Tell all the world of Jesus
13 What wondrous love is this
14 Jesus shall reign
14 Jesus, the name high over all

Revelation 6
2 A mighty fortress is our God
2 A safe stronghold our God is still
2 God is our fortress and our rock
2 Join all the glorious names
2 O Jesus, King, most wonderful
2 You are crowned with many crowns
9 All hail the power of Jesus' name
10 Joy to the world
10 Judge eternal, throned in splendour
11 Jerusalem the golden
11 The victory of our God is won
12 Songs of thankfulness and praise
16 Father in heaven, our voices we raise
16 We will crown him (Father in heaven)

Revelation 7
Here from all nations
3 Father in heaven, grant to your children

4 Take me, Lord, just as I am
9 All hail the power of Jesus' name
9 Alleluia, sing to Jesus
9 And he shall reign
9 Father in heaven, our voices we raise
9 For all the saints who from their labour
9 Here from all nations
9 Jerusalem the golden
9 Oh for a thousand tongues to sing
9 The victory of our God is won
9 We will crown him (Father in heaven)
10 Ye/you servants of God, your master proclaim
11 God of God, the uncreated
11 Of the Father's love begotten
11 You holy angels bright
12 Angel voices ever singing
12 Majesty
12 Now to him who is able
12 Ye/you servants of God, your master proclaim
13 How bright these glorious spirits shine
13 Who are these like stars appearing
14 I believe there is a God
14 In heavenly armour we'll enter the land
14 It's your blood that cleanses me
14 Let us draw near to God
14 O happy band of pilgrims
14 Only by grace
14 The battle belongs to the Lord
14 The Church's one foundation
14 The victory of our God is won
14 There is only one Lord
15 I will seek your face, O Lord
15 My God, how wonderful you are
16 To you, O Lord, our hearts we raise
17 All heaven declares
17 Christian soldiers, onward go
17 Father in heaven, our voices we raise
17 Lord of the church, we pray for our renewing
17 No weight of gold or silver
17 Oft in danger, oft in woe
17 Such love
17 We will crown him (Father in heaven)

Revelation 8

1 When the Lord in glory comes
2 When the Lord in glory comes
3 Praise to our God
4 Hail to the Lord's anointed
4 Jesus shall reign

Revelation 9

13 My hope is built on nothing less
13 We have a gospel to proclaim

Revelation 10

1 O love that wilt not let me go
6 Alleluia, raise the anthem
6 Come, ye faithful, raise the anthem

Revelation 11

11 Breathe on me, breath of God
13 Glory in the highest, to the God
15 And he shall reign
15 Come and see the shining hope
15 Come sing the praise of Jesus
15 Hail to the Lord's anointed
15 In the tomb so cold
15 Jesus comes with clouds descending
15 Lo! He comes with clouds descending
15 Soldiers of the cross, arise
15 The day thou gavest, Lord, is ended
15 The Son of God proclaim
16 In the bleak mid-winter
16 Ye/you servants of God, your master proclaim
17 Ride on, ride on in majesty
19 When the Lord in glory comes

Revelation 12

1 Once in royal David's city
5 Thy/your kingdom come, O God
7 Lift up your heads, you gates of brass
7 Who honours courage here
10 The price is paid
10 There is a redeemer
11 I believe there is a God
11 In heavenly armour we'll enter the land
11 It's your blood that cleanses me
11 Only by grace
11 Soldiers of Christ, arise
11 The battle belongs to the Lord
11 There is only one Lord

Revelation 13

8 Alleluia, raise the anthem
8 Come, ye faithful, raise the an
   them

Revelation 14

1 The God of Abraham praise
3 Alleluia, sing to Jesus
3 Lord of the church, we pray for our
   renewing
5 Jesus the saviour comes
5 My hope is built on nothing less
6 We have a gospel to proclaim
7 Christ is the world's light, he and
   none other
7 I, the Lord of sea and sky
7 To God be the glory
7 We believe in God the Father
7 You are the God of our fathers
13 For all the saints who from their
   labour
13 Jerusalem, my happy home
14 All hail the power of Jesus' name
14 Christ triumphant
14 Come, you thankful people, come
14 I cannot tell why he whom angels
   worship
14 The head that once was crowned
14 You are crowned with many
   crowns

Revelation 15

2 Alleluia, sing to Jesus
2 Holy, holy, holy, Lord God
   almighty
2 I will sing the wondrous story
3 God of eternity, Lord of the ages
3 Great and wonderful your deeds
3 King of the universe, Lord of the
   ages
4 Holy, holy, holy, Lord God
   almighty
4 You are beautiful beyond
   description
5 Great and wonderful are your
   deeds

Revelation 16

5 Holy, holy, holy, Lord God
   almighty
5 There is a redeemer
7 Great and wonderful your deeds
18 When the Lord in glory comes
20 In the bleak mid-winter

Revelation 17

14 Ascended Christ
14 Christ the Lord is risen again
14 Give to our God immortal praise
14 He became poor
14 He came to earth, not to be served
14 He is Lord
14 Hosanna, hosanna, hosanna
14 Jesus, King of kings
14 Judge eternal, throned in
   splendour
14 King of kings .. glory, alleluia
14 King of kings, Lord of lords, lion
14 Let all mortal flesh keep silence
14 Look, ye saints, the sight is
   glorious
14 No more weeping (Paschal
   procession)
14 The head that once was crowned
14 The King of glory comes (King of
   Kings)
14 The victory of our God is won

Revelation 18

5 Creator of the earth and skies
14 Be thou my vision/Lord be my
   vision

Revelation 19

Crown him with many crowns
1 All creation join to say
1 All praise to Christ, our Lord and
   king
1 Alleluia, praise the Lord
1 Alleluia, raise the anthem
1 Alleluia, sing to Jesus
1 Christ the Lord is risen again
1 Christ the Lord is risen today
1 Come, ye faithful, raise the anthem
1 For all the saints who from their
   labour
1 Halle, halle, hallelujah
1 He is risen
1 Jesus Christ is risen today
1 Jesus comes with clouds
   descending
1 Let all mortal flesh keep silence
1 Let us praise the Lord our God
1 Lo! He comes with clouds
   descending
1 Lord, enthroned in heavenly
   splendour
1 Love's redeeming work is done
1 Sing praises to the Lord
1 Word of justice

2 Great and wonderful your deeds
3 Sing praises to the Lord
3 Word of justice
5 Come, praise the Lord
6 As with gladness men of old
6 Halle, halle, hallelujah
6 He came to earth, not to be served
6 Jesus comes with clouds
    descending
6 Jesus is king
6 Judge eternal, throned in
    splendour
6 Let us rejoice and be glad
6 Lo! He comes with clouds
    descending
6 O give thanks to the Lord, for his
    love
6 Rejoice, the Lord is King
6 Sing a new song of thanksgiving
6 Sing praises to the Lord
6 The Lord is King! lift up thy voice
6 Wake, O wake, and sleep no longer
6 Word of justice
7 Here, O my Lord, I see thee face to
    face
7 Let us praise the Lord our God
7 The trumpets sound, the angels
    sing
8 Come, praise the name of Jesus
9 Here, O my Lord, I see thee face to
    face
9 In memory of the Saviour's love
9 In the quiet consecration
10 Come, worship God who is
    worthy
11 A mighty fortress is our God
11 A safe stronghold our God is still
11 God is our fortress and our rock
11 Welcome, happy morning
12 At the name of Jesus
12 Crown him with many crowns
12 Father in heaven, our voices we
    raise
12 Jesus shall reign
12 The head that once was crowned
12 We will crown him (Father in
    heaven)
12 You are crowned with many
    crowns
13 At the name of Jesus
13 Behold, the great creator makes
13 Christmas for God's holy people
13 Come to us, creative Spirit
13 God has spoken, by his prophets
13 I believe there is a God

13 I bind myself to God today
13 It's your blood that cleanses me
13 Jesus, hope of every nation
13 O come, all ye/you faithful
13 Songs of thankfulness and praise
13 The darkness turns to dawn
13 The Son of God proclaim
13 To him we come
13 When things began to happen
15 He walks among the golden lamps
15 Thy/your kingdom come, O God
16 All hail the power of Jesus' name
16 Christ the Lord is risen again
16 He became poor
16 Hosanna, hosanna, hosanna
16 In your arms of love
16 Jesus, King of kings
16 King of kings . . . glory, alleluia
16 King of kings, Lord of lords, lion
16 No more weeping (Paschal
    procession)
16 The head that once was crowned
16 The King of glory comes (King of
    Kings)
16 The victory of our God is won
17 See the feast our God prepares

Revelation 20
    Lord, enthroned in heavenly
    splendour
2 O God most high
4 Christ is made the sure foundation
4 Come, O/thou long-expected
    Jesus
4 Hail the day that sees him rise
4 Jesus lives! Thy/Your terrors now
4 Low in the grave he lay (Christ
    arose)
4 The head that once was crowned
6 Church of God, elect and glorious
6 Forth in the peace of Christ
6 Jesus lives! Thy/Your terrors now
6 The head that once was crowned
11 Great God, what do I see and hear
11 In the bleak mid-winter
11 Loved with everlasting love
11 Songs of praise the angels sang

Revelation 21
1 In the bleak mid-winter
1 It came upon the midnight clear
1 Loved with everlasting love
1 Songs of praise the angels sang
2 Children of the heavenly king
2 Christ is made the sure foundation

2 City of God, Jerusalem
2 God is our strength and refuge
2 I'm not ashamed to own/name my
  Lord
2 It came upon the midnight clear
2 Jerusalem, my happy home
2 Jerusalem on high
2 Jerusalem the golden
2 O Christ the great foundation
2 The Church's one foundation
2 Wake, O wake, and sleep no longer
2 You choirs of new Jerusalem
3 Word of justice
4 Come, you thankful people, come
4 From you all skill and science flow
4 Here from all nations
4 How bright these glorious spirits
  shine
4 O Father of the fatherless (Father
  me)
4 O love that wilt not let me go
4 Soon and very soon
4 There is a land of pure delight
4 Today, if you hear his voice
5 Christ on whom the Spirit rested
5 Jesus, the very thought of thee
5 Lord God, your love has called us
  here
5 O Lord, all the world belongs to
  you
6 Christ is surely coming
6 Glorious things of thee/you are
  spoken
6 God of heaven
6 Holy Spirit, truth divine
6 How good is the God we adore
6 Jesus, lover of my soul
6 Jesus, the joy of loving hearts
6 Lord of the church, we pray for our
  renewing
7 All-creating heavenly Giver
7 Born of the water
7 Stand up! stand up for Jesus
8 Come, you thankful people, come
8 King of the universe, Lord of the
  ages
10 Jerusalem, my happy home
12 For all the saints who from their
  labour
12 Wake, O wake, and sleep no longer
12 We trust in you, our shield
14 The victory of our God is won
19 Christ is made the sure foundation
23 As with gladness men of old
25 There is a land of pure delight

Revelation 22
1 Father in heaven, our voices we
  raise
1 God is our strength and refuge
1 No weight of gold or silver
1 River, wash over me
1 To you, O Lord, our hearts we raise
1 We will crown him (Father in
  heaven)
2 Jerusalem the golden
3 Father in heaven, our voices we
  raise
3 Love divine, all loves excelling
3 We will crown him (Father in
  heaven)
4 Come, praise the name of Jesus
4 Hail the day that sees him rise
4 Jerusalem on high
4 Lord, speak to me that I may speak
4 My God, accept my heart this day
4 The Church's one foundation
4 We love the place, O God
4 When the Lord in glory comes
4 You holy angels bright
5 And he shall reign
5 As with gladness men of old
5 Be thou my vision/Lord be my
  vision
5 Christ is made the sure foundation
5 Christ on whom the Spirit rested
5 There is a land of pure delight
7 Christ is surely coming
7 Come, let us worship the Christ
7 Come, you thankful people, come
7 Jesus comes with clouds
  descending
7 Jesus, where'er thy people meet
7 Lo! He comes with clouds
  descending
7 Lord Jesus, when your people
  meet
7 Oh for a heart to praise my God
7 We are his children
9 Come, worship God who is worthy
10 God is working his purpose out
12 Christ is surely coming
12 Sing a new song of thanksgiving
12 We are his children
13 All heaven declares
13 Christ upon the mountain peak
13 God has spokenóby his prophets
13 God of heaven
13 How good is the God we adore
14 For all the saints who from their
  labour

264

12

FINDING THE MATERIAL YOU NEED

Psalms, Hymns and Spiritual Songs –
The State of the Art

PSALMS

Many of the best songs and hymns begin from the Psalms. As we have observed, psalms are neglected in many churches because of an earlier insistence on one style of singing, and because of their exclusion from the reading Lectionary. But hope is at hand. Iona have recently published *Psalms of Patience, Protest and Praise*[1]. Kevin Mayhew publications have psalms among the variety of materials they are bringing out for churches. So does the Roman Catholic St Thomas More Centre. And *Psalms for Today*[2] and *Songs from the Psalms*[3] have now supplanted their predecessor *Psalm Praise*[4] (except in Australia!). These latter books contain all sorts of psalm material – from Taizé and song style through hymn style, to pointing and classical. They also have spoken psalms with rhythmic responses. This takes the hopelessness out of psalm-*saying* by congregations either using standard Bibles (which were designed for personal use or for a single reader), or using psalms from the *Liturgical Psalter* (which were designed for chanting). Finally, Norman Warren and friends have

[1] *Psalms of Patience, Protest and Praise*, published 1994 by Wild Goose Publications, Iona.
[2] *Psalms for Today*, published 1990 by Hodder & Stoughton Ltd, London.
[3] *Songs from the Psalms*, published 1990 by Hodder & Stoughton Ltd, London.
[4] *Psalm Praise*, published 1973 by The Church Pastoral Aid Society, London.

devised *Responsorial Psalms*[5] Here, the congregation only have a small amount to learn and remember, while the singers or soloist supply the 'meat' (as with much of the Taizé material).

HYMNS AND SONGS

Mission Praise[6] is the highest-selling hymn/song book according to the book shops poll, but *Hymns Ancient and Modern*[7] still has the lion's share of the traditional market. The first *Mission Praise* was compiled for a Billy Graham crusade, and therefore had to be put together in haste. But it struck the right chord at the right moment, and offered so much of the lighter material that contemporary worship needed. Young people brought up on *Youth Praise*[8] – and even *CSSM* choruses[9] – were wanting informality in church. English choruses were supplemented by material coming out of charismatic renewal – essentially from the United States at this time. As with the early *Songs of Fellowship*[10], the songs were good but the hymn versions were were often older even than the 'received' versions in current hymn books and there were archaisms which had previously been eliminated even by *Hymns Ancient and Modern*. *Mission Praise* has since been revised, and in scale is most impressive. Kingsway publish an annual *New Songs*[11] book with the latest worship songs from the United Kingdom and the United States, the latter drawing heavily on the Vineyard repertoire.

---

[5]*Responsorial Psalms*, published 1994 by HarperCollins*Publishers* Ltd, London.
[6]*Mission Praise*, published 1984, 1988, 1990 by HarperCollins*Publishers* Ltd, London.
[7]*Hymns Ancient and Modern*, (various editions) published by The Canterbury Press, Norwich.
[8]*Youth Praise*, published 1964 by the Church Pastoral Aid Society, London.
[9]*CSSM Choruses*, published 1921, 1936 by the Children's Special Service Mission (now Scripture Union).
[10]*Songs of Fellowship*, (various editions) published by Kingsway's Thankyou Music, Eastbourne.
[11]*New Songs*, published 1990 onwards by Kingsway's Thankyou Music, Eastbourne.

BUILDING BRIDGES

Iona has distinctive material which is a bridge between the formal tradition and the current worship song repertoire; it includes many 'a cappella' songs and prayer chants. Much of it is quick to learn for singers and congregation. The same can be said of St Thomas More Centre music, notably that by Christopher Walker and Bernadette Farrell. You don't have to go to the source books for all this material; much of it is being absorbed into wider books like *Psalms for Today, Songs from the Psalms,* and *Let's Praise! (1* and 2)[12].

One of the stumbling blocks to the use of worship songs in traditional churches has been the lack of readily available choral settings. Competent choirs baulk at singing unison all the time; able accompanists respect good arrangements. *Sing Mission Praise*[13] – a substantial book of vocal arrangements of worship songs – is therefore most welcome. The Royal School of Church Music has already sponsored such a volume, but of more limited extent[14]. *Hymns Ancient and Modern* have produced *Worship Songs Ancient and Modern*[15] – though their definition of 'songs' covers the contemporary hymns which the *Ancient and Modern New Standard*[16] hymn book notably lacked in any quantity. We wait to see if these will be combined in a future edition.

NEW APPROACHES

The better of the Jubilate hymn revisions are creeping slowly but surely into other books. This will save some excellent but ageing material that would otherwise be dropped (and some that has already been dropped by *Ancient and Modern New*

[12]*Let's Praise! 1 and 2,* published 1988 and 1994 by HarperCollins*Publishers* Ltd, London.
[13]*Sing Mission Praise,* published 1995 by HarperCollins*Publishers* Ltd, London.
[14]*Anthems from Worship Songs,* published 1994 by The Royal School of Church Music.
[15]*Worship Songs Ancient and Modern,* published 1992 by The Canterbury Press, Norwich.
[16]*Hymns Ancient and Modern New Standard,* published 1992 by The Canterbury Press, Norwich.

Standard). The current (second) edition of *Hymns for Today's Church*[17] is milder than the first in terms of revision, though it pays more regard to inclusive language (with reference to people, not to God). Revisions aside, *Hymns for Today's Church* still remains the largest collection of contemporary hymnody in one book (though the Methodist *Hymns and Psalms*[18] does a good job for that denomination). Its sister publication, *Church Family Worship*[19] is widely plundered for useful material (not least for its responsive prayers), and owned by many ministers and musicians as a 'use to choose' book because of its thematic sections, .

The latest radical leap from the Jubilate stable is into song-style hymnody. *Hymns for the People*[20] is described by its editor, David Peacock, as 'the hymn book for music groups'. One of the reasons why many churches have virtually abandoned hymnody is that music designed for organ accompaniment and four part choir is entirely unsuitable for the modern worship group. So congregations led by singers and instruments such as guitars, synthesisers etc. are starved of the nourishment of hymnody. As I have argued above, Christians learn their theology from hymns and songs because they are memorable and often repeated. Many songs were designed – quite properly – for 'heart response' and do not have the hymn's capacity to teach and nourish. Ministers and worship leaders no longer aided by traditional organ and four-part choir should look at *Hymns for the People* if they feel they are in danger of losing their hymn repertoire.

FOR CHILDREN

In the children's area, there remains *Junior Praise*[21], now augmented by *Junior Praise 2*[22]. Then there's *Children's Praise*[23],

[17]*Hymns for Today's Church*, published 1982 by Hodder & Stoughton Ltd, London.
[18]*Hymns and Psalms*, published 1983 by The Methodist Publishing House.
[19]*Church Family Worship*, published 1986 by Hodder & Stoughton Ltd, London.
[20]*Hymns for the People*, published 1993 by HarperCollins*Publishers* Ltd, London.
[21]*Junior Praise*, published 1986 by HarperCollins*Publishers* Ltd, London .
[22]*Junior Praise 2*, published 1992 by HarperCollins*Publishers* Ltd, London.
[23]*Childrens' Praise*, published 1991 by HarperCollins*Publishers* Ltd, London.

for the non-readers/under 8's – no words edition, and *Spring Harvest Kid's Praise*[24] – not to be confused with the American *Kid's Praise*. The *Ishmael* (Ian Smail) *Song Books*[25] for children/all-age congregations also offer Bible verses set to music – picking up in modern idiom the motivation of many *CSSM* choruses.

THE ETHNIC TREND

There's everything to be gained by understanding other world cultures. *World Praise*[26] – a gem of a book – is ideal as a link between Christians in the first and the third world. There are songs here that are a breath of fresh air for all occasions, but particularly benefit the missionary/partnership event. Geoff Weaver of the Church Missionary Society is largely responsible for the collection. *World Praise Combined*[27] has now arrived on the scene, timed for the World Baptist Conference in Argentina and substantially increasing the ethnic repertoire.

SEASONAL BOOKS

Oxford University Press have just published a wonderful and erudite collection of Christmas Carols[28], and a smaller (cheaper!) edition. This is for choir, rather than the congregation. Stainer & Bell and Novello have re-entered this market, too. Iona – in a quite different idiom – offer *The Innkeeper: twenty Christmas Carols*[29]. *Carol Praise*[30] is still the most accessible (and comprehensive) and now has the added attraction

[24]*Spring Harvest Kid's Praise*, published 1994 by ICC Studios, Eastbourne.
[25]*Ishmael Song Books*, published by Kingsway's Thankyou Music, Eastbourne.
[26]*World Praise*, published 1993 by HarperCollins*Publishers* Ltd, London.
[27]*World Praise Combined*, published 1995 by HarperCollins*Publishers* Ltd, London.
[28]*The New Oxford Book of Carols*, published 1993 by Oxford University Press, Oxford.
[29]*The Innkeeper: Twenty Christmas Carols*, published 1994 by Wild Goose Publications, Iona.
[30]*Carol Praise*, published 1987 by HarperCollins*Publishers* Ltd, London.

of Sue Merryweather's *Play Carol Praise*[31] – instrumental accompaniments for the church or school 'orchestra' (photo-copiable with permission!). If you have a four-part choir, get one of the remaining stock of *Carols for Today*[32] (currently a music bargain in paperback); it is due to be superseded, but may not re-emerge for a year or two. The supplement can now only be obtained from the Norman Nibloe mail order list based in Haywards Heath[33].

SUBSCRIPTIONS AND ELECTRONIC BOOKS

Kingsway, like Oxford University Press and Stainer & Bell in quite a different culture, have occasional material. A subscription brings you the *Worshipping Church Resource* once a quarter. This includes twelve new songs with piano and choral arrangements. Word have a similar package.

Another way of obtaining fresh songs will be NoteStation. Already installed in secular music shops in central London, NoteStation consoles provide an electronic source for free listening and personal selection of material before printing out the music and charging you appropriately. With the advent of on-line hymn and song music (now only a few years away), it will be possible to select and purchase music via computer and modem.

WorshipMaster™[34] follows hard on the heels of their Hodder's brilliant *BibleMaster*™[35]. The drawback with *WorshipMaster*™ is its high up-front cost, and the fact that its contents bear no direct relation to any existing music book.

[31]*Play Carol Praise*, published 1990 by HarperCollins*Publishers* Ltd, London.
[32]*Carols for Today*, published 1987 by HarperCollins*Publishers* Ltd, London.
[33]34 Sussex Road, Haywards Heath, West Sussex RH16 8XF.
[34]*WorshipMaster*™, published 1993 by Hodder & Stoughton Ltd, London/Oxford University Press, Oxford.
[35]*BibleMaster*™, published 1992 by Hodder & Stoughton Ltd, London.

13

FIRST LINE INDEX TO HYMNS, SONGS AND PSALMS

in currently published UK editions

A&M	*Hymns A&M New Standard Edition*[1]		editions are given in brackets)
BPW	*Baptist Praise and Worship*[2]	NEH	*New English Hymnal*[11]
CFW	*Church Family Worship*[3]	O&N	*Hymns Old and New*[12]
CP	*Carol Praise*[4]	PFT	*Psalms for Today*[13]
H&P	(Methodist) *Hymns and Psalms*[5]	SF	*Songs of Fellowship*[14] (including hymns)
HFP	*Hymns for the People*[6]	SFP	*Songs from the Psalms*[15]
HTC	*Hymns for Today's Church*[7] ('s' indicates song supplement)	WP	*World Praise*[16]
		WSAM	*Worship Songs Ancient and Modern*[17]
JP	*Junior Praise*[8]		
LP	*Let's Praise! 1 and 2*[9]	(Ps.)	Psalm derivation(s)
MP	*Mission Praise*[10] (combined edition: numbers for earlier		

[1]*Hymns Ancient and Modern New Standard*, published 1983 by The Canterbury Press, Norwich.

[2]*Baptist Praise and Worship*, published 1991 by Oxford University Press, Oxford.

[3]*Church Family Worship*, published 1986 by Hodder & Stoughton Ltd, London.

[4]*Carol Praise*, published 1987 by HarperCollins*Publishers* Ltd, London.

[5]*Hymns and Psalms*, published 1983 by The Methodist Publishing House, London.

[6]*Hymns for the People,* published 1993 by HarperCollins*Publishers* Ltd, London.

[7]*Hymns for Today's Church*, published 1982 by Hodder & Stoughton Ltd, London.

[8]*Junior Praise*, published 1986 by HarperCollins*Publishers* Ltd, London.

[9]*Let's Praise! 1 and 2*, published 1988, 1994 by HarperCollins*Publishers* Ltd, London.

[10]*Mission Praise,* published 1982, 1986, 1990 by HarperCollins*Publishers* Ltd, London.

[11]*New English Hymnal,* published 1989 by The Canterbury Press, Norwich.

[12]*Hymns Old and New*, published 1989 by Kevin Mayhew, Bury St Edmunds.

[13]*Psalms for Today*, published 1990 by Hodder & Stoughton Ltd, London.

[14]*Songs of Fellowship*, published 1991 by Kingsway's Thankyou Music, Eastbourne.

[15]*Songs from the Psalms*, published 1990 by Hodder & Stoughton Ltd, London.

[16]*World Praise*, published 1993, 1995 by HarperCollins*Publishers* Ltd, London.

[17]*Worship Songs Ancient and Modern*, published 1992 by The Canterbury Press, Norwich.

First Line	Book Reference
A baby was born in Bethlehem	CP 1, WP 1.
A boy gave to Jesus five loaves	JP 1.
A brighter dawn is breaking	NEH 102.
A charge to keep I have	H&P 785.
A child is born for us	CP 2.
A child is born for us today	CP 3, CP 4, HFP 1.
A child is born in Bethlehem	CP 5.
A child this day is born	CP 7.
A Christmas round	WSAM 15.
A debtor to mercy alone	HTC 449.
A glorious company we sing	H&P 787.
A great and mighty wonder	A&M 43, BPW 140, CP 6, H&P 70, HTC 49, NEH 21, O&N 3.
A heavenly splendour from on high	NEH 154.
A man there lived in Galilee	A&M 334, O&N 24.
A messenger named Gabriel	CP 8, HTC 73.
A mighty fortress is our God (Ps. 25)	A&M 114, HFP 96, HTC 523, MP 2 (MP2 284), SF 25.
A mighty mystery we set forth	BPW 403, H&P 579.
A naggy mum, a grumpy Dad	JP 302.
A new commandment that I give to you	BPW 470, CFW 445, HTC S26, JP 303, MP 1 (MP2 283), O&N 29, SF 22.
A purple robe, a crown of thorn	HFP 2, HTC 122, JP 304, WSAM 3.
A round for peace	WSAM 2.
A safe stronghold our God is still (Ps. 25)	A&M 114, BPW 375, H&P 661, HFP 96, HTC 523, MP 2 (MP2 284), O&N 32, SF 25.
A song was heard at Christmas	CP 9, HTC 75.
A sovereign protector I have	BPW 325.
A special star in the sky	JP 305.
A star in the sky	CP 10.
A stranger once did bless the earth	A&M 335.
A Virgin most pure, as the prophets do	H&P 93.
A wiggly waggly worm, a slippery slimy	JP 306.
Abba, Father	BPW 326, CFW 399, JP 2, LP 1, MP 3 (MP1 1), SF 1.
Abide with me, fast falls the eventide	A&M 13, BPW 515, H&P 665, HFP 3, HTC 425, MP 4 (MP1 2), NEH 331, O&N 2, SF 2.
Above the voices of the world	MP 5 (MP2 285).
According to thy gracious word	NEH 270.
Across the desert sands	CP 11.
Advent entrance song (Come to set us)	CP 74, LP 23.
After darkness, light	H&P 186.
Again the Lord's own day is here	A&M 20.
Ah, holy Jesus, how have you offended	BPW 215, H&P 164, HTC 123, NEH 62.
Ah Lord God	MP 6 (MP2 286), SF 3.
Alas! and did my Saviour bleed	HTC 124.
All around me, Lord	JP 7, MP 10 (MP2 291).
All-creating heavenly Giver	HTC 489.
All creation join to say	CFW 259, HFP 4, HTC 150.

All creatures of our God and King (Ps. 145)	A&M 105, BPW 28, CFW 283, H&P 329, HFP 5, HTC 13, MP 7 (MP2 287), NEH 263, O&N 5.
All earth was dark	MP 8 (MP2 288).
All for Jesus, all for Jesus	BPW 332, H&P 251, HTC 469, NEH 272.
All glory be to God on high	HTC 606.
All glory, laud, and honour (processional)	A&M 328, CFW 202, HFP 6, HTC 120, MP 9 (MP2 289), O&N 12.
All glory, laud/praise and honour	A&M 60, BPW 216, CFW 202, H&P 160, HFP 6, HTC 120, MP 9 (MP2 289), NEH 509, O&N 12.
All glory to God in the sky	H&P 400.
All hail, adored Trinity	NEH 145.
All hail, King Jesus	CP 12, MP 11 (MP1 3), SF 7.
All hail the Lamb	MP 12 (MP3 648), SF 8.
All hail the power of Jesus' name (Ps. 9)	A&M 140, BPW 29, H&P 252, HFP 7, HTC 587, LP 2, MP 13 (MP1 51), NEH 332, O&N 13, SF 9.
All hail the power of Jesus' name (revised)	HTC 203, O&N 13, WP 172/173.
All heaven declares (Ps. 10)	LP 234, MP 14 (MP3 649), SF 10, WP 174.
All heaven rings with joyful songs	CP 13.
All heaven waits	MP 15 (MP2 290), SF 11.
All-holy Father, king of endless glory	HTC 391.
All I am will sing out (Jag vill ge dig)	LP 3.
All is made for the glory of God	WP 153
All my heart this night rejoices	CP 14, H&P 91, HFP 8, HTC 76.
All my hope on God is founded	A&M 336, BPW 327, H&P 63, HTC 451, MP 16 (MP2 292), NEH 333, O&N 14.
All my life, Lord	MP 17 (MP2 297).
All my soul to God I raise (Ps. 25)	PFT 25a.
All over the world	JP 5, MP 18 (MP2 293), O&N 15, SF 12.
All people that on earth do dwell (Ps. 100)	A&M 100, BPW 2, CFW 367, H&P 1, HFP 9, HTC 14, JP 4, LP 235, MP 201 (MP1 6), NEH 334, O&N 16, SF 13.
All praise to Christ, our Lord and King	HTC 204.
All praise to our redeeming Lord	BPW 401, H&P 753, MP 19 (MP2 294).
All praise to thee, for thou, O King	A&M 337, H&P 253, NEH 335.
All Scriptures are given	CFW 608.
All shall be well	BPW 243, HFP 10, HTC 149.
All the kings of the earth	WP 140, (WP1 71).
All the riches of his grace	MP 21 (MP1 8), O&N 20.
All the way, all the way	CFW 207, CP 15.
All the way my Saviour leads me	MP 22 (MP2 296).
All things are possible to them	H&P 723.
All things bright and beautiful	A&M 116, BPW 116, CFW 266, H&P 330, HFP 11, HTC 283, JP 6, MP 23 (MP2 298), NEH 264, O&N 21, SF 14.

Amazing grace	BPW 550, CFW 158, H&P 215, HFP 16, HTC 28, JP 8, LP 6, MP 31 (MP1 10), O&N 25, SF 19, WP 175.
Amen, Alleluia!	WP 8, (WP1 6).
Amen, we praise your name, O God	WP 9, (WP1 5).
Among us our beloved stands	BPW 427.
An army of ordinary people	MP 32 (MP2 301), SF 20.
An upper room did our Lord prepare	A&M 434, BPW 429, H&P 594,WSAM 4.
And are we yet alive	H&P 707.
And art thou come with us to dwell	H&P 415.
And can it be	BPW 328, CFW 389, H&P 216, HFP 17, HTC 588, LP 8, MP 33 (MP1 11), O&N 26, SF 21.
And can it be (revised version)	HTC 452.
And did those feet in ancient time	A&M 294, NEH 488, O&N 27.
And didst thou travel light, dear Lord	A&M 339.
And he shall reign	LP 237.
And now, O Father, mindful of the love	A&M 260, H&P 593, HTC 392, NEH 273, O&N 28.
And we know that all things	JP 310.
Angel voices ever singing	A&M 163, BPW 1, H&P 484, HFP 18, HTC 307, MP 34 (MP2 304), NEH 336, O&N 31, SF 24.
Angels from the realms of glory	A&M 39, BPW 155, CFW 661, CP 21, H&P 92, HFP 19, HTC 77, JP 10, MP 35 (MP2 302), O&N 30, SF 23.
Angels, praise him	CFW 272, HTC S32.
Answer me (Ps. 4)	LP 239.
Are you humbly grateful	JP 309.
Arglwydd, arwain drwy'r anialwch	BPW 652.
Arglwydd, gad im dawel orffwys	BPW 648.
Arise, my soul, arise	H&P 217.
Arise, shine (Behold, the darkness)	CP 32, MP 36 (MP1 12).
Arise, shine (Darkness like a shroud)	CP 76, HFP 70, LP 27, MP 110 (MP3 658), SF 78.
Arm of the Lord, awake, awake	H&P 433.
Around the throne of God a band	A&M 320, NEH 191.
As David took no rest until (Ps. 132)	PFT 132.
As I hold out my hand	LP 242.
As Jacob with travel was weary one day	A&M 435, H&P 444,WSAM 5.
As Joseph was awaking	CP 22.
As man and woman we were made	BPW 506, H&P 364.
As now the sun's declining rays	NEH 242.
As pants the hart for the cooling stream	A&M 226, H&P 416, NEH 337.
As sons of the day and daughters	HTC 490.
As the bridegroom to his chosen	A&M 340, H&P 30.
As the deer longs for streams	WSAM 6.
As the deer pants for the water (Ps. 42)	LP 240, MP 37 (MP2 303), SF 27, SFP 42d.
As the disciples, when thy Son had left	A&M 341.
As water to the thirsty (Ps. 84)	HFP 20, HTC 470.

Be bold, be strong	CFW 542, JP 14, LP 11, MP 49 (MP2 312), SF 37.
Be careful little hands what you do	JP 312.
Be gracious to me, Lord (Ps. 57)	PFT 57a.
Be holy in all that you do	JP 314.
Be it my only wisdom here	H&P 786.
Be known to us/O Lord, you gave in love	H&P 597, HTC 410,WSAM 80.
Be merciful to me, O God (Ps. 56)	PFT 56a.
Be still and know that I am God (Ps. 46)	SFP 46c, SFP 46e.
Be still and know that I am God (Ps. 46)	BPW 280,JP 22, LP 245, MP 48 (MP1 16), O&N 42, SF 41.
Be still, for the presence of the Lord	BPW 5, HFP 26, LP 13, MP 50 (MP3 652), SF 40, WP 176.
Be thou/O Lord my guardian (Ps. 17)	A&M 217,CFW 124, HTC 374, NEH 64, O&N 45, WSAM 9.
Be thou my vision/Lord be my vision (Ps. 42)	
	A&M 343, BPW 521, H&P 378, HFP 175, HTC 545, MP 51 (MP1 17), NEH 339, O&N 46, SF 42.
Beauty for brokenness (God of the poor)	LP 244.
Because he died and is risen	CFW 568.
Because he lives	MP 52 (MP1 18), O&N 159.
Because the Lord is my shepherd (Ps. 23)	HFP 27, LP 243, SFP 23f.
Because thou hast said, do this for my	H&P 598.
Because your love is better than life (Ps. 63)	
	CFW 79, MP 53 (MP1 19), SFP 63d.
Before Jehovah's awesome/aweful throne (Ps. 83, 100)	
	A&M 197, H&P 61, HTC 15.
Before the ending of the day	A&M 6, HTC 276, NEH 241, O&N 41.
Before the eternal King and Priest	HTC 397.
Before the heaven and earth	CFW 206, CP 29, HFP 29, HTC 612.
Before the Lord my soul is bowed (Ps. 131)	PFT 131a.
Before the throne of God above	HTC 453.
Before we take the body of our Lord	WSAM 8.
Begin, my tongue, some heavenly theme	H&P 2.
Begone, unbelief; My Saviour is near	H&P 667.
Behold a little child	H&P 143.
Behold how pleasant it shall be (Ps. 133)	PFT 133b.
Behold, I tell you a mystery	CFW 563, CP 31.
Behold the amazing gift of love	H&P 666.
Behold, the darkness (Arise, shine)	CP 32, MP 36 (MP1 12), SF 38.
Behold, the great creator makes	A&M 44, HTC 50, NEH 23.
Behold the Lord	LP 246.
Behold, the mountain of the Lord	BPW 617, H&P 50.
Behold the servant of the Lord	H&P 788.
Behold the temple of the Lord	H&P 808.
Behold us, Lord, a little space	H&P 376.
Behold, what manner of love the Father	JP 15.
Being of beings, God of love	H&P 690.
Believe not those who say	H&P 708.
Belize boogie (The Lord was born)	LP 202.

278

Blest be the everlasting God	H&P 669.
Blest be the tie that binds	BPW 472, H&P 754, MP 60 (MP2 311), SF 49, WP 177.
Blest by the sun, the olive tree	NEH 512.
Blow upon the trumpet (Ps. 98)	CP 37, HFP 31, HTC 186.
Born as a stranger	CP 38, CP 39.
Born by the Holy Spirit's breath	BPW 281, H&P 279, HTC 225, MP 61 (MP2 314).
Born in song	H&P 486, HFP 32.
Born in the night, Mary's Child	BPW 156, CP 40, H&P 95, JP 313, MP 62 (MP2 315).
Born of the water	HFP 33, HTC 382, LP 249.
Bread is blessed and broken	WSAM 11.
Bread of heaven, on you we feed	A&M 271, HTC 398, NEH 276, O&N 52.
Bread of life	LP 250.
Bread of the world in mercy broken	A&M 270, BPW 428, H&P 599, HFP 34, HTC 396, NEH 277, O&N 53.
Break forth into joy	MP 63 (MP1 23).
Break thou/now the bread of life	BPW 98, CFW 614, H&P 467, HFP 35, MP 64 (MP2 316), SF 50.
Breathe on me, breath of God	A&M 157, BPW 282, CFW 326, H&P 280, HFP 36, HTC 226, LP 16, MP 67 (MP1 25), NEH 342, O&N 54, SF 51.
Breathe on me, Spirit of Jesus	LP 253.
Brief life here is our portion	NEH 326.
Bright the vision that delighted (Ps. 11)	A&M 96, BPW 71, H&P 445, HTC 578, NEH 343, O&N 55.
Brightest and best of the sons	A&M 47, BPW 190, CP 41, H&P 123, HTC 338, MP 65 (MP2 317), NEH 49.
Bring a psalm	SF 52.
Bring songs of joy to God the Lord (Ps. 33)	PFT 33a.
Bring to the Lord a glad song (Ps. 149)	BPW 30, CFW 54, HFP 37, HTC 336, LP 17, PFT 149a, SFP 149a.
Bring your Christingle with gladness	JP 315.
Bring your tributes to the Lord of hosts (Ps. 29)	SFP 29c.
Broken for me	CFW 40, HFP 38, HTC S6, LP 18, MP 66 (MP2 318), O&N 56, SF 53.
Brother, let me be his servant	O&N 57, SF 54.
Brother, sister, let me serve you	BPW 473.
Brothers and sisters, in Jesus our Lord	JP 21.
Brothers and sisters, of God we sing	WP 157.
By blue Galilee Jesus walked of old	JP 23.
By Christ redeemed, in Christ restored	H&P 600.
By every nation (Easter (Ps. 117)	HTC 579, LP 19.
By flowing waters of Babylon (Ps. 137)	SFP 137b.
By gracious powers	BPW 117.
By his redeeming love	WSAM 7.
By rivers of sorrow we sat (Ps. 137)	PFT 137a.
By the Babylonian rivers (Ps. 137)	WP 14 (WP1 9).

By the waters of Babylon (Ps. 137)   WP 15.
By your cross   LP 251.
By your side (Ps. 55)   LP 252, SF 55.
Calypso Carol (See him lying on a bed)   BPW 174, CFW 656, CP 257,
   H&P 118, HFP 253, HTC 91,
   MP 589 (MP2 553), O&N 444,
   SF 491.

Can I forget bright Eden's grace   H&P 417.
Can we/man by searching find out God   A&M 438, H&P 76, HTC 426.
Can you be sure that the rain will fall   JP 316.
Can you count the stars shining in the   JP 317.
Can you imagine how it feels to know   JP 318.
Captain of Israel's host, and Guide   H&P 62.
Captains of the saintly band   A&M 299, NEH 215.
Caring, sharing   CFW 448.
Carpenter, carpenter, make me a tree   BPW 118.
Cast your burdens onto Jesus   LP 255, WP 17.
Cause me to come to thy river   MP 68 (MP2 319), SF 56.
Celebrate Jesus   SF 57, WP 180.
Celebration song (in the presence)   CFW 334, LP 92, MP 341
   (MP1 108), SF 244.

Change my heart, O God   LP 20, MP 69 (MP2 321), SF 58,
   WP 178.

Child in a stable   CP 43.
Child in the manger   BPW 158, CFW 652, CP 42,
   HFP 39, HTC 51, MP 71 (MP3
   657), O&N 62.

Child of gladness, child of sorrow   CP 44, CP 45.
Child of the stable's secret birth   H&P 124, HTC 53, NEH 43.
Children, join the celebration   JP 320.
Children of Jerusalem   H&P 163, JP 24, MP 70 (MP4 801).
Children of the heavenly King   A&M 213,CFW 556, HTC 566,
   NEH 344, O&N 63.

Children of the King (I see perfection)   LP 73, MP 292 (MP3 693).
Christ be my leader by night as by day   JP 319.
Christ, above all glory seated   H&P 189.
Christ arose (Low in the grave he lay)   BPW 256, H&P 202, HFP 191,
   HTC 158, LP 122, MP 453
   (MP1 450), SF 378.

Christ be beside me   WSAM 12.
Christ be my leader by night as by day   H&P 709.
Christ be the Lord of all our days   HTC 256.
Christ be with me   NEH 278.
Christ, enthroned in highest heaven   NEH 327.
Christ for the world we sing   A&M 344.
Christ, from whom all blessings flow   CFW 463, H&P 764, HTC 491.
Christ in majesty ascending   HFP 40.
Christ in me is to live   CFW 140.
Christ in the stranger's guise   WSAM 13.
Christ is alive! let Christians sing   BPW 244, H&P 190, HFP 41.
Christ is all to me   WP 18.
Christ is ascending! let creation sing   HFP 42.
Christ is born for us today   CP 46.
Christ is born to be our King   CP 47.
Christ is born within a stable   CFW 666, CP 48.

Christ is going to the Father	HFP 43.
Christ is made the sure foundation	BPW 474, CFW 483, H&P 485, HFP 44, HTC 559, MP 73 (MP1 27), NEH 205, O&N 66.
Christ is our cornerstone	A&M 161,CFW 482, HTC 564, NEH 206, O&N 67.
Christ is risen	WP 25 (WP1 15).
Christ is risen! hallelujah/alleluia	BPW 245, HFP 45, LP 257, MP 74 (MP2 322), SF 60.
Christ is surely coming	CFW 598, CP 49, HFP 46, MP 75 (MP2 323).
Christ is the answer	MP 72 (MP1 29).
Christ is the heavenly food that gives	A&M 439.
Christ is the King! O friends rejoice	A&M 345, BPW 475, HFP 47, HTC 492, NEH 345, O&N 68.
Christ is the world's Light, he and none	A&M 440, BPW 34, H&P 455, HFP 48, HTC 321.
Christ is the world's Redeemer	H&P 219.
Christ is the world's true light (Ps. 27)	A&M 346, BPW 618, H&P 456, HTC 323, NEH 494.
Christ of the upward way	BPW 522.
Christ on whom the Spirit rested	HTC 228.
Christ, our King before creation	H&P 75, HTC 428.
Christ, the fair glory of the holy angel	A&M 321, NEH 190.
Christ the Lord is risen again	A&M 79, H&P 192, HFP 49, HTC 153, NEH 105, O&N 69.
Christ the Lord is risen today	BPW 246, CFW 258, H&P 193, HTC 150, MP 76 (MP2 324), SF 61.
Christ the Way of life	MP 78 (MP4 802).
Christ triumphant	BPW 306, CFW 300, HFP 50, HTC 173, JP 25, LP 21, MP 77 (MP1 28), O&N 70, SF 62, WSAM 14.
Christ upon the mountain peak	A&M 441, BPW 195, H&P 155, HFP 52, HTC 115, NEH 177.
Christ was born on Christmas Day	CP 50.
Christ, when for us you were baptised	A&M 442, BPW 405, H&P 129.
Christ, who knows all his sheep	A&M 347.
Christ who welcomed little children	BPW 497.
Christ, whose glory fills the skies (Ps. 19)	A&M 4,CFW 134, H&P 457, HFP 51, HTC 266, MP 79 (MP2 320), O&N 71.
Christ's is the world	WP 19.
Christian, do you not hear the Lord	HTC 472.
Christian, dost thou see them	A&M 55, NEH 65.
Christian people, raise your song	A&M 443, BPW 430, H&P 601.
Christian, seek not yet repose	HTC 355.
Christian soldiers, onward go (Ps. 3)	CFW 530, HTC 524.
Christians, awake, salute the happy morn	A&M 36, BPW 159, CP 51, H&P 96, HFP 53, HTC 78, MP 80 (MP2 325), NEH 24, O&N 65, SF 59.
Christians, join in celebration	CFW 458.
Christians, lift up your hearts (House)	A&M 445.
Christians, lift up your hearts (Praise)	A&M 444, HTC 229.

Come, Holy Ghost, all-quickening fire	H&P 282.
Come, Holy Ghost, our hearts inspire	A&M 448, BPW 97, H&P 469, NEH 348.
Come, Holy Ghost, our souls inspire	A&M 93, H&P 283, HTC 589, MP 90 (MP1 36), NEH 138, O&N 84, WSAM 97.
Come, Holy Ghost, thine influence shed	H&P 602.
Come Holy Spirit	LP 256.
Come, Holy Spirit, heavenly Dove	H&P 297.
Come into his presence singing	HTC S2, O&N 85.
Come into the Holy of holies	SF 69.
Come, join to praise our God	CFW 354.
Come, let us all unite and sing	H&P 31.
Come, let us anew our journey pursue	H&P 354.
Come let us bow down in worship	MP 91 (MP2 328).
Come let us celebrate the day	WP 111 (WP1 57).
Come, let us glorify the Lord	CP 65.
Come, let us join our cheerful songs	A&M 144, BPW 6, CFW 555, H&P 810, HFP 62, HTC 206, MP 93 (MP1 37), O&N 86, SF 70.
Come, let us join our friends above	H&P 812.
Come, let us kneel before him	CP 66.
Come, let us praise the Lord (Ps. 95)	BPW 119, LP 259, MP 92 (MP3 653), SFP 95g.
Come let us sing (Hooke)	MP 95 (MP3 656).
Come, let us sing for joy (Ps. 95)	LP 24, SF 71, SFP 95h.
Come let us sing for joy to the Lord	JP 324.
Come let us sing of a wonderful love	BPW 330, H&P 691, JP 29, MP 94 (MP1 35), SF 72.
Come, let us sing out with joy (Ps. 95)	SFP 95d.
Come, let us sing to the Lord (Ps. 95)	CFW 393.
Come, let us to the Lord our God	H&P 33.
Come, let us use the grace divine	H&P 649.
Come, let us, who in Christ believe	H&P 755.
Come, let us with our Lord arise	A&M 449, H&P 575, HTC 375, NEH 254.
Come, let us worship Christ	HFP 63, HTC S10, LP 262, MP 96 (MP2 329).
Come, let us worship our Redeemer (Ps. 95)	CP 68, MP 97 (MP3 654).
Come, let us worship the Christ of creation	HTC 207.
Come, light of the world	HFP 64, LP 263.
Come listen to my tale	JP 30.
Come, Lord Jesus	CP 67, O&N 88.
Come, Lord, to our souls come down	A&M 348, H&P 470.
Come, most/thou Holy Spirit, come	CFW 327, HTC 227.
Come, my soul, thy suit prepare	H&P 546.
Come, my way, my truth, my life	H&P 254.
Come now, everlasting Spirit	BPW 285.
Come now, O Prince of peace	WP 23 (WP1 13).
Come now with awe	CP 72, MP 98 (MP3 655).
Come now with joyful	WP 21.
Come, O Fount of every blessing (Ps. 108)	H&P 517, HTC 337.
Come, O Holy Spirit, come	WP 160 (WP1 79).
Come, O thou all-victorious Lord	H&P 418.
Come, O thou Traveller unknown	A&M 243, H&P 434, NEH 350.

Come, O/thou long-expected Jesus	A&M 31, CP 70, HFP 57, HTC 52, MP 102 (MP2 335).
Come on and celebrate	JP 325, LP 25, MP 99 (MP2 330), SF 73.
Come on, let us sing to the Lord	CP 69.
Come on, let's go up and go	JP 31.
Come, praise the Lord (Ps. 134)	CFW 486, HTC 609, PFT 134b, O&N 90.
Come, praise the name of Jesus	BPW 331, HTC 538.
Come, pure hearts, in sweetest measures	A&M 300.
Come quickly, Lord, to rescue me (Ps. 70)	PFT 70,WSAM 16.
Come, rejoice before him (Ps. 100)	LP 260, SFP 100h.
Come, rejoice before your maker (Ps. 100)	BPW 35, CFW 96, HTC 17,PFT 100a.
Come, rejoice in God (Ps. 100)	LP 261, SFP 100i.
Come rejoicing, faithful men	NEH 505.
Come ride with kings	CP 71.
Come, risen Lord, and deign to be	A&M 349, H&P 605, NEH 279.
Come, risen Lord, as guest	HTC 399.
Come see the beauty of the Lord	MP 100 (MP2 331), SF 74.
Come, sing of the springtime	BPW 247.
Come, sing praises to the Lord (Ps. 95)	CFW 115, SFP 95f.
Come sing the praise of Jesus	CFW 250, HTC 208, MP 101 (MP2 332).
Come, sinners, to the gospel feast	H&P 460.
Come, thou everlasting Spirit	H&P 298.
Come, thou/most Holy Spirit, come	A&M 92,CFW 327, H&P 284, HTC 227, NEH 139.
Come, thou/O long-expected Jesus	A&M 31, BPW 139, CP 70, H&P 81, HFP 57, HTC 52, MP 102 (MP2 335), NEH 3.
Come, thou Redeemer of the earth	NEH 19.
Come to be our hope, Lord Jesus	LP 264, WP 159 (WP1 78).
Come to Jesus, he's amazing	JP 33.
Come to set us free (Advent entrance)	CP 74, LP 23.
Come to the waters	MP 104 (MP1 38), O&N 93.
Come to us, creative Spirit	H&P 377, HTC 308.
Come walk with us	WP 52.
Come, watch with us	MP 105 (MP4 805).
Come, we that love the Lord	BPW 525, H&P 487.
Come with all joy to sing to God (Ps. 95)	CFW 205, HTC 16, PFT 95a.
Come with me, come wander	BPW 333.
Come, workers for the Lord	A&M 350, H&P 380.
Come, worship God who is worthy (Ps. 95)	BPW 36, CFW 606, HTC 18, PFT 95b.
Come, ye faithful, raise the anthem	A&M 145, BPW 269, H&P 813, HFP 12, HTC 205, MP 103 (MP4 806), NEH 351.
Come, ye/you faithful, raise the strain	A&M 76, BPW 248, H&P 194, HTC 160, NEH 106, O&N 94.
Come, you thankful people, come	A&M 289, BPW 120, CFW 526, H&P 355, HFP 65, HTC 284, JP 32,

	MP 106 (MP2 333), NEH 259, O&N 95, SF 75.
Comes Mary to the grave	HFP 66, HTC 152, WSAM 17.
Command thy blessing from above	H&P 488.
Commit thou all thy griefs	H&P 672.
Commit your way to God the Lord (Ps. 37)	PFT 37a.
Consider how he loves you (Sweet Perfume)	LP 265.
Counting, counting, one, two, three	JP 326.
Crackers and turkeys and pudding	JP 327.
Cradle, O Lord, in your arms everlasting	BPW 619.
Cradle rocking, cattle lowing	CFW 649, CP 73.
Cradled in a manger, meanly	H&P 98, MP 107 (MP4 807).
Create in me a clean heart	MP 108 (MP2 334), SF 76.
Create in me a pure heart (Ps. 51)	LP 267.
Create in us clean hearts (Ps. 51)	LP 266.
Creation creed (The Lord is a mighty)	LP 201.
Creator of the earth and skies	A&M 351, H&P 419, HFP 67, HTC 320, NEH 152.
Creator of the starry height	A&M 23.
Creator of the stars of night	NEH 1.
Creator Spirit, by whose aid	BPW 286, H&P 285.
Creator Spirit, come, inspire	HFP 68, HTC 232.
Crown him with many crowns (Ps. 77)	A&M 147, BPW 37, CFW 198, H&P 255, HFP 69, HTC 174, LP 36, MP 109 (MP1 39), NEH 352, O&N 97, SF 77, WP 179.
Crown with love, Lord, this glad day	A&M 450.
Daniel was a man of prayer	JP 36.
Dark the night	WSAM 18.
Darkness like a shroud (Arise, shine)	CP 76, HFP 70, LP 27, MP 110 (MP3 658), SF 78.
Day by day, dear Lord	H&P 671, WSAM 19.
Day of wrath and doom impending	NEH 524.
Dear Lord and Father of mankind	A&M 115, BPW 84, H&P 673, HFP 71, HTC 356, JP 37, MP 111 (MP1 40), NEH 353, O&N 98, SF 79.
Dear Lord, to you again our gifts	A&M 352.
Dear Master, in whose life I see	BPW 337, H&P 522.
Dearest Jesu, we are here	A&M 269.
Deck yourself, my soul, with gladness	A&M 257, H&P 606, HTC 400, NEH 280.
Deep and wide, deep and wide	JP 35.
Deep in the shadows of the past	H&P 447.
Delight yourself in the Lord (Ps. 37)	LP 268, MP 112 (MP2 337), SFP 37c, WP 181.
Delight yourselves in the Lord	MP 113 (MP2 338), WP 181.
Did you ever talk to God above	JP 329.
Ding dong! Merrily on high	CFW 667, CP 77, JP 38, MP 114 (MP2 336), O&N 99.
Ding, dong, ring out the carillon	CP 78.
Disposer supreme, and Judge of the earth	A&M 298, NEH 216.
Do not be afraid	MP 115 (MP1 41), O&N 100.
Do not be worried and upset	MP 117 (MP1 42).

Do something new, Lord	SF 80.
Do you want a pilot	JP 40.
Dona nobis pacem II (Grant to us) (Ps. 85)	LP 52, WSAM 2.
Don't be afraid	LP 269.
Don't build your house on the sandy land	JP 39.
Don't know much about the ozone layer	JP 328.
Dost thou truly seek renown	NEH 81.
Down from his glory	MP 116 (MP4 808).
Down from the height	CP 75.
Downtrodden Christ	HTC 125.
Doxology Canon	WSAM 20.
Draw me closer	SF 81.
Draw near and take the body of the Lord	HTC 401.
Draw near to God	MP 118 (MP2 339).
Draw nigh, and take the body of the Lord	NEH 281.
Drop down, ye heavens, from above	NEH 501.
Drop, drop, slow tears	NEH 82.
Early morning, come prepare him	A&M 451.
Early on Sunday	BPW 249.
Earth has many a noble city	A&M 48, CFW 93, O&N 102.
Earth, rejoice, our Lord is King	H&P 811.
Earth was waiting, spent and restless	BPW 141, HTC 54.
Easter Canon	WSAM 21.
Easter song (By every nation, race and tongue) (Ps. 148)	HTC 579, LP 19.
Easter song of praise	WSAM 22.
El-Shaddai	MP 119 (MP2 341), SF 82.
Emmanuel, Emmanuel, his name is called	CFW 642, CP 81, MP 121 (MP3 659), SF 83.
Emmanuel, Emmanuel, we call your name	CFW 642, CP 81, MP 121 (MP3 659), SF 83.
Emmanuel, Emmanuel, wonderful counsellor	LP 28.
Emmanuel, God is with us (Ps. 46)	SFP 46d, CP 79.
Emmanuel, God with us	MP 120 (MP2 342).
Emmanuel .. he is here	CP 80.
Empty he came	CP 82, HTC 127.
Enter in to his great love	SF 84.
Enthrone thy God within thy heart	H&P 692.
Ere God had built the mountains	H&P 32.
Ere I sleep, for every favour	H&P 638.
Eternal depth of love divine	H&P 34.
Eternal Father, Lord of life	HTC 295.
Eternal Father, strong to save	A&M 292, BPW 587, CFW 350, H&P 379, HTC 285, MP 122 (MP2 340), NEH 354, O&N 104.
Eternal God and Father	LP 29.
Eternal God, we come to you	MP 123 (MP2 343), SF 85.
Eternal God, we consecrate	A&M 452.
Eternal light, eternal light	BPW 85, H&P 458, HTC 454.
Eternal light, shine in my heart	HFP 72, HTC 339.
Eternal Monarch, King most high	NEH 128.
Eternal Power, whose high abode	H&P 49, NEH 207.
Eternal ruler of the ceaseless round	A&M 353, BPW 477, NEH 355, O&N 105.

Eternal Son, eternal love	H&P 766.
Even if I don't like the way things went	JP 330.
Everlasting Father	WSAM 24.
Everlasting love	WSAM 24.
Every day if you go astray	JP 331.
Every nation, praise the Lord (Ps. 117)	CFW 97.
Every star shall sing a carol	A&M 354, BPW 162.
Everybody join in singing this song	JP 332.
Everyone in the whole wide world	JP 333.
Everything is yours, Lord	WP 138.
Everywhere he walks with me	JP 334.
Everywhere the skies declare (Ps. 19)	SFP 19d.
Exalt the Lord our God	MP 124 (MP2 344), SF 87.
Exalted, you are exalted	SF 86.
Exult, creation round God's throne	WSAM 23.
Facing a task unfinished	MP 126 (MP2 346), SF 88.
Fair waved the golden corn	NEH 260.
Fairest Lord Jesus	BPW 334, HTC 209,WSAM 26.
Faith of our Fathers, taught of old	NEH 479.
Faithful cross, above all other	NEH 517.
Faithful one, so unchanging	LP 270, SF 89.
Faithful Shepherd, feed me (Ps. 23)	CFW 571, HTC 29, NEH 282, O&N 106.
Faithful vigil ended	A&M 453, BPW 191, CFW 562, CP 83, HTC 55, MP 125 (MP3 660), NEH 44.
Falling, falling, gently falling	BPW 287, CFW 315.
Far beyond our mind's grasp	BPW 432, WP 60.
Father all-loving	A&M 355.
Father all-powerful	A&M 355.
Father almighty, we your humble servants	HTC 402.
Father, although I cannot see	HTC 455, MP 127 (MP2 347).
Father and God, from whom our world	HTC 357.
Father be with her/his/their family	JP 335.
Father eternal, Lord of the ages	HTC 1, NEH 356.
Father, for our friends we pray	JP 336.
Father God, I give all thanks	SF 91.
Father, God, I love you	MP 129 (MP1 56).
Father God, I wonder (I will sing)	JP 337, LP 30, MP 128 (MP2 348), SF 92.
Father God in heaven (Kum ba yah) (Ps. 102)	
	BPW 589, CFW 171, HFP 73, HTC 358, LP 33,WSAM 27.
Father God in heaven, hallowed be thy name	
	H&P 518.
Father God, the Lord, Creator	MP 130 (MP2 350).
Father God we worship you	SF 93.
Father God, we worship you, evermore	CP 84.
Father God, we worship you, you make us	MP 131 (MP2 345).
Father, hear the prayer we offer	A&M 113, BPW 523, CFW 85, H&P 436, HTC 360, JP 41, MP 132 (MP1 43), NEH 357, O&N 109.
Father, here I am	SF 94.
Father, I can call you Father	SF 90.
Father I have sinned	LP 272.

288

Father, I place into your hands	JP 42, MP 133 (MP1 45), O&N 110, SF 97.
Father, I want you to hold me	LP 271.
Father, if justly still we claim	H&P 299.
Father in heaven, grant to your children	BPW 38, H&P 3, HFP 74, HTC 2, LP 273, WP 38 (WP1 19), WSAM 25.
Father in heaven, have mercy upon us	WP 72.
Father in heaven, how we love you	LP 32, MP 135 (MP3 661), SF 96, WP 182.
Father in heaven, our voices we raise	LP 31, MP 134 (MP3 662), SF 95.
Father, in high heaven dwelling	H&P 640.
Father, in whom thy saints are one	NEH 196.
Father, in whom we live	H&P 4.
Father, in your presence kneeling	BPW 498, CFW 10.
Father, it is right and fitting	BPW 433.
Father, lead me day by day	H&P 790, JP 43.
Father, let us dedicate (Ps. 115)	CFW 73, HTC 257.
Father, Lord of all creation	A&M 356, BPW 620, O&N 111.
Father, make us one	MP 137 (MP2 349), SF 98.
Father most holy, merciful and loving	A&M 94, H&P 5, HTC 3, NEH 144, O&N 112.
Father, never was love so near	MP 138 (MP3 663).
Father, now behold us	CFW 11, HTC 384.
Father of all, whose laws have stood	BPW 335, HTC 539.
Father of all, whose powerful voice	H&P 21.
Father of everlasting grace	H&P 300.
Father of glory, whose heavenly plan	BPW 604.
Father of heaven, whose love profound	A&M 97, H&P 519, HTC 359, NEH 358, O&N 113.
Father of Jesus Christ – my Lord	H&P 693.
Father of mercies, in your word (Ps. 143)	A&M 167, BPW 99, CFW 601, HTC 247.
Father of mercy, God of consolation	NEH 323.
Father of peace, and God of love	H&P 218.
Father on high to whom we pray (Ps. 102)	BPW 499, HTC 296.
Father, see thy children	NEH 283.
Father, sending your anointed Son	MP 136 (MP2 351).
Father, Son and Holy Ghost	H&P 791.
Father, we adore you (fountain of life)	SF 100.
Father, we adore you, lay our lives	BPW 39, CFW 191, HTC S5, JP 44, O&N 114, SF 99, WSAM 28, WP 183.
Father, we adore you, you've drawn us	MP 140 (MP2 352), SF 101.
Father, we give you thanks, who planted	H&P 603.
Father, we love you	JP 45.
Father, we love you, we worship	BPW 41, CFW 336, MP 142 (MP1 46), O&N 116, SF 102, WP 184.
Father, we praise thee, now the night	H&P 633, NEH 149.
Father, we thank thee who hast planted	A&M 357.
Father, we thank you for the light	A&M 454, H&P 561.
Father, we thank you now for planting	BPW 434, NEH 284.
Father welcomes all his children	BPW 408, O&N 115.
Father, who in Jesus found us	A&M 358, H&P 607, O&N 117.

Father, who on man dost shower	H&P 341.
Father, whose everlasting love	H&P 520.
Father whose mighty word	BPW 591.
Father, you are my portion	SF 103.
Father, your church with thankfulness	H&P 650.
Father, your love is precious	MP 141 (MP2 354), SF 104.
Father, your word is like a light	JP 338.
Fear not for I am with you	LP 35, SF 105.
Fear not, for I bring all people good	CP 85.
Fear not, rejoice and be glad	CFW 516, MP 144 (MP1 47), O&N 119, SF 106.
Fierce raged the tempest	A&M 225, CFW 362, H&P 144.
Fight the good fight with all your might	A&M 220, BPW 524, CFW 546, H&P 710, HFP 75, HTC 526, MP 143 (MP1 49), NEH 359, O&N 120, SF 107.
Fill now/thou my life, O Lord my God	A&M 200, BPW 569, H&P 792, HFP 76, HTC 541, MP 146 (MP1 48), O&N 121, SF 108.
Fill the place, Lord	MP 145 (MP2 355).
Fill thou/now my life, O Lord my God	A&M 200, BPW 569, H&P 792, HFP 76, HTC 541, MP 146 (MP1 48), O&N 121, SF 108.
Fill your hearts with joy and gladness (Ps. 147)	BPW 40, CFW 513, HFP 77, HTC 30, JP 339, MP 147 (MP2 353), O&N 122, PFT 147a.
Filled with the Spirit's power	A&M 359, H&P 314, HTC 233.
Finished the strife of battle now	A&M 455.
Fire of God, titanic Spirit	HTC 234.
Firmly I believe, and truly	A&M 118, CFW 145, HTC 429, NEH 360, O&N 123.
First of the week and finest day	HTC 376.
Fisherman, come and fish for men	BPW 196.
Fling wide the gates (Ps. 24)	CFW 291, CP 86, PFT 24b.
Fling wide your doors (Ps. 24)	LP 36, SFP 24h.
Follow me, says Jesus	JP 46.
Food to pilgrims	WP 35.
For all the love that from our earliest	BPW 371.
For all the saints who from their labour	A&M 305, BPW 478, CFW 550, H&P 814, HTC 567, MP 148 (MP1 51), NEH 197, O&N 125, SF 109.
For all thy saints, O Lord	A&M 308, NEH 224.
For all your boundless gifts (Ps. 87)	PFT 87.
For God so loved the world (Kendrick)	LP 274, MP 149 (MP3 664).
For God so loved the world (Londonderry)	CFW 402, HFP 78.
For his name is exalted	MP 150 (MP2 357), SF 110.
For I'm building a people of power	BPW 483, CFW 469, JP 47, LP 37, MP 151 (MP1 50), O&N 126, SF 111.
For Mary, mother of our Lord	A&M 360, NEH 161.
For me to live is Christ	BPW 410.
For the beauty of meadows, of grandeur	BPW 42.
For the beauty of the earth	A&M 104, BPW 121, CFW 182,

H&P 333, HFP 79, HTC 298, JP 48,
MP 152 (MP2 356), NEH 285,
O&N 128, SF 112, WP36 (WP1 20).

For the bread which you have broken   A&M 456, CFW 46, HFP 80,
HTC 403.

For the foolishness of God is wiser   JP 340.

For the fruits of his creation   A&M 457, BPW 123, CFW 522,
H&P 342, HFP 82, HTC 286,
MP 153 (MP1 52), O&N 129.

For the healing of the nations   A&M 361, BPW 621, H&P 402,
O&N 130.

For the Lord is marching on   SF 113.

For the might of your arm   BPW 479, H&P 435, MP 154 (MP4 809).

For this purpose   BPW 372, CFW 255, CP 88, LP 39,
MP 155 (MP2 358), SF 114.

For thou, O Lord, art high   MP 158 (MP1 53), SF 115.

For unto us a child is born (Burt)   MP 156 (MP2 359), SF 116.

For unto us a child is born (Hadden)   CP 89, MP 157 (MP3 665).

For we see Jesus   SF 117.

For your holy book we thank you   H&P 471.

For your mercy and your grace   CFW 72, HTC 258, O&N 132.

For your wonderful deeds   SF 118.

Forgive our sins as we forgive   A&M 362, BPW 83, H&P 134,
HFP 83, HTC 111, NEH 66.

Forgotten for eternity (Ps. 13)   SFP 13b.

Forth in the peace of Christ   A&M 458, BPW 607, HTC 542,
LP 38, NEH 361.

Forth in thy / your name, O Lord, I go   A&M 239, BPW 526, H&P 381,
HTC 306, MP 159 (MP1 55),
O&N 131.

Forty days and forty nights   A&M 56, BPW 218, H&P 130,
HTC 103, MP 160 (MP2 360),
NEH 67, O&N 133.

Forward, be our watchword   BPW 527.

Free to serve   WP 37 (WP1 21).

Freedom and life are ours   BPW 528, HFP 84, HTC 544.

Freedom is coming   BPW 622.

Freedom is coming (Oh freedom is coming)   LP 156.

Freely, for the love he bears us   MP 161 (MP4 810).

From all who live beneath the skies (Ps. 117)   A&M 98, CFW 419, H&P 489,
HTC 580, SF 119.

From deep despair to you I call (Ps. 130)   HFP 81, SFP 130d.

From east to west, from shore to shore   CP 90, H&P 99, NEH 20.

From fears and phantoms of the night (Ps. 91)   HFP 251.

From glory to glory advancing   A&M 276, NEH 286, O&N 136.

From heaven above I come to bring   CP 87.

From heaven above to earth I come   H&P 100.

From heaven to here   WSAM 13.

From heaven you came (The Servant King)   BPW 529, CFW 449, CP 91,
HFP 85, JP 341, LP 40, MP 162
(MP2 361), SF 120, WP 185.

From my knees to my nose   JP 342.

From the distant east and the farthest   CP 92.

From the eastern mountains   A&M 327, NEH 50.

From the Father's throne on high	CP 93.
From the rising of the sun (Ps. 113)	BPW 43, CFW 139, JP 49, MP 163 (MP1 54), O&N 138, SF 121, SFP 113b.
From the sun's rising (Ps. 122)	HFP 86, LP 41, MP 164 (MP3 666), SF 122.
From the very depths I cry (Ps. 130)	SFP 130e.
From time beyond my memory (Ps. 71)	PFT 71a, SFP 71a.
From you all skill and science flow	A&M 286, H&P 389, HTC 310.
Gabi, gabi (Praise the Father) (Ps. 107)	LP 164, WP40.
Gabriel's message does away	NEH 4.
Gather us in	WSAM 29.
Get together, get together	WP 39.
Get up out of bed	JP 343.
Girls and boys, leave your toys	CFW 668, CP 94, JP 344.
Give God thanks for he is gracious (Ps. 107)	PFT 107.
Give him the glory (lift your voice)	LP 110.
Give me a heart	MP 165 (MP4 811).
Give me a new heart, O God (Ps. 51)	LP 275.
Give me a sight, O Saviour	MP 166 (MP1 57).
Give me joy in my heart	A&M 459, CFW 446, H&P 492, HTC S11, O&N 140.
Give me life, Holy Spirit	SF 123.
Give me oil in my lamp, keep me burning	BPW 530, JP 50, MP 167 (MP1 58).
Give me the faith	H&P 767, MP 168 (MP2 362).
Give me wings of faith to rise	BPW 307, H&P 815, NEH 225.
Give praise for famous men	HTC 568.
Give praise to the Lord	WP 123.
Give rest, O Christ, to thy servant	NEH 526.
Give thanks to God, for he is good (Ps. 136)	SFP 136b.
Give thanks to God, the Lord of all (Ps. 136)	PFT 136a.
Give thanks to the Lord	JP 345, MP 169 (MP3 667), SF 125.
Give thanks with a grateful heart	LP 42, MP 170 (MP4 812), SF 124, WP 186.
Give to me, Lord, a thankful heart	BPW 531, H&P 548.
Give to our God immortal praise (Ps. 100, 136)	A&M 460, BPW 47, H&P 22, HTC 31, MP 171 (MP2 363).
Give us, O God, the grace to see	BPW 594.
Give us the wings of faith to rise	A&M 324.
Glad music fills the Christmas sky	CP 95, CP 96, HFP 87, HTC 82.
Gloria	WP 43 (WP1 23).
Gloria, gloria	BPW 44.
Gloria in excelsis Deo	WSAM 15.
Glorious Father we exalt you	MP 172 (MP3 670), SF 126.
Glorious things of thee/you are spoken (Ps. 127)	A&M 172, BPW 480, CFW 183, H&P 817, HTC 494, MP 173 (MP1 59), NEH 362, O&N 143, SF 127.
Glory and honour	LP 44.

Glory and praise to God (Ps. 19)	H&P 581, PFT 19b.
Glory be to God in heaven	CFW 24, HTC 581, MP 175 (MP2 364).
Glory be to Jesus	A&M 66, HFP 88, HTC 126, NEH 83, O&N 144.
Glory, glory, glory, glory be to God	WP 43.
Glory, glory, glory to God	CP 97.
Glory, glory, glory to the King (Ps. 24)	CP 98, SFP 24i.
Glory, glory, halleluiah	WP 154.
Glory, glory in the highest	MP 174 (MP3 668), SF 128.
Glory in the highest heaven	A&M 277, CP 99.
Glory in the highest, to the God	CFW 25, HFP 89, HTC 582, LP 43, NEH 363.
Glory, love, and praise, and honour	A&M 461, NEH 287.
Glory to God (Peru)	LP 282, O&N 146, WP 42 (WP1 22).
Glory to God (Taizé)	LP 283.
Glory to God, glory to God (France)	WP 44.
Glory to God, all heaven with joy	A&M 462.
Glory to God in the highest	JP 51, MP 177 (MP2 365).
Glory to God, give the glory to him	WP 100.
Glory to God, within the church	BPW 605.
Glory to thee, O God	A&M 363, O&N 148.
Glory to thee, who safe has kept	NEH 233.
Glory to the Lord of love	WP 45.
Glory to you, my God, this night (Ps. 63)	A&M 10, BPW 108, H&P 642, HTC 274, JP 52, MP 176 (MP2 366), NEH 244, O&N 147.
Go forth and tell	BPW 570, CFW 506, H&P 770, HFP 90, HTC 505, LP 46, MP 178 (MP1 61), O&N 164.
Go forth for God	NEH 321.
Go in Jesus' name	WP 67.
Go, labour on, spend, and be spent	H&P 794.
Go, tell it on the mountain	BPW 571, CFW 424, CP 100, H&P 135, JP 65, MP 179 (MP3 672), O&N 170.
God be in my head (Ps. 105)	A&M 236, BPW 592, H&P 694, HFP 91, HTC 543, NEH 328, O&N 149.
God, be merciful to me (Ps. 51)	PFT 51a.
God, be praised at early morn	WP 124.
God be with you till we meet again	H&P 651.
God brings us comfort where his anger	HFP 92.
God came among us, he became a man	CP 101, MP 180 (MP3 673).
God everlasting, at your word (Ps. 90)	PFT 90b.
God everlasting, wonderful and holy	A&M 463, NEH 288.
God forgave my sin	CFW 293, HTC S12, JP 54, MP 181 (MP1 60), O&N 150, SF 129.
God from on high hath/has heard	A&M 38, H&P 102.
God, give us a new heart	WP 26 (WP1 16).
God has chosen me	LP 276.
God has exalted him	CFW 294, CP 102, SF 130.
God has given us a book full of stories	BPW 200.
God has made me, and he knows me	JP 346.

God has spoken – by his prophets (Ps. 62)	BPW 100, H&P 64, HFP 94, HTC 248.
God has spoken to his people (Ps. 131)	CFW 611, CP 103, HTC 13, LP 53, MP 182 (MP2 367), SF 131.
God holds the key	MP 183 (MP2 368).
God in his love for us lent us	JP 347.
God in his love for us lent us this	H&P 343, WSAM 30.
God is a name my soul adores	H&P 24.
God is building a house	MP 184 (MP2 369).
God is good (Ps. 132)	CFW 377, JP 55, LP 49, MP 185 (MP2 370), SF 132.
God is great, amazing	WP 187.
God is here! As we his people	A&M 464, H&P 653, HTC 560.
God is here, God is present	SF 133.
God is hope and God is now	BPW 373.
God is in his temple	BPW 7, H&P 494, MP 186 (MP4 813).
God is King – be warned, you mighty (Ps. 82)	PFT 82.
God is King! The Lord is reigning (Ps. 93)	PFT 93b.
God is King – the nations tremble (Ps. 99)	PFT 99a.
God is light	A&M 364.
God is love (Personent hodie)	BPW 45, CFW 368, H&P 220, HFP 93, HTC 311, LP 50, O&N 152.
God is love, and where true love is	A&M 465, H&P 757, NEH 513.
God is love, let heaven adore him	A&M 365, BPW 374, CFW 386, H&P 36, MP 187 (MP2 371), NEH 364, O&N 153.
God is my great desire (Ps. 63)	PFT 63a.
God is my strong salvation (Ps. 27)	PFT 27a.
God is our Father	SF 134.
God is our fortress and our rock (Ps. 25)	A&M 114, HFP 96, HTC 523, MP 2 (MP2 284), SF 25.
God is our guide, our light	JP 56.
God is our refuge and defence	BPW 375.
God is our refuge and strength (Ps. 46)	PFT 46b.
God is our strength and refuge (Ps. 46)	BPW 308, CFW 77, CP 106, HFP 95, HTC 527, LP 47, MP 188 (MP2 372), PFT 46a.
God is so good	CFW 396, JP 53.
God is the King of all the earth (Ps. 47)	PFT 47b.
God is the strength of my life (Show us) (Ps. 118)	LP 48.
God is with the righteous (Ps. 1)	SFP 1f.
God is working his purpose out (Ps. 135)	H&P 769, HTC 191, JP 57, MP 189 (MP2 373), NEH 495, O&N 154, SF 135.
God loves you, and I love you	JP 348.
God loves you so much	JP 349.
God made me for himself to serve him (Ps. 14)	HTC 361.
God moves in a mysterious way	A&M 112, BPW 122, H&P 65, MP 193 (MP2 375), NEH 365, O&N 155.

God of Abraham, lead us	LP 277.
God of all ages	MP 190 (MP3 669).
God of all comfort	SF 136.
God of all mercy	JP 350.
God of all power, and truth, and grace	H&P 726.
God of all-redeeming grace	H&P 727.
God of almighty love	H&P 793.
God of concrete, God of steel	A&M 366.
God of eternity, Lord of the ages (Ps. 80)	HTC 495.
God of freedom, God of justice	BPW 623.
God of glory (Ps. 137)	CFW 337, CP 104, LP 51, MP 191 (MP2 376), SF 137.
God of God, the uncreated (Ps. 113)	CP 105, HTC 56.
God of gods, we sound his praises	BPW 46, CFW 561, HFP 98, HTC 340 PFT 156A.
God of grace and God of glory	A&M 367, BPW 572, H&P 712, HTC 324, MP 192 (MP2 378), SF 139.
God of grace, I turn my face (Ps. 138)	LP 278, SF 138.
God of heaven	LP 279.
God of hosts, you chose a vine (Ps. 80)	PFT 80.
God of light and life's creation	CFW 505, HTC 561,WSAM 31.
God of love and truth and beauty	A&M 368, H&P 403.
God of mercy, God of grace (Ps. 67, 85)	A&M 179, BPW 48, CFW 527, HFP 97, HTC 293, NEH 366, O&N 156, WSAM 32.
God of my salvation, hear	H&P 729.
God of the morning, at whose voice	BPW 9.
God of unexampled grace	H&P 166.
God our Father and creator	HTC 562.
God our Father, bless your people	HTC 496.
God rest you/ye merry, gentlemen	BPW 163, CP 108, H&P 103, HFP 99, HTC 84, NEH 25, O&N 157.
God save and bless our nation	HTC 325.
God save our gracious Queen (revised)	HTC 326, O&N 158.
God save our gracious Queen (traditional)	A&M 293, BPW 712, CFW 68, HTC 592, MP 194 (MP2 374), NEH 489.
God sent his Son	WP 46, (WP1 58).
God sent his Son	JP 58, MP 52 (MP1 18), O&N 159.
God so loved the world he sent to us	JP 59.
God speaks – the Lord of all the earth (Ps. 50)	PFT 50b.
God speaks, and all things come to be	H&P 23.
God, that madest earth and heaven	A&M 12, H&P 641, NEH 245, O&N 161.
God the Father caused to be	CFW 320.
God the Father, name we treasure	A&M 466, HTC 385.
God the Father of creation (Ps. 125)	BPW 376, CFW 277, HTC 427.
God the Father throned in splendour	BPW 50.
God told Joshua to take Jericho	JP 351.
God was there before the world was made	JP 352.
God, we praise you	LP 45.
God, we praise you! God, we bless you	BPW 49, CFW 536, HTC 341.

God who created this Eden of earth	A&M 369.
God, who hast caused to be written	A&M 467, H&P 472.
God who made the earth	BPW 377, JP 63, O&N 162.
God who spoke in the beginning	A&M 468.
God/Thou, whose almighty word	CFW 416, H&P 29, HFP 100, HTC 506, MP 699 (MP1 244), SF 557.
God, whose city's sure foundation	NEH 199.
God, whose farm is all creation	A&M 370, BPW 124, H&P 344, HTC 282, JP 61, O&N 163.
God whose love is everywhere	JP 353.
God whose love we cannot measure	HFP 101.
God whose praise is sung in Zion (Ps. 65)	PFT 65a.
God whose Son was once a man	JP 62, MP 195 (MP2 380).
God will arise because the weak (Ps. 12)	PFT 12a.
God, you have giv'n us power to sound	A&M 469, H&P 345.
God, your glory we have seen in your Son	H&P 459.
God's fire	WP 102 (WP1 53).
God's glory fills the heavens (Ps. 19)	PFT 19c.
God's holy ways are just and true (Ps. 111)	PFT 111A.
God's not dead, no, he is alive	JP 60.
God's Spirit is in my heart	BPW 574, CFW 422, H&P 315, O&N 160.
Going up to Jerusalem	JP 354.
Good Christian people, rise and sing	CP 111.
Good Christian(s) men/all rejoice	BPW 164, CP 107, H&P 104, HFP 102, HTC 85, MP 196 (MP2 379), SF 140.
Good Christians all, rejoice and sing	A&M 85, BPW 250, H&P 191, HTC 154, NEH 107.
Good Christians all, rejoice with heart	BPW 164, H&P 104, HFP 102, HTC 85, MP 196 (MP2 379), SF 140.
Good is our God who made this place	A&M 371.
Good Joseph had a garden	H&P 195.
Good King Wenceslas looked out	CP 109, O&N 168.
Good thou art, and good thou dost	H&P 37.
Grace is when God gives us	JP 355.
Gracious Spirit, dwell with me	H&P 286.
Gracious Spirit, Holy Ghost	A&M 154, BPW 288, CFW 476, H&P 301, HFP 123, HTC 474, MP 198 (MP2 377), NEH 367.
Grant, O Lord, a peaceful respite	BPW 648.
Grant to us your peace (Dona nobis) (Ps. 85)	LP 52, SFP 85b.
Grant us your peace, for you alone	BPW 624.
Granted is the Saviour's prayer	H&P 287.
Great and marvellous (Pitcher)	SF 141.
Great and marvellous (Prosch)	SF 142.
Great and wonderful are thy wondrous	SF 143.
Great and wonderful are your deeds	LP 55.
Great and wonderful your deeds	CFW 335, HTC 605.
Great God of power and might	WP 119.
Great God of wonders, all thy ways	H&P 38, MP 197 (MP4 814).
Great God, we praise the mighty love	HTC 299.
Great God, we sing that mighty hand	H&P 356.

Hallelujah, my Father	CFW 224, CP 19, MP 206 (MP1 66), O&N 180, SF 152.
Hallelujah, praise the Lord (Ps. 111)	SFP 111b.
Hallelujah! sing to Jesus	MP 207 (MP1 67), SF 153.
Hallelujah, sing to the Lord	MP 208 (MP3 674).
Hands that have been handling	A&M 278.
Hang on, stand still	JP 356.
Happiness is to know the Saviour	JP 70.
Happy are they, they who love God	A&M 176, CFW 125, H&P 711, HTC 473, NEH 369, O&N 181.
Happy Christmas, everybody	CFW 639, CP 114.
Happy day of great rejoicing	CP 112.
Happy is the one (Ps. 32)	LP 57, SFP 32b.
Happy the home that welcomes you	H&P 366, HTC 300.
Happy the man that finds the grace	H&P 674.
Happy the souls to Jesus joined	H&P 816.
Hark, a herald voice is calling	NEH 5.
Hark, a thrilling voice is sounding	A&M 24, HTC 192.
Hark, my soul! it is the Lord	A&M 244, H&P 521, HTC 472, MP 209 (MP2 381), O&N 184.
Hark, the glad sound	H&P 82, HFP 170, JP 68, MP 210 (MP2 385), O&N 185.
Hark the glad sound! – the Saviour comes	A&M 30, BPW 143, CFW 217, HTC 193, NEH 6, SF 154.
Hark! the herald-angels sing	A&M 35, BPW 165, CFW 660, CP 115, H&P 106, HFP 108, HTC 59, JP 69, MP 211 (MP2 384), NEH 26, O&N 186, SF 155.
Hark! the sound of holy voices	A&M 304, NEH 226, O&N 187.
Hark! the voice of love and mercy	HTC 128.
Hark what a sound, and too divine for	H&P 236.
Have faith in God, my heart	A&M 372, BPW 336, H&P 675, HTC 431.
Have mercy, Lord	WP 30 (WP1 18).
Have mercy, Lord, as you promise (Ps. 51)	SFP 51c.
Have mercy on me O God (Ps. 51)	PFT 51b.
Have mercy on us, Lord	WP 82 (WP1 43).
Have thine own way, Lord	MP 212 (MP2 386), SF 156.
Have you ever seen the Lord	WP 54.
Have you got an appetite	JP 357.
Have you heard the raindrops drumming	JP 71.
Have you not heard	HTC 386.
Have you seen the little Child	CP 116.
Have you seen the pussy cat	JP 72.
He became poor	LP 286.
He brought me to his banqueting house	JP 73.
He came down that we may have love	LP 287, WP 56 (WP1 27).
He came to earth, not to be served	LP 289, SF 161.
He comes to us as one unknown	WSAM 33.
He gave his life (Selfless love)	BPW 435, CFW 34, HFP 109, HTC 405, LP 56, MP 214 (MP2 387).
He gave me beauty for ashes	MP 213 (MP2 395), SF 162.
He gave me eyes so I could see	BPW 125, JP 74.
He gives me strength	JP 360.

He has arisen, alleluia! (Ps 102)	WP 104 (WP1 51).
He has shown you (Ps. 103)	LP 58, MP 215 (MP3 675).
He healed the darkness of my mind	HFP 110, LP 290.
He holds the key to our salvation	CP 119, SF 163.
He is born, our Lord and Saviour	CP 117, MP 216 (MP3 676), WP 189.
He is exalted, the King is exalted	LP 288, MP 217 (MP3 677), SF 164, WP 188.
He is here, he is here	MP 218 (MP1 68).
He is Lord	BPW 378, CFW 295, H&P 256, HTC S7, JP 75, LP 59, MP 220 (MP1 69), O&N 190, SF 165, WP 190.
He is lovely	LP 291.
He is our peace	SF 166.
He is risen	LP 60, WP 58 (WP1 26).
He lives, he lives, Christ Jesus lives	BPW 379.
He lives in us, the Christ of God	BPW 554, HFP 111, HTC 457.
He made me (he gave me eyes)	BPW 125.
He made the stars to shine	JP 76.
He made the water wet	JP 359.
He paid a debt he did not owe	JP 77.
He sat to watch o'er customs paid	NEH 189.
He shall reign	SF 170.
He stood before the court	HFP 112, HTC 129.
He that is down needs fear no fall	A&M 218, H&P 676,WSAM 34.
He that is in us	LP 61, MP 219 (MP2 388), SF 171.
He walked where I walk	MP 221 (MP3 678), SF 172.
He walks among the golden lamps	HTC 177.
He wants not friends that hath thy love	A&M 183, H&P 495, NEH 371.
He was born a little child	WP 57 (WP1 28).
He was pierced for our transgressions	HFP 114, LP 292, MP 222 (MP3 684), SF 173.
He who bore witness by a good confession	NEH 220.
He who created light	HFP 115.
He who dwells	MP 223 (MP3 679).
He who made the starry skies	CP 118.
He who would valiant be	HTC 590, JP 80, MP 224 (MP2 389), NEH 372, O&N 195, SF 174.
Head of the church, our risen Lord	H&P 547.
Head of thy church triumphant	H&P 818.
Head of thy church, whose Spirit fills	H&P 316.
Heal me, hands of Jesus	HFP 113, HTC 319.
Heal us, Immanuel! Hear our prayer	H&P 390.
Healing God, almighty Father	MP 226 (MP2 391).
Healing grace	SF 157.
Hear how the bells	CP 121.
Hear me, O Lord, and respond to my prayer (Ps. 86)	HFP 116, PFT 86a.
Hear me, O Lord, in my distress (Ps. 143)	PFT 143a.
Hear my cry, O God (Ps. 61)	MP 227 (MP2 392), O&N 188.
Hear my cry, O Lord (Ps. 61)	SFP 61c.
Hear my prayer, O Lord (Ps. 102)	SFP 102b.
Hear, O Lord our cry	SF 158.

Hear, O Shepherd	SF 159.
Hear the bells	WSAM 10.
Hear the chimes as they ring	CP 120.
Hear the skies around	CP 122.
Hear us, O Lord, from heaven	H&P 346.
Hear us, O Lord, have mercy on us	NEH 507.
Heavenly Father, I appreciate you	SF 160.
Heavenly Father, may your blessing	H&P 473.
Heavenly Father, we would sing out	JP 358.
Heavenly hosts in ceaseless worship	HFP 117, HTC 570.
Heaven is singing for joy	WP 31.
He is risen, risen, risen	WP 58.
Help me to understand it, Lord	LP 294.
Help us, O Lord, to learn	A&M 373, CFW 615, H&P 474, HTC 493, NEH 370, O&N 191.
Help us to help each other, Lord	A&M 374, CFW 439, HFP 118, HTC 540, O&N 192.
Her virgin eyes saw God incarnate	A&M 310, NEH 182.
Here from all nations	BPW 309, CFW 577, HFP 119, HTC 571.
Here from the world we turn	MP 228 (MP4 815).
Here he comes robed in majesty	CFW 57.
Here I am	LP 63, MP 229 (MP2 393), SF 167
Here I am, ready for you	WP 59.
Here I am, the one who turned	WP 79.
Here I stand at the door	LP 293.
Here in this place	LP 295, WSAM 29.
Here is bread	LP 296.
Here is love	SF 168.
Here, Lord, we come to you	HTC 327.
Here, Lord, we take the broken bread	BPW 440, H&P 604, HTC 404.
Here, O my Lord, I see thee face to face	A&M 274, BPW 436, H&P 608, HFP 120, HTC 406, MP 230 (MP2 394).
Here we are	SF 169.
Here within this house of prayer	HTC 568.
Here within your presence	WP 10.
He's got the whole world in his hands	CFW 189, H&P 25, JP 78, LP 62, MP 225 (MP2 390), O&N 194.
He's great, he's God, Jesus Christ	JP 79.
Hevenu shalom	JP 81, MP 231 (MP2 396).
Hey you, do you love Jesus	JP 361.
Hey! Hey! Anybody listening	JP 362.
High in the heavens, eternal God	H&P 26.
Higher, higher	SF 175.
Hills of the north, rejoice	A&M 470, BPW 311, H&P 237, NEH 7, O&N 196.
His eyes will guide my footsteps	HTC 301.
His hands were pierced	MP 232 (MP1 70).
His name is higher than any other	CFW 640, MP 233 (MP1 71), SF 176.
His name is wonderful	BPW 385, MP 234 (MP1 72), O&N 197, SF 177.
His name was Saul of Tarsus	JP 363.
His voice is the sea	SF 178.

301

How blest the poor who love the Lord	BPW 197.
How bright these glorious spirits shine	A&M 306, HTC 572, NEH 227.
How brightly shines the morning star	NEH 27.
How can I be free from sin	LP 302.
How can I repay the Lord (Ps. 116)	PFT 116b.
How can we sing with joy (Ps. 119)	BPW 86, HFP 124, HTC 362.
How can we sinners know	H&P 728.
How did Moses cross the Red Sea	JP 83.
How do thy mercies close me round	H&P 562.
How do we start (That the world may)	LP 303.
How firm a foundation (Ps. 69)	BPW 380, HFP 125, HTC 430, MP 243 (MP1 76), O&N 202.
How glad are those with peace of mind (Ps. 32)	
	PFT 32a.
How glorious Zion's courts appear	H&P 448.
How good a thing it is (Ps. 133)	CFW 116, HTC 497, PFT 133a.
How good is the God we adore (Ps. 143)	BPW 338, CFW 84, HFP 126, HTC 450, MP 244 (MP1 77), O&N 203.
How good it is to give thanks (Ps. 92)	SFP 92c.
How good it is to sing (Ps. 147)	SFP 147d.
How good, Lord, to be here	H&P 156.
How gracious are their feet	H&P 449.
How great is God almighty (Ps. 48)	CFW 313, SFP 48b.
How great is our God	JP 82, MP 245 (MP2 401), O&N 204.
How great is the goodness (Ps. 31)	SFP 31b.
How great thou art (O Lord my God)	BPW 62, O&N 370.
How happy are thy servants, Lord	H&P 609.
How I love you (you are the one) (Ps. 190)	LP 69, MP 246 (MP2 398), SF 190.
How long, O Lord (Ps. 13)	HFP 128, LP 304, SFP 13c.
How long will you forget me (Ps. 13)	CFW 222, PFT 13a.
How lovely is thy dwelling-place	MP 247 (MP2 399).
How lovely is thy dwelling-place	MP 248 (MP3 685), SF 191.
How lovely is your dwelling-place (Ps. 84)	LP 70, SFP 84d.
How lovely is your dwelling-place (Ps. 84)	SFP 84e.
How lovely is your dwelling-place (Ps. 84)	PFT 84a.
How lovely is your dwelling-place (Ps. 84)	PFT 84c.
How lovely on the mountains	BPW 310, CFW 421, CP 125, JP 84, LP 71, MP 249 (MP1 79), O&N 205, SF 192.
How many are against me, Lord (Ps. 3)	PFT 3a.
How pleased and blest was I	BPW 10, H&P 497.
How precious, O Lord	MP 252 (MP2 400), SF 193.
How shall I sing that majesty	A&M 472, H&P 8, NEH 373.
How shall they hear	HTC 507, MP 250 (MP2 402).
How sure the Scriptures are	HFP 127, HTC 249.
How sweet the name of Jesus sounds (Ps. 194)	
	A&M 122, BPW 339, H&P 257, HFP 129, HTC 211, MP 251 (MP1 78), NEH 374, O&N 206, SF 194.
How wonderful, the things	WP 12 (WP1 33).
How wonderful this world of thine	H&P 336.
How you bless our lives	SF 195.

Humbly in your sight   WP 65 (WP1 30).
Hush, do not cry   CP 128.
Hush, little baby; peace, little boy   CP 129.
Hush you, my baby   CP 127.
Hushed was the evening hymn   H&P 523, JP 85, MP 253
     (MP2 403).

I am a lighthouse   JP 87, SF 196.
I am a new creation   CFW 359, LP 74, MP 254
     (MP2 404), SF 197, WP 193.

I am a sheep, baa, baa   JP 373.
I am a wounded soldier   MP 255 (MP3 687), SF 198.
I am like a house with two windows   JP 366.
I am not ashamed   SF 199.
I am not mine own   MP 256 (MP2 405).
I am not skilled to understand (Ps. 54)   H&P 221, HTC 432, MP 257
     (MP2 406).

I am not worthy, holy Lord   HTC 407.
I am so glad that our Father in heaven   JP 88.
I am the bread (Jesus the Lord said: I)   BPW 202.
I am the bread of life   H&P 611, MP 261, O&N 207.
I am the bread of life .. remember me   WSAM 35.
I am the bread, the bread   MP 260 (MP3 686).
I am the church   JP 367.
I am the God that healeth thee   SF 201.
I am the resurrection and the life   JP 368.
I am the way, the truth and the life   JP 89.
I am trusting in you   MP 259 (MP2 432).
I am trusting thee/you, Lord Jesus   BPW 340, CFW 406, HFP 130,
     HTC 433, JP 86, MP 258 (MP1 81),
     SF 202.

I am waiting for the dawning   MP 262 (MP4 816).
I am weak but thou art strong   MP 263 (MP1 82).
I believe in God the Father   CFW 404, HFP 131, HTC 434.
I believe in Jesus   LP 305, MP 264 (MP3 688), SF 203.
I believe there is a God (Ps. 53)   LP 306.
I bind myself to God today   HTC 5.
I bind unto myself today   H&P 695, NEH 159, O&N 211.
I bless the Christ of God   HTC 435.
I call to your (My soul waits) (Ps. 130)   LP 75, SFP 130f.
I can almost see   SF 204.
I can run through a troop   JP 90.
I cannot count your blessings   MP 265 (MP3 692).
I cannot tell why he whom angels worship   BPW 381, H&P 238, HFP 135,
     HTC 194, MP 266 (MP1 83),
     O&N 212, SF 205.

I cast all my cares upon you   JP 369.
I come to you for shelter, Lord (Ps. 31)   PFT 31a.
I come with joy to meet my Lord   A&M 473, BPW 437, CFW 16,
     H&P 610, HFP 132, HTC 408,
     WSAM 36.

I confess that Jesus Christ is Lord   MP 267 (MP2 407).
I cried out for heaven to hear me (Ps. 77)   PFT 77.
I danced in the morning   A&M 375, JP 91, NEH 375,
     O&N 213.
I delight greatly in the Lord   MP 268 (MP2 408), SF 206.

I do not hold life so dear	LP 307.
I do not know what lies ahead	JP 92, MP 269 (MP2 409).
I exalt you	SF 207.
I exalt you, mighty Lord	WP 144.
I find my refuge in the Lord (Ps. 11)	PFT 11.
I found him cradled	WSAM 88.
I get so excited, Lord	MP 270 (MP2 410), SF 209.
I give you all the honour	MP 271 (MP2 412), SF 210.
I give you now	SF 211.
I gotta home in gloryland that outshines	JP 97.
I greet thee, who my sure Redeemer art	H&P 391.
I have a destiny	SF 212.
I have a dream, a man once said	BPW 625.
I have a friend who is deeper	JP 370.
I have decided	LP 76.
I have decided to follow Jesus	JP 98, MP 272 (MP1 84).
I have found	SF 213.
I have made a covenant	SF 214.
I have no strength but yours (Ps. 7)	SFP 7b.
I have seen the golden sunshine	JP 99.
I hear the sound of rustling	MP 274 (MP1 88), O&N 221, SF 216.
I hear the sound of the army of the Lord	JP 100, MP 273 (MP2 413), SF 217.
I hear the words of love	HTC 436.
I heard the voice of Jesus say	A&M 247, H&P 136, MP 275 (MP1 85), NEH 376, O&N 220, SF 215.
I hunger and I thirst (Ps. 63)	H&P 730, HTC 409.
I just want to praise you (Lord, I lift)	SF 219.
I just want to praise you, lift my hands	MP 276 (MP2 411), SF 218.
I know I'll see Jesus some day	MP 277 (MP4 817).
I know it was your love for me	LP 308.
I know not why God's wondrous grace	BPW 532, MP 279 (MP1 89), SF 220.
I know that my Redeemer lives – what joy	H&P 196, O&N 223.
I know that my Redeemer lives, and ever	H&P 731.
I know that my Redeemer lives, comfort	BPW 251, HFP 133, HTC 169, MP 278 (MP1 86).
I know that my Redeemer lives crowned	BPW 516.
I know whom I have believed	MP 279 (MP1 89).
I lift my eyes to the quiet hills (Ps. 121)	BPW 595, MP 281 (MP2 416), PFT 121b.
I lift my eyes to you (Ps. 123)	PFT 123a.
I lift my eyes up to the mountains	SF 221.
I lift my hands (I will serve no foreign god)	SF 223.
I lift my hands (Most of all)	MP 280 (MP2 414), SF 222.
I lift my soul to you (Ps. 25)	LP 309.
I lift my voice to praise your name	SF 224.
I lift up mine eyes to the hills	H&P 498.
I lift up my eyes to the hills (Ps. 121)	PFT 121d.
I live, I live because he is risen	MP 282 (MP2 415), SF 225.
I'll trust you Lord	WP 141
I look out through the doorway	JP 371.
I look to the hills	MP 283 (MP3 689).
I look up to the mountains (Ps. 121)	LP 81, SFP 121f.

I long to praise the Lord — WP 73.
I love my Lord — MP 284 (MP1 90).

I love the Lord, he heard my voice (Ps. 116) — PFT 116a.
I love the name of Jesus — MP 285 (MP1 91), O&N 225.
I love to think, though I am young — CFW 194.
I love you, I love you Jesus — LP 77.
I love you, I love you – the earth — WP 143.
I love you, Lord, and I lift my voice — MP 287 (MP1 87), SF 226.
I love you Lord Jesus — JP 372.
I love you, Lord, my strength (Ps. 18) — PFT 18b.
I love you, my Lord — SF 227.
I love you, O Lord, my rock (Ps. 18) — SFP 18c.
I love you, O Lord, you alone (Ps. 18) — BPW 341, CFW 248, HFP 134, HTC 475, LP 78, MP 286 (MP3 691), PFT 18a.

I love you with the love of the Lord — SF 228.
I may never march in the infantry — JP 101.
I met Jesus at the crossroads — JP 102.
I met you at the cross — JP 103.
I need thee every hour — BPW 533, H&P 524, MP 288 (MP1 92).

I offer up my song (Ps. 143) — LP 310.
I praise you, Lord, with all my heart (Ps. 9) — PFT 9, SFP 9.
I really want to worship you (You laid) — LP 230, MP 795 (MP2 644), SF 633.
I receive you, O Spirit of love — MP 289 (MP2 417).
I receive your love — BPW 342, MP 290 (MP2 418), SF 248.

I rejoiced to hear them say (Ps. 122) — PFT 122a.
I rest in God alone (Ps. 62) — LP 79, MP 291 (MP3 690), SFP 62c.
I see perfection (Children of the King) — LP 73, MP 292 (MP3 693).
I see the Lord — SF 249.
I see the mountains far away (Ps. 121) — PFT 121a.
I seek you, Lord God, I yearn (Ps. 63) — SFP 63c.
I serve a risen Saviour — JP 113, MP 295 (MP1 94).
I set the Lord before my eyes (Ps. 16) — PFT 16a.
I should be getting to know you (Ps. 128) — LP 311.
I sing a new song — MP 294 (MP2 420).
I sing a song of the saints of God — BPW 481, JP 115.
I sing the almighty power of God — H&P 334, MP 293 (MP2 419).
I stand amazed in the presence — MP 296 (MP2 421).
I stand before the presence — MP 297 (MP2 422).
I tell you (Leben) — LP 80.
I, the Lord of sea and sky — LP 312.
I to the hills will lift mine eyes — BPW 126, H&P 496.
I trust in thee, O Lord — MP 299 (MP1 95).
I've come to a time when I must change — JP 383.
I've found a friend — MP 352 (MP1 113).
I've got peace like a river — JP 120, MP 353 (MP1 114).
I've got that joy, joy, joy, joy — JP 121.
I vow to thee, my country — A&M 295, O&N 246.
I waited, I waited on the Lord (Ps. 40) — LP 313, SFP 40c.
I waited patiently for the Lord (Ps. 40) — SFP 40b.
I wanna sing — SF 258.
I want a principle within — H&P 422.

I want Jesus to walk with me	LP 314, WSAM 40.
I want the Spirit of power within	H&P 291.
I want to be a history maker	SF 259.
I want to give my all (I want to serve)	LP 82.
I want to learn to appreciate you	MP 298 (MP2 423).
I want to live for Jesus ev'ry day	JP 122.
I want to love you, Lord	JP 374.
I want to see your face	MP 300 (MP3 703).
I want to serve the purpose of God	LP 315, SF 260.
I want to serve you (I want to give)	LP 82.
I want to serve you, Lord	MP 303 (MP3 700).
I want to sing	LP 83.
I want to tell you	JP 375.
I want to thank you	MP 301 (MP3 694).
I want to walk with Jesus Christ	CFW 141, HTC S16, JP 124, MP 302 (MP2 444), SF 261.
I want to worship the Lord	MP 304 (MP1 93).
I was glad when they said to me (Ps. 122)	CFW 559, SFP 122c.
I was lost but Jesus found me	JP 125.
I was made to praise you	SF 262.
I was once in darkness	SF 263.
I was sinking deep in sin	MP 450 (MP4 824).
I will build my church	LP 84, MP 305 (MP3 695), SF 264.
I will call (so shall I be saved)	SF 265.
I will call upon the Lord (The Lord liveth)	MP 306 (MP1 96), SF 266.
I will change your name	SF 267.
I will come and bow down (Ps. 16)	CP 130, LP 85, SFP 16c.
I will dwell in his secret place (Ps. 91)	SFP 91b.
I will enter his gates with thanksgiving (Ps. 100)	
	BPW 11, MP 307 (MP1 97), O&N 248, SF 268, SFP 100e.
I will exalt you O God my King (Ps. 145)	PFT 145b.
I will give thanks to the Lord most high (Ps. 7)	
	PFT 7.
I will give thanks to thee	MP 308 (MP1 98), SF 269.
I will give thanks to you (Ps. 57)	SFP 57b.
I will give you praise	MP 309 (MP3 696), SF 270.
I will lift up my eyes (Ps. 121)	SFP 121h.
I will lift up my eyes to the hills (Ps. 121)	PFT 121c.
I will live within the shadow (Ps. 91)	SFP 91c.
I will magnify thy name	MP 310 (MP3 702), SF 271.
I will make you fishers of men	JP 123.
I will pour out my Spirit on all flesh	H&P 292.
I will praise you all my life	SF 272.
I will praise you Lord with all my heart (Ps. 138)	
	SFP 138b.
I will praise you with the harp (Ps. 71)	SFP 71b.
I will rejoice, I will rejoice	MP 311 (MP2 424), SF 274.
I will rejoice in you and be glad	MP 312 (MP2 428), SF 273.
I will rise and bless you, Lord	SF 275.
I will seek your face, O Lord	LP 316, SF 276.
I will sing about your love	CFW 81, MP 314 (MP2 425).
I will sing, I will sing a song	CFW 517, HTC S15, JP 126, MP 313 (MP1 99).
I will sing of the Lord for ever (Ps. 89)	SFP 89b.

I'm going to shine, shine, shine	JP 392.
I'm going to stand up, I'm going to	JP 380.
I'm going to take a step of faith	JP 381.
I'm gonna thank the Lord	SF 230.
I'm in love with you	SF 231.
I'm not alone	SF 235.
I'm not ashamed to own/name my Lord	BPW 343, H&P 677, HTC 448, MP 323 (MP1 100), O&N 229.
I'm redeemed	MP 324 (MP2 430).
I'm singing for my Lord ev'rywhere I go	JP 105.
I'm special because God has loved me	JP 106, MP 325 (MP2 431), SF 236.
I'm very glad of God	JP 107.
Immanuel, God is with us, Immanuel	SF 232.
Immanuel, O Immanuel	LP 318, MP 326 (MP3 699), SF 233.
Immortal, invisible (Ps. 36, 104)	A&M 199, BPW 383, CFW 267, H&P 9, HFP 137, HTC 21, LP 88, MP 327 (MP1 103), NEH 377, O&N 227, SF 234.
Immortal Love, for ever full (Ps. 46)	A&M 133, BPW 198, H&P 392, HTC 105, MP 328 (MP4 819), NEH 378, O&N 228.
In a byre near Bethlehem	BPW 199.
In a stable	WP 70 (WP1 35).
In a stable, in a manger	CP 134.
In Adam we have all been one	A&M 474, H&P 420.
In all my vast concerns with thee	H&P 72.
In awe and wonder, Lord our God	HFP 138.
In Christ shall all be made alive	HTC 459.
In Christ there is no east or west	A&M 376, BPW 482, CFW 429, H&P 758, HTC 322, MP 329 (MP2 435), NEH 480, O&N 231, WP 194.
In everything that I do, show me	JP 391.
In full and glad surrender	HTC 557, MP 330 (MP1 104), O&N 233.
In heavenly armour we'll enter the land	HFP 140, LP 90, MP 639 (MP2 579), SF 237.
In heavenly love abiding (Ps. 23)	BPW 555, H&P 678, HFP 141, HTC 458, MP 331 (MP1 106), O&N 234, SF 238.
In him we live and move	MP 332 (MP2 433), SF 239.
In humble gratitude, O God	A&M 377.
In loving-kindness Jesus came	MP 333 (MP4 820).
In majesty he comes	SF 240.
In memory of the Saviour's love	HTC 412.
In moments like these	MP 334 (MP2 434), SF 241.
In my hour of grief or need (Ps. 10)	PFT 10.
In my life, Lord	BPW 348, CFW 495, LP 89, MP 335 (MP1 105), SF 242, WP 195.
In my need Jesus found me	JP 109, MP 336 (MP2 436).
In our day of thanksgiving one psalm	A&M 284, H&P 660, NEH 208, O&N 235.
In our work and in our play	JP 108.
In silent pain the eternal Son	HFP 142, WSAM 39.

308

It takes an almighty hand to make	JP 395.
It was a man who was born	HTC 456.
It was in Judah's land	CP 142.
It was Jesus who taught his disciples	JP 397.
It was on a starry night when the hills	JP 396.
It was raining (light a candle)	LP 91.
It's a happy day	JP 118, SF 255.
It's a song of praise	JP 398.
It's an adventure following Jesus	JP 399.
It's easy to be a believer	JP 400.
It's good, Lord, to be here	BPW 201.
It's me, it's me, it's me, O Lord	JP 119.
It's not very nice saying, Na na na na	JP 401.
It's rounded like an orange	JP 402.
It's the little things that show our	JP 403.
It's the presence of your Spirit	SF 256.
It's your blood that cleanses me	LP 322, MP 351 (MP3 701), SF 257.
Jag vill ge dig o Herre (All I am will)	LP 3.
Jehovah Jireh	LP 94, MP 354 (MP3 710), SF 284.
Jehovah Jireh, God will provide	JP 404, SF 283.
Jerusalem! How glad I was (Ps. 122)	PFT 122b.
Jerusalem man, walking from his homeland	JP 405.
Jerusalem, my happy home	A&M 187, HTC 569.
Jerusalem on high	HTC 565.
Jerusalem the golden	A&M 184, BPW 312, HTC 573, NEH 381, O&N 254.
Jerusalem, thou city blest	NEH 228.
Jesu, Lord of life and glory	NEH 68.
Jesu, meek and lowly	NEH 85.
Jesu, the very thought is sweet	NEH 291.
Jesus, a stranger	LP 324.
Jesus at your name	MP 355 (MP2 446).
Jesus bids us shine	JP 128.
Jesus calls us here to meet him	BPW 12.
Jesus calls us! – in/o'er the tumult	A&M 312, H&P 141, HTC 104, MP 359 (MP1 116), NEH 200, O&N 255.
Jesus came – the heavens adoring	HTC 195.
Jesus, child of Mary	CP 143.
Jesus Christ gives life and gladness	HFP 145.
Jesus Christ is alive today	JP 129, MP 358 (MP1 117).
Jesus Christ is risen	NEH 111.
Jesus Christ is risen today	A&M 77, BPW 252, CFW 242, HFP 146, HTC 155, JP 130, MP 357 (MP2 447), NEH 110, O&N 256, SF 285.
Jesus Christ is the Lord of all	LP 325.
Jesus Christ is waiting	BPW 534.
Jesus Christ, my heart's true captain	BPW 409.
Jesus Christ our great Redeemer	CP 145, MP 356 (MP3 706).
Jesus Christ our living Lord	WP 75 (WP1 41).
Jesus Christ, sovereign King (Ps. 133)	LP 326.
Jesus Christ, the hope of the world	WP 121.
Jesus Christ the Lord is born	CFW 671, CP 146, HFP 147, HTC 83, JP 131.

	MP 373 (MP2 454), NEH 112, O&N 262, SF 296.
Jesus, Lord, Redeemer	H&P 199.
Jesus, Lord, we look to thee	A&M 380, H&P 759, NEH 481.
Jesus, Lord, we pray	A&M 475, H&P 365, HTC 302.
Jesus' love is very wonderful	CFW 374, JP 139.
Jesu, lover of my soul (Ps. 69)	A&M 123, NEH 383, O&N 263.
Jesus, lover of my soul (Ps. 69)	BPW 345, H&P 528, HFP 154, HTC 438, MP 372 (MP1 120), SF 297.
Jesus loves me! – this I know	HTC 303, JP 140.
Jesus, loving Lord	WP 167.
Jesus my Lord	MP 374 (MP1 121).
Jesus, my Lord, how rich thy grace	A&M 381, H&P 147.
Jesus, my Lord, let me be	A&M 476.
Jesus, my Lord, my God, my all	HTC 476, NEH 384, O&N 264.
Jesus, my strength, my hope	H&P 680.
Jesus, my Truth, my Way	H&P 734.
Jesus, name above all names	BPW 55, CFW 226, CP 149, JP 141, MP 375 (MP1 122), O&N 265, SF 298.
Jesus knows the inmost heart	WP 93.
Jesu, our hope, our heart's desire	A&M 86, HTC 178.
Jesus, our Lord, our King and our God	A&M 382.
Jesus, our Master, on the night	NEH 293.
Jesus, priceless treasure (Ps. 119)	H&P 259, HTC 461.
Jesus, Prince and Saviour	JP 407, MP 377 (MP2 456).
Jesus put this song into our hearts	CFW 423, JP 408, LP 130, MP 376 (MP2 457), SF 299, WP 197.
Jesus, remember me	BPW 221, LP 328.
Jesus, restore to us again	LP 332.
Jesus said that whosoever will	JP 142.
Jesus, Saviour, ever mild	H&P 527.
Jesus, Saviour, holy child	CP 150, HFP 155.
Jesus, Saviour of the world	CFW 356, HTC 607.
Jesus, Saviour, Lord	WP 129
Jesus, send me the helper	JP 409.
Jesus, send more labourers	LP 330, SF 300.
Jesus shall reign (Ps. 72)	A&M 143, BPW 313, CFW 415, H&P 239, HFP 156, HTC 516, LP 97, MP 379 (MP1 123), NEH 388, O&N 266, SF 301, WP 198.
Jesus shall take the highest honour	LP 331, MP 378 (MP3 705), SF 302.
Jesu, son of Mary	A&M 281, NEH 329.
Jesus, stand among us at the meeting	MP 381 (MP1 124), SF 303.
Jesus, stand among us in thy/your risen power	
	BPW 88, H&P 530, HFP 157, MP 380 (MP1 125), HTC 364, O&N 268, SF 304.
Jesus, sun and shield art thou	H&P 261.
Jesus take me as I am	MP 382 (MP1 127), SF 305.
Jesus, the conqueror, reigns	H&P 262.
Jesus, the first and last	H&P 735.
Jesus, the gift divine I know	H&P 318.

Jesus the good shepherd is	H&P 263.
Jesus, the joy of loving hearts (Ps. 143)	BPW 439, H&P 258, HFP 158, HTC 413, MP 383 (MP1 128), O&N 269.
Jesus the Liberator	WSAM 44.
Jesus the Lord is seeking me	WP 69 (WP1 37).
Jesus, the Lord of love and life	BPW 507.
Jesus the Lord said	WP 78 (WP1 40) HTC 294, MP 384 (MP2 458)
Jesus the Lord said: I am the bread	BPW 202, H&P 137, WSAM 45.
Jesus, the name above all names	SF 306.
Jesus, the name high over all	H&P 264, HFP 159, HTC 213, MP 385 (MP1 126), SF 307.
Jesus the Saviour comes!	HFP 160.
Jesu, the very thought of thee	A&M 120, NEH 385, O&N 271.
Jesus, the very thought of thee	H&P 265, HTC 478, MP 386 (MP1 129), SF 308.
Jesus, the word bestow	H&P 768.
Jesus, these eyes have never seen	A&M 245, NEH 389, O&N 270.
Jesu, thou joy of loving hearts	A&M 255, NEH 292.
Jesus, thou soul of all our joys	H&P 761.
Jesus, thy boundless love to me	H&P 696.
Jesus, thy far-extended fame	H&P 148.
Jesus, thy wandering sheep behold	H&P 772.
Jesus, to your table led	H&P 613.
Jesus, transfigured, we scarcely can	BPW 203.
Jesus, united by thy grace	H&P 773.
Jesus was born in a stable	CP 151.
Jesus was the Son of God	JP 411.
Jesus, we are here (Jesu tawa pano)	LP 333, WP 74 (WP1 38).
Jesus, we celebrate your victory	LP 334, MP 387 (MP3 707), SF 309.
Jesus, we enthrone you	BPW 52, LP 98, MP 388 (MP1 131), SF 310, WP 196.
Jesus, we follow thee	H&P 583.
Jesus, we look to thee	H&P 760.
Jesus, we thus obey	A&M 477, H&P 614.
Jesus, we want to meet	WSAM 83.
Jesus, where'er thy people meet	A&M 162, H&P 549, HTC 371, NEH 390, O&N 272.
Jesus, whose all-redeeming love	A&M 383.
Jesus will never, ever	JP 412.
Jesus, you are changing me	LP 335, MP 389 (MP2 459), SF 311.
Jesus, you are the power	MP 390 (MP3 709).
Jesus, you are the radiance	LP 99, MP 391 (MP2 460), SF 312.
Jesus, you have lifted me	LP 100.
Jesus, your blood and righteousness	H&P 225, HTC 460.
Jesus, your name is power	LP 336.
Join all the glorious names	BPW 557, H&P 78, HTC 214, MP 392 (MP2 461), SF 313.
Joseph was sold as a slave	JP 413.
Joshua fit the battle of Jericho	JP 143.
Journey to Bethlehem, worship your King	CP 152.
Joy and triumph everlasting	NEH 229.
Joy is the flag flown high from	JP 144.
Joy, joy, ring out your joy (Ps. 95)	SFP 95i.

Joy to the world (Ps. 96, 98)	BPW 315, CFW 664, CP 153, H&P 77, HFP 161, HTC 197, LP 102, MP 393 (MP3 708), O&N 273, SF 314, WP 199.
Joy, wonderful and free (Argentina)	WP 88.
Jubilate (O shout to the Lord) (Ps. 100)	LP 154.
Jubilate Deo (Ps. 100)	BPW 13, O&N 274.
Jubilate, everybody (Ps. 100)	BPW 14, JP 145, MP 394 (MP1 130), O&N 274, SF 315, SFP 100g,WSAM 46.
Judge eternal, throned in splendour	BPW 627, CFW 62, H&P 409, HFP 162, HTC 329, MP 395 (MP4 822), NEH 490, O&N 275.
Just as a lost and thirsty deer (Ps. 42)	HFP 163, SFP 42c.
Just as I am	A&M 246, BPW 346, CFW 411, H&P 697, HFP 164, HTC 440, LP 101, MP 396 (MP1 132), NEH 294, O&N 277, SF 316, WP 200.
Just as I am, your child to be	JP 146.
Just like you promised	SF 317.
Keep me shining, Lord	JP 147.
Kids under construction	JP 414.
King forever	SF 318.
King of glory, King of peace (Ps. 145)	A&M 194, BPW 53, CFW 157, H&P 499, HFP 165, HTC 603, MP 397 (MP2 462), NEH 391, O&N 278.
King of kings and Lord of lords	JP 148.
King of kings . . glory, alleluia	CP 154, LP 103, MP 398 (MP2 463).
King of kings, Lord of lords, lion	LP 104, SF 319.
King of the universe, Lord of the ages	HFP 166, HTC 22.
Kings came riding from the east	CP 155.
Kneels at the feet of his friends	BPW 606.
Kum ba ya, my Lord	H&P 525, O&N 279.
Kum ba yah (Father God in heaven) (Ps. 65)	
	CFW 171, HFP 73, HTC 358, LP 33.
Kum ba yah, my Lord, Kum ba yah	JP 149.
Kyrie eleison	BPW 454.
Kyrie eleison (Look around you) (Ps. 67)	LP 113.
Lamb of God, Holy One, Jesus Christ	SF 320.
Lamb of God, I look to thee	H&P 738.
Lamb of God whose dying love	H&P 550.
Land of hope and glory (Glory in the highest)	
	A&M 277, CP 99.
Large creatures, small creatures	JP 415.
Laud, O Sion, thy salvation	NEH 521.
Laudate Dominum (O praise the Lord God) (Ps. 117)	LP 153.
Laudate omnes gentes	BPW 19.
Laughter and song (Ps. 126)	PFT 126a.
Lead kindly Light	A&M 215, H&P 67, MP 399 (MP2 464), NEH 392, O&N 280.
Lead me from death to life	BPW 628.

Lead us, heavenly Father (revised versions)	CFW 111, 365, HTC 525.
Lead us, heavenly Father (traditional version)	
	A&M 224, BPW 597, H&P 68, HFP 167, HTC 595, MP 400 (MP2 465), NEH 393, O&N 281, SF 321.
Leader of faithful souls, and guide	H&P 819.
Led like a lamb (You're alive)	BPW 254, CFW 253, HFP 168, JP 151, LP 105, MP 402 (MP1 282), SF 322.
Let all in heaven and earth unite (Ps. 29)	PFT 29a.
Let all mortal flesh keep silence	A&M 256, BPW 441, H&P 266, HTC 61, NEH 295, O&N 282.
Let all that is within me	MP 401 (MP1 133).
Let all the earth hear his voice	CP 158, MP 403 (MP3 718).
Let all the world in every corner sing (Ps. 68)	
	A&M 202, BPW 54, CFW 49, H&P 10, HTC 342, MP 404 (MP1 135), NEH 394, O&N 283.
Let bells peal forth the universal fame	NEH 395.
Let creation bless the Father	HTC 312.
Let earth and heaven agree	H&P 226.
Let earth and heaven combine	H&P 109.
Let every Christian pray	A&M 478, H&P 305, HTC 230.
Let everything that has breath (Ps. 150)	PFT 150b.
Let God arise (Ps. 68)	CFW 534, CP 159, LP 127, MP 405 (MP2 467), SF 323.
Let God arise, and let his enemies (Ps. 68)	SFP 68b.
Let God arise! his enemies be gone (Ps. 68)	PFT 68a.
Let God be gracious to us and bless us (Ps. 67)	
	PFT 67c.
Let God speak	SF 324.
Let God, who called the worlds to be (Ps. 50)	
	PFT 50a.
Let him to whom we now belong	H&P 698.
Let it be to me	LP 337, MP 406 (MP3 711).
Let me have my way among you	MP 407 (MP1 134), O&N 284, SF 325.
Let me tell you how I need you	WP 85.
Let my spirit rejoice in your love	WP 91 (WP1 47).
Let our choirs new anthems raise	NEH 219.
Let our praise to you	LP 106, MP 408 (MP2 468), SF 326.
Let praises ring, let praises ring	CP 160, SF 327.
Let saints on earth together sing	A&M 182, HTC 574, MP 409 (MP2 466), NEH 396.
Let the beauty of Jesus	MP 410 (MP1 136).
Let the desert sing	CP 156-7, HTC 198.
Let the hearts of those who seek (Ps. 105)	SFP 105b.
Let the heavens shout for joy	LP 107.
Let the Lord's people, heart and voice	A&M 479.
Let the people praise you, O God (Ps. 67)	HFP 169, LP 339, SFP 67e.
Let the round world with songs rejoice	NEH 214.
Let the world sing Jesus reigns	LP 107.
Let there be glory and honour	SF 328.
Let there be light	BPW 630.

Let there be love	BPW 484, CFW 58, LP 108, MP 411 (MP1 137), SF 329.
Let there be peace on earth	BPW 629, O&N 285.
Let those with voices sing (Ps. 45)	PFT 45.
Let trumpets sound	HFP 170, MP 210 (MP2 385).
Let us acknowledge the Lord	MP 413 (MP2 469).
Let us break bread together	A&M 480, BPW 443, H&P 615, MP 414 (MP2 470), O&N 286, SF 330, WSAM 47.
Let us draw near to God	LP 338.
Let us employ all notes of joy	A&M 273.
Let us gladly with one mind (Ps. 118)	BPW 56, CFW 280, HTC 23.
Let us go to the house of the Lord (Ps. 122)	LP 340, SF 331, SFP 122d.
Let us greet one another	LP 341, WP 92.
Let us love and sing and wonder	HFP 171, HTC 215.
Let us praise God together	CFW 438, HTC S18, JP 152, O&N 287.
Let us praise his name with dancing	SF 332.
Let us praise the Lord our God (Ps. 99)	LP 342, WP 11 (WP1 7).
Let us praise the Lord with our voices	WP 125.
Let us praise the Lord triumphant	BPW 649.
Let us rejoice and be glad	LP 343.
Let us sing the King Messiah	BPW 631.
Let us sing to the God of salvation (Ps. 95)	BPW 15, CFW 186, HFP 172, SFP 95e.
Let us sing to the Lord a song of praise	WP 34 (WP1 17).
Let us talents and tongues employ	A&M 481, CFW 29, HTC 414, WSAM 48. WP 94.
Let us with a gladsome mind (Ps. 136)	A&M 204, CFW 280, H&P 27, HTC 23, JP 154, MP 415 (MP2 471), NEH 397, O&N 288, SF 333.
Let your living water flow	SF 334.
Let's go and tell our friends	JP 416.
Let's just praise the Lord	MP 412 (MP1 138).
Let's praise God together	JP 417.
Let's talk about Jesus	JP 150.
Life and light and joy are found	H&P 382.
Life is great! so sing about it	A&M 482.
Lift high the cross, the love of Christ	A&M 72, BPW 575, H&P 170, HTC 508, MP 417 (MP1 139), O&N 289, SF 335.
Lift Jesus higher	MP 416 (MP2 472).
Lift up your eyes	WP 6.
Lift up your heads, eternal gates (Ps. 24)	PFT 24a.
Lift up your heads, O ye gates	SF 338.
Lift up your heads, O you gates (Ps. 24)	CP 162, SF 337, SFP 24e.
Lift up your heads to the coming King	CFW 208, CP 161, LP 109, MP 418 (MP2 473), SF 336.
Lift up your heads, you gates of brass (Ps. 24)	H&P 227, HTC 509.
Lift up your heads, you mighty gates (Ps. 24)	A&M 483, CP 163, H&P 240,

Lift up your hearts to the Lord (Ps. 98)   NEH 8.
CP 164, HTC 366, SFP 98d.
Lift up your hearts to things above   H&P 820.
Lift up your hearts! We lift them, Lord   A&M 241, H&P 405, NEH 398,
O&N 290.

Lift your heart and raise your voice   CP 165.
Lift your voice and sing (Give him glory)   LP 110.
Light a candle (it was raining)   LP 91.
Light a flame   SF 339.
Light beyond shadow   WSAM 49.
Light has dawned   LP 111, MP 422 (MP3 719), SF 341.
Light of gladness, Lord of glory   CFW 154, HTC 277.
Light of the lonely pilgrim's heart   NEH 399.
Light of the minds that know him   HTC 477, NEH 400.
Light of the world (You are the light)   LP 227.
Light of the world, shine your light   SF 342.
Light of the world, thy beams I bless   H&P 681.
Light of the world, Jesus shining   WSAM 49.
Light shining in the darkness   CP 167.
Light the candles round the world   CP 168.
Lighten a darkness   SF 340.
Lighten our darkness   CFW 593, HTC 278, LP 112.
Light's abode, celestial Salem   A&M 185, NEH 401, O&N 291.
Light's glittering morning fills the sky   A&M 329, HTC 157.
Lights to the world (The earth was dark)   CFW 447, CP 291, HFP 270,
LP 198, MP 643 (MP3 747).

Like a candle flame   MP 420 (MP3 712).
Like a flicker in the darkness   CP 169.
Like a gently breeze   SF 343.
Like a mighty river flowing   BPW 632, CFW 407, HFP 179,
HTC 32, LP 344, MP 419
(MP1 145), O&N 292.

Like a river glorious   HTC 463, MP 421 (MP1 140),
O&N 293, SF 344.

Like a shepherd I will feed you   LP 346.
Like the deer, athirst and questing (Ps. 42)   PFT 42a.
Like the murmur of the dove's song   HFP 173, WSAM 50.
Lion of Judah on the throne   CP 170, SF 345.
Listen to my prayer, Lord (Ps. 61)   BPW 556, HTC 365, PFT 61a,
SFP 61a.

Listen to the shouts of praises   BPW 222.
Little children, wake and listen   CP 171.
Little donkey, little donkey   CFW 644, CP 172.
Live, live, live   JP 153.
Living Lord (Lord Jesus Christ)   A&M 391, BPW 444, CFW 390,
HFP 178, HTC 417, LP 119,
MP 435 (MP2 480), O&N 302,
SF 357, WSAM 51.

Living Lord, turn your face   WP 155.
Living under the shadow of his wing   CP 166, MP 423 (MP2 474), SF 346.
Lo, from the desert homes   A&M 316.
Lo, God is here, let us adore   H&P 531, NEH 209.
Lo! He comes with clouds descending   A&M 28, BPW 314, CFW 599,
CP 144, H&P 241, HFP 149,
HTC 196, MP 424 (MP1 141),

Lo, I am with you to the end of the world	NEH 9, O&N 296, SF 347. BPW 109.
Lo, in the wilderness, a voice	A&M 384, NEH 170.
Lo, round the throne, a glorious band	A&M 303.
Long ago and far away	CP 173.
Long ago, prophets knew	A&M 484, H&P 83, NEH 10.
Long ago there was born	JP 418.
Long, long ago before our time began	JP 419.
Long, long ago it happened	CP 174.
Long time ago in Bethlehem	CFW 645, CP 175.
Look and learn	WP 95 (WP1 48).
Look and see the glory of the King	SF 348.
Look around you (Kyrie eleison) (Ps. 67)	LP 113.
Look away to Bethlehem	CP 177.
Look, Lord, in mercy as we pray	HTC 498.
Look to the skies, there's a celebration	CFW 657, CP 178, MP 425 (MP3 717).
Look, ye saints, the sight is glorious	H&P 201, HTC 179, MP 426 (MP2 475), SF 349.
Lord all-knowing (Ps. 139)	CFW 394, PFT 139b.
Lord and Father, King forever	SF 350.
Lord, as I wake I turn to you (Ps. 5)	A&M 485, CFW 162, H&P 634, HFP 174, HTC 267, NEH 236, PFT 5, WP 97, (WP1 46).
Lord, as the day begins	HTC 268.
Lord, as we rise to leave the shell	A&M 385, BPW 608.
Lord be my vision/Be thou my vision	A&M 343, BPW 521, HFP 175, HTC 545, LP 114, MP 51 (MP1 17), NEH 339, SF 42.
Lord, be thy word my rule	A&M 232, HTC 250.
Lord, bless Africa	WP 112.
Lord, bring the day to pass	H&P 347.
Lord, by whose breath all souls and seed	A&M 485.
Lord Christ, the Father's almighty Son	A&M 386.
Lord Christ, we praise your sacrifice	A&M 487, H&P 532, HTC 132.
Lord Christ, when first thou cam'st	A&M 387.
Lord Christ, who on thy heart didst bear	A&M 388, H&P 394, O&N 297.
Lord Christ whose love has brought us he	BPW 16.
Lord, come and heal your church	LP 115, MP 427 (MP3 716), SF 351.
Lord, dismiss us with thy/your blessing	H&P 652, JP 155, O&N 298.
Lord, enthroned in heavenly splendour	A&M 263, H&P 616, HTC 416, MP 431 (MP2 476), NEH 296, O&N 299, SF 352.
Lord everlasting	CP 176.
Lord, for the years	BPW 535, CFW 88, HFP 176, HTC 328, LP 116, MP 428 (MP1 142), O&N 300.
Lord, forgive me	WP 96 (WP1 49).
Lord from whom all blessings flow	BPW 485.
Lord, give us your spirit	H&P 319.
Lord God, by whom all change is wrought	H&P 39.
Lord God, heavenly King	SF 353.
Lord God, in whom all worlds	H&P 384.
Lord God of hosts, within whose hand	NEH 162.
Lord God, the Holy Ghost	H&P 306.

Lord God, thou art our maker and our end	A&M 389.
Lord God, we give you thanks for all	A&M 488.
Lord God, we see thy power displayed	A&M 390.
Lord God, your love has called us here	A&M 489, H&P 500, HTC 480.
Lord have mercy (Russia)	WP 86 (WP1 44).
Lord have mercy (Ghana)	WP 87 (WP1 45).
Lord, have mercy (Kyrie Eleison)	BPW 454.
Lord have mercy, Lord have mercy (Ghana)	WP 30.
Lord have mercy, Lord have mercy	MP 429 (MP2 482), O&N 301.
Lord have mercy on us	MP 430 (MP2 481).
Lord, have mercy on us	LP 118, SF 354.
Lord, hear our prayer for this new year	H&P 357.
Lord, hear the praises of thy faithful	NEH 160.
Lord, help me to know your presence	LP 347.
Lord, here is one to be baptised	H&P 584.
Lord, how majestic is your name (Ps. 8)	PFT 8a.
Lord, how majestic you are	LP 348, SF 355.
Lord, I believe a rest remains	H&P 736.
Lord, I have made thy word my choice	A&M 490, H&P 475.
Lord, I love you	MP 432 (MP3 715).
Lord, I was blind; I could not see	BPW 558, H&P 423, HFP 177, HTC 437, MP 433 (MP2 477).
Lord, I will celebrate your love	SF 356.
Lord, if at thy command	H&P 771.
Lord, in the strength of grace	BPW 411, H&P 800.
Lord, in this, thy mercy's day	NEH 69.
Lord, in thy name thy servants plead	NEH 126.
Lord, in your mercy, remember me	WP 145 (WP1 72).
Lord, it belongs not to my care	A&M 242, H&P 679, NEH 402.
Lord, it is eventide	MP 434 (MP2 478).
Lord Jesus Christ (Living Lord)	A&M 391, BPW 444, CFW 390, H&P 617, HFP 178, HTC 417, JP 156, LP 119, MP 435 (MP2 480), NEH 297, O&N 302, SF 357, WSAM 51.
Lord Jesus Christ, be present now	A&M 491.
Lord Jesus Christ, invited guest	HTC 297.
Lord Jesus, for my sake you come	BPW 224, HTC 133.
Lord Jesus here I stand	SF 358.
Lord Jesus, in the days of old	H&P 645.
Lord Jesus, let these eyes of mine	HTC 549.
Lord Jesus, once a child	H&P 585.
Lord Jesus, once you spoke to men	A&M 392, BPW 598, HTC 112.
Lord Jesus, think of me (Ps. 102)	A&M 129, H&P 533, HTC 316, NEH 70, O&N 303.
Lord Jesus, we must know you	BPW 609.
Lord Jesus, when your people meet	HTC 371.
Lord Jesus, you are faithful	JP 420.
Lord Jesus, you have promised	WSAM 52.
Lord, keep my heart tender	SF 359.
Lord, let your grace descend on those	BPW 412, H&P 587.
Lord, look upon this helpless child	H&P 586.
Lord, make me a mountain	JP 421, MP 436 (MP2 483).
Lord, make me an instrument	MP 437 (MP1 144), SF 360.

Lord, make your word my rule	HTC 250.
Lord, may we see your hands	MP 438 (MP1 146).
Lord, now let your servant depart	CP 179.
Lord, now let your servant go	CFW 98, HTC 611, PFT 162b.
Lord, now let your servant go his own	CP 180.
Lord of all beauty, thine the splendour	A&M 106.
Lord of all being, throned afar	H&P 11, MP 439, NEH 403.
Lord of all good, our gifts we bring	A&M 393, H&P 797.
Lord of all goodness	LP 345.
Lord of all hopefulness, Lord of all joy	A&M 394, BPW 517, CFW 86, H&P 552, HTC 101, JP 157, NEH 239, O&N 305.
Lord of all my footsteps (Ps. 17)	PFT 17.
Lord of all power, I give you my will	A&M 395, HTC 547, O&N 306.
Lord of all the saints, we praise thee	NEH 195.
Lord of all, to whom alone	A&M 492.
Lord of beauty, thine the splendour	NEH 265.
Lord of creation, to you be all praise	H&P 699, MP 440 (MP2 479).
Lord of light, whose name shines brighter	H&P 796.
Lord of light, your name outshining	BPW 610.
Lord of lords and King eternal	A&M 396.
Lord of lords, King of kings	SF 361.
Lord of love, you come to bless	WP 137.
Lord of our growing years	BPW 514, HTC 259.
Lord of our highest love	H&P 618.
Lord of our life	HTC 529, MP 441 (MP2 484), NEH 404.
Lord of the boundless curves of space	A&M 493, H&P 335, NEH 405.
Lord of the changing year	HTC 261.
Lord of the church, we pray for our renewing	
	BPW 486, HFP 180, HTC 499, MP 442 (MP2 485).
Lord of the cross of shame	HFP 181, HTC 548, MP 443 (MP1 147), O&N 309.
Lord of the home, your only Son	A&M 494, BPW 500, H&P 367.
Lord of the living, in your name assembled	H&P 654.
Lord of the worlds above	A&M 165.
Lord, pour thy Spirit from on high	A&M 282.
Lord, save thy world; in bitter need	A&M 397, H&P 425.
Lord, speak softly to my soul	CP 181.
Lord, speak to me that I may speak	BPW 611, CFW 428, H&P 553, HTC 510, MP 444 (MP1 148).
Lord, teach us how to pray aright	A&M 227, CFW 173, H&P 551, HTC 367, NEH 406, O&N 310.
Lord, teach us to pray	LP 349.
Lord that descendest, Holy Child	A&M 398.
Lord, that I may learn of thee	H&P 737.
Lord, the light (Shine, Jesus, shine)	BPW 347, HFP 182, LP 120, MP 445 (MP3 714), SF 362, WSAM 71, WP 201.
Lord, this thing I ask you (Ps. 131)	PFT 131b.
Lord, thy Church on earth is seeking	H&P 774.
Lord, thy word abideth	A&M 166, CFW 620, H&P 476, HFP 187, HTC 251, MP 446 (MP2 486), NEH 407, O&N 311.

Lord, to you we bring our treasure	A&M 495.
Lord, we are blind; the world of sight	A&M 399.
Lord, we ask now	JP 301.
Lord, we believe to us and ours	H&P 307.
Lord, we believe when we call	LP 350.
Lord, we come	SF 363.
Lord, we come in your name (Ps. 133)	LP 351.
Lord we give you praise	SF 364.
Lord, we have come at your own invitation	BPW 413, H&P 700.
Lord, we long for you	MP 448 (MP3 713), SF 365.
Lord, we long for you (Heal our nation)	LP 352.
Lord, we worship you	SF 366.
Lord, we your church are deaf and dumb	H&P 775.
Lord, we've come to worship you	JP 422.
Lord, while for all mankind we pray	NEH 491.
Lord, who left the highest heaven	CP 182, HTC 97.
Lord, who may dwell (Ps. 15)	PFT 15a.
Lord, who may venture (Ps. 15)	PFT 15b.
Lord, who shall sit beside thee	NEH 175.
Lord, who throughout these forty days	H&P 131.
Lord, will you turn (Ps. 38)	PFT 38.
Lord, you are brilliant	JP 423.
Lord, you are calling	SF 367.
Lord, you are more precious	LP 355, MP 447 (MP2 487), SF 368.
Lord, you are so precious to me	SF 369.
Lord, you are the Light of the World	JP 424.
Lord, you can make our spirits shine	HTC 512.
Lord, you give to us the precious gift	H&P 368.
Lord, you have been our dwelling-place (Ps. 90)	SFP 90d.
Lord, you have given yourself for our	BPW 576.
Lord, you have searched and known my way	BPW 564, H&P 71.
Lord, you left your throne	CFW 108, CP 183.
Lord, you need no house	BPW 349, HFP 183, HTC 546.
Lord, you put a tongue in my mouth	SF 370.
Lord, you sometimes speak in wonders	BPW 101, HFP 184, LP 353.
Lord, you were rich beyond all splendour	CFW 673, CP 184, HFP 185, HTC 63, MP 700 (MP4 840).
Lord, your church on earth	BPW 577, HFP 186, HTC 511, LP 117.
Lord, your glory fills my heart	SF 372.
Lord, your Kingdom bring triumphant	BPW 578.
Lord, your name is holy	SF 373.
Lord, your name is wonderful	SF 374.
Lord, your word shall guide us	BPW 102, CFW 620, HFP 187, HTC 251, LP 121, MP 446 (MP2 486).
Lord, you're faithful and just	SF 371.
Love beyond measure	SF 375.
Love came down at Christmas	BPW 171, CP 187-8, H&P 105, HTC 62, MP 451 (MP2 489), SF 376.
Love divine, all loves excelling	A&M 131, BPW 559, CFW 387,

Love is his word	H&P 267, HFP 188, HTC 217, LP 354, MP 449 (MP1 149), NEH 408, O&N 313, SF 377. BPW 445, HFP 189, HTC 481, LP 133, O&N 314.
Love, joy, peace	JP 425.
Love, joy, peace and patience	JP 158.
Love lifted me	MP 450 (MP4 824).
Love of the Father, love of God the Son	A&M 159, NEH 409.
Love was born at Christmas	CP 186.
Loved with everlasting love	HFP 190, HTC 482, MP 452 (MP2 488).
Love's redeeming work is done	A&M 83, CFW 259, HTC 150, NEH 113, O&N 315.
Loving Jesus, gentle lamb	H&P 738.
Loving Shepherd of your sheep	A&M 134, CFW 147, HTC 305, O&N 316.
Low in the grave he lay	JP 159.
Low in the grave he lay (Christ arose)	BPW 256, H&P 202, HFP 191, HTC 158, LP 122, MP 453 (MP1 150), O&N 317, SF 378.
Lowly Jesus, King of glory	CP 185.
Lullaby, baby, lie still and slumber	CP 190.
Lullaby, little Jesus	CP 189.
Made in God's image	BPW 633.
Magnificat (Come, glorify) (Ps. 147)	LP 356.
Majesty	BPW 57, CFW 339, JP 160, LP 123, MP 454 (MP1 151), O&N 319, SF 379, WSAM 53, WP 203.
Majesty! King of eternity	WP 98.
Make a joyful melody	SF 380.
Make me a captive, Lord	H&P 714, MP 455 (MP1 152).
Make me a channel of your peace	BPW 634, CFW 470, H&P 776, HFP 192, HTC S19, JP 161, LP 124, MP 456 (MP1 153), O&N 320, SF 381, WSAM 54.
Make me a servant, humble and meek	JP 162.
Make me Lord, a dreamer	SF 382.
Make music to the Lord most high (Ps. 92)	PFT 92a.
Make the book live to me, O Lord	JP 163.
Make us one, Lord	SF 383.
Make us worthy, Lord	HTC S20.
Make way, make way	CFW 587, CP 197, JP 427, LP 125, MP 457 (MP2 491), SF 384, WSAM 55.
Maker of earth, to thee alone	NEH 71.
Man of Sorrows, what a name	BPW 350, CFW 237, H&P 228, HFP 195, HTC 130, MP 458 (MP1 154), SF 385.
March on, my soul, with strength	H&P 716.
Martyr of God, whose strength	NEH 217.
Mary and Joseph, praise with them	CP 192.
Mary came with meekness	CP 191, HFP 193.
Mary had a baby, yes Lord	CFW 650, CP 193, O&N 321.
Mary had a little baby	JP 164.

Mary, listen to the angel of the Lord — CP 194.
Mary sang a song — CFW 643, CP 195-6, HFP 194.
Mary, weep not, weep no longer — NEH 174.
Mary's child (Born in the night) — BPW 156, CP 40, MP 62 (MP2 315).

Master, speak! thy servant heareth — BPW 536, H&P 535, MP 459 (MP1 155), SF 386.

Master, we lift our eyes (Ps. 123) — PFT 123b.
Matthew had been sitting in his little — JP 428.
May God be gracious, may we see (Ps. 67) — PFT 67b.
May God be gracious to us (Ps. 67) — HTC 330.
May God be gracious to us and bless (Ps. 67) — SFP 67d.
May God's blessing — MP 460 (MP1 156).
May my life — SF 387.
May our worship be acceptable (Ps. 19) — LP 134, MP 461 (MP3 720), SFP 19f.

May our worship be as fragrance — LP 357.
May the fragrance of Jesus — LP 135, MP 462 (MP2 492), SF 388.
May the grace of Christ our Saviour — A&M 181, BPW 110, CFW 504, H&P 762, HFP 196, NEH 298, O&N 323.

May the Lord answer you (Ps. 20) — SFP 20b.
May the Lord bless you — MP 464 (MP2 490).
May the Lord God hear you pray (Ps. 20) — PFT 20a.
May the Lord God hear your prayer (Ps. 20) — LP 358, SFP 20c.
May the Lord, mighty God — WP 170.
May the mind of Christ my Saviour — BPW 537, H&P 739, HFP 199, HTC 550, JP 165, LP 136, MP 463 (MP1 157), O&N 324.

May the mind of Christ our Saviour — BPW 537, CFW 452, HTC 370.
May the peace of God the Father — WP 101.
May the words of my mouth (Ps. 19) — SFP 19e.
May we be a shining light — SF 389.
May we, O Holy Spirit, bear your fruit — HTC 236.
Maybe you can't draw or sing or be a — JP 429.
Meekness and majesty (This is your God) — BPW 58, CP 198, HFP 197, LP 138, MP 465 (MP2 493), SF 390.

Meet and right it is to sing — H&P 501.
Men and women, let us walk (Ps. 133) — LP 359, WP 139, (WP1 70).
Merciful Lord — WP 118.
Mercy, blessing, favour, grace (Ps. 67) — PFT 67a.
Mighty God — SF 391.
Mighty in victory, glorious in majesty — CP 199, JP 430, MP 466 (MP3 721).
Mighty is our God — JP 431.
Mine eyes have seen the glory of the — H&P 242, O&N 325.
Miserere nobis (Holy Lord, have mercy) — LP 65.
Mister Noah built an ark — JP 167.
M-m-m-m must I really go and visit him — JP 426.
More love, more power — SF 392.
Morning glory, starlit sky — A&M 496, WSAM 56.
Morning has broken — BPW 132, CFW 279, H&P 635, HFP 198, HTC 265, JP 166, LP 137, MP 467 (MP4 825), NEH 237, O&N 326, SF 393.

Moses, I know you're the man — BPW 489, H&P 450, O&N 327.

Moses left his palace	WSAM 57.
Most ancient of all mysteries	NEH 147.
Most glorious Lord of life	NEH 255.
Move Holy Spirit	SF 394.
Mwamba ni Yesu (Who is the rock)	LP 228.
My peace	SF 399.
My dear Redeemer and my Lord	BPW 205.
My faith is like a staff of oak	JP 168.
My faith, it is an oaken staff	H&P 682, O&N 328.
My faith looks up to thee	H&P 683, MP 469 (MP1 158), NEH 72, O&N 329.
My faithful shepherd is the Lord (Ps. 23)	CFW 560.
My Father, for another night	A&M 3, HTC 269.
My goal is God himself	MP 470 (MP4 826).
My God, accept my heart this day	A&M 279, H&P 701, HTC 551, NEH 318, O&N 330.
My God, and is thy table spread	A&M 259, O&N 331.
My God, how wonderful you are	A&M 102, CFW 341, H&P 51, HFP 200, HTC 369, MP 468 (MP2 498), NEH 410, O&N 332, SF 395.
My God, I am thine	H&P 563.
My God, I know, I feel thee mine	H&P 740.
My God, I love thee; not because	A&M 65, H&P 171, NEH 73, O&N 333.
My God, I love you	HTC 479.
My God, I thank you who hast made the	H&P 564, MP 471 (MP4 827).
My God is so big/great	CFW 82, JP 169.
My God, my King, thy various praise	H&P 12.
My God, now is your table spread	HTC 418.
My gracious Lord, I own thy right	H&P 741.
My heart and voice I raise	H&P 268.
My heart is full of admiration	SF 396.
My heart is full of adoration	LP 360.
My heart is full of Christ, and longs	H&P 799.
My heart is ready, O my God (Ps. 108)	PFT 108a.
My heart overflows	MP 472 (MP2 494).
My hope is built on nothing less	HFP 201, HTC 462, MP 473 (MP1 162), O&N 335.
My life is yours, O Lord	MP 474 (MP2 495).
My lips shall praise you (Ps. 23)	LP 361.
My Lord, he is a-coming soon	CFW 588, CP 200.
My Lord, He is the fairest of the fair	MP 475 (MP2 496), SF 397.
My Lord, I did not choose you (Ps. 143)	HFP 202, HTC 107.
My Lord is higher than a mountain	JP 170.
My Lord, my life, my love	NEH 411.
My Lord of light who made the worlds	CFW 342, HFP 203, HTC 4.
My Lord, what love is this	HFP 205, LP 363, MP 476 (MP4 828), SF 398, WP 202.
My Lord, you wore no royal crown	HFP 204, HTC 118, LP 139.
My peace I give unto you	MP 477 (MP2 497).
My peace I leave with you	LP 362.
My prayers rise	WP 107 (WP1 54).
My Saviour, how shall I proclaim	H&P 743.
My saviour met death's oppression	WP 99.

324

My song is love unknown	A&M 63, BPW 204, CFW 215, H&P 173, HFP 206, HTC 136, MP 478 (MP1 160), NEH 86, O&N 337, SF 400.
My soul doth magnify the Lord	MP 479 (MP1 159), O&N 338.
My soul glorifies the Lord	CP 201.
My soul is at rest in God alone (Ps. 62)	PFT 62b.
My soul longs for you (Korea)	WP 22 (WP1 12).
My soul longs for you , O my God (Ps. 63)	SF 401.
My soul, there is a country	A&M 191, NEH 412.
My soul waits (I call to you)	LP 75.
My soul will glorify	WP 106 (WP1 55).
My spirit longs for thee	A&M 57, NEH 299.
My trust I place in God's good grace	HTC 387.
Name of all majesty	CFW 306, HFP 207, HTC 218, LP 140, MP 481 (MP2 499).
National Anthem	A&M 293, BPW 712, CFW 68, HTC 592, MP 194 (MP2 374).
Nature with open volume stands	A&M 497, H&P 174, NEH 87.
Nearer, my God, to thee	H&P 451, MP 482 (MP2 502), O&N 339.
New every morning is the love	A&M 2, H&P 636, HFP 208, HTC 270, JP 171, MP 480 (MP1 161), NEH 238, O&N 341.
New songs of celebration render (Ps. 98, 150)	
	A&M 498, H&P 491, HTC 343.
No fear of God before the eyes (Ps. 36)	PFT 36.
No more weeping (Paschal procession)	LP 142.
No other name	LP 365.
No room for the Saviour	CP 202.
No sorrow, no mourning	WP 158
No use knocking on the window	A&M 400.
No weapon formed, or army or king	CP 203, MP 483 (MP2 500).
No weight of gold or silver	CFW 223, HFP 209, HTC 138.
Noah was the only good man	JP 432.
None other lamb, none other name	H&P 271.
No-one but you, Lord	SF 402.
Not all the blood of beasts	HTC 439.
Not far beyond the sea, nor high	A&M 401, H&P 477.
Not for our sins alone	A&M 229.
Not the grandeur of the mountains	CFW 382, HFP 210.
Not to us be glory given (Ps. 115)	PFT 115.
Not unto us	SF 403.
Not what these hands have done	MP 487 (MP4 829).
Not without a cause	SF 404.
Nothing but the love of Jesus	CFW 398.
Nothing can trouble (Ps. 145)	LP 364.
Now at last	HFP 211.
Now be strong and very courageous	JP 172.
Now Christ is risen	WSAM 21.
Now dawns the Sun of righteousness	MP 484 (MP3 722).
Now evening comes to close the day	CFW 461.
Now from the altar of our hearts	A&M 499.
Now I have found the ground	H&P 684, MP 485 (MP2 501).
Now in holy celebration	NEH 166.

Now in reverence and awe	LP 366.
Now in the name of him who sent	H&P 590.
Now is eternal life	A&M 402, H&P 203, NEH 114.
Now is the healing time decreed	NEH 59.
Now Jesus we obey	BPW 446.
Now join we, to praise the Creator	A&M 500, BPW 612, H&P 348.
Now let us from this table rise	A&M 403, BPW 451, H&P 619, HTC 419, O&N 343.
Now let us learn of Christ	CFW 148, HFP 212, HTC 503, LP 141.
Now let us see your beauty, Lord	BPW 87, H&P 534.
Now lives the Lamb of God	BPW 255, CFW 246, HTC 159.
Now may he, who from the dead	BPW 111.
Now, my soul, thy voice upraising	NEH 88.
Now, my tongue, the mystery telling	A&M 252, O&N 344.
Now praise the protector of heaven	HTC 19.
Now Saul was rejected as king	JP 433.
Now tell us, gentle Mary	CP 204.
Now thank we all our God	A&M 205, BPW 128, CFW 199, H&P 566, HFP 213, HTC 33, JP 175, MP 486 (MP1 163), NEH 413, O&N 345, SF 405.
Now that the daylight fills the sky	NEH 151.
Now the day is over	A&M 19, JP 173.
Now the green blade riseth	A&M 501, BPW 257, H&P 204, JP 174, NEH 115, O&N 346.
Now the silence	WSAM 58.
Now through the grace of God	HTC 390.
Now to him who is able	LP 367.
Now unto him who is able to keep you	BPW 115.
Now unto the King	SF 406.
O be glad in the Lord, and rejoice (Ps. 100)	CFW 443, SFP 100j.
O be joyful in the Lord (Ps. 100)	SFP 100n.
O bless the God of Israel	CFW 585, CP 205, HTC 599.
O bless the Lord (O my soul) (Ps. 103)	SFP 103f, WSAM 59.
O bless the Lord, my soul (Ps. 103, 104)	BPW 129, HTC 34.
O bless the Lord, my soul, I sing (Ps. 104)	PFT 104b.
O bless the Lord, O my soul	LP 369.
O bless the Lord, the God (Ps. 148)	LP 368.
O blessed are those who fear the Lord (Ps. 128)	
	SFP 128c.
O blest creator of the light	NEH 150.
O bread to pilgrims given	H&P 620.
O Breath of Life, come sweeping through	BPW 293, CFW 464, H&P 777, HFP 214, HTC 237, MP 488 (MP1 164), O&N 347, SF 407.
O changeless Christ, for ever new	BPW 206, HTC 108.
O Christ, at your first Eucharist	HTC 420.
O Christ of all the ages, come	HTC 262.
O Christ, our hope, our hearts' desire	NEH 129.
O Christ the great foundation	HTC 502.
O Christ, the healer, we have come	H&P 395, WSAM 60.
O Christ the Lord, O Christ the King	H&P 406, NEH 496.
O Christ, the master carpenter	HTC 135.
O Christ, the same, through all	HTC 263, NEH 258.

O Christ, who art the light and day — NEH 61.
O come, all ye faithful (Processional) — A&M 326.
O come all you children to Bethlehem — CP 210.
O come, all ye/you faithful — A&M 34, BPW 169, CFW 672, CP 206, H&P 110, HFP 215, HTC 65/597, JP 176, MP 491 (MP2 504), NEH 30, O&N 348, SF 408.

O come and dwell in me — H&P 293.
O come and join the dance — MP 489 (MP3 723).
O come and let us to the Lord — H&P 567.
O come and stand beneath the cross — NEH 98.
O come, Christians, wonder — CP 207.
O come let us adore him — MP 490 (MP1 165), SF 409.
O come let us sing out to the Lord (Ps. 95) — PFT 95c.
O come, let us sing to the Lord (Ps. 95) — CFW 493.
O come let us worship — MP 492 (MP2 505).
O come, let us worship and bow down — CP 208.
O come, O come, Emmanuel — A&M 26, BPW 144, CP 209, H&P 85, HFP 216, HTC 66, JP 177, MP 493 (MP2 506), NEH 11, O&N 349, SF 410.

O come, our all-victorious Lord — HTC 441.
O crucified Redeemer — A&M 404, H&P 424.
O day of God, draw nigh — A&M 405, BPW 635.
O dearest Lord, your sacred head — A&M 71, BPW 351, H&P 172, HTC 134, NEH 89.

O Father of the fatherless (Father me) — LP 370.
O Father, send you light (Ps. 43) — SFP 43c.
O Father, we bless your name (Panama) — LP 144.
O Father, whose creating hand — H&P 349.
O food of men wayfaring — NEH 300.
O for a thousand tongues to sing — WP 204.
O for the wings to fly afar (Ps. 55) — PFT 55.
O give thanks to the Lord, all you — BPW 61, JP 434, LP 143, MP 497 (MP1 182), SF 413.
O give thanks to the Lord for he is good (Ps. 136) — SFP 136c.

O give thanks to the Lord, for his love (Ps. 96) — LP 371.
O gladsome light, O grace — NEH 247.
O glorious maid, exalted far — NEH 183.
O God beyond all praising — CFW 47, HFP 219, HTC 36, LP 147, O&N 357.

O God, by whose almighty plan — A&M 406, H&P 396.
O God, by whose design — BPW 508.
O God, defender of the poor (Ps. 4) — PFT 4a.
O God, hear me calling (Ps. 61) — PFT 61b.
O God in heaven, whose loving plan — A&M 407, H&P 369.
O God most high — LP 372.
O God my Creator — SF 414.
O God, O Spirit, known to us — H&P 309.
O God of all creation — BPW 60.
O God of awesome majesty — BPW 66.

O God of Bethel, by whose hand	A&M 216, BPW 599, H&P 442, NEH 416, O&N 358.
O God of earth and altar	H&P 426, NEH 492, O&N 359.
O God of Jacob, by whose hand (Ps. 57)	HTC 35.
O God of our forefathers, hear	H&P 554.
O God of truth, whose living word	A&M 222.
O God our Father, who dost make us one	H&P 778.
O God, our help in ages past (Ps. 90)	A&M 99, CFW 50, H&P 358, HFP 220, HTC 37, MP 498 (MP2 503), NEH 417, O&N 360, SF 415.
O God, thy being who can sound	H&P 54.
O God, thy loving care for man	NEH 221.
O God, thy soldier's crown	NEH 218.
O God, unseen yet ever near	A&M 272, HTC 421.
O God, we thank you that your name (Ps. 75)	PFT 75.
O God, what offering shall I give	H&P 801.
O God, whose loving hand has led	NEH 319.
O God, whose will is life and good	A&M 408.
O God, you are my God (Ps. 63)	PFT 63b.
O God, you give to all mankind	HTC 313.
O gracious Light	WSAM 63.
O gracious Lord, be near me (Ps. 6)	PFT 6.
O happy band of pilgrims	A&M 208, HTC 530, NEH 418, O&N 361.
O happy day that fixed my choice	BPW 539, H&P 702, HTC 442, JP 178, MP 499 (MP1 169), O&N 362.
O heavenly Jerusalem	A&M 322.
O heavenly King, look down from above	H&P 504.
O heavenly Word of God on high	NEH 2.
O holy City, seen of John	A&M 409.
O Holy Father, God most dear	A&M 410.
O Holy Ghost, thy people bless	A&M 155.
O Holy Spirit breathe on me	BPW 294, CFW 316, MP 500 (MP1 170).
O Holy Spirit, come to bless	CFW 475, HTC 238.
O Holy Spirit, giver of life	HTC 239.
O Holy Spirit, Lord of grace	A&M 152, H&P 310, NEH 419, O&N 363.
O I will sing unto you with joy	SF 417.
O Jerusalem, look toward the east	NEH 510.
O Jesu, Saviour of mankind	NEH 223.
O Jesus Christ, within me grow	BPW 540, H&P 742.
O Jesus, I have promised	A&M 235, BPW 352, H&P 704, HFP 221, HTC 531, LP 374, MP 501 (MP1 172), NEH 420, O&N 365, SF 418.
O Jesus, King, most wonderful	BPW 353, H&P 269, HTC 484, NEH 386.
O joy of God, we seek you in the morning	HTC 422.
O kind creator, bow thine ear	NEH 60.
O King enthroned on high	A&M 158, H&P 311, NEH 421, O&N 366.

O King most high of earth and sky	NEH 131.
O Lamb of God (Philippines)	WP 24 (WP1 14).
O Lamb of God (Zimbabwe)	WP 64 (WP1 31).
O leave your sheep	CP 212.
O let the Church rejoice (Ps. 147)	CFW 467, PFT 147b.
O let the heart beat high with bliss	NEH 153.
O let the Son of God enfold you	MP 502 (MP2 508), SF 419.
O lift us up, strong Son of God	H&P 427.
O Light and Truth of God (Ps. 43)	PFT 43a.
O little one sweet, O little one mild	H&P 111, NEH 31.
O little town of Bethlehem	A&M 40, BPW 170, CFW 647, CP 213-6, H&P 113, HFP 222, HTC 88, MP 503 (MP2 509), NEH 32, O&N 367, SF 420.
O Lord, all the world belongs (Ps. 82)	BPW 636, LP 148, O&N 368.
O Lord and Master of us all	H&P 717.
O Lord, come quickly when I call (Ps. 141)	PFT 141.
O Lord, enlarge our scanty thought	H&P 568.
O Lord, give me an undivided heart	SF 421.
O Lord, have mercy on me	MP 504 (MP2 510), SF 422.
O Lord, have mercy on us (Brazil)	WP 130 (WP1 66).
O Lord, have mercy upon us (Philippines)	WP 41.
O Lord, hear my prayer (Ps. 130)	SFP 130g.
O Lord, hear my prayer (Ps. 130)	BPW 600, LP 149, SF 423.
O Lord, hear my prayer (Ps. 130 France)	WP 113.
O Lord, how lovely is the sight	BPW 17.
O Lord, how many are my foes (Ps. 3)	SFP 3b.
O Lord, I bring myself to you (Ps. 143)	SFP 143b.
O Lord, I turn my mind to you	MP 531 (MP3 726).
O Lord, I want to sing your praises (Ps. 63)	LP 373.
O Lord Jesus, enfold me	WP 122.
O Lord most Holy God	MP 505 (MP2 511), SF 424.
O Lord my God, O Lord my God (Ps. 22)	HFP 223, LP 375, SFP 22c.
O Lord my God, when I in awesome wonder	BPW 62, JP 179, MP 506 (MP1 173), SF 425, WP 206.
O Lord, my God, you know (Ps. 139)	LP 376, WSAM 61.
O Lord my love, my strength (Ps. 144)	HTC 485.
O Lord, my rock, to you I cry (Ps. 28)	PFT 28.
O Lord my shepherd, lead me (Ps. 23)	PFT 23b.
O Lord of every shining constellation	A&M 411, BPW 130, HTC 314.
O Lord of heaven and earth and sea	A&M 287, BPW 387, CFW 498, H&P 337, HTC 287, NEH 422.
O Lord of hosts, all heaven possessing	NEH 423.
O Lord of life, thy quickening voice	H&P 637.
O Lord of the Kingdom where losing is	BPW 316.
O Lord, our God, how majestic	MP 507 (MP2 512), SF 426.
O Lord our God, you are a great God	SF 427.
O Lord our God, arise	NEH 497.
O Lord our Governor (Ps. 8)	PFT 8c.
O Lord our guardian and our guide (Ps. 17)	CFW 124, HTC 374.
O Lord, our Lord, how excellent	SF 428.
O Lord, our Lord, how majestic (Ps. 8)	CP 217, LP 150, MP 508 (MP3 727), SFP 8d.
O Lord, the clouds are gathering	HFP 224, LP 151, MP 509 (MP3

	728), SF 429.
O Lord, the God who saves me (Ps. 88)	PFT 88.
O Lord, the mansions (Ps. 84)	PFT 84b.
O Lord, the refuge (Ps. 90)	HFP 225, LP 377, SFP 90c.
O Lord, we long to see your face	A&M 412.
O Lord, who came from realms above	HFP 226, HTC 552, MP 525 (MP1 174).
O Lord, who gave the dawn its glow	BPW 650.
O Lord, you are my confidence	WP 33.
O Lord, you are my God	SF 430.
O Lord, you are my light	MP 510 (MP2 513), SF 431.
O Lord, you are the centre (Ps. 16)	LP 378.
O Lord, you gave in love divine	HTC 410.
O Lord, you know my mind (Ps. 139)	SFP 139c.
O Lord, your tenderness	LP 152, MP 511 (MP2 517), SF 433.
O Lord, you're beautiful	MP 513 (MP2 514), SF 432.
O Lord, you're great, you are fabulous	JP 435.
O Lord, you've done great things	MP 512 (MP2 516).
O love divine, how sweet thou art	A&M 124, NEH 424.
O love divine, what hast thou done	H&P 175.
O love, how deep, how broad, how high	A&M 119, BPW 207, H&P 229, NEH 425, O&N 371.
O love of God, how strong and true	BPW 388, H&P 42, MP 514 (MP2 515).
O love that wilt not let me go	BPW 541, H&P 685, HFP 227, HTC 486, MP 515 (MP1 171), SF 434.
O loving Lord, you are forever seeking	BPW 354, H&P 798.
O magnify the Lord	SF 435.
O magnify the Lord with me (Ps. 34)	LP 379.
O Master Christ, draw near to take	HTC 553.
O Master, let me walk with thee	H&P 802.
O, most merciful	NEH 301.
O my Lord, you are most glorious	SF 436.
O my Saviour, lifted	A&M 248, MP 516 (MP2 518), O&N 376, SF 437.
O my soul	WSAM 59.
O people, listen (Ps. 49)	PFT 49b.
O perfect love, all human thought	A&M 280, BPW 509, H&P 370, MP 517 (MP2 520), NEH 320, O&N 388.
O praise God in his holiness	H&P 502.
O praise God in his sanctuary (Ps. 150)	PFT 150c.
O praise him, O praise him	H&P 503.
O praise our great and glorious Lord	NEH 116.
O praise the Lord God (Ps. 117)	LP 153, NEH 426.
O praise the Lord – O my soul (Ps. 104)	SFP 104f.
O praise the Lord, the mighty God	CP 211.
O praise ye the Lord (Ps. 148, 150)	A&M 203, CFW 490, HFP 257, HTC 354, MP 518 (MP2 519), NEH 427, O&N 389, SF 445.
O Prince of peace, whose promised birth	CP 218, HTC 89.
O put your trust in God (Ps. 42)	PFT 42b.
O quickly come, dread judge of all	NEH 13.

O raise your eyes on high and see	A&M 502.
O righteous Lord (Ps. 4)	LP 380, SFP 4b.
O sacred head, once wounded	A&M 68, BPW 223, H&P 176, HTC 139, MP 520 (MP2 521), NEH 90, O&N 390, SF 446.
O Sacrifice of Calvary	HTC 424.
O Saviour Christ, I now confess	MP 519 (MP4 830).
O send your light forth and your truth	BPW 18, H&P 537.
O shout to the Lord (Jubilate) (Ps. 100)	PFT 100c.
O shout to the Lord in triumph (Ps. 100)	LP 154, SFP 100f.
O sing a song of Bethlehem	A&M 413, WSAM 62.
O sing out to the Lord a new song (Ps. 96)	SFP 96d.
O sing to the Lord	WP 16.
O sing to the Lord a new song (Ps. 96)	PFT 96b.
O sing to the Lord a new song (Ps. 98)	PFT 98c.
O sing to the Lord, O sing God a new song	WP 15.
O sinner man, where will you run to	JP 194.
O Son of God, eternal Love	NEH 428.
O sons and daughters, let us sing	A&M 74, H&P 205.
O soul, are you weary and troubled	MP 712 (MP1 249), O&N 392.
O Spirit of the living God	BPW 579, H&P 322, HFP 228, HTC 513.
O splendour of God's glory bright	H&P 461.
O strength and stay upholding all	A&M 7, NEH 248, O&N 393.
O taste and see that the Lord is good (Ps. 34)	CFW 28, LP 381, SF 447, SFP 34c.
O teach me what it meaneth	MP 521 (MP2 522).
O thou, in all thy mighty so far	NEH 429.
O thou not made with hands	A&M 174, H&P 656, NEH 430.
O thou, who at thy Eucharist didst pray	A&M 265, H&P 779, HTC 420, NEH 302, O&N 397.
O thou who camest from above	A&M 233, BPW 355, H&P 745, HFP 226, HTC 596, MP 525 (MP1 174), NEH 431, O&N 398, SF 451.
O thou, who dost accord us	NEH 75.
O thou who makest souls to shine	HTC 512.
O thou who this mysterious bread	H&P 621.
O thou who through this holy week	NEH 96.
O thou, whom once they flocked to hear	H&P 150.
O Trinity, most blessed light	A&M 5, NEH 54.
O Trinity, O Trinity	HFP 229, HTC 6.
O vision blest of heavenly light	NEH 176.
O what a gift	CFW 33, H&P 270, MP 526 (MP1 176), O&N 402.
O what their joy and their glory must be	A&M 186, NEH 432.
O when the saints go marching in	JP 195.
O word immortal of eternal God	NEH 303.
O word of God above	NEH 211.
O Word of God incarnate	H&P 478, MP 527 (MP1 177).
O worship the King (Ps. 104)	A&M 101, BPW 63, CFW 351, H&P 28, HFP 230, HTC 24, LP 155, MP 528 (MP1 178), NEH 433, O&N 405, SF 456, WP 205.

O worship the Lord in the beauty	A&M 49, BPW 22, CFW 92, CP 219, H&P 505, HFP 231, HTC 344, MP 529 (MP1 179), NEH 52, O&N 406, SF 457.
Of all the Spirit's gifts to me	A&M 503, H&P 320.
Of the Father's love begotten (Ps. 148)	A&M 33/325, BPW 145, H&P 79, HTC 56, NEH 33, O&N 354.
Of the glorious body telling	NEH 268.
Off to David's town they go	CP 220.
Oft in danger, oft in woe (Ps. 119)	A&M 210, CFW 530, H&P 715, HTC 524, MP 533 (MP2 524), NEH 434, O&N 356.
Oh for a closer walk with God	A&M 231, HTC 368, MP 494 (MP1 166), NEH 414, O&N 351.
Oh for a heart to praise my God	A&M 230, BPW 538, H&P 536, HFP 217, HTC 483, MP 495 (MP1 167), NEH 74, O&N 352, SF 411.
Oh for a thousand tongues to sing	A&M 125, BPW 59, H&P 744, HFP 218, HTC 219, LP 145, MP 496 (MP1 168), NEH 415, O&N 353, SF 412.
Oh freedom is coming (Freedom is coming)	LP 156.
Oh heaven is in my heart	LP 382, SF 416, WP 207.
Oh how blest the hour, Lord Jesus	H&P 655.
Oh how good is the Lord	CFW 376, O&N 364.
Oh, how he loves you and me	JP 436.
Oh, I will sing unto you with joy	MP 530 (MP2 507).
Oh, isn't it good (Ps. 133)	LP 146, WP 115 (WP1 61).
Oh no! the wine's all gone	JP 437.
Oh! Oh! how good is the Lord	JP 180, MP 532 (MP2 527).
Oh, oh, oh, oh	JP 438.
Oh that mine eyes might closed be	H&P 555.
Oh that you would bless me	SF 448.
Oh the bitter shame and sorrow	H&P 538, HTC 487, MP 524 (MP2 523).
Oh the deep, deep love of Jesus	HTC 465, MP 522 (MP2 525).
Oh the joy of your forgiveness	SF 449.
Oh, the joy of your forgiveness	MP 534 (MP3 724).
Oh, the Lord looked down from his window	JP 184.
Oh, the love that drew salvation's plan	JP 181.
Oh the valleys shall ring	CP 221, MP 523 (MP2 526), SF 450.
Oh, we are more than conquerors	SF 455.
Oh what a day for singing	CP 225.
Oh what a mystery I see	MP 535 (MP3 725).
Oh what shall I do, my Saviour to praise	H&P 569.
Oh where do you think baby Jesus was born	CP 222.
Oh yes I am, oh yes I am	JP 439.
Old man Noah built an ark	JP 440.
Omnipotent Redeemer, our ransomed souls	H&P 440.
On a hill far away	MP 536 (MP1 175), O&N 377.
On a night when all the world	CP 224.
On all the earth thy Spirit shower	H&P 321.
On Calvary's tree	CFW 227, JP 183.
On Christmas night	H&P 115, JP 441, MP 537 (MP4

	831), O&N 380.
On earth an army is marching	LP 157.
On Jordan's bank, the Baptist's cry	A&M 27, BPW 147, CFW 581, CP 226, H&P 84, HTC 601, JP 186, MP 538 (MP2 528), NEH 12, O&N 382.
On the day of Pentecost	A&M 504.
On the eve of Christmas	H&P 116.
On the journey to heaven	WP 80.
On the mountain, in the valley	WP 116.
On the road to Damascus	JP 442.
On this day, the first of days	NEH 256.
On this high feast day	NEH 168.
On this very special night	CP 227.
Once in royal David's city	A&M 46, BPW 172, CFW 646, CP 228, H&P 114, HFP 232, HTC 67, JP 185, MP 539 (MP2 530), NEH 34, O&N 378, SF 438.
Once on a mountain top	H&P 157.
Once, only once, and once for all	A&M 261, NEH 304, O&N 379.
Once there was a house, a busy little	JP 444.
Once upon a time it was many years ago	JP 443.
One and two and three and four	JP 445.
One day when heaven	JP 187, MP 540 (MP1 180).
One holy apostolic church	HTC 514.
One is the body	LP 383.
One more step along the world I go	BPW 356, H&P 746, JP 188, WSAM 64.
One must water, one must weed	CFW 471.
One shall tell another (New wine)	CFW 30, CP 230, MP 541 (MP2 531), SF 439.
One there is, above all others	BPW 560, H&P 149, MP 542 (MP2 532).
One thing I ask, one thing I seek (Ps. 84)	LP 385, SF 440.
One thing I know, that Christ has healed	HFP 233.
One, two, three, Jesus loves me	JP 189.
One who is all unfit to count	H&P 539.
Only a boy called David	JP 190.
Only begotten, word of God eternal	NEH 210.
Only by grace	LP 386, SF 441.
Only one thing I ask (Ps. 84)	LP 384.
Only the fool will say (Ps. 53)	PFT 53, SFP 53.
Onward, Christian soldiers	A&M 333, CFW 551, H&P 718, HTC 532, MP 543 (MP4 832), NEH 435, O&N 383, SF 442.
Open, Lord, my inward ear	H&P 540.
Open my eyes that I may see	MP 544 (MP2 533), O&N 385.
Open our eyes, Lord	BPW 359, CFW 612, LP 158, MP 545 (MP1 181), O&N 386, SF 443.
Open the gates of righteousness (Ps. 118)	PFT 118a.
Open this book that we may see your word	BPW 103.
Open thou mine eyes	MP 546 (MP1 205).
Open your eyes, see the glory	LP 159, MP 547 (MP3 729), SF 444.

Our blest Redeemer, ere he breathed	A&M 151, H&P 312, MP 548 (MP2 529), O&N 399.
Our confidence is in the Lord (Ps. 452)	LP 387, SF 452.
Our eyes have seen the glory	JP 191, MP 549 (MP2 535).
Our Father, by whose name	A&M 505, H&P 371.
Our Father God, thy name we praise	BPW 104.
Our Father in heaven (Marsh)	MP 550 (MP2 534).
Our Father in heaven (Mayor)	LP 388.
Our Father in heaven (Rolinson)	LP 389.
Our Father which art in heaven	MP 661 (MP2 586), O&N 400.
Our Father who is in heaven (Caribbean)	JP 191, MP 552 (MP2 537), WP 117 (WP1 62).
Our Father, whose creative love	H&P 372.
Our God eternal, reigning (Ps. 90)	PFT 90a.
Our God has turned to his people	CP 229.
Our God is an awesome God	SF 453.
Our God, our help in ages past	BPW 389.
Our great Redeemer, as he breathed	HTC 241.
Our harvest day is over for yet another	JP 193.
Our Lord, his passion ended	A&M 91, H&P 323.
Our Saviour Christ once knelt in prayer	HTC 116.
Out of darkness let light shine (Ps. 80)	HTC 447.
Out of my bondage	MP 551 (MP2 536).
Out of our failure to create (Ps. 130)	PFT 130a.
Out of the depths I cry (Ps. 130)	PFT 130c.
Out of the depths I cry to thee	H&P 429.
Out of your great love	SF 454.
Over desert, hill and valley	CP 223.
Palms of glory, raiment bright	A&M 307, NEH 230.
Panama praise (O Father, we bless)	LP 144.
Paschal procession (No more weeping)	LP 142.
Pass through the gates	CP 231.
Passover God, we remember your faithful	BPW 447.
Patiently waiting for you, O Lord	WP 120.
Peace be with you, Christian people	WP 7 (WP1 4).
Peace be with you, peace be with you	WP 108 (WP1 56).
Peace be with you all, we sing	HFP 234, LP 390.
Peace, I give to you	JP 196, MP 553 (MP2 538).
Peace is flowing like a river	MP 554 (MP1 183), O&N 408, SF 458.
Peace like a river	SF 459.
Peace, perfect peace	BPW 561, HTC 467, MP 555 (MP1 184), O&N 410.
Peace, perfect peace, is the gift of	BPW 112, O&N 411.
Peace to you	LP 391, MP 556 (MP3 730), SF 460.
People walking in the dark	CP 232.
Personent hodie (God is love)	BPW 45, CFW 368, H&P 220, HFP 93, HTC 311, LP 50, O&N 152.
Peter and James and John in a sailboat	JP 197.
Peter and John went to pray	JP 198, MP 598 (MP1 199), O&N 412.
Peter feared the cross for himself	A&M 414.
Play your pipe, bang your drum	CP 233.
Pour out, I will pour out my spirit	LP 392.

Praise the Lord, praise the Lord (Ps. 148)	SFP 148d.
Praise the Lord, rise up rejoicing	A&M 416.
Praise the Lord, sing him a new song (Ps. 150)	
	SFP 150f.
Praise the Lord who reigns above	H&P 55.
Praise the Lord with joyful cry (Ps. 150)	H&P 508, PFT 150a.
Praise the Lord, you heavens (Ps. 51, 148)	A&M 195, CFW 284, H&P 15, HFP 240, HTC 583, NEH 437, O&N 421.
Praise the name of Jesus	CFW 401, MP 566 (MP1 189), SF 468.
Praise to God, almighty maker	BPW 414, H&P 582.
Praise to God and peace on earth	CP 237.
Praise to God in the highest	BPW 69.
Praise to God the Father	CP 238.
Praise to God, whose word was spoken	NEH 438.
Praise to our God	CP 239.
Praise to the Holiest in the height	A&M 117, BPW 562, H&P 231, HFP 241, HTC 140, MP 563 (MP1 191), NEH 439, O&N 423, SF 469.
Praise to the living God	H&P 56.
Praise to the Lord (Ps. 34)	SFP 34d.
Praise to the Lord our God	JP 205.
Praise to the Lord, sing alleluia (Ps. 148)	LP 165.
Praise to the Lord, the almighty (Ps. 103)	A&M 207, BPW 68, CFW 89, H&P 16, HFP 242, HTC 40, MP 564 (MP1 192), NEH 440, O&N 424, SF 470.
Praise to the mighty Lord	CP 240.
Praise we now the Word of grace	A&M 417, O&N 425.
Praise we offer, Lord of glory	HTC 346.
Praise ye the Lord, praise ye the Lord	SF 471.
Praise ye the Lord, tis good to raise	H&P 338.
Praise ye the Lord, ye servants of the	H&P 509.
Praise you, Lord	BPW 390, MP 565 (MP2 541), SF 472.
Pray for the church, afflicted	H&P 556.
Pray that Jerusalem may have	H&P 510, NEH 441.
Prayer is like a telephone	JP 448.
Prayer is the soul's sincere desire	H&P 557, HTC 372, MP 567 (MP1 190), NEH 442.
Prayer to a heart of lowly love	BPW 601.
Prepare the way (Clear the road)	LP 22, SF 63.
Prepare the way for Jesus to return	CP 241.
Prepare the way of the Lord	CP 242, SF 473.
Prepare the way, the way for the Lord	CP 243.
Prince of peace, counsellor	LP 166.
Prince of peace, you are	SF 474.
Pull back the veil on the dawn of creation	BPW 208.
Purify my heart	LP 393, SF 475, WP 209.
Put on the sword of the Spirit	CFW 541.
Put peace into each other's hands	BPW 637, HFP 243.
Put thou thy trust in God	A&M 223, O&N 428.
Put your hand in the hand of the man	JP 206.

Ring the bells, ring the bells	CP 253.
Rise and hear! The Lord is speaking	A&M 509.
Rise and shine, and give God his glory	JP 210.
Rise up, O men of God	A&M 418, O&N 437.
Rise up, you champions of God	SF 486.
Risen Lord, whose name we cherish	HTC 500, LP 173.
River, wash over me	LP 174, MP 581 (MP2 548), SF 487.
Roar the waves	HTC 289.
Rock of ages, cleft for me (revised)	HTC 444.
Rock of ages, cleft for me (traditional)	A&M 135, BPW 545, H&P 273, HFP 250, HTC 593, MP 582 (MP1 197), NEH 445, O&N 438, SF 488.
Roll the stone, roll the stone	JP 449.
Round me falls the night	A&M 18, HTC 279, NEH 249, O&N 439.
Royal sons of a royal king	CP 254
Safe in the hands of God (Ps. 27)	SFP 27b
Safe in the shadow of the Lord (Ps. 91)	CFW 395, HTC 445, MP 583 (MP2 549), PFT 91a, WSAM 68.
Said Judas to Mary, now what will you do	JP 211.
Saints of God, lo, Jesu's people	NEH 179.
Salvation is found in no-one else	CFW 397.
Sanna	LP 395, WP 126 (WP1 63).
Saul had made	JP 450.
Save me, O God, hear my prayer (Ps. 54)	PFT 54.
Saviour, again to thy dear name (Ps. 105)	A&M 15, CFW 553, H&P 643, HTC 281, MP 584 (MP4 833), NEH 250, O&N 441.
Saviour, and can it be	H&P 541.
Saviour, blessed Saviour	H&P 274.
Saviour Christ, in praise we name him	HTC 216.
Saviour Christ, in mercy come	BPW .
Saviour eternal, health and life	NEH 502.
Saviour from sin, I wait to prove	H&P 747.
Saviour of the world	JP 216, MP 585 (MP2 550).
Saviour, thy dying love	MP 586 (MP2 551).
Saviour, who didst healing give	NEH 194.
Search for the infant born in a stable	BPW 209.
Search me, O God (Ps. 139)	JP 212, LP 396, MP 587 (MP1 200), O&N 442, SFP 139e.
See amid the winter's snow	BPW 173, CP 256, H&P 117, HFP 252, HTC 90, JP 213, MP 588 (MP2 552), O&N 443, SF 489.
See, Christ was wounded for our sake	BPW 229, HTC 137.
See him come	SF 490.
See him lying on a bed of straw	BPW 174, CFW 656, CP 257, HFP 253, HTC 91, JP 214, MP 589 (MP2 553), O&N 444, SF 491, WSAM 69.
See him on the cross of shame	MP 592 (MP2 554).
See his glory	SF 492.
See how great a flame aspires	H&P 781.
See Israel's gentle Shepherd stand	H&P 588.
See, Jesus, thy disciples see	H&P 763.

338

See the conqueror mounts in triumph	A&M 88, HTC 181, NEH 132, O&N 446.
See the dawn appearing	CP 258.
See the feast our God prepares	CFW 17, HFP 262.
See the man walking, see the man walking	JP 451.
See this bread	LP 398.
See, to us a child is born	CP 259, JP 452.
See where our great High Priest	H&P 622.
Seek ye first the Kingdom of God	BPW 357, CFW 168, H&P 138, JP 215, MP 590 (MP1 201), O&N 445, SF 493, WSAM 70.
Seek ye the Lord all ye people	MP 591 (MP1 202).
Selfless love (He gave his life)	BPW 435, CFW 34, HFP 109, HTC 405, LP 56, MP 214 (MP2 387).
Send forth the gospel	BPW 584, MP 593 (MP2 555).
Send me, Jesus	WP 151 (WP1 75).
Send me, Lord (Thuma mina)	LP 177, WP 151 (WP1 74).
Send me out from here, Lord	CFW 425, LP 176, MP 594 (MP2 556).
Send more labourers	LP 178.
Send out the gospel! Let it sound	HTC 517.
Sent away to a cattle shed	CP 255.
Sent by the Lord am I	LP 399, WP 131 (WP1 67).
Sent forth by God's blessing, our true	A&M 510, BPW 448, WSAM 67.
Servant of all, to toil for man	H&P 383.
Servant of God, remember	NEH 80.
Servants of the living Lord (Ps. 113)	PFT 113a.
Set my spirit free	MP 595 (MP2 557), SF 494.
Shall we not love thee, mother dear	NEH 184.
Shalom, my friends	BPW 114, JP 217, O&N 448.
Shalom, shalom	LP 400.
She danced amid the city lights	WP 132.
Shepherd divine, our wants relieve	A&M 228, H&P 558.
Shepherds came, their praises bringing	BPW 192, CFW 670, CP 260, HFP 254, HTC 74.
Shepherds, leave your drowsy sheep	CP 262.
Shepherds, leave your flocks	CP 263.
Shepherds, wake to news of joy	CP 264.
Shepherds watch and wise men wonder	BPW 175.
Shine bright, dazzle, dazzle	JP 453.
Shine thou upon us, Lord	H&P 560.
Shout aloud, girls and boys	CP 265.
Shout for joy and sing (Ps. 100)	SFP 100k.
Shout for joy and sing, let your praises	SF 495.
Shout for joy and sing, serve the Lord (Ps. 100)	LP 179.
Shout for joy and sing your praises (Ps. 100)	LP 401, SF 496.
Shout for joy, loud and long	CFW 260, HTC 348.
Shout it in the street	H&P 782.
Shout, shout joyfully (Ps. 100)	LP 180, SFP 100m.
Shout with joy to God (Ps. 66)	SFP 66b.
Show me how much you love me (Ps. 119)	LP 402, SFP 119f.
Show me the way (When I'm confused)	LP 222.
Show me your hands	LP 397, WSAM 72.

Show us your strength (Ps. 118)	LP 48.
Show us your ways, O Lord (Ps. 25)	H&P 133, SFP 25b.
Show your power, O Lord	LP 181, MP 596 (MP3 734), SF 497.
Silent, I have waited (Ps. 39)	PFT 39.
Silent night, holy night	BPW 176, CFW 648, CP 266, H&P 112, HFP 255, HTC 95, JP 219, MP 597 (MP2 558), NEH 35, O&N 449, SF 498.
Silent the earth when God arose (Ps. 76)	PFT 76.
Silver and gold (Ps. 34)	MP 598 (MP1 199), O&N 142.
Silver star shining out over Bethlehem	CP 267.
Sing a new song, alleluia (Ps. 149)	CFW 535, SFP 149b.
Sing a new song of glory (Ps. 96)	PFT 96a.
Sing a new song of thanksgiving	CP 268.
Sing a new song, sing a new song	H&P 332.
Sing a new song to the Lord (Ps. 98)	CFW 420, CP 271, H&P 57, HTC 349, JP 454, MP 599 (MP1 203), O&N 450, PFT 98b, WSAM 73.
Sing a song, a joyful song	CFW 654, CP 269.
Sing, all creation, sing to God (Ps. 100)	PFT 100b.
Sing alleluia forth in duteous praise	A&M 188.
Sing alleluia to the Lord	CFW 565, CP 270, HTC S22, LP 182, MP 601 (MP1 204), SF 499.
Sing alleluya forth ye saints on high	NEH 446.
Sing and celebrate, Christ is risen	JP 457.
Sing and celebrate, God gave Jesus	JP 456.
Sing choirs of heaven	WSAM 22.
Sing glory, glory	CFW 254, CP 272.
Sing hallelujah to the Lord	CFW 565, CP 270, HTC S22, LP 182, MP 601 (MP1 204), O&N 451, SF 499.
Sing heaven, shout for joy	CP 273.
Sing his praises	CFW 378.
Sing hosanna! (Give me oil in my lamp)	BPW 530, MP 167 (MP1 58).
Sing how the age-long promise	NEH 156.
Sing lullaby	CP 274, HTC 92.
Sing merrily to God (Ps. 81)	PFT 81.
Sing my soul, sing to God	WP 13 (WP1 8).
Sing, my tongue, the glorious battle	A&M 59, BPW 226, H&P 177, HTC 142, NEH 78.
Sing, my tongue, the Saviour's glory	BPW 449, H&P 624.
Sing of his victory	WP 134 (WP1 68).
Sing of the Lord's goodness (Ps. 149)	HFP 256, LP 183, WSAM 77.
Sing out to the Lord a new song (Ps. 96)	SFP 96c.
Sing praise and bless the Lord (France)	WP 90.
Sing praise to God the Father	JP 455.
Sing praise to God who reigns above	A&M 193, H&P 511, NEH 447.
Sing praise to the Lord (Ps. 148, 150)	BPW 70, CFW 490, HFP 257, HTC 354, LP 184, MP 518 (MP2 519).
Sing praises to our God (Ps. 47)	SFP 47d.
Sing praises to the Lord	LP 403.
Sing praises unto God	SF 500.
Sing, sing, sing to the Lord	WSAM 74.

Sing to God new songs of worship (Ps. 98)	CFW 249, HTC 352, LP 187, MP 600 (MP2 560), PFT 98a, SFP 98a.
Sing to him in whom creation	H&P 324, NEH 142.
Sing to the great Jehovah's praise	H&P 360.
Sing to the Lord a joyful song	H&P 17.
Sing to the Lord, be joyful in praise	SF 501.
Sing to the Lord glad hymns of praise	NEH 316.
Sing to the Lord with a song (Ps. 96)	LP 185, SFP 96e.
Sing to the Lord with joyful voice	H&P 61.
Sing to the world	LP 186.
Sing unto the Lord a new song	SF 502.
Sing we a song of high revolt	A&M 419, BPW 638.
Sing we of the blessed mother	NEH 185.
Sing we praise to God the King (Ps. 93)	CFW 333.
Sing we the King who is coming to reign	BPW 318, H&P 244, JP 218, MP 602 (MP1 206).
Sing we the praises of the great	A&M 315.
Sing we the song of those who stand	H&P 821.
Sing ye faithful, sing with gladness	NEH 448.
Singabahambayo (On earth an army)	LP 157.
Sion's daughters, sons of Jerusalem	NEH 212, NEH 522.
Six hundred years old was the preacher	JP 458.
Siya Hamba (we are marching)	LP 215.
Sleep, Lord Jesus	BPW .
Sleepers, wake! the watch-cry pealeth	A&M 32.
Small wonder the star	CP 261.
So freely flows the endless love	LP 189, MP 603 (MP2 561), SF 503.
So I've made up my mind	CFW 143.
So we're marching along	CFW 543, JP 459.
Soft the evening shadows fall	CP 275.
Soften my heart, Lord, I want to meet	LP 405, SF 504.
Soften my heart, Lord, soften my heart	LP 188, MP 606 (MP3 738), SF 505.
Softly, a shepherd is singing	CP 276.
Soldiers marching	CP 278.
Soldiers of Christ, arise	A&M 219, BPW 580, CFW 529, H&P 719, HFP 258, HTC 533, MP 604 (MP1 207), NEH 449, O&N 454, SF 506.
Soldiers of the cross, arise	HTC 534.
Soldiers, who are Christ's below	A&M 302, NEH 450, O&N 455.
Some people laugh, some people sing	JP 462.
Some trust in chariots (Ps. 20)	SFP 20d.
Someone's brought a loaf of bread	JP 220.
Sometimes a light surprises	A&M 108, H&P 571.
Sometimes I'm naughty	JP 460.
Sometimes problems can be BIG	JP 461.
Son of God, eternal Saviour	A&M 132, BPW 639, HTC 102, NEH 498.
Son of God, if thy free grace	H&P 720.
Son of God, this is our praise song	SF 507.
Son of the Lord most high	A&M 420, BPW 210, H&P 152.
Songs of gladness, songs of gladness	CP 277.
Songs of praise the angels sang	A&M 196, H&P 512, HFP 259, HTC 350, NEH 451, O&N 457.

Songs of thankfulness and praise	A&M 53, HTC 98, NEH 56, O&N 458.
Sons of the Holy One, bright	NEH 192.
Soon and very soon	CFW 566, CP 279, JP 221, LP 190, MP 605 (MP1 208).
Sorry, Lord, for all the things	JP 463.
Soul of my Saviour, sanctify	NEH 305.
Souls of men, why will ye scatter	A&M 251, HTC 443, MP 607 (MP2 559).
Sound on the trumpet (Ps. 126)	CP 280, SFP 126d.
Sovereign Lord, I am yours	LP 404.
Sovereign Lord, in all the earth (Ps. 8)	SFP 8e.
Sovereign Lord, Sovereign Lord	HTC S9, SF 508.
Speak forth your word, O Father	BPW 581.
Speak, Lord, in the stillness	BPW 105, CFW 174, HFP 260, HTC 253, MP 608 (MP2 562).
Spies were sent out to view	JP 464.
Spirit, breathe on us	SF 509.
Spirit divine, attend/inspire our prayer	CFW 309, H&P 327, HFP 261, HTC 240, MP 614 (MP2 563).
Spirit of faith, by faith be mine	HFP 263, WSAM 75.
Spirit of faith, come down	H&P 325.
Spirit of God, descend upon my heart	H&P 313.
Spirit of God divine	MP 610 (MP2 564).
Spirit of God most high (Ps. 133)	CFW 480, HFP 264, HTC 242.
Spirit of God, please fill me	JP 465.
Spirit of God, rest on your people	LP 406.
Spirit of God, show me Jesus	LP 191, MP 609 (MP3 736).
Spirit of God, unseen as the wind	BPW 295, CFW 609.
Spirit of God within me	BPW 296, H&P 294, HTC 243.
Spirit of holiness	CFW 323, HTC 246, MP 611 (MP2 565), WSAM 76.
Spirit of Jesus	WP 110.
Spirit of mercy, truth and love	A&M 89, NEH 143, O&N 459.
Spirit of the living God (Armstrong)	BPW 298, CFW 317, HTC S23, JP 222, MP 613 (MP1 209), SF 511, WSAM 78.
Spirit of the living God (Iverson)	H&P 295, O&N 460, SF 510.
Spirit of the living God, move among us	BPW 299, CFW 318, HTC S24.
Spirit of the living God . . . fill me anew	MP 612 (MP3 737).
Spirit of truth, essential God	H&P 480.
Spirit of wisdom, turn our eyes	H&P 385.
Spouse of Christ, whose earthly conflict	NEH 523.
Spread, O spread, thou mighty word	NEH 482.
Spread the table of the Lord	BPW 450, H&P 625.
Spring has come for us today	HTC 160.
Stand, soldier of the cross	H&P 591.
Stand up and bless the Lord (Montgomery)	A&M 201, H&P 513, HTC 351, MP 615 (MP1 210), NEH 452, O&N 462, SF 512.
Stand up and bless the Lord (Silver)	JP 224, MP 616 (MP2 566).
Stand up, clap hands	CFW 274, JP 225.
Stand up! stand up for Jesus	A&M 221, H&P 721, HTC 535, MP 617 (MP1 211), NEH 453, O&N 463, SF 513.

Teach me your way (Undivided heart) (Ps. 25)

 LP 195, SFP 86b.

Tell all the world of Jesus BPW 582, CFW 434, HFP 267,

 HTC 521, LP 196.

Tell his praise in song and story (Ps. 34) BPW 563, HTC 41, PFT 34a.

Tell me the old, old story H&P 232, JP 227, MP 628

 (MP2 572).

Tell me the stories of Jesus H&P 153, JP 228, MP 629

 (MP2 573).

Tell me, why do you weep CFW 590, CP 287.

Tell my people I love them MP 630 (MP2 574).

Tell out my soul A&M 422, BPW 391, CFW 187,

 CP 285, H&P 86, HFP 268,

 HTC 42, JP 229, LP 197, MP 631

 (MP2 215), NEH 186, O&N 475,

 SF 520.

Ten thousand times ten thousand A&M 189, HTC 576, O&N 476.

Thank you for ev'ry new good morning JP 230.

Thank you for the cross LP 411, MP 632 (MP3 739), SF 522.

Thank you for the love that our mums JP 467.

Thank you, God, for sending Jesus JP 233, MP 638 (MP2 571).

Thank you Jesus BPW 392, JP 235, MP 633

 (MP1 216), SF 523.

Thank you, Jesus, for your love MP 634 (MP2 578).

Thank you Lord MP 635 (MP2 575).

Thank you, Lord, for this fine day JP 232, SF 524.

Thank you, Lord, for this new day BPW 643.

Thank you Lord, for your presence MP 636 (MP2 576).

Thank you O Lord of earth and heaven (Ps. 75)

 HTC 43.

Thank you, thank you, Jesus JP 231.

Thanks be to God (Kendrick) CFW 539, MP 637 (MP2 577),

 SF 521.

Thanks be to God who gives us LP 412.

Thanks be to God whose church on earth H&P 570.

Thanks to God whose word was spoken (Ps. 33)

 A&M 423, BPW 106, CFW 621,

 H&P 483, HTC 255.

That mighty resurrected Word H&P 658.

The advent of our God NEH 14.

The advent of our King A&M 25, O&N 479.

The angel Gabriel from heaven came BPW 177, CP 286, H&P 87,

 O&N 480.

The battle belongs to the Lord HFP 140, LP 90, MP 639

 (MP2 579), SF 237.

The bells ring out at Christmas-time CP 288.

The best book to read is the Bible JP 234.

The Bread of life WSAM 79.

The brightness of God's glory HTC 221.

The children of the Hebrews NEH 508.

The Church of Christ in every age BPW 613, H&P 804.

The Church of God a Kingdom is A&M 169, NEH 483, O&N 482.

The Church triumphant in thy love NEH 198.

The Church's one foundation A&M 170, BPW 393, H&P 515,

 HTC 501, MP 640 (MP1 217),

	NEH 484, O&N 483, SF 525.
The Church's one foundation (Bilbrough)	SF 526.
The darkness turns to dawn	CP 289-290, HTC 68.
The day draws on with golden light	NEH 100.
The day of resurrection	A&M 75, H&P 208, HTC 161, NEH 117, O&N 486.
The day thou gavest/you gave us (Ps. 527)	A&M 16, BPW 319, CFW 436, H&P 648, HFP 269, HTC 280, JP 236, MP 641 (MP1 218), NEH 252, O&N 487, SF 527.
The deer longs for pure flowing streams	WP 147.
The duteous day now closeth	A&M 17, H&P 647, NEH 253.
The earth and its fulness (Ps. 24)	LP 413, SFP 24g.
The earth is the Lord's (Ps. 24)	LP 128, MP 642 (MP3 748), SF 528, SFP 24f.
The earth is the Lord's and all that is in it (Ps. 24)	
	PFT 24c.
The earth is yours, O God (Ps. 65)	CFW 514, HTC 290, SFP 65c.
The earth was dark (lights to the world)	CFW 447, CP 291, HFP 270, LP 198, MP 643 (MP3 747).
The eternal gates lift up their heads	NEH 133.
The eternal gifts of Christ the King	A&M 297, NEH 213.
The everlasting Lord is King (Ps. 97)	PFT 97.
The family table	WSAM 80.
The fields are white unto harvest time	JP 237.
The first day of the week	A&M 424, H&P 576.
The first nowell the angel did say	BPW 178, CFW 109, CP 292, H&P 119, HFP 271, HTC 93, JP 238, MP 644 (MP2 580), NEH 36, O&N 489, SF 539.
The fool whose heart declares (Ps. 14)	PFT 14.
The glory of our King was seen	H&P 161.
The God of Abraham praise	A&M 331, BPW 131, H&P 452, HTC 9, MP 645 (MP2 581), NEH 148, O&N 490, SF 530.
The God of heaven thunders (Ps. 29)	SFP 29b.
The God of love my shepherd is (Ps. 23)	A&M 110, H&P 43, NEH 77, O&N 491.
The God we seek	CP 293.
The God who rules this earth	A&M 425.
The God who sent the prophets	H&P 454.
The God whom earth and sea and sky	A&M 309, O&N 492.
The grace of life is theirs	BPW 210, H&P 373.
The grace of the Lord	CFW 358.
The great creator of the worlds	A&M 511.
The great God of heaven is come down	NEH 37.
The great love of God	H&P 45.
The greatest thing in all my life	JP 239, MP 646 (MP1 219).
The growing limbs of God the Son	NEH 45.
The hands of Christ, the caring hands	HFP 272, HTC 141, WSAM 81.
The head that once was crowned	A&M 141, BPW 274, CFW 287, H&P 209, HFP 273, HTC 182, MP 647 (MP1 220), NEH 134, O&N 493, SF 531.
The heavenly child in stature grows	A&M 50, O&N 494.

The heavenly Word, proceeding forth	A&M 253, NEH 269.
The heavens declare the glory (Silver) (Ps. 19)	
	HTC 254, MP 648 (MP2 598).
The heavens declare thy glory, Lord (Ps. 19)	A&M 168, H&P 481.
The heaviness of travel	CP 294.
The highest and the holiest place	NEH 165.
The holly and the ivy are dancing	H&P 88.
The holly and the ivy, for they are both	CP 295, O&N 495.
The journey of life	BPW 542, CFW 210, JP 468.
The joy of the Lord is my strength	JP 240.
The King is among us	BPW 20, CFW 6, LP 199, MP 650 (MP1 222), SF 532.
The King of glory comes (King of Kings)	LP 104, O&N 496, SF 319.
The King of love my Shepherd is (Ps. 23)	A&M 126, BPW 394, CFW 27, H&P 69, HFP 274, HTC 44, JP 241, MP 649 (MP1 221), NEH 457, SF 533, SFP 23d.
The King shall come when morning dawns	BPW 320.
The Kingdom is upon you	A&M 512.
The Kingdom of God	BPW 321, H&P 139, HFP 275, HTC 333, LP 194, MP 651 (MP2 582).
The Lamb's high banquet we await	NEH 101.
The law of Christ alone can make us free	BPW 640, H&P 407.
The Law of God is life to choose (Ps. 1)	PFT 1b.
The light of Christ has come	CFW 8, CP 296, MP 652 (MP1 223), O&N 498.
The light of the morning is breaking	BPW 146.
The little baby Jesus is asleep	CP 297.
The Lord ascendeth up on high	H&P 210, NEH 135.
The Lord has given	MP 653 (MP2 583), SF 534.
The Lord has led forth (Ps. 105)	CFW 121, LP 200, MP 654 (MP3 741), SF 535, SFP 105a.
The Lord has need of me	JP 242.
The Lord is a great and mighty King	CFW 59, MP 655 (MP1 224).
The Lord is a mighty King	LP 201.
The Lord is building Jerusalem (Ps. 147)	SFP 147e.
The Lord is full of compassion (Ps. 103)	PFT 103c.
The Lord is here	WSAM 82.
The Lord is King he is mighty in battle	CFW 537, CP 299, MP 657 (MP3 742).
The Lord is King! I own his power	BPW 543.
The Lord is King! lift up thy/your voice (Ps. 58, 97)	
	A&M 107, BPW 322, CFW 290, H&P 58, HFP 276, HTC 183, MP 656 (MP2 226), O&N 499.
The Lord is marching out	LP 131, SF 536.
The Lord is my light (Ps. 27)	LP 414, WP 148 (WP1 76).
The Lord is my shepherd (Ps. 23)	PFT 23c.
The Lord is my shepherd (Ps. 23)	H&P 44, JP 244.
The Lord is my shepherd, he knows (Ps. 23)	
	SFP 23e.
The Lord is my strength	MP 658 (MP1 225).
The Lord is my strength and my song	LP 416.
The Lord is risen indeed	A&M 84, JP 469, NEH 118,

	O&N 501.
The Lord Jehovah reigns	H&P 59.
The Lord made man, the Scriptures tell	HTC 143.
The Lord my pasture shall prepare	A&M 111, NEH 458.
The Lord my shepherd rules my life (Ps. 23)	
	CFW 137, HFP 278, HTC 45, LP 203, PFT 23a, SFP 23a, SFP 23a.
The Lord reigns (Ps. 97)	LP 417, MP 659 (MP2 584), NEH 266, SFP 99b.
The Lord was born (Belize boogie)	LP 202.
The Lord whom earth and sea and sky	NEH 181.
The Lord will come (Ps. 72)	A&M 29, H&P 245, NEH 15, O&N 504.
The Lord your God is in your midst	LP 415, SF 538.
The Lord's day	WSAM 83.
The Lord's my shepherd, I'll not want (Ps. 23)	
	A&M 426, BPW 395, JP 243, NEH 459, HFP 279, H&P 70, HTC 591, MP 660 (MP1 227), SF 537,
The Lord's prayer	MP 661 (MP2 586).
The love of Christ who died for me	MP 662 (MP4 834).
The majesty of mountains (Ps. 104)	PFT 104c, SFP 104c.
The maker of the sun and moon	NEH 38.
The Most Excellency is Jesus	WP 149.
The most important thing for us	JP 470.
The nations are waiting	SF 539.
The new commandment	CFW 445, HTC S26.
The people that in darkness sat	A&M 52.
The people who in darkness walked	CP 298, HTC 71.
The price is paid	CFW 233, LP 206, MP 663 (MP2 587), SF 540.
The promises of God are pure (Ps. 12)	PFT 12b.
The prophets spoke in days of old	A&M 513.
The race that long in darkness pined	H&P 89, NEH 57, O&N 505.
The right hand of God is writing	H&P 408, LP 418, WP 150 (WP1 73).
The royal banners forward go	A&M 58, BPW 228, H&P 179, NEH 79.
The saint who first found grace to pen	NEH 163.
The Saviour died, but rose again	H&P 233.
The Saviour, when to heaven he rose	H&P 211.
The Saviour's precious blood	H&P 410.
The Servant King (From heaven you came)	BPW 529, CFW 449, CP 91, HFP 85, LP 40, MP 162 (MP2 361), SF 120.
The shepherd guards his sheep	CP 300.
The shepherds found the stable	JP 471.
The sinless one to Jordan came	NEH 58.
The sky shall unfold	CP 301.
The Son of consolation	NEH 167.
The Son of God proclaim (Ps. 67)	A&M 427, BPW 455, H&P 627, HFP 280, HTC 415, O&N 513.

The Son of God rides out to war	HTC 577.
The song of the supper	WSAM 86.
The spacious firmament on high	A&M 103, H&P 339, NEH 267, O&N 514.
The Spirit came, as promised	BPW 297, CFW 314, HTC 244.
The Spirit lives to set us free	JP 472, MP 664 (MP2 588), O&N 515.
The Spirit of the Lord	LP 205, MP 665 (MP3 746), SF 548.
The star in the east shone bright	CP 302.
The stars danced, the angels sang	CP 303.
The steadfast love of the Lord (Ps. 37)	CFW 373, JP 250, MP 666 (MP1 229), O&N 517, SF 549, SFP 37b.
The story has broken	CP 304.
The strife is past/o'er, the battle done	A&M 78, BPW 261, CFW 243, H&P 214, HFP 281, HTC 163, MP 670 (MP2 585), NEH 119, O&N 518.
The sun is sinking fast	A&M 14.
The time was early evening	WSAM 86.
The trumpets sound, the angels sing	HFP 282, LP 419, MP 667 (MP4 835), SF 550.
The victory of our God is won	HFP 283.
The virgin Mary had a baby boy	CFW 655, CP 305, HTC S25, JP 251, O&N 519.
The voice of God goes out to all	H&P 140.
The will of God to mark my way (Ps. 119)	CFW 607, HFP 277, PFT 119a.
The wise man built his house upon	JP 252.
The wise may bring their learning	CFW 105, CP 306, JP 253, O&N 520.
The word of God is living and active	CFW 610, JP 474.
The Word of the Lord is planted	JP 473.
The works of the Lord are created	HTC 26.
The world was in darkness	MP 668 (MP4 836).
Thee we adore, O hidden Saviour	A&M 254, NEH 308.
Thee will I love, my God and King	H&P 40.
Thee will I praise with all my heart	H&P 41.
Then I saw a new heaven and earth	MP 669 (MP2 589).
Then the glory	WSAM 84.
There are hundreds of sparrows	BPW 565, CFW 275, JP 246.
There are moments	WP 55.
There he stood, Goliath, mighty man	JP 475.
There in God's garden stands the tree	A&M 514.
There is a book (who runs may read)	H&P 340.
There is a fountain	HTC 144, MP 671 (MP3 744).
There is a green hill far away	A&M 137, BPW 230, CFW 219, H&P 178, HFP 284, HTC 148, JP 245, LP 204, MP 674 (MP1 230), NEH 92, O&N 507, SF 542.
There is a land of pure delight	A&M 190, BPW 323, H&P 822, HTC 575, NEH 460, O&N 508.
There is a name I love to hear	MP 672 (MP1 232), SF 543.
There is a Redeemer	CFW 228, CP 307, HFP 285, LP 207, MP 673 (MP2 590), SF 544, WP 212.

There is no condemnation	MP 675 (MP2 594).
There is no love like the love of Jesus	MP 676 (MP2 591).
There is no moment of my life (Ps. 139)	BPW 133, CFW 164, H&P 428, HFP 286, PFT 139a.
There is none holy as the Lord	MP 677 (MP1 231).
There is none like you	LP 420.
There is no-one else like you	JP 476.
There is only one Lord	LP 421.
There is power in the name of Jesus	LP 422, SF 545.
There is singing in the desert	CFW 133.
There once was a man called Daniel	JP 477.
Therefore the redeemed	MP 685 (MP2 593), SF 541.
Therefore we lift our hearts	MP 686 (MP1 228).
There's a bright sky over Bethlehem	CP 308.
There's a city to build, there are walls	CFW 492.
There's a friend for little children	CFW 572.
There's a light upon the mountains	BPW 149, H&P 246, MP 679 (MP2 592).
There's a new life in Jesus	JP 249.
There's a quiet understanding	MP 678 (MP1 233), O&N 509, SF 546.
There's a Saviour to see on Christmas	CP 309.
There's a song for all the children	CFW 572, HTC 304, JP 478, MP 680 (MP4 837).
There's a song of exaltation	JP 247.
There's a sound on the wind	MP 681 (MP1 235), SF 547.
There's a spirit in the air	A&M 515, BPW 300, H&P 326, HTC 245, WSAM 85.
There's a way back to God	JP 248, MP 682 (MP1 234).
There's a wideness in God's mercy	BPW 573, H&P 230, MP 683 (MP4 838), NEH 461, O&N 510.
There's no greater name than Jesus	BPW 396, HTC S27, MP 684 (MP1 236), O&N 511.
These are the facts as we have received them	
	HFP 287, HTC 162, MP 687 (MP2 595).
These were the words	CP 310.
They killed him as a common thief	LP 423, WSAM 87.
They say he's wonderful	CFW 519.
They that wait upon the Lord	MP 688 (MP2 596).
They who stand in awe of God (Ps. 112)	HFP 288.
They whose course on earth is o'er	NEH 462.
Thine arm, O Lord, in days of old	A&M 285, H&P 397, NEH 324.
Thine be the glory, risen conquering Son	A&M 428, CFW 263, H&P 212, HFP 316, HTC 167, MP 689 (MP1 238), NEH 120, O&N 522, SF 551.
Thine for ever! God of love	A&M 234, HTC 556, NEH 463, O&N 523.
Thine, O Lord, is the greatness	SF 552.
Think big: an elephant	JP 479.
Think of a world without any flowers	BPW 134, CFW 276, H&P 572, JP 254.
This child from God above	H&P 589.
This Child, secretly comes in the night	HFP 289, JP 480, MP 690 (MP3

	743).
This day above all days	HTC 164.
This day God gives me	A&M 516.
This day, the first of days was made	NEH 53.
This earth belongs to God (Ps. 24)	CFW 584, CP 312, HFP 290, LP 208, SFP 24d.
This is a catchy song	JP 481.
This is the day of light	A&M 21, HTC 380, O&N 528.
This is the day the Lord hath/has made (Ps. 96, 118)	
	A&M 22, BPW 21, CFW 201, H&P 577, HTC 379, NEH 257, O&N 529.
This is the day, this is the day (Ps. 118)	CFW 319, H&P 578, HFP 291, HTC S28, JP 255, MP 691 (MP1 239), O&N 530, SF 553, SFP 118b.
This is the truth which we proclaim	CFW 2, HTC 388.
This is the word of God's decree (Ps. 110)	PFT 110.
This is what our Saviour said	MP 692 (MP2 597).
This is your God (Meekness and majesty)	BPW 58, CP 198, HFP 197, LP 138, MP 465 (MP2 493), SF 390.
This joyful Eastertide	BPW 258, H&P 213, HTC 165, JP 256, NEH 121, O&N 531.
This little light of mine, I'm gonna let	JP 258.
This night a miracle happened	CP 313.
This stone to thee in faith we lay	H&P 659.
This, this is the God we adore	H&P 277.
Those who rely on the Lord (Ps. 125)	PFT 125.
Thou art before me, Lord, thou art	H&P 543.
Thou art coming, O my Saviour	HTC 202.
Thou art my God	MP 694 (MP1 240).
Thou art the Christ, O Lord	A&M 317, NEH 172.
Thou art the everlasting Word	BPW 397, MP 693 (MP2 599).
Thou art the way; by thee alone	A&M 128, H&P 234, HTC 113, MP 695 (MP2 605), NEH 464, O&N 535.
Thou art worthy	HTC S30, MP 696 (MP1 242), O&N 536, SF 554.
Thou didst leave thy throne	A&M 250, BPW 179, CFW 108, H&P 154, MP 697 (MP1 237), NEH 465, O&N 537, SF 555.
Thou God of truth and love	H&P 374.
Thou/God, whose almighty word	A&M 180, BPW 591, CFW 416, H&P 29, HFP 100, HTC 506, MP 699 (MP1 244), NEH 466, O&N 538, SF 557.
Thou hallowed chosen morn of praise	NEH 122.
Thou hidden love of God, whose height	H&P 544.
Thou hidden source of calm repose	H&P 275.
Thou Judge of quick and dead	H&P 247.
Thou, Lord, hast given thyself	MP 698 (MP1 243).
Thou, O Lord, art a shield about me	SF 556.
Thou Shepherd of Israel, and mine	H&P 750.
Thou to whom the sick and dying	NEH 325.

Thou who dost rule on high   H&P 386.

Thou who wast rich   HFP 185, HTC 63, MP 700 (MP4 840).

Thou whom shepherds worshipped, hearing   A&M 54.

Thou wilt keep him in perfect peace   MP 701 (MP1 245), O&N 539.

Though the world has forsaken God   JP 257.

Three days on   WSAM 88.

Three-in-One and One-in-Three   CFW 346, HTC 12, O&N 540.

Through all our days we'll sing   HTC 145.

Through all the changing scenes (Ps. 34)   A&M 209, BPW 544, CFW 576, H&P 73, HFP 292, HTC 46, MP 702 (MP1 246), NEH 467, O&N 541.

Through Mary of Nazareth   CP 314.

Through our God we shall do valiantly (Ps. 108)   CFW 540, CP 315, LP 209, MP 703 (MP2 600), SF 558, SFP 108b.

Through the love of our God   MP 704 (MP2 601).

Through the night of doubt and sorrow   A&M 211, BPW 546, CFW 128, H&P 441, HTC 466, NEH 468, O&N 543.

Thuma mina (Send me, Lord)   LP 177.

Thy ceaseless, unexhausted love   H&P 48.

Thy faithfulness, Lord, each moment   H&P 805.

Thy hand, O God, has guided (Ps. 78)   A&M 171, BPW 398, CFW 130, H&P 784, HFP 315, HTC 536, MP 705 (MP1 247), NEH 485, O&N 545.

Thy Kingdom come, O God (Ps. 68)   A&M 177, CFW 67, H&P 783, HTC 334, NEH 499, O&N 546.

Thy Kingdom come! on bended knee   A&M 178, NEH 500.

Thy love, O God, has all mankind created   H&P 411.

Thy loving-kindness is better (Ps. 63)   MP 706 (MP1 241), O&N 547.

Thy way, not mine, O Lord   HTC 555, O&N 548.

Timeless love! We sing the story (Ps. 89)   CFW 372, H&P 60, HTC 47, MP 707 (MP1 250), PFT 89a.

Tis good, Lord, to be here   A&M 318, NEH 178, O&N 549.

Tis the gift to be simple   WSAM 89.

To be in your presence   LP 424.

To Christ, the Prince of peace   A&M 127, O&N 550.

To God be the glory   BPW 566, CFW 412, H&P 463, HFP 293, HTC 584, JP 259, LP 210, MP 708 (MP1 248), SF 559, WP 213.

To God our great salvation (Ps. 145)   PFT 145a.

To God's loving-kindness   CFW 5.

To him we come   BPW 547, CFW 152, HFP 294, HTC 518, LP 211, MP 709 (MP2 602).

To him who is able   LP 212, MP 710 (MP2 603).

To him who sits on the throne   SF 560.

To lead a blameless life, O Lord (Ps. 26)   PFT 26.

To mercy, pity, peace and love   NEH 469.

To mock your reign, O dearest Lord   A&M 517.

To people of goodwill   CP 316.

To the Lord I looked in patience (Ps. 40)	PFT 40a.
To the name of our salvation	A&M 121, H&P 80, HTC 222, O&N 552.
To the name that brings salvation	NEH 470.
To thee, O Lord, our hearts we raise	A&M 291, H&P 362, NEH 261.
To thee our God we fly	A&M 330, NEH 127.
To those who rule our land (Ps. 72)	PFT 72.
To us a child of royal birth	A&M 45, CP 317, HTC 64.
To you, before the end of day	H&P 639.
To you, O Lord, I lift up my soul (Ps. 25)	SFP 25c.
To you, O Lord, our hearts we raise	CFW 510, HTC 291.
Today, if you hear his voice	LP 425.
Today the Christ is born	CP 311.
Tonight, while the world	MP 713 (MP3 745).
Touch me, God's Spirit eternal	WP 84.
Trotting, trotting through Jerusalem	H&P 162.
True-hearted, whole-hearted	MP 711 (MP2 604).
Trust and obey (When we walk)	BPW 548.
Turn the hearts of the children	CFW 190.
Turn your eyes upon Jesus	JP 260, MP 712 (MP1 249), O&N 392.
Twelve men went to spy in Canaan	JP 261.
Twin princes of the courts of heaven	NEH 164.
Two little eyes to look to God	JP 262.
Tydi, a roddaist liw i'r wawr	BPW 650.
Tydi, a wnaeth y wyrth, O! Grist, Fab	BPW 651.
Undivided heart (Teach me your way)	LP 195.
Unless the Lord builds the house (Ps. 127)	LP 426.
Unless the Lord constructs (Ps. 127)	SFP 127c.
Unless the Lord has built (Ps. 127)	PFT 127b.
Unto the hills around (Ps. 122, 144)	HTC 48.
Unto the silent hills I raise	BPW 602.
Unto thee, O Lord	SF 561.
Unto us a boy is born	BPW 181, CFW 671, H&P 127, HFP 147, HTC 83, JP 263, MP 714 (MP2 606), NEH 39.
Unto you, O Lord	SF 562.
Up from the depths I cry to God (Ps. 130)	PFT 130b.
Upon the day of Pentecost	H&P 328.
Upon thy table, Lord, we place	A&M 429, H&P 628.
Veni Sancte Spiritus (Holy Spirit, come)	LP 67.
Victim divine, thy grace we claim	H&P 629, NEH 309.
Victory is on our lips	MP 715 (MP1 252).
Virgin-born, we bow before thee	A&M 311, NEH 187, O&N 555.
Wait for the Lord	BPW 148.
Wake, O wake, and sleep no longer	HTC 199.
Wake, O wake, with tidings thrilling	H&P 249, NEH 16.
Walk in the light: so shalt thou know	H&P 464, O&N 515.
Walking in a garden	A&M 518, NEH 123.
Wandering like lost sheep we were going	JP 482.
We are a chosen people	MP 716 (MP2 607), SF 563.
We are a land divided (Ps. 60)	PFT 60.
We are a people of power	LP 213, SF 565.
We are all together	SF 564.
We are being built into a temple	CFW 491, SF 566.

We are called to be God's people	BPW 583.
We are gathering together	MP 727 (MP1 251), O&N 558.
We are here to praise you	LP 214, MP 717 (MP2 608), SF 567.
We are his children	LP 427.
We are in God's army	SF 568.
We are marching in the great procession	MP 718 (MP2 609).
We are marching in the light of God	BPW 487, LP 215, WP 135, (WP1 69).
We are moving on	MP 719 (MP2 610).
We are one body in the Lord	CFW 120.
We are on the Lord's road	WP 136
We are soldiers of the King	JP 483.
We are standing	SF 569.
We are the hands of God	SF 570.
We are your people, Lord by your grace	A&M 519.
We are your people who are called	SF 571.
We believe in God Almighty	CFW 613, HFP 295, HTC 10.
We believe in God the Father	HFP 296, LP 129, MP 720 (MP2 611), SF 572.
We believe this is Jesus	CP 319.
We break this bread	HFP 297, LP 428, MP 721 (MP3 750), SF 573.
We bring the sacrifice of praise	MP 722 (MP2 612), SF 574.
We cannot measure how you heal	WSAM 90.
We come as guests invited	CFW 35, HFP 298, HTC 602, MP 723 (MP2 613).
We come to praise you, Father (Ps. 145)	SFP 145d.
We come unto our fathers' God	BPW 488, H&P 453, MP 724 (MP2 614).
We cry hosanna, Lord	CFW 209, MP 725 (MP2 615), O&N 559.
We declare that the Kingdom of God	CP 318, LP 126, SF 575.
We declare that there's only one Lord	SF 576.
We declare your majesty	LP 216, MP 726 (MP2 616), SF 577.
We do not know how to pray as we ought	H&P 545, WSAM 91.
We extol you	SF 578.
We exalt you, mighty Lord	WP 144
We find thee, Lord, in others' need	A&M 430, O&N 560.
We give God thanks for those who knew	CFW 453, HFP 299, HTC 318.
We give immortal praise	A&M 520, BPW 72, H&P 18, HTC 11.
We give you thanks, dear Lord	BPW 511.
We hail thy presence glorious	A&M 266, NEH 310.
We have a gospel (Fulda)	A&M 431, BPW 585, CFW 433, H&P 465, HFP 300, HTC 519, LP 220, MP 728 (MP2 617), NEH 486.
We have a king who rides a donkey	JP 264.
We have come as the family of God	LP 429.
We have come into his house	CFW 117, HTC S29, MP 729 (MP1 253), O&N 561.
We have come into this place	SF 579.
We have come to Mount Zion	SF 580.
We have heard a joyful sound	JP 266, MP 730 (MP1 255).
We have heard, O Lord our God (Ps. 44)	LP 431, PFT 44, SFP 44.

We have reason to rejoice	CP 320.
We know that all things	SF 581.
We know that Christ is raised	HTC 389.
We limit not the truth of God	BPW 107.
We look into your heavens (Ps. 19)	PFT 19a.
We love the Jesus stories	BPW 211.
We love the place, O God (Ps. 26, 84)	A&M 160, CFW 497, HFP 301, HTC 558, MP 731 (MP2 618), NEH 471, O&N 563.
We love to praise you Jesus	JP 265.
We need to grow, grow, grow, grow	JP 484.
We place you on the highest place	SF 584.
We pledge to one another	BPW 512.
We plough the fields, and scatter	A&M 290, BPW 135, CFW 509, H&P 352, HFP 302, HTC 292, JP 267, MP 732 (MP2 619), NEH 262, O&N 564, SF 585.
We praise thy name, all-holy Lord	NEH 158.
We praise, we worship you, O God	BPW 490, H&P 443.
We praise you, Lord, for Jesus Christ	A&M 521.
We praise you, we bless you	MP 733 (MP2 620).
We pray for peace	H&P 413.
We pray thee, heavenly Father	A&M 264, NEH 311, O&N 565.
We really want to thank you, Lord	CFW 494, JP 268, MP 734 (MP1 256), SF 586.
We remembered on the road	WSAM 92.
We rest on thee, our shield	HFP 303, HTC 446, MP 735 (MP2 621), SF 587.
We saw thee not	HTC 121.
We see the Lord	MP 736 (MP1 257), O&N 567.
We shall be as one	SF 588.
We shall draw water joyfully	LP 430.
We shall overcome	JP 270.
We shall stand	LP 217, MP 737 (MP3 751), SF 589.
We share a new day's dawn	HTC 271.
We sing the glorious conquest	A&M 313, NEH 155, O&N 568.
We sing the praise of him who died	A&M 138, BPW 231, H&P 182, HTC 146, MP 738 (MP1 258), NEH 94, O&N 569.
We thank you – Ahsante	WP 2.
We thank you – Imela	WP 68 (WP1 34).
We thank you for the memories	BPW 491.
We three kings of Orient are	CFW 99, CP 321, JP 271, MP 740 (MP2 622), O&N 570.
We trust in you, our shield	HFP 303, HTC 446, MP 735 (MP2 621), SF 587.
We turn to you, O God of every nation	A&M 522, BPW 641, H&P 412.
We were not there in Bethlehem	CP 322.
We were not there to see you come	HTC 121.
We will crown him (Father in heaven)	LP 31, MP 134 (MP3 662), SF 95.
We will glorify	SF 590.
We will honour you	SF 591.
We will lay our burden down	WSAM 93.
We will praise, we will praise	CFW 375, JP 485.
We will sing of our Redeemer	MP 739 (MP1 259).

We will tell each generation (Ps. 78)	PFT 78.
We wish you a merry Christmas	CP 324.
We worship and adore you	CP 323, SF 592.
We worship God	HFP 304, LP 218.
We would extol thee, ever-blessed Lord	A&M 206.
We your people	LP 219, MP 741 (MP3 752).
Welcome, Child of Mary	CP 326.
Welcome, happy morning	HTC 166.
Welcome, Jesus, Child of Mary	CP 328.
Welcome the Christ child	CP 327.
Welcome to another day	HTC 272.
Welcome to Christ's family	CFW 14.
Welcome to the family, we're glad that	BPW 415.
Welcome, welcome, Saviour born	CP 330.
Welcome your King	CP 329.
We'll praise him on the trumpet	JP 486.
We'll sing a new song	CFW 297, CP 325, MP 742 (MP1 260), SF 582.
We'll walk the land (Let the flame burn)	MP 743 (MP4 841), SF 583.
We're following Jesus	JP 487.
We're going to shine like the sun	LP 432.
We're told he was born at a Bethlehem inn	WP 114 (WP1 60).
Were you there when they crucified	A&M 523, BPW 232, H&P 181, JP 269, MP 745 (MP2 623), NEH 93, WSAM 94.
We've a story to tell	BPW 586, JP 272, MP 744 (MP1 261).
What a friend we have in Jesus	BPW 603, CFW 179, H&P 559, HFP 305, HTC 373, JP 273, MP 746 (MP1 262), O&N 571, SF 593, WP 214.
What a mighty God	JP 491, LP 223, MP 747 (MP3 749).
What a mighty God we serve	WP 161 (WP1 80).
What a wonderful change	MP 748 (MP1 263).
What a wonderful Saviour is Jesus	CFW 567, JP 274.
What Adam's disobedience cost	A&M 524, H&P 430.
What can I give to the King	CP 331.
What child is this	MP 749 (MP2 624), NEH 40, O&N 572.
What colours God has made	JP 488.
What do you give a God	JP 489.
What does the Lord require	A&M 432, H&P 414.
What drives the stars	JP 490.
What is our calling's glorious hope	H&P 749.
What joy to hear the pilgrims say (Ps. 122)	SFP 122e.
What kind of love is this	MP 750 (MP3 753).
What made a difference in the life	JP 492.
What offering shall we give	HTC 439.
What purpose burns within our hearts	BPW 551.
What riches on this earth (Ps. 49)	PFT 49a.
What shall I do my God .. loving	H&P 46.
What shall I do my God .. my Saviour	H&P 47.
What shall I render to my God	H&P 703.
What shall our greeting be	H&P 806.

What shall we offer our Good Lord	H&P 807.
What sweet of life endureth	NEH 330.
What wondrous love is this	LP 433, WSAM 95 WP 163.
When all the world to life is waking	NEH 240.
When all your mercies, O my God (Ps. 89)	A&M 109, BPW 361, CFW 383, H&P 573, HFP 306, HTC 39, MP 751 (MP4 842), NEH 472, O&N 574.
When came in flesh the incarnate word	NEH 17.
When Christ was born in Bethlehem	NEH 203.
When Christ was lifted from the earth	A&M 525, HTC 335.
When Easter to the dark world came	H&P 200.
When fear and grief had barred the door	BPW 259.
When God breathes his Spirit in my life	JP 497.
When God delivered Israel (Ps. 126)	SFP 126c.
When God from heaven to earth came down	CFW 663, CP 332.
When God of old came down from heaven	A&M 90.
When he comes	MP 752 (MP2 625).
When he was baptised in Jordan	BPW 234.
When I am sad and sorrowful	WP 109 (WP1 59).
When I behold Jesus/what kind of love	WP 164 (WP1 81).
When I consider	WP 97.
When I feel the touch	MP 753 (MP1 264), SF 594.
When I lift up my voice (Ps. 142)	LP 434, SFP 142b.
When I look into your holiness	MP 754 (MP2 626), SF 595, WP 216.
When I look towards the hills (Ps. 121)	SFP 121e.
When I needed a neighbour, were you there	A&M 433, JP 275, O&N 576.
When I survey the wondrous cross	A&M 67, BPW 233, CFW 238, H&P 180, HFP 307, HTC 147, JP 277, LP 221, MP 755 (MP1 265), NEH 95, O&N 578, SF 596, WP 215.
When I'm afraid I will trust in God (Ps. 56)	SFP 56b.
When I'm confused (Show me the way)	LP 222.
When I'm feeling lonely	JP 493.
When, in our music, God is glorified	H&P 388.
When Israel broke their cruel chains (Ps. 114)	PFT 114.
When Israel was in Egypt's land	JP 276.
When Jesus came to Jordan	A&M 526, H&P 132.
When Jesus led his chosen three	HTC 117.
When Jesus the healer passed through	H&P 151.
When Jesus walked upon this earth	HTC 317.
When morning gilds the skies	A&M 146, BPW 73, H&P 276, HTC 223, JP 278, MP 756 (MP1 266), NEH 473, O&N 579, SF 597.
When my bitter foes surround (Ps. 43)	PFT 43b.
When my love to Christ grows weak	H&P 183.
When my sorrows cover me (Ps. 69)	LP 436, SFP 69b.
When our confidence is shaken	H&P 686.
When peace like a river	MP 757 (MP3 757).
When shepherds watched and angels sang	CFW 659, CP 333.

When the angel came to Mary	CP 334.
When the Church of Jesus	BPW 614.
When the dark clouds are above you	JP 494.
When the King shall come again	CFW 594, CP 335, HFP 308, HTC 200.
When the Lord came to our land	CFW 100, CP 336.
When the Lord, he turned again (Ps. 126)	SFP 126e.
When the Lord in glory comes	HTC 201, JP 280, MP 758 (MP2 628).
When the Lord turned again (Ps. 126)	PFT 126b.
When the road is rough and steep	JP 279.
When the Spirit of the Lord	CFW 472, LP 224, SF 598.
When the stars in their flight	WP 89.
When the sun is darkened	CP 337.
When the trumpet of the Lord	JP 281, MP 759 (MP1 268).
When the waters cover me (Ps. 69)	PFT 69a.
When things began to happen	HFP 309, HTC 69.
When this land knew (Ps. 85)	CFW 55, PFT 85a.
When to our world the Saviour came	MP 761 (MP2 627).
When we are down you raise us up	WSAM 96.
When we look up to the sky	JP 495.
When we walk with God (Ps. 1)	SFP 1d.
When we walk with the Lord	BPW 548, H&P 687, MP 760 (MP1 269), SF 599.
When you prayed beneath the trees	HFP 310, WSAM 98.
When you're feeling good	JP 496.
Where cross the crowded ways of life	BPW 626, H&P 431.
Where do Christmas songs begin	BPW 180, CP 338.
Where high the heavenly temple stands	A&M 130, HTC 184.
Where is this stupendous stranger	A&M 527, NEH 41.
Where love and loving-kindness dwell	A&M 528.
Where restless crowds are thronging	BPW 642.
Where shall my wondering soul begin	H&P 706.
Where the appointed sacrifice	NEH 312.
Where the Lord walks	MP 763 (MP2 630).
Where the Spirit is, there's freedom	WP 27.
Where you go, I will go	SF 600.
Wherefore, O Father, we thy humble	A&M 275, NEH 313.
Where's everybody going	CP 339.
Wherever I am I will praise you Lord	JP 283.
Wherever I am I'll praise him	JP 282, MP 762 (MP1 267).
Whether you're one	JP 284, SF 601.
While shepherds watched	A&M 37, BPW 182, CFW 658, CP 341-4, H&P 120, HFP 311, HTC 94, JP 285, MP 764 (MP2 629), NEH 42, O&N 580, SF 602.
Whitsuntide round	WSAM 97.
Who are these like stars appearing	A&M 323, NEH 231, O&N 581.
Who are we who stand and sing	A&M 529.
Who can cheer the heart like Jesus	MP 765 (MP1 270).
Who can ever say they understand	SF 603.
Who can measure heaven and earth	HTC 27.
Who can sound the depths (Ps. 82)	HFP 312, LP 225, MP 766 (MP3 754), SF 604.

Who does Jesus love	CFW 144.
Whoever lives beside the Lord	WP 162.
Who fathoms the eternal thought	H&P 432.
Who honours courage here	HTC 537.
Who is he in yonder stall	CP 340, MP 767 (MP1 271), SF 605.
Who is like unto thee	MP 768 (MP1 272), SF 606.
Who is on the Lord's side	BPW 615, H&P 722, JP 287, MP 769 (MP1 274), SF 607.
Who is the rock (Mwamba ni Yesu)	LP 228, WP 105 (WP1 52).
Who is this child	CP 346.
Who is this that grows like the dawn	SF 608.
Who is this, so weak and helpless	NEH 474.
Who put the colours in the rainbow	CFW 518, JP 288, O&N 584.
Who took fish and bread, hungry people	JP 286.
Who would true valour see	A&M 212, BPW 362, H&P 688, HTC 590.
Who's the king of the jungle	JP 289.
Why, God, have you forsaken me (Ps. 22)	PFT 22a.
Why, impious Herod, should'st thou fear	NEH 46.
Why in the dawning (Ps. 52)	PFT 52.
Wide, wide as the ocean	CFW 357, JP 292, O&N 585.
Will you come and follow me	BPW 363, LP 437, WP 165.
Will your anchor hold in the storms	BPW 549, H&P 689, JP 290, MP 770 (MP1 275).
Wind, wind blow on me	MP 771 (MP2 631), SF 609.
Winds through the olive trees	CP 345.
Winter has gone	WP 166 (WP1 82).
Wise men, seeking Jesus	H&P 128.
Wise men, they came to look for wisdom	CP 347, HTC 100.
With all my heart (Ps. 119)	LP 435, MP 772 (MP3 755), SF 610.
With all my heart I seek (Ps. 119)	PFT 119b.
With all your heart rejoice (Ps. 21)	PFT 21.
With a song in my heart	WP 83.
With Christ we share a mystic grave	NEH 317.
With gladness we worship, rejoice	H&P 19.
With glorious clouds encompassed round	H&P 184.
With golden splendour and with roseate	NEH 171.
With harps and viols	MP 773 (MP2 632).
With heart and hands (Ps. 101)	PFT 101.
With Jesus in the boat we can smile	JP 291.
With joy we meditate the grace	A&M 530, BPW 275, H&P 235, MP 774 (MP4 843).
With joyful shouts acclaim (Ps. 100)	PFT 100d.
With loving hands	HTC 106.
With my heart I worship you	MP 775 (MP2 634).
With my whole heart	SF 611.
With solemn faith we offer up	NEH 314.
With wonder, Lord, we see (Ps. 8)	A&M 531, CFW 271, H&P 353, PFT 8b.
With wonder, Lord	WSAM 99.
Within a crib my Saviour lay	CP 348, HTC 70.
Within our darkest night	LP 439.
Within the veil	MP 778 (MP1 273).
Witness, both earth and heaven now	BPW 416.
Won, the victor's crown	HTC 185.

You are the Holy One	SF 626.
You are the King of glory	BPW 74, CFW 211, CP 352, JP 296, MP 790 (MP1 279), SF 627.
You are the light of the world	LP 227.
You are the Lord (Ps. 71)	LP 444.
You are the mighty King	LP 229, MP 791 (MP2 642), SF 628.
You are the one (How I love you)	LP 69, MP 246 (MP2 398), SF 190.
You are the rock of my salvation (Ps. 95)	LP 445.
You are the Vine	MP 792 (MP2 643), SF 629.
You are the way, to you alone	HTC 113.
You are to be praised O God (Ps. 65)	PFT 65b.
You are worthy, Lord you are worthy	HTC 30, MP 794 (MP2 646), SF 630.
You are worthy, you are worthy	BPW 75.
You can trust his promises	LP 447.
You can weigh an elephant's auntie	JP 501.
You can't catch a plane	JP 502.
You can't stop rain from falling down	BPW 567, JP 297, O&N 594.
You choirs of new Jerusalem	HTC 168.
You created the wind and the ocean	WP 146.
You did not wait for me	SF 631.
You did this mighty deed, O Christ	BPW 651.
You gates, lift up your heads on high	BPW 276.
You gave us, Lord, by word and deed	BPW 89.
You have been a shelter, Lord (Ps. 90)	LP 448.
You have been given	SF 632.
You have changed my sadness (Ps. 30)	SFP 30b.
You holy angels bright (Ps. 42)	BPW 23, HFP 313, HTC 353.
You laid aside your majesty	LP 230, MP 795 (MP2 644), SF 633.
You laid the foundations of earth (Ps. 102)	PFT 102a.
You, living Christ, our eyes behold	A&M 533, NEH 487.
You, Lord, have the message (Ps. 19)	LP 446.
You make my heart feel glad	SF 634.
You, O Lord, rich in mercy	LP 231, SF 635.
You purchased men	SF 636.
You sat down	LP 449, SF 639.
You servants of God (Ps. 134)	A&M 149, BPW 76, HFP 314, HTC 520, MP 784 (MP1 278), SF 620.
You servants of the Lord (Ps. 134)	CP 353, HTC 598.
You shall go out with joy	CFW 118, CP 354, MP 796 (MP1 281), O&N 595, SF 640, WSAM 100.
You will show me the path of life (Ps. 16)	SFP 16d.
Your hand, O God, has guided (Ps. 98)	A&M 171, BPW 398, CFW 130, H&P 784, HFP 315, HTC 536, JP 298, MP 705 (MP1 247).
Your Kingdom come (Ps. 10)	BPW 644, CFW 67, CP 355, HTC 334.
Your Kingdom come, O Lord	WP 168 (WP1 84).
Your light, O God, was given to earth	H&P 387.
Your love is to me	MP 797 (MP2 645).
Your loving-kindness is better than life (Ps. 63)	SFP 63e.
Your mercy flows	SF 637.

14

WRITING BIBLE PRAYERS

Using Scripture passages to create responsive material

In the past, Christian congregations learned most of their doctrine from hymns. This is a bold statement; but true when you think about it. Hymns, often-repeated, and retained in the mind because of their rounded form, their rhyming structure and their association with memorable melodies, were best placed as a vehicle of teaching.

But now, the traditional (or even contemporary) hymn is less prominent; not gone completely, and not perhaps for ever, but in many places the song is king. The four-part choir and organ which were needed to sustain the old hymn tune arrangements are no longer there. Great new hymns abound; but are used mostly in North America. At best, there is a waiting period in the United Kingdom while the music catches up with the words.

A few songs are full of doctrine. But most were written for another purpose; to fulfil the genuine need for 'heart-worship', formerly lacking in our services – partly because the Psalms had been lost. Heart-worship songs do not *need* to be doctrinal (in fact, too much detail would destroy them). Compared with the hymns, the sermon is a poor second in terms of teaching and nourishment. The hymn goes on teaching and feeding the Christian mind even when the preacher has gone home and the Bible reading is no longer remembered. Now, more than ever, we need *prayers steeped in Scripture*, as a counterpart to our songs.

The old *Book of Common Prayer* of the Church of England had this advantage; its prayers were full of Bible texts, strategically placed and beautifully interpreted. Sadly, the Prayer Book was never officially revised for nearly four hundred years. In the meantime, language moved on and, for the most part now, has left the old book behind.

Historically, many Free churches glad to shake off the rigidity of Prayer Book services nevertheless retained some of its prayers. Some suspected 'vain repetition' as being unscriptural, but fell into the trap of the minister's cliché – vain repetition indeed!

Christians of all denominations and none are beginning to rediscover the joys of using Scripture passages as prayers – most helpfully using material that has been thought out beforehand. Better still, they are discovering the blessings of *responsive* (technically 'responsorial') prayers – which allow worshippers to enter into prayerful Bible worship for themselves. And such prayers can be good for us as worship leaders too; especially since it encourages us to make ourselves less prominent and to put Scripture centre-stage.

'LITURGY'

Historically, the word 'Liturgy' refers to the prayer(s) used at The Lord's Supper, The Communion, The Eucharist, The Mass – so many names for the love-feast of Jesus! More generally, 'liturgy' has come to be used for all prayers which are pre-formed (not extempore); and especially for any prayer or service which makes provision for the people to join in praying.

PRECEDENTS

Those who still have reservations need to realise how many 'rounded forms' of prayer text there are in the Bible. This is easily seen, for example in the New Testament, if you open a modern translation, such as the Good News Bible, or the New International Version, and notice the paragraphs of text with loose-ended lines. Some of these are quotations familiar to the recipients of the letters, others are affirmations of faith, doxologies etc. Many Old Testament prayers, too, have a 'rounded form' which has enabled them to be received, learned, and used as vehicles of worship to God, for instance, Solomon's prayer at the dedication of the Temple (2 Chronicles 6). Such worship had an element of 'drama' – celebrating the deliverances of God – which vehicle Christians also employ in the service of the Lord's Supper/Holy Communion. Many of the psalms are of such a form as would meet the liturgical and dramatic needs of worship (for example, Psalm 24 and Psalm 118).

HOW TO DO IT

Let the Bible passage suggest the kind of prayer which you could derive from it. For instance, Psalm 51 lends itself to creating a confession of sin – and, if developed carefully, a declaration of God's forgiveness. 1 Corinthians 15 provides an original affirmation of faith ('Creed'). The end of Ephesians 3 is a wonderful Gloria ('doxology') at the climax of a worship service. There are great possibilities for greetings ('Peace') at the beginning of most of the Epistles, and several obvious passages on which to base a Blessing/Benediction at the end of them. Many examples will be found in *Bible Praying*[1].

When creating responsive prayers, here are some ways of treating the text which have proved invaluable in developing worship (prayer) material:

USE 'TRIGGER' PHRASES

There will be those who find reading difficult, especially younger children. A consistent 'trigger' phrase throughout the prayer will help to bring them in, and so enable them to participate fully (as 'O God, in your unfailing love' in the example below).

[1]*Bible Praying*, published 1992 by HarperCollins*Publishers* Ltd, London.

Example:

CONFESSION *From Psalm 51*
The sacrifices of God are a broken spirit; a broken and a contrite heart, O God, you will not despise. O God, in your unfailing love:
have mercy on us.

We know our transgressions, and our sin is ever before us; against you only have we sinned and done evil in your sight. O God, in your unfailing love:
have mercy on us.

According to your great compassion blot out our transgressions, wash away all our iniquities and cleanse us from our sin. O God, in your unfailing love:
have mercy on us.

Cleanse us, and we shall be clean,
wash us, and we shall be whiter than snow;
through Jesus Christ our Lord. Amen.

Another sort of 'trigger' phrase is that which brings an '**Amen**' from the people. Only certain triggers will do this adequately. For instance:

. . . through Jesus Christ our Lord. **Amen.**
. . . for ever and ever. **Amen.**
. . . (we pray) in your glorious (wonderful etc.) name. **Amen.**
. . . Thank you, Lord. **Amen.**

USE CAREFUL PRINTING

It used to be said, 'Only the best is good enough for God'. This led unfortunately to Christians setting impossible objectives and, in the musical world, forcing worshippers into other people's cultural preferences. Now the ethic is more, 'Only the fastest is good enough for God' – as witness the bad overhead projection stencil which abandons punctuation to the confusion of the reader. We dare not forget the Reformation maxim that to be 'understood of the people' matters. Hence clarity of meaning in printing is all-important for people of the word.

Here are some principles for setting out modern prayer material:

- the people's response should be in bold type – even the Amen at the end of the minister's prayer (if it is to be printed at all).
- the minister's part should be right and left justified (flush with both margins on both sides – see examples here). But the people's part is in 'sense-equivalent' lines:

i.e. *not like this!*   *but like this:*

Cleanse us, and	**Cleanse us,**
we shall/	**and we shall be clean,**
be clean, wash/	**wash us,**
us, and we shall be	**and we shall be**
whiter/	**whiter than snow;**
than snow; through Jesus/	**through Jesus Christ**
Christ our Lord. Amen.	**our Lord. Amen.**

Sense-equivalent lines enable people:

a) To read as they think.
b) To breath at the right point and avoid making nonsense of the text.
c) To keep together.

USE A FINAL 'PEOPLE'S' PARAGRAPH

One of the disadvantages of continually repeated responses is a creeping feeling of banality about it if you have too many paragraphs. So let there be at the most only three or four petitions and replies. Another disadvantages of repeated brief responses is that a congregation or worship gathering may feel deprived if they are not given the chance to say more than a simple phrase (especially if they are Anglicans, and are used to saying a whole prayer together – for instance, the Confession). For this reason it is wise to end responsive prayers with a full paragraph which all can say together. This satisfies the articulate, and acts as an effective confirmation of what has gone before.

USE RHYTHMIC LINES

One of the reasons why reading the Psalms together from the Bible, or from traditional psalters (including the *Liturgical Psalter* from the Anglican *Alternative Service Book 1980*), is unsatisfactory and unfulfilling is this. Unlike hymns and songs, these psalm versions do not have rhythm to help the people keep together. Psalms in the NIV, GNB etc. are designed for reading; and the ASB psalms are intended for chanting. Neither version works at all well for a congregation reading together.

Examples of psalm versions set for reading together may be found in *Psalms for Today*[2], *Songs from the Psalms*[3], *Church Family Worship*[4], *Prayers for the People*[5], or the 'L' psalms in *The Dramatised Bible*[6]. These psalms have rhythm and careful sentence length.

Example:

FROM PSALM 116 *(sections only)*
I love the Lord because he heard my voice:
The Lord in mercy listened to my prayer.

Because the Lord has turned his ear to me:
I'll call on him as long as I shall live.

---

[2]*Psalms for Today*, published 1990, Hodder & Stoughton Ltd, London.
[3]*Songs from the Psalms*, published 1990, Hodder & Stoughton Ltd, London.
[4]*Church Family Worship*, published 1988, Hodder & Stoughton Ltd, London.
[5]*Prayers for the People*, published 1992, HarperCollins*Publishers* Ltd, London.
[6]*The Dramatised Bible*, published 1989, HarperCollins*Publishers* Ltd, London.

What shall I give the Lord for all his grace?
I'll take his saving cup and pay my vows.

Within the congregation of his saints:
I'll offer him my sacrifice of praise.

Praise the Lord:
Amen, amen!

In this particular example both leader's and people's parts are in rhythm – so there could be several leaders. Usually, with one leader, only the people's part of a psalm or prayer needs to be rhythmic.

USE QUESTIONS

A very effective way of involving a congregation in worship is to base questions on a chosen Bible passage – especially prayers of approach, affirmations of belief, or thanksgiving prayers:

Example:

CREED *From Isaiah 44*
We believe in God who made all things:

Did he stretch out the heavens, spread out
the earth and form us in the womb?
He did!

Is he the Lord almighty, our king and our
redeemer?
He is!

Are we his own people, called by his name?
We are!

Does he pour out his spirit upon us as on a
dry and thirsty land?
He does!

We believe in one God, the almighty,
Father, Son and Holy Spirit. Amen.

INDICATING THE SOURCE

It may seem obvious, but if we are to teach people to look to the Bible for help in their praying we should make it clear where we are getting these prayers from! This can be done by placing the Bible reference at the top, and/or by announcing where the prayer comes from before it is used: 'Let's praise God loudly as we respond to this declaration of faith based on the prophecy of Isaiah, chapter forty-four.'

FINDING EXAMPLES, AND PASSAGES TO START FROM

The indexes at the back of *Bible Praying* and of the Leader's edition of *Prayers for the People* give easy access to suitable prayers, and list texts which lend themselves to prayer arrangement. Looking through a modern Bible for printed text set in loose-ended lines, as poetry, is also a direct way to discover suitable passages.

USING 'PRAISE SHOUTS'

The Psalms are full of brilliant coupled lines which are imme-diately adaptable as Praise Responses. These can be used anywhere; but most effectively prior to singing:

Example:

PRAISE *from Psalm 100*
Shout for joy to the Lord, all the earth,
serve the Lord with gladness.

Come before him with joyful songs,
give thanks to him,
and praise his name. Amen.

HYMN
Praise, my soul, the King of heaven,
to his feet your tribute bring . . . *etc.*

Further examples of prayers of this type will be found in subsequent sections of this book.

15

BIBLE PRAYERS: RESOURCES SECTION

*Containing two short services and a variety of
prayers based on passages of Scripture*

Bible resource sections follow: *A Word Service*, a communion
service – *The Lord's Supper*, and a more general resource selection – Bible Prayers for Worship. It is not expected that
worship leaders will want to use uncritically all these
prayers. They may simply serve as examples of what might
be done to meet a local need. The sequences of all three
sections are generally based upon a common pattern of
worship-flow:

Greeting/Peace
Approach to God/Preparation for worship
Confession of sins
Assurance of forgiveness
Exhortation to praise
Psalms
Introduction to Readings
Readings
Conclusion to Readings
Affirmation of faith
Intercession – for others, for ourselves
Thanksgiving
Thank-offering
Act of Remembrance
Acclamation/Doxology/Ascription

Renewal of promises/Act of Commitment/Dedication
Blessing/Benediction
Dismissal

This suggested pattern may be found helpful when preparing
services from scratch. Not every element need be there, of
course, but the list could act as a good check that worship
opportunities had been offered.

These prayers may be freely reproduced for local or conference use under the conditions outlined on p. iv. Some of them
have appeared in *Spring Harvest* song books and in other
published worship or books of prayers; most have been
devised or developed recently.

I have indicated within the services where psalm versions,
hymns or songs might feature. You would not normally want
musical items at all those points. In fact, the services can be
used effectively without any music at all. The 'psalm version'
could well be a song or hymn based on a psalm. Psalm
versions can be appropriately used adjacent to the Bible
reading.

Titling and numbering of the prayers helps to indicate the
order of worship to a congregation. Titles also present a
problem – as we found when preparing prayer material for
Spring Harvest. 'Absolution' may suit Anglicans, but looks
suspiciously 'priestly' to others; in which case 'Assurance of
Forgiveness' or 'Receiving God's Forgiveness' might provide
sensible alternatives. So it is worth checking on people's preferences and sensitivities when producing local service sheets
or overhead projection material. Certainly, my titles here are
not sacrosanct – so please change at will!

A WORD SERVICE

Bible Prayers for a Congregational Service

1. INVITATION TO PRAISE
From Psalm 98
Sing to the Lord, all the world,
for the Lord is a mighty God.

Sing a new song to the Lord,
for he has done marvellous things.

Proclaim his glory among the nations,
**and shout for joy
to the Lord our king.**

HYMN OR SONG(S)

2. GREETING
From Romans 1 etc.
Grace and peace to you from God our
Father and from the Lord Jesus Christ.
Amen.

3. APPROACH (MORNING)
From Psalm 118
Lord,
this is the day you made;
we rejoice and are glad in it:
help us and bless us
as we come into your presence –
we praise you and exalt you,
we celebrate and thank you;
for you are our God
and your love endures for ever.
Amen.

4. APPROACH (EVENING)
From Psalm 134
Lord,
your servants come
in the evening of the day
to worship in your presence.
We lift up our hands to praise you
    in this holy place.
Lord, maker of heaven and earth,
we bless you now. **Amen.**

SONG(S)

5. CONFESSION OF SINS
From Psalm 51
**Lord God, be gracious to us
because of your great love for us;
in your great mercy
wash away our sins –
for we are weighed down by them,
and we know we have failed;**

we have offended against you
and done evil in your sight:
**create in us a pure heart,
put a loyal spirit in us,
and give us again the joy
    that comes from your salvation.
Amen.**

6. ASSURANCE OF FORGIVENESS
From Psalm 103
The love of God for those who seek
him is as great as the heavens are high
above the earth: as far as the east is
from the west he removes *your* sins
from *you,* and he will remember them
no more. **Amen.**

7. EXHORTATION TO PRAISE
From Revelation 19
Let us rejoice and be glad,
and give God the glory. Amen.

PSALM VERSION

8. BEFORE READING
From 2 Samuel 22
You are our lamp, O Lord;
you turn our darkness into light.

READING(S) FROM SCRIPTURE

9. AFTER READING
From Mark 4
Those who have a mind to hear,
let them hear!

SONG(S) IN RESPONSE TO READING

10. AFFIRMATION OF FAITH
From 1 Corinthians 8 and 12
We believe in one God and Father;
from him all things come.

We believe in one Lord Jesus Christ;
through him we come to God.

We believe in one Holy Spirit;
**in him we are baptised
    into one body.**

**We believe and trust in one God,
Father, Son and Holy Spirit. Amen.**

OR

11. AFFIRMATION OF FAITH
From Ephesians 3
Let us declare our faith in God:

We believe in God the Father,
from whom every family
in heaven and on earth
is named.

We believe in God the Son,
who lives in our hearts through faith,
and fills us with his love.

We believe in God the Holy Spirit,
who strengthens us with power
from on high.

We believe in one God;
Father, Son and Holy Spirit. Amen.

12. THE LORD'S PRAYER
From Matthew 6 and Luke 11
Our Father in heaven,
hallowed be your name,
your kingdom come,
your will be done,
on earth as in heaven.
Give us today our daily bread.
Forgive us our sins
as we forgive
those who sin against us.
Lead us not into temptation
but deliver us from evil.

For the kingdom, the power,
and the glory are yours,
now and for ever. Amen.

13. BEFORE PRAYER
From Hebrews 4
Let us approach God's throne with confidence:
we shall receive mercy,
and find grace to help us in our need.
Amen.

SONG(S) LEADING INTO PRAYER

14. FOR PEOPLE IN NEED
From Psalm 31
Be merciful, Lord,
to all those in trouble:
those who are ill or weary,
those who are deep in sorrow,
those whose life is ebbing away,
those who are without friends,
those who are forgotten by the world:

Lord, we trust them to your care;
in Jesus' name. **Amen.**

15. FOR OURSELVES
From Isaiah 33
Lord, be gracious to us,
for we long for you:
be our strength every day,
our salvation in time of trouble,
our greatest treasure in life,
and our reward in heaven;
through Jesus our redeemer. **Amen.**

16. THANKSGIVING
From Isaiah 63
Our God,
we thank you for all your kindness,
and we praise you
for all the good things you have done
     for us:
you are our saviour –
in our distress you share our sorrows,
in your love and mercy
     you redeem us;
through Jesus Christ our Lord. **Amen.**

17. THANK OFFERING
From 1 Chronicles 29
Lord, we bring these gifts to honour
your holy name:
they came from your hands
and they all belong to you. Amen.

OR

18. THANK OFFERING
From 2 Corinthians 8
Thank you, Lord Jesus Christ,
that, though you were rich,
yet for us you became poor
that we, through your poverty,
might become rich.
By your grace
let our riches supply
     the needs of others,
so that we may not have too much,
and they may not have too little;
for your name's sake. **Amen.**

OR

19. THANK OFFERING
From Philippians 4
To our God and Father,
who meets all our needs

according to his glorious riches
in Christ Jesus,
be glory for ever and ever. **Amen.**

SONG(S) OF DEVOTION, THANKFULNESS OR PREPARATION

ADDRESS/SERMON

20. DOXOLOGY
From Romans 16
**Glory to God
who alone is all wise;
through Jesus Christ, for ever! Amen.**

HYMN/SONG

21. DISMISSAL (EVENING)
From Exodus 33
Lord God almighty, you have revealed
your goodness to us and proclaimed
your name among us:
show us your glory.

You have mercy upon us, and compassion; you forgive our sins:
**hide us in the cleft of the Rock,
cover us with your hand.**

You know us by name; we have found
favour in your sight:
**now let your presence go with us,
and give us rest. Amen.**

22. THE GRACE
From 2 Corinthians 13
The grace of our Lord Jesus Christ,
and the love of God,
and the fellowship of the Holy Spirit,
be with us all evermore. **Amen.**

OR

23. BENEDICTION
From Jude
Now to him who is able to keep us
from falling and to present us faultless
before his glorious presence with great
joy – to the only God our Saviour be
glory, majesty, power and authority,
through Jesus Christ our Lord, before
all ages, now, and for evermore!
Amen.

OR

24. BLESSING
From Numbers 6
The Lord bless you and keep *you*, the
Lord make his face to shine upon *you*,
the Lord be kind and gracious to *you*,
the Lord look upon *you* with favour,
and give *you* peace. **Amen.**

CHOIR/MUSIC GROUP

THE LORD'S SUPPER

Bible prayers for a Communion Service

1. GREETING ONE ANOTHER
From Philippians 4
We greet you all in Christ Jesus:
**the grace of the Lord Jesus Christ
be with you. Amen.**

2. APPROACHING GOD
From Psalm 26
Lord God,
we are here to worship you –
let your love guide us,
and your faithfulness lead us;
we come to ask your forgiveness,
to gather round your table,
to bring you our thanksgiving,
and to proclaim your redemption:
receive the praise of your people.
Amen.

3. PRAISING TOGETHER
From Psalm 96
Sing to the Lord a new song:
proclaim his salvation each day.

Declare his glory to all:
**he is great and worthy of praise.
Amen.**

4. PREPARING FOR WORSHIP
From Psalm 51
**God of unfailing love and mercy,
wash away our wickedness
and cleanse us from our sin;
create in us a pure heart,
and strengthen our spirits within us;
restore to us
    the joy of your salvation –
open our lips,
    and we will praise you. Amen.**

5. HEARING JESUS'
COMMANDMENTS
From Mark 12
Jesus said: Love the Lord your God
with all your heart and with all your
soul and with all your mind and with
all your strength; and love your neighbour as yourself:

**Lord,
we have broken your commandments:
forgive us, and help us to obey. Amen.**

6. CONFESSING OUR SINS
From Amos 2
**Lord God almighty,
we have rejected your law,
and have not obeyed your
commandments;
we have sinned
and dishonoured your holy name:
have mercy on us;
for Jesus' sake. Amen.**

OR

7. CONFESSING OUR SINS
From 1 John 1
**God our Father,
you have taught us
that if we say we have no sin
we deceive ourselves
and the truth is not in us:
we humbly confess our sins to you,
and we ask you to keep your promise
    to forgive us our sins
and to cleanse us
    from all unrighteousness;
through Jesus Christ our Lord.
Amen.**

8. RECEIVING GOD'S
FORGIVENESS
From Psalm 6
The Lord God be merciful to *you* and
heal *you*; the Lord turn his face
towards *you* and deliver *you*; the Lord
save *you* in his unfailing love; through
Jesus Christ. **Amen.**

9. PRAYING FOR OTHERS
From Hebrews 4, Ephesians 3 etc.
Let us approach God's throne with
confidence:
**we shall receive mercy,
and find grace to help
    in time of need.**

For those in need . . .
Upon . . . have mercy, Lord:
we entrust them to your care.

For the world . . .
In . . . Lord, let peace and justice rule:
let your love prevail.

For the Church . . .
O God, you are able to do immeasurably more than all we ask or think by the power that is at work among us: . . .

To God be glory in the Church and in Christ Jesus:
for ever and ever. Amen.

10. SAYING A PSALM TOGETHER
From Psalm 36
Your love, O Lord, reaches the heavens:
**your faithfulness extends to the
  skies.**

Your righteousness is like the towering mountains:
your justice is like the great deep.

How precious is your love, O Lord:
we find shelter under your wings!

We feast on the food you provide:
**we drink
  from the river of your goodness.**

For with you is the fountain of life:
in your light we see light. Amen.

11. READING FROM THE OLD TESTAMENT
Before – from Jeremiah 9
Let us hear God's word:
let us listen to the Lord.

After – from 1 Kings 22
Let the people mark these words:
the Lord has spoken!

12. READING FROM AN EPISTLE
Before – from 1 Corinthians 1
To the church of God, dedicated in Christ Jesus and called to be holy.
Amen

After – from Revelation 1-7
Hear what the Spirit is saying to the churches:
thanks be to God. Amen.

13. READING FROM A GOSPEL
Before – from Revelation 1
The word of God and the testimony of Jesus Christ, from the Gospel of/ *according to* . . . **Amen.**

After – from 1 Peter 1
This is the Gospel we proclaim:
thanks be to God. Amen.

14. AFFIRMING OUR FAITH
From Ephesians 3
We declare our faith in God:

**We believe in God the Father,
from whom every family
in heaven and on earth is named.**

**We believe in God the Son,
who lives in our hearts through faith,
and fills us with his love.**

**We believe in God the Holy Spirit,
who strengthens us
  with power from on high.**

**We believe in one God;
Father, Son and Holy Spirit. Amen.**

15. SHARING THE PEACE OF CHRIST
From 2 Corinthians 13
The God of love and peace be with you. **Amen.**

From Romans 15
Welcome one another as Christ has welcomed you:
to God be the glory. Amen.

16. GIVING THANKS TO GOD
From Ruth 2
The Lord be with you:
the Lord bless you.

From Psalm 107
Let us give thanks to the Lord:
his mercy lasts for ever.

He satisfies the thirsty:
**he fills the hungry
with good things.**

[From Ephesians 5
In the name of our Lord Jesus Christ we give thanks for everything to God the Father:]

Father, we thank you for all your
goodness, especially that/*for* . . .

From Isaiah 6
O God, high and exalted, yet present
among us, with angels and saints in
heaven we cry to each other:
**Holy, holy, holy,
the Lord almighty is holy,
his glory fills the world. Amen.**

*From Colossians 1, Hebrews 13 and
Psalm 50*
Father, in your presence we declare the
mystery of your love for us and
honour you with our sacrifice of praise
and thanksgiving. So we prepare your
way before you:
show us your salvation.

From 1 Corinthians 11
Our Lord Jesus Christ in the night he
was betrayed, took bread, and when
he had given thanks, he broke it and
said,
'This is my body, given for you;
do this to remember me'.

From 1 Corinthians 10 and John 6
We break this bread:
to share in the body of Christ.

In the same way, after supper, he took
the cup, saying,
'This cup is the new covenant
   in my blood;
do this, whenever you drink it,
to remember me.'

From 1 Corinthians 10
We drink this cup:
to share in the blood of Christ.

From 1 Corinthians 12 and Revelation 22
Whenever you eat this bread and
drink this cup you proclaim the Lord's
death until he comes:
Amen. Come, Lord Jesus.

AND/OR

From Revelation 5
**Worthy is the Lamb who was slain,
to receive power and wealth,
wisdom and strength,
honour and glory and praise. Amen.**

From Romans 5 and John 6
Eternal Father, pour out your love into
our hearts by the Holy Spirit whom
you have given to us, and let this bread
and wine be for us the body and blood
of Christ, food of our eternal life.
Amen.

17. THE LORD'S PRAYER
From Matthew 6 and Luke 11
**Our Father in heaven,
hallowed be your name,
your kingdom come,
your will be done,
on earth as in heaven.
Give us today our daily bread.
Forgive us our sins
as we forgive
   those who sin against us.
Lead us not into temptation
but deliver us from evil.**

**For the kingdom, the power,
and the glory are yours,
now and for ever. Amen.**

18. HEARING GOD'S INVITATION
From James 4
Come near to God, and he will come
near to you. **Amen.**

From John 6
Jesus said, 'If you come to me you will
never go hungry.' **Amen.**

From John 6
Jesus said, 'If you believe in me you
will never be thirsty.' **Amen.**

THE COMMUNION MINISTRY

20. GIVING GOD THE GLORY
From Romans 16
**Glory to God,
who alone is all-wise;
through Jesus Christ, for ever! Amen.**

21. SHARING GOD'S BLESSING
From Psalm 129
The blessing of the Lord be upon you:
**we bless you in the name of the Lord.
Amen.**

22. DEPARTING TOGETHER
From John 20
Jesus said, 'As the Father has sent me, so I am sending you.' Go in the name of Christ. **Amen.**

OR

23. DEPARTING TOGETHER
From Isaiah 55
Let us go out with joy:
let us depart in peace. Amen.

24. DEPARTING TOGETHER (EVENING)
From Exodus 33
The presence of the Lord go with you:
the Lord give us rest. Amen.

BIBLE PRAYERS FOR WORSHIP:
A RESOURCE SELECTION

Prayers from this selection may be transcribed for local use under the conditions outlined on p. iv

GREETING ONE ANOTHER

1. GREETING ONE ANOTHER
From Ruth 2
The Lord be with you:
the Lord bless you!

2. GREETING ONE ANOTHER (EVENING)
From Psalm 134
All of you who serve the Lord; you who come in the evening of the day to worship in his house, you who lift up your hands in his holy place, and praise the Lord: (may) the Lord, the maker of heaven and earth, bless you! **Amen.**

3. GREETING ONE ANOTHER
From John 14
Peace to you all – not as the world gives; Jesus' peace to you all:
Our hearts will not be troubled, we shall not be afraid. Amen.

4. GREETING ONE ANOTHER
From Romans 1
Grace and peace to you from God our Father and from the Lord Jesus Christ. **Amen.**

5. GREETING ONE ANOTHER
From Romans 15
Welcome one another as Christ has welcomed you:
to God be the glory. Amen.

6. GREETING ONE ANOTHER
From Romans 15
The God of peace be with you all.
Amen.

7. GREETING ONE ANOTHER
From 1 Corinthians 1
(*Here the local name is supplied.)
To the church of God in . . .*, to those sanctified in Christ Jesus and called to be holy, to all those everywhere who call on the name of our Lord Jesus Christ – their Lord and ours: grace and peace to you from God our Father and the Lord Jesus Christ. **Amen.**

8. GREETING ONE ANOTHER
From 2 Corinthians 13
The God of love and peace be with you. **Amen.**

9. GREETING ONE ANOTHER
From Galatians 1
Grace and peace be with you from God our Father and the Lord Jesus Christ, who gave himself for our sins according to the will of our God and Father; to whom be glory for ever and ever. **Amen.**

10. GREETING ONE ANOTHER
From Galatians 6
Peace and mercy to the people of God.
Amen.

11. GREETING ONE ANOTHER
From Ephesians 2
Peace to those who are near, and peace
to those who are far away:
through Christ
we all approach the Father
by the one Holy Spirit. Amen.

12. GREETING ONE ANOTHER
From Ephesians 6
Grace to all who love our Lord Jesus
Christ with an undying love. **Amen.**

13. GREETING ONE ANOTHER
From Ephesians 6
Peace to our brothers and sisters, and
love with faith from God the Father
and the Lord Jesus Christ. **Amen.**

14. GREETING ONE ANOTHER
From Philippians 1
From God our Father and the Lord
Jesus Christ, grace and peace to you:
grace and peace to all!

15. GREETING ONE ANOTHER
From Philippians 4
Rejoice in the Lord! **Amen.**

16. GREETING ONE ANOTHER
From Philippians 4
We greet you all in Christ Jesus:
The grace of the Lord Jesus Christ
be with you.

17. GREETING ONE ANOTHER
From Philippians 4
The grace of the Lord Jesus Christ be
with your spirit. **Amen.**

18. GREETING ONE ANOTHER
From 2 Thessalonians 1
Grace and peace to you from God our
Father and the Lord Jesus Christ.
Amen.

19. GREETING ONE ANOTHER
From 2 Timothy 1
Grace, mercy and peace from God the

Father and Christ Jesus our Lord.
Amen.

20. GREETING ONE ANOTHER
From 2 Timothy 4
The Lord be with your spirit:
grace and peace be with you. Amen.

21. GREETING ONE ANOTHER
From Titus 1
Grace and peace from God the Father
and Christ Jesus our Saviour. **Amen.**

22. GREETING ONE ANOTHER
From Jude
You are loved by God the Father and
kept by Jesus Christ:
mercy, peace and love
  be ours for ever. Amen.

23. GREETING ONE ANOTHER
From 1 Peter 5
Peace to all of you who are in Christ:
let us greet one another with love.

24. GREETING ONE ANOTHER
From Philemon 1
Grace to you and peace from God our
Father and the Lord Jesus Christ.
Amen.

25. GREETING ONE ANOTHER
From 1 Peter 1
Grace and peace be yours in full
measure. **Amen.**

26. GREETING ONE ANOTHER
From 2 Peter 1
Grace and peace be yours in full
measure through the knowledge of
God and of Jesus our Lord. **Amen.**

27. GREETING ONE ANOTHER
From 2 John
Grace, mercy and peace from God the
Father and from Jesus Christ, the
Father's Son, be with you in truth and
love. **Amen.**

28. GREETING ONE ANOTHER
From 2 John
Peace to you . . . greet your friends by
name. **Amen.**
(We greet one another)

29. GREETING ONE ANOTHER
From Revelation 22
The grace of the Lord Jesus be with God's people. **Amen.**

30. GREETING ONE ANOTHER
From Revelation 1
Grace and peace to you from Jesus Christ, who is the faithful witness, the first-born from the dead. **Amen.**

31. GREETING ONE ANOTHER
From Revelation 1
Grace and peace to you from him who is, and who was, and who is to come. **Amen.**

32. GREETING ONE ANOTHER
From Titus 1
Grace and peace to you from God our Father and Jesus Christ our Saviour. **Amen.**

33. GREETING ONE ANOTHER
From Revelation 1
Grace and peace to you from Jesus Christ, who is the faithful witness, the first-born from the dead. **Amen.**

34. GREETING ONE ANOTHER
From Revelation 1
Grace and peace to you from God who is, and who was, and who is to come, and from Jesus Christ, the faithful witness, the first-born from the dead. **Amen.**

35. EASTER/ADVENT RESPONSE
From Ephesians 5
Wake up, sleepers, rise from death:
**the light of Christ
will shine upon us.**

DRAWING NEAR TO GOD

36. DRAWING NEAR TO GOD (COMMUNION)
From Psalm 26
Lord God,
we are here to worship you –
let your love guide us,
and your faithfulness lead us;
we come to ask for your forgiveness,
to gather round your table,
to bring you our thanksgiving,
to proclaim your redemption:
receive the praise of your people.
Amen.

37. DRAWING NEAR TO GOD (MORNING)
From Psalm 143
Lord God,
as we remember days gone by,
and think about
    all you have done for us,
our souls thirst for you
and we lift our hands to you in prayer.
Answer us now, Lord,

don't hide yourself from us;
remind us this morning
    of your constant love:
for we put our trust in you,
through Jesus Christ our Lord. **Amen.**

38. DRAWING NEAR TO GOD (MORNING)
From Psalm 143
O Lord God,
make us to hear your voice
    in the morning,
for in you shall be our trust;
show us the way
    that we should walk in,
for we lift up our souls to you;
teach us to do
    the thing that pleases you,
for you are our God.
Let your loving Spirit lead us
into the place of righteousness,
for your name's sake. **Amen.**

HEARING GOD'S COMMANDMENTS

39. THE TEN COMMANDMENTS
From Exodus 20/Deuteronomy 5, etc.
Let us hear the decrees, and the laws of the Lord, learn them, and be sure to follow them:

'You shall have no other gods but me':
Lord, help us to love you
with all our heart, all our soul,
all our mind and all our strength.

'You shall not make for yourself any idol':
Lord, help us to worship you
in spirit and in truth.

'You shall not dishonour the name of the Lord your God':
Lord, help us to honour you
with reverence and awe.

'Remember the Lord's day and keep it holy':
Lord, help us to celebrate Christ
risen from the dead,
and to set our minds on things above,
not on things on the earth.

'Honour your father and your mother':
Lord, help us to live as your servants,
giving respect to all,
and to love our brothers and sisters
in Christ.

'You shall not murder':
Lord, help us to be reconciled
one with another,
and to overcome evil with good.

'You shall not commit adultery':
Lord, help us to realise
that our body is a temple
of the Holy Spirit.

'You shall not steal':
Lord, help us to be honest
in all we do,
and to care for those in need.

'You shall not be a false witness':
Lord, help us
always to speak the truth.

'You shall not covet anything which belongs to your neighbour':
Lord, help us to remember
Jesus said,

'It is more blessed to give
than to receive',
and help us to love our neighbours
as ourselves;
for his sake. Amen.

40. JESUS' COMMANDMENTS
From Mark 12
Jesus said: Love the Lord your God with all your heart and with all your soul and with all your mind and with all your strength; and love your neighbour as yourself:
Lord,
we have broken your
commandments –
forgive us, and help us to obey;
for your name's sake. Amen.

41. JESUS' COMMANDMENTS
From Matthew 22 and John 13
We pray for strength to keep Jesus' commandments:

'Love the Lord your God with all your heart, with all your mind, with all your soul, and with all your strength':
Lord, help us to obey.

'Love your neighbour as yourself':
Lord, help us to obey.

'Love one another as I have loved you':
Lord, help us to obey.

In your mercy strengthen us
and move our hearts
to do your will. Amen.

42. FULFILLING THE COMMANDMENTS
From Romans 13
The commandments: do not commit adultery, do not commit murder, do not steal, do not desire what belongs to another – these and all others are summed up in one command: love your neighbour as yourself:
Lord, help us to love our neighbours
and to do them no wrong,
that we may obey your law. Amen.

381

43. THE GREATEST
COMMANDMENT
From 1 John 4 and Psalm 139
Love one another, for love is of God,
and whoever loves is born of God.
O God, search our hearts;
see if there is any offence in us,
and lead us in the way everlasting.
Amen.

CONFESSING OUR SINS

44. CONFESSING OUR SINS
From 2 Kings 22
Lord, we have not obeyed your word,
nor heeded what is written
    in the Scriptures:
we repent with all our heart,
and humble ourselves before you.
In your mercy forgive us:
grant us your peace
and the strength to keep your laws;
through Jesus Christ our Lord. **Amen.**

45. CONFESSING OUR SINS
From Ezra 9
O God,
we are too ashamed and disgraced
    to lift up our faces to you,
because our sins
    are higher than our heads,
and our guilt
    has reached to the heavens.
O Lord, you are righteous;
we are before you in our guilt,
not one of us
    can stand in your presence.
Forgive us; in Jesus' name. **Amen.**

46. CONFESSING OUR SINS
From Nehemiah 9
O our God,
the great, mighty and awesome God,
gracious and merciful;
you keep your covenant of love –
you have acted faithfully,
while we have done wrong.
We did not follow
    your commandments
or pay attention to your warnings;
even while we were enjoying
    your great goodness
we did not serve you,
or turn from our evil ways;
because of our sin

our happiness is taken away –
our enemy rules
    even our souls and bodies
and we are in great distress.
Forgive us and restore us
for your name's sake. **Amen.**

47. CONFESSING OUR SINS
From Job 40-42
Lord, you are without equal;
everything under heaven is yours:
we are unworthy
and have to answer to you.
We confess our lack of understanding
and repent of all our sin.
Lord, our ears have heard of you,
and now our eyes have seen you
in Jesus our Redeemer. **Amen.**

48. CONFESSING OUR SINS
From Psalm 51
Lord God, have mercy on us,
according to your steadfast love;
and in your abundant mercy,
blot out our transgressions:
cleanse us from our sin,
create in us a clean heart and life,
and continually renew a right spirit
    within us. **Amen.**

49. CONFESSING OUR SINS
From Psalm 51
O God, in your goodness have mercy
on us, wash us clean from our guilt:
purify us from our sin.

We know our faults well:
our sins hang heavy upon us.

Against you only have we sinned:
we have done evil in your sight.

So you are right to judge us:
you are justified in condemning us.

Remove our sin and we will be clean:
wash us,
and we will be whiter than snow.

Hide your face from our sins:
wipe out all our guilt
through Jesus Christ our Lord.
Amen.

50. CONFESSING OUR SINS
From Psalm 51
The sacrifices of God are a broken
spirit; a broken and contrite heart, O
God, you will not despise. O God, in
your unfailing love:
have mercy on us.

We know our transgressions, and our
sin is ever before us; against you only
have we sinned and done what is evil
in your sight. O God, in your unfailing
love:
have mercy on us.

According to your great compassion
blot out our transgressions, wash
away all our iniquity and cleanse us
from our sin. O God, in your unfailing
love:
have mercy on us.

Cleanse us, and we shall be clean;
wash us,
and we shall be whiter than snow;
through Jesus Christ our Lord.
Amen.

51. CONFESSING OUR SINS
From Psalm 101
Lord God, our hearts are guilty,
we have been dishonest,
we have looked on evil,
we have clung to our selfish ways.
We have talked about others
    behind their backs
with haughty eyes and a proud heart.
Lord, forgive us and help us;
renew us in righteousness
    every morning:
make our lives faithful
and our talk blameless
that we may live in your presence
    for ever;
through Jesus Christ our Lord. **Amen.**

52. CONFESSING OUR SINS
From Psalm 106
O Lord our God,
we have not obeyed your commands,
we have not always done
    what is right;
in our weakness we have sinned,
we have done wrong
we have acted wickedly;
we have forgotten
    your many kindnesses
and we have rebelled against you:
O Lord, forgive us and save us
bring us back and restore us;
that we may give thanks
    to your holy name
and glory in your praise. **Amen.**

53. CONFESSING OUR SINS (EVENING)
From Psalm 109
O Lord, we need you:
our hearts are wounded,
our days fade like evening shadows,
we are weak and despise ourselves;
for we have sinned against you.
Forgive us, O Lord,
and in your constant love save us;
through Jesus our redeemer. **Amen.**

54. CONFESSING OUR SINS
From Psalm 119
Lord, we are to blame,
for we have not followed your law,
we have not kept
    your commandments,
we have not sought for you
    with all our heart,
we have not walked in your ways,
nor have we fully obeyed you;
Lord, we long to be faithful
    and obedient:
do not put us to shame.
Give us upright hearts,
teach us obedience
and do not forsake us for ever. **Amen.**

55. CONFESSING OUR SINS
From Psalm 130
Out of the depths, O Lord, we cry to
you. O Lord, hear our voice:
listen to our cry for mercy.

If you kept a record of our sins, who
could stand before you? O Lord, hear

our voice:
listen to our cry for mercy.

But you offer forgiveness, and therefore we fear you, O Lord, hear our voice:
listen to our cry for mercy.

We wait for you, O Lord, and in your promise we put our hope. O Lord, hear our voice:
listen to our cry for mercy.

We long for you, O Lord, more than the sleepless long for the morning, O Lord, hear our voice:
listen to our cry for mercy.

O God, we put our trust in you,
because with you
   there is unfailing love
and full redemption
   from all our sins,
through our Saviour Jesus Christ.
Amen.

56. CONFESSING OUR SINS
From Psalm 130
O Lord, we cry to you
   from the depths of our being:
let your ears be open
   as we plead for mercy.
If you kept a record of our sins
none of us could stand before you;
but you alone can forgive us,
therefore we come to you in awe.
Lord, we wait for you
and in your promise we put our
   hope;
through our saviour Jesus Christ.
Amen.

57. CONFESSING OUR SINS
From Psalm 142
Lord, we have sinned:
we lift up our voice to you
and cry for mercy.
There is no-one else
   to whom we can go:
save us from our sins
and from temptations
   that are too strong for us.
Set us free,
that we may praise your name;
through Jesus Christ our Lord.
Amen.

58. CONFESSING OUR SINS
From Psalm 143
O Lord, hear our prayer
   as we cry for your mercy;
in your faithfulness
   and righteousness
come to help us.
Do not bring us to judgement,
for no-one is innocent before you.
Answer us now, Lord;
do not hide yourself from us,
show us the way we should go,
rescue us from our enemy.
Teach us to do your will,
and by your good Spirit
lead us in a safe path,
for your name's sake. Amen.

59. CONFESSING OUR SINS
From Psalm 143
Lord, we have failed you:
darkness overtakes us,
our spirits tremble
and our hearts are dismayed;
your face is hidden from us,
and we wait for your word of love.
Hear our prayer,
listen to our cry for mercy;
in your faithfulness
   and righteousness
come to our relief.
Do not bring us to judgement –
for no-one living
   is righteous before you;
show us the way we should go,
teach us to do your will
and let your Spirit lead us;
through Jesus Christ our Lord.
Amen.

60. CONFESSING OUR SINS
From Isaiah 6
O Lord our God,
enthroned on high,
filling the whole earth
   with your glory:
holy, holy, holy is your name.
Our eyes have seen the King,
the Lord almighty;
but our lips are unclean.
We cry to you in our sinfulness
to take our guilt away,
through Jesus Christ our Lord.
Amen.

61. CONFESSING OUR SINS
From Isaiah 43
O Lord our God,
we confess
    that we have not called upon you,
we have not been generous
    in our giving,
nor have we honoured you;
but we have wearied you
    with our wrong-doing
and burdened you with our offences:
blot out our transgressions
and remember our sin no more,
for your name's sake. Amen.

62. CONFESSING OUR SINS
From Isaiah 57
O God,
you are eternal,
    and your name is holy;
you live in a high and holy place –
yet also with the humble
    and penitent:
revive our spirits,
    renew our hearts.
We confess our greed
    and our wilful ways:
you have punished us,
you have hidden your face from us.
O God, forgive us,
through Jesus Christ our Lord.
Amen.

63. CONFESSING OUR SINS
From Isaiah 59
O God,
our offences are many in your sight,
and our sins testify against us;
our wrong-doing is ever with us,
and we acknowledge our iniquities;
we have rebelled against you
and acted treacherously towards you,
turning our backs on you:
O God, forgive us,
through Jesus Christ our Lord.
Amen.

64. CONFESSING OUR SINS
From Isaiah 64
Sovereign Lord,
we have continually sinned
    against you;
we have become unclean,

all our righteous acts
    are like filthy rags;
we shrivel up like leaves,
and our sins sweep us away.
Yet, O Lord, you are our Father:
do not remember our sins for ever.
We are your people:
look upon us, we pray,
and forgive us;
through Jesus our redeemer. Amen.

65. CONFESSING OUR SINS
From Jeremiah 14
O Lord,
we acknowledge
    our own wickedness
and the guilt of our society;
we have sinned against you.
For the sake of your name
do not despise us;
remember your covenant with us
    in Jesus our redeemer,
and forgive us our sin;
for his name's sake. Amen.

66. CONFESSING OUR SINS
From Lamentations 5
Remember, O Lord,
    your people in their sorrow;
look, and see our disgrace:
joy is gone from our hearts;
our dancing has turned to mourning,
we are no longer proud –
the crown has fallen from our head,
for we have sinned.
You, O Lord, reign for ever,
your throne endures
    to every generation:
do not forget us now,
do not forsake us for long:
forgive us, restore us and renew us;
through our redeemer, Jesus Christ.
    Amen.

67. CONFESSING OUR SINS
From Daniel 9
O Lord our God, you brought your
people out of slavery with a mighty
hand, and made for yourself a name
which endures to this day:

We have sinned, we have done wrong.
O Lord, hear:
O Lord, forgive!

In keeping with all your righteous acts, turn away your anger from your people. O Lord, hear:
O Lord, forgive!

Our sins have made us despised by those around us. O Lord, hear:
O Lord, forgive!

We do not come before you because we are righteous; but because of your great mercy: O Lord; hear:
O Lord: forgive!

O Lord our God, do not delay
but send your Holy Spirit
to revive your church,
because your people
bear the name of Christ. Amen.

68. CONFESSING OUR SINS
From Amos 2
Lord God almighty,
we have rejected your law,
and have not obeyed
your commandments;
we have ignored
the needs of the poor,
and denied justice to the oppressed.
Lord, we have sinned
and dishonoured your holy name:
have mercy on us;
for Jesus' sake. Amen.

69. CONFESSING OUR SINS
From Jonah 2
O Lord our God,
in distress we call to you;
from the depths we cry for help –
the storm swirls around us,
our troubles threaten to engulf us.
We feel we have been banished
from your sight,
but we look again
towards your loving peace.
We have clung to worthless things
and forfeited the grace
that could have been ours:
We are trapped under a weight of sin
O Lord, we call to you:
forgive us and restore us,
through Jesus our redeemer. Amen.

70. CONFESSING OUR SINS
From 1 Corinthians 13
Let us confess our lack of love, and our need of grace:

When we lose patience,
when we are unkind,
when we are envious,
when we are rude or proud,
when we are selfish or irritable,
and when we will not forgive:
have mercy on us, O God.
Help us not to delight in evil,
but to rejoice in the truth;
help us always to protect, to trust,
to hope and to persevere
so that we may see you face to face,
and learn to love as you love us;
in Jesus Christ our Lord. Amen.

71. CONFESSING OUR SINS
From Ephesians 5 and 6
This prayer may be led by a representative of those named; a parent, a child, a father, a mother, a husband, a wife,
(*The bracketed section may be omitted)
O God, the Father of us all, we come to you in sorrow, for we have often failed you:
Lord, forgive us, and help us to obey.

You have taught us: 'Honour your father and mother, that it may go well with you and that you may enjoy long life on the earth.' We have often failed you:
Lord, forgive us, and help us to obey.

You have taught us as children: 'Obey your parents in the Lord, for this is right.' We have often failed you:
Lord, forgive us, and help us to obey.

You have taught us as fathers: `Do not exasperate your children; instead, bring them up in the training and instruction of the Lord.' We have often failed you:
Lord, forgive us, and help us to obey.

You have taught us as mothers to live with sincere faith and bring our children to Christ. We have often failed you:
Lord, forgive us, and help us to obey.

[You have taught us as husbands: `Love your wives as you love yourselves.' We have often failed you:
Lord, forgive us, and help us to obey.

You have taught us as wives: 'Respect your husbands.' We have often failed you:
Lord, forgive us,
   and help us to obey.]

You have taught us as the Christian family: 'Submit to one another out of reverence for Christ.' We have often failed you:
Lord, forgive us, and help us to obey.

Father, help us all to hear your word, and to obey it; for Jesus' sake. Amen.

72. CONFESSING OUR SINS
From 1 John 1
O God,
you have taught us
that if we say we have no sin

we deceive ourselves
and the truth is not us:
we humbly confess our sins to you;
and we ask you to keep your promise
to forgive us our sins
and to cleanse us
   from all unrighteousness;
through Jesus Christ our Lord.
Amen.

73. CONFESSING OUR SINS AND RECEIVING GOD'S FORGIVENESS
From 2 Samuel 12
Why have you rejected the word of the Lord by doing evil in his sight?
We have sinned against the Lord.

The Lord has taken away your sin; you will not die. **Amen.**

RECEIVING GOD'S FORGIVENESS

74. RECEIVING GOD'S FORGIVENESS
From Nehemiah 9
The Lord our God is a forgiving God, gracious and merciful, slow to anger and full of love; because of his great compassion he will not abandon us. You were disobedient and rebelled against him, yet from heaven he hears you in your distress, he forgives your sin and delivers you; through Jesus Christ our Lord. **Amen.**

75. RECEIVING GOD'S FORGIVENESS
From Psalm 6
The Lord God be merciful to you and heal you; the Lord turn his face towards you and deliver you; the Lord save you in his unfailing love; through Jesus Christ. **Amen.**

76. RECEIVING GOD'S FORGIVENESS
From Psalm 130
If God kept a record of your sins you could not stand; but with him there is forgiveness – therefore fear him, wait for him, put your hope in him. His love for you has not failed, and he has redeemed you from all your sins; through Christ, our Lord. **Amen.**

77. RECEIVING GOD'S FORGIVENESS
From Isaiah 40 and 38
Hear God's tender words of comfort for you: 'Your struggles are ended, your sin is paid for'. God will show you his glory, and you will receive the grace of forgiveness at his hand:

The Lord restore your health, the Lord bring you salvation and let you live; the Lord in his love keep you from destruction and put your sins behind his back for ever. **Amen.**

78. RECEIVING GOD'S FORGIVENESS
From Isaiah 41
Let us receive forgiveness in the name of our God.

We are God's servants –
he has chosen us and not rejected us:
we will not fear, for he is with us,
nor be afraid, for he is our God -
he will strengthen us and help us;
he will uphold us with
   his righteous right hand;
through Jesus Christ our Lord.
Amen.

79. RECEIVING GOD'S FORGIVENESS
From Isaiah 43
The Lord, your redeemer, the Holy One, blots out your transgressions and remembers *your* sins no more; for his name's sake. **Amen.**

80. RECEIVING GOD'S FORGIVENESS
From Isaiah 49
Hear the assurance of God's forgiveness:

In the time of his favour the Lord answers you; in the day of salvation he helps you; the Lord comforts you, he has compassion on you; he has not forsaken you, nor has he forgotten you. Lift up your eyes and look around: the Lord is your saviour and your redeemer; in Christ you are forgiven. **Amen.**

81. RECEIVING GOD'S FORGIVENESS
From Isaiah 53
Receive God's forgiveness through our Lord Jesus Christ: he covers your weaknesses and carries your sorrows; he was pierced for your transgressions and crushed for your iniquities; he took your punishment upon himself to bring you peace: by his wounds you are healed. **Amen.**

82. RECEIVING GOD'S FORGIVENESS
From Amos 5
Seek good and not evil and you shall live; hate evil, love good, and the Lord will be with you: God almighty has mercy upon you; through Jesus our Redeemer. **Amen.**

83. RECEIVING GOD'S FORGIVENESS
From Colossians 2
God has rescued us from the power of darkness, and brought us safe into the kingdom of his dear Son: in Christ our sins are forgiven, we are set free. **Amen.**

84. RECEIVING GOD'S FORGIVENESS
From Hebrews 10
Draw near with a sincere heart and a sure faith: you are purified from your guilt and washed clean through the blood of Christ. Hold on to this hope, and trust the promises of God. **Amen.**

PRAISING GOD

85. PRAISING GOD (BEFORE HYMN, PSALM, SONG)
From Psalm 70
Praise to the Lord, our God:
praise his glorious name for ever.

Let the earth be filled with his glory:
Amen. Amen.

86. PRAISING GOD (BEFORE HYMN, PSALM, SONG)
From Psalm 113
Praise the Lord, you servants of the Lord:
Praise his name!

His name be praised, now and for ever:
From the east to the west praise the name of the Lord!

87. PRAISE SHOUT
From Isaiah 12
All God's people, rejoice and shout aloud:
great is the Holy One, our Saviour! Amen.

88. PRAISING GOD'S GLORY
From Isaiah 23 and 24
Lord Almighty, you bring low all pride and glory, you humble the famous in the earth; you stretch out your hand over the sea and make the nations tremble. To you we raise our voices, and shout for joy; we acclaim your majesty, we give you praise, we exalt your name. From the ends of the earth we proclaim:
Glory to the righteous One,

who reigns among us
for ever and ever! Amen.

89. PRAISING GOD'S GLORY
From Isaiah 25
O Lord, we exalt and praise your
name, for you are faithful to us and
have done marvellous things – things
promised long ago:
you are our God –
we trust in you, and you save us;
through Jesus our redeemer. Amen.

90. PRAISING GOD (BEFORE HYMN, PSALM, SONG)
From Revelation 19
Praise God!
The Lord our almighty God is king!

Rejoice and be glad:
praise his greatness! Amen.

91. BEFORE READING
From 2 Samuel 22
You are our lamp, O Lord:
you turn our darkness into light.
Amen.

92. BEFORE READING
From Psalm 130
We wait eagerly for the Lord:
in his word we trust.

93. BEFORE READING
From Jeremiah 9
Let us hear God's word:
let us listen to the Lord.

94. AFTER READING
From 1 Kings 22
All you people, mark these words:
the Lord has spoken. Amen.

95. AFTER READING
From Nehemiah 8.6
Praise the Lord, the great God:
Amen. Amen.

96. AFTER READING
From 1 Peter 1
After a Reading:
The word of the Lord remains for ever.
Amen.

After a Gospel Reading:
This is the Gospel we proclaim.
Amen.

97. AFTER READING
From Revelation 1
Happy are those who read these
words aloud.
Happy are those who hear
and take them to heart

98. AFTER READING
From Revelation 1
After a Reading:
Happy are those who read these
words:
Happy are those who hear them.

After a Gospel Reading:
This is the word of God and the testimony of Jesus Christ. **Amen.**

99. AFTER READING
From Revelation 1-7
Hear what the Spirit is saying to the
churches:
thanks be to God. Amen.

For sets of Communion responses see the
Communion Service resources (p. 381).

AFFIRMING OUR FAITH

100. RESPONSE BEFORE AFFIRMATION
Before an appropriate affirmation, hymn or
song. From 1 John 5
Who can defeat the world?
Only the one who believes
that Jesus is the Son of God.

101. AFFIRMING OUR FAITH
From Psalm 126
We declare our faith in God:

Who brought us out from slavery?
The Lord! Thank you, Jesus.

Who filled our hearts with joy?
The Lord! Thank you, eternal Spirit.

Who has done great things for us?
The Lord! Thank you, Father.

Who gives us joy instead of tears; who
gives us songs instead of weeping;
who blesses us with all good things?
The Lord our God:
Father, Son and Holy Spirit. Amen.

102. AFFIRMING OUR FAITH
From Psalm 145
We believe in God
who is gracious and compassionate,
slow to anger and rich in love.

We believe in God,
whose kingdom is everlasting,
who dominion endures for ever.

We believe in God,
who is faithful to all his promises,
and loving towards all he has made.

We believe in God,
who opens his hand
and satisfies the needs
of all things living. Amen.

103. AFFIRMING OUR FAITH
From Isaiah 43
We believe in the Lord God,
the Holy One,
Father, Son and Holy Spirit;
we are his witnesses
and his servants.
He alone is the Lord,
apart from him there is no saviour;
he has revealed and saved
and proclaimed;
he is our creator, our redeemer
and our king;
it is he
who blots out our transgressions
and remembers our sins no more.
Amen.

104. AFFIRMING OUR FAITH
From Isaiah 44
We believe in one God
who made all things;
he alone stretched out the heavens
and spread out the earth:
he formed us in the womb.
He is our king and our redeemer –
the Lord almighty.

We belong to the Lord –
we are his people
and are called by his name;
he pours out his Spirit upon us

as water on a thirsty land.

We believe in one God, the almighty,
Father, Son and Holy Spirit. Amen.

105. AFFIRMING OUR FAITH
From Isaiah 44
We believe in one God who made all
things:

Did he stretch out the heavens, spread
out the earth, and form us in the
womb?
He did!

Is he the Lord almighty, our king and
redeemer?
He is!

Are we his own people, called by his
name?
We are!

Does he pour his Spirit on us as on a
dry and thirsty land?
He does!

We believe in one God,
the Almighty,
Father, Son and Holy Spirit. Amen.

106. AFFIRMING OUR FAITH
From Isaiah 53
We believe in Jesus Christ,
the suffering Servant,
the Son of God;
he took upon himself
our weaknesses
and carried our sorrows;
he was wounded for our sins
and beaten for our wickedness;
he was led as a lamb to the slaughter,
as a sheep before the shearers
he did not open his mouth;
he was put to death for our sins –
the sacrifice
by which we are forgiven;
he bore the sin of many
and prayed for our forgiveness.
Amen.

107. AFFIRMING OUR FAITH
From Romans 1
We believe in the Gospel,
promised by God long ago
through the prophets,
written in the Holy Scriptures.

We believe in God's Son,
our Lord Jesus Christ:
as to his humanity,
born a descendant of David,
shown with great power
   to be the Son of God
by his raising from death. Amen.

108. AFFIRMING OUR FAITH
From Romans 1, 4 and 8
Let us proclaim our faith:

We believe in God the Father,
whose eternal power
   and divine nature
are clearly seen
in the creation of the world.

We believe in God the Son,
who died for our sin,
and rose again for our justification.

We believe in God the Holy Spirit,
who bears witness with our spirit
that we are the children of God.

We believe in one God:
Father, Son and Holy Spirit. Amen.

109. AFFIRMING OUR FAITH
From 1 Corinthians 8 and 12
We believe in one God and Father;
from him all things come.

We believe in one Lord Jesus Christ;
through him we come to God.

We believe in one Holy Spirit;
in him we are baptised
into one body.

We believe and trust in one God,
Father, Son and Holy Spirit. Amen.

110. AFFIRMING OUR FAITH
From 1 Corinthians 8 and 12
There is one God and Father:
from him all things come.

There is one Lord Jesus Christ:
through him we come to God.

There is one Holy Spirit:
in him we are baptised
into one body.

We believe in one God:
Father, Son, and Holy Spirit. Amen.

111. AFFIRMING OUR FAITH
From 1 Corinthians 12
We believe in one Lord Jesus Christ,
one faith, one baptism,
one God and Father of us all,
who is in all and over all
and through all. Amen.

112. AFFIRMING OUR FAITH
From 1 Corinthians 12
Let us affirm our faith in the unity and
the diversity of God:

We believe in the one Holy Spirit
giver of gifts of various kinds.

We believe in one Jesus Christ
Lord of various kinds of service.

We believe in one almighty Father
working in various ways.

We believe in one God
Father, Son and Holy Spirit. Amen.

113. AFFIRMING OUR FAITH
From 1 Corinthians 15
Let us declare our faith in the resurrec-
tion of our Lord Jesus Christ:

Christ died for our sins
in accordance with the Scriptures;
he was buried;
he was raised to life on the third day
in accordance with the Scriptures;
afterwards he appeared
   to his followers,
and to all the apostles:
this we have received,
and this we believe. Amen.

114. AFFIRMING OUR FAITH
From 2 Corinthians 1
All God's promises are 'yes' in Christ;
through him we give glory to God and
say, 'Amen':

It is Christ
to whom we belong.

It is the Father
who assures us of our salvation
and anoints us for his service.

It is the Spirit
by whom we are sealed in love
   for evermore.

We believe in one God:
Father, Son, and Holy Spirit. Amen.

115. AFFIRMING OUR FAITH
From 2 Corinthians, 4 and 5
We speak because we believe:

God,
who raised the Lord Jesus Christ
    to life,
will also raise us up with Jesus,
and take us together
    into his presence.

Though outwardly
    we are wasting away,
inwardly we are being renewed
    day by day;
we live by faith, and not by sight.
Amen.

116. AFFIRMING OUR FAITH
From Galatians 2
We have been crucified with Christ
and we no longer live,
but Christ lives in us.
The life we live in the body
we live by faith in the Son of God,
who loved us
    and gave himself for us. Amen.

117. AFFIRMING OUR FAITH
From Ephesians 2
Let us declare our faith in the resurrec-
tion and reign of Christ:

By his mighty power,
God raised from the dead
our Lord Jesus Christ
and seated him
    at his right hand in heaven,
far above all rule and authority,
power and dominion,
and every title that can be given,
not only in the present age
but also in the age to come.
God placed all things under his feet
and appointed him
to be head over everything
    for the Church,
        which is his body,
the fulness of him who fills
    everything everywhere
    and always. Amen.

118. AFFIRMING OUR FAITH
From Ephesians 3
Let us declare our faith in God:

We believe in God the Father,
from whom
every family in heaven and on earth
    is named.

We believe in God the Son,
who lives in our hearts through faith,
and fills us with his love.

We believe in God the Holy Spirit,
who strengthens us with power
    from on high.

We believe in one God;
Father, Son and Holy Spirit. Amen.

119. AFFIRMING OUR FAITH
From Ephesians 4
As God's people, let us declare our
faith:

There is one body and one Spirit,
just as we were called to one hope;
one Lord, one faith, one baptism:
one God and Father of all,
who is over all, and through all,
and in all. Amen.

120. AFFIRMING OUR FAITH
From Philippians 2
Let us affirm our faith in Jesus Christ
the Son of God:

Though he was divine,
he did not cling to equality
    with God,
but made himself nothing.
Taking the form of a slave,
he became as we are;
as a man he humbled himself,
and was obedient to death –
even the death of the cross.
Therefore God has raised him
    on high,
and given him
    the name above every name:
that at the name of Jesus
every knee should bow,
and every voice proclaim
that Jesus Christ is Lord,
to the glory of God the Father. Amen.

121. AFFIRMING OUR FAITH
From Philippians 2
Did Christ Jesus share the very nature of God?
He did!

Did he make himself nothing, taking the very nature of a slave?
He did!

Did he humble himself, becoming obedient to death – even the death on a cross?
He did!

Has God exalted him to the highest place of all and given him the name that is above every name?
He has!

Will every knee bow to him, in heaven, on earth and under the earth?
They will!

And will every tongue confess that 'Jesus Christ is Lord'?
We shall:
Jesus Christ is Lord! Amen.

122. AFFIRMING OUR FAITH
From Philippians 2
(Getting gradually quieter:)
Equal with God:
 Jesus is Lord.
Emptied himself:
 Jesus is Lord.
Came as a slave:
 Jesus is Lord.
Found as a man:
 Jesus is Lord.
Humbly obeyed:
 Jesus is Lord.
Went to his death:
 Jesus is Lord.
Death on a cross:
 Jesus is Lord.

(Getting gradually louder:)
God raised him up:
 Jesus is Lord.
Gave him the name:
 Jesus is Lord.
Higher than all:
 Jesus is Lord.
Every knee bow:
 Jesus is Lord.
All tongues confess:

'Jesus is Lord!'.

Glory to God! **Amen!**

123. AFFIRMING OUR FAITH
From Philippians 3
(Sisters and brothers . . .)
Do we belong to heaven?
We do!

Are we waiting for the Saviour to come from there?
We are!

Who is he?
The Lord Jesus Christ!

Can his power bring all things under his control?
It can!

Will he transform our humble bodies so that they may be like his glorious body?
He will!

Alleluia! **Amen!**

124. AFFIRMING OUR FAITH
From Colossians 1
Let us confess our faith in the Son of God:

Christ is the image of the
 invisible God,
the first-born over all creation.
By him all things were created:
things in heaven and on earth,
visible and invisible,
thrones, powers, rulers,
 and authorities;
all things were created by him
 and for him.

He is before all things
and in him all things hold together.

He is the head of the body,
 the Church;
he is the beginning,
and the first-born from the dead.
Amen.

125. AFFIRMING OUR FAITH
From Colossians 2
God has rescued us
 from the power of darkness,
and brought us safe
into the kingdom of his dear Son:

393

in Christ our sins are forgiven,
we are set free. Amen.

126. AFFIRMING OUR FAITH
From 1 Thessalonians 4
We believe
   that Jesus died and rose again;
we believe
   that God will take with Jesus
those who have died in him;
the Lord himself will come,
the dead in Christ will rise:
so we shall ever be with the Lord.
Amen.

127. AFFIRMING OUR FAITH
From 2 Thessalonians 2 and 3
Let us affirm the teaching to which we
hold:

We believe in God the Father
who loved us,
and by his grace gave us
eternal encouragement
   and good hope.

We believe in God the Son
who assures our hearts
and strengthens us
   in every good deed and word;
whose grace is with us all.

We believe in God the Holy Spirit,
the Lord of peace,
who gives us peace
   at all times and in every way.

We believe in one God:
Father, Son and Holy Spirit. Amen.

128. AFFIRMING OUR FAITH
From 1 Timothy 3
Let us proclaim the mystery of our faith:

We believe in one Lord Jesus Christ –
he was revealed in the flesh,
attested by the Spirit,
seen by apostles,
proclaimed to the nations,
believed in throughout the world,
and taken up to glory. Amen.

129. AFFIRMING OUR FAITH
From Titus 2 and 3
We believe the grace of God has
dawned upon us with healing for all
the world, and so we rejoice to declare

our faith in him:

We trust in God the Father,
who has revealed his love
   and kindness to us,
and in his mercy saved us,
not for any good deed of our own.
but because he is merciful.

We trust in Jesus Christ,
who gave himself up for us
to free us from our sin,
and set us apart for himself –
a people eager to do good.

We trust in the Holy Spirit,
whom God poured out on us
   generously
through Christ our saviour,
so that justified by grace
we might become heirs
with the hope of eternal life. Amen.

130. AFFIRMING OUR FAITH
From Titus 3
Let us declare our faith in God's salva-
tion:

God our Saviour saved us
not because of righteous things
   we had done,
but because of his mercy.
He saved us
through the washing of rebirth
and renewal by the Holy Spirit,
whom he poured out on us
   generously
through Jesus Christ our saviour;
so that,
   having been justified by his grace,
we might become heirs
with the hope of eternal life.

This is a trustworthy saying. Amen.

131. AFFIRMING OUR FAITH
From Hebrews 1
God who spoke to our ancestors
   through the prophets
many times and in many ways,
in these last days has spoken to us
   by his Son,
whom he appointed
   heir of all things,
through whom he made the worlds:

The Son is the radiance
   of God's glory,

the likeness of God's being;
he sustains all things
  by his powerful word;
he achieved the forgiveness of sins
and sat down at the right hand
  of the Majesty in heaven. Amen.

132. AFFIRMING OUR FAITH
Hebrews 4
Let us hold firmly to the faith we
profess:

**We have a great High Priest
in the very presence of God
Jesus, God's Son:
he can feel sympathy
  with our weakness;
for he was tempted
  in every way that we are,
but did not sin.**

133. AFFIRMING OUR FAITH
From 1 Peter 3
Let us confess our faith in Christ:

**Christ died for sins
once for all,
the just for the unjust,
to bring us to God:
he was put to death in the body,
but made alive by the Spirit;
he has gone up on high,
and is at God's right hand,
ruling over angels
  and the powers of heaven. Amen.**

134. AFFIRMING OUR FAITH
From 1 John
**We believe in God the Father,
who reveals his love to us in Christ.**

**We believe in God the Son,
who pours out his Holy Spirit on us.**

**We believe in the Holy Spirit,
who teaches us God's truth.**

**We believe in one God:
Father, Son, and Holy Spirit. Amen.**

135. AFFIRMING OUR FAITH
From 1 John 5
We believe in Jesus Christ the Son of
God, and we have this truth in our
hearts:
**God has given us eternal life,
and this life is in his Son.**

Whoever has the Son has life:
**whoever does not have
  the Son of God
does not have life.**

We believe that the Son of God has
come:
**he has given us wisdom
to know the true God. Amen.**

136. AFFIRMING OUR FAITH
From Revelation 1
Let us declare our faith in God:

**We believe in God the Father;
the almighty,
who was, and is, and is to come.**

**We believe in Jesus Christ;
the faithful witness,
the first-born from the dead,
the King of kings,
who loves us,
and has freed us from our sins
  by his blood.**

**We believe in the Spirit;
giver of many gifts,
proceeding from the throne on high.**

**We believe in one God:
Father, Son, and Holy Spirit. Amen.**

137. AFFIRMING OUR FAITH
From Revelation 1
We believe in Jesus Christ, before
whom we fall down and worship but
need not be afraid:
**He is the first and the last,
the living one;
he has authority over death
and the world of the dead.**

He was dead:
**but now he is alive for ever and ever.
Amen.**

138. AFFIRMING OUR FAITH
From Revelation 1
**We believe in one God and Father
whom we serve as a kingdom
    and priests;
to whom be glory and power for ever.**

**We believe in Jesus Christ,
who was raised from death,
who loves us,**

and has freed us from our sins
    by his blood.

**We believe in one Holy Spirit
who declares the word of God
    to the Churches.**

We believe in the Father,
the Son and the Holy Spirit:
one God, the almighty,
the Lord, the first and the last,
who is, who was and who is to come.
Amen.

139. AFFIRMING OUR FAITH (ADVENT)
From Revelation 1
**We believe in Jesus Christ:
he is the faithful witness,
he is the first-born from the dead,
he is the ruler of the powers
    of the world.**
He loves us –
he has loosed us from our sins
    by his blood.
He has made us a kingdom of priests
to serve our God.
He is coming on the clouds,
every eye will see him –
even those who pierced him.
All the peoples on earth will mourn
    because of him.
So shall it be. Amen.

140. AFFIRMING OUR FAITH
From Revelation 2
**We believe in Jesus Christ
before whom we fall down
    and worship
but need not be afraid:
he is the first and the last,
the living one;
he has authority over death
and the world of the dead,
for he was dead, but now is alive
    for ever and ever. Amen.**

141. AFFIRMING OUR FAITH
From Revelation 4, 5 and 22
We believe in God the Father, who
created all things:
**by his will they were created
and have their being.**

We believe in God the Son, who was
slain; with his blood he purchased us
for God:
**from every tribe and language
and people and nation.**

We believe in God the Holy Spirit; the
Spirit and the Bride say, 'Come!'
Even so, come, Lord Jesus! Amen.

142. AFFIRMING OUR FAITH
From Revelation 4 and 5
We say together in faith:
**Holy, holy, holy
is the Lord God Almighty,
who was, and is, and is to come.**

We believe in God the Father, who
created all things:
**by his will they were created
and have their being.**

We believe in God the Son, who was
slain:
**with his blood,
he purchased us for God,
from every tribe and language
    and people
and nation.**

We believe in God the Holy Spirit –
the Spirit and the Bride say, 'Come!'

Even so, come, Lord Jesus!
Amen.

PRAYING FOR OTHERS (*Sample Selection*)

143. INVITATION TO PRAYER
From Lamentations 3
Let us open our hearts to God in
heaven and pray. **Amen.**

144. FOR THE NEEDY, THE WORLD, AND THE CHURCH
From Hebrews 4, Ephesians 3 etc.
Let us approach God's throne with
confidence:

we shall receive mercy,
and find grace to help
in time of need. Amen.

For those in need . . .
Upon . . . have mercy, Lord:
we entrust them to your care.

For the world . . .
In . . . Lord, may peace and justice
rule:
let your love prevail.

For the Church . . .
O God, you are able to do immeasurably more than we ask or think by the
power that is at work among us: . . .

To God be glory in the Church and in
Christ Jesus:
for ever and ever. Amen.

145. INTERCEDING FOR OUR LAND
From Psalm 85
O God, our saviour,
you have been merciful to our land,
you have made us prosperous
    in the past,
you have forgiven us our sins
and pardoned our wrong-doing:
bring us back to faith,
make us strong again;
show us your constant love
and give us your saving grace,
help us to listen
    to what you are saying

and to leave our foolish ways,
so that we might receive your peace.

Lord, help us to honour you,
so that your healthful presence
may remain in our land:
then your love and our loyalty
    will meet,
our justice and your peace embrace;
our faith reach up from the earth
and your goodness look down
    from heaven;
you will bless us,
and our righteousness
    will prepare your way before you;
through Jesus Christ our Lord. Amen.

146. PRAYING ABOUT MISSION
From Isaiah 61
Sovereign Lord, you have anointed us
with your Spirit, and have sent us to
preach good news to the poor, to bind
up the broken-hearted, to announce
freedom to the captives and release for
the prisoners of darkness; to proclaim
your grace and your judgement, to
provide for those who mourn. Bless all
to whom we go; bring your beauty
into their lives – joy instead of
mourning, praise instead of despair;
through us, make them like trees you
have planted – rooted in righteousness, that they may display your
splendour; through Jesus Christ our
saviour. Amen.

PRAYING FOR OURSELVES (*Sample Selection*)

147. PRAYING FOR GOD'S PRESENCE
From Isaiah 33
Lord,
be gracious to me,
for I long for you;
be my strength every morning,
and my help in time of trouble.
Thank you, Lord. Amen.

148. PRAYING FOR HOLINESS
From Isaiah 35
Lord God,
lead us in the way of holiness,
cleanse us for our journey,
and teach us to be wise;
guard your redeemed,

crown your ransomed ones
    with everlasting joy;
let sorrow and sighing flee away
and gladness overtake us;
in Jesus Christ our saviour. Amen.

149. PRAYING FOR GOD'S RENEWING
From Isaiah 40
Lord, everlasting God, creator of the
ends of the earth, you never grow tired
or weary and no one can fathom your
wisdom: when we feel weak increase
in us your power, when we are tired
refresh us, when we stumble and fall
lift us up. Lord, you are our hope:
renew us and strengthen us now and

always. **Amen.**

150. PRAYING FOR OURSELVES (ADVENT)
From Mark 13
When the skies grow dark and buildings fall, then hear us:
have mercy on us, Lord.

When deceivers come and the nations rise in anger, then hear us:
have mercy on us, Lord.

When the famines begin, and when the earth shakes to bring the future to birth, then hear us:
have mercy on us, Lord.

When we stand for a witness, when we are arrested and betrayed, then hear us:
have mercy on us, Lord.

When the sun is darkened and the moon fails to give us light, and the stars fall from the sky, then hear us:
have mercy on us, Lord.

When you come in your great power and glory with your angels from heaven, have mercy on us, Lord:
gather us from the four winds,
from the ends of the earth,
to be with you for ever. Amen.

OFFERING GOD OUR GIFTS

151. OFFERING GOD OUR GIFTS
From 1 Chronicles 29
Lord, we bring these gifts to honour your holy name:
they came from your hands
and they all belong to you. Amen.

152. OFFERING GOD OUR GIFTS
From 2 Corinthians 8
Thank you, Lord Jesus Christ,
that, though you were rich,
yet for us you became poor
that we, through your poverty,
might become rich.

By your grace
let our riches
    supply the needs of others,
so that we may not have too much,
and they may not have too little;
for your name's sake. **Amen.**

153. OFFERING GOD OUR GIFTS
From Philippians 4
To our God and Father,
who meets all our needs
according to his glorious riches
    in Christ Jesus,
be glory for ever and ever. Amen.

GIVING THANKS TO GOD

154. GIVING THANKS TO GOD
From Isaiah 59
We thank you, God our Father, that your arm is strong to save, and your ear ready to hear; we thank you that as you promised you have come to save your people who repent of their sins; we thank you that your Spirit is upon us and will not leave us, and we thank you that your word will not depart from us, nor from our children, nor from their children, from this time on for ever. **Amen.**

155. THANKING GOD FOR UNITY IN THE SPIRIT
From 1 Corinthians 12
We thank God for our unity in diversity.

There are different kinds of gifts:
but the same Spirit.

There are different kinds of service:
but the same Lord.

There are different kinds of working:
but the same God.

Praise to God almighty,
Father, Son and Holy Spirit,
who works in us
in all these ways. Amen.

156. THANKING GOD FOR EVERYTHING
From Ephesians 5
We give thanks for everything to God the Father:
in the name of our Lord Jesus Christ.
Amen.

157. THANKING GOD FOR JESUS' EXALTATION
From Philippians 2.9-11
We praise you, our God,
because you exalted your Son Jesus
    Christ
to your right hand in glory,
and gave him
    the name above every name,
that at the name of Jesus
    every knee should bow.

Accept our worship, our love
    and thanksgiving;
and grant that we,
with those of every tongue,
may confess that Jesus Christ is Lord,
to your glory and honour. **Amen.**

158. THANKING GOD FOR HIS PROMISES
From Revelation 2 and 3
Hear the promises of Jesus the first and the last, the living one, who was dead but now is alive for ever and ever, who has authority over death and the world of the dead:

Those who win the victory will eat from the tree of life:
thank you, Lord Jesus.

Those who win the victory will not be hurt by the second death:
thank you, Lord Jesus.

Those who win the victory will be given a new name:
thank you, Lord Jesus.

Those who win the victory will receive authority from the Father:
thank you, Lord Jesus.

Those who win the victory will be clothed in white, and their names will remain in the book of the living:
thank you, Lord Jesus. Amen.

PRAISING GOD FOR HIS GLORY (*Ascription/Doxology*)

159. PRAISING GOD FOR HIS GLORY (BEFORE SONG)
From Exodus 15
Who is like you, O Lord, our God –
majestic in holiness, awesome in glory,
working wonders?
In your unfailing love
    you will lead your redeemed;
in your strength you will guide us.

Let us sing to the Lord for he is highly exalted:
the Lord will reign for ever and ever.
Amen.

160. PRAISING GOD FOR HIS GLORY
From Ephesians 3
Now to God the Father who is able to do immeasurably more than all we ask or think, by the power of the Spirit at work in us:
to him be the glory in the Church
and in Christ Jesus
throughout all generations
for ever and ever! Amen.

161. PRAISING GOD FOR HIS GLORY
From Philippians 4
To our God and Father,
who meets all our needs
according to his glorious riches
    in Christ Jesus,
be glory for ever and ever. **Amen.**

162. PRAISING GOD FOR HIS GLORY
From Jude
Now to him who is able to keep us from falling and to present us before his glorious presence without fault and with great joy – to the only God our Saviour be glory, majesty, power and authority, through Jesus Christ our Lord, before all ages, now, and for evermore! **Amen.**

163. PRAISING GOD FOR HIS GLORY
From Revelation 5
You are worthy, O Lord our God:
to receive glory and honour
and power.

For you created all things:
**and by your will they existed
and were created.**

You are worthy, O Christ, for you were slain:
**and by your blood you ransomed us
for God.**

From every tribe and tongue and people and nation:
**you made us a kingdom of priests
to serve our God.**

To him who sits upon the throne, and to the Lamb:
**blessing and honour,
glory and might,
for ever and ever! Amen.**

DEDICATING OURSELVES TO GOD'S SERVICE

164. DEDICATION
From Deuteronomy 26
Choose for yourselves this day whom you will serve:
We will serve the Lord!

You are witnesses against yourselves that you have chosen to serve the Lord:
Yes, we are witnesses.

Serve no other gods; yield your hearts to the Lord your God:
**We will serve the Lord our God,
and obey him. Amen.**

165. ACT OF COMMITMENT
From Philippians 3
Lord,
whatever we once thought gain,
we offer you for the sake of Christ:
we long for him – to be found in him,
and, through faith in him
to gain the righteousness
    that comes from you alone;
we want to know him,
the power of his resurrection
and the fellowship of his suffering;
to die to ourselves
that we might rise with him
    to eternal life. **Amen.**

ASKING FOR GOD'S BLESSING

166. ASKING FOR GOD'S BLESSING
From 1 Kings 8
Praise to the Lord, who has given rest to his people:
**not one word of his promises
    has failed.**

May the Lord your God be with you:
may he never leave us or forsake us.

May he turn *your* hearts to him, to walk in his ways and to keep his commandments:
**may the words we have prayed
    before the Lord our God
be near him day and night.**

Let all the people of the earth know the Lord is God:
there is no other! Amen.

167. ASKING FOR GOD'S BLESSING (COMMISSIONING)
From Job 29
Rescue the poor who cry for help, assist the orphans who have no-one to save them, bless the dying, make the widow's heart sing; put on justice as your clothing, righteousness as your robe; be eyes to the blind and feet to the lame; care for the needy, and champion the stranger; in the name of Christ destroy the power of the evil one, and the blessing of God almighty, Father, Son and Holy Spirit be upon you wherever you go. **Amen.**

168. ASKING FOR GOD'S BLESSING
From Psalm 5
The Lord lead you in his righteousness, the Lord make his way clear before you, the Lord spread his protection over you, the Lord surround you

with his love as with a shield; and the blessing of God almighty, the Father, the Son, and the Holy Spirit, be with you always. **Amen.**

169. ASKING GOD'S BLESSING (BAPTISM/CONFIRMATION)
From Psalm 84
The Lord be your sun and your shield; the Lord withhold no good thing from you as you walk before him in innocence; and the blessing of God almighty, the Father, the Son, and the Holy Spirit, be with you always. **Amen.**

170. ASKING FOR GOD'S BLESSING
From Psalm 129
The blessing of the Lord be upon you: **we bless you in the name of the Lord. Amen.**

171. ASKING FOR GOD'S BLESSING
From Isaiah 11
The Spirit of the Lord rest upon you: the Spirit of wisdom and understanding, the Spirit of counsel and power, the Spirit of knowledge and the fear of the Lord; may you delight in the Lord, now and always. **Amen.**

172. ASKING FOR GOD'S BLESSING
From Isaiah 26
Trust in the Lord, your eternal Rock, and he will keep your mind in perfect peace. Keep faith with him, walk with him, wait for him, desire him; reach out to him in the night, seek for him in the morning: and his blessing be upon *you* always. **Amen.**

173. ASKING FOR GOD'S BLESSING
From Isaiah 40
The Lord *your* shepherd tenderly care for *you*, gather *you* in his arms, carry *you* close to his heart and gently lead *you*; and the blessing of God the Father, God the Son, and God the Holy Spirit, be with *you* always. **Amen.**

174. ASKING FOR GOD'S BLESSING
From Isaiah 57
The Lord guide *you* and restore his comfort to *you*; the Lord bring praise to *your* lips; the Lord send *you* peace wherever *you* go; the Lord in his mercy heal *you*; and the blessing of God almighty, the Father, the Son and the Holy Spirit, be with *you* now and always. **Amen.**

175. ASKING FOR GOD'S BLESSING
From Isaiah 57
The Lord look upon *your* need and heal *you*; the Lord guide *you*, the Lord restore comfort to *you*, the Lord give *you* his peace. Amen.

176. ASKING FOR GOD'S BLESSING
From Isaiah 61
The Sovereign Lord anoint *you* with his blessing that *you* may preach good news to the poor, bind up the brokenhearted, proclaim freedom for the captives and release for those who are in darkness; that *you* may declare the Lord's favour and his judgement, and comfort those who mourn; so may the grace of our God, Father, Son and Holy Spirit, be upon *you* always. **Amen.**

177. ASKING FOR GOD'S BLESSING
From Isaiah 61
The Sovereign Lord anoint you with his blessing: proclaim good news to the poor, go and bind up the brokenhearted, announce freedom for the captives and release for those who are in darkness, declare the Lord's favour and his judgement, comfort all who mourn; and the grace of our God, Father, Son and Holy Spirit, be upon you always. **Amen.**

178. ASKING FOR GOD'S BLESSING
From Isaiah 65
The Lord make you glad and fill you with delight, the Lord grant you long life that you may enjoy the work of your hands, the Lord hear you before you call to him, the Lord answer you while you are still praying; the Lord bless you among his people and give you peace. **Amen.**

179. ASKING FOR GOD'S BLESSING
From Philippians 1
Live lives worthy of the gospel of Christ, stand together, defend the faith, do not be afraid; trust your Saviour, follow him, suffer for him: and the blessing of our God, Father, Son and Holy Spirit be upon *you* now and always. **Amen.**

180. ASKING FOR GOD'S BLESSING
From Philippians 2
Be united in Christ, enjoy the comfort of his love, the fellowship of his Spirit, the tenderness and compassion of our God; and the blessing of God almighty, the Father, the Son and the Holy Spirit, be with *you* always. **Amen.**

181. ASKING FOR GOD'S BLESSING
From Philippians 2
Shine like stars in a darkened world, hold out the word of life, be glad and rejoice in the Lord Jesus; and the blessing of God the Father, God the Son and God the Holy Spirit be with *you* always. **Amen.**

182. ASKING FOR GOD'S BLESSING
From Philippians 3
Forget what lies behind; reach out for what is yet to come, press on to win the prize – God's heavenward call in Jesus Christ. And the blessing of God almighty, Father, Son and Holy Spirit, be upon *you* always. **Amen.**

183. ASKING FOR GOD'S BLESSING
From Philippians 4
Rejoice in the Lord always, let everyone know your gentleness, do not be anxious, make your needs known to God; and the peace of God guard *your* hearts in Christ Jesus. **Amen.**

184. ASKING FOR GOD'S BLESSING
From Philippians 4
Rejoice in the Lord always, show gentleness to everyone; do not be anxious, make your needs known to God by prayer, with thanksgiving: and the peace of God guard *your* heart and mind in Christ Jesus. **Amen.**

185. ASKING FOR GOD'S BLESSING
From Philippians 4
Whatever is true, whatever is honourable, whatever is just, whatever is pure, whatever is lovely, whatever is gracious; if there is anything excellent, or anything worthy of praise: think on these things; and the God of peace be with *you* always. **Amen.**

186. ASKING FOR GOD'S BLESSING (RESPONSIVE)
From Philippians 4
May God meet all your needs from his glorious riches in Christ Jesus:
to God our Father be glory
for ever and ever. Amen.

GOING OUT FROM WORSHIP (*Dismissal*)

187. GOING OUT FROM WORSHIP
From Exodus 33
Lord God almighty, you have revealed your goodness to us and proclaimed your name among us:
now let your presence go with us,
and give us rest. Amen.

188. GOING OUT FROM WORSHIP
From Exodus 33
The presence of the Lord go with you:
the Lord give us rest. Amen.

189. GOING OUT FROM WORSHIP
From 1 Corinthians 16
Love to all of you in Christ Jesus:
the grace of the Lord Jesus
be with us all. Amen.

190. GOING OUT FROM WORSHIP
From Philippians 1
Rejoice and pray in the Spirit:
Jesus will set us free!

Hope in God and believe; have courage:
we are not ashamed!

Let Christ be exalted in you:
**for us to live is Christ, to die is gain.
Amen.**

191. GOING OUT FROM WORSHIP
From 2 Timothy 2
Salvation is in Jesus Christ:
and eternal glory:

If we die with him,
we shall live with him.

If we endure,
we shall reign with him. Amen.

192. GOING OUT FROM WORSHIP
From 2 Timothy 2
Be strong through the grace that is ours in union with Christ Jesus; take your part in suffering as his loyal soldier; remember him who was raised from the dead, Jesus Christ, our Lord and Saviour. **Amen.**

193. GOING OUT FROM WORSHIP
From Revelation 22
Jesus says, 'Behold I am coming soon!'
The Spirit and the bride say, 'Come!':
All who hear say, 'Come!'

Jesus, the faithful witness says, 'Yes, I am coming soon.'
Amen. Come, Lord Jesus.

The grace of the Lord Jesus be with all God's people. **Amen.**

MISCELLANEOUS

Other prayers based on Scripture will be found in Bible Praying[1]; other responsive material in Prayers for the People[2]

194. WEDDING RESPONSE
From Song of Songs 8
ᴹClose your heart to every love
but mine.
ᵂHold no-one your arms but me.

195. BAPTISM RESPONSE
From Matthew 28
All authority in heaven and on earth has been given to Jesus. As he has commanded, we baptise you in the name of the Father, and of the Son, and of the Holy Spirit.
**Obey him:
he will be with you always. Amen.**

[1]*Bible Praying*, published 1992 by HarperCollins*Publishers* Ltd, London.
[2]*Prayers for the People*, published 1992 by HarperCollins*Publishers* Ltd, London.

16

A SEASONAL SELECTION
OF OTHER PRAYERS

While the use of Bible passages as the basis for liturgical prayers has obvious advantages – and may appeal to those who are otherwise suspicious of written prayer forms, there is no reason why liturgies should be uniquely Bible based. I have gathered here a selection of prayers which have been found useful, many of them widely reproduced in local church leaflets and in national church service books (for instance, the Church of England's *Patterns for Worship*[1] and *A Service of the Word*[2]). Most of them are arranged in responsive ('responsorial') form so as to enable congregational participation. They may be freely reproduced under the conditions outlined on p. iv.

Most of the responsorial prayers here have 'trigger' phrases and consistent responses, for example:

Lord, in your mercy:
forgive us and help us.

OR

. . . gracious Lord:
we give you thanks and praise.

---

[1]*Patterns for Worship*, published 1989 by Church House Publishing, London.
[2]*A Service of the Word*, published 1993 by Church House Publishing, London.

This is an excellent way to make congregational praying accessible to those who cannot read easily – or at all. They soon know *when* a response is invited, and *what* that response should be. There is a slight danger of boredom if the response is repeated too often in the prayer, or frustration if the congregation is not allowed to say anything else. Early experiment with drafts of *Church Family Worship*[3] identified this latter problem, and a rhythmic congregational conclusion was added to each prayer. This was a compromise, but a good one, since it also had the effect of providing a resolution to the thoughts of the prayer.

Other prayers featured here are without responses, but where set in 'loose ended' text are meant for optional congregation use or, if not in bold type, for saying by the minister alone.

EPIPHANY AND LENT

1. CONFESSION OF SINS
Epiphany

Lord Jesus Christ, wise men from the east worshipped and adored you; they brought you gifts – gold, incense, and myrrh:

We too have seen your glory, but we have often turned away, Lord, in your mercy,
forgive us and help us.

We too have gifts, but we have not fully used them or offered them to you. Lord in your mercy,
forgive us and help us.

We too have acclaimed you as King, but we have not served you with all our strength. Lord, in your mercy,
forgive us and help us.

We too have acknowledged you as God, but we have not desired holiness. Lord, in your mercy,
forgive us and help us.

We too have welcomed you as Saviour, but we have failed to tell others of your grace. Lord, in your mercy,
forgive us and help us.

**Make our trust more certain,
make our love more real,
make our worship more acceptable to you;
for your glory's sake. Amen.**

2. CONFESSION
Lent, general

Almighty God, our Father, we come to you with humble hearts, to confess our sins:

For turning away from you, and ignoring your will for our lives: Father, forgive us,
save us and help us.

For behaving just as we wish, without thinking of you: Father forgive us,
save us and help us.

For failing you – not only by what we do, but also by our thoughts and words: Father, forgive us,
save us and help us.

[3]*Church Family Worship*, published 1986 by Hodder & Stoughton, London.

For letting ourselves be drawn away from you by temptation in the world about us: Father, forgive us,
save us and help us.

For acting as if we were ashamed to belong to your dear Son Jesus: Father, forgive us.
save us and help us.

**Father, we have often failed you,
and we humbly ask
   your forgiveness:
help us so to live
that others may see your glory;
through Jesus Christ our Lord.
Amen.**

3. DEDICATION
Lent, commitment
O God,
we are your children, and you love us;
so deep is your love
that nothing we have done,
   or thought to do,
shall take away the peace you give;
so strong is your love
that no passing trouble
   shall tear us from your arms;
so precious is your love
that all our life shall be lived out
   in your service –
and yours shall be the glory;
through Jesus Christ our Lord. **Amen.**

4. DEDICATION
Lent, prayer, commitment
Lord Jesus Christ,
we give ourselves into your hands.
Grant us grace to see you,
to know your way,
to feel you near.
Find us now in the quiet,
and hold us fast
   in the haste of the day;
for your glory's sake. **Amen.**

5. THANKSGIVING
Mothering Sunday, family occasions
We thank God for giving us other people to be part of our lives:

For parents, and the love which brought us to birth: we praise you, O Lord,
and bring you thanks today.

For mothers who have cherished and nurtured us: we praise you, O Lord,
and bring you thanks today.

For fathers who have loved and supported us: we praise you, O Lord,
and bring you thanks today.

For brothers and sisters with whom we have shared our home: we praise you, O Lord,
and bring you thanks today.

For children, entrusted to our parental care: we praise you, O Lord,
and bring you thanks today.

For other relatives and friends who have been with us in our hopes and our joys: we praise you, O Lord,
and bring you thanks today.

For all who first spoke to us of Jesus, and have drawn us into the family of our Father in heaven: we praise you, O Lord,
and bring you thanks today.

**Help us to live
as those who belong to one another
   and to you,
now and always. Amen.**

6. BLESSING
Family occasions
God the Father keep you in his care, the Lord Jesus Christ be your constant friend, and the Holy Spirit guide you in all you do, now and always. **Amen.**

PASSIONTIDE AND EASTER

7. CONFESSION OF SINS
Palm Sunday, Passiontide
On Palm Sunday, the crowds worshipped Jesus; on Good Friday they shouted for him to die. Let us who also worship him, confess that we sometimes reject him, and ask his forgiveness:

Lord Jesus Christ, you come to us in peace, but we shut the door of our mind against you. In your mercy:
forgive us and help us.

You come to us in humility, but we prefer our own proud ways. In your mercy:
forgive us and help us.

You come to us in judgement, but we cling to our familiar sins. In your mercy:
forgive us and help us.

You come to us in majesty, but we will not have you to reign over us. In your mercy:
forgive us and help us.

Lord, forgive our empty praise,
fill our loveless hearts;
come to us,
and make our lives your home
for ever. Amen.

8. CONFESSION OF SINS
Passiontide
Lord Jesus Christ, we confess we have failed you as did your disciples; and we ask for your mercy and your help:

When we are tempted to betray you for the sake of selfish gain: Christ, have mercy;
Lord, forgive us and help us.

When we do not keep watch in prayer, and will not share the pain of your suffering: Christ, have mercy;
Lord, forgive us and help us.

When we allow the world to silence you, and run away from those who abuse you: Christ, have mercy,
Lord, forgive us and help us.

When we will not confess your name, and fear the consequences of being known to belong to you: Christ have mercy;
Lord, forgive us and help us.

When we spurn your dying love, and will not offer you the sacrifice of our lives: Christ, have mercy;
Lord, forgive us and help us.

Cleanse us from our sins
by your precious blood,
and graciously restore us
to your service;
for your praise and glory. Amen.

9. CONFESSION
Good Friday, General
Almighty God, we confess that too often we have taken the easy way of the world, rather than your way, and so have grieved your heart of love.

We have been slow to admit that we are not our own, but belong to you: in your mercy,
forgive us and help us.

We have been unwilling to see that we are bought with the price of Christ's blood: in your mercy,
forgive us and help us.

We have been unprepared to live out our lives as your servants: in your mercy,
forgive us and help us.

Raise us by the power of your love,
and fill us with the joy of your Spirit;
through Jesus Christ our Lord.
Amen.

10. CONFESSION OF SINS
Easter
O Jesus Christ, risen master and triumphant Lord, we bow before you in sorrow for our sins, and confess to you our weakness and unbelief:

We have lived by our own strength, and not by the power of your resurrection. In your mercy, forgive us:
Lord, hear us and help us.

We have lived by the light of our own eyes, as faithless and not believing. In your mercy, forgive us:
Lord, hear us and help us.

We have lived for this world alone, and doubted our home in heaven. In your mercy, forgive us:
Lord, hear us and help us.

Lift our minds above earthly things,
set them on things eternal;
show us your glory and your power,
that we may serve you gladly
all our days.
Amen.

---

11. AT COMMUNION
Especially Easter

Lord Jesus Christ, we are your disciples with whom you desire to eat; and we come to your table. Our hearts were burning within us as you talked with us on the way and opened the Scriptures to us. Now in your name we break bread, and give thanks and receive it: open our eyes, confirm our faith and fill us with your grace, that we may believe and declare to all: 'It is true! The Lord has risen'. **Amen.**

12. CONFESSION
Ascension, Advent, heaven

O God, our Father in heaven, we confess to you our failure to live as children of your grace and heirs of your promises:

When we make this world's goods our treasure, and are mindless of your kingdom and your reward: in your mercy,
Father, forgive us and help us.

When we forget that here we have no enduring city, and fail to look for the city which is to come: in your mercy,
Father, forgive us and help us.

When we measure worth by the standards of this passing age and reject your eternal truth: in your mercy,
Father, forgive us and help us.

When we lose the vision of Christ and no longer run to win the prize of your call to heaven: in your mercy,
Father, forgive us and help us.

Father,
you have raised us up
 together with Christ:
set our hearts and minds
 on things above,
where he is seated in glory
at your right hand for evermore.
Amen.

ASCENSION, PENTECOST, MISSION AND MINISTRY

13. CONFESSION OF SINS
Ascension, general

Lord Jesus Christ,
crucified, risen and ascended for us:
we have not loved you
 as our Redeemer,
nor obeyed you as our Lord;
we have not brought our prayers
 to you,
nor heeded your tears
 shed over the world.
Forgive us, we pray;
breathe into us a new spirit of service,
and make us joyfully obedient
 to your will:
for your glory's sake. **Amen.**

14. CONFESSION OF SINS
Pentecost, renewal

Almighty God,
we confess that we have sinned
 against you:
for we have denied
 your saving presence
 in our lives,
and we have grieved your Holy Spirit.

Come to us in the fire of your love,
and set our minds
on the things of the Spirit,
that we may share his gifts
 and bear his fruit
in love and joy and peace;
through Jesus Christ our Lord. **Amen.**

15. FOR THE HOLY SPIRIT
Pentecost, prayer for healing or renewal,
before an address/sermon

Come, Holy Spirit:
speak to us of Jesus,
heal us and renew us,
warm our hearts
 with love for one another,
strengthen our wills to obey;
bring glory to the name
 of our mighty God. **Amen.**

16. FOR COURAGE
Mission, commitment

Our heavenly Father,
your Son left his glory
 for the sorrow of our world:
grant us the strength

to leave behind our comfort
   and security,
to take up the cross of our Saviour
and follow where he leads;
for his name's sake. **Amen.**

17. THANKSGIVING AND DEDICATION
Mission, prayer for healing
Almighty God,
we thank you for your mercy
   and your grace:

you are our light in darkness,
our strength in weakness,
and our comfort in sorrow.
You heal our bodies and our minds,
you ease our pain,
you lift our anxieties
and give us hope.
So fill us with your Spirit's power
that we may take your healing love
to a world in need,
and bring glory to your name:
through Jesus Christ our Lord. **Amen.**

HARVEST, ALL SAINTS, THE CHURCH

18. CONFESSION OF SINS
Rogation, Harvest, creation
O God our Father, we confess that we
have often used your gifts carelessly,
and acted as though we were not
grateful. Hear our prayer, and in your
mercy forgive us and help us:

When we enjoy the fruits of the
harvest, but forget they come from
you – then, Father, in your mercy,
forgive us and help us.

When we are full and satisfied, but
ignore the cry of the hungry and those
in need – then, Father, in your mercy,
forgive us and help us.

When we are thoughtless, and do not
treat with respect or care the
wonderful world you have made –
then, Father, in your mercy,
forgive us and help us.

When we store up goods for ourselves
alone, as if there were no God and no
heaven – then, Father, in your mercy,
forgive us and help us.

**Grant us thankful hearts
and a loving concern for all people;
through Jesus Christ our Lord.
Amen.**

19. THANKSGIVING
Harvest, general
Thank you, O God,
for the good things
you so richly provide;
thank you for your wisdom
   given when we ask you;
thank you for your love for us,

unasked and undeserved.
Give us ever thankful hearts,
and always
   a sense of how much we owe you,
then help us to serve you
in obedience and love;
through Jesus Christ our Lord. **Amen.**

20. THANKSGIVING
Church anniversary
Lord God, we thank you for our
heritage of faith:

For the vision of apostles and evange-
lists who brought it to us, gracious
Lord,
we give you thanks and praise.

For the courage of martyrs and
teachers who secured it for us,
gracious Lord,
we give you thanks and praise.

For the devotion of preachers and
pastors who proclaimed it to us,
gracious Lord,
we give you thanks and praise.

For the love of families and friends
who nourished it within us, gracious
Lord,
we give you thanks and praise.

For the freedom to speak of it in the
world about us, and to share it with
our neighbours, gracious Lord,
we give you thanks and praise.

**Lord God, we thank you
   for our heritage of faith:
give us the will and the strength
to pass it on to others**

for glory of your name;
**through our Saviour Jesus Christ.
Amen.**

21. FOR THE BODY OF CHRIST
Ministry, rededication
O God our Father, you grant your people gifts, that we may work together in the service of your Son:

Bless those who lead, that they may be strong and true, yet be humble before you: Lord, through your Spirit,
answer our prayer.

Bless those who teach, that they may enlighten our understanding, yet be taught by your wisdom: Lord, through your Spirit,
answer our prayer.

Bless those who offer healing, that they may extend your touch of grace, yet always know your healing presence: Lord, through your Spirit,
answer our prayer.

Bless those through whom you speak, that they may proclaim your word in power, yet have their ears open to your gentle whisper: Lord, through your Spirit,
answer our prayer.

Bless those who administer, help, and organise, that they may be diligent in their duty, yet seek your kingdom first: Lord, through your Spirit,
answer our prayer.

**Grant that as one Body
we may grow up into him
who is the head of the Church,
Jesus Christ our Lord. Amen.**

22. FOR OUR NATIONAL LEADERS
General
Almighty God,
we pray for our Queen
and all leaders of our country,
that they may govern us wisely
  and well;
we pray for one another,
that we may live and work together
in love, mutual understanding
  and peace,
through Jesus Christ our Lord. **Amen.**

ADVENT AND CHRISTMAS

23. CONFESSION
Advent
We must give account of our stewardship: let us ask forgiveness for our sin and failure.

Lord, we have not used your gifts wisely: forgive us for being unprofitable; in your mercy,
hear us and help us.

Lord, we have not kept brightly burning the light you entrusted to us: forgive us for being unprepared; in your mercy,
hear us and help us.

Lord, we have sometimes ended the day in anger or bitterness: forgive us for being unrepentant: in your mercy,
hear us and help us.

**Renew our vision,
restore our watchfulness,
make us faithful as you are faithful,
that when you come in glory
we may hear you say:**

**'Enter into the joy of your Lord.'
Amen.**

24. ABOUT BEING READY
Advent
Lord Jesus Christ, whose advent all shall see: let your coming be with triumph, but not to our shame; let your coming be with glory, but not to our surprise; let your coming be with justice, but not to our judgement. Make our love burn bright for you, our loyalty endure, and our faith increase; that with you we may rejoice on that day, and so enter into your eternal kingdom. **Amen.**

25. GREETING
Christmas, carol services
Welcome, everybody! At Christmas time we delight again to hear the story of the journey to Bethlehem, the song of the angels, the surprise of the shepherds, and their joy as they found Jesus in the manger. And because he

was born to poverty, we remember at this season all who are hungry or cold. And because he became a refugee, we remember the stranger and the homeless among us. And because he felt the pain of life and death, we remember those who are ill, or anxious, or bereaved. And because we know he came for our salvation, let us in heart and mind go once again to Bethlehem, to hear again the message of the angels and worship afresh the Son of God. **Amen.**

26. THE GREATEST PRESENT
Christmas – children
O God our Father, we praise you for Christmas – our happiness and presents, our families and the friends we see again; and for this greatest present of all we thank you: for the gift of Jesus at Bethlehem to be our saviour and our king. **Amen.**

27. BLESSING
Christmas, carol services
The joy of the angels, the wonder of the shepherds, and the peace of the Christ child, fill your hearts this Christmas time; and the blessing of God the Father, God the Son, and God the Holy Spirit, be with you now and always. **Amen.**

AT HOLY COMMUNION

28. INTRODUCTION
Holy Communion
In memory now we travel back two thousand years; in faith Christ comes to us across the ages. We break bread, as he did, and remember his body broken for us; we pour out wine, as he did, and remember his blood poured for us to the ground. We hold out our hands to receive his grace; we eat to feed on his love, and drink to pledge our loyalty; we rise to take up our cross; we go out to serve him in his world. **Amen.**

29. FAMILY COMMUNION PRAYER
God our Father, we give you our thanks (at this season especially for . . .) and we rejoice to praise you through Jesus Christ our Lord:
**Through him you made us;
through him you set us free
   from sin and death.
Through him you gave us
   your Holy Spirit,
and called us into one family.**

So, Father, by the same Spirit, let us who take this bread and wine, receive the body and blood of Christ.

For when the time came for him to be lifted up to die and so to enter his glory, he gathered his disciples and took bread and gave thanks to you; then he broke it and gave it to them saying, 'Take, eat: this is my body which is given for you; do this to remember me'.

After supper he took the cup and gave thanks. He gave it to them saying, 'Drink this, all of you: this is my blood of the new covenant, shed for you and for many that sins may be forgiven; do this every time you drink it, to remember me'.

Now as we look for his coming, we celebrate with this bread and wine his one perfect sacrifice; proclaiming his death for our salvation and rejoicing in the power of his resurrection, until we share the fellowship of his eternal kingdom.

**Father,
accept the thanks and praise
   of your children
in this sacred feast;
renew us by your Holy Spirit,
and make us one
in Christ Jesus our Lord. Amen.**

AND/OR, OPTIONAL ENDING

With the whole family in heaven and on earth we praise and adore you, saying:
**Holy, holy, holy Lord,
God of power and might,
heaven and earth are full
   of your glory.
Hosanna in the highest. Amen.**

411

17

SPOKEN PSALMS
FOR WORSHIP

*Examples of psalms arranged for
congregational response*

An earlier chapter has encouraged us to reconsider our use of the Psalms in congregational worship. As was pointed out there, the Psalms is often the 'Cinderella' of the Bible books, in that every other book is scheduled for reading by the Lectionaries of the mainstream churches. Traditionally, psalms have been sung and therefore excluded from 'lectern' readings. Many churches attempt either to *say* prayer book versions, which are usually arranged for chanting, or Bible versions, which understandably lack the rhythm needed to carry a congregation along in unity.

The 'Spoken Psalms' printed here reflect the probable use of the Psalms in Hebrew worship. They make sensible division between the minister's or worship leader's part, and the response of the congregation (bold type). To add variety and action, the parts are sometimes subdivided ('*A*', '*B*', and '*C*' etc.). In some examples – for instance Psalms 24 and 118 – parts can be given to individual readers/actors. In Psalm 24, below, the enquirer '*E*' should stand up in the body of the congregation; in Psalm 118 the Worshipper '*W*' can begin at the door of the room or building, and advance through the congregation as the psalm progresses.

These psalm versions may be freely reproduced for local use under the conditions outlined on p. iv. An entire set of texts representing all one hundred and fifty psalms (including each section of Psalm 119) is in course of preparation.

Spoken Psalms for Worship

Psalm 8

The congregation may divide at 'A', 'B', and 'C'

O Lord, our Lord:
**how great is your name
in all the world!**
^AYour glory fills the skies;
^Byour praise is sung by children;
^Cyou silence your enemies.

I look at the sky your hands have made, the moon and stars you put in place:
Who are we that you care for us?

You made us less than gods:
to crown us with glory and honour.

You put us in charge of creation:
^Athe beasts of the field.
^Bthe birds of the air.
^Cthe fish of the sea.
O Lord, our Lord:
**how great is your name
in all the world! Amen.**

Psalm 24

'E' – enquirer; 'D' – director; or these lines may also me said by the minister/leader.

The earth is the Lord's, and everything in it:
the world, and all who live here.

He founded it upon the seas:
and established it upon the waters.

^EWho has the right to go up the Lord's hill; who may enter his holy temple?
**Those who have clean hands
and a pure heart,
who do not worship idols
or swear by what is false.**

They receive blessing continually from the Lord:
**and righteousness
from the God of their salvation.**

Such are the people who seek for God;
**who enter the presence
of the God of Jacob.**

^DFling wide the gates, open the ancient doors:
that the king of glory may come in.

^EWho is the king of glory?
**The Lord, strong and mighty,
the Lord mighty in battle.**

^DFling wide the gates, open the ancient doors:
that the king of glory may come in.

^EWho is he, this king of glory?
**The Lord almighty,
he is the king of glory. Amen.**

Psalm 33

Sing joyfully to the Lord, you righteous:
**it is right that his people
should praise him.**

Praise the Lord with the harp:
make music to him on the strings.

Sing to the Lord a new song:
play skilfully, and shout for joy.

For the word of the Lord is right and true:
and all his work is faithfulness.

The Lord loves righteousness and justice:
his endless love fills the earth.

By the word of the Lord the skies were formed:
his breath created moon and stars.

Let all the earth fear the Lord:
the people of the world revere him.

For he spoke, and it came to be:
he commanded, and all was made.

The Lord holds back the nations:
he thwarts their evil intent.

God's purposes are sure:
his plans endure for ever.

Happy is the nation whose God is the Lord:
happy the people he makes his own.

The eyes of the Lord are on those who fear him:
who trust in his unfailing love.

We wait in hope for the Lord:
he is our help and shield.

In him our hearts rejoice:
we trust his holy name.

May your constant love be with us, Lord:
as we put our hope in you. Amen.

Psalm 36

Your love, O Lord, reaches the heavens:
your faithfulness
 extends to the skies.

Your righteousness is towering like the mountains:
your justice is like the great deep.

How precious is your love, O God:
we find shelter under your wings!

We feast on the food you provide:
we drink from the river
 of your goodness.

For with you is the fountain of life:
in your light we see light. Amen.

Psalm 40

Happy are those who trust in God:
who do not worship idols.

Sacrifice and offering you do not desire:
but you want my ears to be open.

So I said, 'Lord I come:
obedient to your word.'

I delight to do your will, O God:
and keep your teaching in my heart.

I'll tell the world your saving news:
you know my lips will be sealed.

I have not hid your righteousness:
but speak of your all your salvation, Lord.

I do not hide your faithful love:
but share your mercy with them all.

May all who come to you be glad; may all who know your saving power for ever say:
How great is the Lord! Amen.

Psalm 46

The congregation may divide at 'A', 'B', and 'C'. 'V' – voice of God

God is our refuge and strength:
an ever-present help in trouble.

Therefore we will not fear:
^Athough the earth should shake,
^Bthough mountains fall into the sea,
^Athough the waters surge and foam,

^Bthough the mountains shake and roar.

The Lord almighty is with us:
^ALLthe God of Jacob is our fortress.

There is a river whose streams make glad the city of God, the holy place where the Most High dwells:
^AGod is within her, she will not fall;
^BGod will help her at break of day.

Nations are in uproar, kingdoms fall:
^AGod lifts his voice –
^Bthe earth melts away.

The Lord Almighty is with us:
^ALLthe God of Jacob is our fortress.

Come and see what God had done:
his devastation on the earth!

He stops the wars throughout the world:
^Ahe breaks the bow
 and shatters the spear –
^Bhe sets the shield on fire.

^VBe still, and know that I am God: I will be exalted over the nations, I will be exalted over the earth.

The Lord Almighty is with us:
^ALLthe God of Jacob is our fortress.
Amen.

Psalm 47

Clap your hands, all you nations:
shout to God with cries of joy.

How awesome is the Lord most high:
the King who rules
 the whole wide earth!

God has ascended to his throne:
with shouts of joy and sound of trumpets.

Sing praises to our God, sing praises:
sing praises to our King, sing praises.

For God is king of all the earth:
sing to him a psalm of praise.

God is seated on his throne:
he rules the nations of the world.

The leaders of the nations come:
as subjects of our holy God.

The lords of earth belong to God:
he reigns supreme. Amen.

Psalm 65

O God, it is right for us to praise you,
because you answer our prayers:

You care for the land and water it:
and make it rich and fertile.

You fill the running streams with water:
and irrigate the land.

You soften the ground with showers:
and make the young crops grow.

You crown the year with goodness:
and give us a plentiful harvest.

The pastures are filled with flocks:
the hillsides are clothed with joy.

The fields are covered with grain:
they shout for joy and sing. Amen.

Psalm 66

The congregation may divide at 'A', 'B', and 'C'.

Praise your God with shouts of joy:
all the earth, sing praise to him.

Sing the glory of his name:
ᴬoffer him your highest praise.

Say to him: How great you are:
ᴮwonderful the things you do!

All your enemies bow down:
ᶜall the earth sings praise to you.

Come and see what God has done:
**ᴬcausing mortal men to fear –
ᴮfor he turned the sea to land,
ᶜled his people safely through.**

We rejoice at what he does –
**ᴬruling through eternity,
ᴮwatching over all the world,
ᶜkeeping every rebel down.**

Praise our God, you nations, praise:
**ᴬlet the sound of praise be heard!
ᴮGod sustains our very lives:
ᶜkeeps our feet upon the way.**

Once, you tested us, O God –
ᴬsilver purified by fire—

Let us fall into a trap,
ᴮplaced hard burdens on our backs –

Sent us through the flame and flood:
ᶜnow you bring us safely home.

I will come to worship you:
**ᴬbring to you my offering,
ᴮgive you what I said I would,
ᶜwhen the troubles threatened me.**

All who love and honour God:
**ᴬcome and listen, while I tell
what great things he did for me
ᴮwhen I cried to him for help,
when I praised him with my songs.**

When my heart was free from sin:
ᶜthen he listened to my prayer.

Praise the Lord who heard my cry:
**ᴬᴸᴸGod has shown his love to me!
Amen.**

Psalm 67

May God be gracious to us and bless us:
and make his face to shine upon us.

Let your ways be known upon earth:
your saving grace to every nation.

Let the peoples praise you, O God:
let the peoples praise you.

Let the nations be glad:
and sing aloud for joy.

Because you judge the peoples justly:
and guide the nations of the earth.

Let the peoples praise you, O God:
let all the peoples praise you.

Then the land will yield his harvest:
and God, our God, will bless us.

God will bless us:
**and people will fear him
to the ends of the earth. Amen.**

Psalm 80

Hear us, O Shepherd of Israel, leader of your flock:
**hear us from your throne
above the cherubim.**

Shine forth, awaken your strength, and come to save us:
**Bring us back, O God, and save us,
make your face to shine upon us.**

O Lord God almighty, how long will you be angry with your people's prayers?

**You have given us sorrow to eat
and tears to drink.**

You have made us a source of
contention to our neighbours, and our
enemies insult us:
**Bring us back, O God, and save us,
make your face to shine upon us.**

Return to us, O God Almighty
look down from heaven and see.

Look on this vine that you planted
with your own hand, this child you
raised for yourself:
**Let your hand rest upon the people
you have chosen.**

Then we will not turn away from you:
**revive us,
and we shall praise your name.**

**Bring us back, O God, and save us,
make your face to shine upon us.
Amen.**

Psalm 93

The Lord reigns, robed in majesty:
he arms himself with power.

The earth is firmly set in place:
it can never be moved.

Your throne was founded long ago:
before all time began.

The oceans raise their voice, O Lord:
and lift their roaring waves.

The Lord is mightier than the sea:
he rules supreme on high.

His laws stand firm through endless
days:
his praise for evermore. Amen.

Psalm 95

*'M' – first minister/leader; 'N' – second
minister/leader.*

ᴹCome, let's joyfully praise our God,
acclaiming the Rock of our salvation;
ᴺcome before him with thanksgiving,
and greet him with melody:
**Our God is a great God –
a king above all other gods.**

The depths of the earth are in his
hands:
the mountain peaks belong to him.

The sea is his – he made it;
his own hands prepared the land.

ᴹCome, bow down to worship him;
ᴺkneel before the Lord who made us.
**We are his people,
the sheep of his flock.**

If you listen to his voice, you shall
know his power today. **Amen.**

Psalm 96

*The congregation may divide at 'A',
and 'B'.*

Sing to the Lord a new song:
ᴬ**sing to the Lord, all the earth.**

Sing to the Lord, praise his name:
ᴮ**proclaim his salvation each day.**

Declare his glory among the nations:
ᴬ**his marvellous deeds
among the peoples.**

Great is the Lord, and worthy of
praise:
ᴮ**honour him above all gods.**

Splendour and majesty surround him:
ᴬ**power and beauty fill his temple.**

Praise the Lord all people on earth:
ᴮ**praise his glory and might.**

Give him the glory due to his name:
ᴬ**bring an offering into his temple.**

Worship the Lord in his beauty and
holiness:
ᴮ**tremble before him all the earth.**

Say to the nations:
ᴬᴸᴸ**The Lord is king!**

Let the heavens rejoice and the earth
be glad:
ᴬ**let all creation sing for joy.**

For God shall come to judge the
world:
ᴮ**and rule the people with his truth.**
ᴬᴸᴸ**Amen.**

Psalm 97

*The congregation may divide at 'A', and
'B'.*

The Lord is king:
ᴬᴸᴸ**the Lord is king!**

Let the whole wide earth rejoice:
ᴬ**let the islands all be glad.**

Thunder-clouds encircle him:
ᴮ**truth and justice are his throne.**

Fire shall go before the Lord:
ᴬ**burning up his enemies.**

Lightning strikes the darkened world:
ᴮ**all the people see and fear.**

Mountains melt before our God:
ᴬ**he is Lord of all the earth.**

Skies proclaim his righteousness:
ᴮ**nations see his glory now.**

Idol-worshippers are shamed:
ᴬ**gods bow down before the Lord.**

Let Jerusalem rejoice:
ᴮ**in your faithful judgements, Lord!**

Sovereign of the universe:
ᴬ**mightier still then all the gods!**

Yet you help your saints, O Lord:
ᴮ**saving them from wicked men.**

Light will shine upon the good:
ᴬ**gladness fills the righteous heart.**

Now recall what God has done:
ᴬ**thank him**
ᴮ**praise him,**
ᴬᴸᴸ**and rejoice! Amen.**

Psalm 98

O sing to the Lord a new song:
for he has done marvellous things.

His right hand and his holy arm:
have brought a great triumph to us.

He lets salvation be known:
his righteousness
  seen by the world.

His glory is witnessed by all:
to us he continues his love.

Rejoice in the Lord, all the earth:
and burst into jubilant song.

Make music to God with the harp:
with songs
  and the sound of your praise.

Sing praises to God as your king:
with trumpets and blast of the horn.

Let rivers and streams clap their hands:
the mountains together sing praise.

The Lord comes to judge the whole earth:
in righteousness
  God rules the world. Amen.

Psalm 99

The congregation may divide at 'A', and 'B'.

The Lord reigns:
ᴬ**let the nations tremble!**

He sits enthroned on high:
ᴮ**let the earth shake!**

Great is the Lord our God:
ᴬ**exalted over all the world.**

Let the nations praise his awesome name, and say:
ᴬ**God is holy!**

Praise the Lord and worship at his feet:
ᴮ**God is holy!**

Exalt the Lord your God, and worship on his holy mountain:
ᴬᴸᴸ**The Lord our God is holy! Amen.**

Psalm 100

Rejoice in the Lord, all the earth:
worship the Lord with gladness.

Remember the Lord is our God:
we are his flock and he made us.

Come to his temple with praise:
enter his gates with thanksgiving.

The love of the Lord will not fail:
God will be faithful for ever. Amen.

Psalm 103

Praise the Lord, my soul:
all my being, praise his holy name!

Praise the Lord, my soul:
and do not forget
  how generous he is.

He forgives all my sins:
and heals all my diseases.

He keeps me from the grave:
and blesses me with love and mercy.

The Lord is gracious and compassionate:
slow to become angry,

and full of constant love.

He does not keep on rebuking:
he is not angry for ever.

He does not punish us as we deserve:
or repay us for our wrongs.

As far as the east is from the west:
so far
 does he remove our sins from us.

As kind as a Father to his children:
so kind is the Lord
 to those who honour him.

Praise the Lord, all his creation:
praise the Lord, my soul! Amen.

Psalm 104

O Lord our God, you are very great:
you are clothed with splendour
 and majesty.

You make winds your messengers:
and flashes of fire your servants.

How many are your works:
the earth is full of your creatures!

When you hide your face, they are afraid:
when you take away their breath, they die.

When you send your Spirit they are created:
and you renew the face of the earth. Amen.

Psalm 105

Give thanks to the Lord, praise his name:
tell the nations what he has done.

Sing to him, sing praise to him:
tell of all his wonderful deeds.

Glory in his holy name:
let all who worship him rejoice.

Go to the Lord for help:
and worship him for ever.

Remember the wonders he does:
the miracles he performs.

He is the Lord our God:
he judges the whole wide earth.

He keeps his word and covenant:
for a thousand generations.

The covenant with Abraham:
the oath he swore to Israel.

He brought them out of Egypt:
and none of them was lost.

He gave a cloud for covering:
a pillar of fire by night.

He gave them bread from heaven:
and water from the rock.

He brought his people out rejoicing:
his chosen ones with shouts of joy.
Praise the Lord! Amen.

Psalm 107

Give thanks to the Lord, for he is good:
his love endures for ever.

Repeat these words in praise to the Lord, all those he has redeemed:
his love endures for ever!

Some sailed the ocean in ships:
they earned their way on the seas.

They saw what the Lord can do:
his wonderful deeds in the deep.

For he spoke and stirred up a storm:
and lifted high the waves.

Their ships were thrown in the air:
and plunged into the depths.

Their courage melted away:
they reeled like drunken men.

They came to the end of themselves:
and cried to the Lord in their trouble.

He brought them out of distress:
and stilled the raging storm.

They were glad because of the calm:
he brought them safely to harbour.

Let them give thanks to the Lord:
for his unfailing love. Amen.

Psalm 111

Praise the Lord:
praise the Lord!

With my whole heart I will thank the Lord: in the company of his people.
Great are the works of the Lord:
those who wonder, seek them.

Glorious and majestic are his deeds:

his goodness lasts for ever.

He reminds us of his works of grace:
he is merciful and kind.

He sustains those who fear him:
he keeps his covenant always.

All he does is right and just:
all his words are faithful.

They will last for ever and ever:
and be kept in faith and truth.

He provided redemption for his people, and made an eternal covenant with them:
holy and awesome is his name!

The fear of the Lord is the beginning of wisdom; he gives understanding to those who obey:
to God belongs eternal praise! Amen.

Psalm 113

Praise the Lord:
praise the Lord!

You servants of the Lord, praise his name:
let the name of the Lord be praised, both now and evermore!

From the rising of the sun to the place where it sets:
the name of the Lord be praised!

The Lord is exalted above the earth:
his glory over the heavens.

Who is the Lord our God?
He is throned in the heights above –

Yet he bends down:
yet he stoops to look at our world.

He raises the poor from the dust:
and lifts the needy from their sorrow.

Praise the Lord:
Amen.

Psalm 116

I love the Lord because he heard my voice:
the Lord in mercy listened to my prayers.

Because the Lord has turned his ear to me:

I'll call on him as long as I shall live.

The cords of death entangled me around:
the horrors of the grave came over me.

But then I call upon the Lord my God:
**I said to him:
'O Lord, I beg you, save!'**

The Lord our God is merciful and good:
the Lord protects the simple-hearted ones.

The Lord saved me from death and stopped my tears:
he saved me from defeat and picked me up.

And so I walk before him all my days:
and live to love and praise his holy name.

What shall I give the Lord for all his grace?
I'll take his saving cup, and pay my vows.

Within the congregation of his saints:
I'll offer him my sacrifice of praise.

Praise the Lord:
Amen, amen!

Psalm 117

Praise the Lord, all you nations:
praise him, all you people!

Great is his love towards us:
his faithfulness shall last for ever.

Praise the Lord:
Amen.

Psalm 118
*'M' – minister; 'W' – worshipper,
advancing from the back; 'C' –
choir/chorus; 'D' – director in flat tone.*

ᴹGive thanks to the Lord, for he is good:
his love endures for ever.

ᴹAll those who fear the Lord shall say:
His love endures for ever.

ᵂOpen for me the gates of the Temple;
I will go in and give thanks to the Lord.

^MThis is the gate of the Lord, only the righteous can come in.

^WI will give thanks because you heard me; you have become my salvation.

^CThe stone which the builders rejected as worthless turned out to be the most important of all:
^{ALL}**The Lord has done this –**
what a wonderful sight it is!

^MThis is the day of the Lord's victory – let us be happy, let us celebrate:
^{ALL}**O Lord save us,**
O Lord, grant us success.

^MMay God bless the one who comes in the name of the Lord:
^{ALL}**The Lord is God—**
he has been good to us!

^MFrom the Temple of the Lord, we bless you.

^DWith branches in your hands, start the procession and march round the altar:

^WYou are my God and I will give you thanks:
^{ALL}**You are my God,**
and I will exalt you.

^MGive thanks to the Lord, for he is good:
^{ALL}**His love endures for ever. Amen.**

Psalm 122

I was glad when they said to me:
let us go to the house of the Lord!

Pray for the peace of Jerusalem:
may those who love our land
be blessed.

May there be peace in your homes:
and safety for our families.

For the sake of those we love we say:
Let there be peace! Amen.

Psalm 124
The congregation may divide at 'A', and 'B'.

If the Lord had not been on our side – now let Israel say:
If the Lord
had not been on our side –
^A**when enemies attacked us,**

^B**when their anger flared against us,**
^{ALL}**they would have swallowed us**
alive.

The flood would have engulfed us,
^A**the torrent**
would have swept over us,
^B**the waters would have drowned us.**

Praise the Lord, who has not given us up to their teeth:
^A**We have escaped like a bird from**
the snare:
^B**the snare is broken and we are free.**
^{ALL}**Our help**
is in the name of the Lord,
who made heaven and earth. Amen.

Psalm 126

When the Lord brought us back from slavery:
we were like those who dream.

Our mouths were filled with laughter:
our tongues with songs of joy.

Then those around us said, 'The Lord has done great things for them':
The Lord has done great things
for us,
and we are filled with joy.

Those who sow in tears
shall reap with songs of joy. Amen.

Psalm 128
'M' – minister.

The pilgrim's song:
Blessed are those who fear the Lord,
who walk in his ways.

You will eat the fruit of your work; blessings and prosperity will be yours:
Blessed are those who fear the Lord,
who walk in his ways.

Your wife will be like a fruitful vine within your house; your children will be like young olive trees around your table:
Blessed are those who fear the Lord,
who walk in his ways.

^MMay the Lord bless you all the days of your life; may you have prosperity; may you live to see your children's children:
Peace be with you. Amen.

Psalm 134

You servants of the Lord, who stand in
his temple at night:
praise the Lord!

Lift your hands in prayer to the Lord:
in his sanctuary, praise the Lord!

May the Lord who made the heavens
and earth bless you from Zion:
Amen!

Psalm 136

*The congregation should divide at 'A',
and 'B'.*

Give thanks to God, for he is good:
his love shall last for ever!

^A**Give thanks to him,
the God of gods:**
ᴬᴸᴸ**his love shall last for ever!**

^B**Give thanks to him,
the Lord of lords:**
ᴬᴸᴸ**his love shall last for ever!**

For God alone works miracles:
ᴬᴸᴸ**his love shall last for ever!**

^A**The skies were made
at his command:**
ᴬᴸᴸ**his love shall last for ever!**

^B**He spread the seas upon the earth:**
ᴬᴸᴸ**his love shall last for ever!**

^A**He made the stars to shine at night:**
ᴬᴸᴸ**his love shall last for ever!**

^B**He made the sun to shine by day:**
ᴬᴸᴸ**his love shall last for ever!**

^A**He brought us out from slavery:**
ᴬᴸᴸ**his love shall last for ever!**

^B**He leads us onward by his grace:**
ᴬᴸᴸ**his love shall last for ever!**

He saves us from our enemies:
ᴬᴸᴸ**his love shall last for ever!**

Give thanks to God, for he is good:
ᴬᴸᴸ**his love shall last for ever!**
Amen!

Psalm 143 and Psalm 51

O Lord, I spread my hands out to you:
I thirst for you like dry ground.

Teach me to do your will, for you are
my God:

let your good Spirit lead me in safety.

You require sincerity and truth in me:
fill my mind with wisdom.

Create in me a pure heart, O God:
and renew a faithful spirit in me.

Do not cast me from your presence:
or take your Holy Spirit from me.

Give me again the joy of your
salvation:
and make me willing to obey. Amen.

Psalm 147

*The congregation may divide at 'A', 'B',
and 'C'.*

O praise the Lord, sing out to God:
ᴬᴸᴸ**such praise is right and good.**

The Lord restores Jerusalem:
^A**he brings the exiles home.**

He heals all those with broken hearts:
^B**he bandages their wounds.**

He counts the number of the stars:
^C**he calls them each by name.**

How great and mighty is the Lord:
^A**immeasurably wise!**

He raises up the humble ones:
^B**and brings the mighty down.**

Sing hymns of triumph to his name:
^C**make music to our God!**

He spreads the clouds across the sky:
^A**he showers the earth with rain.**

He sends the animals their food:
^B**he feeds the hungry birds.**

His true delight is not the strong:
^C**but those who trust his love.**

Extol the Lord, Jerusalem:
^A**let Zion worship God!**

For God shall keep your people safe:
^B**and bring your harvest home.**

He gives commandment to the earth:
^C**his will is quickly done.**

He spreads like wool the falling snow:
^A**how cold the frosty air!**

He sends the wind, the warming rain:
^B**and melts the ice away.**

His laws he gives to Israel:
ᶜand Judah hears his word.

He does not favour other lands:
ᴬᴸᴸso, praise the Lord. Amen!

Psalm 148
*The congregation may divide at 'A',
and 'B'.*

Praise the Lord!

Praise the Lord from the heavens:
praise him in the heights above.

Praise him, all his angels:
ᴬpraise him, all his heavenly host.

Praise him, sun and moon:
ᴮpraise him, all you shining stars.

Let them praise the name of the Lord:
ᴬᴸᴸPraise the Lord!

Praise the Lord from the earth:
ᴬpraise him, great sea creatures.

Praise him, storms and clouds:
ᴮpraise him, mountains and hills.

Praise him, fields and woods:
ᴬpraise him, animals and birds.

Praise him, rulers and nations:
ᴮpraise him, old and young.

Let them praise the name of the Lord:
ᴬᴸᴸPraise the Lord! Amen.

Psalm 149

Praise the Lord:
praise the Lord!

Sing a new song to the Lord:
let the people shout his name!

Praise your maker, Israel:
hail your king, Jerusalem.

Sing and dance to honour him:

**praise him
with the strings and drums.**

God takes pleasure in his saints:
crowns the meek with victory.

Rise, you saints, in triumph now:
sing the joyful night away!

Shout aloud and praise your God!
Hold aloft the two-edged sword!

Let the judgement now begin:
kings shall fall and tyrants die.

Through his people, by his word:
God shall have the victory!

Praise the Lord:
praise the Lord! Amen.

Psalm 150

Praise the Lord!

Praise God in his sanctuary:
praise his strength beyond the skies!

Praise him for his acts of power:
**praise him
for his surpassing greatness.**

Praise him with the sounding of the trumpet:
praise him with the harp and lyre.

Praise him with tambourine and dancing:
praise him with the strings and flute.

Praise him with the clash of cymbals:
praise him with resounding cymbals.

Let everything that has breath praise the Lord:
Praise the Lord! Amen.

18

SENTENCES ABOUT GIVING

This collection is reproduced courtesy of Robert Watson,
Vicar of Holy Trinity, Knaphill
The themes correspond to those in Church Family
Worship[1], Prayers for the People[2], *and*
The Dramatised Bible[3].

There is a reformed tradition of using Scripture sentences at the moment when money thank-offerings are dedicated. For instance, in the *Book of Common Prayer* service of Holy Communion there is a selection of twenty texts about giving. The archaism of the translation means that very few of these options have been used – mainly 'Let your light so shine (before men,) that they (/all) may see your good works, and glorify your Father (which is) in heaven' – Matthew 5 (brackets mine). There is obviously much to be said for the practice, for it reminds worshippers that giving to the work of evangelism and ministry, as well as to all the practical funds that make those things possible, relies upon our dedicated support. Robert Watson, who sent me this list, speaks of its teaching potential, and tells me that his church has never needed a stewardship campaign!

For convenience, the texts are grouped under thematic and seasonal subheadings, which also correlate with those to be found in various books, notably *Church Family Worship*[1], *Prayers for the People*[2], and *The Dramatised Bible*[3].

[1]*Church FamilyWorship*, published 1986 by Hodder & Stoughton Ltd, London.
[2]*Prayers for the People*, published 1992 by HarperCollins*Publishers* Ltd, London.
[3]*The Dramatised Bible*, published 1989 by HarperCollins*Publishers* Ltd, London.

JANUARY – FEBRUARY

1. New Year, Thanksgiving for the Old Year

You, Lord, are all I have, and you give me all I need; my future is in your hands. How wonderful are your gifts to me; how good they are! *Psalm 16.5-6*

With all his abundant wealth through Christ Jesus, my God will supply all your needs. To our God and Father be the glory for ever and ever! Amen. *Philippians 4.18-20*

Give to the Lord freely and unselfishly, and he will bless you in everything you do. *Deuteronomy 15.10*

2. Epiphany, The Wise Men, The Escape to Egypt

Opening their treasures they offered him gifts. *Matthew 2.11*

Celebrate your festivals and give God what you solemnly promised him. *Nahum 1.15*

Jesus said, 'Pay God what belongs to God.' *Mark 12.17*

3. The People of God, Covenant and Unity

Do not forget to do good and to help one another, because these are the sacrifices that please God. *Hebrews 13.16*

Paul said of the Macedonians, 'They gave as much as they could, and even more than they could. Of their own free will they begged us and pleaded for the privilege of having a part in helping God's people.' *2 Corinthians 8.3, 4*

The people had given willingly to the Lord, and they were happy that so much had been given. *1 Chronicles 29.9*

4. Following Jesus, Jesus' Teaching

The Lord Jesus himself said, 'There is more happiness in giving than in receiving.' *Acts 20.35*

Be concerned above everything else with the Kingdom of God and with what he requires of you, and he will provide you with all these other things. *Matthew 6.33*

Jesus said, 'The measure you use for others is the one that God will use for you.' *Luke 6.38*

MARCH – APRIL

5. The Life of Prayer, Forgiveness

I ask you God . . . let me be neither rich nor poor . . so give me only as much good as I need. [If I have more I might say that I do not need you. But if I am poor I might steal and bring disgrace on my God.] *Proverbs 30.7-9*

If you refuse to listen to the cry of the poor, your own cry for help will not be heard. *Proverbs 21.13*

Kindness shown to the poor is an act of worship. *Proverbs 14.31*

God said to Moses, 'Never come to worship me without bringing an offering.' *Exodus 23.15*

6. The Family, Parents and Children, Mothering Sunday

As often as we have the chance, we should do good to everyone, and especially to those who belong to our family in the faith. *Galatians 6.10*

The families gave free-will offerings to the Lord [for the rebuilding of the house of God] – as much as they were able to give. *Ezra 2.68, 69*

7. Palm Sunday
Others offered their gifts from what they had to spare of their riches; but she, poor as she was, gave all she had to live on. *Luke 21.4*

Bring the full amount of your tithes to the Temple, so that there will be plenty of food there. Put me to the test and you will see that I will open the windows of heaven and pour out on you in abundance all kinds of good things. *Malachi 3.8-10*

8. Passiontide, Good Friday, Easter Eve
The Son of God loved me and gave his life for me. *Galatians 2.20*

9. Easter, Resurrection
You have been raised to life with Christ, so set your hearts on the things that are in heaven, where Christ sits on his throne at the right-hand side of God. *Colossians 3.1*

O God, I will offer you what I have promised; I will give you my offering of thanksgiving, because you have rescued me from death and kept me safe from defeat. And so I walk in the presence of God, in the light that shines on the living. *Psalm 56.12-13*

MAY – JUNE

10. God's Creation
'All the silver and gold of the world is mine' . . . the Lord Almighty has spoken. *Haggai 2.8*

[John answered] 'No-one can have anything unless God gives it to him.' *John 3.27*

The person who sows few seeds will have a small crop; the one who sows many seeds will have a large crop. *2 Corinthians 9.6*

11. Jesus is Lord, Ascension
Jesus said, 'No servant can be the slave of two masters; he will hate one and love the other; he will be loyal to one and despise the other. You cannot serve both God and money'. *Luke 16.13*

Because of God's great mercy to us I appeal to you: offer yourselves as a living sacrifice to God, dedicated to his service and pleasing to him. This is the true worship that you should offer. *Romans 12.1*

12. The Holy Spirit
God gives you his Holy Spirit. *1 Thessalonians 4.8*

Freely you have received, freely give. *Matthew 10.8*

13. The Holiness and Majesty of God, Trinity
Let Almighty God be your gold, and let him be silver, piled high for you. Then you will also trust in God and find that he is the source of your joy. *Job 22.25, 26*

'No-one is to appear before me without an offering,' says the Lord. *Exodus 34.20*

Preparing for Worship

JULY – AUGUST

14. Sea Theme, Holidays
Every Sunday each of you must put aside some money, in proportion to what you have earned. *1 Corinthians 16.2*

Jesus said, 'Give to others, and God will give to you. Indeed, you will receive a full measure, a generous helping, poured into your hands – all that you can hold.' *Luke 6.38*

15. God's Love to Us, Our Response
Give because you want to, not because you have to. *2 Corinthians 9.5*

Jacob said, 'Please accept this gift which I have brought for you; God has been kind to me and given me everything I need.' *Genesis 33.11*

16. Invitation to Faith
God loved the world so much that he gave his only Son, so that everyone who believes in him may not die but have eternal life. *John 3.16*

What can I offer the Lord for all his goodness to me? I will bring an offering to the Lord, to thank him for saving me. In the assembly of all his people I will give him what I have promised. *Psalm 116.12-14*

17. The Witnessing Church, the World-wide Church
Be generous, and you will be prosperous. Help others, and you will be helped. *Proverbs 11.25*

Paul said of the Macedonians, 'First they gave themselves to the Lord; and then, by God's will they gave themselves to us as well.' *2 Corinthians 8.5*

We seem poor, but we make many people rich; we seem to have nothing, yet we really possess everything. *2 Corinthians 6.10*

SEPTEMBER – OCTOBER

18. The Caring Church, Healing
Since you have plenty at this time, it is only fair that you should help those who are in need. Then, when you are in need and they have plenty, they will help you. In this way both are treated equally. *2 Corinthians 8.14*

Whenever you possibly can, do good to those who need it. *Proverbs 3.27*

19. God's Gifts to the Church, Renewal
Thanks be to God for his inestimable gift! *2 Corinthians 9.15*

You are so rich in all you have: in faith, speech, and knowledge, in your eagerness to help and in your love for us. And so we want you to be generous also in this service of love. *2 Corinthians 8.7*

20. The Church: Anniversary, Commitment, Giving
Jacob pledged to God, 'I will give you a tenth of everything you give to me.' *Genesis 28.22*

Take to the one place of worship your offerings and the gifts that you have promised the Lord. *Deuteronomy 12.26*

If you are eager to give, God will accept your gift on the basis of what you have to give, not on what you do not have. *2 Corinthians 8.12*

426

Each of you is to bring a gift as you are able, in proportion to the blessings that the Lord your God has given you. *Deuteronomy 16.16-17*

21. Harvest Thanksgiving

Celebrate the Harvest Festival, honour the Lord your God, by bringing him a freewill offering in proportion to the blessing he has given you. *Deuteronomy 16.10*

Honour the Lord by making him an offering from the best of all that your land produced. *Proverbs 3.9*

Do not deceive yourselves, no-one makes a fool of God. A person will reap exactly what he sows. *Galatians 6.7*

Now I bring to the Lord the first part of the harvest that he has given me. *Deuteronomy 26.10*

NOVEMBER – DECEMBER

22. Christian Character and Conflict, Our Work, Schools

King David said,'I will not offer to the Lord my God sacrifices that have cost me nothing.' *2 Samuel 24.24*

Keep your lives free from the love of money, and be satisfied with what you have. For God has said,' I will never leave you; I will never abandon you.' *Hebrews 13.5*

[Jesus said,] 'Watch out and guard yourselves from every kind of greed; because a person's true life is not made up of the things he owns, no matter how rich he may be.' *Luke 12.15*

23. Heaven, God's Peace

O God, I will offer you what I have promised; I will give you my offering of thanksgiving, because you have rescued me from death and kept me from defeat. *Psalm 56.12-13*

Do not store up riches for yourselves here on earth, where moths and rust destroy, and robbers break in and steal. Instead, store up riches for yourselves in heaven, where moths and rust cannot destroy, and robbers cannot break in and steal. For your heart will always be where your riches are. *Matthew 6.19-21*

What did we bring into the world? Nothing! What can we take out of the world? Nothing! *1 Timothy 6.7*

24. Christ's Coming, Judgement

One day the Master will say to us, 'Give a complete account of your handling of my property.' *Luke 16.2*

Remember it is the Lord your God who gives you the power to become rich. He does this because he is still faithful today to the covenant that he made with your ancestors. *Deuteronomy 8.18*

25. God's Word to Us, Proclamation

The man who is being taught the Christian message should share all the good things he has with his teacher! *Galatians 6.6*

26. Christmas

You know the grace of our Lord Jesus Christ; rich as he was, he made himself poor for your sake, in order to make you rich by means of his poverty. *2 Corinthians 8.9*

THROUGHOUT THE YEAR

27. At a Baptism

You must present as the Lord's portion the best and holiest part of everything given to you. *Numbers 18.29*

St Paul urged, 'Let not those who are rich in the things of this life be proud, but let them place their hope, not in such an uncertain thing as riches, but in God, who generously gives us everything for our enjoyment. Let them do good; let them be rich in good works, generous and ready to share with others. In this way they will store up for themselves a treasure which will be a solid foundation for the future. And then they will be able to win the life which is true life.' *1 Timothy 6.17-19*

28. At Holy Communion/The Lord's Supper

Each one should give, then, as he has decided, not with regret or out of a sense of duty; for God loves the one who gives gladly. *2 Corinthians 9.7*

As the offering began, the people sang praise to the Lord. *2 Corinthians 29.27*

Among your people I will praise you for what you have done. In the presence of those who worship you, I will offer the sacrifices I promised. *Psalm 22.25*

29. At Local Festivals, For the Peace of the World

Giving thanks is the sacrifice that honours me, and I will surely save all who obey me. *Psalm 50.23*

God is able to give you more than you need, so that you will always have all you need for yourselves and more than enough for every good cause. *2 Corinthians 9.8*

When you give to the poor, it is like lending to the Lord, and the Lord will pay you back. *Proverbs 19.17*

19

RESTORING
MEANING

Bringing out the colour in traditional texts

When I arrived in Tonbridge in 1989 I discovered there was a Wednesday morning Prayer Book Communion. After ten years or more of creating new liturgy and revising and translating hymns, psalms and carols, I abhorred the prospect of conducting this service in old language every week. I arranged for one of my colleagues to lead, and wondered how soon I might phase it out. Then he left (not as a consequence!) and I found myself obliged to conduct the service I had avoided.

Despite my critical attitude, God blessed that time on a Wednesday, and I gained a great love for the people. I gave my dislike for the old service into God's hands, and was thus enabled to minister the Communion with a growing gentleness towards those present. We started praying with each one who came forward to receive Communion. Some reported hearing counsel from God in those prayers. Many responded who had not experienced this sort of ministry before, and would not have sought it. Those who led found the task thrilling and rejuvenating. There was often ministry afterwards because people asked for it – prayer and counselling. The service was completed by Bible Study (after coffee). Numbers had never been great, but were four or five times greater now.

I hadn't planned any of this. But God obviously had; and not only to bless the congregation, I believe, but to teach me a lesson. I had to forget my prejudices; I had to trust God for each different opportunity as it arose.

To the reader of my earlier chapter on modernising language, this may seem strangely inconsistent. Is the author contradicting himself? Well, yes to the extent that God often works paradoxically. I am sure the principle of a liturgy 'understood of the people' is right; after all, it was part of the *raison d'être* of the 1662 Prayer Book itself. In the seventeenth century, the language of that book was indeed the language of the people. But in the present day where the old language *has* to be retained for pastoral reasons, then we must make it live if we can.

The justifications for retaining this particular liturgy are twofold. For one thing, there are some for whom adjustment to the new is no longer possible by reason of age, blindness, deafness etc.; they must be pastorally served. But also, there is not, at the present time, a Communion service available in print and authorised for Church of England use that is comparably *penitential* to the 1662 rite.

One of the key reasons for changing the Sunday liturgy of the Communion service is that a *celebratory* rite was needed. In the 1662 service of Holy Communion we are *still* confessing our sins and repenting up to the end of the service! This just doesn't work for an Easter morning celebration, or similar. But, by the same token, there are occasions when we actually *need* a penitential rite – I believe. A mid-week morning service can be one such occasion.

I have found that the mid-week service often caters for those who have significant burdens – frequently of guilt – to bring to the Lord. Some will come because marriage partners or other family members are unsympathetic to their faith, and consequently resistant to Sunday attendance. What an opportunity for a service which can express healing and forgiveness, and the assurance of love from God!

We learned – as no doubt others have – to intersperse the prayers with gentle exhortation and explanation; we learned to use more ministers, and so to take time over each person receiving Communion as we prayed for them. Hence their expectation of this service is immensely heightened; and it has become for us all – ministers and congregation alike – 'rivers of living water'.

I decided that, if I was not to reject the archaic language, I would have to learn to express its meaning. And I discovered that this could be done simply through an awareness of the sentence construction – which is very different from contemporary syntax. Most importantly, qualifying words frequently come before, rather than after, the noun or verb qualified. For example, in the 'Prayer for the Church Militant' the words 'of thy goodness' qualify 'to comfort and succour'. So the sentence should be read:

> And we most humbly beseech thee/
> of thy goodness, O Lord, to comfort and succour

Reading it the other way makes nonsense of the first line, and deprives the second of its full meaning:

> And we most humbly beseech thee of thy goodness,
>   O Lord,/
> to comfort and succour

Another literary device of the older liturgies, prayers and collects is 'parallelism'. Take, for example this excerpt for the prayer for the sovereign:

> **A** that she
> **B** knowing *whose* minister she is
> **C** may above all things seek . . .

> **A** and that we
> **B** duly considering *whose authority* she hath
> **C** may faithfully serve . . .

If this parallelism is not recognised by the minister and not interpreted correctly in speaking the prayer, the sense will be lost, and the language will lose its force.

I have set out below, prayers from the 1662 Communion. They are arranged in 'sense-equivalent' lines, much as the prayers of today would be, but with further line divisions in order to take full account of the qualifying words. The parallelisms of the text are indicated by the letters '**A**', '**B**' etc., so that proper emphasis can be given. I hope this will be of direct help to Anglican clergy charged with using this service. (And, in the Anglican world now, lay ministers as well as priests are often involved). It should also be of assistance to any minister or worship leader who has to interpret prayers which use a similar archaic form. Pauses come only at the end of each line, and at the bar lines '/'.

FOR THE QUEEN *Note the royal allusions*
    Almighty God,
    whose kingdom* is everlasting and power* infinite:
    have mercy upon the whole church:
    and so rule* the heart of thy chosen servant Elizabeth,
    our Queen and Governor,
A that she . .
B (knowing whose minister she is)
C . . may above all things seek thy honour and glory:
A and that we and all her subjects . .
B (duly considering whose authority she hath)
C may faithfully serve, honour, and humbly obey her,
    in thee, and for thee,
    according to thy blessed word and ordinance;
    through Jesus Christ our Lord, who
    with thee and the Holy Ghost liveth and reigneth*,
    ever one God, world without end. **Amen.**

FOR THE CHURCH MILITANT
    Almighty and everliving God/ who
    by thy holy Apostle hast taught us
    to make prayers and supplications, and
    to give thanks, for all (men):
    we humbly beseech thee
A most mercifully to accept our alms and oblations
A and to receive these our prayers,
      which we offer unto thy Divine Majesty;
    beseeching thee to inspire continually
    the universal church

with the spirit of truth, unity and concord:
and grant,
that all they that do confess thy holy Name may agree
    in the truth of thy holy Word,
and live in unity, and godly love.
We beseech thee/ also to save and defend
    all Christian Kings, Princes and Governors;
    and specially thy servant Elizabeth our Queen
that under her we may be godly and quietly governed:
and grant unto her whole Council,
and to all that are put in authority under her
that they may
    truly and indifferently minister justice,
B   to the punishment of wickedness and vice, and
B   to the maintenance of thy true religion, and virtue.

Give grace, O heavenly Father,
    to all Bishops and (Curates)
that they may
C   both by their life and doctrine set forth
    thy true and lively Word,/ and
C   rightly and duly administer/ thy holy Sacraments:
and to all thy people give/ thy heavenly grace;
and specially to this congregation here present; that,
with meek heart and due reverence they may
    hear and receive
thy holy Word;
truly serving thee in holiness and righteousness
all the days of their life.
And we most humbly beseech thee
of thy goodness, O Lord, to comfort and succour
all them, who in this transitory life are in trouble,
    sorrow, need, sickness, or any other adversity.

And we also bless thy holy Name for
all thy servants departed this life in thy faith and fear;
beseeching thee to give us grace so to follow
    their good examples,
that/ with them we may be partakers/ of thy heavenly kingdom:
grant this, O Father, for Jesus Christ's sake,
    our only Mediator and Advocate. **Amen.**

ABSOLUTION
    Almighty God, our heavenly Father,/ who
    of his great mercy hath promised/ forgiveness of sins

to all them that
with hearty repentance and true faith turn unto him;
have mercy upon you;
A   pardon and deliver you from all your sins;
A   confirm and strengthen you in all goodness;/and
A   bring you to everlasting life;
through Jesus Christ our Lord. **Amen.**

PRAYER OF HUMBLE ACCESS

A   We do not presume to come to this thy Table,
      O merciful Lord,
   trusting in our own righteousness,
B   but in thy manifold and great mercies.
A   We are not worthy
   so much as to gather up the crumbs under thy Table.
B   But thou art the same Lord,
   whose property is/ always to have mercy:
   Grant us therefore, gracious Lord,
C   so to eat the flesh of thy dear Son Jesus Christ,
C   and to drink his blood,
D   that our sinful bodies may be made clean
      by his body,
D   and our souls washed
      through his most precious blood,
E   and that we may ever more dwell in him,
E   and he in us. **Amen.**

EUCHARISTIC PRAYER

Almighty God, our heavenly Father, who
of thy tender mercy didst give/
   thine only Son Jesus Christ
to suffer death upon the Cross for our redemption;
who made there
A   by his one oblation of himself/ once offered
a full, perfect, and sufficient/ sacrifice, oblation,
   and satisfaction,
for the sins of the whole world;
A   and did institute,/ and in his holy Gospel command us to continue,
a perpetual memory of that his precious death,
   until his coming again
hear us, O merciful Father,
   we most humbly beseech thee; and grant that we . . .

receiving these thy creatures of bread and wine,
B   according to thy Son/our Saviour/Jesus Christ's holy institution,

B   in remembrance of his death and passion,

        . . . may be partakers/ of his most blessed Body
           and Blood:/who,

C   in the same night that he was betrayed, took Bread;/ and,

D   when he had given thanks, he brake it,
           and gave it to his disciples,
    saying

E   Take, eat;/ this is my Body which is given for you:

F   do this in remembrance of me.

C   Likewise/ after supper he took the Cup;/ and,

D   when he had given thanks, he gave it to them,/ saying,

E   Drink . . ye all . . of this;
    for this is my Blood of the New Testament,
    which is shed for you and for many
        for the remission of sins:

F   do this, . . as oft as ye shall drink it, . . in remembrance
        of me. **Amen.**

AFTER COMMUNION
    O Lord and heavenly Father,
    we/ thy humble servants/
    entirely desire thy fatherly goodness
        mercifully to accept
    this our sacrifice of praise and thanksgiving;
    most humbly beseeching thee to grant,/ that

A   by the merits and death of thy Son Jesus Christ,/and

A   through faith in his blood,
    we and all thy whole church may obtain
    remission of our sins, and all other benefits
        of his passion.

    And here/ we offer and present unto thee, O Lord,
    ourselves, our souls and bodies,
    to be a reasonable, holy, and lively sacrifice unto thee;
    humbly beseeching thee,
    that all we, who are partakers of this
        holy Communion,
    may be fulfilled with thy grace
        and heavenly benediction.
    And although we be
      unworthy, through our manifold sins,
    to offer unto thee any sacrifice,
    yet we beseech thee to accept

this our bounden duty and service;
not weighing our merits, but pardoning our offences,
through Jesus Christ our Lord;
by whom, and with whom
in the unity of the Holy Ghost,
all honour and glory be unto thee . . . O Father Almighty . . .
world without end. **Amen.**

Almighty and everliving God,
we most heartily thank thee, for that thou dost
vouchsafe to feed
us,/who have duly received the most precious
Body and Blood
of thy Son/ our Saviour/Jesus Christ;
and dost assure us thereby
A of thy favour and goodness towards us; and,
A that we are very members incorporate in the
mystical body of thy Son,
which is the blessed company of all faithful people;
A and are also heirs through hope
of thy everlasting kingdom,
by the merits of the most precious death and passion of thy
dear Son.
And we most humbly beseech thee,
O heavenly Father,
so to assist us with thy grace,
that we may continue in that holy fellowship, and
B do all such good works as thou hast prepared for us
to walk in;
through Jesus Christ our Lord,
to whom,/with thee and the Holy Ghost,/
be all honour and glory, world without end. **Amen.**

These excerpts from the Book of Common Prayer *are printed in this form by permission of Cambridge University Press. They are arranged in this way for the express purpose of literary explanation, and they do not constitute a complete and authorised service.*

20

LECTIONARY/RESOURCES CROSS-REFERENCE

Sunday Themes Linked to Church Family Worship
(CFW)[1], Prayers for the People (PFP)[2] *and the*
Dramatised Bible (DB)[3]

Many ministers and worship leaders of the Church of England and some other churches will at some time follow the Sunday themes of the Lectionary (as set out in the *Alternative Service Book 1980*. It is useful to know what resources are available in these books, especially when an all-age worship service is included in this sequence. The selections marked with an asterisk (*) below have the more precise correspondence with the Lectionary themes. In these cases, chapters of *Church Family Worship* or *Prayers for the People*, can form the basis of a less formal service.

9 before Christmas: The Creation
CFW numbers 264-284*; PFP Chapter 10; DB page 425: *God's Creation*

8 before Christmas: The Fall
CFW numbers 155-180; PFP Chapter 5; DB page 422–3: *The Life of Prayer, Forgiveness*

7 before Christmas: The Election of God's People: Abraham
CFW numbers 528–553*; PFP Chapter 22; DB page 432–4: *Christian Character and Conflict, Our Work, Schools*

6 before Christmas: The Promise of Redemption: Moses
CFW numbers 110–131*; PFP Chapter 3; DB page 421: *The people of God, Covenant and Unity*

[1]*Church Family Worship*, published 1986 by Hodder & Stoughton Ltd, London.
[2]*Prayers for the People*, published 1992 by HarperCollins*Publishers* Ltd, London.
[3]*The Dramatised Bible*, published 1989 by HarperCollins*Publishers* Ltd, London.

5 before Christmas: The Remnant of Israel
CFW numbers 110–131; PFP Chapter 3; DB page 421: *The people of God, Covenant and Unity*

Advent 1: The Advent Hope
CFW numbers 579–599*; PFP Chapter 24; DB page 434–6: *Christ's Coming, Judgement*

Advent 2: The Word of God in the Old Testament
CFW numbers 600–621*; PFP Chapter 25; DB page 436: *God's Word to Us, Proclamation*

Advent 3: The Forerunner
CFW numbers 622–673; PFP Chapter 26; DB page 437: *Christmas*

Advent 4: The Annunciation
CFW numbers 622–673; PFP Chapter 26; DB page 437: *Christmas*

Christmas 1: The Incarnation
CFW numbers 622–673, 71–90*; PFP Chapter 26, 1; DB page 437, 420–1: *Christmas/New Year, Thanksgiving for the Old Year*

Christmas 2, year 1: The Holy Family
CFW numbers 622–673, 71-90*; PFP Chapter 26, 1; DB page 437, 420–1: *Christmas/New Year, Thanksgiving for the Old Year*

Christmas 2, year 2: The Holy Family/The Wise Men
CFW numbers 71–90, 91–131*; PFP Chapter 1, 2; DB page 420–421: *Thanksgiving for the Old Year/The Wise Men, The Escape to Egypt*

Epiphany 1: Revelation: The Baptism of Jesus
CFW numbers 91–131; PFP Chapter 2; DB page 420–1: *Epiphany, The Wise Men, The Escape to Egypt*

Epiphany 2: Revelation: The First Disciples
CFW numbers 132–154*; PFP Chapter 4; DB page 421–2: *Following Jesus, Jesus' Teaching*

Epiphany 3: Revelation: Signs of Glory
CFW numbers 15–47; PFP Chapter 28; DB page 419: *At Holy Communion/The Lord's Supper*

Epiphany 4: Revelation: The New Temple
CFW numbers 481–507; PFP Chapter 20; DB page 431–2: *The Church: Anniversary, Commitment, Giving*

Epiphany 5: Revelation: The Wisdom of God
CFW numbers 155–180; PFP Chapter 5; DB page 422–3: *The Life of Prayer, Forgiveness*

Epiphany 6: Revelation: Parables
CFW numbers 132–154; PFP Chapter 4; DB page 421–2: *Following Jesus, Jesus' Teaching*

9 before Easter: Christ the Teacher
CFW numbers 132–154; PFP Chapter 4; DB page 421–2: *Following Jesus, Jesus' Teaching*

8 before Easter: Christ the Healer
CFW numbers 437–461; PFP Chapter 18; DB page 430: *The Caring Church, Healing*

7 before Easter: Christ the Friend of Sinners
CFW numbers 388–412; PFP Chapter 16; DB page 428–9: *Invitation to Faith*

Lent 1: The King and the Kingdom: Temptation
CFW numbers 155–180; PFP Chapter 5; DB page 422–3: *The Life of Prayer, Forgiveness*

Lent 2: The King and the Kingdom: Conflict
CFW numbers 528–553*; PFP Chapter 22; DB page 432–4: *Christian Character and Conflict, Our Work, Schools*

Lent 3: The King and the Kingdom: Suffering
CFW numbers 219–238; PFP Chapter 8; DB page 424–5: *Passiontide, Good Friday, Easter Eve*

Lent 4: The King and the Kingdom: Transfiguration
CFW numbers 181–199*; PFP Chapter 6; DB page 423–4: *The Family, Parents and Children, Mothering Sunday*

Lent 5: The King and the Kingdom: The Victory of the Cross
CFW numbers 219–238; PFP Chapter 8; DB page 424–5: *Passiontide, Good Friday, Easter Eve*

Palm Sunday: The Way of the Cross
CFW numbers 200–218*; PFP Chapter 7; DB page 424: *Palm Sunday*

Easter Day: Easter
CFW numbers 239–263; PFP Chapter 9; DB page 425: *Easter, Resurrection*

Easter 1, year 1: The Upper Room/The Bread of Life
CFW numbers 239–263; PFP Chapter 9; DB page 425: *Easter, Resurrection*

Easter 1, year 2: The Upper Room/The Bread of Life
CFW numbers 15–47; PFP Chapter 28; DB page 419: *At Holy Communion/The Lord's Supper*

Easter 2, year 1: The Emmaus Road
CFW numbers 239–263; PFP Chapter 9; DB page 425: *Easter, Resurrection*

Easter 2, year 2: The Emmaus Road
CFW numbers 366–387*; PFP Chapter 15; DB page 427–8: *God's Love to Us, Our Response*

Easter 3, year 2: The Lakeside
CFW numbers 239–263; PFP Chapter 9; DB page 425: *Easter, Resurrection*

Easter 3, year 1: The Lakeside
CFW numbers 239-263; PFP Chapter 9; DB page 425: *Easter, Resurrection*

Easter 4, year 2: The Charge to Peter
CFW numbers 239–263; PFP Chapter 9; DB page 425: *Easter, Resurrection*

Easter 4, year 1: The Charge to Peter
CFW numbers 239–263; PFP Chapter 9; DB page 425: *Easter, Resurrection*

Easter 5, year 1: Going to the Father
CFW numbers 285–306*; PFP Chapter 11; DB page 425–6: *Jesus is Lord, Ascension*

Ascension 1: The Ascension of Christ
CFW numbers 285–306*; PFP Chapter 11; DB page 425–6: *Jesus is Lord, Ascension*

ok*Preparing for Worship*

Pentecost: Pentecost
CFW numbers 307–327*; PFP Chapter 12; DB page 426: *The Holy Spirit*

Trinity: The Trinity
CFW numbers 328–347*; PFP Chapter 13; DB page 427: *The Holiness and Majesty of God, Trinity*

Pentecost 2, year 1: The People of God
CFW numbers 110–131*; PFP Chapter 3; DB page 421: *The people of God, Covenant and Unity*

Pentecost 2, year 2: The Church's Unity and Fellowship
CFW numbers 110–131*; PFP Chapter 3; DB page 421: *The people of God, Covenant and Unity*

Pentecost 3, year 1: The Life of the Baptised
CFW numbers 1–14, 481-507; PFP Chapter 27, 20; DB page 419, 431–2: *At a Baptism/The Church Anniversary, Commitment, Giving*

Pentecost 3, year 2: The Church's Confidence in Christ
CFW numbers 1–14, 481-507; PFP Chapter 27, 20; DB page 419, 431–2: *At a Baptism/The Church Anniversary, Commitment, Giving*

Pentecost 4, year 1: The Freedom of the Sons of God
CFW numbers 155–180; PFP Chapter 5; DB page 422—3: *The Life of Prayer, Forgiveness*

Pentecost 4, year 2: The Church's Mission to the Individual
CFW numbers 388–412*; PFP Chapter 16; DB page 428: *Invitation to Faith*

Pentecost 5, year 1: The New Law
CFW numbers 437–461; PFP Chapter 18; DB page 430: *The Caring Church, Healing*

Pentecost 5, year 2: The Church's Mission to All
CFW numbers 413–436*; PFP Chapter 17; DB page 429: *The Missionary Church, The Worldwide Church*

Pentecost 6: The New Man
CFW numbers 388–412*; PFP Chapter 16; DB page 428-9: *Invitation to Faith*

Pentecost 7: The More Excellent Way
CFW numbers 437–461; PFP Chapter 18; DB page 430: *The Caring Church, Healing*

Pentecost 8: The Fruit of the Spirit
CFW numbers 462–480; PFP Chapter 19; DB page 430-1: *God's Gifts to the Church, Renewal*

Pentecost 9: The Whole Armour of God
CFW numbers 528–553; PFP Chapter 22; DB page 432–4: *Christian Character and Conflict, Our Work, Schools*

Pentecost 10: The Mind of Christ
CFW numbers 200–218; PFP Chapter 7; DB page 424: *Palm Sunday*

Pentecost 11: The Serving Community
CFW numbers 437–461*; PFP Chapter 18; DB page 430: *The Caring Church, Healing*

Pentecost 12: The Witnessing Community
CFW numbers 413–436*; PFP Chapter 17; DB page 429–450: *The Missionary Church, The Worldwide Church*

Pentecost 13: The Suffering Community
CFW numbers 219–238*; PFP Chapter 8; DB page 424–5: *Passiontide, Good Friday, Easter Eve*

Pentecost 14: The Family
CFW numbers 181–199; PFP Chapter 6; DB page 423–4: *The Family, Parents and Children*

Pentecost 15: Those in Authority
CFW numbers 48–70*; PFP Chapter 29; DB page 419–420: *At Local Festivals, For the Peace of the World*

Pentecost 16: The Neighbour
CFW numbers 437–461, 528–553*; PFP Chapter 18, 22; DB page 430, 432–4: *The Caring Church, Healing, Christian Character and Conflict, Our Work, Schools*

Pentecost 17: The Proof of Faith
CFW numbers 132–154; PFP Chapter 4; DB page 421–2: *Following Jesus, Jesus' Teaching*

Pentecost 18: The Offering of Life
CFW numbers 481–507; PFP Chapter 20; DB page 431–2: *The Church: Anniversary, Commitment, Giving*

Pentecost 19: The Life of Faith
CFW numbers 132–154, 388–412*; PFP Chapter 16, 4; DB page 421–2, 428–9: *Invitation to Faith, Following Jesus, Jesus' Teaching*

Pentecost 20: Endurance
CFW numbers 528–553*; PFP Chapter 22; DB page 432–4: *Christian Character and Conflict, Our Work, Schools*

Pentecost 21: The Christian Hope
CFW numbers 239–263, 554–578; PFP Chapter 23, 9; DB page 434, 425: *Heaven, God's Peace/ Easter, Resurrection*

Pentecost 22: The Two Ways
CFW numbers 388–412; PFP Chapter 16; DB page 428–9: *Invitation to Faith*

Last after Pentecost: Citizens of Heaven
CFW numbers 554–578*; PFP Chapter 23; DB page 434: *Heaven, God's Peace*

21

BIBLE
VISUAL AIDS

Using the approach of the Bible itself

We live in a visual age, where verbal communication alone no longer satisfies. Advertising agencies revel in pictorial challenges to the mind; even pop songs spawn a video to promote them. In the churches, preachers and speakers respond to this by using pictures of one sort or another. Indeed pictures are far more uniting than printed words for an all-age congregation.

Visual aids which employ words are of limited use, as their usefulness is determined by age-range and literacy. Word-oriented visual aids are no use to children or adults who cannot read. They are also limited in terms of memorability. Pictures, logos, icons, symbols etc. are far more memorable, do not require reading, and are therefore more useful as visual aids. Symbols are often more visible than words in a large building.

Preachers/speakers who use visual aids in all-age worship are strongly recommended to employ pictures or symbols, and not words. Even single letters are better than words! We could have learned this from the Bible where objects, pictures and symbols are given prominence as a way of communication, not only by prophets, psalmists and letter writers, but also by Jesus himself in the Gospels.

Given the Bible precedent and the current need, it is worth rediscovering for ourselves what our predecessors knew as 'object' lessons. I have witnessed other ministers using a

442

whole range of objects to put their point over – from electric shavers to church brasses. But why do we bother with these things when there are other more immediate and theologically more pertinent visual images available in the texts of the Bible itself? The simplest way is to use the articles themselves – this would obviously be possible with Mark 6. Bags, belts, money etc. can be obtained without difficulty. Of course, it will not be possible to produce many of these items in church! The barns for instance of Luke 12 are nevertheless 'visual', and will make excellent picture illustration – a small barn, a bigger barn etc.

What if you can't draw?
Some ministers involve members of the congregation in the creation of visual aids. This serves the purpose if you are able to dream up your ideas in time. On the other hand, you may not always get what you want! If someone has spent hours on a visual aid for you, you feel obliged to use it.

Alternatively, the local Christian book shop, or an agency like the Church Pastoral Aid Society will sell you books of ready-made art work. In fact you may well have art work in stock for your parish magazine that will do. Simply enlarge it several times on a photocopier until it reaches the size you need. The last print can be on a colour in order to give variety. An excellent source is the Good News Bible editions that contain drawings by the Swiss artist Annie Vallotton. (Note: the edition which includes the Apocrypha has more drawings!) The Bible Society who control the copyright for these drawings make no charge for their use in service sheets. The basis is that not more than three or four are included for any one service of each sheet and that the italic quotation below each drawing is also normally included.

If churches do this on a regular basis, they might consider paying a small donation to the Bible Society, whose address is: Bible Society, Stonehill Green, Westlea, Swindon SN5 7DG (telephone 01793 418100, fax 01793 418118).

On each occasion of use there needs to be reference to the

Good News Bible, from which the illustrations are drawn.

The Bible Society approve a similar arrangement for the use of the Annie Valotton drawings on overhead projector stencils, or blown up drawings for visual aids. The Annie Valotton drawings are obtainable on software from: Christian Clip Art, 12 Crundale Crescent, Cardiff CF4 5PY, telephone 01222 758484.

Standardise

It makes sense to standardise your visual aid format, because on a future occasion you may wish to use the pictures/symbols in different combinations. Art shops stock stiff coloured card in standard sizes which are excellent for background. Foreground can be your own cut-out, or coloured photocopy paper from your enlargement.

Standardise on orientation, too. Vertical 'portrait' format is the better orientation. It's easier for children to hold (if that is sometimes your intention), they'll go higher, and more of them will fit into a row.

Over the years a collection built up in this way, and with care, will provide visual aids at a moment's notice – even when you choose subject/story/passage first; looking through your collection you will probably find some that will fit, even if you have to supplement what you have in stock from time to time.

Useful Hints

1. Always deploy visual aids from the audience's left to the audience's right; that's the way people read (unless you're in China) and the mind is therefore adjusted to take in and remember information in that direction. Incidentally, this also applies to making points with your hand or finger in the air – 'One', 'Two', 'Three', should flow from their left to their right.

2. It is always best to make your preaching point first, and then expose the visual aid. While the visual aid remains

hidden, you have the audience's attention because of their curiosity about what will appear next. The visual aid should normally be used to clinch the point – unless of course it is complex, like a box which is opened to reveal more interest.

3. Keep your hands free of papers or microphones when using visual aids that need holding. A neck microphone is useful for moving around – even for interviewing people. Notes can be written on the back of visual aids if you are using cards rather than physical objects.

4. Use your visual aids to recapitulate on the points you have made.

5. Be careful not to spend too long on one picture or symbol. Attention will wander. In fact, the more you say about a visual aid, the more blurred the meaning.

Overhead projection
Overhead projection view-foils are in some ways less controllable than objects or cards. They also divert attention from your facial expressions rather more (this may be what you want!). In all-age services you cannot involve the children in the same way, and it is always best to have a carefully instructed assistant helping you. This will save you looking at the screen to adjust the frame. When you turn to the screen your words will get lost unless you have a neck microphone. Both screen and projector surface can dazzle and distract you; you need to be able to see the expressions of the audience and make easy eye-contact.

Video
Good video (with smaller audiences – unless you have expensive equipment) can be very effective – especially since it allows you to think ahead! A whole new generation of cartoon or sitcom style discussion starters are becoming available on video. Some of these are an excellent way of

making people think at the start of a presentation. We look forward to the era of the large flat screen and of inexpensive video projection.

The Church Pastoral Aid Society, Scripture Union, the National Society, and the Bible Society are useful sources of this kind of video[1].

Drama

Books of dramatic illustration of Christian concepts, and contemporary settings for Bible parables and truths are available in paperback from Christian book shops. The *Riding Lights* and other theatre groups have been exponents of this genre. *The Dramatised Bible*[2] will be found useful for illustration purposes.

Best of all is to have your own drama group, mime group, or dance drama group (or all three!). Part of their objective will be to be flexible and adaptable enough to match a theme and prepare a performance at reasonably short notice. They will also have a repertoire of their own to offer.

[1] See the address list on pp. 102–107.
[2] *The Dramatised Bible*, published 1989 by HarperCollins*Publishers* Ltd, London.

22

DRAMATISED BIBLE READINGS

Using dramatised stories from the Bible in worship is nothing particularly new; it is an excellent way of presenting the gospel to all generations. In recent years *The Dramatised Bible*[1] has made preparing such readings very much easier – not least because of the permission given to photocopy in sufficient numbers for the cast of any reading.

What surprised me as editor of *The Dramatised Bible* was how much of the Bible uses the device of 'reported speech' and so lends itself to dramatic presentation. For instance, we would not immediately think of the book Jeremiah in this way. And yet Jeremiah has a narrative form quite as amenable to dramatic presentation as, say, Genesis. It is the Hebrew tradition of story-telling which makes the task so inviting and the outcome so effective.

In fact we have encouragement to dramatise from the Bible itself. It seems that the Hebrew people in Temple worship used drama to rehearse the acts of God in their history – notably the crossing of the Red Sea and their deliverance from the slavery of Egypt. Such dramatic presentations were not entertainment – though they would have been marvellously entertaining. And they were far more than visual aids – though Hebrew faith did require each generation to recall, before the next, God's saving interventions, so that his mercy

---

[1] *The Dramatised Bible*, published 1989 by HarperCollins*Publishers* Ltd, London.

447

and his demands would not be forgotten. The Hebrew dramas had a teaching role, and they were acts of worship too – precedents of our own 'anamnesis', or calling to mind of the saving work of Christ in the drama we term, according to our Christian tradition 'The Lord's Supper'/'the Holy Communion'/'the Eucharist'/'the Mass'.

Evidence for a more extended use of drama in Hebrew worship comes from the Psalms. We have only to look at Psalm 118 to see that it is neither a hymn nor merely a meditation. There are obvious solo parts and choral parts. And there are even 'stage' instructions embedded in the text. For example, verse 27, 'With palm branches in your hands march round the altar' – which, in some traditions, we blindly sing as though the psalm were homogeneous. It does not take much imagination to see that what we are dealing with is the script of a drama or the libretto of an opera, set in the context of a magnificent act of worship. Here the intending (and noble?) worshipper approaches the door of the Temple and asks to enter to give thanks for God's deliverance. The ministers/ priests tell him righteousness is a prerequisite of an approach to God. And the drama progresses from there. Permeating the drama are the resonant choruses of the Hebrew liturgy:

Leader:	Let Israel say:
All:	His love endures for ever!
Leader:	Let the House of Aaron say:
All:	His love endures for ever!
Leader:	Let those who fear the Lord say:
All:	His love endures for ever!

Finally, the worshipper is admitted ('Blessed is he who comes in the name of the Lord') and the celebration begins ('With branches in your hands . . .'). As long as we consider the Old Testament dour and prosaic, its exciting suggestions for our own worship practice will be missed.

The New Testament is full of vivid narrative. For the most

part dramatising comes easily and is obviously appropriate. *The Dramatised Bible* also sets in responsive form some of the teaching material. For instance, where Jesus' words are cast in the rabbinical style which preserved them through the oral period until they became written elements of the Gospels:

Teacher: Blessed are the poor in spirit:
Students: For theirs is the kingdom of heaven.

. . . the teaching of Jesus indeed – but thereafter used in this sort of 'catechetical' pattern by Christians from the very beginning.

Even Paul has his own rabbinical style of 'question and answer'. This readily lends itself to dramatic presentation, thereby becoming much clearer in its meaning.

Question: Is God unjust?
Answer: Not at all!
. . . etc.

Using dramatised readings brings the text of Scripture to life, and gives people empathy with the characters. Similarly, the hearers are drawn into the presentation. As the story moves from voice to voice it is very difficult for attention to wander! Even young children, who naturally grow restive during a long and uneventful reading, find their interest and imagination caught up in the narrative as the scriptures are presented in dramatised form.

It also makes the content of the reading more memorable – not least to those who have participated. Much depends on audibility; so care needs to be taken in larger buildings. Where appropriate, a microphone with a wide field that will pick up all the speakers should be used; or separate microphones might be considered. This sort of preparation will enable the minister/leader to involve people whose voices are not so strong or otherwise indistinct.

A strong voice should be cast for any 'key' character, such as the frequent 'Narrator'. It is worth noting that more male

than female characters speak in the Bible. However, when using dramatised readings, a good balance can still be obtained by deploying female voices for narration, for 'Person', 'Person 2', 'Reader 1', 'Reader 2' etc. In the non-narrative, teaching passages it is vital to have a contrast between the speakers.

Where Voices 1-3, Persons 1-3 etc. are used, participants should stand together in a group. Where 'The Lord', or 'God', speaks as a prophetic utterance and not in direct conversation it is best for the reader to be unseen, or at least to stand apart from the rest.

There will be occasions – both formal and informal – when participants can add actions to a dramatised presentation from the Bible. Then, prior agreement over what is to be done is a safeguard against unintended comic accidents! And a rehearsal will be necessary unless the actors are very confident and experienced. At the rehearsal it is sensible to have someone watching who is able to assess the drama's impact on the proposed audience, and for the cast to listen and respond to that person's objective criticism.

A wide range of ready adapted readings can be found in *The Dramatised Bible* and *The Dramatised Bible Readings for Festivals*[2]. The principles used in arranging Bible passages for dramatic reading are essentially simple and can be applied to almost any Bible passage.

In the reading that follows, **bold type** indicates words which need to be inserted for purposes of direction, and *italic type* indicates words which need to be omitted in order to make the drama immediate and fresh.

[2]*The Dramatised Bible Readings for Festivals*, published 1991 by HarperCollins*Publishers* Ltd, London

THE LAST SUPPER

From Luke 22.14–34

Narrator
When the hour came, Jesus and his apostles reclined at the table. *And he said to them:*

Jesus
I have eagerly desired to eat this Passover with you before I suffer. For I tell you, I will not eat it again until it finds fulfilment in the kingdom of God.

Narrator
After taking the cup, he gave thanks *(PAUSE) and said:*

Jesus
Take this and divide it among you. For I tell you I will not drink again of the fruit of the vine until the kingdom of God comes.

Narrator
And he took bread, gave thanks and broke it, and gave it to them *saying:*

Jesus
This is my body given for you; do this in remembrance of me.

Narrator
In the same way, after the supper he took the cup, *saying:*

Jesus
This cup is the new covenant in my blood, which is poured out for you. *(PAUSE)* But the hand of him who is going to betray me is with mine on the table. The Son of Man will go as it has been decreed, but woe to that man who betrays him.

Narrator
They began to question among themselves which of them it might be who would do this. *(PAUSE)* Also a dispute arose among them as to which of them was considered to be greatest. *(PAUSE) Jesus said to them:*

Jesus
The kings of the Gentiles lord it over them; and those who exercise authority over them call themselves 'Benefactors'. But you are not to be like that. Instead, the greatest among you should be like the youngest, and the one who rules like the one who serves. For who is greater, the one who is at the table or the one who serves? Is it not the one who is at the table? But I am among you as one who serves. You are those who have stood by me in my trials. And I confer on you a kingdom, just as my Father conferred one on me, so that you may eat and drink at my table in my kingdom and sit on thrones, judging the twelve tribes of Israel. *(PAUSE)*

(To Peter)
Simon, Simon, Satan has asked to sift you as wheat. But I have prayed for you, Simon, that your faith may not fail. *(PAUSE)* And when you have turned back, strengthen your brothers.

[Narrator]
But he replied:

Peter
Lord, I am ready to go with you to prison and to death.

[Narrator]
Jesus answered:

Jesus
I tell you, Peter, before the cock crows today, you will deny three times that you know me.

This dramatised reading is based on the New International Version of the New Testament. Versions vary in their suitability. The Good News Bible and other more colloquial versions on the whole make better drama. But in especially hallowed passages, and at more dignified or traditional occasions, the sonority of NIV or, say, NRSV, captures the tone required.